Birds of JAPAN

HELM FIELD GUIDES

Birds of JAPAN

MARK BRAZIL

H E L M
LONDON • OXFORD • NEW YORK • NEW DELHI • SYDNEY

Author's dedication

To the natural history heroes who inspired me and helped me along my path:
Sir Peter Scott (1909–1989)
"Johnny" Morris OBE (1916–1999)
Sir David Attenborough (1926–)
Richard Mabey (1941–)

HELM
Bloomsbury Publishing Plc
50 Bedford Square, London, WC1B 3DP, UK

BLOOMSBURY, HELM and the Helm logo are trademarks of Bloomsbury Publishing Plc

First published in the UK in 2018

A catalogue record for this book is available from the British Library

Library of Congress Cataloguing-in-Publication data has been applied for

ISBN: PB: 978-1-4729-1386-9; eBook: 978-1-4729-1387-6

4 6 8 10 9 7 5 3

Photographs by Mark Brazil

Typeset in Humanist BT Light
Printed and bound in India by Replika Press Pvt. Ltd.

CONTENTS

PREFACE

Since first visiting Japan in February 1980 I have been intrigued by the Japanese avifauna and have long wished to produce a modern, illustrated field guide dedicated to the birds of this fascinating archipelago. Finally, here it is!

In studying the fascinating cross-section of Palearctic, Nearctic and Oriental species that occur regularly in Japan, along with the Eurasian, Pacific and New World vagrants that occasionally visit, I became engrossed in understanding their status and distribution (described in detail in *The Birds of Japan* 1991). I was drawn into deeper explorations of individual species (various papers on a range of species and a monograph on one of them: *The Whooper Swan* 2003), then into the wildlife of Asia (*Wild Asia: Spirit of a Continent* 2000) and ultimately the avifauna of the larger region of East Asia (*Field Guide to the Birds of East Asia* 2009). The significance of regional field guides is that they open the eyes of local birdwatchers to the possibilities beyond their own national borders, and provide information on species that may one day appear on their own local or national patch. Nevertheless, larger, heavier volumes are difficult to carry in the field, and Japan is much visited on its own, hence there was a clear need for a more compact volume covering just the Japanese archipelago.

Japan has consistently produced excellent bird photographers and, generation by generation, cadres of dedicated ornithologists and conservationists. Surprisingly, however, in light of its large population size and considerable avian diversity, Japan has produced relatively few birdwatchers or birders. In recent years, however, several Japanese-language field guides have been published, all of them photographic, with the obvious pitfalls of that medium. Many of us still find bird illustrations to be more useful and much more attractive.

Field guides are at best works in progress. In compiling this one, I have adopted the latest published taxonomic decisions available, but I have also opted to err on the side of inclusiveness, on the basis that a number of taxa currently recognised as subspecies will no doubt be confirmed as full species before long. Additional species are recorded in Japan each year, and species considered one-off vagrants just a few years ago are now regularly found. For this reason I have included all vagrants recorded in the country in the main body of the text.

Our ornithological knowledge grows steadily as research and publications continue unabated; new discoveries are made, new understandings are reached; taxonomy shifts and changes. However, each project must have its cut-off date, and mine was December 2016. Nevertheless, even during the final phase important new records came to light, so these are mentioned in an appendix.

I hope that using this book in the field will enhance your birding, and that you will also be critical and tease out its insufficiencies, ambiguities and inaccuracies, whether in text, illustrations or maps. To help improve this guide for the future, please contribute your knowledge, updated information and experience. Contact me via my website, www.japannatureguides.com.

Throughout my life, I have been fortunate in having been influenced and impressed by a number of significant figures, not merely those in public life or in the media who inspire us all, but those who personally supported or encouraged my interests and endeavours in natural history, bird biology and conservation during my childhood, education and later life. I dedicate this book to those who went before, with fond memories of their guidance and inspiration: Dennis Brazil, Michael Dowell, Arthur Jacobs, Ryozo Kakizawa, Sueharu Matano, Dick Orton, Richard Richardson, Masaru Takada, Shinji Takano, Mary and Ray Turner, and Masayuki Yabuuchi.

Mark Brazil Ebetsu, Hokkaido, January 2018

ACKNOWLEDGEMENTS

The success of *Birds of East Asia* (2009), and the subsequent iBook of that title, has been very gratifying, and has made it possible to proceed with this condensed, updated and improved volume focusing entirely on Japan.

Many friends and colleagues have contributed directly or indirectly to these projects through their field experience in the region. Some provided their experience of Asian vagrants elsewhere, and some provided relevant literature, valued insights into taxonomy and critical reviews of drafts – I thank them all.

The many colleagues who helped with *Birds of East Asia* have been thanked there, so here I would like to mention by name those friends and colleagues who have been particularly helpful during the development and preparation of this guide.

I am indebted to Desmond Allen, Craig Brelsford, Neil Davidson, Angus Macindoe, Dr Katsura Mikami, Yann Muzika, and Takeshi Ogura, each of whom gave generously of their time and experience, who reviewed drafts, and who helped improve the latest manuscript.

I also thank those who contributed significantly to my previous work and hence indirectly to this one: Yosuke Amano, Haruhiko Asuka, Chris Cook, Dr Yuzo Fujimaki, Masao Fukagawa, Atsunori Fukuda, Takashi Hiraoka, Hiroshi and Marie-Jo Ikawa, Hiroshi Ikenaga, Himaru Iozawa, Norio Kawano, Kazunori Kimura, Shinji Koyama, Fumikazu Masumoto, Dr Shigeru Matsuoka, Akiyo Nakamichi, Yuji Nishimura, Toshikazu Onishi, Shigeo Ozawa, Dr Akiko Shoji, Yuko Sasaki, Fumio Sato, Tomokazu Tanigawa, Satoshi Tokorozaki, Masahiro Toyama, Osao and Michiaki Ujihara, Dr Takeshi Yamasaki, Mike Yough, and members of the *Kantori* e-mail group.

I thank the original team of artists whose work from *Birds of East Asia* has been reproduced here (Per Alström, Carl D'Silva, Martin Elliott, Kim Franklin, Ren Hathway, Hans Larsson, Dave Nurney, Derek Onley, Christopher Schmidt, Brian Small, the late Laurel Tucker, Jan Wilczur, Tim Worfolk and Bill Zetterström). In particular, I thank Alan Harris, not only for his significant involvement in *Birds of East Asia*, but also for helping so much in tailoring this volume specifically to Japanese species and subspecies and for painting many new plates.

The extensive use of new artwork by Alan Harris for this book has been supported by Bloomsbury and a number of private sponsors. I would like to thank them all: especially Dr Robert Berry and Ms Gail D'Alton (plate 94), Mavis Brazil (plate 121), Dennis Brazil (in memoriam, plate 169), Ethel Cebra (plates 17 and 123), YY Chin (plates 2 and 99), Chris Cook (plate 127), Kathy Emrich and Bob Sherwood (plate 95), Japan Nature Guides (plate 72), Bob Kleiger (plates 126 and 161), Takeyoshi Matsuo (plate 3), and Yann Muzika (plate 119).

At Bloomsbury, I thank Nigel Redman for commissioning the project, and Jim Martin and Anna MacDiarmid for navigating it to its successful conclusion, while Julian Baker and Susan McIntyre tackled the complex task of re-designing the plates and maps, and laying out the book with tremendous skill.

Whilst my friends and colleagues have done their utmost to rescue me from glaring errors and mistakes, any inaccuracies that remain are entirely mine. To all who have been involved – and to any I may have inadvertently overlooked – my deepest thanks.

Finally, I thank my wife, Mayumi Brazil, for her understanding, support and encouragement throughout yet another book project.

USING THIS FIELD GUIDE

THE SCOPE OF THE GUIDE

This book describes in detail the 633 species of birds accepted by The Ornithological Society of Japan (2012) as having been reliably recorded in the country in their most recent checklist (*Check-list of Japanese Birds, 7th revised edition*). It also includes species recorded and supported by publication or unequivocal photographs since. I have included species for which records are considered to be questionable or not officially published to an appendix. Furthermore, I have attempted to include all species (including established introductions, vagrants and recently extinct species) known to have occurred in Japan based on published records prior to late 2016 – in all, 747 species.

Geographical scope

The Japanese archipelago extends for over 3,000 km off the coastline of East Asia. It consists of four main islands, Hokkaido, Honshu, Shikoku and Kyushu, but in addition there are chains of islands stretching between Kyushu and Taiwan, and from Tokyo south for 1,200 km via the Izu Islands to the Ogasawara (Bonin) and Iwo (Volcano) Islands. These subsidiary island chains are of particular ornithological importance.

To the north-east of Hokkaido, several islands, the Habomai Group, Shikotan, Kunashiri and Etorofu, were an integral part of Japanese territory until 1945, and these Northern Territories remain Japanese to the Japanese people to this day. Geologically, Kunashiri and Etorofu are recognised as part of the Kuril Island archipelago, while the Habomai group of islands and Shikotan appear as remnants of a once much larger Nemuro Peninsula. Controlled by Russia since 1945, these islands are considered politically to be part of the Kuril Island chain administered by Sakhalin. Thus political debate affects Japan's borders, and not only with Russia to the north-east, but also to the west and south with South Korea, Taiwan and China. Not wishing for politics to intrude into ornithology, in this volume I have opted to include all of those islands considered at this time to be Japanese by the Japanese people, regardless of these disputes. Thus Japan, as delimited here, extends from north to south (Cape Soya Hokkaido to Minami Iwo-jima) from 45°31'10.6"N 141°55'36.6"E to 24°14'04.3"N 141°27'44.6"E, and from east to west (northern cape of Etorofu to western Yonaguni-jima) 45°30'30.0"N 148°52'41.3"E to 24°26'57.9"N 122°56'02.2"E.

As many of the names for the regions, island groups and island names may be unfamiliar, though vital in terms of understanding avian distribution in Japan, these are shown on the endpaper map.

Taxonomy

The species recorded in this *Field Guide to the Birds of Japan* are described and illustrated following *Birds of East Asia* (Brazil 2009) and the International Ornithological Congress World Bird List (Gill & Donsker 2016), and taking into account the latest published list for Japan (The Ornithological Society of Japan 2012) and subsequent publications, with some minor adjustments to give balance to the plates. Ornithological taxonomy is undergoing considerable flux, making it difficult to provide an order that will be familiar to all. I have strayed from those authorities where I am aware of more recently published papers describing newly accepted species or taxonomic arrangements. Recent taxonomic reviews published by the British and American Ornithologists' Unions have been particularly helpful, as ornithological societies in the region tend to follow rather than lead taxonomic trends. Finally, names of genera, and taxonomic order have been updated as much as possible in line with Gill and Donsker (2017).

Included in the species accounts is information on subspecies. Taxonomic changes are continually altering the playing field, and it is difficult to reach agreement over which taxa are accepted at the specific or subspecific levels at any given time. Changes will undoubtedly occur, even as this book goes to press. I make no pretence of being an authority on taxonomy. Nevertheless, in compiling this work I have been forced to make decisions, often on the basis of limited information. Although personally tending towards the conservative, I have generally argued in favour of splitting the more recognisable 'suspect' taxa as full species, or I have flagged potential splits by using distinct English names.

A number of subspecies occur in Japan that may one day be recognised specifically, perhaps including even very common taxa such as the Oriental Crow (as *Corvus orientalis*), a close relative of the Carrion Crow *C. corone*. There are those who decry the subspecies concept completely as it is currently applied to birds, suggesting that all distinct populations should be considered separately, in which case many more species would be recognised. With that caveat in mind, I have included mention of all those subspecies known to have been recorded in Japan and, where field criteria exist for separation, I have included such details as space permits.

SPECIES ACCOUNTS

The majority of the book comprises the species accounts with their associated distribution maps, and facing them the 189 plates (pp. 24–407). The final plate draws attention to the taxa presumed or known to be extinct, and highlights the need for continued conservation of habitats and species in Japan. The species accounts and layouts are standardised and, I hope, largely self-explanatory.

Each species is given an English name and a scientific name. By convention, the generic name begins in upper case and is followed by the specific name in lower case, thus Olive-backed Pipit is *Anthus hodgsoni*. I have also included subspecific names, as these distinctions will appeal to readers interested in species identification and species limits, and are also of particular interest to birders from Europe and North America seeking to identify birds out of range that may differ subtly from subspecies in those areas. Thus, both subspecies of Olive-backed Pipit are listed, as *Anthus hodgsoni hodgsoni* and *A. h. yunnanensis*, though it should be noted that it is not always possible to identify an individual to subspecies level in the field.

Vernacular and scientific names are based on Gill and Wright (2006) and Gill and Donsker (2016), but with minor variations. Scientific names are generally slow to change, although a number of significant revisions have been adopted here, especially where previous genera are now recognised as polyphyletic, and with respect to gender endings (following David & Gosselin 2002a, 2002b). English names continue to vary considerably from one book to the next, and while convention may sway first one way then another, it is ultimately the author's responsibility to choose.

The length (**L**) of each species is followed by wingspan (**WS**) and mass (**WT**) when available. Size ranges are derived from the major available published sources, principally Takagawa *et al.* (2011), but also del Hoyo et al. (1992–2013), *Handbook of the Birds of the World*, except where these volumes have been superseded by newer works (for example, Svensson *et al.* 1999; Ferguson-Lees & Christie 2005; Sibley 2014), separating those for males and females where relevant. Whilst the interpretation of such measurements in the field may be questionable, they are invaluable for comparative purposes.

Each species account comprises several sections (where information is relevant or available). Status and Distribution (**SD**) describes the range of the species, and provides information on each subspecies. If no subspecies are listed, then the taxon is considered monotypic. Indication is also given of where accidentals/vagrants have been recorded. Some terms, such as 'resident', though unavoidable for brevity, may be somewhat misleading, as they do not imply 'sedentary' – for while birds may be present year-round in a given area, they may be represented by different populations, even different subspecies, at different seasons. An indication of the most likely months of occurrence is given, but this should be considered guidance only and not definitive. Habitat and Habits (**HH**) provides information on which typical habitats a species prefers when breeding, on migration or in winter, and any uniquely distinguishing habits or unusual behaviours are described. In the Identification (**ID**) section, a summary is given of current knowledge of field identification criteria, beginning with information relevant to all individuals, followed by that for males, females, recognisably different winter and summer, and age-related plumages. Particular attention is paid to the field separation of subspecies. The Bare Parts (**BP**) section includes information on bill shape, size and coloration; eye colour and any associated features; and the structure, coloration and any special features of the legs. Sounds and Vocalisations (**SV**) includes summarised descriptions and transliterations of common calls and songs, as well as any physical sounds produced, such as wing-whirring or drumming. Transcribing calls and songs is not easy, especially with information coming via several languages. Cultural and individual differences influence the ways in which we hear and transcribe sounds; however, some attempt seems worthwhile. Call and song descriptions use simple English transliteration based on personal experience. I have made no attempt to define differences in stress or pitch. Transcriptions of vocalisations, however good they are, are only really easy to recognise *after* one has heard the bird, not before; nevertheless they serve as a guide for retrospective identification. Sound recordings of most species included here can be found in the digital edition of *Birds of East Asia*. Taxonomic Notes (**TN**) indicate any recent changes that might cause confusion. And, finally, Alternative Names (**AN**) are given where these are in common use.

The 189 plates, with illustrations of 747 species, essentially follow the currently accepted taxonomic order, with minor adjustments. The plates, situated alongside the text, present the maximum amount of information in the space available. Just as the text has often had to rely on abbreviation to achieve this aim, so many images have been reproduced quite small. Some change of scale within plates is inevitable, when including flight images and behavioural vignettes, but these changes should be self-evident. The artists have endeavoured to illustrate each of the main variations in plumage relating to sex, age and subspecies. Where a species has several subspecies, those more widely differing have been selected for illustration. A range of poses has been chosen to indicate important behavioural characteristics.

DISTRIBUTION AND DISTRIBUTION MAPS

Within the text, for brevity's sake, short forms are commonly used. Thus, for example, *mainland Japan* is used to refer to the four main islands of Hokkaido, Honshu, Shikoku and Kyushu; *Nansei Shoto* refers to all of the islands south-west of Kyushu and north of Taiwan; *Izu/Ogasawara* refers to all of the islands south of Tokyo; *Sea of Japan islands* refers to the offshore islands frequented by birders in search of vagrants, from Tsushima off northern Kyushu and the Oki Islands and Mishima off south-western Honshu, Hegura-jima off Ishikawa Prefecture and Tobishima off Yamagata Prefecture, to Teuri-jima, Rebun, and Rishiri off north-west Hokkaido (see endpaper map).

Distribution maps are provided only for those species occurring regularly in Japan. The shape of Japan does not lend itself easily to mapping, so maps of varying scales have been used: a small-scale map for species ranging throughout the country, a larger-scale map for species with ranges that occur only on mainland Japan, and yet larger-scale maps for species whose ranges are restricted to certain groups of islands. Necessities of space and scale have rendered these maps small; however, they do provide a visual overview of where to look for each of these species. Because of the scale of the maps, no attempt has been made to map the occurrence of accidentals or rare migrants to the region. Colour codes on maps are: green for year-round or resident, red for summer or breeding range, blue for winter range, yellow for on migration, and pink for scarce.

BIRD IDENTIFICATION

With over 700 species recorded in Japan, bird identification may seem at first daunting, but as with the development of any skill, a combination of pleasant effort and practice bring about competence; ultimately, time in the field is what counts, both for enjoyment of birding and for developing proficiency.

Keen field observation and writing field notes, supplemented by study of a field guide such as this, will help you to hone your identification skills through processes of recognition, comparison and elimination. First, it helps to be mindful of the season and time of day, and to recognise the habitat in which a bird is seen – whether it is in coniferous or deciduous forest, on a wet mudflat or a rocky shore. It then helps to recognise prominent and distinctive forms of behaviour – ways of foraging or flying, for example. All can help significantly in assigning a sighting to a particular species.

Placing a bird in the correct family is the first step to its identification, thus learning the families to which birds belong is invaluable. Seasonality, habitat, habits and range may quickly eliminate many unlikely species.

A quick eye, a sharp ear and attention to detail will help in teasing apart the differences between a bird that hops or one that runs from a bird that forages from leaves and another that feeds on tree trunks or branches. Paying attention to the ways in which a bird flies, swims, walks, flicks its wings, bobs its tail or sings, can aid considerably in identification.

Having learned the main families, take time to become familiar with the commonest species – duck, crow, dove, bulbul, starling and bunting. Knowing these, their sizes, patterns and behaviour, will provide you with an instant benchmark against which to compare all subsequent sightings. When faced with a mystery bird, first determine its size in relation to your familiar six, then consider its body shape – is it elongated and slender, like a wagtail, or is it plump, like a Hawfinch or grosbeak? Starting at the head, examine the bill size and shape; is it short and blunt (finch-like) or short and hooked (shrike-like)? Is it short but fine, perhaps an insectivorous flycatcher, or warbler? Is it long, thin, thick, straight or curved, and how does the bird use its bill? Having confirmed the shape and size of the bill, consider the pattern of the head; crown-stripes, eye-stripes, ear patches or the absence of these features are each relevant. Then look to the upperparts. Can you see any distinctive or conspicuous patches of contrasting colour on the back, rump or wings? Are there any wingbars? Observe the underparts carefully too, to see how they compare with the upperparts, and note whether they are plain, barred or streaked, and whether they are pale, dark or distinctively patterned. Note also any details of the tail, in particular its length relative to the wings. If the bird is flying, note the shape of its wings, whether the wings are long or short, narrow or broad, rounded or pointed; and whether they move in a steady blur, a series of distinct slow beats or several rapid beats interspersed with glides. At the same time, note whether the tail is forked, notched, square-tipped, rounded or wedge-shaped, and whether there are distinctive or contrasting patterns on the wings, rump and tail. Where and how a bird flies, forages and perches are also useful keys to identification.

As your skills develop, you will learn to recognise an increasing number of species against which anything new can be referenced mentally. You will begin to recognise that whereas some species have only one plumage, the males, females, adults and juveniles of others differ from each other and through the seasons. Over time you will build up a recognition pattern of features that make most species distinctive, even when seen in silhouette or in poor light. This combination of characters is known as the bird's '*jizz*', a kind of subliminal *gestalt* of what the bird looks like and how it moves. With time, you may want to learn more about moult, about how and when birds change their plumage in a steady sequence from juvenile to first-winter, to first-summer, then to non-breeding adult and breeding adult. Some species achieve this sequence in less than a year from hatching and breed at barely one year old. Other species take a number of years to reach adult plumage and may not breed until they are several years old. Understanding bird behaviour, whether it is flight, foraging, displaying or nesting, may add to your enjoyment of birdwatching.

A very important means of locating and identifying birds is by their vocalisations or other sounds. Sounds of walking over dry leaf litter, whistling wings, the hard tapping of a bill on wood – all these and many more incidental or deliberate sounds can help locate a bird you may not otherwise notice and may even be vital clues to its identity.

Birds essentially have two types of vocalisations – calls and songs. Calls may be used for contact, recognition, to indicate changing behaviour (such as taking flight) or alarm. Songs are a more prolonged series of notes, some of which may sound particularly melodious to our ears, and are particularly used by passerines to define territories and to attract mates. Tracking down each and every call or song to its maker is time-consuming, requiring a painstaking and patient approach. The availability of high-quality recordings of bird songs in particular makes learning bird sounds an easier and more enjoyable pastime these days. One can now learn relevant vocalisations prior to going into the field, facilitating more rapid recognition.

AVIAN TOPOGRAPHY AND TERMINOLOGY

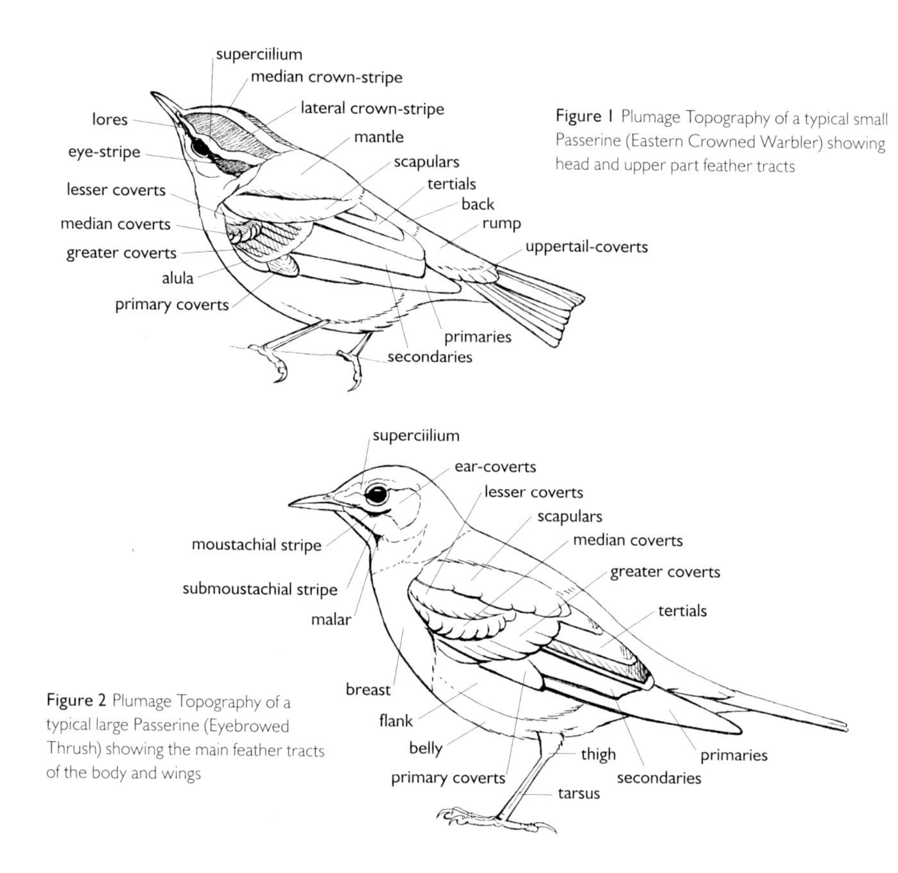

Figure 1 Plumage Topography of a typical small Passerine (Eastern Crowned Warbler) showing head and upper part feather tracts

Figure 2 Plumage Topography of a typical large Passerine (Eyebrowed Thrush) showing the main feather tracts of the body and wings

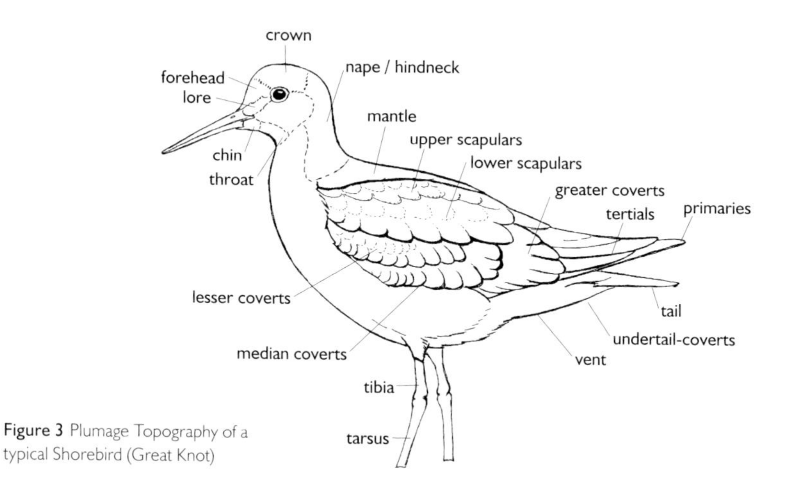

Figure 3 Plumage Topography of a typical Shorebird (Great Knot)

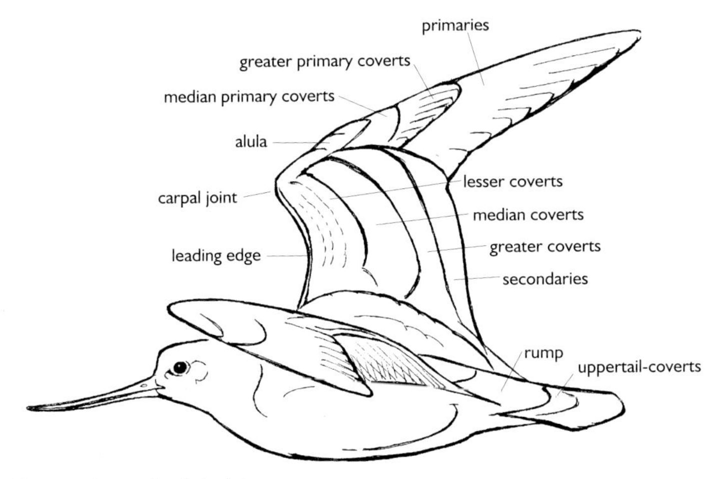

Figure 4 Plumage Topography of a typical Shorebird in flight (Terek Sandpiper)

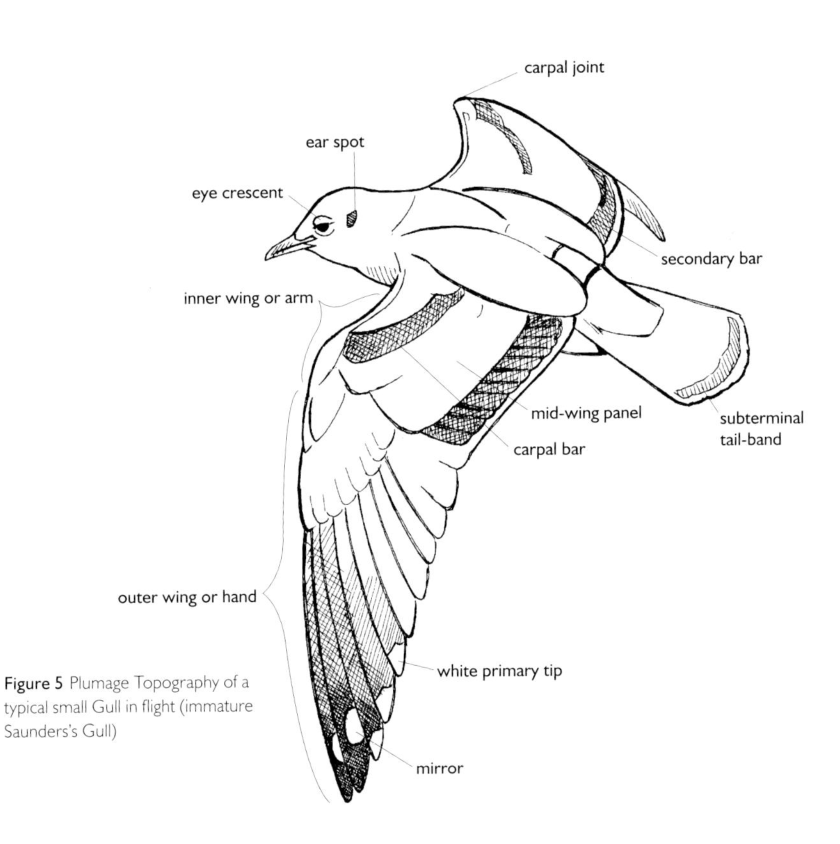

Figure 5 Plumage Topography of a typical small Gull in flight (immature Saunders's Gull)

JAPANESE GEOGRAPHY, CLIMATE AND BIOGEOGRAPHY

Figure 6 Map of Japan showing major biomes.

The more than 3,000 km-long Japanese archipelago spans a wide range of climatic zones and ecosystems. Japan's main terrestrial habitats span towering volcanoes (the highest being Mt Fuji in central Honshu, at 3,776 m), high-altitude peaks in the Japanese Alps, nearly 20 of them rising to over 3,000 m, to low coastal areas including lagoons and swamps. The extremely mountainous nature of the country helps drive its regional and seasonal climatic variation and the distribution of various biomes and hence species. Meanwhile, offshore, significant warm currents flow north along the southern coasts of Japan, whilst a major cold current flows south out of the Bering Sea and along the north-eastern coast of the country. These, other minor currents and regions of mixing of cold and warm currents all influence the distribution of marine planktonic organisms and hence of the fish and birds that are part of the marine food web, and influence the onshore climate, and the flora and fauna there.

It is frequently said that Japan has four clear seasons, but if we count them as follows – winter, spring, rainy season (the early-summer monsoon period), summer, typhoon season (spanning summer into autumn, July to September in Okinawa and Kyushu, August to October further north) and autumn, then in fact we can experience six seasons with very different characteristics. Each of them impacts the environment and has a profound influence on the flora and fauna of the country.

Northern parts of Japan, especially Hokkaido, experience very prolonged, severe winters dominated by cold airflows from continental Asia to the north-west and north, leading to low average temperatures, frozen lakes and rivers, locally heavy snowfalls and, along the shore of the Sea of Okhotsk, extensive sea-ice during late winter. Northern Japan experiences long sub-Arctic winters, and short, mild to warm summers. It has habitats typically considered boreal. In contrast, southern regions of Japan, especially the Nansei Shoto and the Ogasawara Islands, are subtropical year-round. These areas are affected by warm airflows from the south, south-east and south-west, and are warm to hot and humid throughout the year, with high average rainfall. Much of mainland Japan (Kyushu, Shikoku and Honshu) south of Hokkaido belongs to the temperate climate zone, but with the northern parts having longer winters and shorter summers and southern and western parts having shorter winters and longer, hotter and humid summers. Japan also spans different climatic zones from east to west. The Sea of Japan coastal climatic zone is characterised by heavy snowfalls in winter, and mild summers, whereas the Pacific coastal zone typically experiences colder, clearer winter weather with little or no snow, but hot and humid summers.

A typical scene in mid-winter in eastern Hokkaido.

Japan's scenery is dominated by mountains. These support alpine habitats at increasing elevation from north to south. The Daisetsu Mountains of central Hokkaido with Japanese Stone Pine *Pinus pumila* in the foreground.

At higher elevations there are permanent snow fields with areas of stony tundra and alpine flower meadows between them.

Japan's habitats vary from north to south in a pattern that is mirrored in elevation, from higher to lower levels. Above the tree-limit (about 1,500 m in the higher mountains of Hokkaido, and about 2,500–3,300 m in central Honshu), there is rocky, or stony, tundra-like, high-alpine habitat. Few birds frequent this habitat in Hokkaido, but in certain areas of central Honshu it is home to species such as Rock Ptarmigan and Alpine Accentor. This habitat is dominated by prolonged periods of winter freezing, with only brief, intense summers. Above this there is only bare rock. Just below the tundra/alpine zone, and overlapping with the upper reaches of mountain forest, there is commonly a belt of hardy Japanese Stone Pine *Pinus pumila*. This habitat supports a range of species, among them Eurasian Nutcracker, Siberian Rubythroat, Alpine Accentor, Japanese Accentor and Pine Grosbeak (Hokkaido only).

Caldera Lake Shikotsu, Hokkaido, with the volcanic peaks of Tarumae and Fuppushi in the background, surrounded by mixed taiga or boreal forest.

Much of the mid-elevation mountain slopes of Hokkaido (as low as sea level in eastern Hokkaido) and northern and central Honshu support mixed taiga/boreal-like forests. These include Erman's Birch *Betula ermanii*, spruce and fir species. These habitats support a range of species, including: Eastern Buzzard, Hazel Grouse (Hokkaido only), Black Woodpecker (Hokkaido and northernmost Honshu), White-backed Woodpecker, Great Spotted Woodpecker, Japanese Pygmy Woodpecker, Brown-headed, Japanese, White's and Siberian thrushes, Japanese Robin, Red-flanked Bluetail and Sakhalin Leaf Warbler.

At middle elevations in the mountains of central Honshu (here at Kamikochi in the Northern Alps of Nagano Prefecture), the forest resembles boreal forest, but with greater species diversity, including native larches.

The dominant forest habitat of south-western lowland Hokkaido, and throughout northern and central Honshu at middle to lower elevations, is mixed temperate forest. The diversity of tree species here is very considerable, including many familiar and unfamiliar species. The most recognisable, for those from outside the region, will be the pines, larches, oaks, elms, maples, magnolias, azaleas and mountain cherries. These forests support a high diversity of resident and summer migrant birds, among them various owls, cuckoos, thrushes, flycatchers and warblers, as well as Copper Pheasant, Japanese Sparrowhawk, Grey-headed Woodpecker (Hokkaido only) and Japanese Green Woodpecker (mainland Japan south of Hokkaido).

Cool temperate forest in Aomori Prefecture, northern Honshu.

The warmer areas of mainland Japan, from central Honshu west to Shikoku and Kyushu, support very mixed forests, some of which are typically temperate deciduous, as in cool temperate forests further north, but with an increasing proportion of broadleaved evergreen trees and tall bamboos to the west and south. These forests support many of the same species as further north, but with the addition (or higher densities) of species such as Grey-faced Buzzard, Ruddy Kingfisher, Japanese Paradise Flycatcher and, very locally, Japanese Night Heron, Fairy Pitta and Dollarbird.

Warm temperate forest in Kyoto, central Honshu.

The Nansei Shoto (south-west islands), or Ryukyu archipelago, and the Ogasawara Islands support a very distinctive flora with many endemic species. The stature of forest in these areas is low, but tree species diversity is high. The year-round mild climate of these areas supports many resident avian endemic species and unique subspecies, among them Pryer's Woodpecker (Okinawa only), Amami Woodpecker (Amami only), Okinawa Rail (Okinawa only), Ryukyu Green Pigeon, Ryukyu Scops Owl, Lidth's Jay, Amami Thrush, Ryukyu Robin and Bonin Island Honeyeater.

Subtropical forest on the island of Amami Oshima, Kagoshima Prefecture.

Dry grassland habitat at Kirigamine Kogen, Nagano Prefecture, with bushes and dwarf bamboo.

In certain parts of Japan there are restricted areas of "grassland" habitat. These may be either dry or wet, and range from high-altitude meadow-like grasslands with considerable amounts of dwarf bamboo, commonly dominant around upper volcanic slopes and other areas exposed to strong winds, as diverse vegetation around alpine ponds or peat swamps, or as reedbeds around wetlands at lower elevations. These grassland areas may support Green Pheasant, Latham's Snipe, Common Cuckoo, Meadow Bunting, Stejneger's Stonechat, Long-tailed Rosefinch and Chestnut-eared Bunting.

Few species take advantage of stands of bamboo grass (e.g. *Sasa veitchii*), but two that do are the native Japanese Bush Warbler and the now well-established introduced Red-billed Leiothrix.

Japan's surviving reedbeds are home to a range of species, among them Eurasian Bittern, Yellow Bittern, Eastern Marsh Harrier, Red-crowned Crane (Hokkaido), Ruddy-breasted Crake, Marsh Grassbird, Oriental Reed Warbler, Black-browed Reed Warbler and Japanese Reed Bunting (Honshu). The reed and grass fringes of wetlands support various warblers locally in Hokkaido, among them Sakhalin Grasshopper Warbler, Middendorff's Grasshopper Warbler and Lanceolated Warbler, and at the interface between such grassland areas and woodland or agricultural areas in mainland Japan south of Hokkaido there may also be Green Pheasant and Chinese Bamboo Partridge.

The grassland area of Senjougahara (at 1,400 m) in Nikko National Park, Tochigi Prefecture.

The native wetland habitats of Japan range from alpine ponds and peat swamps, montane streams, short, fast-flowing rivers, freshwater lakes and reservoirs, to fresh and brackish coastal lagoons, and estuaries. While the first of these are mostly sterile from an avian perspective, as one descends towards lower elevations species such as Great Cormorant, Mandarin Duck, Long-billed Plover (gravel-bedded rivers), Crested Kingfisher, Common Kingfisher, Brown Dipper, Japanese Wagtail and Grey Wagtail are increasingly likely, depending on the substrate. Lake Biwa in central Japan is not only Japan's largest lake, but also one of the world's oldest surviving ancient lakes. Elsewhere, from Hokkaido to Kyushu there are very much younger volcanic caldera lakes. Lakes at low elevations in Hokkaido and northern and western Honshu support considerable numbers of wintering or migratory waterfowl, among them swans, geese and ducks. Coastal estuaries and mudflats support large numbers of herons, egrets, spoonbills, gulls and ducks (including, for example, many Falcated Duck in western Japan), and at certain seasons a wide range of migratory shorebirds, especially in western Japan. In southern Japan especially, estuaries and mudflats attract wintering Black-faced Spoonbill and Saunders's Gull.

Wetlands range from high altitude to coastal. Here, on the island of Amami Oshima, in the northern Nansei Shoto, riverine wetlands include mudflats and even mangrove forest.

Roughly 70 percent of Japan is mountainous, and perhaps half of the remaining 30 percent is developed for industry and urbanisation, leaving a relatively small proportion of the country suitable for agriculture. Japanese crops range from apples and citrus fruits to pineapples, from potatoes to sugarcane, and include tea, rushes, sugar beet and silkworms, but still the most common, in terms of area, is rice. Japan was once rich in inland river-plain wetlands and coastal wetlands, but most of these have been lost as a result of land reclamation. However, extensive areas of wet rice cultivation provide alternative homes for certain wetland species.

Rice cultivation on Sado Island, Niigata Prefecture. Mountains and forest are never far away in the Japanese landscape.

Agricultural areas, particularly rice fields, support many commensal species, and where rice fields are retained wet, or where they are farmed organically or at low intensity, they support several endangered species. Common species here include Green Pheasant, Black-eared Kite (ubiquitous in most habitats), a range of egrets and herons, various shorebirds on migration, Carrion and Large-billed crows, White-cheeked Starling, buntings and finches in winter. Very locally one can find Crested Ibis (Sado Island), Oriental Stork (Hyogo Prefecture), Greater Painted-snipe, Hooded Crane and White-naped Crane using farmland year-round or in winter.

Of Japan's approximately 126 million residents, approximately 78 percent live in urban areas (45% in Tokyo, Osaka and Nagoya). The urban environment is very densely developed, leaving rather little habitat, even for commensal species. Large-billed Crow, Rock Dove, White-cheeked Starling, Brown-eared Bulbul and Eurasian Tree Sparrow are the most widespread resident species in the largely asphalt, concrete and glass desert of the urban environment. City parks, however, attract surprising numbers of birds, especially during winter and on migration, when they support wintering waterfowl, thrushes and buntings.

As in most major Japanese cities the central business district reaches for the sky. Despite extensive urban sprawl and very dense patterns of development, Japan's urban environment includes parks and, in some areas, street trees.

Japan's coastline is largely rocky, but here and there one can find sand beaches, as here on Minami-shima, in the Ogasawara Islands.

The very extensive coastline of Japan (c 29,000 km) ranges from areas in the north that experience almost Arctic conditions, blasted by wintry northern winds, and strongly influenced by winter storms, sea-ice and the cold, south-flowing Oyashio current, to those in the south that experience almost subtropical conditions, lapped by warm seas and strongly influenced by typhoons, tropical storms and the warm, north-flowing Kuroshio current.

Rocky shores especially are the domain of Temminck's, Pelagic and Red-faced Cormorant (eastern Hokkaido only), and Harlequin Duck. Where there are sheltered bays there may be winter gatherings of Whooper Swan or Bewick's Swan, and numerous other waterfowl, and where there are eelgrass beds Brent Goose. Offshore, migrant seabirds such as divers, grebes, sea duck, and Streaked Shearwater may be found, depending on the season. In warmer regions, there are Pacific Reef Egret and Blue Rock Thrush (north to south-west Hokkaido), and in the southernmost regions, particularly in the Nansei Shoto and Ogasawara Islands, there are offshore coral reefs and seagrass beds, coral sand beaches, and at some river mouths, small areas of mangrove forest.

The remote Ogasawara Islands provide important breeding sites for seabirds and support the endemic Bonin Island Honeyeater.

The Japanese archipelago consists of several large, densely inhabited islands, a number of smaller inhabited islands and many thousands of very small islands and rocky islets, the majority of which are uninhabited. Most of the inshore islands are eroded fragments of the larger main islands, whereas the more distant ones are oceanic, the tips of submarine volcanoes that have never been connected to the main islands.

The larger islands in the Sea of Japan, from Tsushima north to Rishiri, are well-known migrant traps, where numerous vagrants to Japan have appeared. Smaller islands provide breeding grounds for significant numbers of seabirds. Teuri-jima off west Hokkaido, for example, supports a very large Rhinoceros Auklet colony, while islands off south-east Hokkaido support Leach's Storm Petrel and very small numbers of Tufted Puffin. Others, especially off western Honshu and off Kyushu, provide breeding sites for Japanese Murrelet. Further south, subtropical islets support colonies of Brown Booby, Sooty Tern, Black-naped Tern, Roseate Tern and Brown Noddy. Islands in the chain between the Izu and Bonin Islands support important populations of Short-tailed Albatross, Black-footed Albatross, Bryan's Shearwater, Tristram's Storm Petrel, Matsudaira's Storm Petrel and Bonin Petrel.

The Japanese archipelago not only spans climatic and biogeographic extremes, it also serves as a bridge between north-east Asia and south-east Asia. A major bird migration route, the East Asian-Australian Flyway, extends along the continental coast of Asia, linking regions as far apart as south-east Australia and New Zealand with Kamchatka, Yakutia, Chukotka and Alaska. Many regular summer and winter visitors and passage migrants to Japan move along this flyway or its various branches – following the line of the Japanese archipelago branching in Kyushu to the Korean Peninsula or through the main Japanese islands, branching again in Hokkaido, with some species migrating by way of the Kuril Islands and others via Sakhalin into north-east Russia. Kyushu, in particular, is known as a 'crossroads of migration'. There, for example in autumn, one can find Chinese Sparrowhawk migrating from Korea to south-east Asia over Kyushu to Amami and Okinawa, and at the same time see Oriental Honey Buzzard migrating from eastern Japan to China by way of Kyushu. Wherever the flyways cross water, wherever there are headlands, capes or offshore islands, there are regular places of landfall for tired migrants, and these make excellent places to search for common migrants and vagrants.

Whilst the annual movements of millions of birds through the region provide seasonal excitement for birders, the arrival of vagrants adds spice to the mix. Vagrants arrive in Japan from various directions, including North America; perhaps these are migrants that have overshot and reached north-eastern Russia and continued south in Asia rather than returning. Vagrants also arrive in Japan from the west, straying on migration or being blown in by storms. Furthermore, young birds of a number of species are known for their 'reverse migrations', in which they follow the opposite compass direction from the norm, some ending up in Japan. Then there are several species from ranges so far west that even though they have been recorded from the region it is tempting to speculate that they must have been escapees from Asia's enormous bird trade. The arrival of such non-migratory species as the North African Moussier's Redstart and East Africa's Grey Crowned Crane are extreme examples; they and several other species presumed to have been isolated escapes have been omitted.

Unfortunately, the huge trade in captured wild birds, of a wide range of species, in China and, to a lesser extent, in Korea and Japan, must bring out-of-range records, especially of passerines, into question. There is simply no way of knowing how many such passerine 'vagrants' are truly wild or escaped cage birds. Nevertheless, the birder's skill is field identification, and as a means to that end, this field guide covers as many species as possible – wild, well-established and introduced.

ORGANISATIONS

The Ornithological Society of Japan

An academic research organisation that publishes academic journals and occasional checklists; it adjudicates the official list of Japanese birds.

Address: OSJ Bureau, Shunkosha Co, Ltd, Lambdax Building, 2-4-12 Ohkubo, Shinjuku-ku, Tokyo 169-0072, Japan

E-mail: secretary@ornithology.jp and osj@shunkosha.com

Website: http://ornithology.jp/en/

Japan Bird Research Association

A membership, research and bird conservation organisation.

Address: 1–29–9 Sumiyoshi, Fuchu, Tokyo 183–0034, Japan.

Phone: +81-42-401-8661

E-mail: br@bird-research.jp

Website: www.bird-research.jp/

Yamashina Institute for Ornithology

A membership research and bird conservation organisation.

Address: 115 Konoyama Abiko, Chiba 270-1145, Japan

Phone: +81-4-7182-1101

E-mail: bird@yamashina.or.jp

Website: www.yamashina.or.jp/hp/english/

Wild Bird Society of Japan

A membership birdwatching and bird conservation organisation.

Address: 3-9-23 Nishi-gotanda, Shinagawa-ku, Tokyo 141-0031 Japan

Phone: +81-3-5436-2633 Fax: +81-3-5436-2635

Website: www.wbsj.org/en/

Japan Association for the Preservation of Birds

A membership birdwatching and bird conservation organisation.

Address: 3rd floor, the 10th Tanaka Bldg, 54-5, Wada, 3-chome, Suginami-ku, Tokyo 166-0012, Japan

Phone: +81-3-5378-5691 Fax: +81-3-5378-5693

Website: www.jspb.org

Japan Nature Guides

Publishes pocket guides and nature books related to Japan. Provides access to information on the natural history of Japan and on when and where to go to watch birds, mammals and other wildlife. It facilitates visits throughout the archipelago.

E-mail: enquiries@japannatureguides.com

Website: www.japannatureguides.com

REFERENCES

Brazil, M.A. 1991. *The Birds of Japan*. Christopher Helm, London.

Brazil, M.A. 2009. *Field Guide to the Birds of East Asia*. Christopher Helm, London.

David, N. & Gosselin, M. 2002a. Gender agreement of avian species. *Bulletin of the British Ornithologists' Club* 122 (1): 14–49.

David, N. & Gosselin, M. 2002b. The grammatical gender of avian genera. *Bulletin of the British Ornithologists' Club* 122 (4): 257–282.

del Hoyo, J., Elliot, A. & Sargatal, J. (eds). 1992–2013. *Handbook of the Birds of the World*. Volumes 1 to 16 & Special Volume. Lynx Edicions, Barcelona.

del Hoyo, J. & Collar, N. J. 2014. *HBW and BirdLife International Illustrated Checklist of the Birds of the World*. Volume 1: Non-passerines. Lynx Edicions, Barcelona.

del Hoyo, J. & Collar, N. J. 2016. *HBW and BirdLife International Illustrated Checklist of the Birds of the World*. Volume 2: Passerines. Lynx Edicions, Barcelona.

Dickinson, E. C. (ed). 2003. *The Howard and Moore Complete Checklist of the Birds of the World*. Third Edition. Christopher Helm, London.

Ferguson-Lees, J. & Christie, D. A. 2005. *Raptors of the World. A Field Guide*. Christopher Helm, London.

Gill, F. & Wright, M. 2006. *Birds of the World. Recommended English Names*. Christopher Helm, London.

Gill, F. & Donsker, D. (eds). 2016. IOC World Bird List (v 6.4). doi: 10.14344/IOC.ML.6.4

Gill, F. & Donsker, D. (eds). 2017. IOC World Bird List (v 7.3). doi 10.14344/IOC.ML.7.3.

Ikenaga, H., Kawakami, K. & Yanagisawa, N. 2014. Check-list of Japanese Birds 7th Revised Edition species and subspecies presently unaccepted. *Japanese Journal of Ornithology* 63 (1): 134–149 [in Japanese].

Maki, H., Onishi, T. & Iozawa, H. 2014. *A Photographic Guide to the Birds of Japan*. Nihon no Chorui 650 Heibonsha; Tokyo [in Japanese].

Robson, C. 2000. *A Guide to the Birds of Southeast Asia*. New Holland, London.

Sibley, D. A. 2014. *The North American Bird Guide. 2nd Edition*. Knopf; New York.

Svensson, L., Mullarney, K., Zetterström, D. & Grant, P. J. 2009. *Collins Bird Guide. 2nd Edition*. HarperCollins, London.

Takagawa, S., Ueta, M., Amamo, T., Okahisa, Y., Kamioki, M., Takagi, K., Takahashi, M., Hayama, S., Hirano, T., Mikami, O., Mori, S., Morimoto, G. & Yamaura, Y. 2011. JAVIAN Database: a species-level database of life history, ecology and morphology of bird species in Japan. *Bird Research* 7: R9-R12 (and its electronic database 20121010).

The Ornithological Society of Japan. 2012. *Check-list of Japanese Birds, 7th revised edition*. The Ornithological Society of Japan, Sanda.

Wild Bird Society of Japan. 2015. *A Field Guide to the Birds of Japan. 4th Edition*. Wild Bird Society of Japan, Tokyo [in Japanese].

Hazel Grouse *Tetrastes bonasia*

L 36 cm; WS 48–54 cm; WT 350–400 g

SD *T. b. vicinitas* widespread resident Hokkaido. **HH** Evergreen coniferous, mixed and, sometimes, broadleaf deciduous forests, from lowlands to *c.*1,100 m. Forages on ground and on buds, berries and fruits in trees. Typically secretive. Flies readily, but usually not far when disturbed. Roosts beneath snow in winter. **ID** Small, plump and small-headed. Grey-brown, finely barred white and grey, chestnut on scapulars, and chestnut and white on flanks. ♂ has prominent black chin and throat bordered white, small erectile crest and small red eyebrow wattle; white scapular lines visible at rest and in flight, and grey-brown tail has broad black subterminal band (except central feathers) with white tips. ♀ lacks crest and has brown throat diffusely marked white. **BP** Bill short with arched culmen, blackish-grey; narrow white ring, eyes dark brown; legs feathered (buff), toes greyish-pink. **SV** Calls from trees, remarkably sibilant and high-pitched, recalling an exceptionally loud passerine: *tsi tsi tsi tseee* or *tsst-tsst, tse tssssssssss*, also softer murmuring from ground. Loud wing-whirring on take-off. **TN** Formerly *Bonasa bonasia*. **AN** Hazelhen.

Rock Ptarmigan *Lagopus muta*

L 37 cm; WS 58 cm; WT 430–550 g

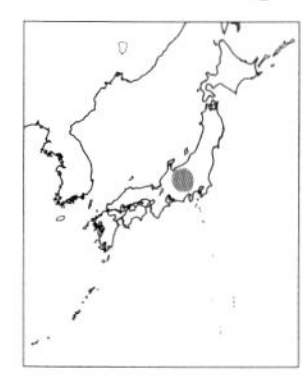

SD *L. m. japonica* threatened by combination of warming climate and predators advancing into its range on certain high peaks in the Japanese Alps, C Honshu. **HH** Alpine zone, at or above the tree-line, above 2,500 m. Moves slowly amongst lichen-covered rocks and dwarf vegetation; often confiding. In winter forms small flocks and seeks shelter at tree-line. **ID** Stocky, with white wings (primary shafts black), white belly and legs year-round. Breeding ♂ grey-brown, with black and white vermiculated pattern giving overall greyish appearance; tail black; belly, wing-coverts, vent, outertail-feather tips all white. ♀ warm tawny-brown with fine black, grey and white bars and spots; wings mainly white; lacks black lores. Non-breeding adult: all white with black tail concealed by long white uppertail-coverts. ♂ has distinctive black eyestripe and lores. Red eyebrow wattles prominent in winter and summer. **BP** Bill slender, even delicate, black; eyes black; legs and toes feathered white year-round, claws blackish. **SV** Throaty series of coughing or snoring croaks, *kuh kuh kwa guwaa*, from ground, but also when flushed, and sometimes by ♀. During aerial display flight ♂ rises on rapidly beating wings, then descends stiff-winged while giving throaty rattled cackle, *ahrrrr-ka-ka-ka-ka-ka;* ♀ has softer *gweeaa* call.

Japanese Quail *Coturnix japonica*

L 20 cm; WT 84–123 g

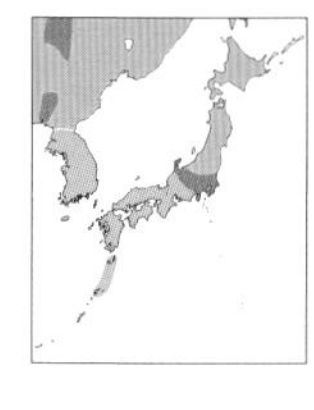

SD Now scarce, breeds Hokkaido, N Honshu, winters south to Nansei Shoto. **HH** Wet and dry meadows, dry grassland, agricultural land. Secretive, exploding into flight when disturbed. **ID** Small, plump, short-tailed, brown gamebird with long creamy supercilia (both sexes). ♂ has plain reddish-brown face, chin and throat, whereas ♀ is mottled grey-brown; well camouflaged. ♂ washed rufous on chest, white on belly, streaked rufous and cream on flanks; ♀ spotted on upper breast, white on belly. In flight, pale brown and rather uniform, with darker flight-feathers and tail barred paler brown. **BP** Bill short, grey; eyes dark brown; legs dull flesh. **SV** ♂ calls loud, rasping: *kextsu, kera keh,* or *guku kr-r-r-r;* ♀ softer *pipipipii;* also a muffled *pirrr* on take-off.

Chinese Bamboo Partridge *Bambusicola thoracicus*

L 28–33 cm; WT 200–350 g

SD Introduced; widespread, common, Honshu (south of Miyagi), also Sado, Tsushima, Izu and Iwo Is. **HH** Evergreen broadleaf forests with dense underbrush, woodlands and parks in lowlands and low hills. Sociable, but secretive. ♂♂ often chorus at dawn and dusk. **ID** Large, plump partridge with distinctive pale blue-grey forehead, supercilia and upper breast; chin, face and neck-sides bright rufous-chestnut. Upperparts mid-brown with chestnut, black and white spots on mantle and wing-coverts, rump greyish-brown, tail finely barred, outer tail-feathers rufous-brown, conspicuous in flight. Blue-grey lower neck, buff on lower breast, belly, flanks and vent, heavily spotted black on flanks. **BP** Bill grey-black; eyes dark brown; tarsi greenish-grey, ♂ has tarsal spurs. **SV** Highly vocal, pairs duet loudly: *chottokoi chottokoi*, or *pippyu kwai pippyu kwai* with calls rising to a crescendo.

Taiwan Bamboo Partridge *Bambusicola sonorivox*

L 27–31 cm; WT 200–342 g

SD Introduced; established resident, C Honshu (Hyogo Prefecture). **HH** As Chinese Bamboo Partridge (CBP). **ID** Resembles CBP, but generally darker, with more extensive and darker grey on face, neck and breast, with rufous restricted to chin, and deeper orange-brown underparts with chestnut, not black, flank spots. **BP** As CBP. **SV** As CBP.

ad ♂
Hazel Grouse
ad ♂
ad ♀
Rock Ptarmigan
ad ♂ sum
ad ♂ win
ad ♂ sum
ad ♂ win
ad ♀ win
ad ♀ sum
ad ♀
ad ♂
Japanese Quail
Chinese Bamboo Partridge calling
ad
Chinese Bamboo Partridge
ad
Taiwan Bamboo Partridge

Copper Pheasant *Syrmaticus soemmerringii* ♂ L 125 cm, WT 940–1350 g; ♀ 55 cm, WT 745–1000 g

SD Endemic: Honshu, Kyushu, Shikoku. *S. s. scintillans* N & W Honshu; *S. s. subrufus* Pacific side C & SW Honshu, Shikoku; *S. s. intermedius* northern side of SW Honshu, also Shikoku; *S. s. soemmerringii* N & C Kyushu; and *S. s. ijimae* C & S Kyushu. **HH** Mixed broadleaf evergreen and coniferous montane forests, shady areas from low to mid elevations. **ID** ♂ elegant, chestnut with extremely long (48–98 cm) cinnamon tail with dark brown and fawn bands. Bare facial skin red; lacks wattles. ♀ smaller, shorter-tailed (14–19 cm); dark brown with large pale scales on flanks, belly and vent; white tip to tail. ♂♂ become darker and richer chestnut from north to south. *S. s. scintillans*: broad white fringes to belly and flanks, narrow white fringes to rump and uppertail-coverts. *S. s. subrufus*: deeper chestnut than nominate; lacks white fringing; rump more golden. *S. s. soemmerringii*: amber fringes to rump and uppertail-covert tips. *S. s. ijimae*: deeper chestnut, lacks white fringes; large white rump and uppertail-covert patch. **BP** Bill grey-black; eyes dark brown; legs grey. **SV** ♂ guttural *guru guru*, indistinct hoarse *ko-ko ko* calls and high-pitched *heese!* in aggression or if flushed. During late winter/early spring, ♂ produces deep drumming sounds with its wings. ♂♀ give quiet *kyup* calls while feeding.

Common Pheasant *Phasianus colchicus* ♂ L 75–89 cm, WT 707–1990 g; ♀ L 53–62 cm, WT 0.545–1.453 kg, WS 70–90 cm

SD Introduced; scarce, Hokkaido (*P. c. pallasi*), possibly native on Tsushima (*P. c. karpowi*). Uncertain subspecies introduced to Iwo, Izu and Nansei Shoto. **HH** Farmland, lowland dry scrub and woodland edge. **ID** ♂ hood and ear-tufts greenish-black, with blue, green or purple sheen; warty red facial wattle extends to forehead, chin and cheeks; complete or partial white collar. Brown to copper-bronze mantle scaled white; large powder-grey wing panel; lower back and rump grey-green, the loose feathers puffed and drooping; tail long, dark grey-brown with prominent transverse black bands. ♀ cryptic, with shorter tail with dark brown bands. *P. c. pallasi*: paler crown and reduced facial wattle. **BP** Bill short, arched, horn-coloured; eyes yellow (♂) or dull orange (♀); tarsi greyish-green. **SV** ♂'s loud, guttural *hok-kok* display call, given repeatedly from prominent low perch or ground, is typically followed by noisy wing-drumming. A loud, harsh crowing *kerrch-krch!* When flushed bursts from cover with noisy wing-whirring and screechy, rattling *kr-krk-krk krk krk*. **AN** Ring-necked Pheasant.

Green Pheasant *Phasianus versicolor* ♂ L 80 cm, WT 850–1100 g; ♀ L 60 cm, WT 600–970 g

SD Endemic: Honshu, Sado, Izu Is, Shikoku, Kyushu, Yakushima and Tanegashima. *P. v. robustipes* N Honshu and Sado; *P. v. tohkaidi* C & W Honshu and Shikoku; *P. v. tanensis* southern C Honshu and islands south of Honshu and Kyushu; *P. v. versicolor* extreme SW Honshu, Kyushu and Goto Is. **HH** Woodland and grassland edges, brush and parkland. **ID** Darker, more compact than Common Pheasant, with shorter, broader tail (27–42.5 cm) commonly held more cocked. ♂ hood bluish-purple with prominent ear-tufts, rounded red facial wattles; lacks white collar. Neck, mantle, breast and flanks deep bottle green. Wing-coverts, lower back and rump pale powder grey; tail long (but shorter with more prominent outer tail feathers than Common), pale grey-brown banded dark. ♀ smaller, shorter-tailed (21–27.5 cm); cryptically coloured, with dark brown feathers fringed pale brown, affording darker, heavily scaled pattern to entire body and wings than ♀ Common. White crescent below eye, scales on body and bands on tail more prominent and more uniform than in slightly smaller ♀ Copper Pheasant, and lacks latter's white-tipped tail. **BP** Bill pale horn (♂) or grey (♀); large red wattles, eyes pale yellow (♂) or dark brown (♀); legs pinkish-grey. **SV** ♂ *ko-kyok* calls (higher and hoarser than Common) are commonly followed by noisy wingbeats. **TN** Formerly within Ring-necked Pheasant *P. colchicus* (e.g. OSJ). **AN** Japanese Green Pheasant.

Indian Peafowl *Pavo cristatus* ♂ L 180–230 cm, WS 130–160 cm, WT 4000–6000 g; ♀ L 90–100 cm,WS 80–130 cm, WT 2750–4000 g

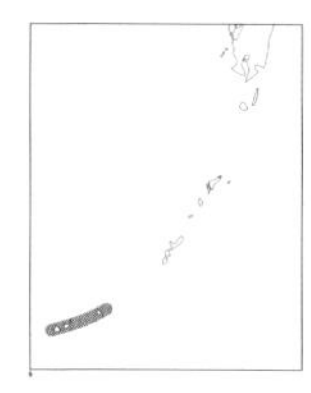

SD Introduced; established Sakishima Is (Miyako to Yonaguni), S Nansei Shoto, and Satsuma Iwojima, N Nansei Shoto. **HH** Social and polygamous; inhabits rural farmland, forest edge. **ID** ♂ bluish-purple head, neck and breast, small fan crest, and enormously long green 'train' (elongated uppertail-coverts; 140–160 cm). Smaller ♀ shares fan crest; drabber dark grey-brown, with short (32.5–37.5 cm) dark-grey tail lacking 'train'. In flight, wings short, broad with chestnut (♂) or brown (♀) primaries. **BP** Bill short, blackish-grey; eyes dark brown; tarsi grey. **SV** Very loud nasal wailing *erWAAH*; also loud rustling made by rattling tail quills.

Copper Pheasant
scintillans
ad ♂
ad ♀
ad ♂ ijimae
Common Pheasant
pallasi
ad ♀
ad ♂
Green Pheasant
tokhaidi
ad ♀
ad ♂
Indian Peafowl
Peafowl and pheasant to indicate scale
ad ♀
ad ♂
(not to scale with pheasants)

Lesser Whistling Duck *Dendrocygna javanica* L 40 cm; WT 450–600 g

SD Accidental Ryukyu Is. (formerly resident). **HH** Swamps, mangroves and wet ricefields; crepuscular. Perches in trees and walks well on land. **ID** Slightly larger than Eurasian Teal, but long neck and upright stance very different from dabbling ducks. Greyish-buff face and neck, darker on crown. Upperparts dark blackish-brown with warmer rufous-brown fringes to coverts and mantle. Underparts paler rufous-brown, flanks and belly warmer. Dark wings with bright chestnut patch on lesser and median coverts and uppertail-coverts, and short blackish-brown tail. **BP** Bill small, dark grey; inconspicuous yellow eye-ring, eyes black; long tarsi and toes blackish-grey. **SV** In flight gives sibilant, shrill, oft-repeated whistled *sweesik*.

Swan Goose *Anser cygnoides* L 81–94 cm; WS 165–185 cm; WT 2800–4200 g

SD Vulnerable. Very rare and declining migrant and winter visitor (not annual) mainly to northern Japan, but has reached south to Ryukyu Is. **HH** Wetlands surrounded by grasslands or flooded vegetation, occasionally wet ricefields and tidal mudflats. **ID** Long-bodied, slender, with long, uniquely bicoloured neck. Long bill and head profile recall Whooper Swan, and feeds on land in similar fashion. Neck appears longer than other geese because of habit of craning neck upwards. Crown and stripe on nape dark chestnut, with buffy cheeks and breast, and white foreneck. Upperparts mid to dark brown, underparts grade from buff to dark brown; flanks, vent, rump, tail tip and undertail white. **BP** Bill long, black with narrow white border at base; eyes brown; tarsi and toes pinkish-orange. **SV** Honking and cackling *gahan gahan gagagaga* in flight, like domestic geese ('Chinese Goose' derived from this species).

Taiga Bean Goose *Anser fabalis* L 90–100 cm; WS 180–200 cm; WT ♂ 5100 g, ♀ 4600 g

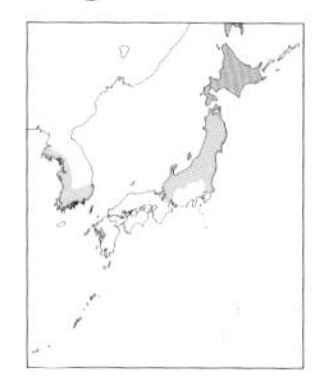

SD *A. f. middendorffi* is a winter visitor (Sep–Apr) that migrates into Japan via Sakhalin and Hokkaido to winter in N & C Honshu; rare winter visitor south to Shikoku, Kyuyshu and Nansei Shoto. OSJ records *A. f. curtus* as accidental to N Honshu and Ogasawara Is. **HH** Large lakes, marshy wetlands and agricultural land; rivers when staging. **ID** Large and long-winged, with very dark head and neck contrasting with paler underparts. Larger than Tundra Bean Goose. Pale buff fringes to scapulars and wings. Tail dark grey-brown with crescentic white base and narrow white tips. Lower neck, breast and belly paler grey-brown with darker scalloping on flanks; vent, uppertail base and undertail white. Taiga has long, somewhat slender bill and a Whooper Swan-like head and bill shape. In flight, mantle, upperwing, rump and underwing all dark (cf. Greylag), whilst white fringes to tertials and scapulars make back more patterned than Greater White-fronted. Whilst both Taiga and Tundra clearly differ in proportions from Greater White-fronted, in flight they may be confused; however, both have pale, unbarred bellies. Juvenile Greater White-fronted (lacks white facial blaze) best separated by plain, drab blackish-yellow bill and voice. Poorly known *A. f. curtus* is very small. **BP** Bill mostly black, with yellow-orange patch near tip (unlike young of other *Anser*). Taiga bill is relatively long and slender. Eyes hazelnut or dark brown; tarsi orange. **SV** Generally lower, slower and hoarser than other geese. Taiga has a rather deep, somewhat buzzy honking *gahahaan* or *gangh-gangh*, and gives a staccato *kakako* contact call in flight.

Tundra Bean Goose *Anser serrirostris* L 78–89 cm; WS 140–175 cm; WT 2800–4200 g

SD Winters (Sep–Apr) largely in N Honshu, migrating there via Hokkaido; rare winter visitor further south. **HH** Large lakes, marshy wetlands and agricultural land; rivers when staging. **ID** Large and long-winged, with very dark head and neck contrasting with paler underparts. Pale buff fringes to scapulars and wings. Tail dark grey-brown with crescentic white base and narrow white tips. Lower neck, breast and belly paler grey-brown with darker scalloping on flanks; vent, uppertail base and undertail white. Compared with Taiga Bean Goose, Tundra has shorter, thicker neck, rounder head and stubbier bill, giving strongly sloping profile; appears 'glum-faced'. In flight, mantle, upperwing, rump and underwing all dark (cf. Greylag), whilst white fringes to tertials and scapulars make back more patterned than Greater White-fronted. **BP** Bill mostly black, with yellow-orange patch near tip (unlike young of other *Anser*). Bill is short, deep-based, with prominent 'grin' line. Eyes hazelnut or dark brown; tarsi orange. **SV** Generally lower, slower and hoarser than other geese. Tundra gives a more metallic *gyahahaan*, which sounds more muffled or hollow than Taiga.

Lesser Whistling Duck
ads
(not to scale with geese)
Swan Goose
ad
ad
Taiga Bean Goose
middendorffi
ad
Taiga Bean Goose flock with
single Swan Goose
Tundra Bean Goose
ad

Greylag Goose *Anser anser*

L 75–90 cm; WS 147–180 cm; WT 2000–4500 g

SD *A. a. rubrirostris* (Eastern Greylag Goose) accidental winter visitor (Oct–Apr). **HH** Lakes, rivers, wet ricefields. **ID** Large, heavy, rather uniform pale grey-brown goose, size similar to Taiga Bean, but neck shorter and thicker, head larger and paler, bill shorter and stouter. Broad pale tips to mantle and coverts form barred pattern. Deep dark grooves on neck; dark bars on flanks and some dark spots on belly, but never as extensive as Greater White-fronted Goose. Young very similar, but upperparts scalloped rather than neatly barred. In flight, pale grey primary and lesser coverts contrast with dark grey-brown median coverts and back; rump noticeably pale grey, and grey-brown tail has white base and broad white band at tip; underwing-coverts also pale, contrasting strongly with darker remiges. **BP** Bill dull pink; weak pink eye-ring, irides black; tarsi and toes dull pink. **SV** Varied shrill, high-pitched notes and deep raucous honks: *ahng ahng ahng* (deeper, more barked than Bean). Frequently gives clanging calls in flight.

Greater White-fronted Goose *Anser albifrons*

L 65–78 cm; WS 130–165 cm; WT 1800–2500 g

SD *A. a. albifrons* winters south to Honshu (Oct–Mar), migrates through Hokkaido (Sep/Oct and Apr/May). Occasional larger individuals may originate in N America. **HH** Highly gregarious, foraging and roosting at large lakes, reservoirs, marshy wetlands, flooded vegetation, agricultural land. Typically roosts (often in tens of thousands) at lakes and forages on snow-free fields. **ID** Compact, mid-sized brownish-grey goose with rather short neck, prominent white face patch and strong flank line; black transverse bars across pale breast and belly form individually variable barcode-like pattern (often lacking in young). Young Lesser and Greater White-fronted and Greylag, have darker grey faces than adults. **BP** Relatively chunky deep-based bill, dull pink, bright pink or orange with white nail (dull yellow with dark nail in young, paler than Bean), surrounded at base and onto forehead by white blaze (cf. Lesser), developing late in first winter; eyes black; tarsi and toes orange. **SV** Very vocal; repetitive, abrupt yapping or musical honking, *kyow-yow-yow*, rapid, high-pitched jerky laughing *widawink widawink*… in flight, and deeper *calls* when flushed.

Lesser White-fronted Goose *Anser erythropus*

L 53–66 cm; WS 115–135 cm; WT 1400–2500 g

SD Vulnerable. Rare, very small numbers winter (Oct–Mar) N Honshu, migrating via Hokkaido. **HH** Typically singly or in family groups amongst other geese (often Greater White-fronted Goose) at wetland roosts and on agricultural land, but foraging movements (walking and pecking) faster than other geese, thus often near leading edge of moving flocks. **ID** Smallest, most delicate grey goose, largest just reach size of smallest Greater, but with smaller head, higher forehead, smaller more colourful bill and shorter, thicker neck, more prominent white blaze and distinctive yellow eye-ring. Plumage like Greater, but darker-backed, belly bars fewer, less distinct and not extending as far onto sides as Greater; head rounder, wings longer and narrower, primaries extend well beyond tail tip. 1st-winter noticeably darker brown and more compact than young Greater. **BP** Bill short, delicate, bright pink; narrow white blaze extends on forehead as triangular wedge when seen front on (reduced or absent in juvenile and bordered by narrow black line), higher on crown than Greater and more neatly rounded; prominent narrow yellow orbital in adult and juvenile, eyes black; tarsi and toes yellowish-orange. Beware – some Greater show more prominent eye-rings and more extensive white shields. **SV** Calls higher pitched, sharp and squeaky, more yelping than Greater: *kyuru-kyu kyu kyukyu* or *plewewew-whew!*

Bar-headed Goose *Anser indicus*

L 71–76 cm; WS 140–160 cm; WT 2000–3000 g

SD Accidental, winter/spring, N Honshu, Hokkaido. **HH** Freshwater swamps, lakes and rivers. **ID** Large, very pale grey goose, with distinctive white head and face, white stripe on sides of plain dark-grey neck and two black crescents, one across rear crown to eyes, the other shorter, around upper nape; hindneck dark greyish-black. Body pale grey with blackish-grey patch on flanks. Young have greyer neck, white face and solid black rear crown (no bars). In flight, long wings largely pale grey, contrasting with black secondaries and primary tips, otherwise pale, but dark flank patch visible. **BP** Bill dull yellow-orange with black nail; eyes black; tarsi and toes dull yellowish-orange. **SV** Low, nasal honking *gaaaa gaaaa gaaaa*.

Greylag Goose
ad
ad
juv
Greater White-
fronted Goose
ad
juv
ad
ad
Lesser White-
fronted Goose
juv
ad
Bar-headed Goose
ad
ad
juv

Snow Goose *Anser caerulescens* L 66–84 cm; WS 132–165 cm; WT 2800–4500 g

SD Once abundant winter visitor to N & C Japan, recovering from near extermination. Small flocks winter annually in N Honshu, migrating via south-central Hokkaido. Mostly **Lesser Snow Goose** *A. c. caerulescens*; **Greater Snow Goose** *A. c. atlanticus* is vagrant. **HH** Lakes, marshes, agricultural land. **ID** Adult: small, all-white with black primaries. 1st-winter: dingy grey upperparts and neck. Accidental dark morph (N American 'Blue Goose') is largely blue-grey with white head and wing-coverts; intermediates occur between 'blue' and white extremes. 'Blue Goose' recalls Emperor, but has clear-cut white hindneck, dark foreneck and much larger bill. **Greater** is larger, heavier, with longer, deeper bill and obvious 'grin'. **BP** Bill pink with prominent black 'grin' (cutting edge) between gape and tip; eyes black; tarsi pink. **SV** Calls include: deep *angk-ak-ak-ak* alarm, a repetitive, soft nasal monosyllabic *whouk* or upward-inflected heron-like *heenk*, and low-pitched grunts when foraging.

Emperor Goose *Anser canagicus* L 66–71 cm; WS 119 cm; WT 2300–3200 g

SD Accidental winter visitor. **HH** Rocky shores, sandy coasts, coastal marshes/wetlands. **ID** Small, stocky, uniquely patterned. Adult: largely dark silver-grey, with black chin, throat and foreneck; head, hindneck and tail white, head may be stained rusty-orange. Head rounded with high forecrown. Young: neck and head grey and entire plumage has rounded pale fringes; scalloped pattern recalls young grey geese, though entirely blue-grey. In flight, all-dark; grey wings, blackish rump and white tail. **BP** Bill small, pink (ad), or greyish-pink (juv); eyes black; legs and feet bright orange. **SV** Low grunting sounds on ground, and rapid, high-pitched double or triple honks *kurahha kurahha* or *kla-ga kla-ga* on take-off and in flight; also *urru guup rugu* in alarm.

Cackling Goose *Branta hutchinsii* L 56–68 cm; WS 115–130 cm; WT 2000 g

SD Aleutian Goose *B. h. leucopareia* recovering from near extinction. Scarce, but winters annually and in increasing numbers (Oct–Apr) in N Japan. *B. h. minima* occasionally recorded. **Taverner's Goose** *B. h. taverneri* accidental. **HH** Lakes, marshes and agricultural land. **ID** Small, dark grey-brown goose, slightly larger than Brent. Head (rather square) and neck black with white chin and cheeks, and white ring at base of neck (sometimes distinct, or incomplete and occasionally lacking). Upperparts dark ashy grey-brown with buff fringes to mantle, scapulars and coverts. Slightly paler on breast and belly, white on vent. In flight very dark, only vent and rump white. Wingbeats rather fast and wings held forwards. *B. h. minima* slightly smaller than **Aleutian**, with darker brown breast (purplish cast) and back, short neck, barely visible collar (sometimes absent), more rounded head, small bill and relatively long legs. Occasional larger individuals are possibly **Taverner's**. **BP** Small black bill tapers to narrow tip; eyes black; tarsi black. **SV** Rather high-pitched, squeaky *yeek* or *uriik*, and deeper nasal *guwa guwa*. **AN** Lesser Canada Goose.

Canada Goose *Branta canadensis* L 68–114 cm; WS 119–152 cm; WT 2300–4500 g

SD *B. c. moffitti* introduced and established in Honshu (Ibaraki, Kanagawa, Yamanashi, Shizuoka and Aichi prefectures). *B. c. parvipes* (apparently wild) vagrant to Hokkaido. **HH** Lakes and rivers. **ID** Medium to large, black-necked, white-cheeked grey-brown goose, with paler and greyer lower neck/breast. In flight, contrast between black neck and paler body/wings obvious, as is white rump against black tail. **BP** Short to long black bill; eyes black; tarsi black. **SV** Repetitive deep nasal honks and distinctive bisyllabic *gah-hut*, with clear pitch change from low to high. **AN** Greater Canada Goose.

Brent Goose *Branta bernicla* L 56–61 cm; WS 110–120 cm; WT 1500–2250 g

SD *B. b. nigricans* (Black-bellied Brent Goose) winters (mid Oct–late Apr) Hokkaido and N Honshu; rare further south. **HH** Saltwater; shallow bays, coastal lagoons, estuaries, and along sandy shores; very rare inland, occasionally joins other geese at lakes or on agricultural land. **ID** Very small, dark, with strongly contrasting white on flanks, tail and vent. Head and neck black, as are upperparts and breast, albeit fringed grey, giving frosted appearance. Adult has prominent broad white necklace on throat, broadest at front, with dark flecks. Juvenile lacks white necklace and has broad pale tips to upperwing-coverts. In flight, only white vent and uppertail-coverts prominent. Wings pointed, slightly swept back; flight fast, often low, and usually in large straggling flocks, less linear than larger geese. **BP** Bill very short, dark blackish-grey; eyes black; short tarsi black. **SV** Deep, rolling, guttural bark-like *gurururu* or *guwawa*. Flocks maintain constant low murmuring or gargling sounds. **AN** Black Brant.

Snow Goose
caerulescens
ad blue phase
ad blue phase
atlanticus
ad
ad blue
phase
juv
blue phase
ad white
phase
juv white
phase
Emperor Goose
stained ad
ad
ad
juv
Canada Goose
parvipes
ad
Cackling Goose
leucopareia
ad
minima
ad
Brent Goose
ad
juv

Black Swan *Cygnus atratus*

L 110–140 cm; WS 160–200 cm; WT 3700–8750 g

SD Introduced, scarce; recorded Hokkaido to Kyushu. **HH** Castle moats, rivers, lakes. **ID** Black, with extremely long, slender neck, raised 'crinkly' wing feathers and white primaries. **BP** Bill, and bare skin extending to eyes, waxy red, with subterminal white band; eyes red; tarsi dark grey or pinkish-grey.

Mute Swan *Cygnus olor*

L 125–160 cm; WS 200–240 cm; WT 8000–16000 g

SD Introduced; also accidental. Established from SW Hokkaido to C & W Honshu and S Kyushu. **HH** Shallow lakes, rivers, castle moats. Confiding; can be aggressive. **ID** Graceful S-shaped neck. Adult: white, head and neck sometimes tinged rusty-orange. Juvenile: grey-brown, whitening with age, some cygnets all-white. On water, wings form high cushion-like dome, tail longer than congeners, more pointed and typically cocked. **BP** Bill deep orange-red with black tip, nostril, base and knob (ad, larger in ♂), or black, fading to dull grey-pink, lacks knob (juv); eyes black; legs and feet black. **SV** Snake-like hissing, grunts and explosive snorting *nyeeorrr*. Runs heavily and noisily across water for take-off, flight audible, laborious wing beats make loud rhythmic throbbing sound.

Trumpeter Swan *Cygnus buccinator*

L 150–180 cm; WS 230–260 cm; WT 7300–12500 g

SD Accidental; Hokkaido, Honshu (Oct–Apr), has wintered. **HH** Ice-free lakes, lagoons, rivers; occasionally farmland. **ID** Resembles Whooper Swan. Feathering on forehead extends forward to point (cf. dark-billed Whistling Swan). Adult: white. 1st-winter: grey-brown on mantle, wings, head and neck. **BP** Bill long, straight and rather angular, black with dark red wedge at base and on lower cutting edge, exposed when beak open (red 'lips' or gape line sometimes lacking); bare black facial skin. 1st-winter's bill is dull pink, but black-based and black-tipped; eyes black; tarsi olive-brown (juv), or black (ad). **SV** Soft nasal honking call is less barking than Whooper Swan's.

Bewick's Swan *Cygnus (columbianus) bewickii*

L 120–140 cm; WS 167–225 cm; WT 6000–8000 g

SD Common winter visitor (Oct–mid April), migrating via Hokkaido to Honshu. **HH** Ice-free lakes and farmland. **ID** Smaller, more compact than Whooper Swan; neck shorter, head rounder, profile gentler. Head peaks at mid-crown; feathering on forehead rounded. Adult: all-white, sometimes with rusty-orange staining, especially on head and foreparts. 1st-winter: dark grey, whitening with age. On water, folded primaries cover horizontal tail. More agile on land than Whooper or Mute. **BP** Bill black with some yellow; pattern is individually variable. Bill shorter, slightly more concave, and proportionately broader-tipped than Whooper's. Culmen often partly, or entirely, black to feathers; may have rounded deep yellow patch from eyes towards nostril. Yellow patch smaller, more rounded, less wedge-shaped than Whooper's. Commonly has narrow yellow wedge at base of lower mandible. 1st-winter bill deep reddish-pink, then black, yellow portion initially white. Eyes brown, occasionally blue or grey; tarsi and toes black. **SV** Higher-pitched, more yapping than Whooper (some overlap). Calls, given singly or doubled, a nasal *koho* or *koho koho*. **AN Tundra Swan** when lumped with following species.

Whistling Swan *Cygnus (columbianus) columbianus*

L 120–150 cm; WS 167–225 cm; WT 4300–9600 g

SD Rare winter visitor; usually among Bewick's Swan (BS). **HH** As BS. **ID** Generally larger than BS. **BP** Bill black, larger, deeper based, less concave than BS, culmen all-black with yellow pre-orbital teardrop. Entirely black-billed individuals (scarce) resemble larger Trumpeter, when rounder head shape and rounded feather line on forehead distinguish it. Rare hybrid Bewick's x Whistling either intermediate or resembles either parent. Eyes brown, occasionally blue or grey; tarsi and toes black. **SV** Call higher-pitched, more musical *klooo* or *kwooo* than BS.

Whooper Swan *Cygnus cygnus*

L 140–165 cm; WS 205–243 cm; WT 8000–12000 g

SD Common winter visitor (Oct–mid-April), Hokkaido, N Honshu; has occasionally bred Hokkaido. **HH** Bays, rivers and ice-free lakes, occasionally farmland. **ID** Large, long-necked; upper neck held vertically, head horizontally, crown peak near rear of head. Adult: white, often tinged rusty-orange on head, neck and breast. 1st-winter: grey, whitening with age. On water, folded primaries cover horizontal tail. **BP** Bill (ad) largely black with extensive yellow wedge from featherline to at least nostrils. Bill initially pink (juv), whitens, then becomes yellow by late winter. Eyes brown, but blue and grey not uncommon; tarsi and feet black. **SV** Frequent bugling calls resemble Bewick's, but louder, deeper, and in threes and fours: *a-hoo a-hoo a-hoo*. Family and flock members use soft *hu-hu* contact calls. Displaying pairs duet, giving strong bugling calls.

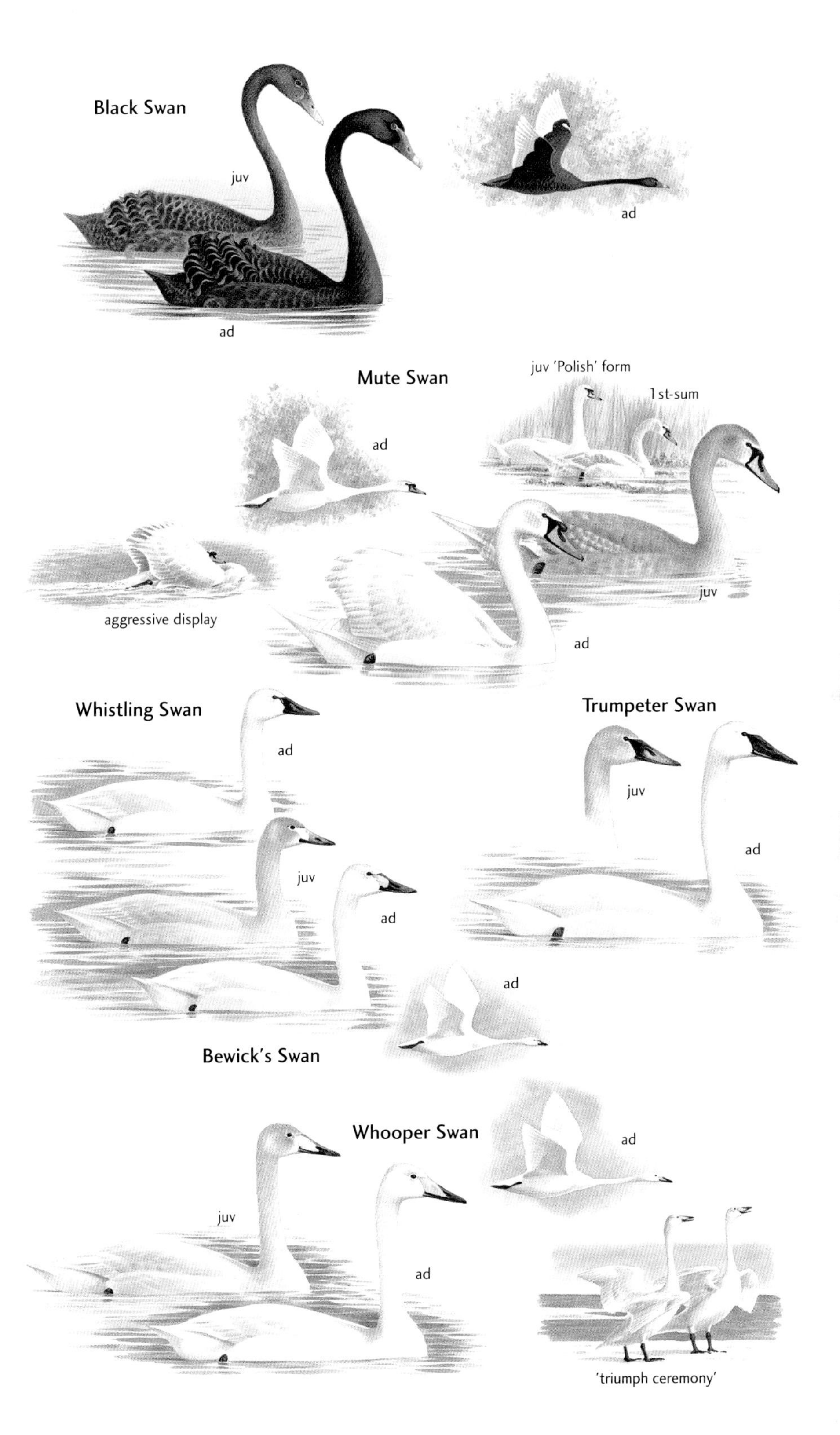

Black Swan
juv
ad
ad
Mute Swan
juv 'Polish' form
1st-sum
ad
aggressive display
juv
ad
Whistling Swan
ad
juv
ad
Trumpeter Swan
juv
ad
ad
Bewick's Swan
Whooper Swan
ad
juv
ad
'triumph ceremony'

Common Shelduck *Tadorna tadorna*

L 56–65 cm; WS 100–133 cm; WT 700–900 g

SD Winters (Oct–Apr) locally S Japan (especially Kyushu); scarce elsewhere. **HH** Coastal mudflats, wetlands. Walks on mudflats or in shallow water, sieving food from water and wet mud. **ID** Large, plump, black, white and chestnut duck, with goose-like proportions, though head larger, neck shorter and legs longer. Adult: blackish-green head and scapulars, and white body with broad dark chestnut band on chest and upper back. Flight-feathers, scapulars, belly stripe and tail black, secondaries with green gloss, tertials chestnut. Juvenile/1st-winter: grey head, neck and upperparts, and white-tipped flight-feathers forming trailing edge to wing. In flight, clearly pied; wings long, pointed, white coverts contrast with black remiges, wingbeats strong and fast. **BP** Bill short, broad (especially tip), deep red (ad ♂ with prominent knob on forehead), or dull pinkish-red (♀ lacks knob); eyes black; tarsi and toes pale pink. **SV** ♂ gives sibilant single- or double-noted whistled *suwees-suwees* on water or in aerial pursuit, also a rapid, somewhat goose-like, guttural growling; ♀ gives nasal quacking *gaggagagaga*... Wings emit dull whistle in flight.

Ruddy Shelduck *Tadorna ferruginea*

L 60–70 cm; WS 110–135 cm; WT 1000–1400 g

SD Rare winter visitor. **HH** Agricultural land (walks well and grazes like a goose), coastal wetlands. **ID** Large orange-brown duck, larger than smallest geese. Body bright orange-chestnut, paler peach on upper neck and head; sometimes white around eyes or bill base. ♂ (breeding) has narrow black collar; ♀ has paler head and lacks collar. Dark flight-feathers (black primaries, green-glossed secondaries) contrast strongly with white forewing and white underwing-coverts. Young have greyer forewing. **BP** Bill blackish-grey; eyes black; tarsi black. **SV** Calls include loud, nasal honking, somewhat goose-like *aakh* or *aang-aang*, an abrupt *pok-pok-pok* and rolling *ahrrrr*.

Mandarin Duck *Aix galericulata*

L 41–47 cm; WS 65–75 cm; WT 444–650 g

SD Breeds along upland rivers (C & N Honshu) and lowland lakes and streams (Hokkaido). Winters C Honshu to Kyushu. **HH** Secluded forested rivers and streams, where nests in tree cavities. On migration and in winter forms flocks; winters at ponds and lakes with well-vegetated and wooded margins, or along fast-flowing rivers; roosts in trees and often feeds onshore. **ID** Slightly smaller than Eurasian Wigeon, with large, maned head and long tail. Breeding ♂ gaudy; largely orange-brown, forehead green, hindcrown orange; white stripe from eye arcs back over head-sides with prominent orange 'whiskers' and 'mane' making head appear even larger, and sweeping creamy white band from eyes to tip of mane. Enlarged orange tertials form distinctive 'sails' rising vertically over lower back. Vertical black and white stripes on breast-sides contrast with purplish-black breast and orange-brown flanks. ♀ mostly grey and olive-brown, with neat white spectacles around eyes and white line behind eyes on plain grey head; white also at bill base. Eclipse ♂ resembles ♀, but has bright pink bill. In flight, appears large-headed, with plain dark grey-brown wings, blue-green speculum with white trailing edge to secondaries; ♂'s chestnut tertials visible. **BP** Bill reddish-pink (♂ all year) or grey (♀) with white nail; eyes black; tarsi orange. **SV** ♂ gives rather varied high, melodious, upwardly inflected whistles: *kehp kehp*, or *pyui*, and rather high, hoarse *ghett* calls, whereas ♀ gives deeper clucking *kyu* or *kwa* calls.

Cotton Pygmy Goose *Nettapus coromandelianus*

L 31–38 cm; WT 380–403 g

SD *N. c. coromandelianus* vagrant, Yonagunijima, Taramajima (S Nansei Shoto), Osaka (W Honshu). **HH** Freshwater ponds, well-vegetated streams and wet ricefields. **ID** Tiny, very pale goose-like duck with black cap. Breeding ♂ white and green, with plain white face, black crown, black band on breast and lower neck. ♀ less contrasting, browner instead of blackish-green, and lacks black breast-band and white wing-band. ♀, young and eclipse ♂ all have black stripe from bill to ear-coverts. In flight, wings largely bottle-green with broad white band on remiges (♂) or greyish-black with white trailing edge to secondaries (♀). **BP** Black bill is tiny; eyes dark reddish-brown (♂) or brown (♀); tarsi black. **SV** ♂ gives rather low, nasal *wuk wirrarakwuk*, ♀ gives a weak *quack*; groups utter babbling *nyar-nyar-nyar*. **AN** Cotton Teal.

Common Shelduck
juv
ad ♂
juv
ad ♀
ad ♂
Ruddy Shelduck
ad ♂
breeding
ad ♀
ad ♂
breeding
Mandarin Duck
ad ♀
ad ♂
ad ♀
ad ♂
Cotton Pygmy Goose
ad ♂
juvenile
♂
eclipse
ad ♀
ad ♂
ad ♀

Gadwall *Mareca strepera*

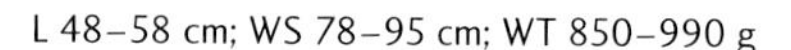
L 48–58 cm; WS 78–95 cm; WT 850–990 g

SD *M. s. strepera* breeds locally E Hokkaido; winters widely C Honshu to Kyushu. **HH** Well-vegetated wetlands in summer; shallow freshwater lakes, coastal lagoons and rivers on migration and in winter. **ID** Rather dark, slightly smaller and noticeably slimmer than Mallard, with more rounded head and smaller bill. Breeding ♂: dull brownish-grey head, dark grey body with pale breast scalloping, black tail-sides, vent, rump and tail-coverts. Chestnut patch and white square visible on closed wing. Eclipse ♂ resembles ♀, but has plain grey tertials and retains wing pattern. ♀: dull blackish-brown (like ♀ Falcated, but has white patch on closed wing), with dark tertials; tail and vent brown, not black. Floats higher than Mallard; feeds more like wigeon. In flight, wings narrower than Mallard; ♂ has prominent white speculum, black and chestnut patches on upperwing; ♀ also has white speculum (less conspicuous, even absent), but lacks chestnut patch; belly white but less clean-cut than Eurasian Wigeon. **BP** Bill dark greyish-black (♂), or grey culmen with orange sides speckled grey (♀); eyes black; tarsi reddish-orange. **SV** ♂ gives high-pitched whistle and low croaking *kua*; ♀ a repetitive rather high-pitched quacking *gaa-gaa-gaa* or *ge-ge-ge* recalling Mallard, but more nasal. In flight, harsh *gerssh gerssh*.

Falcated Duck *Mareca falcata*

L 46–53 cm; WS 78–82 cm; WT ♂ 580–710g, ♀ 422–700 g

SD Breeds only Hokkaido; winters (Oct–mid-Apr) Honshu, Shikoku, Kyushu. **HH** Breeds at well-vegetated lakes and marshes; winters at lakes, rivers, coastal wetlands. **ID** Breeding ♂: unmistakable; pale grey, with large head, forehead and crown all dark metallic chestnut; face-sides, 'whiskers' and 'mane' glossy green, contrasting with white chin and cheek bar, and black and white neck bars. Small white spot at base of culmen unique; breast and flanks finely vermiculated black and white, tail black but sides yellowish-white, largely obscured by long elegant drooping (falcated) black tertials with pale grey fringes. ♀: resembles blackish-brown ♀ Eurasian Wigeon (without white belly), with squarer, plain grey head; underparts scalloped chestnut and dull brown, exposed tertials grey-fringed. Eclipse ♂: resembles ♀, but has darker head and pale grey forewing and may retain long tertials. In flight, ♂ has prominent pale grey forewing and blackish secondaries; ♀ has grey forewing and whitish greater covert bar; short rounded tail. **BP** Bill (♂♀) blackish-grey; eyes black; tarsi blackish-grey. **SV** ♂ disyllabic *foo-ee* and whistle-and-buzz *foo-ee-brurururu*; ♀ a hoarse quacking.

Eurasian Wigeon *Mareca penelope*

L 43–54 cm; WS 71–85 cm; WT 640–720 g

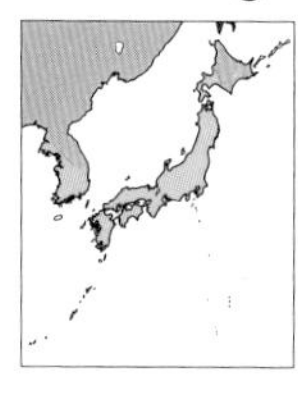

SD Abundant winterer (mid-Sep–late Apr) throughout Japan. **HH** Lakes, coastal lagoons, rivers and estuaries; often grazes onshore. **ID** Medium-sized, compact, with rather short neck, large rounded head and small bill. Breeding ♂: head bright chestnut with creamy-buff blaze. Breast vinaceous. Upperparts and flanks pale to mid grey, finely vermiculated with white; white rear flanks contrast with pointed black tail. Adult ♀: rather uniform dark rufous-brown, best identified by shape. Eclipse ♂: like ♀, but forewings white. In flight (fast and agile) wings pointed, slightly swept back at tips; note large head on narrow neck and pointed tail; adult ♂ has large white forewing patch and dark green speculum; both sexes have a prominent white belly patch, and dusky-grey axillaries and underwing-coverts (unlike American Wigeon). **BP** Bill (♂♀) pale blue-grey with black tip, lacking black at gape; eyes black; tarsi dark grey. **SV** ♂: high, whistled *fee-oo*, often preceded by brief low note (*wu-fee-oo*) and more subdued whistles. ♀: crackling, quacking *gwa gwa gurrerr*.

American Wigeon *Mareca americana*

L 46–58 cm; WS 76–89 cm; WT 680–770 g

SD Rare but annual winter visitor (Oct–mid-Apr, occasionally May). **HH** Joins Eurasian Wigeon (EW) at lakes, rivers, coastal wetlands, occasionally on sea. **ID** Similar to EW, with larger head, steeper forehead, more bulging nape. Breeding ♂: greyer head and neck than EW; speckled grey face, prominent glossy dark green crescent from eyes to nape, and white or buff (not cream/yellow) blaze. Breast, flanks and back pinkish-brown, lacking grey of EW. ♀: paler grey head, especially forehead and lores, and darker blackish-grey patch around eye, affording more masked appearance than EW, with darker rufous flanks. In flight, ♂♀ have prominent white belly and ♂ a white forewing, but axillaries and underwing-coverts white (grey in EW), and ♀ has white bar on greater coverts. Confusing hybrids with EW reported fairly frequently. **BP** Bill short, pale blue-grey with black tip; eyes black; tarsi dark grey. Essentially as EW, but narrow black border at gape lacking in EW. **SV** ♂: distinctive bi- or trisyllabic whistle *wiwhew* resembling EW. ♀: a low growling *warr warr warr*.

ad ♀
ad ♂
ad ♂
Gadwall
ad ♀
Falcated Duck
ad ♂
ad ♂
ad ♀
ad ♀
Eurasian Wigeon
ad ♀
ad ♂
ad ♀
ad ♂
American Wigeon
ad ♀
ad ♀
ad ♂
ad ♂
ad ♂
Eurasian Wigeon ×
American Wigeon hybrid

Mallard *Anas platyrhynchos* L 50–60 cm; WS 81–95 cm; WT ♂ 911–1500 g, ♀ 690–1316 g

SD Commonest large dabbling duck; the origin of many domesticated forms. *A. p. platyrhynchos* breeds in small numbers in C Honshu and Hokkaido. Winters (mainly Oct–Apr) throughout most of Japan south of Hokkaido (where scarce in winter). **HH** Breeds at wetlands; on migration and in winter occurs in flocks at ponds, lakes, rivers, wet ricefields, estuaries and on the sea; often in large numbers with other dabbling ducks. **ID** Large, stocky, with large head and bill and short tail. Breeding ♂ has glossy dark bottle-green head, separated from purplish-chestnut chest by narrow white collar. Body pale grey, 'stern' black, tail white with upcurled black central uppertail-coverts; white-bordered blue speculum visible on closed wing. Eclipse ♂ resembles ♀, but retains ochre bill and black rump. ♀ is brown, streaked, with dark crown and eye-stripe darker than face, belly pale brown. In flight, wings broad and blunt, wingbeats rather slow, heavy and shallow (slower than most other dabbling ducks, but see Eastern Spot-billed Duck); blue speculum with white borders prominent in both sexes; underwings pale, greyish-white, belly lacks white patch. **BP** Bill dull yellow-ochre in ♂, orange with black culmen and centre in ♀; eyes black; tarsi orange. **SV** ♂ gives soft rasping, nasal *kwehp* and sometimes soft teal-like whistled *piu*. ♀ gives archetypal loud quack, *gwaa kuwa kuwa* and laughing, descending series, *quek quek quek quek quak quak*.

Eastern Spot-billed Duck *Anas zonorhyncha* L 54–61 cm; WS 83–91 cm; WT 750–1350 g

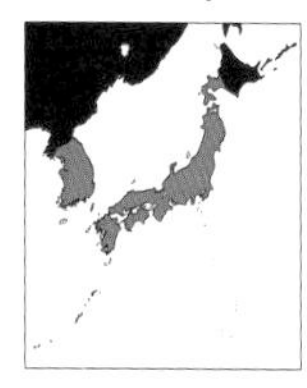

SD Quite common, widespread and largely resident throughout most of Japan; summer visitor (May–Sep) to Hokkaido. **HH** Wetlands, from lakes and ricefields, agricultural ditches and streams to smallest urban ponds, even in city centres. Winters with other dabbling ducks at ponds, lakes, rivers, and wet ricefields. **ID** The largest and heaviest dabbling duck; stocky, with large head and long bill. Sexes similar; very dark above and below, with pale face and black 'stern'. Crown, eye-stripe and lower cheek bar dark ashy-brown; supercilia whitish. Closed wing shows small area of blue speculum and white tertials. In flight, brown wings have dark blue or purple speculum with narrow white borders, usually only hind border prominent; underwings white. Flight heavy with slower beats than most dabbling ducks except Mallard. **BP** Black bill is long, broad, especially at tip, which has large yellow spot; eyes dark reddish-brown; tarsi bright orange. **SV** Mallard-like, but stronger. ♀'s series of quacking *gwe gwe gwe* calls often louder and in descending series. **TN** Formerly within Spot-billed Duck *A. poecilorhyncha*. **AN** Chinese Spot-billed Duck.

Philippine Duck *Anas luzonica* L 48–58 cm; WS 84 cm; WT 725–977 g

SD Vulnerable. Accidental to S Nansei Shoto. **HH** Lowland lakes, mangrove-lined estuaries and marshes, with other waterfowl. **ID** Medium-sized dabbling duck (sexes alike) with black crown, nape and eye-stripe; rufous-brown supercilia, face and upper neck. Dark grey-brown upperparts, pale greyish-buff breast and dark grey-brown underparts with some pale feather fringes affording scalloped appearance to flanks. Rump and vent black, tail dark grey. In flight, pale underwing with dark trailing edge to grey secondaries, and bright green speculum bordered above and below with black and white (also visible on closed wing). **BP** Bill bluish-grey; eyes dark brown; tarsi dark greenish-brown. **SV** Resembles harsh Mallard, similar to quacks of Eastern Spot-billed Duck.

Mallard
ad ♀
ad ♂
ad ♀
ad ♂
eclipse ♂
Eastern Spot-billed Duck
ad ♂
ad ♀
ad ♂
Philippine Duck
ad
ad

Blue-winged Teal *Spatula discors* L 35–41 cm; WS 58–69 cm; WT 266–410 g

SD Accidental winter visitor. **HH** Brackish or saline wetlands. **ID** Size of Garganey, with similar relatively long bill. Breeding ♂: dark slaty blue-grey head with prominent white facial crescent; breast and underparts warm orange-brown with black spots and vermiculations; upperparts darker brown, elongated tertials fringed orange-brown, rear flanks white, undertail-coverts and tail black. ♀ (and eclipse ♂): duller grey-brown with pale buff fringes to most body-feathers and upperparts; dark eye-stripe splits white eye-ring, white loral spot connected to white chin. Eclipse ♂: more distinct ghost of facial crescent. In flight, ♂'s bright blue forewing contrasts with dark grey primaries, and dark green speculum bordered in front by bold white bar; underwing white with a broad black leading edge and white axillaries (compare Garganey). ♀ has similar wing pattern, but blue forewing less bright and white bar narrower. Similar Garganey ♂ has silver, not blue, forewing, narrow green speculum bordered above and below with white; ♀ has grey forewing and similar speculum pattern to ♂. ♀ Garganey has darker eye-stripe, and pale loral spot separated from whitish chin. **BP** Bill rather long, dark blackish-grey; eyes black; tarsi dull ochre. **SV** ♂ gives thin whistled *peeew* or *tui*, whilst ♀ utters coarse, nasal quacking recalling Northern Shoveler; also *tui* or *tsi tsi* calls.

Northern Shoveler *Spatula clypeata* L 43–56 cm; WS 73–82 cm; WT 410–1100 g

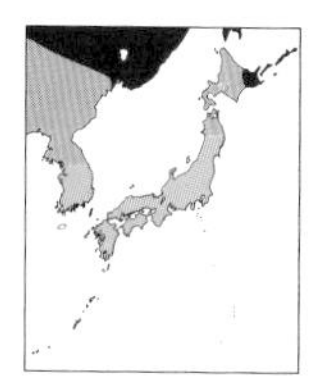

SD Small numbers may breed (May–Aug) in Hokkaido; winters (mid-Sep–late Apr) Honshu, Shikoku, Kyushu. **HH** Breeds at well-vegetated shallow wetlands; on migration and in winter at lakes and coastal lagoons. **ID** Quite large dabbling duck with larger bill than any other duck. Short neck and large bill give it a front-heavy look. Breeding ♂ has distinctive dark bottle-green head, white breast and chestnut flanks and belly. ♀ resembles ♀ Mallard, but smaller, with much larger bill, and green speculum on closed wing. Eclipse ♂ resembles ♀, but has grey head with pale crescent in front of eye, and retains wing pattern. In flight, ♂ has prominent blue forewing and green speculum with bold wedge of white in front; white underwing-coverts contrast with blackish flight-feathers. ♀ in flight has grey forewing, no white trailing edge to dull green speculum, and darker belly than Mallard. **BP** Bill deep-based, long, broadly spatulate at tip, black in ♂, greyer with orange cutting edges in ♀ and eclipse ♂; eyes bright yellow in ad ♂, dull orange-yellow in ♀ and brown in juvenile; legs bright orange. **SV** ♂ generally quiet, but gives strange nasal rattling *took took* on take-off and quiet, hoarse *kue* or *kusu* notes in display; ♀ gives soft, low, staccato, descending, somewhat Mallard-like quacking, *gaa-gaa-gaa-gaa...* or *kwe-kwe-kwe-kwe...* and a wheezy *kerr-aesh*.

Northern Pintail *Anas acuta* L ♂ 61–76 cm, ♀ 51–57 cm; WS 80–95 cm; WT 760–1250 g

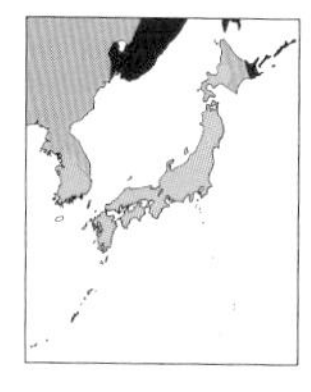

SD Winters (mid Sep–mid Apr) widely and in large numbers. **HH** Ponds, lakes, rivers, wet ricefields, shallow bays and coastal lagoons. **ID** Slimmer and more elegant than other medium-sized dabbling ducks, with long slender neck and long narrow tail. Breeding ♂: dark chocolate head and nape, white foreneck and narrow stripe up neck-side, creamy white breast and belly, grey flanks, black vent and tail with extremely long (c. 10 cm), pointed central rectrices; tail-sides white. ♀ greyer brown, much more slender and longer-necked than ♀ Mallard. Eclipse ♂ resembles ♀, but with adult ♂ upperwing. Wings long and narrow with wingtips swept back; flight agile and fast, often in lines. Grey wings have green speculum with broad hind border (♂), or dark speculum with broad white trailing edge (♀). Underwing of ♂♀ grey with pale bars. **BP** Bill slender, pale blue-grey with black culmen, tip, cutting edges and band at base (♂), or plain grey (♀); eyes black; tarsi dark grey. **SV** Generally quiet, but displaying ♂s give various calls, in particular a low, Eurasian Teal-like whistle, a rolling *furrr-furrr*, and a quieter *kishiin*, audible only at close range. ♀ gives somewhat crow-like *cr-r-r-rah*, a soft, hoarse, somewhat Mallard-like quacking *guegue kuwa kuwa* or low *kwuk*; and in flight a four-note descending series, *keersh-kursh-kurrh-kurrh*.

Blue-winged Teal
ad ♀
ad ♀
ad ♂
ad ♂
Northern Shoveler
ad ♀
ad ♀
ad ♂
ad ♂
ad ♀
ad ♂
ad ♂
Northern Pintail
ad ♀

Garganey *Spatula querquedula*

L 37–41 cm; WS 59–67 cm; WT 220–520 g

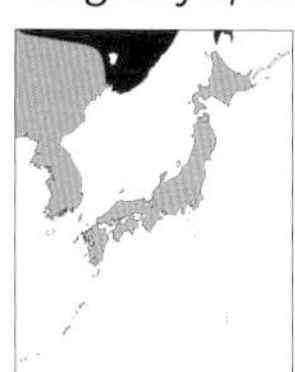

SD Uncommon migrant (Mar–May, Sep/Oct). **HH** Well-vegetated pools, lakes, coastal lagoons. **ID** Slightly larger than Eurasian Teal (ET), head squarer, bill heavier and more prominent, tail slightly longer. Breeding ♂: head, dark at distance, purplish-brown with silvery superciliary stripe extending down neck-sides. Dark brown, finely speckled breast contrasts with pale grey flanks, vermiculated black. Tertials grey, black and white, elongated and droop over flanks; vent and tail brown. ♀ like ♀ ET, but pale supercilia contrasts more strongly with dark crown and very dark eye-stripe, and pale loral spot separated from buffy-white chin. Eclipse ♂ resembles ♀, but has whiter supercilia, darker eye-stripe, whiter lores and dark line on cheek. In flight (faster, more direct than ET), ♂ has pale silvery-grey forewing, dark green speculum bordered front and aft by bold white bars; also, pale grey belly contrasts markedly with dark breast, as does very dark leading edge to underwing with pale grey axillaries and rest of underwing. ♀ in flight: note face pattern, broad white trailing edge to secondaries, recalling Northern Pintail, and paler 'hand' than ET. **BP** Bill rather long, dark blackish-grey; eyes orange-brown to dark brown; tarsi dark grey or black. **SV** ♂ gives hard, wooden clicking or rattling croak *kar-r-r...*; ♀ a soft croaking *kwak* or *ke*, and erratic series of harsh, high-pitched quacks: *graash-graash-graash-graash*.

Baikal Teal *Sibirionetta formosa*

L 39–43 cm; WS 65–75 cm; WT 430–440 g

SD Vulnerable. Once abundant, now scarce. Winters (Oct–Apr) south of Hokkaido. **HH** Lakes and large ponds, wet ricefields and shallow wetlands. Makes mass aerial manoeuvres on approaching and leaving roost. **ID** Noticeably larger and longer-tailed than Eurasian Teal (ET), and smaller-billed than Garganey, with more peaked hindcrown than other teals. Breeding ♂ has unique head pattern; breast pinkish-brown with black spots and grey flanks with vertical white bar (longer and narrower than Green-winged Teal). ♀ has distinctive pale round loral spot, often with dark border, dark crown and eye-stripe (from rear of eye) contrasting with paler brown supercilia and head-sides. May have pale vertical bar or wedge extending onto cheek from pale chin and throat. Eclipse ♂ resembles ♀, but generally more rufous-brown. In flight, forewing grey, ♂'s greenish-black speculum has prominent rufous frontal border and broad white rear border; ♀ has only white rear border and no midwing-bar (cf. ET). **BP** Bill small, black or dark grey; eyes black; tarsi greenish-grey (♂) or greyish-black (♀). **SV** ♂ gives various deep clucking calls: *klo-klo-klo*; *wot-wot-wot*, or *proop*, and ♀ a harsh, jerky, low *quack*.

Eurasian Teal *Anas crecca*

L 34–38 cm; WS 53–59 cm; WT 320–330 g

SD *A.c. crecca* is common, wintering (Sep–May) throughout Japan (though scarce in Hokkaido except on migration). **HH** Ponds, lakes, rivers and wet ricefields. **ID** Small, compact with rounded head and small bill. Breeding ♂ has chestnut head with long, broad dark-green eye patch bordered by buff lines, creamy breast spotted black, grey neck and flanks finely vermiculated black and white, tertials pale grey-brown and hang loosely slightly over tail-sides, which are cream, vent black; broad horizontal bars, white above black, at edge of closed wing. ♀ plain, dark brown, heavily scalloped on flanks, face generally clean with dark eye-stripe. Eclipse ♂ resembles ♀. Flight rapid and agile, leaps from water, turns and twists frequently even in dense flocks. Grey wings, green speculum with prominent white borders; at distance appears dark with short, broad white upperwing-bar. **BP** Bill small, dark grey; eyes black; tarsi dark grey or black. **SV** ♂ sharp, rattled *kyireek*, and fluty *piri piri*; ♀ short, gruff *graurk* and descending series of raspy nasal quacks *gwee gwe gwe gwe* or *peeht pat pat pat*. **TN** Sometimes lumped as Common Teal *A. crecca* with following species, e.g. OSJ.

Green-winged Teal *Anas carolinensis*

L 34–38 cm; WS 58 cm; WT 350 g

SD Rare, but annual winter visitor. Records typically of ♂s. **HH** Rivers, pools and lakes. **ID** Closely resembles Eurasian Teal, but ♂ has less distinct buffy 'frame' to eye patch, lacks bold white horizontal bar at sides but has prominent vertical white bar on breast-sides, and breast darker and buffier. ♀ virtually identical to Eurasian, but may show more contrast between crown, eye-stripe, dark cheek patch and general ground coloration of face. In flight, grey wings with green speculum, but borders usually more rusty, less white than Eurasian. **BP** Bill small, dark grey; eyes black; tarsi dark grey or black. Occasional (♂) hybrids may have vertical *and* horizontal white bars. **SV** Seemingly as Eurasian Teal. **TN** Formerly within Common Teal *A. crecca*, e.g. OSJ.

Garganey
ad ♂
ad ♀
ad ♀
ad ♂
Baikal Teal
ad ♀
ad ♀
ad ♂
ad ♀
ad ♂
ad ♂
Eurasian Teal
ad ♀
ad ♂
ad ♀
ad ♂
Green-winged Teal
ad ♂

Red-crested Pochard *Netta rufina* L 50–60 cm; WS 85–90 cm; WT 830–1320 g

SD Very rare winter visitor (Nov–Mar) Honshu southwards. **HH** Reed-fringed lakes, reservoirs, lagoons, coastal marshes and bays. **ID** Bulky with large head. Breeding ♂: bright rusty-orange head, crown paler. Black neck, breast, central belly, tail and vent contrast with buffy-grey flanks and brown back. ♀: pale, plain grey-brown; grey-brown crown and nape, and whitish face (recall smaller Black Scoter ♀). Eclipse ♂ like ♀, but has red eyes and bill and larger, redder-brown crown. Floats higher than other diving ducks. In flight, ♂♀ have long, prominent white wing-bar contrasting with black tips to remiges, and grey-brown or blackish upperwing-coverts; underwing pale greyish-white; ♂ has chestnut axillaries, pale flanks and black belly stripe. **BP** Bill slender, waxy red with yellow nail (♂) or grey with buff tip (♀); eyes red (♂) or brown (♀); tarsi orange-red, webs black. **SV** ♂ rasping, sneezing *gyi* or *byiii* and subdued *rerr-rerr;* ♀ barking *wrah-wrah-wrah…* or growling *keurr-keurr;* otherwise silent.

Canvasback *Aythya valisineria* L 48–61 cm; WS 74–90 cm; WT 1150–1250 g

SD Rare, probably annual, winter visitor (Sep–May) to C & N Japan. **HH** Lakes, coastal lagoons, and bays. **ID** Larger, longer necked and longer-billed than Common Pochard, with flatter head and long sloping forehead. Breeding ♂: blackish-chestnut head and neck, black breast and 'stern'; pale grey wings and body (can appear white). ♀: head pale brown, breast, body, wings and tail pale grey-brown. In flight, wings pale grey (♂), or mid to dark grey (♀), underwing very pale grey to white, axillaries white; neck appears longer and thicker than other *Aythya*. **BP** Bill long, deep at base, slender at tip, black or dark grey (lacks Common Pochard's pale subterminal band); eyes red (♂) or dark brown (♀); tarsi dark grey. **SV** ♂ gives *wikku wikku wikku,* ♀ a low coarse growling *kururu kururu kururu* or *grrrt grrrt grrrt,* but both generally silent.

Redhead *Aythya americana* L 40–46 cm; WS 74–85 cm; WT 1030–1361 g

SD Winter vagrant to Honshu. **HH** Ponds and lakes. **ID** Mid-sized, body short, back high and rounded; head rounder than Common Pochard. Breeding ♂: bright rufous head and neck, black breast and 'stern', grey upperparts and body. ♀: plain brown, greyer on upperparts, paler on chin. In flight, slow shallow beats, wings broad with some contrast between pale grey flight feathers and darker forewing; underwing pale-grey to white, axillaries white. **BP** Bill blue-grey with white subterminal band and black tip; eyes yellow (♂) or brown (♀/juv); tarsi dark grey. **SV** ♂ occasionally gives a cat-like *myuuou* or *waow;* ♀ gives a harsh *squak* or softer, nasal *grehp*.

Common Pochard *Aythya ferina* L 40–50 cm; WS 67–75 cm; WT 900–1100 g

SD Breeds very locally SE Hokkaido. Winters (Oct–mid-Apr) widely, south of Hokkaido. **HH** Ponds, lakes, coastal lagoons and bays. **ID** Mid-sized with high domed crown, sloping forehead and concave culmen, and short tail. Breeding ♂: dark chestnut head and neck, black breast and 'stern', mid to dark grey upperparts and body. Eclipse ♂: duller brown head and dark brownish-grey breast and stern. ♀: grey-brown head with pale stripe behind eye, pale lores and chin, brownish breast and 'stern', and brownish-grey upperparts and body. Flight strong, direct, rather whirring; wings differ from other *Aythya* in grey wing-bar with little contrast between pale grey flight-feathers and grey forewing, though primary and secondary tips blackish. **BP** Bill black at tip and base with blue band between (♂), or grey at base, blue in middle and black at tip (♀); eyes red/orange (♂) or brown (♀); tarsi grey. **SV** ♂ has soft chattering and series of wheezy whistles; ♀ gives harsh, rattling growl *grrr-grrr* or *kururu kururu*, often in flight.

Baer's Pochard *Aythya baeri* L 46–47 cm; WS 70–79 cm; WT 680–880 g

SD Vulnerable. Accidental or extremely rare winter visitor (mid-Oct–late Mar) mostly to C & W Honshu and Kyushu. **HH** Lakes, ponds, marshes. **ID** Small, compact and very dark; rounded head and bill recall Common Pochard. Breeding ♂: green-glossed black head and neck, blackish-brown upperparts, dark chestnut breast, and paler chestnut and white flanks. Small area of white on vent-sides recalls Ferruginous Duck. Tail short, held low. ♀/1st-winter and eclipse ♂: less clean-cut, blackish-brown head and neck blend into chestnut-brown breast and flanks. In flight, white wing-stripe contrasts strongly with blackish upperwing-coverts and flight-feather tips; underwing largely white, as are belly and vent. **BP** Bill dark grey, bluer towards tip, black nail; eyes white or pale yellow (♂), or brown (♀); tarsi dark grey. **SV** Generally silent, but ♂♀ give harsh *graaaak* in courtship, and *koro koro* (♂) or *kura kura kura* (♀) at other times.

Red-crested Pochard
ad ♀
ad ♂
ad ♂
ad ♀
Canvasback
ad ♀
ad ♂
ad ♀
ad ♂
Redhead
ad ♀
ad ♂
ad ♀
ad ♂
Common Pochard
Baer's Pochard
ad ♀
ad ♂
ad ♂
ad ♀

Ferruginous Duck *Aythya nyroca* L 38–42 cm; WS 60–67 cm; WT 520–580 g

SD Very rare winter visitor (Nov–Mar). **HH** Marshes, freshwater lakes, coastal lagoons. **ID** Compact, dark, with high domed head and conspicuous white undertail-coverts. Breeding ♂: deep, rich chestnut head and breast, and browner flanks (lacks Baer's white flanks), blackish upperparts, rump and tail. Eclipse ♂: duller. ♀: browner, less chestnut. In flight, prominent white wing-bars contrast with blackish upperwing-coverts and wingtips; wing-bar longer and more striking than Tufted or Baer's; underwing, belly and vent white. **BP** Bill dark grey to blue-grey with black nail; eyes white (ad/eclipse ♂) or dark brown (♀/juv); tarsi grey. **SV** ♂: generally silent except during courtship when whistles (*wee-few*) or gives hard nasal *chk-chk-chk*. ♀: low, snoring *ka ka ka ka* or *errr errr errr*.

Ring-necked Duck *Aythya collaris* L 40–46 cm; WS 61–75 cm; WT 690–790 g

SD Winter accidental to Japan's four main islands. **HH** Ponds and lakes. **ID** Recalls Tufted Duck, but larger head has peaked hindcrown, neck longer, different bill and wing patterns, and more prominent tail. Breeding ♂: glossy head with slight rounded crest, black neck, breast, upperparts and 'stern', pale grey flanks with prominent white spur on breast-sides. Purplish-brown neck ring indistinct. ♀: less contrasting, with dark-brown cap, grey cheeks and narrow, broken white eye-ring and lores. In flight, wing-bar grey not white; grey flight-feathers have blackish tips and offer little contrast with black (♂) or dull grey-brown (♀) forewing; underwing pale grey. **BP** Bill dark grey, white at base, with white subterminal band and black tip; eyes orange (ad) or brown (juv); tarsi dark grey. **SV** ♂♀: throaty *kua* or *kwa kwa*, ♀ guttural growling *kerp kerp* ….

Tufted Duck *Aythya fuligula* L 40–50 cm; WS 65–72 cm; WT 1000–1400 g

SD Winters (Oct–late Mar), often in large numbers, south of Hokkaido. **HH** Bays, coastal marshes, lagoons, inland lakes, rivers. **ID** Compact, boldly pied with rounded, crested head with high forehead. Breeding ♂: black with white flanks, head tinged purple; long, dense nuchal crest. Tail short, held low. Eclipse ♂: short crest, grey flanks. ♀: browner, flanks brown, rear crown has short tuft, limited white at bill base (rarely as extensive as Greater Scaup), may show inconspicuous, sometimes more prominent, white undertail-coverts. Resembles ♀ Greater Scaup, but smaller, darker, with different head shape, pale band and broad black tip to bill. In flight, outer primaries mostly dark grey, thus white wing-bar is short; underwing, axillaries and belly white. **BP** Bill blue-grey, tip and nail black; eyes pale yellow (♂) or dull orange-yellow (juv/♀); tarsi grey. **SV** Usually silent. ♂ gives soft whistled *wheeoo* in breeding season, and low *kyu* and *gagaa*. ♀ (like other *Aythya*) has abrupt *krr-krr-krr*…; ♂♀ utter low *gurrrr gurrrr* on take-off and in flight, when wings whistle.

Greater Scaup *Aythya marila* L 40–50 cm; WS 71–80 cm; WT 600–1000 g

SD *A. m. nearctica* winters (Oct–Apr) throughout Japan, locally in very large numbers; some summer. **HH** Bays, harbours, lagoons, lakes, rivers. **ID** Heavy, compact, boldly marked, head lacking crest. Breeding ♂: black head with green gloss, black breast and 'stern', white flanks, grey back. Tail short, held low. ♀: browner; flanks and mantle vermiculated with grey; broad white area at bill base; many show pale patch on ear-coverts in autumn/winter; confusable with Tufted Duck, but larger head rounder and only bill nail is black. Eclipse ♂ like washed-out, slightly browner, breeding ♂. In flight, ♂ has dark grey forewing, long white wing-bar, dark grey outer primaries and black tips to flight-feathers; underwing, axillaries and belly white; ♀ has brownish-grey forewing and back. **BP** Bill uniform blue-grey (♂) or dark grey (♀), with large black nail; eyes yellow; tarsi grey. **SV** Generally silent, but displaying ♂ gives low, hollow hooting; ♀ a more prolonged, deeper growl than Tufted Duck.

Lesser Scaup *Aythya affinis* L 38–48 cm; WS 64–74 cm; WT 800–850 g

SD Winter (mid-Oct–Mar) vagrant. **HH** Ponds, lakes, rivers. **ID** Smaller, with taller, narrower head, and shorter, narrower-tipped bill than similar Greater Scaup; head more angular (crown peak further back). Breeding ♂: head gloss more purplish than green, mantle has broader black barring, flanks appear partly grey due to fine vermiculations. ♀: browner, with grey-vermiculated flanks and mantle, and less white at bill base than ♀ Greater; typically lacks white auriculars of many ♀ Greater in autumn/winter, but may have them in spring/summer. In flight, wing-bar confined to secondaries. Underwing distinctive; lesser and median coverts white, contrasting with grey underwing. **BP** Bill blue-grey, with small black nail; eyes yellow (♂) or orange (juv/♀); tarsi dark blackish-grey. **SV** ♂ gives husky whistling in display; ♀ a guttural *karr karr* or *garf garf*.

Ferruginous Duck
ad ♀
ad ♂
ad ♀
ad ♂
ad ♀
ad ♂
Ring-necked Duck
ad ♂
ad ♀
win
Tufted Duck
ad ♂
ad ♀
ad ♀
ad ♂
ad ♂
ad ♀
Greater Scaup
ad ♀
win
ad ♂
ad ♀
sum
ad ♀
ad ♂
Lesser Scaup
ad ♀
win
ad ♂

Steller's Eider *Polysticta stelleri*

L 43–48 cm; WS 68–77 cm; WT 860 g

SD Very rare winter visitor (Dec–Mar) to Hokkaido and N Honshu. **HH** Rocky coasts, off seaweed-covered shores, occasionally bays. **ID** Smallest eider, with proportionately longer body, smaller, squarer head and much shorter bill; tail longer and often held cocked. Unusual in resembling dabbling ducks in form and bill. Flattish crown, steep forehead and vertical nape. Breeding ♂: white with creamy orange-buff breast, belly and sides; black eye patch, chin, collar, spot on breast-sides, upperparts, 'stern' and tail; rear crown has small greenish-black crest. Black and white tertials droop. Eclipse ♂: blackish-brown with white scapulars; 1st-year ♂: recalls washed-out adult ♀; mottled sooty-brown, with broad white borders to blackish speculum. Wings longer and narrower than other eiders, take-off easier, flight faster; ♂ black with white shoulders, wing-coverts and tips of secondaries; secondaries, primaries and primary-coverts black. ♀: dark with broad white borders to speculum, whitish axillaries and underwing-coverts. **BP** Bill grey, blunt with wedge-shaped tip; eyes black (breeding ♂) or has pale eye-ring (eclipse ♂ and ♀); tarsi dark ochre-grey. **SV** ♀ gives guttural quacking *gaa gaa geah* and loud *cooay*; wings whistle loudly in flight.

King Eider *Somateria spectabilis*

L 55–63 cm; WS 87–100 cm; WT 1750–1850 g

SD Accidental winter visitor to E Hokkaido. **HH** Rocky capes, coasts, harbours. **ID** Large with unusual angular head, bulbous forehead and short bill. ♂: black with white band on upper back and breast, breast salmon-pink; flank bar and large white patch at tail-sides white; crown and nape powder-blue, face greenish, bordered black. Eclipse ♂: dark brown with reduced orange shield and bill. 1st-winter ♂: like eclipse, but breast white. ♀: warm brown, with dark crescents on flanks. Flight heavy, slow, often low over water; appears deep-bellied and very short-necked; ♂ has white upper back separated from white wing-coverts by black shoulders. **BP** Bill orange (♂) with variable-sized shield, blackish-grey (♀/young), with lobe near eye, feathering extending towards nostril and upturned black gape line afford 'smiling' expression; eyes black; tarsi dull ochre. **SV** ♂ gives deep, hollow crooning *yooo hruru ruru* and rolling *arr-arr-arr*; ♀ gives deep quacking *gwaaku gwaaku* and deep, hoarse *gogogogo*….

Pacific Eider *Somateria (mollissima) v-nigrum*

L 60–70 cm; WS 95–105 cm; WT 1915–2218 g

SD Winter accidental to N Japan. **HH** Rocky coasts. **ID** Very large, with long profile, large head, long pointed bill with lobes extending towards eye, and feathering along sides to nostrils. Breeding ♂: white above, black below, rear crown, rear head-sides and upper neck tinged pale grey-green, breast washed peach. Cap black with point extending nearly to nostrils; flanks, tail, vent and flight-feathers black, white back, drooping tertials and round patch near tail base also white. 1st-winter ♂: blackish-brown with white breast/lower neck. ♀: greyish-brown; with finely barred breast and flanks; broad pale fringes to darker mantle. Flight heavy, slow, on short broad wings, rather goose-like, often low over water; appears deep-bellied. ♂ has white back continuous with white wing-coverts, and black flight-feathers; ♀ has brown speculum bordered white and pale grey axillaries, wings otherwise brown. **BP** Bill orange-yellow, paler at nail, with feathering extending in rounded lobe to nostrils; eyes black; tarsi dark grey. **SV** Generally silent except when breeding. **TN** Retained within Common Eider by IOC, not included by OSJ.

Harlequin Duck *Histrionicus histrionicus*

L 38–51 cm; WS 63–70 cm; WT 540–680 g

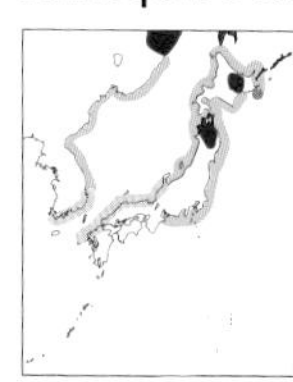

SD Breeds in Hokkaido and N Honshu; winters (Oct–mid Apr) south to C Japan, reaching west to N Kyushu. **HH** Favours turbulent water; breeds along fast-flowing cold rivers with white water and visits rocky coasts; moults in groups away from breeding grounds; winters off rocky capes and rocky coasts, visits bays and harbours. **ID** Uniquely patterned small, dark sea duck, with tiny bill, rounded head, steep forehead, and pointed, often cocked tail. Breeding ♂ essentially steel-blue with chestnut flanks, and attractive white markings outlined black on face, ear-coverts, neck, collar, breast-sides and mantle; white line fringing crown washed with chestnut from eyes back. Despite flamboyant plumage, can look surprisingly dark/monochrome in poor light or at distance. ♀ uniform sooty-brown, with round white spot on ear-coverts, indistinct whitish supraloral and whitish patch below eye. 1st-year ♂ shows elements of adult ♂ facial pattern in otherwise ♀-like plumage, but perhaps not until midwinter. Flight fast and agile on all-dark wings. **BP** Bill pale to dark grey; eyes black; tarsi pinkish-grey. **SV** On breeding grounds ♂ gives high whistled *tiiv* and ♀ soft quacking *koa koa koa* and nasal *ekekekek*…; in winter ♂ gives whistled *feee* and *fee-ah* and ♀ deeper *guwa guwa* calls.

Steller's Eider
ad ♂
ad ♀
ad ♂
ad ♀
King Eider
ad ♂
ad ♀
ad ♀
ad ♂
Pacific Eider
ad ♀
ad ♂
ad ♂
ad ♀
Harlequin Duck
ad ♀
ad ♂
ad ♂
ad ♀

Surf Scoter *Melanitta perspicillata* L 46–55 cm; WS 76–92 cm; WT 900–1000 g

SD Very rare winter visitor (Jan–Mar, exceptionally May), Hokkaido and N Honshu. **HH** Offshore. **ID** Head shape, pattern, and strangely swollen bill with slightly convex profile, all distinctive. ♂: black, with white forehead and nape patches. ♀: blackish-brown with diffuse pale patches before and behind eye, some have pale nape patch. Wings all-dark; primaries darker than those of Black. **BP** Bill large, triangular, swollen at base: orange, black and white with yellow nail (♂), or blackish-grey (♀); eyes white (ad) or dark brown (young); tarsi orange-red. **SV** ♂ occasionally gives low, whistled *puk puk*; ♀ moaning *aa aa aa* or *krrraak krrraak*. Wings whistle in flight.

Siberian Scoter *Melanitta stejnegeri* L 50–58 cm; WS 86–99 cm; WT 1200–1700 g

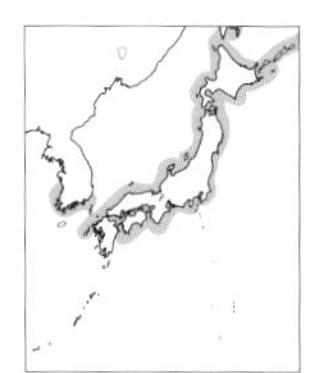

SD Winters (Oct–Mar) along Sea of Okhotsk and Pacific coasts of Hokkaido and Pacific coast of N Honshu. **HH** Coasts, occasionally harbours, inland lakes and rivers. **ID** Largest scoter, with larger head and longer bill than Black. ♂: glossy black, with black flanks, neat white crescent below and behind eye. ♀: blackish-brown with pale oval patches near bill base and behind eye. ♂♀ have large rectangular white wing patches (secondaries) visible on closed wings and in flight. Flight fast and direct, heavier and slower than Black, often in tight groups and straggling lines low over sea. **BP** ♂'s bill is deep pink, red proximally, yellower distally, black on sides at base, with black knob on culmen and large, round 'see-through' nostrils. 1st-winter ♂ lacks knob, deep red or pink areas duller, more orange; ♀'s bill is dark grey to black; eyes pale blue-grey (ad ♂), brown (imm ♂) or dark brown (♀); legs bright pink. **SV** Usually silent, but displaying ♂ gives whistled *fee-er* and low nasal *aah-er*; ♀ a gruff croaking *kraa-ah kraa-ah kraa*. Wings whistle in flight. **TN** Formerly within Velvet Scoter *M. fusca* e.g. OSJ.

White-winged Scoter *Melanitta deglandi* L 50–58 cm; WS 86–99 cm; WT 1200–1700 g

SD Accidental Hokkaido. **HH** Coasts or harbours. **ID** Closely resembles Siberian Scoter, but has brown flanks and orange and black bill. **BP** Bill is orange-tipped with black base and knob; legs bright pink. **SV** Usually silent. **TN** Formerly lumped with previous species within Velvet Scoter *M. fusca*.

Black Scoter *Melanitta americana* L 43–54 cm; WS 70–90 cm; WT 950–1268 g

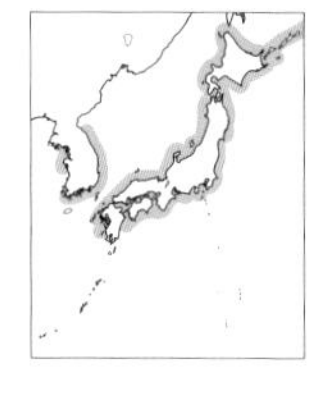

SD Very common (Oct–Mar) off N Japan. **HH** Coastal waters, harbours, occasionally inland lakes. **ID** Dumpy, with small rounded head and rather prominent pointed tail. Adult ♂: black; immature ♂ resembles ♀, but acquires some yellow to bill base. ♀: dark grey-brown with contrasting greyish-white cheeks. Flight fast and direct on somewhat broad, black wings, with paler greyish-brown primaries; often in bunched groups and straggling lines low over sea. **BP** Bill partly black, with swollen base to upper mandible yellow or orange, nostrils small and oval, near front edge of yellow 'shield' (♂); or all black (♀; imm ♂); eyes black; tarsi dark grey. **SV** ♂ highly vocal; haunting, fluting *pyuuu*, *pyeee* or *pyi-feeee*; ♀ gives harsh rasping or growling *ururu┬u* or *kaarrr*. Wings of ♂ whistle in flight.

Long-tailed Duck *Clangula hyemalis* L ♂ 51–58 cm, ♀ 38–47 cm; WS 65–82 cm; WT 650–800 g

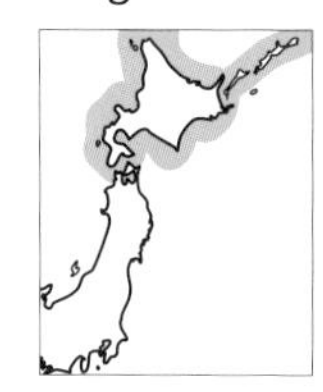

SD Winters (Nov–Apr) commonly around coasts of Hokkaido and N Honshu. **HH** Inshore waters off rocky coasts and sandy shores, occasionally harbours, inland lakes, rivers. **ID** Small, dumpy, with long neck, small head and small bill, and dark wings in all plumages. Sexually and seasonally dimorphic. ♂: distinctive extremely long (10–15 cm) central rectrices; winter/spring ♂ has grey cheeks, dark chestnut ear and breast patches, back and wings, with white head, neck, shoulders, tertials, underparts and most of tail; elongated plumes black. In early summer mainly blackish-brown with white face-patch, flanks and 'stern'. ♀ (winter): white face with dark forehead, crown and ear-patch, dark brown breast and upperparts, 'stern' white; spring ♀ resembles ♂, but lacks long tail, head and neck become duskier. Flight fast and agile on all-dark, narrow, pointed wings, beats only rising to horizontal; elegant in flight, though quite pot-bellied. **BP** Small bill, black with large pink spot near tip (ad ♂), or dark grey (♀/juv) with black tip; eyes dull orange (♂), brownish-orange (♀) or dark brown (juv); tarsi dark grey. **SV** Very vocal during late winter: ♂ gives deep yodelling *ow ow a ow-na a ow-na*; ♀ a weak high quacking *kuwaa* or soft *kak kak kak kak*; pleasant piping chorus maintained by flocks.

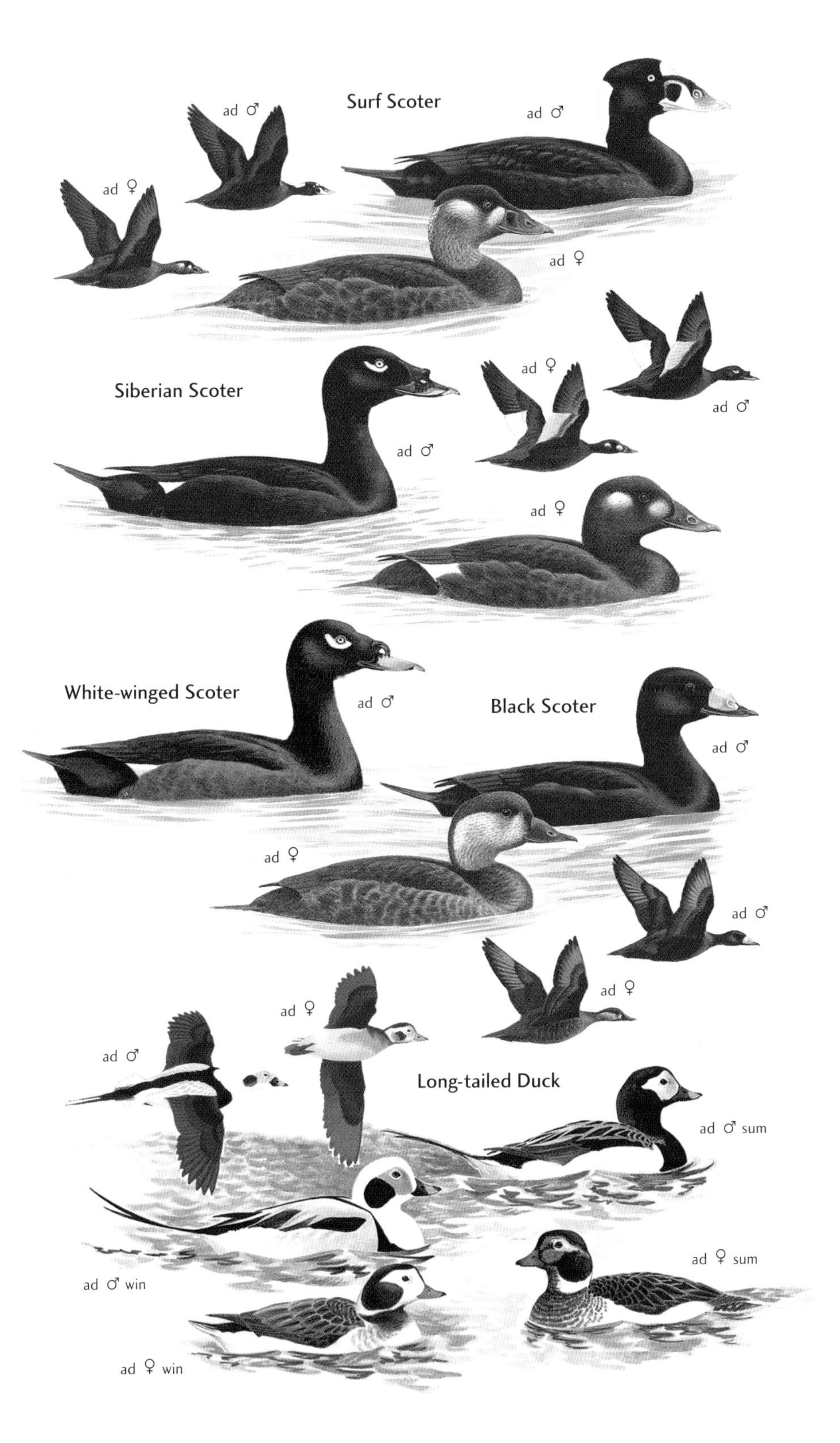
Surf Scoter
ad ♂
ad ♀
ad ♂
ad ♀
Siberian Scoter
ad ♀
ad ♂
ad ♂
ad ♀
White-winged Scoter
ad ♂
Black Scoter
ad ♂
ad ♀
ad ♂
ad ♀
ad ♀
ad ♂
Long-tailed Duck
ad ♂ sum
ad ♀ sum
ad ♂ win
ad ♀ win

Bufflehead *Bucephala albeola* L 33–40 cm; WS 53–61 cm; WT 330–450 g

SD Very rare winter visitor (Nov–Mar) to Pacific coast of Hokkaido and N Honshu. **HH** Offshore or in bays and coastal lagoons. **ID** Smallest diving duck; compact with relatively large head but small bill. Breeding ♂ has black head with purple and green gloss and huge white band from eyes back over head. Upperparts black; breast, scapulars and body white. Eclipse ♂ resembles ♀ but has large white oval on black head. ♀ has sooty-brown head with white ovals below and behind eye; body dark grey. Juvenile like ♀, but face-patch less distinct. In flight, head appears raised, with body angled upwards; adult ♂ very white, with large white patch from speculum across forewing; ♀ has small white speculum and white belly patch; flight rapid on whirring wings. **BP** Bill pale grey; eyes black; tarsi dark grey. **SV** Typically silent, but ♂ sometimes squeals or growls and ♀ gives soft grunting *gururu gururu* or a low *prrk prrk*.

Common Goldeneye *Bucephala clangula* L 40–51 cm; WS 62–77 cm; WT 710–1200 g

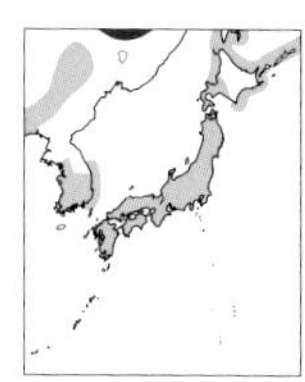

SD *B. c. clangula* winters (mainly Nov–Mar) along shores of Sea of Okhotsk, Pacific and Sea of Japan. **HH** Along coasts, rivers, and at lakes. **ID** Medium-sized diving duck, with large triangular head, high-peaked crown, short neck and compact body. Tail held very low on water. Breeding ♂ has black head with green gloss and white oval on lores. Upperparts and 'stern' black, breast and flanks pure white; scapulars (white with narrow black fringes) droop over flanks. ♀ brown-headed and grey-bodied, with diffuse white collar and whitish belly; white speculum visible on closed wing. Eclipse ♂ like ♀ but has ♂ wing pattern. Flight fast with deep wingbeats and stiff, whirring wings which produce distinct musical whistle. In flight, adult ♂ wings black, with white speculum, forewing and scapulars; ♀ wings greyer with white speculum and smaller forewing patch divided by black line; underwing of both dark. **BP** Bill short, somewhat broad, dark blackish-grey (♂) or mostly black with yellow band near tip (♀); eyes bright yellow (♂), pale yellow (♀) or brown (juv); tarsi dull yellow/orange. **SV** Generally quiet but ♂ gives forced *bee-beeech*, and dry, grating rattle *drrrr*, recalling Garganey, and hoarse, buzzy whistle (*kyi riiku kyi riiku*) in display (common in winter quarters from Mar), whilst ♀ gives *Aythya*-like low guttural *arr arr arr* and harsh, dry staccato quacks: *grak grak grak* or *kuwa kuwa kuwa*. In flight, stiff wings produce loud musical whistle.

Barrow's Goldeneye *Bucephala islandica* L 42–53 cm; WS 67–82 cm; WT 737–1300 g

SD Winter vagrant to Hokkaido and Ishikawa. **HH** Lakes and coasts. **ID** Slightly larger than Common Goldeneye (CG), with larger head, steeper forehead, flatter crown, crown peak further forwards, and 'mane' at rear. Breeding ♂: black head with purple gloss, and large white crescent on lores forming point higher than eye. Upperparts like CG, but black more extensive, including black spur on breast-sides, and row of white 'windows' on black scapulars. ♀ like CG, but shares ♂'s head-shape. Eclipse ♂ like ♀ but has ♂ wing pattern. Juvenile distinguishable from CG only by head shape and wing pattern. In flight, adult ♂ wings blacker, with white speculum, divided from white forewing by black line, scapulars have only white spots; ♀ wings also have less white; underwing of both dark; wings emit low whistle, quieter, less musical than CG. **BP** Bill black (♂), or mostly orange with grey base (♀); eyes bright yellow (♂), pale yellow (♀) or brown (juv); tarsi dull yellow/orange with dark webs. **SV** ♂ gives gruff *kakaa* in breeding season and ♀ a low guttural *arr arr arr* and dry staccato quacks: *grak grak grak* (deeper than CG). **TN**: Not included by OSJ.

Smew *Mergellus albellus* L 35–40 cm; WS 56–69 cm; WT 515–935 g

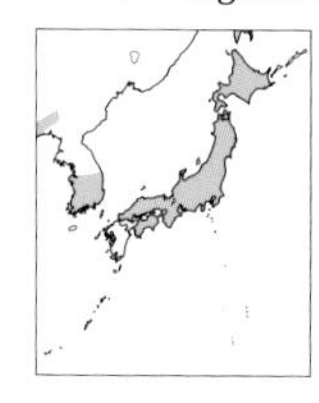

SD Winters (Oct–Apr) from Hokkaido (where may have bred) to Kyushu. **HH** Freshwater pools, lakes and rivers; also at fresh or brackish coastal lagoons. May form dense mixed flocks with other sawbills. **ID** Compact, with slightly tufted head and small bill. Breeding ♂ white, with black 'panda' mask around eyes and on lores, fine black lines on rear crown and breast-sides; mantle/back black, white flanks finely vermiculated grey, 'stern' dark grey. ♀ grey with dark chestnut head, white cheeks and chin. Eclipse ♂ brown-headed, grey-bodied, with white crest and breast. In flight, adult ♂ distinctly pied, black flight-feathers and mantle contrasting with white scapulars and forewing; ♀ greyer, with smaller white forewing and mostly white underparts. **BP** Bill dark grey; eyes black; legs grey. **SV** Breeding ♂ gives a frog-like husky *eruru eruru eruru ukuu* and ♀ a gruff, crackling *krrr* or *grrr*. **TN** Formerly in *Mergus*.

Bufflehead
ad ♂
ad ♀
ad ♂
ad ♀
ad ♂
ad ♀
ad ♂
Common Goldeneye
ad ♀
ad ♂
ad ♀
Barrow's Goldeneye
ad ♀
ad ♂
ad ♂
ad ♀
ad ♂
Smew
ad ♀

Hooded Merganser *Lophodytes cucullatus*

L 42–50 cm; WS 56–70 cm; WT 453–879 g

SD N American vagrant to Hokkaido. **ID** Larger and longer-billed than Smew with steep forehead and unique erectile crest; long tail. Breeding ♂ largely black with white chest, chestnut flanks and large white fanned crest with black margin; tertials black with white fringes. ♀ plain grey-brown, but size, head shape and tertial pattern distinctive (cf. Red-breasted). Wingbeats fast and shallow, wings appear narrow and dark with small white area on inner secondaries; underwing and axillaries pale grey. **BP** Bill black (breeding ♂), dark grey (eclipse) or dull ochre-yellow with grey tip and culmen (juv./♀); eyes bright yellow (♂), or orange to dull yellow (♀/juv); legs dull pinkish-orange. **SV** Wings trill in flight. **TN** Formerly in *Mergus*. Not included by OSJ.

Common Merganser *Mergus merganser*

L 51–68 cm; WS 78–94 cm; WT 1500–1700 g

SD *M. m. merganser* breeds in Hokkaido, winters in N & C Japan. **HH** Forest with rivers and lakes; winters mainly on larger rivers and freshwater lakes and lagoons, sometimes in very large flocks (1,000s). **ID** Largest sawbill, with smooth crest. Breeding ♂ has black head and upper neck glossed green, black mantle, white neck, breast and underparts flushed pink or peach; tail grey. ♀ (and eclipse ♂) like large ♀ Red-breasted, but has pale chin and neat demarcation between dark brown head and whitish neck. Wingbeats shallow, neck held straight, recalling grebe or diver. Wing pattern distinctive: ♂ has extensive, almost undivided white innerwing patch, and white scapulars; ♀ has large white, undivided speculum. **BP** Bill long, thick-based with darker well-hooked tip, red (ad) or orange (juv); eyes dark brown (ad) or white (juv); tarsi reddish-orange. **SV** ♂ gives deep, muffled *krroo-kraa*, ♀ short, deep *kar-r-r kar-r-r*; clearer notes given by both sexes in wide, circular display flights. In normal flight, gives fast chuckling *chakerak-ak-ak-ak*. **AN** Goosander.

Red-breasted Merganser *Mergus serrator*

L 48–66 cm; WS 67–82 cm; WT 900–1200 g

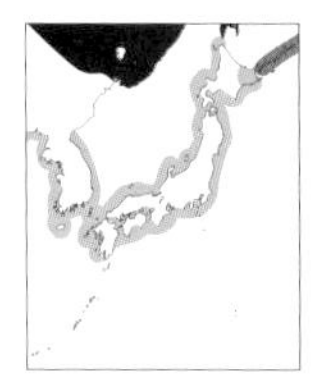

SD Winters (Oct–Apr) mainly in N Japan. **HH** Winters at sea, along coasts, occasionally at coastal lagoons and on lakes. **ID** Slim, elegant, with long thin neck, rather vertical forehead and wispy crest. Floats low in water with neck erect, recalling grebe or diver. Breeding ♂ has bottle-green head, white neck ring, ginger-brown neck to black chest, sides black with unique white spots, black mantle and grey/white flanks, and grey 'stern'. ♀ has mid-brown head grading into grey neck and body (unlike Common Merganser). In flight, note long slim neck; adult ♂ has large white patch on inner wing divided by two fine black lines. ♀ has rather dark forewing, white patch divided by single black line, and white belly. **BP** Bill long, very slender, deep red with dark culmen (ad ♂) or orange-red (juv/♀), small terminal nail hook; eyes red (♂), orange (♀) or orange-brown (juv); tarsi dull orange. **SV** Displaying ♂ gives hiccupping and sneezing *chika pitcheew*, purring *ja-aah* or *kwa kwa* and more metallic *koroo* or *yeow*. ♀'s harsh grating calls resemble Common Merganser, but higher pitched, *prrek prrek* or *grak grak*. Both sexes also call in wide, circular display flights in spring.

Scaly-sided Merganser *Mergus squamatus*

L 52–62 cm; WS 70–86 cm

SD Vulnerable. Very rare, but annual, winter visitor recorded from Hokkaido to Nansei Shoto, but mostly in C & W Honshu and Kyushu. **HH** Winters on fast-flowing rivers, sometimes on lakes and reservoirs, usually singly or in groups of 2–3. **ID** Large, boldly marked sawbill, with long, double, wispy hindcrest. Breeding ♂ has longer glossy green head than Red-breasted, flatter crown; neck and mantle black, breast and flanks white, rump and tail grey; flank feathers have grey fringes forming large scales, finer at rear, and grey vermiculations on lower back and rump. ♀ like large ♀ Red-breasted, but with neater neck pattern (more like Common Merganser) and fewer grey scales on flanks. Wing pattern like Red-breasted; ♂ has large white patch on inner wing divided by two fine black lines, ♀ has smaller white patch divided by single black line, thus differing from otherwise similar Common Merganser. **BP** Bill long, thick, bright red with yellow tip; eyes dark brown; tarsi reddish-orange. **SV** Like Red-breasted, but also makes deep, hoarse hiss. **AN** Chinese Merganser.

Hooded Merganser
ad ♂ hood displayed
ad ♀
ad ♀
ad ♂
ad ♂

Common Merganser
ad ♀
ad ♀
ad ♂
ad ♂

Red-breasted Merganser
ad ♀
ad ♀
ad ♂
ad ♂

Scaly-sided Merganser
ad ♀
ad ♀
ad ♂
ad ♂

Red-throated Loon *Gavia stellata*

L 53–69 cm; WS 91–110 cm; WT 988–2460 g

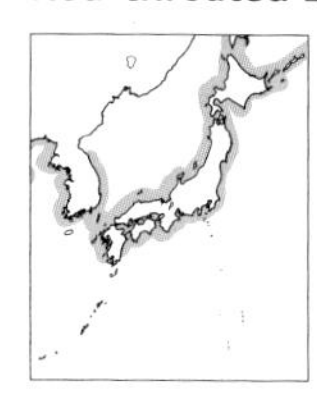

SD Commonest; winters (Oct–Apr) around N Japan. **HH** Coastal; may enter bays and harbours; rare inland. **ID** Small, slim, flat-chested, with slim vertical neck, rather flat crown, bill slightly uptilted. Breeding adult: dark rufous throat contrasting with grey face and neck. Much whiter in winter. In flight, slim-necked, head low-slung, appears hunch-backed, toes small; faster, deeper wingbeats than other loons; narrow wings angled back. **BP** Bill slender, upturned to sharp tip, black (breeding) or dark grey; eyes deep red; tarsi dark grey. **SV** Typically silent, though may give flight calls: a short nasal barking *gwaa-gwaa-gwaa-gwaa...* or a more prolonged goose-like cackling *gark gark gark gargark gaagarag.* **AN** Red-throated Diver.

Black-throated Loon *Gavia arctica*

L 62–75 cm; WS 100–130 cm; WT 2600 g

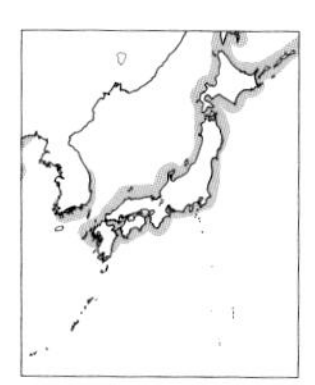

SD *G. a. viridigularis* winters (Oct–Apr) mainly around N Japan. **HH** Coastal; sometimes bays and harbours; uncommon/rare inland. **ID** Larger, heavier than Red-throated (RTL), very like Pacific (PL). Sits low in water, full-chested, neck thicker than RTL, longer than PL, held in S-curve, head angular with steep forehead. Distinctive white flank-patch separates it from very similar PL in all plumages. Summer adult has black throat-patch with green gloss (purple in PL), and clear black and white stripes on neck and breast-sides (bolder than PL). In winter, head and neck darker than RTL, dark cap extends to eye, cheeks white, but back and neck-sides mid-grey (border darkest), forming strong contrast between front and back of neck, which is only half white. Juv/1st-winter: browner, with pale, scaled pattern on back and scapulars. In flight, toes rather prominent; slower, shallower wingbeats than RTL. **BP** Bill dagger-shaped, horizontal, thick, blackish-grey, darkest at tip; eyes deep red (breeding) or black; tarsi dark grey. **SV** Typically silent. **AN** Black-throated Diver.

Pacific Loon *Gavia pacifica*

L 63–66 cm; WS 91–112 cm; WT 1700 g

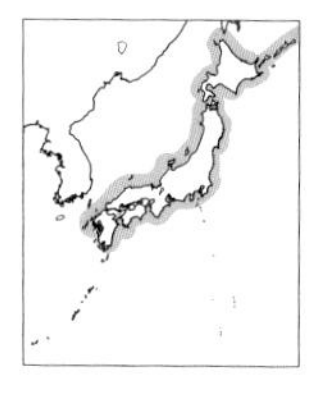

SD Winters (Oct–Apr) along Pacific coasts. **HH** As Black-throated Loon (BTL). **ID** Very similar to BTL, but slightly smaller, head less angular, more rounded, bill thinner. Holds head more level than BTL. Summer adult: noticeably paler crown/nape than BTL, white stripes on neck and breast-sides narrower; black throat-patch glossed purple. Winter adult: as BTL, but upperparts darker grey and typically narrow dark 'choker' on throat contrasts with white chin and neck, but variably distinct, and sometimes absent. Flanks typically dark, though occasionally shows small area of white. Juv/1st-winter: usually have dark brown 'choker'. **BP** Bill black (ad breeding) or grey with blackish culmen and tip (juv/non-breeding); eyes deep red; tarsi dark grey. **SV** Typically silent. **AN** Pacific Diver.

Common Loon *Gavia immer*

L 69–91 cm; WS 122–148 cm; WT 2780–4480 g

SD Winter vagrant, Hokkaido. **HH** Coasts, harbours. **ID** Large, heavily built with thick neck. Head angular with steep forecrown and forecrown bump. Breeding adult: black head and neck, white-striped chin bar and neck patch. Upperparts blackish-grey with extensive white chequers on shoulders and back, elsewhere fine white spots. Winter adult: larger than BTL and PL with pale patch around eyes. Partial white collar on neck-sides in all except breeding adults. White chin and fore throat contrast strongly with dark border to rear neck. Juv/1st-winter: light, scaly pattern on upperparts. Flight heavy, slow and goose-like, with thick neck, thick bill and large toes. **BP** Bill heavy, dagger-shaped, black (breeding) or blue-grey with dark culmen and tip (juv/non-breeding); eyes blood red (breeding) or dark brown; tarsi dark grey. **SV** Typically silent. **AN** Great Northern Diver.

Yellow-billed Loon *Gavia adamsii*

L 76–91 cm; WS 135–152 cm; WT 4050–6400 g

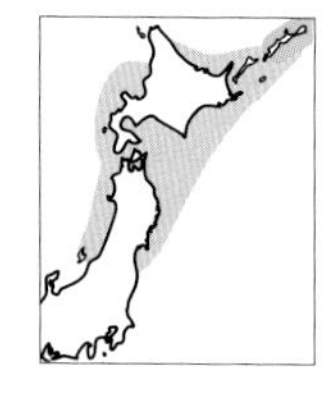

SD Scarce winter visitor to Hokkaido, N and C Honshu. **HH** Inshore waters, bays, harbours. **ID** Largest, most heavily built loon, with thick neck and bill, which is usually held upwards. Head shape like Common Loon (CL). Summer adult: larger and cleaner neck-patch and white markings on upperparts than CL. Winter adult: paler, particularly around eyes and ear-coverts, with little contrast on neck. Frequently has mottled look to face, even at distance. Juv/1st-winter: like adult, but light scaly pattern on upperparts, pale head and neck, dark ear-coverts. In flight, like CL. **BP** Bill dagger-shaped with wedge-shaped tip, ivory or yellowish, less yellow in winter (ad) or pale horn with grey basal half of culmen (juv); eyes blood red (breeding) or dark reddish-brown; tarsi black. **SV** Typically silent. **AN** White-billed Diver.

Red-throated Loon
ad sum
ad sum
ad win
juv
ad win
Black-throated Loon
ad sum
ad sum
ad win
juv
ad win
Pacific Loon
ad sum
characteristic 'snorkelling' posture
ad sum
ad win
juv
ad win
Common Loon
ad sum
ad sum
juv
ad win
ad win
Yellow-billed Loon
ad sum
ad sum
juv
ad win
ad win

Laysan Albatross *Phoebastria immutabilis* L 79–81 cm; WS 195–203 cm; WT 2300–2800 g

SD Winter breeder (Oct–May) on remote islands in the Izu/Ogasawara chain. **HH** In non-breeding season commonest albatross off E Japan. **ID** Heavily built; pied plumage superficially resembles that of large gull; does not change with age. Head, neck, rump and underparts white, otherwise dark. Dark smudge below and around eye. Upperwing, mantle, upper rump and tail very dark blackish-brown. In flight, white shafts to upper primaries visible; underwing pattern variable, but broad leading edge, trailing edge and primaries always black, with small to large black patch on carpal and closer to body. **BP** Bill large, dark pink or deep yellow with dark grey tip (ad), or all dark (juv); eyes black; legs greyish-pink. **SV** Mostly silent, but on breeding grounds emits groaning sounds during slow, elaborate courtship dance. **TN** Formerly in *Diomedea*.

Black-footed Albatross *Phoebastria nigripes* L 68–74 cm; WS 193–213 cm; WT 3000–3600 g

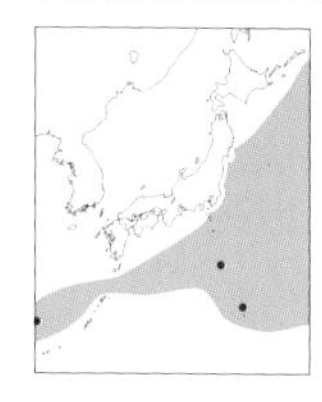

SD Winter breeder (Oct–May) on several remote Japanese islands (Torishima, Ogasawara and Senkaku). **HH** In non-breeding season occurs off Japan's Pacific coast. **ID** Darkest of the three breeding albatrosses in the region (except imm Short-tailed Albatross), appearing longer-winged. Dark sooty-brown, slightly paler on underparts, with white around bill base and below eye. Uppertail-coverts, vent and undertail-coverts white. Some have pale on belly and breast, and may be confused with imm Short-tailed, but have dark collar and dusky-pink bill. Juvenile also all dark, with all-dark tail, rump and vent. In flight, note white shafts to primaries at all ages. Pale ad/juv differs from juv/imm Short-tailed in lacking pale patches on inner secondaries and by black, or at most dusky-pink, bill. **BP** Bill long, thick, black or dusky pinkish-grey with dark tip; eyes dark greenish-brown; tarsi blackish-grey. **SV** Generally silent, but at sea and on breeding colonies sometimes gives long, extended groaning *uuwoouu* or short, continuous *uuuu*. At sea bickers over food with sheep-like bleating and shrill whistles. Simple courtship display dance also incorporates bill-snapping and groaning calls. **TN** Formerly in *Diomedea*.

Short-tailed Albatross *Phoebastria albatrus* L 84–94 cm; WS 213–229 cm; WT Av 5300 g

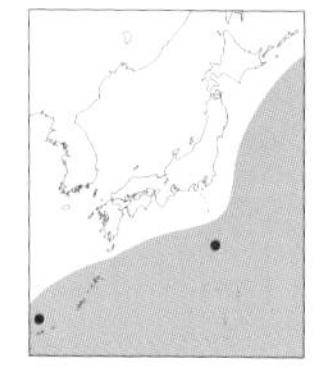

SD Vulnerable. N Pacific albatross recovering from near extinction in early 20th century; breeds during winter (Oct–May) only on remote Izu (Torishima) and Senkaku Is (East China Sea). In non-breeding season disperses north past Honshu and E Hokkaido. **HH** Breeds on open flats or scree slopes with grass on oceanic islands. **ID** Largest, rarest and most spectacular of the region's albatrosses. Wings and tail broader, and bill larger and more obviously pink than other species. Adult plumage (acquired after 12+ years) largely white with golden crown and face, and dusky grey-brown nape; black primaries (with white shafts), secondaries, tertials and outer wing-coverts; shoulders and inner secondaries white; tail black. White mantle, rump and uppertail-coverts readily distinguishes adult from other albatrosses. Juvenile is entirely very dark brown for several years, then becomes increasingly pale. As subadult, look for large pink bill, and pale or white patch on inner secondaries. **BP** Bill pink with grey tip; eyes black; tarsi dull greyish-pink. **SV** At breeding colonies gives loud braying *bwaaaaa* or *bwiiaaaa* or *u uuu u* (lower than Black-footed), and a loud clattering of mandibles in display (lower and slower than Black-footed); otherwise largely silent. **TN** Formerly in *Diomedea*. **AN** Steller's Albatross.

Laysan Albatross
Black-footed Albatross
ad lighter
ad darker
ad
ad
ad
imm
imm
ad
imm
imm
Short-tailed Albatross
young imm
young imm

Northern Fulmar *Fulmarus glacialis*

L 45–50 cm; WS 102–112 cm; WT ♂ *c* 700g, ♀ *c* 835 g

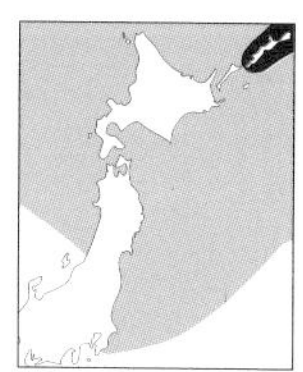

SD *F. g. rodgersii* is largest and commonest of large petrels in NW Pacific and Sea of Okhotsk. During post-breeding dispersal reaches NE Japan, mostly E Hokkaido and N Honshu, rarely further south (Oct–Apr). **HH** In non-breeding season exclusively pelagic, but occasionally seen from shore. An opportunistic and versatile feeder, taking carrion, fish offal from fishing fleets and macro-plankton. **ID** Superficially gull-like; compact, with large head, short, thick neck, broad, rounded wings and stubby bill. Dark form sometimes mistaken for Flesh-footed Shearwater. Adult may be dark, light or very light, but all three have dark tail and dark smudge around eye. The darkest are plain grey-brown with paler inner primaries. Light adults have white head, neck, upper tail and underparts; wings and uppertail-coverts mid-grey with pale and dark speckling; primaries darker, with white patch on innermost. Very light adults are mostly white, with a little grey on upperwing. Floats high on water; takes off with pattering run across water. Glides on broad, stiff wings, interspersed with rapid shallow beats. **BP** Tubenose bill is yellowish-horn, stubby and deep with prominent nostrils; eyes black; tarsi pinkish-grey. **SV** Highly vocal on breeding grounds, gives deep, guttural cackling *aark aak aak*, accelerating in duet, and also squabbles noisily, grunting and cackling in flocks at sea or when feeding.

Cape Petrel *Daption capense*

L 38–40 cm; WS 81–91 cm; WT 340–480 g

SD S Hemisphere species accidental in Japan (*D. c. capense*). **HH** Pelagic. Commonly follows ships. **ID** Northern Fulmar-like in proportions, but distinctively pied. Hood, mantle and tail-band black; mantle and rump white, heavily spotted black. Upperwing black with large white patches on inner primaries and inner secondaries. **BP** Bill short, tube-nosed, black; eyes black; tarsi black. **SV** Gives short, sharp whistles and harsh rattling calls at sea. **TN** Not included by OSJ.

Providence Petrel *Pterodroma solandri*

L 40 cm; WS 95–105 cm; WT 500 g

SD Vulnerable. Scarce migrant mostly in deep waters east of Japan, north to Hokkaido during Jun–Nov. **HH** Pelagic. **ID** Large, thickset gadfly petrel. Rather dark, grey and brown; head darker, often giving hooded appearance, but paler around base of stubby bill and on chin, and underparts slightly paler than breast and head. M pattern across upperwing, and dark blackish-grey tail (broadly tipped darker), both contrast with dull upperparts, though M can be inconspicuous at distance. Mantle and undersides of primaries and secondaries may be mottled or entirely pale; white bases to primaries and greater primary-coverts form two neat crescents on otherwise uniform dull-grey underwing, creating skua-like white flash at base of primaries. **BP** Bill short, thick, black; eyes black; tarsi grey. **SV** Generally silent at sea. **AN** Solander's Petrel.

Juan Fernandez Petrel *Pterodroma externa*

L 43 cm; WS 95–97 cm; WT 500 g

SD Vulnerable. A post-typhoon accidental migrant to Honshu and Okinawa. **HH** Pelagic. **ID** Large grey and white gadfly petrel, with rather typical grey upperparts and prominent black M pattern on upperwings. Black cap extends below eyes and is continuous with back, lacking white collar of White-necked Petrel, but bordered at sides by white extending from throat. Tail grey, but sometimes has basal off-white horseshoe. Underparts entirely white. Underwing largely white, with black tips and leading edge to otherwise white primaries, a narrow black trailing edge to wing, and very short black bar from carpal towards body (cf. Stejneger's). **BP** Bill short, black; eyes black; tarsi grey. **SV** Generally silent at sea.

Cape Petrel
Northern Fulmar
dark morph
light morph
darkest variant
dark morph
Juan Fernandez Petrel
Providence Petrel
fresh
worn

Kermadec Petrel *Pterodroma neglecta* L 38–39 cm; WS 92 cm; WT 509 g

SD *P. n. neglecta* is a scarce migrant to the N Pacific; very small numbers occur (most frequent Sep) over deep waters east of Honshu north to Hokkaido. **HH** Pelagic. **ID** Polymorphic gadfly petrel with obvious skua-like wing flashes (bases to inner webs of primaries) on upper and underside of wing in pale and dark morphs, and rather short, square tail. Dark morph mostly plain dark grey-brown, recalls similar Providence Petrel, but is brown rather than grey, and lacks white underwing greater primary-coverts crescent. Pale morph is grey-brown with paler head, and very pale grey or off-white lower breast and belly. Typically has a fleck of white between base of stubby black bill and eye. Flight (in moderately calm conditions) leisurely, with deep wingbeats followed by long glides, rising and banking in broad arcs. **BP** Bill stubby, black; eyes black; tarsi pinkish-orange. **SV** Generally silent at sea.

Hawaiian Petrel *Pterodroma sandwichensis* L 40–43 cm; WS 90–91 cm; WT 434 g

SD Vulnerable. Accidental to N & C Honshu, Japan. **HH** Pelagic. **ID** Rather large, long-winged, dark greyish-brown and white gadfly petrel, similar to Juan Fernandez Petrel. Forehead white, crown and nape black, the cap extending below eyes and onto neck and upper breast-sides; mantle and back pale grey to greyish-brown (slightly paler than head and wings), wings and tail dark slaty-grey. Slight M mark on wings. Underparts largely white, with broad black markings close to leading edge (carpal and primary-coverts), rather broad black tips to white-based primaries, and narrow black trailing edge; axillaries white, only rarely showing any dark markings. **BP** Bill short, black; eyes black; tarsi bluish-flesh. **SV** Generally silent at sea. **TN** Formerly within Dark-rumped Petrel *P. phaeopygia* (e.g. WBSJ, OSJ).

Mottled Petrel *Pterodroma inexpectata* L 33–35 cm; WS 74–82 cm; WT 247–441 g

SD Common summer migrant (Jun–Aug) to deeper waters of N Pacific north to Bering Sea, but rare west into Japanese waters; nevertheless, it should be looked for during any summer pelagic off E & NE Japan. **HH** Pelagic. **ID** Very distinctive, rather heavy gadfly petrel. Almost entirely pale or mid-grey on upperparts, with strong dark grey M on upperwings. Underwing white with strong black bar from carpal almost to the axillaries. The most obvious feature is the dark grey belly patch, which contrasts well with the white underwings and vent (though can be surprisingly difficult to see even at moderate range); neck- and breast-sides also grey. **BP** Short, stout black bill contrasts with white lores and chin; black patch around black eye; tarsi flesh-coloured with distal webs black. **SV** Generally silent at sea.

White-necked Petrel *Pterodroma cervicalis* L 43 cm; WS 95–100 cm; WT 380–545 g

SD Vulnerable. Very rare in Japanese subtropical waters, e.g. off Ogasawara Is (mid-Jul–late Nov). **HH** Pelagic. **ID** Large grey and white gadfly petrel, resembling Juan Fernandez Petrel, but appears heavier and shorter-winged at sea, and upperparts more brown-toned. Dark grey or black cap, pale grey mantle and innerwing, and dark grey tail. Neck and underparts white; the white hind-collar, separating black cap from grey upperparts, further distinguishes it from Juan Fernandez. Underwing mostly white, with black border to forewing and on secondary and primary tips. **BP** Bill short, black; eyes black; tarsi grey. **SV** Generally silent at sea. **TN** Not currently included by OSJ.

Kermadec Petrel
pale morph
intermediate morph
dark morph
dark morph
intermediate morph
Hawaiian Petrel
worn
fresh
White-necked Petrel
fresh
worn
Mottled Petrel
fresh
worn

Black-winged Petrel *Pterodroma nigripennis*

L 28–30 cm; WS 63–71 cm; WT 140–200 g

SD Migrant to NW Pacific (Jun–Nov), typhoon-blown accidental to Hokkaido and S Honshu; should be looked for during summer and autumn pelagic trips off E & NE Japan. **HH** Pelagic. **ID** Grey, black and white gadfly petrel with strong underwing pattern. Upperparts entirely pale or mid-grey with strong dark grey M on upperwings recalling Mottled Petrel, but lacks grey belly patch of that species, and is smaller with less towering flight. Underwing closely resembles Bonin Petrel, white with very strong black bar from carpal almost to axillaries (but has much narrower black primary-coverts patch), and prominent black trailing edge to underwing (not noticeable in Mottled), but cap is less black and head and neck-sides paler, greyer than Bonin. **BP** Bill stout and black, lores and chin white; eyes black with white eyebrow and small black mask; tarsi black. **SV** Generally silent at sea.

Bonin Petrel *Pterodroma hypoleuca*

L 30–31 cm; WS 63–71 cm; WT *c.* 182 g

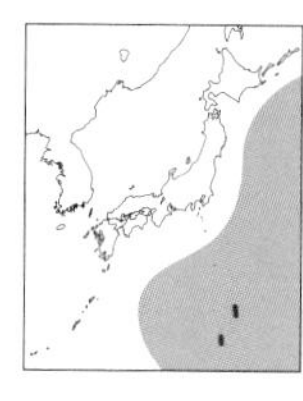

SD The only gadfly petrel that breeds in Japan. Breeds (Nov–May) on outer islands south from Ogasawara (Bonin) Is. Outside the breeding season it disperses across NW Pacific and is occasionally reported from Nansei Shoto north through Japanese waters to Kuril Is. **HH** Pelagic. **ID** Small, graceful gadfly petrel, similar to Black-winged; dark-grey upperparts with darker, blackish-grey wings. Mask and neck-sides blacker than Black-winged. Lores, chin, foreneck and underparts pure white. Distinctive underwing pattern with broad black primary-coverts patch and strong black carpal bar extending towards, but not reaching, flanks; undertail-coverts white. **BP** Bill short, black; eyes black; tarsi pink, toes blackish-pink. **SV** Generally silent at sea.

Stejneger's Petrel *Pterodroma longirostris*

L 26–31 cm; WS 53–66 cm

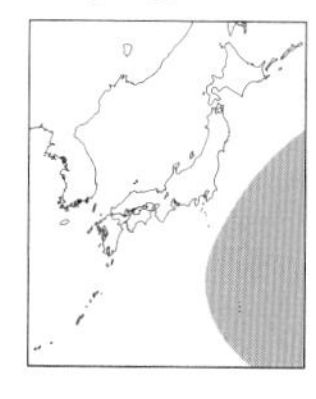

SD Vulnerable. Though only rarely recorded off the Japanese coast, from Okinawa to N Honshu, this migrant to NW Pacific occurs in very large numbers just east of Japanese waters (May–Sep/Oct), and should be looked for after typhoons during any summer or autumn pelagic off E Japan. **HH** Pelagic. **ID** Small grey, black and white gadfly petrel with very strong M mark on upperparts and very pale trailing edge to inner wing. Very similar to Black-winged Petrel, but eye-patch less obvious, paler grey on upperparts and has more prominent dark grey M on upperwings. Underwing white, with only small black carpal patch and inconspicuous black trailing edge. **BP** Bill black; eyes black; tarsi dark grey. **SV** Generally silent at sea.

Cook's Petrel *Pterodroma cookii*

L 25–30 cm; WS 65–66 cm; WT *c.* 200 g

SD Accidental off Pacific coast, to be looked for after typhoons during any summer or autumn pelagic off E Japan. **HH** Pelagic. **ID** Small, lightweight *Pterodroma*; head and back pale grey, contrasting with bold dark M across upperwings; tail may have dark tip. Underwings mostly white (unlike other relatives). **BP** Black bill is thin; eyes black; tarsi dark grey. **SV** Generally silent at sea. **TN** Not currently included by OSJ.

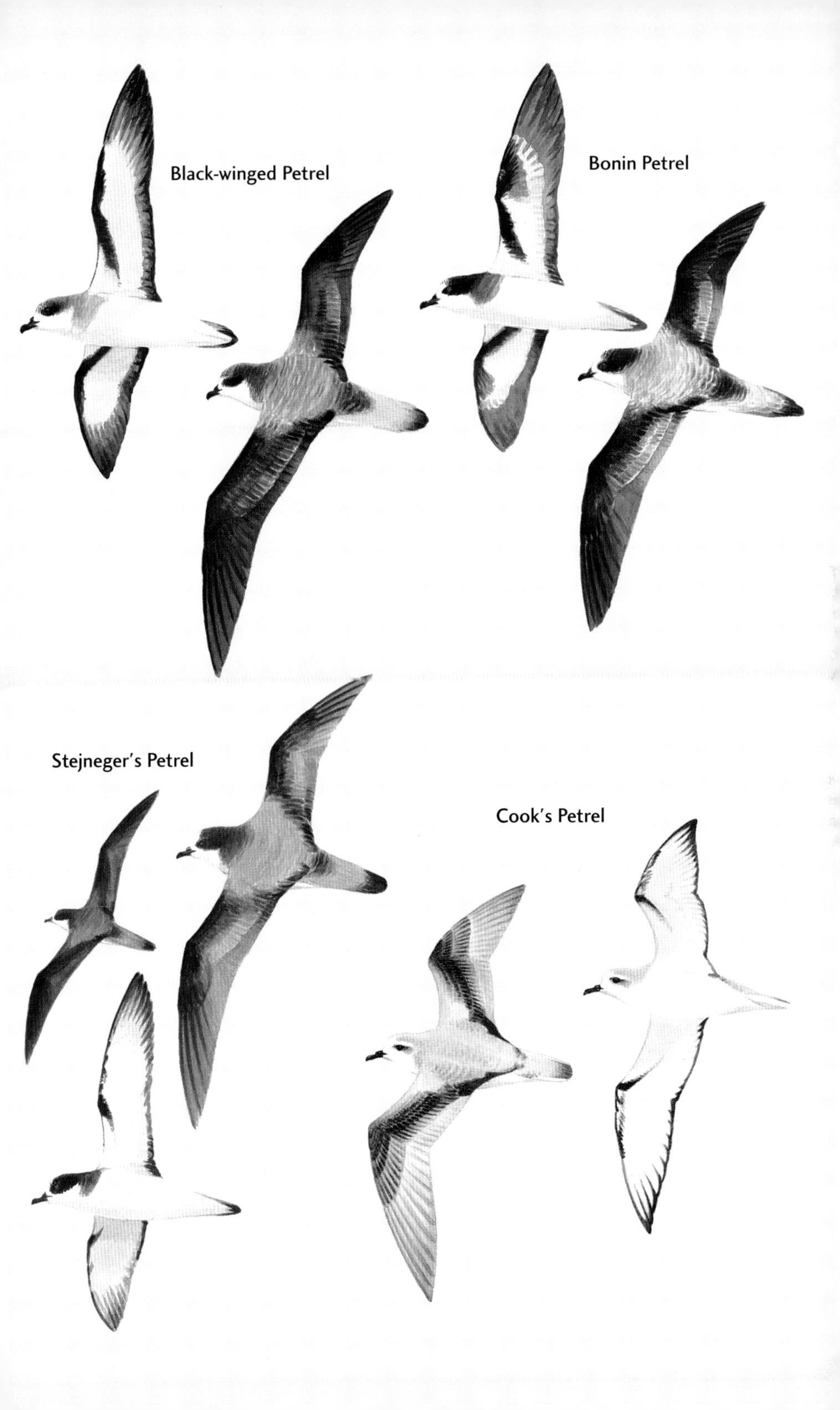
Black-winged Petrel
Bonin Petrel
Stejneger's Petrel
Cook's Petrel

Streaked Shearwater *Calonectris leucomelas*

L 48–49 cm; WS 122 cm; WT 440–545 g

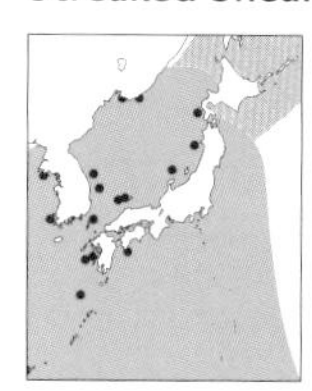

SD Most frequent in warm-water regions of NW Pacific, around Japan where it breeds (Mar–Nov) colonially on islands from south-west Hokkaido to the Nansei Shoto. Forages at considerable distance from breeding colonies. Disperses after breeding, mostly southwards. **HH** Pelagic. The commonest shearwater in sight of land, and after typhoons; during fog and heavy rain sometimes recorded inland. Burrow-nester on forested offshore islands, visited only at night. **ID** Large, long-winged shearwater (largest in region), with broad wings, white underparts and underwings, and prominent pale or white head at distance. Plain mid-brown hindneck, mantle, wings, rump and tail, with pale fringes to secondaries, some wing-coverts and mantle, producing impression of dark M across paler wings and mantle, and pale V on uppertail-coverts in worn plumage. Head and neck flecked white to almost entirely white (age-related?); face and underparts all white. Flight steady with slow flaps, gull-like on angled wings, interspersed with long glides; pale underwing, dark carpals, white body, long thick neck and pale head diagnostic. **BP** Bill grey/pink with dark tip; eyes dark brown or black; tarsi pinkish-grey, feet do not reach tail tip. **SV** Noisy growling at colony, with returning ♂ giving *pee wee pee wee* and ♀ deeper, more vigorous *guwaae guwaae* calls.

Wedge-tailed Shearwater *Ardenna pacifica*

L 38–46 cm; WS 97–105 cm; WT 320–510 g

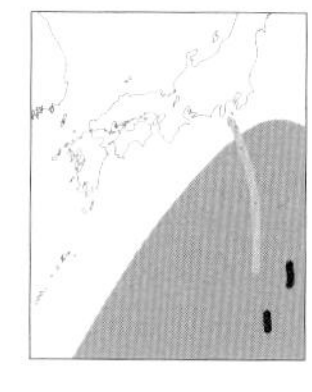

SD Replaces Streaked Shearwater in tropical waters. Breeds (late Mar–early Oct) only on Ogasawara and Iwo Is. Ranges north to Izu Is; a very rare visitor to waters further north off Honshu and the Nansei Shoto. **HH** Pelagic. **ID** Mid-sized shearwater with pale and dark morphs, both with long wedge-shaped tail. Dark morph entirely dark brown (including underwing); pale morph (predominates in Japan) resembles Streaked, mid-brown above with pale underparts, but lacks Streaked's pale head and face. Underwing-coverts all white, leaving only primaries and secondaries dark. Flight rather lazy with short glides on bowed wings held forwards, interspersed by slow flaps; less graceful than other shearwaters. **BP** Bill dark grey; eyes black; tarsi pink. **SV** At breeding sites gives deep moaning *uu-oo uu-oo* or *vuu oo vuu oo*. Silent at sea. **TN** Formerly in *Puffinus*.

Buller's Shearwater *Ardenna bulleri*

L 46–47 cm; WS 97–99 cm; WT 342–425 g

SD Vulnerable. Rare, usually with flocks of Short-tailed Shearwater. Most frequently encountered off E Honshu (Aug–Oct), but reaches as far north as E Hokkaido. **HH** Pelagic. **ID** Medium to large, slender-bodied grey, black, and white shearwater with striking *Pterodroma*-like pattern to upperparts. Between Short-tailed and Sooty shearwaters in size, but more slender with longer tail, broader-based wings and neatly patterned plumage. Upperparts have striking M pattern, with blackish-grey crown, nape and tail, and dark grey flight-feathers; very dark wing-coverts contrast with pale grey hindneck, mantle, shoulders and greater coverts, rump and uppertail-coverts. Underparts clean white. Flight is graceful, languid, and buoyant, recalling smaller albatrosses, with long effortless glides low over water even in completely calm conditions. **BP** Bill grey with dark culmen and tip; eyes black; tarsi dark grey. **SV** Generally silent at sea. **TN** Formerly in *Puffinus*. **AN** New Zealand Shearwater.

Streaked Shearwater
Buller's Shearwater
fresh
worn
Wedge-tailed Shearwater
dark morph
dark morph
pale morph
intermediate
morph
pale morph

Sooty Shearwater *Ardenna grisea*

L 43–51 cm; WS 94–109 cm; WT 650–978 g

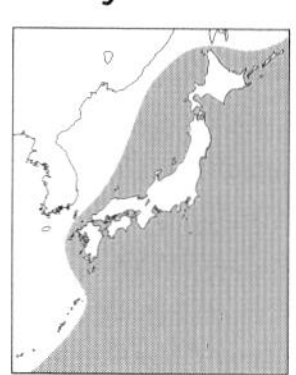

SD Abundant, northbound migrant in early summer (Apr–May) off the Pacific coast; smaller numbers migrate via the Sea of Japan. **HH** Pelagic. **ID** Medium-sized, blackish-brown. Long, narrow, pointed wings with silvery-grey to white (individually variable in extent) on underwing-coverts contrasting strongly with dark brown axillaries and flight-feathers. Broadest and brightest white is on primary-coverts, contrasting with dark primaries. Whitish secondary-coverts form bar that gradually narrows towards body. Separation from Short-tailed Shearwater often impossible, except at close range. Crown flat, the forehead gently sloping to bill. Neck short, wingtips extend beyond short tail. Bill longer than Short-tailed and head less rounded. Flight powerful, smooth and rather direct, banking strongly; wings angled back in strong wind; body stocky, more uniformly tubular than Short-tailed, thus looks dumpy at rear. In calm weather, gives 3–7 quick, stiff-winged flaps, followed by glide of 3–5 seconds. In moderate breeze flight lacks sudden changes in direction; flaps briefly then arcs up in longer glide. In strong winds, glides without flapping, arcing up very high followed by long downward glide. **BP** Bill long (almost as long as head), fairly stout at base with 'pinched-in' middle and heavy hooked tip, dark-grey with black culmen and tip; eyes black; tarsi dark grey. **SV** Feeding groups can be noisy, giving a raucous, nasal *aaaa*. **TN** Plate 24 shearwaters all formerly in *Puffinus*.

Short-tailed Shearwater *Ardenna tenuirostris*

L 40–43 cm; WS 95–100 cm; WT 480–800 g

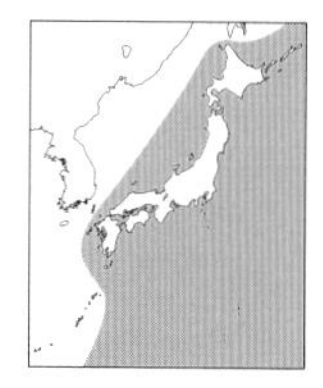

SD Abundant migrant, passing Japan's Pacific coast northbound in early summer (Apr–May) during a loop migration around N Pacific, smaller numbers migrate via Sea of Japan. Enormous flocks gather off SE & E Hokkaido and off Sea of Okhotsk coast (Apr–Jun). **HH** Pelagic. **ID** Dark brownish-grey shearwater closely resembling Sooty. Adult: generally like Sooty, but the underwing-coverts, though pale grey or brownish-grey with a silvery sheen (light-dependent, and usually brightest on median secondary-coverts, not median primary-coverts), are usually darker and more uniform (rarely all dark). In flight, appears duller than Sooty (though some, confusingly, have uniform silvery wing linings, including most underwing-coverts and bases to flight-feathers), with toes extending noticeably beyond tail. Juvenile (late autumn/winter): entirely pale grey underwings and brown underparts, especially pale on breast, neck and throat, contrasting with dark crown and ear-coverts. Usually shows pale throat and short neck; bill appears shorter and more slender than Sooty. Wings shorter and narrower than Sooty, with more even width, and wingtips appear slightly more rounded. Flight action highly variable (Sooty rather consistent), faster, more erratic, with longer periods of flapping, more mechanical wingbeats, usually less arcing and gliding, and frequent changes of direction. Characteristically rocks side-to-side while flapping. **BP** Bill short (clearly shorter than head), dark grey with black culmen and tip; eyes black; tarsi dark grey. **SV** Generally silent. **AN** Slender-billed Shearwater.

Flesh-footed Shearwater *Ardenna carneipes*

L 40–47 cm; WS 99–107 cm; WT 510–765 g

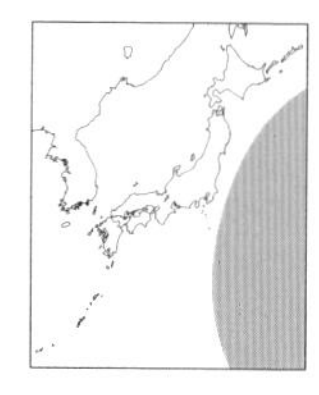

SD Mostly recorded off Pacific coast in early summer (May–Jun). Relatively scarce compared with previous two species. **HH** Pelagic. **ID** Stocky, dark brown shearwater with large head and full chest. Most easily distinguished by uniform dark upperwing and underwing-coverts, slightly pale grey flight-feathers (below) and leg and bill colour. Darker and noticeably broader-winged than Sooty. At rest resembles Wedge-tailed, but larger with paler bill, and wingtips extend beyond tail. Flight laboured, almost gull-like, beats deeper and slower than Sooty. Beware dark-morph Northern Fulmar for which it is often mistaken, but Flesh-footed much darker brown (not milky grey), with longer, narrower wings, smaller head and slender-bodied jizz, and longer, more slender bill with obvious dark tip. Wings lack prominent pale panel at base of primaries of Northern Fulmar. **BP** Bill nearly as long as head, straw-coloured to pink with dark grey tip (bill conspicuously bicoloured even at distance); eyes black; tarsi pinkish-grey often obvious against dark tail. **SV** Generally silent, but gives sharp, high squeals during feeding frenzies. **AN** Pale-footed Shearwater.

Pink-footed Shearwater *Ardenna creatopus*

L 45–48 cm; WS 109–118 cm; WT 576–879 g

SD Vulnerable. Vagrant, E Honshu. **HH** Pelagic. **ID** Dull brown shearwater recalling Flesh-footed, with dusky head and uniformly dark upperparts and upper wings. Lighter-morph adults have pale underwings, darker adults have mottled underwings. **BP** Bill pinkish with dark tip; eyes black; tarsi dull pinkish. **SV** Generally silent.

Sooty Shearwater
Short-tailed Shearwater
fresh
fresh
Pink-footed Shearwater
Flesh-footed
Shearwater

Christmas Shearwater *Puffinus nativitatis* L 35–38 cm; WS 71–81 cm; WT 324–340 g

SD Accidental to N, C & S Honshu coasts. **HH** Pelagic. **ID** Small, slender, uniformly dark-brown shearwater. Resembles Wedge-tailed Shearwater but smaller, with rounded tail. Upperparts and underparts uniform dark brown, like small Short-tailed Shearwater, but long narrow wings lack silvery-grey underwing. **BP** Bill black; eyes black; tarsi dark brown. **SV** Generally silent at sea. **AN** Kiritimati Shearwater; Christmas Island Shearwater.

Newell's Shearwater *Puffinus newelli* L 33 cm; WS 71–81 cm; WT 324–340 g

SD Accidental to S Honshu. **HH** Pelagic. **ID** A boldly black-and-white *Puffinus* shearwater; very dark above, dark cap extends to below eye, pure white below, with white extending from neck round to ear, and from flanks wrapping prominently on to sides of rump. The undertail-coverts are dark (see Manx Shearwater). Rapid wingbeats interspersed with short glides; underwing is white with broad black margins. **BP** Bill black; eyes black; legs dark pink, toes pinkish-grey. **SV** Generally silent at sea.

Manx Shearwater *Puffinus puffinus* L 30–38 cm; WS 76–89 cm; WT 350–575 g

SD Accidental to S Honshu. **HH** Pelagic. **ID** Medium-sized shearwater with uniform sooty-black upperparts (can appear brownish-black in strong light), extending below eyes to lores and auriculars, and onto neck- and breast-sides, and in some to axillaries. Underparts white, including undertail-coverts. On water shows clean white flanks; wingtips extend beyond tail. In flight, tends to flap more (and glide less) with extremely rapid, stiff, almost auklet-like wingbeats interspersed by longer glides, unlike congeners; shears and banks in stronger winds. Differs from congeners in being larger, with white undertail-coverts and black lores. **BP** Bill grey with dark culmen and tip; eyes black; tarsi dark grey. **SV** Generally silent at sea.

Bryan's Shearwater *Puffinus bryani* L *c.* 25 cm

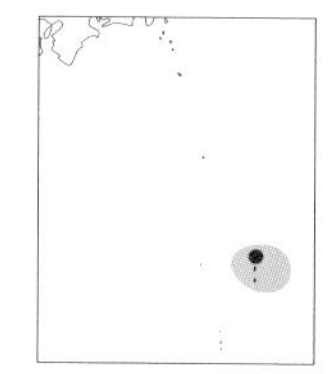

SD Critically Endangered. Breeds only on Ogasawara Is. **HH** Pelagic. **ID** Smallest of all *Puffinus* shearwaters. Slate-black above, white below and on lores, above eyes and on ear coverts. Wings broadly rounded at tip, tail long. Undertail-coverts blackish. **BP** Bill dark grey; eyes black. **SV** Generally silent at sea.

Bannerman's Shearwater *Puffinus bannermani* L 27–33 cm; WS 64–74 cm; WT 150–230 g

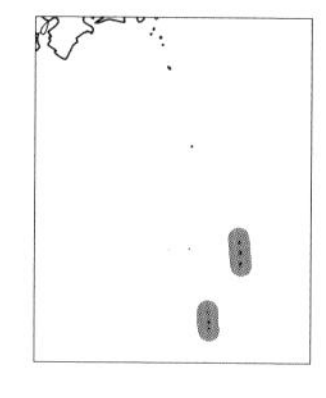

SD Endangered. A local and uncommon endemic, seemingly restricted to vicinity of its remote breeding grounds, on Ogasawara and Iwo Is, where occurs year-round, though has reached Nansei Shoto. **HH** Pelagic. **ID** Second-smallest shearwater in region. Forehead rather vertical like Short-tailed Shearwater, but crown appears flatter. Bill plain and two-toned, with slate-black upperparts (mantle, rump and upperwing-coverts may show paler fringes) and white chin to undertail-coverts; dusky blackish-grey neck- and breast-sides. White at bill base below lores, white spot in front of eyes suggesting supercilia, pale grey mottling around eyes and ear-coverts, white face below eye, white flanks and dark undertail-coverts. At rest, wingtips fall close to or short of tail tip. Wings rather broad and round-tipped; underwing white with broad dusky margin at rear and tip, whilst leading edge also dark and broad, especially on inner wing. Undertail dark with white, or at least pale, central rectrices. Flight rapid, with fast wingbeats and short glides. Previously considered conspecific with Atlantic **Audubon's Shearwater**, but has paler, greyer head and hind-collar, contrasting with black mantle and whiter face; mottled blackish-grey underwing-coverts, neck- and breast-sides; and paler fringes to upperparts. **BP** Bill dark grey with blue base; eyes black; tarsi and toes dark blue-grey, webs pink. **SV** Generally silent at sea. **TN** Formerly part of Audubon's Shearwater *P. lherminieri*, e.g. OSJ; also considered as Tropical or Baillon's Shearwater *P. bailloni*.

Christmas Shearwater
Newell's Shearwater
Bryan's Shearwater
Manx Shearwater
fresh
worn
Bannerman's Shearwater

Bulwer's Petrel *Bulweria bulwerii*

L 26–28 cm; WS 68–73 cm; WT 78–130 g

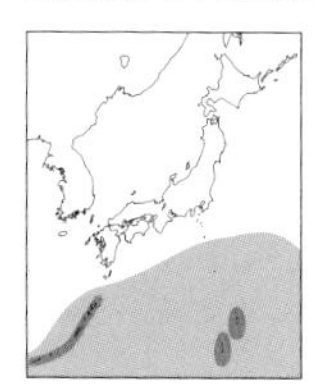

SD Breeds on remote islands off S Japan (e.g. Izu, Ogasawara and Iwo Is). Reasonably common (Apr–Oct) around outer Japanese islands south from Ogasawara Is and the Nansei Shoto. Less common northwards to Izu Is. Recorded from mainland coasts or inland only after typhoons. **HH** Pelagic. **ID** Long-winged and long-tailed dark petrel with small head, intermediate between shearwaters and storm petrels. Entirely blackish-brown, with only slightly paler diagonal upperwing-coverts bar. Slightly larger and longer-tailed than Tristram's Storm Petrel, with which it may be confused, though wings broader, and tail pointed when closed but wedge-shaped when open (not forked). Flight also differs from Tristram's, being graceful, somewhat shearwater-like, but lighter, erratic, buoyant, even tern-like, suddenly changing speed and direction, employing loose, deep wingbeats, and often gliding on arched wings. **BP** Bill short, rather heavy, black; eyes black; tarsi pale pink, webs black distally. **SV** Gives hoarse barking *hroo hroo hroo*, guttural *krsh krsh* notes and moans, but only at nest.

Wilson's Storm Petrel *Oceanites oceanicus*

L 15–19 cm; WS 38–42 cm; WT 34–45 g

SD *O. o. exasperatus* occurs occasionally off Japan's Pacific coast. **HH** Pelagic. **ID** Dark blackish-brown plumage relieved only by pale panel on greater upperwing-coverts, variably narrow to broad, and by broad square white rump and extensively white undertail-coverts. Tail square, but may appear notched. Flight bounding, wings outstretched, skipping, pattering, walking on water with legs extended, occasionally showing diagnostic yellow webs; flight also often slow and fluttering, with very prolonged glides on flat, depressed wings. Wings short, with indistinct carpal bend, 'arm' short and broad, 'hand' longer, creating broadly triangular wing shape with rounded tip (compare Leach's). Centre of otherwise dark underwing is pale brown, and toes extend well beyond tail tip. Frequently foot-patters along sea surface whilst feeding, with wings and tail raised, revealing white lateral undertail-coverts. **BP** Bill slender, short, black; eyes black; long legs black, toes dark grey, webs yellow. **SV** Generally silent, but foraging groups give harsh, stuttering, chattering *kerr kerr kerr kerr* calls.

Band-rumped Storm Petrel *Oceanodroma castro*

L 19–21 cm; WS 44–46 cm; WT 29–56 g

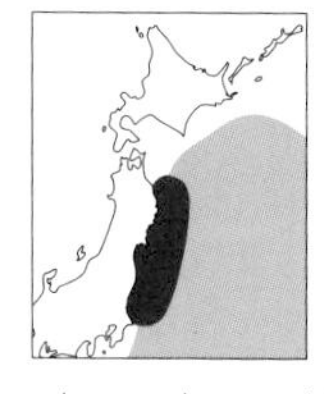

SD Breeds only on islands off Pacific coast of Honshu (mostly May–Oct). **HH** Pelagic. Most frequently encountered storm petrel from NW Pacific ferries. **ID** Largely brownish-black to black, with broad white rump (wider than long), extending to rump-sides (but not vent). In flight, dark brown carpal bar weak and does not reach leading edge, not as pale as Wilson's or as long as Leach's. Most similar to Leach's, but has broader wings; wing-shape intermediate between Leach's and Wilson's. Wings longer (especially 'arm') than Wilson's; tail shorter and squarer, only slightly forked, and toes do not extend to tip. Flight erratic, with many twists and turns, often turning back on its course; less bounding than Leach's, with quicker, shallower beats; glides on bowed wings. **BP** At close range, black bill is stubbier, heavier than other species; eyes black; short tarsi black (not visible in flight). **SV** Highly vocal around colonies: squeaky *chiwee* and repetitive, deep purring *kuwa kuwa gyururuuru* or *kerr wheecha wheecha wheecha wheeeechuh* (deeper and hoarser than Leach's). **TN** May become *Thalobata castro* in the future. Perhaps polytypic. **AN** Madeiran Storm Petrel.

Swinhoe's Storm Petrel *Oceanodroma monorhis*

L 19–20 cm; WS 44–46 cm; WT 38–40 g

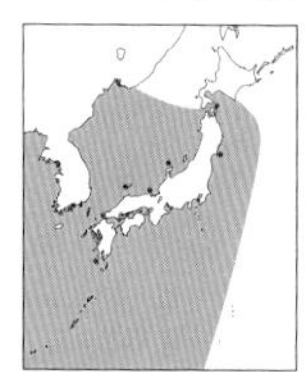

SD Breeds (May–Sep) on a few remote islands around Honshu. Disperses to south and west post breeding. Scarce, vulnerable and enigmatic; most frequently seen from offshore ferries. **HH** Pelagic. **ID** Small all-black storm petrel, with no white rump patch (much smaller than Tristram's and Matsudaira's). Similar in size, structure and wing pattern to Leach's, but blacker, with all-dark rump and only slightly forked tail (note that some Leach's show little white on rump). In flight, dark brown carpal bar less prominent than other species, and 2–3 pale, outer primary shafts may be inconspicuous, except at very close range (cf. Matsudaira's). Wings have long angular shape typical of *Oceanodroma* species. Flight, like Leach's, rather tern- or pratincole-like, powerful, graceful, bounding but erratic, with sudden banks and arcs; also rather fluttering flight interspersed with glides. **BP** Black stubby bill; eyes black; short tarsi and toes black. **SV** Generally silent at sea. **TN** May become *Cymochorea monorhis* in the future.

Bulwer's Petrel
Wilson's Storm Petrel
Swinhoe's Storm Petrel
Band-rumped Storm Petrel

Leach's Storm Petrel *Oceanodroma leucorhoa* L 19–22 cm; WS 45–48 cm; WT 45 g

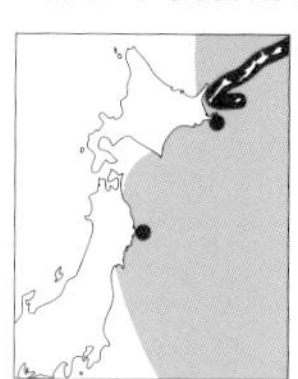

SD *O. l. leucorhoa* breeds (May–Aug) on nearshore islands off SE Hokkaido. In non-breeding season may be encountered anywhere at sea off Pacific coast of Honshu and Hokkaido. **HH** Breeds in burrows. May appear inland during heavy rain and fog. Pelagic outside breeding season. **ID** Slender, fairly large, long-winged storm petrel, largely blackish-brown (slightly paler than Band-rumped or Wilson's), with prominent, long V-shaped white rump, sometimes with dark central feathers, dark vent and all-dark undertail-coverts, thus less bright than Band-rumped. In flight, long wings are pointed, narrower in 'arm' than Band-rumped or Wilson's, with strong carpal angle and very prominent pale-brown carpal bar extending diagonally across entire wing. Flight strong and bounding, wingbeats deep, sometimes glides on bowed wings with carpals held forward, or wings raised; deeply notched tail; some birds show white primary shafts. **BP** Bill short, black; eyes black; tarsi black. **SV** Highly vocal at/near colonies when gives a crooning *uooooo u* from inside burrow and a very rapid, highly repetitive chattering cooing: *oteke-te-toto* or *totte ketto tep top top* and more alarm-sounding *ki ki ki ki kyurururu...* calls in flight over colony; otherwise silent. **TN** May become *Cymochorea leucorhoa* in the future.

Tristram's Storm Petrel *Oceanodroma tristrami* L 24–25 cm; WS 56 cm, WT 70–112 g

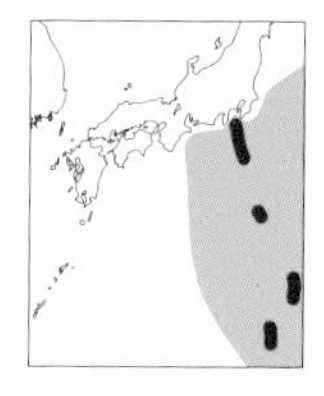

SD Breeds (Oct–Apr) only on Izu, Ogasawara and Iwo Is. Occurs in warm waters around and between breeding areas all year. **HH** Breeds on volcanic islands, otherwise pelagic. **ID** Large, long-winged storm petrel, mostly black with blue-grey to brown tinge; lacks white rump. Similarly all-dark Swinhoe's is smaller. Approaches Bulwer's Petrel in size, but Bulwer's has relatively longer and narrower wings. Wings long and angled at carpal. In flight, brown carpal bar long and prominent, lacks distinctive white primary bases of Matsudaira's Storm Petrel. Tail long and deeply forked. Flight strong, wings held more stiffly and less angled than smaller storm petrels, and much longer than Swinhoe's, which glides less frequently. **BP** Bill longer, more prominent than smaller storm petrels; eyes black; tarsi black. **SV** Breeding colonies are noisy at night; birds in burrows give crooning *auooo koo* notes, and those in flight *keekoo kyukukuku*. **TN** May become *Cymochorea tristrami* in the future.

Matsudaira's Storm Petrel *Oceanodroma matsudairae* L 24–25 cm; WS 56 cm; WT 62 g

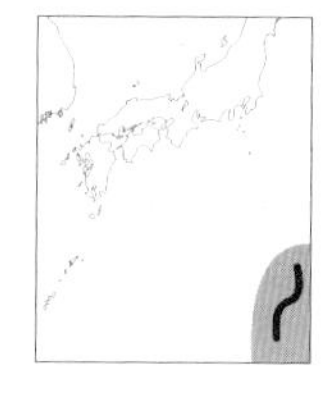

SD Endemic breeder on Ogasawara and Iwo Is (Jan–Jun). In non-breeding season disperses away from Japanese waters. **HH** Breeds on volcanic islands, otherwise pelagic. **ID** Large and long-winged, mostly black with brownish tinge, lacks white rump patch. Carpal bar short and brown; tail long and deeply forked. Much larger than similarly patterned Swinhoe's; closely resembles Tristram's, but carpal bar less distinct and has prominent white bases to outermost 4–5 primaries. Flight strong, purposeful, but slow with wings held more stiffly and less angled than smaller storm petrels; heavier in flight than Swinhoe's or Bulwer's. **BP** Bill black, longer, more prominent than smaller storm petrels; eyes black; black tarsi very long, toes black. **SV** Generally silent at sea. **TN** May become *Loomelania matsudairae* in the future.

Fork-tailed Storm Petrel *Oceanodroma furcata* L 20–23 cm; WS 46 cm; WT 59 g

SD *O. f. furcata* breeds (May–Jun) just north of Japan in N & C Kuril Is. Regular in small numbers off Hokkaido and N Honshu, mostly in winter. **HH** Breeds on remote islands, otherwise pelagic. Occasionally visits harbours after storms. **ID** The only pale grey storm petrel. Head appears overly large, with steep bulging forehead and flat crown, with blackish eye-patch. Relatively stocky and broad-winged, with sooty black underwing- and upperwing-coverts. On upperwing, appears to have double bar, black and pale grey, on inner wing. Rump and longish forked tail are pale grey and tail tip is dark grey to black. In flight, wingbeats fairly shallow, fluttering with erratic zigzags, speed changes and interspersed short glides. **BP** Bill short, black; eye-patch and eyes black; tarsi dark grey. **SV** Generally silent at sea, but at colonies gives soft twittering, chirping and high rasping *skveeee skew skwe*. **TN** May become *Hydrobates furcatus* in the future. **AN** Grey Storm Petrel.

Leach's Storm Petrel
Tristram's Storm Petrel
Matsudaira's Storm Petrel
worn
fresh
Fork-tailed Storm Petrel
typical storm petrel foraging behaviour, pattering on sea surface

Little Grebe *Tachybaptus ruficollis*

L 25–29 cm; WS 40–45 cm; WT 130–236 g

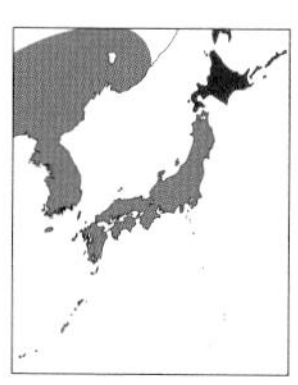

SD *T. r. poggei* year-round south of Hokkaido (where mainly a summer visitor). **HH** Small well-vegetated ponds. Winters at lakes, rivers, occasionally harbours. **ID** Small, short-necked, with rounded, tail-less body. Breeding adult: chestnut cheeks and foreneck, dark chocolate-brown crown, nape and upperparts. Winter adult: brown and buff. Flight low and laboured. Upperwing uniformly brown with narrow white trailing edge; underwing white. **BP** Bill black with yellow gape and pale tip (breeding), or pale horn (non-breeding); eyes white or pale-yellow; tarsi grey. **SV** ♂ gives rapid series of high-pitched *ke-ke-ke* notes, rising to long wavering far-carrying trill *kiri kiri kiri kiririri*. Abbreviated trills given in winter; short, sharp clicks in alarm.

Red-necked Grebe *Podiceps grisegena*

L 40–50 cm; WS 77–85 cm; WT 806–925 g

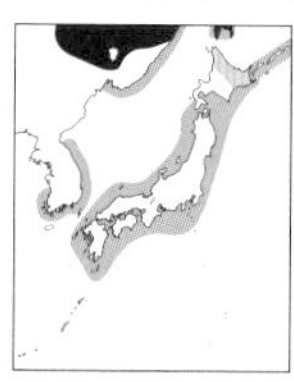

SD *P. g. holbollii* rare Hokkaido breeder (May–Aug). Winters (Sep–Apr) along Pacific coast (commoner north, scarcer south). **HH** Well-vegetated ponds/lakes; winters along coasts, bays, occasionally inland (lakes/rivers). **ID** More compact and darker than Great Crested (GCG), with squarer head and shorter, thicker neck. Winter adult: duskier grey head, face and neck than GCG; dark cap extends to lores; rear ear-coverts pale. Juv/1st-winter: black and white face bars. Flight similar to GCG, but neck shorter and darker. **BP** Bill long, straight, angled below horizontal, yellow base with dark grey culmen and tip (breeding ad) or dull yellow (non-breeding ad/juv); eyes black; tarsi dark grey. **SV** Gull-like wailing, harsh squeals, neighing *kerekerekere*… and mournful *uwaa uwaa* calls.

Great Crested Grebe *Podiceps cristatus*

L 46–51 cm; WS 59–73 cm; WT 596–1490 g

SD *P. c. cristatus* uncommon summer visitor (May–Aug), N Honshu. Winters (uncommon; Oct–Apr) N Honshu to Kyushu; scarce Hokkaido. **HH** Large reed-fringed lakes; courtship displays noisy and elaborate with distinctive head-waving and nodding. Winters along coasts or inland at lakes/rivers. **ID** Large; elegant; long neck, striking white face and eyebrows contrast with black and orange head plumes. Winter adult: paler, lacks head adornments; white supercilium separates black crown from eye and narrow, black loral line. In flight, rapid flickering wingbeats, thin neck and large feet with white on forewing and secondaries. **BP** Bill dagger-like, long, straight, pinkish-horn; eyes dark red; tarsi grey. **SV** Noisy, far-carrying guttural *kuwaa*, rolling *crra-ahrr* and slow series of wooden *breck-breck-breck* calls on breeding grounds.

Slavonian Grebe *Podiceps auritus*

L 31–38 cm; WS 46–55 cm; WT 300–470 g

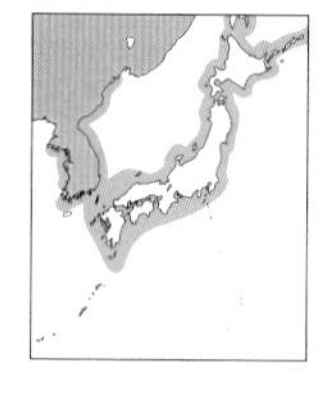

SD *P. a. auritus* winters (Oct–Apr) mostly in N Japan. **HH** More often shallow coastal waters, less frequently on freshwater lakes/rivers than Black-necked (BNG). **ID** Smaller, more compact than Red-necked. Only likely to be confused with BNG. Head appears larger, flatter (than BNG) and triangular with crown peak at rear. Breeding adult: colourful, attractive chestnut with broad golden-yellow band from bill base to rear of head. Winter adult: black cap extends to eyes, contrasting with clean white cheeks and neck-sides. Juv/1st-winter: like winter adult with pale bill. In flight, upperwing pattern similar to Great Crested and Red-necked. **BP** Bill short but strong, black with grey-white tip (ad breeding) or grey with white tip (juv/ad winter), diagnostic bare pink loral stripe between bill and eye in all plumages; eyes deep red; tarsi grey. **SV** Generally silent. **AN** North America: Horned Grebe.

Black-necked Grebe *Podiceps nigricollis*

L 28–34 cm; WS 41–60 cm; WT 265–450 g

SD *P. n. nigricollis* winters (Oct–Apr) from N Japan south to Kyushu. **HH** Commonly occurs inland on lakes/rivers, also at estuaries, infrequently on sea or in harbours. Sometimes gathers in dense foraging flocks of tens to hundreds of individuals. **ID** Mid-sized, rather dark grebe, slightly smaller and thinner-necked than Slavonian, with loose fan of golden-yellow ear plumes. Dumpy, rounded body especially 'bottom' recalls Little. Head rounded, crown peak central; forehead steep. Winter adult: black crown extends as bulge below eyes to cheeks, face less clean than Slavonian; neck dusky. Juv/1st-winter: like winter adult with browner ear-coverts and neck. In flight, lacks Slavonian's white shoulder patch. **BP** Bill slender, pointed, uptilted to tip, black (breeding) or pale grey (juv), with dark tip and culmen (non-breeding); eyes bright red; tarsi dark grey. **SV** Generally silent. **AN** North America: Eared Grebe.

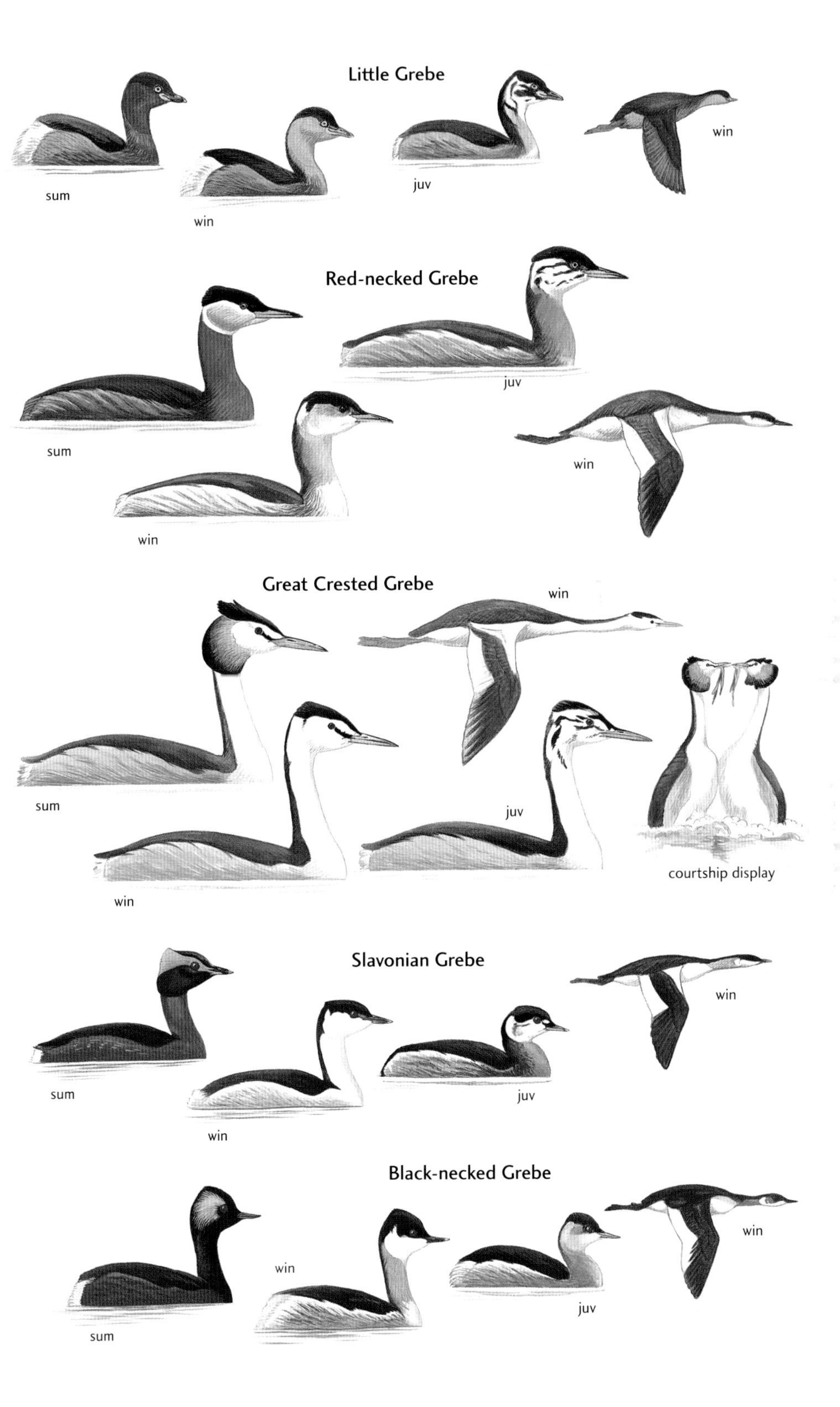
Little Grebe
sum
win
juv
win
Red-necked Grebe
sum
win
juv
win
Great Crested Grebe
win
sum
win
juv
courtship display
Slavonian Grebe
sum
win
juv
win
Black-necked Grebe
sum
win
juv
win

Black Stork *Ciconia nigra* L 95–100 cm; WS 173–205 cm; WT 3000 g

SD Rare visitor mostly in S Japan. **HH** Forages in wetlands and farmland areas. **ID** Very tall, between Grey Heron and Oriental Stork in size. Adult is glossy black (with metallic green/purple sheen), with white belly, thighs, vent and axillaries. Young dark brown where adult is black. Flight strong, with slow shallow beats, but prefers to soar. In flight, white belly and axillaries prominent on otherwise all-black bird. **BP** Bill, lores and extensive eye-ring deep red (ad) or grey-green (juv); eyes black; tarsi dull reddish-pink (ad) or grey-green (juv). **SV** Silent away from breeding grounds.

Oriental Stork *Ciconia boyciana* L 110–115 cm; WS 195–200 cm; WT 5000 g

SD Endangered. Once widespread resident in Japan; following extirpation captive breeding and reintroduction have been successful in N Hyogo Prefecture, Honshu. Elsewhere, from Hokkaido to Okinawa, a rare migrant and winter visitor. **HH** Nests on pole platforms, feeds in shallow wetlands such as wet ricefields. **ID** Very large, between Hooded and White-naped cranes in size. White, with black flight-feathers and primary-coverts. Stands tall with neck erect; lower neck and upper breast-feathers elongated and may blow loosely. Secondaries have prominent greyish-white outer webs. Flight strong, with slow shallow beats, but prefers to soar. In flight, wings distinctly pied. **BP** Black bill is long, deep at base, sharply pointed, lower mandible is upturned at tip; narrow eye-ring, small loral patch, base of lower mandible and gular region are all red; irides whitish-yellow; long tarsi red. **SV** On breeding grounds gives weak *shuu* or *hyuu* prior to loud bill-clattering display when mandibles are pointed upwards, waved and clattered together loudly like castanets.

Black-headed Ibis *Threskiornis melanocephalus* L 65–76 cm; WT 1200 g

SD Rare migrant and winter visitor (Oct–Apr) recorded from Hokkaido to Nansei Shoto, most frequently in the south. **HH** Solitary or in small groups, foraging in flooded grasslands and well-vegetated swamps. **ID** Approaches size of spoonbills. Adult is white, except naked black skin on head and upper neck; wings white. Breeding adult has loose ruff of white feathers on lower neck, grey scapulars, elongated grey tertials and variable yellow wash on breast and mantle; non-breeding adult loses grey coloration and neck ruff. Juvenile has grey feathering on head and white-feathered neck. In flight all-white, with line of bare, pink skin on 'arm' visible on underwing at base of greater wing-coverts (juv has black tips to outermost primaries); black head and neck contrasting with white body and large bill distinguish it from egrets, and decurved bill from spoonbills. **BP** Adult has strong, black, decurved bill; eyes dark red-brown to black; strong black tarsi. **SV** Silent away from breeding grounds.

Crested Ibis *Nipponia nippon* L 55–78 cm; WT 2000–3000 g

SD Endangered. Once common and widespread resident; now very rare due to habitat loss and agricultural intensification. Captive breeding and reintroduction on Sado I has been successful. Birds are breeding in the wild and the population is increasing; stragglers from Sado have reached the Japan Sea coast of Honshu. **HH** Social; nests in small colonies in deciduous treetops, foraging at nearby shallow wetlands and wet ricefields. **ID** Large ibis (size of Black-faced Spoonbill), with unique plumage. Adult is white with delicate peach or salmon-pink cast to flight-feathers, neck and breast; has long loose-feathered nuchal crest. Head, neck and mantle become deep grey when breeding, stained by oily secretion. Young are grey. In flight, wings essentially white, with strong pink cast, especially to undersides of flight-feathers. **BP** Bill strong, decurved, black with red tip and base; bare skin of face and forecrown vermilion; eyes yellow; short tarsi bright red. **SV** Gives staccato *taaa* or *aaa* calls in flight.

Glossy Ibis *Plegadis falcinellus* L 55–65 cm; WS 88–105 cm; WT 485–580 g

SD Vagrant to Okinawa. **HH** Shallow freshwater wetlands. **ID** Large dark ibis. Distinguished by all-dark, chocolate-brown or chestnut plumage, with purple and green gloss; wings metallic-green; lores blue with white border above and below; non-breeder duller with white streaks on head and neck. In flight, recalls dark curlew, with long thin neck, distinctive bill and toes protruding well beyond tail tip. **BP** Bill long, relatively narrow-based and curved, curlew-like, grey-green to dark brown; eyes black; long tarsi dark grey or brown (bill and legs dull yellow in non-breeding season). **SV** Generally silent away from nest, but occasionally gives deep *grunting grrr*, a muffled, nasal moaning, *urnn urnn urnn*, and deep quacking sounds.

Black Stork
ad
juv
ad
ad
ad
ad
Oriental Stork
juv
Black-headed Ibis
ad
juv
Crested Ibis
ad
breeding
ad
ad non-
breeding
sum
win
sum
Glossy Ibis
juv

Eurasian Spoonbill *Platalea leucorodia*

L 80–93 cm; WS 120–135 cm; WT 1130–1960 g

SD *P. l. leucorodia* is rare winter visitor (Oct–Apr) to S Japan; accidental elsewhere. **HH** On migration and in winter, occurs singly or in small groups at pools, lakes or muddy wetlands, where wades slowly, swinging head and bill from side-to-side to sieve food. Frequently occurs with Black-faced Spoonbill in winter. Partly nocturnal, thus often seen roosting during day. **ID** Large, white, with all-white wings. Breeding adult has yellow 'spoon', yellowish throat and band across lower neck/upper breast, and prominent white nape plumes. Non-breeding lacks crest and yellow. Juvenile also lacks crest and has paler bill and legs. Roosting individuals with bill concealed separable from very rare Black-faced by eye being outside the black mask. In flight, neck and legs outstretched, adult is all white whereas juvenile has black tips to outermost primaries; extended neck, large bill and quicker wingbeats interspersed with glides distinguish it from egrets. **BP** Very long dark grey to black bill has transverse ridges with spatulate tip (yellow in summer), bill pink in young; facial feathering extends in front of eye to bill base; gular patch pinkish. Unlike egrets, eyes dark red-orange, not pale yellow; legs dark-grey to black, brownish-pink in juv. **SV** Generally silent away from breeding grounds.

Black-faced Spoonbill *Platalea minor*

L 73–81 cm; WS 110 cm; WT 1580–2200 g

SD Endangered. A rare endemic E Asian species breeder which is gradually increasing thanks to conservation efforts. The population now stands at over 2,500 birds. Small numbers migrate to winter in Kyushu and Nansei Shoto, where they also occasionally summer; rare winter visitor to C Honshu. **HH** Forages singly or in small groups (sometimes with Eurasian Spoonbill in winter), at coastal mudflats, muddy wetlands and lakes, in manner of Eurasian Spoonbill, or by more actively chasing and lunging for prey; partly nocturnal, thus often seen roosting by day. **ID** Smaller than Eurasian, but similarly all white. Adult has black bill with black 'spoon', bare black face. In breeding plumage has yellowish or rusty band on lower neck/upper breast, and prominent nape plumes that may also be tinged yellow. In flight, adult is all white, whereas juvenile has black tips to outermost primaries and black shafts to all primaries; extended neck, large bill and quicker wingbeats interspersed by glides distinguish it from egrets. **BP** Very long dark grey to black bill (ad), or pink bill (juv), has transverse ridges with spatulate tip. Black facial skin extends across forehead, to eyes, and surrounds the bill base, enclosing a small, yellow pre-orbital patch; the chin and gular region are feathered white; eyes dark red-orange; legs dark grey to black. **SV** Generally silent away from breeding grounds.

Eurasian Bittern *Botaurus stellaris*

L 69–81 cm; WS 100–130 cm; WT 867–1940 g

SD Scarce. *B. s. stellaris* breeds locally in Hokkaido and N & C Honshu. Small numbers also winter in Japan. **HH** Extensive wetlands, generally in reedbeds, but at almost any large wetland with vegetation further south in winter, from Honshu to Kyushu, though cryptic and highly secretive. **ID** Large, buff-brown, heavily streaked heron. Neck thicker and shorter than Grey Heron, and short-necked appearance exacerbated by hunched posture. Legs shorter and toes larger than Grey Heron. Occasionally appears at reedbed edge or in ricefields where finely patterned, cryptic ginger-and-buff plumage, combined with blackish-brown crown, nape and moustachial stripe, is distinctive. Abandons hunched posture if disturbed and stretches erect, revealing vertical dark brown stripes on throat and neck. Rarely flies, but when does so resembles large owl with broad rounded wings (though all flight-feathers and primary-coverts narrowly barred blackish and dark ginger), with huge trailing toes. **BP** Bill long, strong, sharply pointed, yellow or green at base/lores; eyes reddish-brown; rather short legs greenish-yellow, very large greenish-yellow toes protrude well beyond tail in flight. **SV** In breeding season ♂ gives very deep, very far-carrying resonant booming call, typically repeated slowly three times: *bwooo bwooo bwooo*. At close range breathy inhalation is audible: *uh-buwooo uh-buwooo uh-buwooo*. In non-breeding season also gives gruff *kau* at night, and when flushed a short, gruff *grek grek*.... **AN** Great Bittern.

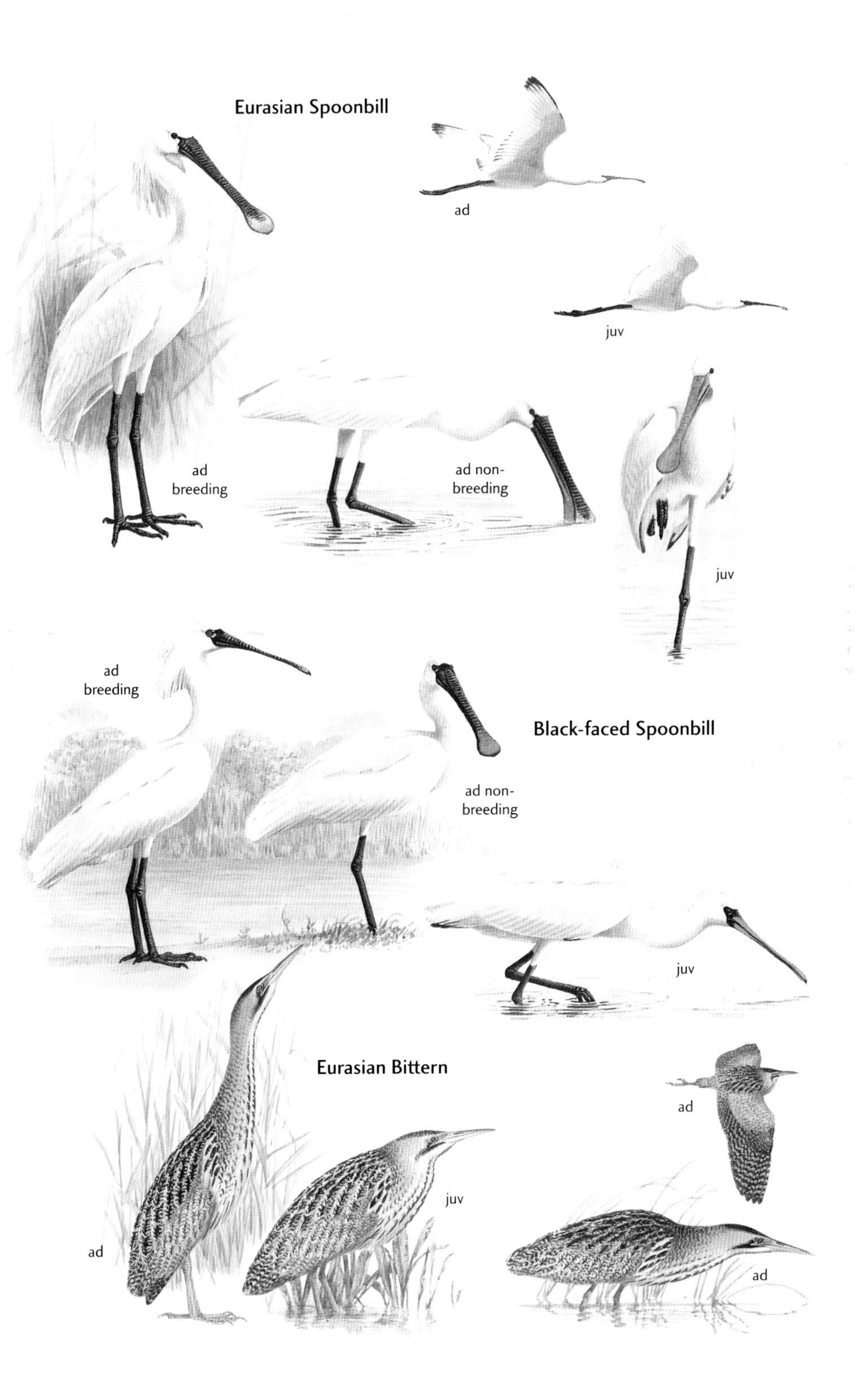
Eurasian Spoonbill
ad
juv
ad
breeding
ad non-
breeding
juv
ad
breeding
Black-faced Spoonbill
ad non-
breeding
juv
Eurasian Bittern
ad
juv
ad
ad

Yellow Bittern *Ixobrychus sinensis* L 30–40 cm; WS 53 cm; WT 115 g

SD Scarce and local summer visitor (May–mid-Oct) mainly in south; scarce or absent in north; has wintered SW Kyushu. **HH** Inland wetlands, lake margins, reedbeds, lotus and ricefields. Bursts from cover, flops across reeds and drops again quickly. **ID** Small, rather plain buff-brown bittern. ♂ has black cap, pale tawny-brown hindneck and mantle, paler foreneck and buff belly. ♀ duller with dark-grey crown with some streaking, pale streaking on back and more distinct streaking on foreneck than ♂. Juvenile dark with vertical brown streaks. In flight, pale buff wing-coverts contrast strongly with blackish-brown flight-feathers and primary-coverts. Tail short, blackish, toes protrude beyond tip. **BP** Bill orange-yellow with dark culmen and tip, lores yellow; eye-ring yellow, eyes yellow; tarsi yellow. **SV** When breeding gives repetitive, pumping *oo oo*, *whoa whoa*, or *wooo wooo* calls by day or night. Flight call is a dry *kik-kik-kik* or raspy *tschek*, lower pitched but recalls Whiskered Tern.

Schrenck's Bittern *Ixobrychus eurhythmus* L 33–40 cm; WS 55–59 cm; WT 170 g

SD Summer visitor (May–Sep) to C & N Honshu, but seemingly in considerable decline, now extremely rare and absent from most (all?) traditional sites since 1980s. **HH** Reedbeds, marshes, occasionally ricefields; solitary and secretive. Behaviour as Yellow Bittern. **ID** Small two-tone bittern (slightly larger than Yellow Bittern). ♂ has dark chestnut face, hindneck, mantle, rump and innerwing-coverts, blackish crown, tail and flight-feathers, with prominent pale buff patch on larger wing-coverts. Underparts warm whitish-buff with dark gular stripe extending to breast. ♀/young differ strikingly: crown dark grey, neck, mantle, wings and tail mid-brown spotted white, and neck, breast and flanks streaked mid-brown on pale buff. In flight, ♂'s pale buff wing-coverts contrast strongly with blackish flight-feathers and primary-coverts, whilst ♀'s white spotted wing-coverts are noticeable. Tail short, blackish, toes and part of legs protrude beyond tip. **BP** Bill dark in ♂ with pink facial skin, ♀/young have black culmen, yellow at base of upper and all-yellow lower mandible, and yellow lores; eyes yellow but black at rear, forming distinct 'C' shape, similar to Cinnamon, but distinct from Yellow; tarsi dull yellow. **SV** Repetitive, rhythmic *oo oo oo* or *gup-gup-gup* calls at night in breeding season recall Yellow Bittern, but tempo is twice as fast; also gives a low, gruff *wek* in flight. **AN** Von Schrenck's Bittern.

Cinnamon Bittern *Ixobrychus cinnamomeus* L 38–41 cm; WS 49 cm; WT 130–148 g

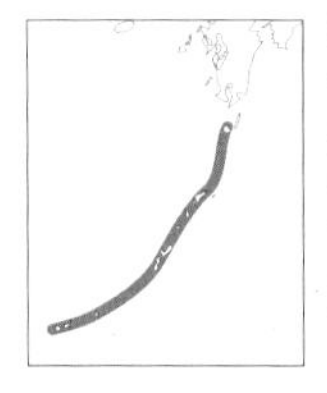

SD Scarce resident in the Nansei Shoto. **HH** Solitary; wetlands including wet rice and rush fields, swamps and wet grasslands, where may be relatively conspicuous; also found in orange and mango orchards in Amami and Yaeyama Is. Flight typically low and slow. **ID** Small and stocky, plain but rich cinnamon-orange bittern. ♂ entirely rich cinnamon, somewhat paler on underparts. ♀ and young resemble ♀ Schrenck's, with dark brown crown, rear neck and mantle, foreneck and breast heavily streaked dark brown, but upperparts dark and pale brown, flecks not white, and flight-feathers cinnamon-rust. ♂ plain cinnamon, tail very short, toes and much of legs protrude beyond tail tip. **BP** Bill yellow with dark culmen, bare lores yellow; eye-ring and eyes yellow, but black at rear, forming distinct 'C' shape, similar to Schrenck's but distinct from Yellow; tarsi yellow. **SV** Flight call, given especially on take-off, deep croaking *kwe kwe* or stuttering *kik-kuk kuk kik kik*. When breeding, at night and at dawn gives an even series of deep *aaa aaa* notes, and mellow *kokokokoko* notes. **AN** Chestnut Bittern.

Black Bittern *Dupetor flavicollis* L 54–66 cm; WS 80 cm; WT 300–420 g

SD *D. f. flavicollis* is accidental (mostly in spring, Mar–May) in the Nansei Shoto and even Honshu. **HH** Rice- and rush fields, swamps and wet grasslands. **ID** Mid-sized, very dark bittern. ♂ almost entirely black, but with yellow throat and foreneck to upper breast with two broken lines of black and chestnut streaks on upper neck to breast. ♀ dark brown where ♂ is black. In flight, appears uniformly dark. **BP** Bill rather deep-based, yellow with grey culmen and dark tip; eyes yellow or pale green; rather short tarsi dull green. **SV** Series of staccato *nyuk-nyuk-nyuk* or deep croaking calls in flight, and a mellow, descending booming on territory, *kwoouh kwoouh* or *booouhh*. **AN** Formerly *Ixobrychus flavicollis*, e.g. OSJ. **AN** Mangrove Bittern.

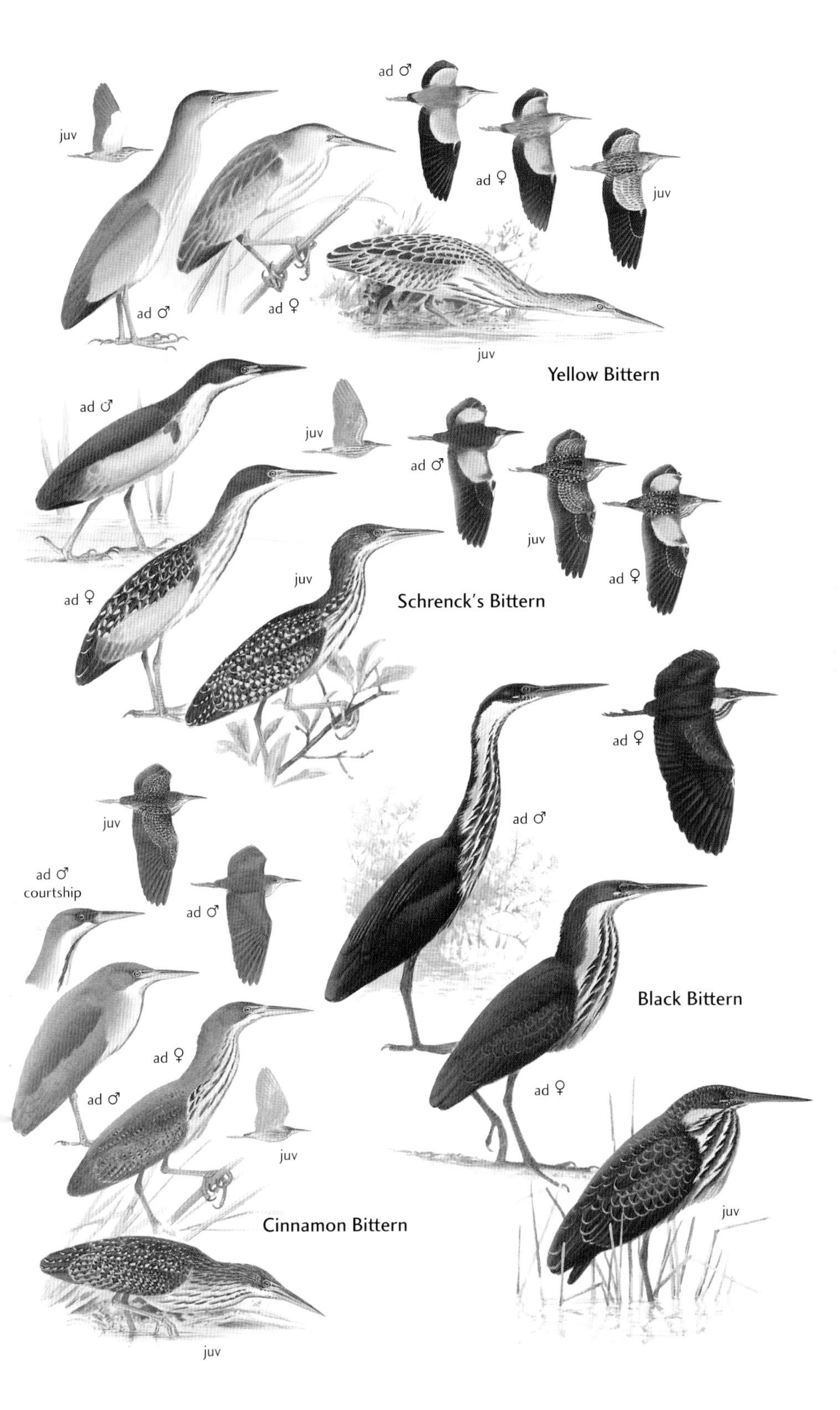
ad ♂
juv
ad ♀
juv
ad ♂
ad ♀
juv
Yellow Bittern
ad ♂
juv
ad ♂
juv
ad ♀
juv
Schrenck's Bittern
ad ♀
juv
ad ♀
ad ♂
ad ♂
courtship
ad ♂
ad ♀
ad ♂
juv
Black Bittern
ad ♀
juv
Cinnamon Bittern
juv

Japanese Night Heron *Gorsachius goisagi* L 49 cm; WS 87 cm; WT 470 g

SD Endangered. Scarce, secretive summer visitor (mid-Apr–mid-Sep), endemic breeder Kyushu, Shikoku, W & C Honshu. May winter, Nansei Shoto. Migrants occur on Sea of Japan islands, e.g. Hegura-jima. **HH** Crepuscular/nocturnal, mature forest, woodland edges. **ID** Stocky, short-necked. Adult: dull chestnut-brown with fine black vermiculations, head and neck-sides rufous-brown to chestnut. Underparts pale buff with dark streaks. Young: black crown, upperparts finely vermiculated dark and mid-brown, more extensively streaked neck, and off-white lores and eye-ring. Very broad wings, blackish flight-feathers brown-tipped, alula and secondary fringes white. **BP** Bill stout, dark grey with greenish-yellow lores (blue when breeding); shorter than Malayan, but has same decurved culmen; eye-ring yellowish-green, irides pale yellow; tarsi dark yellowish-green. **SV** Slow, repetitive, deep owl-like hooting, in early evening: first part of call, *o-bwoo*, only audible at close range, thus heard as *bwoo bwoo bwoo*.

Malayan Night Heron *Gorsachius melanolophus* L 47–51 cm; WT 417–450 g

SD Resident S Nansei Shoto; accidental north to Hokkaido. **HH** Secretive, nocturnal/crepuscular, occasionally diurnal. Mature subtropical forest and forest edge; prefers short shaded vegetation; avoids tangles and dense understorey. **ID** Closely resembles Japanese Night Heron (JNH), but has blacker crown and more prominent nuchal crest. Adult: more rufous-brown face and neck than JNH. Juvenile: paler than JNH with more prominent white spotting on crown, face and nape (see imm Black-crowned); takes c. 2 years to achieve adult plumage (appears first on ear-coverts). Very broad wings, blackish secondaries brown-tipped, whereas primaries white-tipped. **BP** Bill stout, arched, black, blue base to lower mandible, blue lores, gape and eye-ring all more prominent than JNH; irides greenish-yellow; tarsi dull, dark yellowish-green. **SV** Deep, owl-like hoots at dawn and dusk: *whoop whoop* at close range and *toob toob* at distance. Generally repeated in pulsing series of 6–20 notes, at c. 1 per second; several may call simultaneously.

Black-crowned Night Heron *Nycticorax nycticorax* L 58–65 cm; WS 90–100 cm; WT 400–800 g

SD *N. n. nycticorax* resident Nansei Shoto to C Honshu; summer visitor north to N Honshu, scarce Hokkaido. **HH** Noisy colonies in trees above water. Secretive, mostly nocturnal, occasionally diurnal, sometimes confiding. **ID** Mid-sized, very stocky, with large head, short neck and legs. Adult: black crown and back, with long white nuchal plumes. Supraloral stripe, forehead and entire underparts white or very pale grey. Wings and tail pale to mid-grey. Young: dull brown with indistinct, broad pale streaks on mantle/underparts, prominent white spots on wing-coverts, and fine white streaks on crown. Slow floppy wingbeats on short, rounded and strongly bowed wings. **BP** Bill stout, black with grey lores (breeding), yellow-green base with black tip and grey culmen, and green lores (imm); irides dark reddish-orange; tarsi range from dull yellow to orange and pink. **SV** Deep croaking calls at colonies, and deep nasal barking, *kwok*, *goa* or *guap guap* calls in flight.

Nankeen Night Heron *Nycticorax caledonicus* L 55–60 cm; WS 95–110 cm; WT 550–990 g

SD Formerly endemic *N. c. crassirostris* Ogasawara Is, extinct since c.1889; recent vagrant (likely *N. c. hilli* or *N. c. pelewensis*) on Hahajima, Ogasawara. **HH** Wetlands, damp forest edges. **ID** Adult: warm cinnamon-brown with black cap and long nuchal plumes. Young: heavily spotted/streaked brown and white. **BP** Bill black; eyes large with green ring and lores, irides yellow-green (yellow when breeding); short tarsi bright yellow to dusky-ochre. **SV** Deep croaks. **AN** Rufous Night Heron.

Striated Heron *Butorides striata* L 52 cm; WS 52–60 cm; WT 135–300 g

SD *B. s. amurensis* summer visitor (mid-Apr–late Sep) Kyushu, Shikoku, Honshu, rarely Hokkaido. *B. s. javanica* may occur S Nansei Shoto. **HH** Shy, solitary, dense cover, streams, ponds, wet fields, swamps, mangroves. Adopts vertical 'bittern-like' posture if disturbed. **ID** Small, dark heron, with short legs, but long bill. Adult: black crown and loose nuchal crest. Face to underparts mostly pale to dark grey, with white at edge of crown, on chin and in streaks on mid neck to belly. Mantle feathers long, loose, dark grey with green gloss; tail short, blackish-grey. ♂ grey-toned; ♀ browner; juvenile greyish-brown with heavily streaked and spotted underparts. Flight sluggish; wings dark, but upperwing-coverts and secondaries have pale grey or off-white fringes. **BP** Bill long, straight, black; lores and eye-ring greenish-yellow, eyes yellow; tarsi yellow. **SV** Call: sharp, loud *kyeowp*, *pyuu* or *tiuu* at night, also on migration. Song: hard, low *chi-kwowp*, repeated at long intervals.

Japanese Night Heron
ad
juv
ad
juv
Malayan Night Heron
ad
juv
ad
juv

Black-crowned Night Heron
ad courtship
ad breeding
juv
ad
juv
1st summer
2nd winter
Striated Heron
amurensis
Nankeen
Night Heron

Chinese Pond Heron *Ardeola bacchus*

L 42–52 cm; WS 79–90 cm

SD Scarce (Oct–May) S Nansei Shoto; uncommon spring overshoot migrant elsewhere. Has bred Kyushu. **HH** Streams, ditches, wet meadows, damp woodland edges. **ID** Appears dark when foraging, but like dark-backed cattle egret in flight. Adult breeding: rich chestnut head and breast with prominent nape plumes, mantle charcoal-grey with loose plumes covering most of wings at rest. Wings, rump, tail all white. Winter: mantle plain, dull grey-brown; head, neck, breast all whitish, heavily streaked grey-brown. **BP** Bill yellowish with black tip (breeding), or duller with dark upper mandible (winter); bare pale eye-ring, irides yellow; short tarsi yellow. **SV** Call a gruff *kwa* or high-pitched squawk.

Javan Pond Heron *Ardeola speciosa*

L 45 cm; WS 80–100 cm

SD Vagrant, perhaps accidental, S Nansei Shoto. **HH** Wetlands, farmland. **ID** Adult breeding: head and neck creamy brownish-buff, breast deep cinnamon; mantle, scapulars dark slate-grey, wings, tail, belly white. Adult winter: as previous species, but may have white (instead of dusky) tips to primaries. **BP** Bill yellow with a black tip (breeding), or duller with dark upper mandible (winter); eyes yellow; tarsi yellow. **SV** Call a gruff *kwa* or high-pitched squawk.

Eastern Cattle Egret *Bubulcus coromandus*

L 50–60 cm; WS 88–96 cm; WT 340–390 g

SD Mostly summer visitor (Apr–Sep) north to N Honshu; some spring overshoots reach Hokkaido; some winter S Japan. **HH** Nests colonially, roosts socially; often in groups around stock animals; grasslands, drier wetland margins, fields. Walks boldly with pigeon-like head-bobbing. **ID** Smaller than other white egrets, with shorter neck, legs and bill. Adult breeding: bright rusty-orange head, neck, upper breast and mantle plumes. Adult winter: white. In flight, wings rounded and arched, wingbeats deep. **BP** Bill blunt, yellow, with deep reddish-pink base (breeding), or plain yellow (non-breeding), lores yellow; feathered chin extends forwards of nostril; eyes yellow to red; legs short, rather thick, pinkish-orange (breeding), or dark greyish-green or blackish (winter). **SV** Vocal at colonies, and occasionally away from them: a short, gruff, barking *goaa* or *guwaa*. **TN** Formerly within Cattle Egret *B. ibis* (e.g. OSJ).

Grey Heron *Ardea cinerea*

L 90–98 cm; WS 155–175 cm; WT 1000–2000 g

SD *A. c. jouyi* resident throughout Japan's main islands (formerly summer visitor to Hokkaido). **HH** Large, conspicuous breeding colonies (Feb–Jun) in tall trees near rivers, lakes, coasts; roosts in trees. Forages at fresh, brackish, saltwater wetlands. May gather in flocks after breeding. Tall, but often with neck hunched into shoulders. **ID** Adult: pale to mid-grey, with white crown, face, foreneck and underparts; neck- and breast-sides buffy-grey. Black 'bandana' around crown and small nuchal crest. Neck and breast streaked black. Young: greyer on neck, blacker on head than adult. In flight, retracted neck forms conspicuous rounded bulge and appears whitish; wings markedly two-tone, with black flight-feathers and primary-coverts contrasting with grey upper- and underwing-coverts. Flight slow, on deeply bowed wings. **BP** Bill large, stout, dagger-like, varying from pinkish-orange (breeding) to yellow (non-breeding), and dull-grey (imm). Eyes pale to deep yellow. Very long legs flush bright pinkish-orange (breeding), otherwise dull greyish-flesh. **SV** Flight call a deep, hoarse long *fraaank* or bisyllabic *frah-aank*; gives throaty rattling and croaking *kuwaa* or *gua* calls at colonies.

Purple Heron *Ardea purpurea*

L 78–90 cm; WS 110–145 cm; WT 525–1345 g

SD *A. p. manilensis* resident S Nansei Shoto (Yaeyama). Scarce migrant or accidental to offshore islands, mainland Honshu, Hokkaido. **HH** Nests in reeds or trees. Solitary, secretive, crepuscular, foraging in well-vegetated swamps, reedbeds, lake margins. **ID** Tall rakish heron with very slender long neck and bill; often leans forward or sideways with neck curved and head cocked, ready to lunge at prey. Adult: chestnut, black and grey. Prominent black and chestnut stripes from face to chest; crown and nape blackish, mantle and tail dark grey, thighs and lower back plumes also chestnut. Juvenile: browner overall. Flight, jerky, more buoyant than heavier Grey Heron, on deeply arched wings. In flight, neck bulge very conspicuous, more angular than Grey, wings less markedly two-tone as upper and underwing-coverts tinged brown (ad) or all brown (young). **BP** Long, narrow, bayonet-like bill has dark culmen and yellowish sides; eyes yellow; long legs yellowish-brown, but flush pinkish-brown when breeding; large, bunched toes very obvious in flight. **SV** Flight call, a guttural *guwaa* or emphatic *skrech*, is shorter, less resonant than Grey Heron's; also gives growling *graaaau* or nasal gurgling *gurrh* calls.

Chinese Pond Heron
ad courtship
ad breeding
ad non-
breeding
ad
breeding
non breeding
ad breeding
non-
breeding
Javan Pond Heron
ad non-
breeding
ad breeding
ad courtship
ad
breeding
ad
courtship
non-breeding
ad courtship
Eastern Cattle Egret
ad sum
ad
juv
ad
juv
Grey Heron
ad win
ad
Purple Heron
ad
juv
ad
1st-sum
juv

Great Egret *Ardea alba*

L 84–94 cm; WS 140–170 cm; WT 700–1200 g

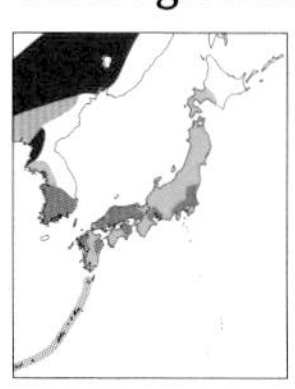

SD *A. a. alba* winter visitor (Oct–Apr) north to N Honshu; spring migrants reach Hokkaido. Increasing winter visitor SW Hokkaido southwards, mainly C Honshu to Kyushu. **Eastern Great Egret** *A. (a.) modesta* summer visitor, some wintering (or resident), breeds Honshu, Shikoku, Kyushu. **HH** Lakes, rivers, wetlands. **ID** Neck has characteristic kink. Leans forward, craning long neck while foraging. Adult: extensive, lacy lower-back plumes, no head/breast plumes. Compared with Grey Heron: *modesta* slightly smaller, *alba* as large as or larger. In flight, feet well beyond tail, toes large; wings forward of mid-line, neck bulges deeply. **BP** Bill long, stout, black, lores blue-green (breeding), yellow with greenish lores (non-breeding); gape line extends behind eye, eyes yellow. Non-breeding *modesta* black tarsi/toes, deep pink tibia when breeding. Non-breeding *alba* pale/bright yellow tarsi/toes, pink or yellow tibia and tarsi when breeding. **SV** Hoarse *crrack* or *guwaa*, dry, grating *grrraah* on taking flight. **TN** Also in *Egretta* and *Casmerodius* (e.g. OSJ).

Intermediate Egret *Ardea intermedia*

L 63–72 cm; WS 105–115 cm; WT 440–630 g

SD A summer visitor (Apr–Oct) north to N Honshu (scarce overshoots reach Hokkaido), some winter Kyushu, Nansei Shoto. **HH** Wetlands, wet ricefields, mangroves, mudflats. **ID** From smaller Little and larger Great by short bill, rounded head, slender neck held in curved S, lacking Great's angular kink and Little's head plumes. Central crown peak gives head characteristic rounded triangular shape. Adult breeding: extensive lacy breast and back plumes. In flight, feet well beyond tail, toes prominent; wings forward of mid-line. **BP** Bill short, yellow, tip black, lores yellow (non-breeding), or largely black with yellow base and greenish-yellow lores (breeding); gape line extends to eye, eyes yellow; long tarsi black. **SV** Hoarse barking *goah-goah* or *graak graak* and more prolonged rasping *graaarsh*.

Little Egret *Egretta garzetta*

L 58–62 cm; WS 88–106 cm; WT 487–605 g

SD *E. g. garzetta* resident north to N Honshu; migrants occasionally reach Hokkaido. **HH** Nests colonially, roosts socially, in dense trees near marshes, lakes, rivers. Wetlands, wet ricefields, streams, shallow coastal lagoons, rarely beaches or rocky shores. Stirs mud or water with feet ('foot-paddling') to disturb prey. **ID** Adult breeding: two nape plumes, lacy breast and lower-back plumes. Scarce dusky form has grey wash to breast, belly, wings, tail. In flight, legs/feet beyond tail; wings set centrally. **BP** Bill long, slender, black, lores yellow to greyish-green (non-breeding), pink or orange (breeding); eyes yellow; long tarsi black (sometimes greenish-black or patchily yellow), toes yellow. **SV** Guttural gargling croaks, *guwa*, bleating *mmyaaaaw* and bizarre gargling *blublublublublub* at colonies, grating, throaty, crow-like *aaah*, or *kra a a ak* when flushed and in flight.

Pacific Reef Egret *Egretta sacra*

L 58–66 cm; WS 90–100 cm; WT 330–700 g

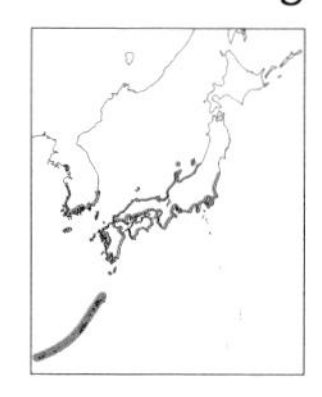

SD *E. s. sacra* resident Nansei Shoto to C Honshu. **HH** Rocky coasts. Vagrants occasionally at other wetland habitats, e.g. estuaries, where confusion possible with other white egrets. Forages using a distinctive crouching, creeping, lunging gait. **ID** Size of Little Egret, but neck shorter, thicker, wings more rounded, and legs shorter – only feet protrude beyond tail in flight. Has few plumes (restricted to lower back) when breeding. Dimorphic. Dark form: commoner than white, blue-grey, with white chin. White form: told from other egrets by stocky proportions and bill shape; immature may be flecked grey. **BP** Bill long, thick, blunt (less sharply pointed than Little, narrowing more continuously from base than Swinhoe's), varies from dark yellowish-grey (dark morph) to pale yellow with dark culmen (white morph); lores blue-grey to yellowish; eyes yellow; strong legs appear short (especially tibia), stout with chunky joints, yellowish-green with large yellow toes. **SV** Deep *gruk* (recalls Northern Raven), down slurred *nyarp*, nasal *gyaaah gyaaah*. **AN** Pacific Reef Heron; Eastern Reef Egret.

Swinhoe's Egret *Egretta eulophotes*

L 65–68 cm; WS 97–114 cm

SD Vulnerable. Accidental migrant, very rare winter visitor, Nansei Shoto to Hokkaido. **HH** Mudflats, river mouths, rocky shores. Distinctive foraging technique: crouching, leaning posture, suddenly darting or dashing forward to lunge at disturbed prey. **ID** Neck thicker, shorter than Little. Extensive erectile plumes on crown and nape, breast and lower-back plumes lacy. Distinguish from Pacific Reef on proportions and behaviour. **BP** Bill thick, symmetrically dagger-shaped, narrowing only near tip, yellow/orange (breeding), blackish with yellow base (non-breeding); lores blue-grey to blue (summer) or yellow (winter); eyes yellow; tarsi shorter and thicker than Little, blackish, variably yellow; yellow-green toes and dark tarsi may contrast, or may grade between yellow-green and blackish. **SV** Guttural croaking *gwa* call on taking flight. **AN** Chinese Egret.

Great Egret
modesta
ad non-breeding
ad breeding
ad non-breeding
Intermediate Egret
ad breeding
ad non-
breeding
ad breeding
ad white
morph
ad dark
morph
juv
Pacific Reef Egret
Little Egret
Swinhoe's Egret

Great White Pelican *Pelecanus onocrotalus* L 140–175 cm; WS 245–295 cm; WT ♂ 9000–15000 g, ♀ 5400–9000 g

SD Accidental visitor to Nansei Shoto. Records from Honshu and Hokkaido may involve escapees from aviaries, which sometimes remain for years associating with other waterbirds, e.g. Grey Herons at heronries. The status of un-ringed birds is not known. **HH** Estuaries, large rivers and lakes. **ID** Huge, white, short-legged, long-necked and long-billed waterbird. Adult has yellow breast patch in summer. Flight-feathers black, forming striking contrast with remainder of white plumage in flight. Juv/1st-winter rather dark brownish-grey, but also have bare pink facial skin. In flight, at all ages has all-dark flight-feathers. **BP** Bill largely yellow with grey culmen and sides to lower mandible, gular or bill pouch yellow or yellowish-orange; bare facial skin extensive, pinkish-orange (only narrow point of feathering in centre of forehead), eyes black; short, stout legs and large feet pink or yellowish-orange. **SV** Usually silent away from colonies, but gives deep grunting calls on taking flight. **AN** Rosy Pelican; Eastern White Pelican.

Spot-billed Pelican *Pelecanus philippensis* L 127–152 cm; WS 250 cm; WT *c.* 5000 g

SD Vulnerable. Accidental to Nansei Shoto. **HH** Occurs on estuaries, large rivers and lakes. **ID** Smallest pelican recorded in Japan. Overall plumage rather dull, greyer even than Dalmatian, with greyish-white head, neck, underparts and wings. Breeding adult develops tufted crest on rear crown and hindneck, a dull pink rump and vent, cinnamon underwing-coverts and spotted bill pouch. Non-breeding adult has shorter crest and paler, pinker bill pouch and face; lacks pink wash. In flight, adult has blackish-grey flight-feathers and tail tip. Young have dark axillaries and underwing-coverts, dark flight-feathers and pale central underwing stripe. **BP** Face mostly feathered, upper mandible dull yellow or pinkish-orange with blue spots, bill rather short for a pelican, pouch pinkish-grey with blue spots and blotches, tip has small hook; bare patch around eye off-white, irides dark, lores bluish-grey; tarsi black. **SV** Generally silent away from breeding colonies.

Dalmatian Pelican *Pelecanus crispus* L 160–180 cm; WS 270–320 cm; WT 10000–13000 g

SD Accidental (October to May) to N, C & W Honshu, Kyushu, and Nansei Shoto. **HH** Estuaries, large rivers, lakes. **ID** Large, dusky-grey pelican. Similar to Spot-billed Pelican, but larger. Adult is grey-tinged white. When breeding has a golden-yellow breast patch, unkempt, curly head plumes and feathered face and forehead. Non-breeding adult lacks yellow breast patch and has paler, duller bill. Juvenile is similar to Great White Pelican, but face feathered and bill darker, greyish-pink. In flight, all flight-feathers are black above, but secondaries, especially, are pale grey below, black only at tips. This and Spot-billed Pelican show whitish medial band against otherwise dusky-grey underwing. **BP** Bill long and black with strongly hooked tip, pouch reddish-orange when breeding, bill pink and pouch yellowish-pink when non-breeding; bare skin around eye pink (less extensive than Great White Pelican with broader band of feathers on centre of forehead), irides pale yellow; short stout legs and large feet dark grey (breeding) or pink (non-breeding). **SV** Although generally silent away from colonies, may call while fishing.

Great White Pelican
ad
ad
juv
ad sum
juv
Spot-billed
Pelican
ad sum
ad
ad
roosting Spot-
billed Pelican
juv
juv
ad
ad
ad sum
juv
Dalmatian Pelican

Red-tailed Tropicbird *Phaethon rubricauda* L 46–96 cm; WS 104–119 cm; WT 600–835 g

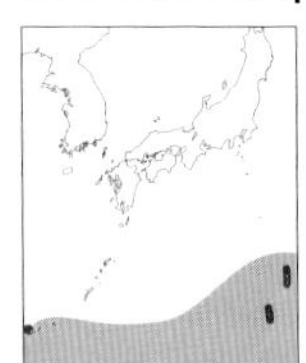

SD *P. r. melanorhynchos* breeds (May–Aug) on remote islands of S Nansei Shoto, Ogasawara and Iwo Is groups. Accidental (typhoon blown) north of breeding range. **HH** Pelagic. Typically flies high over sea, then swoops or plunges for food. **ID** Adult white with black loral crescent, streak behind eye, black shafts to outer primaries and small black area on tertials. Tail short, rounded, white, with two very long (30–35 cm) red central tail-feather shafts (often hard to detect at long range). Juvenile has wide-spaced, coarse blackish-brown bars on largely white upperparts and wing-coverts, wings largely white with narrow black area on primary shafts to tips; lacks tail-streamers. Commonly flies high above sea, hovers and plunges to feed. **BP** Bill prominent, arched and sharply pointed, red (ad) or black (juv), changing with age to yellow then orange; eyes black; tarsi blue/grey with black distal webs to toes. **SV** Screams loudly at nest, giving high, nasal yapping *nyak*, also long rolling call, and in flight a rasping *skrawk* and ratchet-like *ki ki ki*.

White-tailed Tropicbird *Phaethon lepturus* L 37–82 cm; WS 90–95 cm; WT 300 g

SD *P. l. dorotheae* is rare on remote islands of S Nansei Shoto and Ogasawara Is. Accidental north to Japanese main islands, usually after typhoons (April–Sep). **HH** Like Red-tailed Tropicbird. **ID** Adult white, with broad black streak from lores to well behind eye, broad black outer primary bases contrasting with white primary-coverts, and black bar on innerwing-coverts and tertials. Tail short, rounded, with two very long (33–45 cm) white central tail-feather shafts. Juvenile white, with wide-spaced, fine greyish-black bars on upperparts and wing-coverts; wings largely white, with broad black area in primary bases; lacks tail plumes. Smaller than Red-tailed, with faster, more buoyant flight. **BP** Bill short, orange-yellow or yellow; eyes black; short tarsi and toes black. **SV** Harsh tern-like *ki-dit-kit* and squawking *skrech* at colony, and rattling *ki-di ki-di ki-di...* flight call.

Great Frigatebird *Fregata minor* L 85–105 cm; WS 205–230 cm; WT ♂ 1000–1400 g, ♀ 1215–1640 g

SD *F. m. minor* is a rare visitor ranging from Nansei Shoto to Hokakido, most frequently after autumn typhoons (Aug–Nov). **HH** Pelagic. **ID** Large, black, with black axillaries. Adult ♂ black with bronzy-green sheen to upperparts, alar bar slight or absent, small wrinkled red gular pouch and black underparts. ♀ has black cap and head-sides, indistinct brown hind-collar, diagnostic greyish-white throat, and large white, saddle-shaped chest patch extending to breast-sides but not axillaries; black point on belly broadly rounded. Juvenile has combination of elliptical white belly patch and sandy-brown head and breast, and some have short axillary spurs angling outwards. **BP** Bill long, sharply hooked, dark grey (♂), pale blue-grey or pinkish-horn (♀/juv); eyes black (♀ with pink eye-ring); tarsi dark red (♂) or grey (♀/juv). **SV** Silent away from breeding grounds.

Lesser Frigatebird *Fregata ariel* L 71–81 cm; WS 175–193 cm; WT ♂ 625–875g, ♀ 760–955 g

SD *F. a. ariel* is a rare visitor to coastal Japan (exceptionally even to Hokkaido), during or after summer storms and autumn typhoons (May–Nov). **HH** Pelagic. **ID** Smaller than other frigatebirds. Adult ♂ is largely black with blue sheen to upperparts, and narrow white axillary patches or 'spurs' extending to flanks, but not joining across belly; alar bar slight or absent. ♀ has black hood extending to throat, white hind-collar, moderate off-white alar bar, and restricted white breast patch reaching neck- and breast-sides and onto axillaries (triangular and angled outwards), leaving large, pointed-oval black belly patch. Juvenile has whitish-sand or pale rusty-cream hood, blackish-brown breast-band and small, triangular white belly patch extending to axillaries as 'spurs' angled outwards. **BP** Bill long, slim, sharply hooked, dark grey (♂), pale blue-grey or pinkish-horn (♀/young); eyes black, ♀ has pink eye-ring; tarsi dark red (ad) or grey (young). **SV** Silent away from breeding grounds.

White-tailed Tropicbird
ad
juv
Red-tailed Tropicbird
ad
juv
Great Frigatebird
ad ♂
ad ♀
juv
ad ♂
ad ♀
juv
Lesser Frigatebird
ad ♂
ad ♀
juv
juv harasses a Red-tailed Tropicbird

Masked Booby *Sula dactylatra*

L 81–92 cm; WS 150–170 cm; WT 1550 g

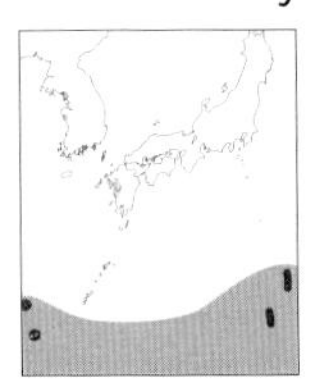

SD *S. d. personata* is a very local summer visitor (mostly Jun–Oct) to southernmost islands of Nansei Shoto; accidental north to Kyushu, Shikoku and C Honshu. **HH** Breeds on remote islands; otherwise pelagic. **ID** Larger, longer-winged and shorter-tailed than other boobies. Adult is mostly white with black face, flight-feathers, primary-coverts and rectrices. Underwing-coverts white. Juvenile is largely brown above with brown hood and white below, resembling Brown Booby, but upper chest is white, white collar separates brown of head from mantle, and white rump separates brown of mantle from tail; underparts white, including underwing-coverts. **BP** Bill pale yellow (ad) or dusky greyish-yellow (juv), with area of bare, black skin around eye and bill base; irides pale yellow (dark in juv); short legs and feet dull grey or olive. **SV** Usually silent except at colonies, where ♂ gives wheezy rising then falling *fuuwheeeoo* and ♀ a loud braying.

Red-footed Booby *Sula sula*

L 66–77 cm; WS 124–152 cm; WT 900–1000 g

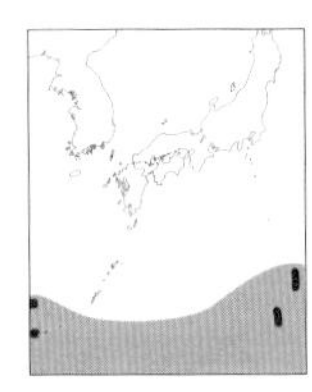

SD *S. s. rubripes* is a very local summer visitor (mostly Jun–Oct) to southernmost islands of Nansei Shoto, Ogasawara and Iwo Is. Accidental to coasts of Kyushu, Shikoku and even north as far as Rishirito, Hokkaido, usually during or after typhoons. **HH** Breeds on remote islands; forages at night far from shore. In non-breeding season pelagic. **ID** Smallest of the three boobies in the region, with proportionately longer tail, shorter slimmer neck, rounder head and slender bill. Polymorphic, but in Japan only the white morph has been recorded. Adult all white with black primaries and secondaries, but white tertials (thus black trailing edge does not reach body), black primary-coverts and all-white tail (see Masked Booby). Underwing pattern same as upperwing, the black under primary-coverts are diagnostic. Juvenile is brown above and below (though vent whitish-brown) with all-dark underwing (compare juv Brown). Flight faster than other boobies. At all ages, slender jizz and smaller size of Red-footed is helpful, especially so in relation to juvenile Brown. **BP** Bill pale blue-grey, with bare pink facial skin at base (ad), or pink with dull-grey tip and grey/pink facial skin (juv); large eyes black; feet dark grey (juv) to bright red (ad). **SV** Both sexes give guttural rattling squawks and screeches, but only at breeding colonies.

Brown Booby *Sula leucogaster*

L 64–74 cm; WS 132–150 cm; WT 724–1550 g

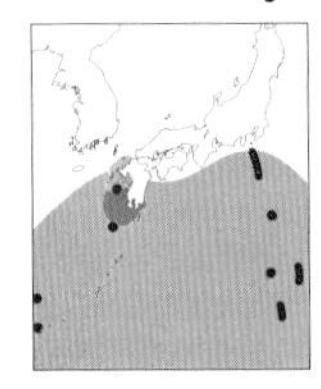

SD *S. l. plotus* occurs year-round in Japanese waters; it is a locally common breeder on offshore islands of S Nansei Shoto, Kyushu, Izu, Ogasawara and Iwo Is. Commonly reaches coasts and bays of Kyushu (often in small flocks) and S Honshu, and may also be encountered off Pacific coast as far north as Hokkaido. *S. l. brewsteri*: recorded once in Yaeyama Is. **HH** Breeds on remote islands and forages over inshore waters. **ID** Adult is mostly dark, chocolate-brown, upper surfaces entirely so, head, neck and upper breast also chocolate-brown, strongly contrasting with white lower chest, belly and undertail-coverts, and white underwing-coverts. No white hind-collar (compare juv Masked Booby). ♀ is larger than ♂. Juvenile is like adult, but mottled brown and white on underparts and has white axillaries and underwing-coverts (see Red-footed). In flight, wings broad-'armed', with sharply pointed 'hand'; tail long, graduating to point, all dark. Upperwing all dark, underwing has broad dark leading and trailing edges, and all-dark primaries/primary-coverts; axillaries and underwing-coverts white. **BP** Bill long, strongly tapered and pointed, lacks obvious nostril; bare facial skin bluish/purple (♂) or yellow (♀); eyes dark brown; short legs and large webbed feet pale to bright yellow (ad) or dark grey (juv). **SV** Usually silent at sea, but at colonies ♂ gives high, sibilant *schweee* and ♀ short, rather guttural grunting and honking *guwa guwa guwa* or *guu guu guu* calls.

Masked Booby
ad
ad
juv
ad white
morph
ad intermediate
morph
Red-footed
ad white
morph
Red-footed Booby
ad brown
morph
juv
ad brown
morph
ad
ad intermediate
morph
ad
ad
juv
Brown Booby

Great Cormorant *Phalacrocorax carbo*

L 80–90 cm; WS 121–149 cm; WT 1400–2400 g

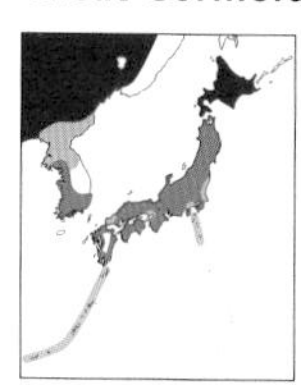

SD *P. c. hanedae* mostly resident Kyushu, Shikoku and Honshu, summer visitor N Honshu and Hokkaido, though status changing as population increases and spreads northwards. **HH** Inland lakes and rivers, but habitat overlap and confusion with Temminck's likely at estuaries and bays. **ID** Adult: black, with long thick neck, white facial patch extending to throat and variable narrow white plumes on crown, nape and head-sides. In late winter/early spring has large white flank patch. Upperwing-coverts and mantle have *bronze sheen* with black fringes; however, beware effects of light and note flight-feathers have greenish sheen. Juvenile: like dull adult, but commonly white or mottled brown and white on underparts. Flight heavy, goose-like with broad wings, but neck short, thick and kinked. **BP** Bill long, thick, pale grey, darker at tip, yellow at base and gape, upper mandible dark grey, lower whitish, and yellow skin angles back from eye to gape, then forms prominent rounded gular patch beneath bill (see Temminck's); eyes dark green; legs and feet greyish-black. **SV** At colonies makes gruff, guttural croaking sounds: *gock gock* or *guwau*, sometimes repeated in growling series. Also gives croaking *kursh kursh kursh* calls.

Temminck's Cormorant *Phalacrocorax capillatus*

L 81–92 cm; WS 152 cm; WT 2600–3300 g

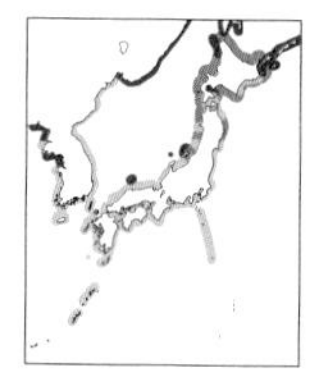

SD Resident Hokkaido, N & C Honshu, and Kyushu; winters southwards. **HH** Favours rocky coasts and rocky islets; sometimes visits coastal lagoons and estuaries. **ID** Large (overlaps with Great), with larger head and more square rear crown; plumage as Great, but white facial patch more extensive. Adult: upperwing-coverts and mantle have deep *green sheen* with black margins, and flight-feathers also have dark green sheen. Facial skin and gular pouch yellow, but less extensive than Great, does not extend beneath bill. Yellow skin forms vertical border just behind eye (always broader than in Great) then extends to sharp point at gape. Juvenile: like dull adult, but commonly white, or mottled brown and white, on underparts, and has yellow lower mandible. In flight appears heavier, more laborious, rear of head squarer than Great. **BP** Bill long, thick, dark blackish-grey (darkest at tip) when breeding, yellow only on gape, but yellow at base of lower mandible when not breeding; eyes dark green; tarsi greyish-black. **SV** Gruff *guwaa*, deep rolling *guwawawa* or *gurururu* calls given only at colonies. **AN** Japanese Cormorant.

Pelagic Cormorant *Phalacrocorax pelagicus*

L 63–76 cm; WS 91–102 cm; WT 1200–2000 g

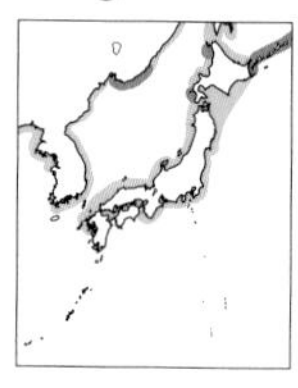

SD *P. p. pelagicus* year-round along Pacific and Sea of Okhotsk coasts of Hokkaido. Winters (Nov–Apr) around Japanese archipelago south to Izu Is. **HH** Breeds and roosts on coastal cliffs, rock stacks and offshore islands; typically forages inshore, wintering in similar habitat. **ID** Small, most slender cormorant with long, thin neck, small rounded head and very thin bill. Overall jizz best separates it from other cormorants. Adult: black with white flank patch (extending onto sides of rump, thus differing from other cormorants' flank patches) and sparse white filoplumes on neck-sides (Mar–May), has purple neck gloss and wispy crests on crown. Lacks white facial patch of larger cormorants. Juvenile: like adult, but has black face. Wingbeats faster than larger species. **BP** Bill slender, pale (even yellow) to dark blackish-grey (can appear extremely pale in sunshine, when easily mistaken for Red-faced Cormorant), and bare facial skin dark reddish and restricted to small area below eye, though when breeding red is brighter and lower mandible may be yellower; irides dark green; tarsi black. **SV** Grunting and groaning calls at colonies.

Red-faced Cormorant *Phalacrocorax urile*

L 71–89 cm; WS 110–122 cm; WT 1600–2100 g

SD Rare breeder on islets and islands off southeast Hokkaido. Rare winter visitor to E Hokkaido; accidental N & C Honshu. **HH** Breeds and roosts on cliffs, rock stacks, rocky islets and islands, typically forages inshore. Winters near colonies, occasionally S & N of breeding areas. **ID** Slightly larger and appears stockier, larger-headed and thicker in neck and bill than Pelagic Cormorant, but there is overlap. Adult: as Pelagic, but when breeding has more prominent, slightly bushier, crest. Bright red bare facial skin more extensive than in Pelagic, extends from base of bill over forehead, around eye to chin. Juvenile: lacks red face, instead has yellowish eye-ring and much paler face than Pelagic. Confusion easily possible with non-breeding pale-billed Pelagic. Wingbeats faster than larger cormorants. **BP** Bill pale yellowish-grey, brighter yellow in adult; breeding adult has blue gape; eyes dark green; tarsi black. **SV** At colonies gives low, weak guttural croaking *kwoon* or *gwoo* calls.

Great Cormorant
ad sum
ad
juv
juv
ad win
Temminck's Cormorant
juv
ad
ad sum
juv
ad win
Pelagic Cormorant
juv
ad sum
Pelagic with
two Temminck's
juv
ad win
Red-faced Cormorant
ad sum
juv
juv
ad
ad win

Western Osprey *Pandion haliaetus* L 54–64 cm; WS 127–174 cm; WT ♂ 1120–1740 g, ♀ 1210–2050 g

SD *P. h. haliaetus* uncommon, summer visitor to Hokkaido and N Honshu, year-round south to N Nansei Shoto, Kyushu, Shikoku and Izu Is. Winters along coasts from C Honshu southwards. **HH** Rivers, lakes, coasts; nests on treetops, crags and cliffs. Soars and hovers over water, stoops steeply then plunges feet first to catch fish. **ID** Long-winged, two-toned, with broad black mask. Upperparts blackish-brown, underparts white with band of dark streaks across upper breast (heaviest in ♀). In flight, head prominent, tail short, wings narrow, long in 'hand' and typically angled at carpal (appears gull-like), with four primary tips separated. Underwing (ad) largely white, with black carpal patch and black fringes to coverts forming dark midwing bar, juvenile has less distinct underwing bar. **BP** Bill black with pale blue-grey base; eyes yellow (ad), or orange (juv); upper legs feathered white, lower tarsi blue-grey. **SV** Short plaintive whistled *cheup cheup*… in display, or series of 4–20 clear notes, with whistles and chirps. Also gives sharp *kew-kew-kew* calls in alarm, and a longer slurred *teeeeaa* whistle.

Black-winged Kite *Elanus caeruleus* L 31–37 cm; WS 77–92 cm; WT ♂ 197–277g, ♀ 219–343 g

SD *E. c. hypoleucus* accidental, Nansei Shoto. **HH** Woodland edges, grassland, cultivation. **ID** Small, falcon-like kite, head rather large with large eyes, broad-based wings and long, notched tail. Adult: pale silver-grey upperparts, clean white underparts contrasting strongly with black eye-patch, upperwing-coverts and underside of primaries. Juvenile: appears scaly, with rufous-tinged crown and breast, and white fringes to dark grey mantle, back and greater coverts. At rest, wingtips extend beyond tail tip. In flight, wings commonly angled back at carpal, 'arm' long, 'hand' appears short. Flight light, buoyant, with fast beats, commonly hovering with legs dangling, or gliding, harrier-like, with wings raised. **BP** Bill small, black, broad-based, with yellow cere; eyes red (ad) or greenish to dull orange (juv); tarsi yellow. **SV** Calls include a chattering *kek-kek-kek*, and *wheep wheep* in alarm.

Black-eared Kite *Milvus lineatus* L 51–66 cm; WS 125–153 cm; WT 630–1240 g

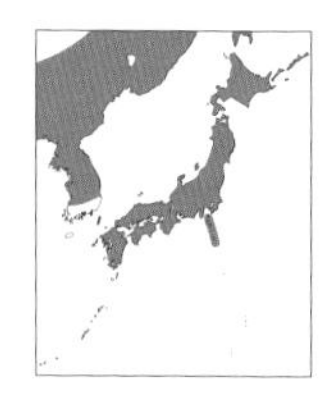

SD Widespread and common resident, except Nansei Shoto, where scarce. **HH** Coasts, lowlands, farmland, woodland, wetlands and habitation, also mountains during summer. A scavenger, not an active hunter. Gathers locally at communal winter roosts. **ID** Large, with long, broad wings, and long tail with shallow fork. Adult: varies from dark, dull, blackish-brown to warmer rufous, generally paler on head and vent, with prominent dark ear-coverts patch. Underparts pale brown with heavy dark streaking. Pale buff spotting on mantle, wing-coverts and streaked underparts, especially in juvenile. In flight, wings held flat, often angled at carpal, but frequent adjustment to trim of wings and especially tail, often twisting and turning when soaring, tip barely notched; primary tips distinct; shows prominent crescent on underwing (pale bases to primaries). **BP** Bill weak, black tip, grey base; eyes brown; legs feathered, feet dull yellow. **SV** Highly vocal in spring, when gives plaintive, tremulous, descending whistle: *pi-rrr* or *piihyorohyorohyoro pyiippippi*. **TN** IOC retains within Black Kite *M. migrans lineatus*.

Oriental Honey Buzzard *Pernis orientalis* L 54–65 cm; WS 128–155 cm; WT ♂ 510–800 g, ♀ 635–1050 g

SD Summer visitor (May–Sep) throughout four main islands, scarcest in Hokkaido. Conspicuous and in flocks on migration at certain capes. **HH** Lowland and montane forests to c. 1,800 m. Feeds on ground and at bee or wasp nests. **ID** Dark, broad-winged, long-tailed raptor with small head and long neck. Pale, intermediate and dark forms; all have small nuchal crest. Upperparts greyish-brown, face plain grey, wings and tail dark greyish-brown; underparts cream with finer dark barring on underside of flight-feathers, through rufous with chest barring, to almost entirely dark brown. Commonly has dark malar and dark gular stripe on pale throat. Face grey (♂) or brown (♀). At rest, wingtips fall short of tail-tip. In flight, black wingtips very rounded, six primary tips distinct; no dark carpal spot; ♂ has three black lines on underside of remiges, broad dark trailing edge to underwing, tail dark with broad pale central band, ♀ has four bands on remiges, narrow trailing edge to underwing and pale tail with two narrow dark bands near base and broader subterminal band. Normal flight involves several flaps followed by long glide with wingtips depressed, soars on flat wings. **BP** Bill slender, small, blackish at tip, paler grey at base; eyes large, dark reddish-brown (♂) or yellow (♀); tarsi feathered, feet yellow. **SV** High, four-note whistled *wee hey wee hey*, or a whistled scream *kleeeur*. **TN** IOC retains as Crested Honey Buzzard *P. ptilorhynchus orientalis*.

Western Osprey
juv
ad
ad
ad
ad
ad
ad
ad
juv
Black-winged Kite
ad
Black-eared Kite
ad
juv
ad
juv
Oriental Honey Buzzard
ad
ad ♀
ad ♂
ad ♂
ad ♀
juv

Cinereous Vulture *Aegypius monachus*

L 100–110 cm; WS 250–295 cm; WT 7000–12500 g

SD Accidental winter visitor to Hokkaido, Honshu, Shikoku, Kyushu and Nansei Shoto. **HH** Mountains, forest, farmland. **ID** Enormous. Adult has small pale brown head, with a long brown neck ruff; bare grey skin (extent variable) on ear-coverts; eye-patch, lores and throat dark brown. Juvenile is blacker, especially on cap, face and ruff. In flight, long, broad wings with 6–7 long 'fingered' primaries recall *Aquila* eagles; underwing dark; tail short, ragged, rounded or wedge-shaped; wingbeats deep and slow, soars on flat wings or with 'hand' drooping and angled back slightly. **BP** Bill heavy, tip black, dull bluish-pink base and gape (bright pink in juv); eyes dark brown; legs heavily feathered; feet whitish-grey. **SV** Hoarse cackling rattle on take-off, various croaks, grunting *kaa* calls, and hisses when approaching food. **AN** Eurasian Black Vulture; Monk Vulture.

Ryukyu Serpent Eagle *Spilornis (cheela) perplexus*

L 50–56 cm; WS 110–123 cm; WT 700–900 g

SD Endemic resident of Ishigaki and Iriomote Is, accidental on Yonaguni I. **HH** Subtropical evergreen broad-leaved forest <500 m, coastal lowlands and farmland. Often soars; perches openly on trees and poles. **ID** Small, pale, with short bushy nuchal crest. Adult crown and loose crest black, upperparts greyish-brown with fine silver-white spotting, wings and tail darkest, blackish-grey primaries white-tipped, tail almost black with narrow white tip and broad central band; underparts paler greyish-brown with light spotting on breast and more extensive, broader grey-white ovals across lower breast, belly, flanks and thighs. Juvenile is pale cream with dark brown flight-feathers and tail, dark brown ear-coverts, cream supercilia, dark brown spots on crown and neck and blotches on mantle and wing-coverts, underparts largely cream with fine brown barring on thighs. Wings and tail generally as Crested; underwing-coverts greyish-brown heavily spotted greyish-white. Juvenile in flight is extremely pale, underwing-coverts mostly white, primaries/secondaries very pale with black tips and two narrow black bands. **BP** Bill short, grey, cere yellow; legs and feet yellow; eye-ring yellow, irides yellow (ad) or white (juv). **SV** Loud, shrill *peeee piee fee feee*. **TN** IOC retains within Crested Serpent Eagle *S. cheela*.

Japanese Hawk-Eagle *Nisaetus (nipalensis) orientalis*

L 70–83 cm; WS 134–175 cm;
WT ♂ 2000–2500 g, ♀ 2500–3500 g

SD Resident, but scarce, throughout the four main islands of Japan. **HH** Heavily wooded or forested mountains to c. 2,000 m. In winter, northern birds make local movements, and higher montane birds may descend. **ID** Large, extremely broad-winged, rather pale eagle, with broad tail with rounded tip. Adult is dark brown with particularly dark ear-coverts, very narrow grey supercilia, heavy streaking on nape and neck-sides. Partly erectile rear crown-feathers form short, broad rounded crest; mantle and wing-coverts dark brown with some pale fringes; white throat with dark mesial stripe and dark striping on upper neck; flanks, belly, thighs, feathered legs and undertail-coverts off-white heavily barred dark rufous-brown. Juvenile is paler tawny-buff, especially on underparts. At rest wingtips extend just beyond tail base. In flight, very broad wings with broadly rounded tips, brown finely barred underwing-coverts, and narrow dark barring across pale underside to flight-feathers, trailing edge strongly curved; tail has 4–5 dark bars on pale background. Juvenile has plain buff-brown underwing-coverts and thighs, breast and belly pale buffy-white. Glides and soars on flat or shallow V-shaped wings. **BP** Bill strong, deep, dark grey with dark grey cere (ad), or dark grey with yellow basal half (juv); eyes golden-yellow to orange (ad) or pale bluish-grey to yellow (juv); legs large, feathered, large feet dull yellow. **SV** Usually silent, but may give various shrill screams and whistles (some likened to Green Sandpiper, others to Little Grebe, including *pippii pippii* or *pyo pyii*) on territory, from perch and in flight. **TN** Formerly *Spizaetus nipalensis*. **AN** Hodgson's Hawk-Eagle. **TN** IOC retains within Mountain Hawk-Eagle *N. nipalensis*.

Cinereous Vulture
ad
ad
juv
Ryukyu Serpent Eagle
juv
ad
ad
Japanese Hawk-Eagle
juv
ad
ad
ad

Greater Spotted Eagle *Clanga clanga* L 63–73 cm; WS 157–179 cm; WT ♂ 1500–2000 g, ♀ 2100–3200 g

SD Accidental, winter; Hokkaido to Nansei Shoto. **HH** Wetlands, farmland, forests. **ID** Dark, compact eagle. Adult: flat crown, spiky nape-feathers, whitish crescent on uppertail-coverts, pale bases to primaries. Dark wings very broad, 'arm' short, secondaries bulge slightly, 'hand' broad with 6–7 long, prominent 'fingers'. Tail broad, rounded, shorter than Golden or Eastern Imperial. Juvenile: creamy spots on upperparts, double wingbars, off-white vent. Juvenile from below like adult, but remiges narrowly barred. At rest appears hunched; wingtips almost reach tail tip. Flight slow, soars with wings flat or slightly arched at carpal. **BP** Bill small, dark grey, cere and short gape line (to eye) yellow, with round nostrils (slit-like in *Aquila* eagles); eyes dark brown; thighs heavily feathered, legs closely feathered, toes yellow. **SV** Staccato yelps: *kleep kleep kleep* or *kyui kyui*. During undulating and swooping aerial display (frequently in late winter), gives repetitive plaintive, barking *kiak-kiak-kiak*…

Steppe Eagle *Aquila nipalensis* L 60–81 cm; WS 165–214 cm; WT ♂ 2500–3500 g, ♀ 2300–4900 g

SD *A. n. nipalensis* accidental, winter. **HH** Wooded hills, open grasslands. **ID** Large, with large head/neck. Adult: rufous nape and pale chin, otherwise dark with pale fringes to mantle and wing-coverts, and prominent baggy 'trousers'. Dark brown underwing-coverts; has dark blackish-brown trailing edge and finely pale-barred dark flight-feathers, all dark-tipped; tail narrowly barred, with dark terminal band. Juvenile: greyish-brown; underparts unstreaked. Wing pattern distinctive: broad white mid-underwing bar and two narrower white bands on upperwing-coverts; trailing edge to wing and terminal tail-band white; uppertail-coverts also have narrow white band. White underwing bar and trailing edge become less prominent with age. At rest, wingtips reach or extend beyond tail tip. Flight sluggish, wingbeats heavy; long broad wings straight and level in powered flight; glides and soars on slightly bowed wings with well-spread 'fingers' (more prominent than Greater), drooping below 'wrist'. **BP** Bill large, dark grey, cere and long gape line yellow (extends to rear of eye); eye brown under heavy brow; thighs and legs feathered, large feet yellow. **SV** Typically silent. **TN** Not included by OSJ.

Eastern Imperial Eagle *Aquila heliaca* L 57–67 cm; WS 176–216 cm; WT 3200–4000 g

SD Vulnerable. Accidental, winter; Hokkaido to Nansei Shoto. **HH** Wetlands, riparian woodland. **ID** Large; head prominent, bill large, deep-based. Adult: dark brown, crown, nape and head-sides straw-coloured, sides of mantle white. Tail (shorter than Golden) grey with broad black band at tip. Juvenile: pale tawny-brown, mantle and wing-coverts dark-streaked, broad pale tips form double wingbar; rump and back plain buff. In flight, adult wings long, plain and dark, broad to base with prominently 'fingered' primaries; tail long, square-ended and two-toned. Wings, narrower than Golden, parallel-edged. Flight deliberate with heavy floppy beats; glides/soars on flat or slightly raised wings with primary tips upcurled. Juvenile has very different wing pattern and bulging secondaries; flight-feathers and tail blackish-brown with pale tips. Pale grey inner primaries form 'window'; underwing- and upperwing-coverts buff, heavily streaked dark brown, and upperwing greater coverts blackish with white fringes forming narrow wing-bar; uppertail-coverts creamy white; thighs and vent plain buff. **BP** Bill large, deep, yellow base, grey tip; eyes yellowish-grey to pale brown; short legs heavily feathered, small feet yellow. **SV** Vocal, especially during aerial display flight – deep quacking barks *kuwa kuwa kuwa* or *owk-owk-owk*…, also a squealing whistled *skiwip*.

Golden Eagle *Aquila chrysaetos* L 78–95 cm; WS 180–234 cm; WT 3200–5500 g

SD Rare local resident *A. c. japonica* breeds Kyushu, Shikoku, C Honshu; accidental Hokkaido to Izu islands. **HH** Mountains, rocky crags, dense forests. **ID** Adult: golden crown and nape contrast with overall dark plumage. At rest, wings reach tail tip. In flight, head and neck prominent; wingbeats slow, deliberate, on long dark wings with broad 'hand', bulging secondaries and narrower bases, with prominently 'fingered' primaries and curved trailing edge to secondaries; tail long, broad, narrow-based. Soars high with wings flat or in shallow V and pressed forwards. Adult: pale upperwing-coverts form upperwing panel; juvenile: even darker; 1st-year: large, white wing patches, conspicuous white tail with black terminal band. **BP** Bill grey with black tip, yellow cere and grey lores; eyes amber to red-brown (ad) or dark brown (juv) under heavy brows; legs heavily feathered, toes yellow. **SV** Weak calls include a whistled *pee-yep*, a deeper barking *kiek-kiek-kiek* or *kra kra*, and a yapping *nyek nyek*.

Greater Spotted Eagle
ad
juv
ad
ad
juv
Steppe Eagle
ad
juv
ad
ad
imm
Eastern Imperial Eagle
ad
juv
ad
ad
juv
Golden Eagle
ad
ad
ad
juv

Grey-faced Buzzard *Butastur indicus*

L 47–51 cm; WS 101–110 cm; WT 380–440 g

SD Common, but locally declining, migrant summering (Apr–Oct) from Kyushu to N Honshu. Some winter in Nansei Shoto. **HH** Montane coniferous and mixed evergreen forests, lowland forest edge, also around agricultural land. On migration, locally common and often in flocks. **ID** Mid-sized, rather slender, buzzard-like hawk. Adult: mid-grey to dark chocolate-brown, all but darkest (almost entirely black) forms have grey-brown head, grey cheeks and white chin, with black gular stripe; crown flat, white supercilia prominent. Upperparts and breast typically mid- to dark brown, lower breast and flanks brown-barred white. Juvenile: more heavily streaked with more contrasting head pattern. Wings and tail longer and narrower than Eastern Buzzard, resembling large sparrowhawk, underwing pale with fine dark barring; pale U on uppertail-coverts, square-tipped tail has three dark bars. Flight generally rather laboured, but on migration often appears quite buoyant, with almost falcon-like glides. **BP** Bill reasonably long with prominent hook, basal half yellow, cere orange-yellow; eyes bright yellow (ad) or brown to pale yellow (juv); tarsi dull yellow. **SV** Rather vocal year-round, but especially prior to nesting. Call, while soaring or perching, a whistled *whick-awee* or tremulous, drawn-out, but strong, *pik-kwee*, the second part prolonged and upslurred. **AN** Grey-faced Buzzard-eagle.

Chinese Sparrowhawk *Accipiter soloensis*

L 25–35 cm; WS 52–62 cm; WT 140–204 g

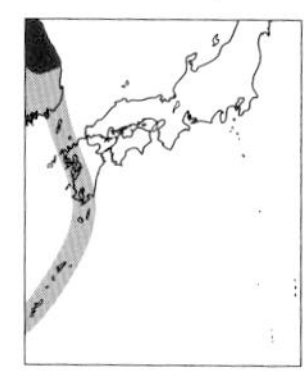

SD Migrants pass through Nansei Shoto, Kyushu and Tsushima; very rare elsewhere. **HH** Forested hills, and open fields near wooded areas. Locally common migrant (May, Sep/Oct); often in flocks. **ID** Pale, mid-sized *Accipiter* with plain grey head (no supercilia) and upperparts, darker wings, mantle and tail, wingtips rather pointed and tail rather short. Underparts white with pale rufous wash or bars. Young resemble Japanese Sparrowhawk, but darker brown with blackish-brown crown, grey face lacking supercilia, and distinct underwing pattern. At rest has long primary projection. Flight fast and agile; often soars. In flight, adult has narrow, rather pointed black wingtips (unique in *Accipiter*), contrasting strongly with mainly white, unbarred underwings with grey trailing edges; undertail very pale with several narrow dark grey bars; tail proportionately short. Juvenile in flight recalls juvenile Eurasian Sparrowhawk, but breast and belly more rufous and underwing-coverts very pale buff and mostly plain; underside of flight-feathers pale with very narrow dark barring. **BP** Bill grey, tip black, swollen cere orange-yellow, reaching forehead and prominent on plain grey face; eyes dark brown to dark red (ad) or yellow (juv); tarsi bright yellow-orange. **SV** Typically silent away from breeding grounds. **AN** Chinese Goshawk.

Japanese Sparrowhawk *Accipiter gularis*

L 23–32 cm; WS 46–58 cm; WT ♂ 92–142 g, ♀ 111–193 g

SD *A. g. gularis* is a summer visitor to Hokkaido, resident in Honshu, Shikoku and Kyushu, C Nansei Shoto and a scarce migrant elsewhere. *A. g. iwasakii* is resident on Ishigaki, Iriomote and Yonaguni Is. **HH** Breeds in deciduous and mixed forests, also urban parks; on migration and in winter (and *A. g. iwasakii*) occurs in subtropical forests. **ID** Japan's smallest *Accipiter*. *A. g. gularis* resembles small, plain Eurasian Sparrowhawk, with long primary projection and four narrow dark bands on largely pale tail (terminal broadest). ♂ dark bluish-grey on face and upperparts; underparts whitish, breast, flanks and belly variably washed and barred brick red. ♀ browner above, whiter below with dark rufous barring, throat white with faint gular stripe. Juvenile browner with rufous streaks on lower neck, barred flanks and breast. *A. g. iwasakii* is darker grey on face and head, browner on wings and tail. At rest, primary projection long and tail has pale bars obviously broader than dark bars. Flight fast and agile, often soars; like larger Eurasian, but wings shorter, 'arm' broader, tips narrower and more pointed, tail shorter; shape recalls Oriental Turtle Dove. Field ID of subspecies uncertain, but *iwasakii* averages smaller and darker above than *gularis*, underside browner; wings blunter and tail more densely barred. **BP** Bill blue-grey with black tip, cere greenish-yellow (young) to yellow (ad); eye-ring yellow; eyes yellow (♀/young ♂), darkening to orange-yellow (*iwasakii*) or dark red (ad ♂ *gularis*); tarsi greenish-yellow (young) to yellow (ad). **SV** High-pitched chattering *kyik kye-kye-kye*, often given on migration, also sharp, ringing *kyip-kyip*.

Grey-faced Buzzard
ad
juv
ad
juv

Chinese Sparrowhawk
ad
juv
ad
juv

Japanese Sparrowhawk
gularis
ad ♀
juv
ad ♂
ad ♂
juv
ad ♀

Eurasian Sparrowhawk *Accipiter nisus* L 28–40 cm; WS 56–78 cm; WT ♂ 105–196 g, ♀ 185–350 g

SD *A. n. nisosimilis* is a widespread and fairly common winter visitor. Some resident (mainly C Honshu to Hokkaido). Northern birds migrate through the archipelago. **HH** Well-forested lower montane areas and wooded lowlands; also wooded urban areas and parks; generally in forest or at edges. **ID** Medium-sized *Accipiter* with rather small head, short, broad, blunt wings and long tail (with four dark bands from above). ♂ small, with slate- to blue-grey upperparts, plain face, rufous cheeks and rufous-barred breast. ♀ large, resembles Northern Goshawk, but slimmer, with dark grey upperparts, white underparts barred grey (lacks gular stripe of Japanese and Chinese sparrowhawks). Large ♀ confusable with Northern Goshawk ♂, but has shorter 'arms' and longer 'hands', tail longer, narrower at base with squarer corners and even slight notch, relatively smaller head, less prominent white vent. Primary projection moderate. In flight, may appear pigeon-like, with gentle undulations on rapid, light flaps interspersed by short glides; less direct than Northern Goshawk, but agile in pursuit of prey, often very close to ground, but also soars over canopy and high on migration. Underwing, including coverts and axillaries, rather strongly barred, tail has three bold dark bars below, and is rather narrow, longer than width of wings, thus wings appear narrower, and tail longer compared with Japanese Sparrowhawk. Juvenile has brown-barred underparts with little or no streaking. **BP** Bill dark grey with yellow cere; eyes yellow-orange to red (♂), or yellow to orange (♀); legs greenish-yellow to yellow, feet yellow. **SV** Generally silent, except when breeding, when gives chattering or cackling *ki ki ki; kee kee kee* or *kekekekekeke* calls, higher-pitched than Northern Goshawk.

Northern Goshawk *Accipiter gentilis* L 46–63 cm; WS 89–122 cm; WT ♂ 894–1200 g, ♀ 1300–1400 g

SD *A. g. fujiyamae* is resident in Hokkaido, Honshu, Shikoku and N Kyushu, and perhaps a partial migrant occurring south to Nansei Shoto. *A. g. albidus* is an accidental winter visitor to Hokkaido and N Honshu. **HH** Forests and plantations. Rather shy, views often distant, but can be territorial and aggressive near nests; in winter may visit areas with concentrations of waterfowl. **ID** Very large, powerful *Accipiter*, reaching size of Eastern Buzzard. Deep chest, long but very broad wings, and long, broad tail, longer neck, more protruding head than Eurasian Sparrowhawk, and has dark crown and ear-coverts, and very prominent white brows. Adult has rather dark grey upperparts, some with brown tones, and white underparts with fine dark-grey barring from breast to belly, undertail-coverts long, white, often conspicuous; grey tail has three broad dark bands; ♀ larger. Juvenile has brown upperparts and buff underparts heavily streaked brown. Rather long primary projection and long undertail-coverts. Flight aggressive, turns and accelerates with remarkable speed in pursuit of prey, also glides and soars over territory; differs from Eurasian Sparrowhawk – short series of relaxed flaps followed by straight glide without losing height. Wingbeats stiff, powerful and steady, wings bulge at secondaries, 'hand' somewhat narrower at tip and clearly 'fingered'. In flight, adult is broad-bodied and plain grey from below; juv/1st-year densely streaked dark brown on buff underparts, underwing narrowly barred, upperwing also barred and has pale bar on greater coverts. Tail broad-based and rounded at tip, long white undertail-coverts bulge and may wrap conspicuously around rump-sides; tail commonly spread when soaring. *A. g. albidus* appears very pale, has very pale grey upperparts and almost white underparts; juvenile is buffy-white with pale to dark-brown streaking, brown tail and remiges, and whitish underparts with dark brown vertical streaks. **BP** Bill well hooked, grey tip, greenish-yellow cere; eyes orange-red (♂), bright orange-yellow (♀) or pale yellow (juv); legs short and thick, yellow. **SV** Generally silent, except when breeding, when gives stronger, deeper, chattering *kya kya kya kya*, *kee kee kee*, or *kyik-kyik-kyik* calls than Eurasian Sparrowhawk.

Eurasian Sparrowhawk
ad ♂
ad ♂
ad ♀
ad ♀
juv ♀
juv ♀
Northern Goshawk
ad ♂
albidus
juv ♀
ad ♀
albidus
ad ♂
fujiyamae
juv ♀

Western Marsh Harrier *Circus aeruginosus*

L 46–63 cm; WS 89–122 cm; WT ♂ 894–1200 g, ♀ 1300–1400 g

SD *C. a. aeruginosus*, accidental to W Honshu. **HH** Wetlands, reedbeds, and open grasslands. **ID** Like Eastern Marsh Harrier, large, bulky with long, broad wings, but ♂ has brown mantle and upperwing-coverts, grey secondaries and primary-coverts and black primaries (tricoloured upperwing); forewing white to cream, head typically very pale fawn and long tail is plain grey. ♀ extremely dark chocolate-brown with paler upperwing-coverts, creamy white crown and chin, dark eyestripe, and plain reddish-brown rump and tail; underparts dark brown, except pale breast-band; axillaries and underwing-coverts dark brown, secondaries dark grey, primaries mid-brown with blackish-brown tips. Juvenile dark blackish-brown, with buttery-yellow crown and throat, pale brown to off-white underwing-coverts and dark brown tail, also without white rump. At rest, wingtips fall just short of tail tip. Flight as Eastern, wingbeats heavy, glides and soars on raised wings, may hover. **BP** Bill short, slender, blue-grey with black tip, and yellow cere; eyes yellow (♂), dull orange (♀), or brown (juv); long tarsi and toes yellow, visible in flight against dark underparts. **SV** Silent away from breeding grounds.

Eastern Marsh Harrier *Circus spilonotus*

L 48–58 cm; WS 119–145 cm; WT ♂ 405–730g, ♀ 540–960 g

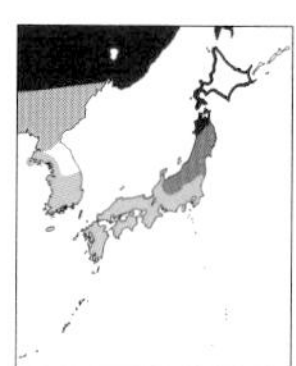

SD Uncommon. Summer visitor to Hokkaido, resident or winter visitor N Honshu, winter visitor south throughout Japan. **HH** Grasslands or marshes with extensive reeds or tall grasses. **ID** Size of Eastern Buzzard, but appears larger; slimmer with long tail and long, broad wings; slower wingbeats add to impression of larger size. Variable ♂ is typically grey and black, somewhat resembling Pied Harrier, but far less neatly marked; mantle and upperwing-coverts dark grey to black, head largely black with white streaks, black extending to neck/chest, or grey with dark face. Underparts white, streaked grey or black on upper chest; underwing white, primary tips black, secondaries mostly plain pale grey sometimes with narrow black bars near tips; upperwing has black coverts (spotted white), primaries and secondaries mostly pale grey, outer primary tips black, others, and secondaries, have some faint black bars; tail unbarred grey with narrow, inconspicuous white rump. ♀ somewhat resembles Hen Harrier; generally dark grey-brown, paler on head, breast and underwing. ♀ and juvenile show much individual variation. ♀ rather rufous-brown on underparts, cooler brown on face (lacks cap and dark eyestripe of Western Marsh), underwing-coverts heavily streaked mid- to dark brown, flight-feathers grey with darker barring; tail has narrow grey bands, and narrow rump patch is white, though some have buff rump or no rump patch. Juvenile warm brown with pale creamy brown head, breast and mantle; underwing largely dark but coverts and axillaries creamy white (see Western Marsh). In flight, wings black-tipped, with 3–4 visible 'fingers'. Wingbeats generally slow, glides frequently holding wings in pronounced V; sometimes hovers with legs dangling before dropping onto prey. **BP** Bill has grey-black tip, yellow base and gape; eyes yellow (♂) or dull orange-brown (♀); long tarsi yellow. **SV** Typically silent, but when breeding gives various calls: *myuaa myuu kyuii* and *ke ke*, also a high-pitched squealing *pishee pishee* (♂) and soft *kyu-kyu* notes (♀).

Pied Harrier *Circus melanoleucos*

L 42–50 cm; WS 110–125 cm; WT ♂ 265–325 g, ♀ 390–455 g

SD Accidental from Hokkaido to Nansei Shoto. **HH** Open areas, marshes, ricefields and reedbeds; habits as other harriers. **ID** Small, slightly built, slender-winged harrier. ♂ unmistakably elegant, pied with pale grey wings and tail; underparts white, underwing white with black primaries, secondaries all white at tips (see Hen Harrier). Can recall larger Eastern Marsh Harrier ♂, but is far more cleanly marked. ♀ resembles ♀ Hen, but greyer, shares white rump, but is darker, more contrasting, with dark greyish-brown upperparts and wings, with pale forewing and dark grey, barred brown remiges; tail grey with 4–5 fine dark bars, the subterminal band being darkest; underwing much paler than ♀ Hen, with pale underwing-coverts and brown streaking, remiges pale with narrow dark grey barring. Juvenile ♂ resembles adult ♀, but has much darker brown upperwings and tail and narrower white rump patch, underparts and underwing-coverts more rufous than adult ♀. Juvenile ♀ is largely dark brown with whitish nape, streaked head, buff rump, no grey in wings and dark, banded tail. Flight lighter than Eastern Marsh or Hen, but also glides and soars on V-shaped wings. **BP** Bill has grey-black tip, yellow base and gape; eyes yellow (♂ bright, ♀ dull) or dark brown (juv); long tarsi yellow. **SV** Usually silent away from breeding grounds, but may give a rapid chattering *wek-wek-wek* or *chak-chak-chak-chak* in alarm.

ad ♂
ad ♂
ad ♂
ad ♀
Western Marsh Harrier
ad ♀
Eastern Marsh Harrier
ad ♂
ad ♀
juv
ad ♀
ad ♂
juv
ad ♀
Pied Harrier
ad ♂
ad ♂
juv ♂
ad ♀
ad ♀

Pallid Harrier *Circus macrourus* L 40–50 cm; WS 100–121 cm; WT ♂ 235–415 g, ♀ 400–550 g

SD Accidental; C & W Honshu. **HH** Open country, dry grassland, cultivation, marshes. **ID** Elegant, recalls small, slim, pale Hen Harrier; long wings narrow to pointed tip. ♂: pale grey, may appear white, head especially pale grey, throat and chest white (lacks Hen's hooded appearance). Long-legged. ♀: bold head pattern with dark eyestripe, dark ear-coverts and prominent pale supercilia, narrow hind-collar; flanks and 'trousers' have diffuse broad double rufous spots. Juvenile: unstreaked orange-buff underparts and underwing-coverts, with bolder face pattern (pale tawny collar contrasting with dark neck and white patch below eye). In flight, ♂ upperwing pale grey with *four* outer primaries solid black; underwing white with black outer primaries forming distinct wedge; tail pale grey with mid-grey barring, white rump narrow and indistinct. ♀ underwing has pale, irregularly barred primaries, contrasting with darker secondaries, which have very narrow grey bars; rump white. Flight buoyant, light with rapid beats and wavering glides (wings in shallow V). **BP** Bill yellow, tip black, cere yellow; eyes pale yellow (ad), grey with brown ring (juv); long tarsi yellow. **SV** Generally silent.

Hen Harrier *Circus cyaneus* L 43–53 cm; WS 100–121 cm; WT ♂ 300–400 g, ♀ 370–700 g

SD Uncommon winter visitor (Oct–Apr), Hokkaido, Honshu, Shikoku and Kyushu, scarce Nansei Shoto and other islands. **HH** Marshes, reedbeds, grasslands, agricultural habitats; habits similar to marsh harriers. **ID** Smaller and slighter than marsh harriers, but larger than other harriers, with long, broad-tipped wings, broader in 'arm' than 'hand', and long tail. ♂: mid-grey above, with grey hood, broad black wingtips, pale grey primaries, secondaries and tail, broad white rump and white underparts below grey chest; underwing white with *six* black primary tips and broad, dark grey trailing edge to inner primaries and secondaries. ♀: dark brown with heavily streaked underparts and pale-fringed upperparts, clearly barred wings and tail both above and below, prominent white rump and pale brown underparts streaked darker. Tail has broad dark grey subterminal band and 3–4 bands on mid-tail. Juvenile: dark-headed, with orange-brown body and underwing. ♀ and juvenile have owl-like facial disc and pale collar. In flight, long-winged rowing action is slow and smooth, glides on flat or slightly raised wings, frequently rocking from side to side, revealing white rump. **BP** Bill grey-black, cere and gape yellow; eyes orange-yellow (♂), brown to pale yellow (♀); long tarsi yellow. **SV** Usually silent away from breeding grounds.

Northern Harrier *Circus hudsonius* L 41–50 cm; WS 97–122 cm; WT ♂ 290–390 g, ♀ 390–600 g

SD N American sister species of Hen Harrier; vagrant Hokkaido and Honshu in winter. **HH** Marshes, agricultural land. **ID** Adult ♂: essentially like Hen, but with *five* black primary tips, covering a smaller area, and trailing edge to secondaries black, not grey. Juvenile: dark-headed, with orange-brown body and underwing, almost orange breast and upperparts (unstreaked). **BP** Bill like Hen; eyes yellow (♂), or brown to yellow (♀); long legs (10% longer than Hen) and feet orange-yellow. **SV** Usually silent. **TN** Formerly a Nearctic race of Hen Harrier; not included by OSJ. **AN** American Harrier.

Montagu's Harrier *Circus pygargus* L 39–49 cm; WS 102–123 cm; WT ♂ 227–305 g, ♀ 254–445 g

SD Vagrant reported in winter. **HH** Marshes, agricultural land. **ID** Small, slender and very long-, narrow-winged harrier; wings reach tail tip when perched (in most harriers, wingtips fall nearly to or short of tail tip). ♂: resembles ♂ Hen Harrier, but black wingtip narrower, has unique black bar across secondaries, and distinct contrast between dark mantle and paler grey flight-feathers; upperwing darker than Pallid with more extensive black on primaries; underwing darker than Hen with more extensive black on underside of primaries and outer secondaries, two black bars on secondaries, and variable rufous streaking on underwing-coverts and flanks. ♀: resembles ♀ Hen and Pallid, but slighter than Hen with inconspicuous narrow white rump, black band on secondaries, underwing cleanly marked with dark trailing edge and clear blackish bands on secondaries, several narrower bands on underside of primaries. Juvenile: unstreaked orange-buff underparts and underwing-coverts, dark secondaries and trailing edge, pale primaries with several black bars, black outer primary tips, and paler face with broader supercilia, reduced dark ear-coverts and crucially lacks distinct dark rear neck and pale collar. In flight, more agile, with narrower wings and more buoyant flight, than Hen. **BP** Bill as Hen; eyes pale orange (ad ♂), yellow (♀) or brown (juv); tarsi yellow, legs shorter than other harriers, thus has lower, more horizontal stance. **SV** Usually silent. **TN** Not included by OSJ.

Pallid Harrier
ad ♂
ad ♂
imm ♂
juv
ad ♀
juv
Hen Harrier
ad ♂
ad ♂
ad ♀
imm ♂
ad ♀
ad ♀
Northern Harrier
ad ♂
ad ♀
ad ♂
juv
Montagu's Harrier
ad ♂
ad ♂
ad ♀
ad ♀
juv

PLATE 46: SEA EAGLES

White-tailed Eagle *Haliaeetus albicilla* L 74–94 cm; WS 193–244 cm; WT ♂ 3075–5430 g, ♀ 4080–6900 g

SD *H. a. albicilla* breeds locally in Hokkaido. Large numbers arrive from Russia to winter (Oct–Apr) in Hokkaido, with some reaching N Honshu and ocasionally further south. **HH** Rocky coasts with cliffs; shallow coastal lagoons, lakes, large rivers and marshes; builds enormous stick nest in trees or on crags. **ID** Large eagle; perches upright, hunched, for long periods, or horizontally on ground or ice, when wingtips reach tail tip. Adult has pale tawny head, broadly rectangular wings, short, conspicuous baggy brown 'trousers', and short, white tail. Neck, mantle and wings have pale fringes, giving 'frosted' appearance. Young more mottled; tail may have white base and dark tip. Becomes progressively 'cleaner' and tail whiter with age. Flight-feathers dark sooty-brown, underwing-coverts more chestnut-brown; young have pale band on underwing-coverts and paler axillaries. In flight, wingbeats shallow and laborious on long, broad wings, with 5–6 'fingered' primaries, series of shallow beats occasionally interspersed with glides on flat or slightly bowed wings; frequently soars, sometimes at considerable height, with wings slightly raised above horizontal. **BP** Bill large, deep, horn to pale yellow with yellow cere (ad) or dark grey (imm); lores whitish; eyes pale yellow (ad) or dark brown (imm); legs feathered, feet yellow. **SV** Rather vocal on territory, a series of gentle barks or yelps, *kyee-kyee-kyee*, or deeper stronger *kra-kra-kra* in alarm, but also calls in winter in alarm or when competing for food.

Steller's Eagle *Haliaeetus pelagicus* L 85–105 cm; WS 195–230 cm; WT ♂ 4900–6000 g, ♀ 6800–9000 g

SD Vulnerable. Locally common winter visitor (Nov–Mar) to Sea of Okhotsk and Pacific coasts of Hokkaido (especially Shiretoko) and inland, particularly in E Hokkaido. Small numbers also reach N and C Honshu; accidental south to Nansei Shoto. **HH** Rocky coasts, large coastal lagoons and river mouths, also ranges inland along rivers and at large lakes and wetlands; congregates at rich food supplies (fish and waterfowl) and locally at roosts. **ID** Very large blackish-brown eagle, with unique wing and tail shape, rather long neck, large dark brown head frosted on crown and neck, with white blaze on forehead. Entire fore-wing, thighs, rump and large diamond-shaped tail of adult white; appears to have large baggy white 'trousers'. ♀ larger with deeper bill. Young variable, initially extremely dark with pale axillaries, underwing covert bar, and enormous pale horn-coloured bill. With age, tail, thighs and forewing whiten steadily, becoming progressively 'cleaner' and tail whiter; white forehead blaze is last to develop (c. 5 years). Wings clearly 'fingered', with 'hand' and base both narrower than midwing, giving distinctive wing shape. In flight, beats often appear laborious, but flight can be extremely active, especially in aerial displays and chases, when 'rows' powerfully like a massive falcon. Soars frequently. **BP** Bill massive, dwarfs that of White-tailed, depth particularly impressive, strongly hooked, deep yellow including gape and lores; eye-ring yellow, irides pale yellow to white; legs massive, white-feathered, large feet yellow. **SV** On wintering grounds, when squabbling over food or roosting site, or when displaying in late winter, gives loud, throaty barking *kyow-kyow-kyow* or *gra-gra-gra* from perch or during aerial display. Louder and deeper than White-tailed. **AN** Steller's Sea Eagle.

Bald Eagle *Haliaeetus leucocephalus* L 70–90 cm; WS 180–230 cm; WT 2500–6300 g

SD Accidental (*H. l. washingtoniensis*) to S Kuril Islands (Kunashiri); likely to reach Hokkaido. **HH** Coasts, large rivers and lakes. **ID** Large, blackish-brown eagle, with large white head. Adult unmistakable. Juvenile very dark, with white only in axillaries, underwing-coverts and base of tail; becomes whiter on belly, underwing, tail and upper back in 2nd year. By 3rd year, head begins to whiten, but has dark band from ear to nape. Juvenile and subadult resemble young Steller's and White-tailed, but structural differences important: neck shorter, tail longer, and has whitish-buff axillaries and contrasting buff and brown bars on underwing-coverts. Long, broad wings have pale grey panel at base of primaries on underside; younger birds have more prominent secondary bulge and extensive white mottling in brown underwing. **BP** Bill large, bright pale yellow (ad), dark grey (juv), with dull yellow base (2nd-year) and bright yellow base (3rd-year); eyes dark brown (juv), dull brown (2nd-year) and off-white (3rd-year/ad); tarsi yellow. **SV** Calls variable, but surprisingly weak; a flat whistled *kah-kah-hah* in flight or perched.

White-tailed Eagle
ad
ad
juv
ad
juv
imm
ad
juv
ad
Steller's Eagle
juv
imm
ad
imm
Bald Eagle
ad
juv
ad

Rough-legged Buzzard *Buteo lagopus* L 53–61 cm; WS 120–153 cm; WT ♂ 730–990 kg, ♀ 845–1152 g

SD Two subspecies: mostly *B. l. menzbieri* but *B. l. kamtschatkensis* has also occurred. Scarce winter visitor to northern Japan, mainly Hokkaido and N Honshu; accidental south to Nansei Shoto. **HH** Montane and coastal grasslands, farmland, and wetlands. **ID** Large, long-winged, and long-tailed; larger and paler than Eastern Buzzard. Adult is grey-brown, with very pale head, variable brown streaking on throat and neck, dark flank patches may merge across belly; prominent black carpal contrasts with whitish primary bases, upperparts dark, contrasting with white tail with black subterminal band (juv tail extensively grey-brown, whitish only at base); narrow black eyestripe. ♂ has darker head and pale breast. ♀ and juvenile have paler head that can appear white. Wings long, but broad-tipped (reaching tail tip at rest). Flight slow, often low, on shallow beats; hovers frequently; glides on flat wings, but may soar on slight dihedral. Upperwing largely dark, but pale band across coverts, large pale area formed by most of primaries being grey-white, and most of uppertail white. Underwing pale, largely white, but prominent dark carpal, flight-feather tips (forming marginal band); undertail white with 2–3 prominent dark terminal bands (♂) or one (♀). Larger *kamtschatkensis* is very similar to *menzbieri*, but throat and upper breast darker, giving hooded appearance; flank patches paler, less extensive; pale panel on upper surface reduced, almost absent, with extensive white tips to body, mantle and scapulars. **BP** Bill has grey tip with yellow cere; eyes yellow or brown (ad), or pale to brownish-grey (juv); legs feathered, toes yellow. **SV** Generally silent in winter, but may give loud, high-pitched *pi-i-aay* alarm calls. **AN** North America: Rough-legged Hawk.

Upland Buzzard *Buteo hemilasius* L 61–72 cm; WS 143–161 cm; WT ♂ 950–1400 g, ♀ 970–2050 g

SD Accidental in winter from Nansei Shoto north to Hokkaido. **HH** Hills, open country and lowland farmland in winter. **ID** Larger with more eagle-like proportions than Eastern Buzzard – wings and tail longer, broader. May also recall Rough-legged. Adult pale morph has whitish head with dark moustachial streak, grey-brown upperparts; underparts whitish with large blackish-brown flank patches, thighs and large black carpal patch (resembling Eastern). Underwing-coverts pale brown, wingtips and trailing edge to underwing black; large grey-white patches at bases of primaries form 'window' on both surfaces of wing, tail greyish-white finely barred near tip. Dark morph is blackish-brown, with pale underside to flight feathers. Tail pale grey-brown with fine barring (lacks subterminal band of Rough-legged); only distinguished from dark Eastern by size/structure. Juvenile is like dark-morph adult. Flight slow, wingbeats deep, glides with 'arms' raised and 'hands' flat, soars with wings in deep V, also hovers. **BP** Bill blue-grey, cere greenish-yellow; eyes whitish or yellowish to golden-yellow; tarsi greyish-yellow to yellow. **SV** Mewing calls resemble Eastern Buzzard, but longer and more nasal *piiyoo piiyoo*; also short, nasal yapping calls.

Eastern Buzzard *Buteo japonicus* L 51–59 cm; WS 109–136 cm; WT 520–970 g

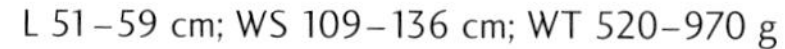

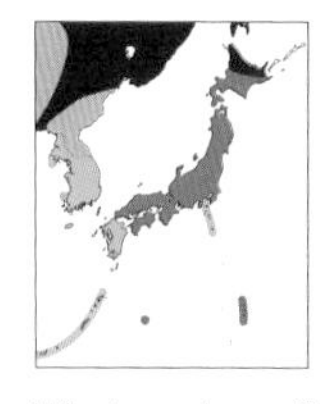

SD *B. j. japonicus* breeds from Hokkaido to Kyushu and winters south to Izu Is and Nansei Shoto. *B. j. toyoshimai* is an endemic resident of the Ogasawara Is. *B. j. oshiroi*, an endemic resident of Daito Is, is probably extinct. **HH** Forests, well-wooded hills, open agricultural areas, even in trees and poles along roadsides in winter. **ID** Compact, broad-winged, typically dark brown above and very pale below, with small bill and feet. Adults are variable, but head typically paler than upperparts; underparts off-white with prominent dark-brown patches on sides/thighs extending to lower chest and contrasting with pale belly and vent. Superficial resemblance to Rough-legged Buzzard, especially in winter when reflection off snow makes Eastern appear whiter below, but upper tail is uniform. Juvenile is more heavily streaked below. Wingbeats slow, stiff, glides on flat wings or with lowered 'hands', commonly soars with wings in shallow V, rides thermals, even hovers for short periods. Underwing flight-feathers pale, coverts pale brown, large carpal patch and primary tips black; undertail pale with fine grey bars. *B. j. toyoshimai* smaller, shorter-winged and usually paler than *B. j. japonicus*, with only small brown patches on underside. *B. j. oshiroi* is smaller, darker, redder and shorter-winged. **BP** Bill small, weak, tip grey, cere yellow; eyes brown (ad) or pale grey to pale brown (juv); tarsi yellow. **SV** Call, given in aerial display, a loud mewing *kiiii-kiiii* or *peeyou*; may be heard year-round. **TN** Formerly Common Buzzard *B. buteo* (e.g. OSJ). **AN** Japanese Buzzard.

Rough-legged Buzzard
kamtschatkensis
ad
ad
ad
ad
juv
juv
Upland Buzzard
ad
ad
ad pale
ad dark
juv
ad
juv
Eastern Buzzard
japonicus
ad
ad
ad
juv
ad toyoshimai
pale form
ad toyoshimai
dark form

PLATE 48: BUSTARDS, RAILS AND CRAKES I

Great Bustard *Otis tarda* ♂ L 90–105 cm, WS ♂ 210–260 cm, WT 5800–18000 g; ♀ L 75–85 cm, WS 170–190 cm, WT 3300–5300 kg

SD Vulnerable. *O. t. dybowskii* accidental in winter (Sep–Apr) from Hokkaido to Nansei Shoto. **HH** Agricultural land. **ID** Large, stout-bodied, goose-sized bird, with large head, long neck and long legs. Bulky, tail short. Head and neck pale grey, upperparts pale to mid orange-brown barred black, tail somewhat darker; underparts white. Enormous ♂ has elongated white facial whiskers on chin and broad chestnut chest band when breeding, loses whiskers and breast-band narrower at other times. ♀ much smaller, lacks chest-band, and is paler, sandier brown, neck thinner and less grey. Take-off requires lumbering run, but flight fast with deep beats, recalling *Aquila* eagles. Wings long, broad, rounded, with prominent 'fingers', largely white with black carpal crescent, primary tips and broad secondary band, secondary wing-coverts concolorous with back, but primary-coverts and flight-feathers mostly greyish-white, forming extensive pale panel contrasting with black primary tips and broad black band on secondary tips. **BP** Bill greyish-horn; eye large, irides dark brown; legs greenish-grey. **SV** Generally silent away from breeding grounds; alarm call is a bizarre short nasal bark.

Little Bustard *Tetrax tetrax* L 40–55 cm; WS 83–91 cm; WT ♂ 794–975 g, ♀ 680–945 g

SD Vagrant to Kyushu. **HH** Dry grasslands, short crop fields. **ID** Small bustard the size of ♀ pheasant, but proportions very different. ♂ (breeding) has grey head, black neck with two white collars, one (narrow) forms V on foreneck, one (broad) around lower neck; sandy to mid-brown upperparts and white from upper breast to vent. ♀/non-breeding ♂ more uniform, lack grey, black and white on head and neck, body and upperparts sandy brown with dark mottling. Wings broad, rounded, wingtips arched and wingbeats rapid and shallow, recalling grouse. Broad white panel across secondaries and inner primaries (wings appear very white); primary tips and crescent on greater coverts black. **BP** Bill short, slightly arched, dull grey, blackish-grey at tip; eyes reddish-brown (breeding ♂), paler brown (♀); long tarsi dull greyish-green. **SV** Essentially silent, except on breeding grounds, but when flushed may give low *ogh* and wings may whistle weakly, but distinctively, in flight.

Swinhoe's Rail *Coturnicops exquisitus* L 12 cm; WT 36 g

SD Very rare, secretive and poorly known visitor to Japan, from Hokkaido to Nansei Shoto (has bred N Honshu). **HH** Breeds in wet meadows and marshes, and winters in similar habitats and wet ricefields. **ID** Very small crake, which may be confused with Baillon's. Upperparts mid- to dark brown, with broad blackish-brown streaks and very fine transverse white bars. Warm brown face and breast finely speckled white, ear-coverts and breast dark brown, belly white. Wings short and rounded; coverts and tertials patterned like upperparts; flight-feathers plain greyish-brown, secondaries form clear white patch in flight. **BP** Bill short, grey with dull yellow base; legs grey. **SV** Range of grunting, squealing and cackling calls, and distinctive hard note repeated like two stones tapped together. Also a fast series of continuous sounds described as *kyo kyoro ru....*

Slaty-legged Crake *Rallina eurizonoides* L 21–25 cm; WS 47.5 cm; WT 90–180 g

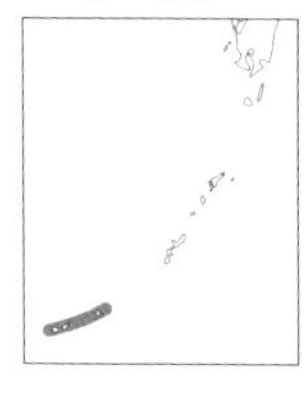

SD *R. e. sepiaria* is resident in S Nansei Shoto. **HH** Shy and retiring in damp forest, forest edge, scrub, marshes and wet fields. **ID** Large crake. Adult has rufous-brown head, neck and breast, plain dark brown upperparts and wings; underparts to undertail-coverts dark blackish-brown or black, narrowly barred white. Juvenile is duller, cooler brown on head and neck, with grey cheeks and white throat. **BP** Bill strong, blackish-grey; eyes red (ad) or brownish-orange (juv); tarsi greenish-grey. **SV** Calls at night from tree perch, a distinctive double *beep-beep* or *kuwa, kuwa*. Also gives hollow, repetitive *pok-pok pok-pok...* and downslurred, nasal *paau paau* notes. In winter also calls at dusk, a prolonged, but slowing, harsh growling *grgrgr ger ger-ker-ker-ker....* In circling display flight after dark, low over lowland forest, gives an evenly repeated *aow aow*. In alarm gives harsh metallic *kik kik kik* or loud *kwek* calls. **AN** Banded Crake.

Species on this plate are not to scale

Okinawa Rail *Gallirallus okinawae*

L 29–33 cm; WS 48–50 cm; WT 340–430 g

SD Endangered. Endemic resident, N Okinawa I (Yambaru). **HH** Dense primary and secondary subtropical evergreen forest, forest edge, forest pools, streams. Forages terrestrially, but roosts in trees. **ID** Large, dark, essentially flightless rail. Adult has distinctive black face with broad white band from eye to neck-sides; underparts slate-grey with extensive fine white barring. Juvenile duller, less clearly marked. **BP** Bill rather thick-based, bright red with yellow-horn tip (ad), or duller red (juv); long, strong legs and feet red. **SV** Typically heard early morning, late afternoon or evening, though also calls at night. Calls include guttural grunting sounds (*kyo kyo kyo; ke ke; gu gu; kururu*) and loud *kwi kwi kwi ki-kwee ki-kwee*, rolling *kikirr krarr* followed by rising *kweeee* until becomes pig-like squeal followed by *ki-kwee-ee ki-kweee-ee kwee ke-kwee*, often in duet, followed by *ki-ki-ki* and *kyip-kyip-kyip* calls. Eerie calls at night sound like hyena yelps. Regularly gives a loud frog-like chirping *kurrrroilT!* (rising at end), and a deep gurgling bubbling, perhaps in agitation or alarm, *gu-gu-gugugugu*. **TN** Formerly *Rallus okinawae*.

Slaty-breasted Rail *Gallirallus striatus*

L 25–30 cm; WT 100–142 g

SD Vagrant Miyako, Okinawa (subspecies uncertain). **HH** Shy, partly nocturnal. Marshes, damp grasslands. **ID** Recalls Eastern Water Rail (EWR), but crown and nape dark chestnut; blackish-olive upperparts including tail and wings covered with fine grey bars; face, neck and breast grey, throat white; blackish-grey belly, flanks and undertail coarsely barred white. **BP** Bill thicker, straighter and slightly shorter than EWR, dull red at base and on lower mandible, greyer tip and culmen; eyes red (no eye-ring), tarsi grey. **SV** Hard *ter rek* or series of metallic *shtik* notes, and buzzing, repeated *kech kech kech* notes rising and falling in strength. **TN** Formerly *Rallus striatus*. **AN** Blue-breasted Banded Rail.

Brown-cheeked Rail *Rallus indicus*

L 23–29 cm; WS 38–45 cm; WT 85–190 g

SD Scarce (overlooked?) summer visitor (May–Sep), N Honshu, Hokkaido. Winters (Oct–Apr) C Honshu southwards. **HH** Swamps, marshes, reedbeds, wet meadows, ricefields. **ID** Adult: upperparts dull olive-brown; face and neck-sides grey-blue, with white supraloral stripe and broad brown eyestripe, breast grey-blue, but with variable brown wash across lower neck/breast; flanks to undertail-coverts blackish with white barring. Juvenile: underparts buff, with black and buff flank barring. Wings broad, relatively long, brown; flight surprisingly strong and fast. **BP** Bill long and slightly decurved, dark red at base and on lower mandible, tip and culmen blackish; eyes deep red; tarsi pinkish-grey. **SV** Low grunts, high squeals and a softer *jip jip jip*, also an abrupt series of piping *kyu kyu kyu* notes. In breeding season utters series of *c*.10 sharp *skrink skrink* or *kyi kyi kyi*… notes. **TN**: Formerly within *R. aquaticus* (e.g. OSJ). **AN** Eastern Water Rail.

Corn Crake *Crex crex*

L 22–25 cm; WS 42–53 cm; WT ♂ 165 g, ♀ 145 g

SD Vagrant, Kyoto, Honshu, and Chichijima, Ogasawara Is. **HH** Damp meadows, dry grasslands. **ID** Recalls water rail, but stouter with stubby bill. Pale blue-grey face, neck and upper chest, remaining plumage yellowish-brown. Dark spots cover upper parts; wings prominently orange-brown; legs dangle noticeably in flight. **BP** The short, stubby bill is dull pinkish; eyes brown; legs and feet dull greyish-pink. **SV** Silent on migration.

White-breasted Waterhen *Amaurornis phoenicurus*

L 28–33 cm; WS 49 cm; WT ♂ 203–328 g, ♀ 166–225 g

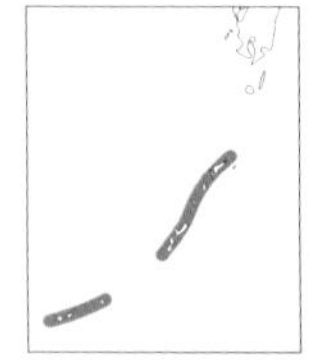

SD *A. p. phoenicurus* resident Nansei Shoto, has strayed north to Japan's main islands, including Hokkaido. **HH** Common, often conspicuous, foraging in open, mangroves, along streams, rivers, wet grassy marshes, wet fields. **ID** Large, size of Common Moorhen. Adult boldly pied; dark slate-grey above, white on face and underparts; lower belly and undertail-coverts cinnamon. Juvenile has grey-white face, foreneck and breast. Restless, flicks cocked tail. **BP** Bill stout, straw yellow, red at base of upper mandible; eyes black; tarsi bright yellow. **SV** Vociferous, wide range of loud calls, at dawn, dusk or at night, often from raised perch. A generally monotonous *u-wok u-wok*, long series of *kru-ak kru-ak kru-ak-a-wak-wak* notes or short nasal *wid* repeated slowly or more gulping *whigh* in rapid series; will also chorus at dawn and dusk with more varied grunts, chuckles and frog-like noises: *kshorr kor kor*… and *korokorororowa*; and cat-like *gyaoo gyaoo*. Also a Ruddy-breasted Crake-like rapid descending trill *kyegegegegegege*, though deeper and more guttural.

Okinawa Rail
ad
juv
Slaty-breasted Rail
ad
juv
Corn Crake
Brown-cheeked Rail
ad
juv
ad
White-breasted Waterhen
ad
juv

Baillon's Crake *Porzana pusilla* L 17–19 cm; WS 33–37 cm; WT ♂ 23–45 g, ♀ 17–55 g

SD *P. p. pusilla* (perhaps a separate species, **Eastern Baillon's Crake**) is a scarce migrant and summer visitor (mid-Apr–late Oct) throughout Japan. **HH** Secretive, in swamps, marshes, wet grasslands and reedbeds. **ID** Tiny with very short wings. Adult is warm mid- or rufous-brown above with irregular large black and narrow white streaks; face, foreneck and breast blue-grey, ear-coverts, hindneck and neck-sides brown; flanks, belly, vent and undertail-coverts narrowly barred black and white. Juvenile is drabber above, lacks blue-grey, instead face brown, chin, throat and belly off-white with brown wash on breast and pale grey-white barring on belly, flanks and undertail-coverts. **BP** Bill rather thick, dull green (ad), or dull yellow with black tip (juv); eyes deep red (ad) or orange-brown (juv); tarsi dull brownish-yellow. **SV** Territorial song is rather weak and does not carry far; a dry descending sputtering trill or rattle, *kokkokko* or *tou tou tou tou*, given at night. In alarm gives sharp *tac* or *tyuik* notes and a low, continuous growling or series of hard notes, *kraa-kraa-kraa-chachachacha*.

Spotted Crake *Porzana porzana* L 19–22 cm; WS 37-42 cm; WT 57-147 g

SD Accidental to Okinawa. **HH** Marshes and damp meadows. **ID** Slightly smaller than similar Eastern Water Rail, but easily separated by short bill, pale face, darkly spotted brown upperparts, fine white spots covering neck, flanks barred with pale grey, and plain buff undertail-coverts. In flight shows white leading edge to brown wings. **BP** Bill short, yellowish with red base; eyes brown; legs and feet greenish. **SV** Silent on migration.

Ruddy-breasted Crake *Porzana fusca* L 19–23 cm; WS 37 cm; WT 60–100 g

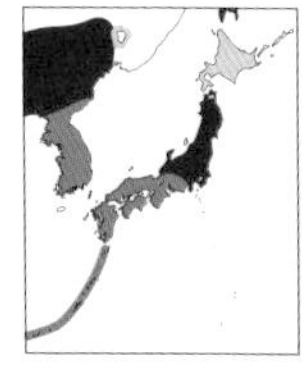

SD *P. f. phaeopyga* is resident in the Nansei Shoto; *P. f. erythrothorax* occurs year-round from Kyushu to S Honshu and is a scarce summer visitor (Apr–Oct) further north to N Honshu and Hokkaido. **HH** Around marshes, ricefields, streams and ditches, occasionally venturing into open. **ID** Medium-sized dark crake; mid- to dark brown from crown to tail and wings, chestnut face and underparts to belly; chin/throat white; lower belly, rear flanks and undertail-coverts black with very narrow white barring. Juvenile is dull olive-brown, with no chestnut, barred like adult, but also has fine white barring on dull olive chest. **BP** Bill dark grey, short; eyes deep red; tarsi red. *P. f. phaeopyga* is slightly darker than *P. f. erythrothorax*, but extremely difficult to separate in field. **SV** Crepuscular, gives brief descending trills with an increasing tempo, commencing with a single hard *kyot*, repeated and speeding up like someone knocking at a door, *kyot kyot kyokkyokyo burururu*; also quiet, clucking *puk* notes while foraging.

Band-bellied Crake *Porzana paykullii* L 20–22 cm; WS 42 cm; WT 96–132 g

SD Accidental to Hokkaido and Nansei Shoto. **HH** Shy, retiring and little-known species of marshes and wet meadows. **ID** Medium-sized short-billed crake, slightly larger than Ruddy-breasted Crake; crown, upperparts and wings dark grey-brown, some with fine barring on upperwing-coverts; flanks, lower breast, belly and undertail-coverts barred black and white. Distinguished from Ruddy-breasted Crake by grey, rather than deep brown, upperparts and wings, and paler orange, rather than red, tarsi. **BP** Bill short, greenish-grey; eyes red; tarsi orange-red. **SV** Rapid wooden purring or drumming call, *tototototo...*, blending into a trilled *urrrrr*, given at dusk, dawn and at night.

Baillon's Crake
Spotted Crake
ad
ad
juv
juv

Band-bellied Crake
Ruddy-breasted Crake
erythrothorax
ad
juv

Watercock *Gallicrex cinerea* ♂ L 42–43 cm; ♂♀ WS 68–86 cm; WT 300–650 g; ♀ L 35–36 cm, WT 200–434 g

SD Summer visitor to S Nansei Shoto. Rare, but regular, in spring on islands in Sea of Japan and through main islands as far north as Hokkaido. **HH** Shy and largely nocturnal; normally occurs in marshes and wet fields, but on migration also on offshore islands with grassland and scrub. **ID** Large, oversized but slender version of Common Moorhen; tail typically cocked. Breeding ♂ mostly slate-blue or dark greyish-black (lacks white flank stripe), mantle and wing-feathers fringed brown. Non-breeding ♂ and smaller ♀ appear orange-buff; plain-faced with large dark eye; underparts have fine darker brown barring, the upperparts with buff fringes to dark-centred scapulars and wing-feathers. Flight strong, tarsi trailing obviously beyond short tail. **BP** Bill orange with yellow tip, and red shield extends to raised horn on forehead (breeding ♂), or yellowish-horn lacking shield (non-breeding ♂, ♀ and juv); eyes deep red (breeding ♂), otherwise brown; tarsi dull red (breeding ♂), otherwise dull green or ochre, toes very long. **SV** Rather noisy when breeding, giving rhythmic series of deep booming *ka-pon ka-pon ka-pon* or *ku-wa ku-wa*, also softer, hollow *youmb youmb youmb* and resonant gulping *tyokh* or *kluck* notes; silent in winter.

Common Moorhen *Gallinula chloropus* L 30–38 cm; WS 50–55 cm; WT ♂ 249–493g, ♀ 192–343 g

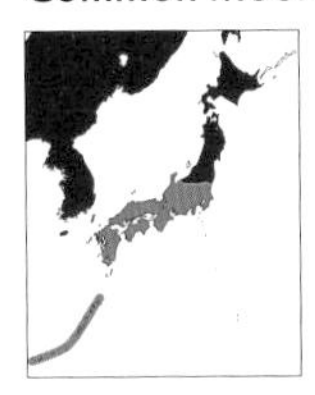

SD *G. c. chloropus* is a summer visitor to N Honshu and Hokkaido, wintering and resident from C Japan south through Nansei Shoto. **HH** Freshwater wetlands, ponds, marshes, ricefields and rivers, usually with extensive and dense fringing vegetation; at times secretive, at others bold and conspicuous, foraging in open on water or on land. **ID** A large dark gallinule. Adult is mostly slate-grey, though upperparts tinged brown, with prominent broken white bar on flanks. Tail quite long, undertail-coverts white with vertical black central stripe, particularly noticeable due to constant flicking of tail; also jerks head back and forth like pigeon. Juvenile is dull grey-brown with whitish chin and throat, white flank bar and undertail-coverts, and same mannerisms as adult. Take-off conspicuous, with long splashing run across water; flight weak, feet trailing prominently. **BP** Adult has stout, bright red bill with yellow tip, and red shield extending up forehead; juvenile has dull, dark brownish-yellow bill; eyes chestnut; tarsi greenish-yellow with orange-red spot near feather edge, toes very long. **SV** Wide vocabulary of various loud, harsh gargling sounds, *pruruk-pruuk-pruuk*, or series of brief guttural *ku ku ku...* notes, an explosive single *krrrruk*, creaking and clucking sounds, and a sharp *keek* or *kit i tit kit i tit* in alarm and in flight.

Eurasian Coot *Fulica atra* L 36–39 cm; WS 70–80 cm; WT 400–1000 g

SD *F. a. atra* is locally resident or a summer visitor to Kyushu, Honshu and Hokkaido, wintering in C & S Japan, but increasingly recorded also in Hokkaido in winter, and reaches Izu and Ogasawara Is. **HH** Standing freshwater bodies, from ponds to large lakes with abundant vegetation, also rivers and river mouths; aggressive during breeding season, when fights and chases are conspicuous, but often gregarious at other times. **ID** Large, stocky, hunched, all-black gallinule, the most aquatic of its group, rarely seen far from water, though may graze onshore; commonly upends and dives for food; constantly nods head. Adult is all black with striking white bill and frontal shield. Juvenile is plain ash-brown with whitish throat and breast. Flight laboured, take-off requires running start, tarsi/toes often dangling, trailing edge of secondaries white. **BP** Adult's bill is white with pinkish tinge, extending up forehead as distinctive shield; juvenile's bill is grey; eyes deep dark red (ad) or dark brown (juv); tarsi dull green, feet grey with prominently lobed toes. **SV** Highly vocal, often noisy, with rich repertoire, especially at night. Explosive *kik kik kik*, also loud *krek*, *tyok* and *kyururu* calls, and shorter guttural *gu-gu-gu* amongst commoner calls. At night and in flight gives nasal trumpeting *neee beeep*.

Watercock
ad ♂
breeding
ad ♀
juv
ad ♂
non-breeding
Eurasian Coot
Common Moorhen
juv
ad
ad
juv

Siberian Crane *Leucogeranus leucogeranus* L 140 cm; WS 210–230 cm; WT 5670–8620 g

SD Critically Endangered. Very rare (not annual) winter visitor (mostly Oct–Feb) to Kyushu, occasionally Nansei Shoto, C & N Honshu, and has occurred in spring/summer (Apr–Aug) in S and E Hokkaido. **HH** Wetlands, including marshes, ricefields, tidal flats and shallow lakes. **ID** Large, all-white crane with red face and black wingtips; at rest, white tertials mostly cover black primaries. Young dark cinnamon, becoming mottled white with age; brown remaining on head, neck and flight feathers through first winter. In flight, solid black wingtips contrast with otherwise white plumage. Flight slow, measured, slow, deep downbeats and quick upbeats, black primaries deeply 'fingered'; legs and neck extended. **BP** Bill yellow-orange; bare facial skin to eye and forecrown red; eyes staring yellow; long tarsi reddish-pink. **SV** Rolling *kuru kuruu kuru kuruu* and soft musical *koonk koonk* in flight, higher pitched than other cranes. Young give thin, high, downslurred whistles *tchyu tchyu tchyu*.... **AN** Siberian White Crane.

Sandhill Crane *Antigone canadensis* L 88–120 cm; WS 160–210 cm; WT ♂ 3750 g, ♀ 3350 g

SD Small numbers of *A. canadensis* winter (Nov–late Mar) annually in SW Kyushu (Izumi), joining large flocks of Hooded Crane; accidental elsewhere from Hokkaido to Ogasawara. **HH** Wetlands and agricultural areas. **ID** Slightly larger than Hooded, but paler grey, with variable warm rusty-brown on upperparts, especially wing-coverts and rump, but may extend to neck and back (though some have essentially none). Forehead and forecrown to rear of eye red, appearing somewhat heart-shaped at front; head and neck pale grey, lacking black, and often paler, even white, below eye, on lores and chin. Young similar, but lack bare red forehead and are browner. Flight feathers blackish, but show little contrast with brown of upperwing coverts; underwing paler grey, only outer primaries blackish. **BP** Bill dark grey above, lower mandible yellowish-horn; eyes yellow; tarsi greyish-black. **SV** A loud rolling, bugling *karr-roo karr-roo* or *kururuu* (similar to Common Crane), but lower, more drawn-out), with juvenile giving sibilant whistled *sweer* notes.

White-naped Crane *Antigone vipio* L 120–153 cm; WS 200–210 cm; WT 4750–6500 g

SD Vulnerable. Historically bred in Hokkaido. Currently a locally common winter visitor (mid-Oct–late Mar) to SW Kyushu (c. 40–50% of world population), and a migrant through W Kyushu and Tsushima. Accidental in winter elsewhere in Japan from Nansei Shoto north to Hokkaido. **HH** Gregarious in non-breeding season, family groups forming large flocks at wetlands and on fallow agricultural land; forms spectacular gatherings with Hooded Crane. Performs brief, but dramatic, courtship displays (duetting and posturing) on wintering grounds **ID** Large, elegant grey and white crane. Head mostly white with dark grey lores and forehead, large red eye patch bordered with dark grey, and dark grey ear spot; neck white with dark grey line forming point below head; breast, underparts and mantle dark grey, scapulars pale grey, coverts whitish-grey, tertials almost white. Flight feathers blackish (primaries have white shafts), forming strong contrast with pale grey upperwing and underwing-coverts. Young similar to adults, but have rusty-brown on head and neck, and wings less white, more grey-brown. **BP** Bill yellowish-horn; eyes yellow; tarsi dull pink. **SV** Various strong bugling *kururuu* or *guruu* calls, stronger and louder than other cranes. Sexes duet on wintering grounds, with ♂ giving deep *kururu* or *gyururu* and ♀ *ko ko ko* or *kuwa kuwa kuwa* calls. Young give high, thin whistle.

Demoiselle Crane *Grus virgo* L 90 cm; WS 150–170 cm; WT 2100–2500 g

SD Extremely rare winter visitor (mostly Oct–Feb) to Kyushu, Shikoku, Honshu and Hokkaido. **HH** Wetlands, ricefields and agricultural land, where mixes with flocks of other cranes. **ID** Very small, slender crane, with fully feathered head. Adult is elegant, pale grey, with black head, neck and breast, extending as chest plumes (black chest separates from Common Crane at distance). Hindcrown pale grey; whitish ear-tufts extend from eye to nape (unique amongst cranes). Pale grey tertials sleek and particularly elongated, drooping very low. 1st-winter has contrast of head less developed and neck less black. In flight, primaries and primary-coverts, secondaries and tail all-dark grey contrasting with paler grey upperparts and tertials, as Common, but black of neck extends to centre of breast. Flight faster, more agile than larger cranes. **BP** Bill yellowish horn at tip, paler at base; eyes blood-red (♂) or orange (♀), dark in juvenile; tarsi pinkish-grey; lacks bare red skin on head. **SV** Trumpeting is shriller, higher than Common, but drier and more wooden, also a rolling trill, *kuu kururuu* or *kd r r r r r kd r r r r r*.... **TN** Formerly *Anthropoides virgo*.

Siberian Crane
ad
ad
juv
Sandhill Crane
juv
ad
White-naped Crane
courtship display
juv
ad
late 1st-win
ad
juv
Demoiselle Crane
ad

Common Crane *Grus grus* L 96–125 cm; WS 180–200 cm; WT ♂ 5100–6100 g, ♀ 4500–5900 g

SD Rare winter visitor (mid-Oct–late Mar). Very small numbers reach SW Kyushu each winter. Accidental elsewhere, from Nansei Shoto to Hokkaido. **HH** Agricultural land, grasslands and around lakes and wetlands. As with other cranes, families remain together throughout autumn migration, winter and spring migration; often join other cranes, and roost in shallow water. **ID** A medium-sized grey crane with black and white head, black foreneck, and broad dark-grey 'bustle' (loose tertials) with some black feathers obscuring tail. Forecrown red; broad white band extends from eye over sides and back of head and neck. Young have brown markings on scapulars/coverts, and buffy-grey head and neck; adult head pattern acquired during first winter; bustle is grey tinged brown. Flight straight, leisurely, slow, deep beats are even, legs and neck extended; flight-feathers blackish, with pale carpal patch on leading edge of wing at base of outer primaries. **BP** Bill dull, greenish-horn, dagger-shaped; eyes yellow (juv) to orange/red (ad); tarsi very long, black. **SV** Pairs utter bugling duet with various *kaw, karrroo, kleeeur* and *kluuer* notes, and a short rolling trill *kr r r reeech*. In flight and on migration gives deep trumpeting *krraw* and rattling *kururuu kururuu* or *k d d dew*. Lone adult may give wooden knocking sound and young a plaintive whistling *peerp peerp*.

Hooded Crane *Grus monacha* L 91–100 cm; WS 160–180 cm; WT ♂ 3280–4870 g, ♀ 3400–3740 g

SD Vulnerable. Locally abundant winter visitor (mid-Oct–early Apr) to SW Kyushu (c. 80% of world population visit Izumi), migrating there via Tsushima and W Kyushu. Small numbers used to winter in SW Honshu; accidental elsewhere from Nansei Shoto north to N Hokkaido. **HH** Wetlands and grasslands, including farmland and lakeshores. Extremely gregarious, forming large, dense flocks. **ID** Very small dark blackish-grey crane with white head and neck (hood). Forehead and lores black; small red forecrown largely covered by black feathering. Young lack black and red of forehead, and have rusty off-white head and neck and somewhat browner plumage than adult. Flight feathers and coverts are blackish with no contrast on upperwing. Hybrids between Hooded and Common Cranes occur most years in Kyushu; variable, but commonly lack black on nape, throat/foreneck more dark grey than black, and shorter-billed than Common. **BP** Bill greenish-horn; eyes deep red; long tarsi greyish-black. **SV** Loud rolling *krrrk*; *kleeer k d d duuur*; or *kuururun*; juvenile keeps contact with family using high-pitched *reeh* or *pyii pyii* calls.

Red-crowned Crane *Grus japonensis* L 138–160 cm; WS 220–250 cm; WT 6000–12000 g

SD Endangered. The once widespread and presumed migratory Japanese population is recovering from near extinction (fewer than 20 birds) in early 20th century; now over 1,500 essentially resident birds are mainly concentrated in E Hokkaido, though range steadily expanding to C and N Hokkaido. Make short-distance movements to winter at provisioned sites, principally in the Kushiro area. Accidental in winter to Honshu, Shikoku and Kyushu. Highly significant in Japanese culture: symbolic of long life (believed to live a thousand years) and happiness. **HH** Extensive wetlands with reedbeds. Non-breeders summer, and occasionally winter, at coastal lagoons, mudflats, lakes, swamps and open fields. In winter, family groups form flocks of 100+ at river roosts and on open agricultural land. **ID** Largest, and arguably the most beautiful, crane. Largely snow white, with black head and neck, broad white band from eye to nape; forehead black, crown red (larger in ♂, but variable in size depending on state of arousal/excitement), and black 'bustle' of loose tertials and black secondaries obscuring tail. Juvenile is cinnamon. Subadult like adult, but lacks red crown and has dark rusty-brown, not black, feathering, although commonly has black tips to primaries. In flight, white primaries deeply 'fingered', black secondaries and tertials contrast with otherwise white plumage. **BP** Bill dark horn, eyes reddish-brown (ad) or black (juv); tarsi blackish-grey to black. **SV** Trumpeting and bugling calls on breeding grounds far-carrying; winter duet *ka, kaa-kaa, ka*, with ♂ giving short first and last notes, particularly in association with dramatic display dances in Feb–Apr; softer *krewip* notes before and during flight. Juvenile uses plaintive high-pitched whistle as a contact call. **AN** Japanese Crane; Manchurian Crane.

Common Crane
ad
juv
ad
ad
Hooded Crane
juv
ad
ad
Red-crowned Crane
juv
adult with chicks
ad
courtship display

Barred Buttonquail *Turnix suscitator*

L 14–17 cm; WT ♂ 35–52 g, ♀ 47–68 g

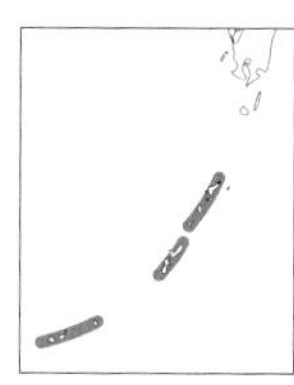

SD *T. s. okinavensis* resident C & S Nansei Shoto (Amami Is to Sakishima). **HH** Dry grassland, scrub, cultivated fields, especially sugar cane. **ID** Small, warm rusty-brown upperparts, paler on wing-coverts. ♀ larger and brighter than ♂. ♀: chin to upper breast black; head speckled black and white, upperparts scaled white, breast-sides barred black. ♂: chin black, breast and sides barred black, face pattern more quail-like, with buff supercilia and malar. Non-breeding duller. Rarely flies. **BP** Bill blue-grey; eyes grey-white; legs blue-grey. **SV** Breeding females court males with prolonged, deep purring *drr-r-r-r-r-r* and series of very deep rhythmic crooning or hooting notes: *hoon-hoon-hoon-hoon-hoon; uhuu uhuu uhuu* or *pwoo pwoo pwoo*.

Eurasian Oystercatcher *Haematopus ostralegus*

L 40–47 cm; WS 72–86 cm; WT ♂ 425–805 g, ♀ 445–820 g

SD *H. o. osculans* uncommon migrant, local winter visitor Hokkaido, N & C Honshu (Sep–Apr); accidental south to Kyushu, Nansei Shoto, Ogasawara Is. **HH** Rocky or sandy shores, mudflats, estuaries, large rivers. **ID** Large, boldly pied shorebird with prominent bright-red bill. Adult: black head, neck and upperparts; extensively white on closed wing. Non-breeding: may develop trace of white half-collar on throat. Juv/1st-winter: mantle and scapulars narrowly barred brown, creating scalloped effect. In flight, broad white wingbar on primaries and secondaries, rump/tail white with black terminal band. **BP** Bill long, thick, red, orange at extreme tip (ad), or blackish at tip (juv); eye-ring and irides red; legs red (breeding), or flesh pink to orange-red. **SV** Very vocal, giving various sharp, shrill piping *pi pi pi, kip, kleep* and *klee-eep* notes.

Black-winged Stilt *Himantopus himantopus*

L 35–40 cm; WS 67–83 cm; WT 160–210 g

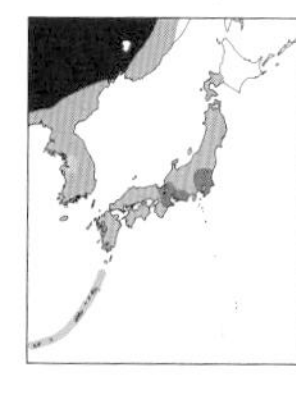

SD Resident C Honshu, also migrant, some winter south to Nansei Shoto; accidental south to Ogasawara; some straggle north as far as Hokkaido. **HH** Shallow coastal wetlands. **ID** Extremely tall and slender. Adult: all-black wings, back glossy black in ♂, brown-tinged in ♀. Tail pale grey. Underparts, rump and wedge extending up back white. Head and neck entirely white, or with variable amounts of black on crown, nape and ear-coverts (♂ usually with more black, ♀ grey). Juvenile: brown-backed, with brown wings and crown. In flight, white back and narrow white band at tips of secondaries; legs from tarsus extend beyond tail. See following species. **BP** Bill needle-like, all black (ad), or with reddish base (juv); eyes dark red (ad) or brown (juv); extremely long flesh-pink legs. **SV** Noisy, but only when breeding: tern-like *kik-kik-kik* or *skyip-skyip-skyip*, and softer *pyu* and *pyuii* notes.

White-headed Stilt *Himantopus leucocephalus*

L 36 cm; WS 67 cm; WT 193 g

SD Accidental. **HH** Shallow wetlands. **ID** Very similar to Black-winged Stilt, but marginally larger with glossy black (♂) or brown (♀) hindneck from rear crown to base of neck. **BP** As Black-winged Stilt, but bill slightly longer, with slightly uptilted tip, legs slightly shorter. **SV** As previous species. **TN** Also treated within previous species.

Black-necked Stilt *Himantopus mexicanus*

L 35–36 cm; WS 74 cm; WT 160 g

SD Vagrant or introduced; has bred Osaka; winter records from Aichi, Kyoto and Nara. **HH** Shallow wetlands. **ID** Very similar to Black-winged Stilt, but ♂ is black from crown to nape, with black face and white patch above eye. ♀ is similar to ♂ but with brown back. Juvenile has face pattern of adult, but with grey nape. **BP/ SV** As previous species. **TN** Also treated within previous species.

Pied Avocet *Recurvirostra avosetta*

L 42–45 cm; WS 67–80 cm; WT 225–397 g

SD Rare migrant or winter visitor (Nov–May) Nansei Shoto north to C Honshu; accidental north to Hokkaido and south to Ogasawara. **HH** Coastal and inland wetlands. Unusual foraging motion, swinging bill from side to side in shallow water; also swims and upends. **ID** Tall, elegant, boldly pied shorebird, with long legs and uniquely upturned bill. Adult is mostly white, with glossy black forehead, crown and nape, scapulars, primaries and carpal bar. Juvenile is brown where adult is black, with extensively brown-mottled mantle and wings. In flight, tarsi extend well beyond tail tip, upperwing white with black scapulars, carpal band and primaries; from below, wings all white except black primaries; flight fast. **BP** Bill black; eyes dark brown; long legs pale greyish-blue. **SV** Commonly utters series of clear, flute-like notes: *klee-ee-klee* or *kluiit kluiit kluiit*; alarm call from ground or in flight *kweep kweep*.

Eurasian Oystercatcher
ad
Barred Buttonquail
ad ♂
ad ♀
Black-winged Stilt
ad ♂
himantopus
White-headed Stilt
ad ♂
leucocephalus
ad ♂
himantopus
ad ♂
leucocephalus
ad ♀
leucocephalus
ad ♀
himantopus
juv
Pied Avocet
ad
Black-necked Stilt
ad mexicanus
ad feeding

Northern Lapwing *Vanellus vanellus*

L 28–31 cm; WS 82–87 cm; WT 128–330 g

SD Scarce to locally uncommon winter visitor to Japan from N Honshu to Kyushu; has bred Honshu; scarce migrant and winter visitor north to Hokkaido and south to Nansei Shoto. **HH** In winter, flocks occur on grasslands and fields, at margins of wetlands and occasionally on mudflats. **ID** Large, sociable and vocal; unique in having crest, deep black breast-band, and broad, rounded wings. Adult has black crown, face, chin, breast-band and long wispy crest. Lores, behind eye, cheeks, belly to flanks white, undertail-coverts dull orange/buff. Upperparts dark metallic green, with purple sheen at bend of wing. In winter has less contrasting face pattern and pale buff fringes to mantle and wing-coverts. Juvenile has shorter crest and pale buff fringes to back and wings. In flight, broad black wings with white-tipped outer primaries, underwing-coverts and rump white, and tail black; feet do not extend beyond tail tip. **BP** Bill short, black; eyes black; legs short, dull brownish-pink. **SV** Very vocal. From ground gives rather cat-like *myuu* and in flight rather nasal *chee-zik chee-zik*, and a higher-pitched plaintive *pee-wit*. ♂'s display flight is impressively aerobatic, with various calls combined into a more complex 'song'.

Grey-headed Lapwing *Vanellus cinereus*

L 34–37 cm; WS 75 cm; WT 240–410 g

SD Resident in C & W Honshu and N Kyushu; scarce or rare further north to Hokkaido or south to Ogasawara and Nansei Shoto. **HH** Wet ricefields, also wet grasslands and marshes; in winter also at riversides. **ID** Large, vocal and boldly marked. Adult is striking, with grey head, neck and upper chest, broad black bar separating grey chest from white belly; brown upperparts; has tiny yellow loral spot. Winter adult has less prominent chest-band. Juv/1st-winter head, upperparts and chest mid-brown vermiculated grey. In flight, black primaries contrast with white secondaries, brown wing-coverts and back; white rump and tail with black subterminal band; feet extend beyond tail tip. **BP** Bill yellow with black tip; eyes reddish-orange, narrow eye-ring yellow; legs long, dull ochre to bright yellow. **SV** Flight call a sharp *kik kik*, and on ground gives plaintive, but insistent, *chee-it chee-it* in alarm, and series of staccato *chyink-chyink-chyink*… notes.

Grey Plover *Pluvialis squatarola*

L 27–31 cm; WS 71–83 cm; WT 180–350 g

SD *P. s. squatarola* is an uncommon migrant throughout coastal Japan and a winter visitor from C Honshu to Nansei Shoto and Ogasawara Is. **HH** On migration and in winter occurs mainly on sand and mudflats, but also at rivers and ricefields and on reclaimed land. May form dense flocks at roost, but usually forages alone or in wide-spaced flocks. **ID** Largest plover, heavy-set, with very large eyes and stout bill. Breeding adult has black face and underparts (mottled white in ♀); white extends from forehead, via supercilia into broad neck-stripe ending at wing bend. Vent and undertail-coverts white. Upperparts largely black, with very prominent white spots and feather tips, affording silver-spangled appearance. Non-breeding adult and young duller, browner or grey, lack distinct supercilia, black eye very prominent on rather plain face. In flight shows white rump and tail (with grey tail barring), prominent white wing-stripe, white underwing with black axillaries distinctive. **BP** Bill black; eyes black; legs dark grey/black. **SV** A mournful trisyllabic *pleee-you-ee* or *tyu-eer-lee*. **AN** North America: Black-bellied Plover.

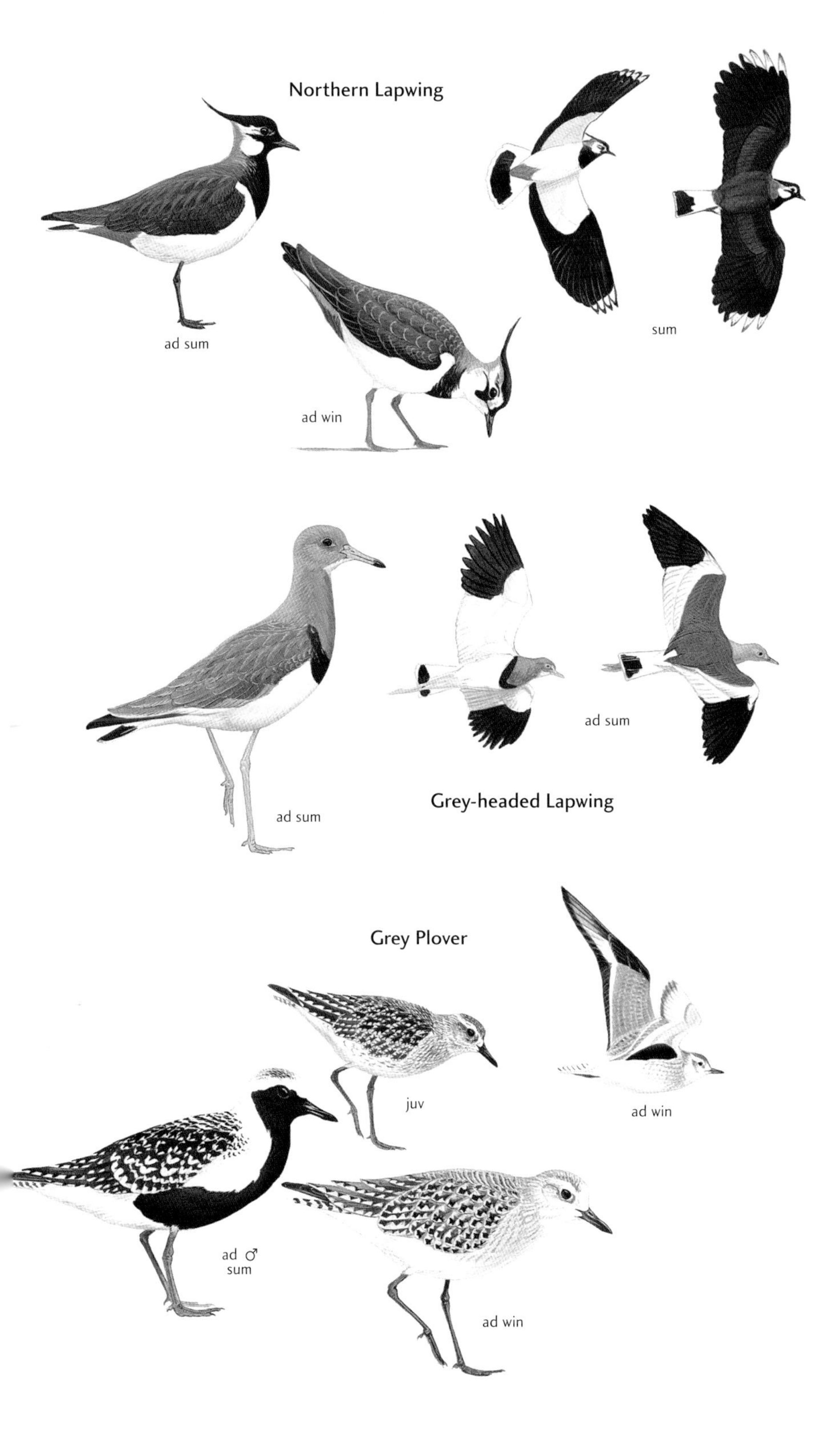
Northern Lapwing
ad sum
ad win
sum
ad sum
ad sum
Grey-headed Lapwing
Grey Plover
juv
ad win
ad ♂
sum
ad win

European Golden Plover *Pluvialis apricaria*

L 26–29 cm; WS 67–76 cm; WT 160–280 g

SD Vagrant to Okinawa and C Honshu. **ID** Similar to Pacific and American Golden Plovers, but larger and stockier, with shorter wings barely extending past tail tip, broader wings with prominent white wingbar in flight, and white (not grey) axillaries and underwing. Breeding plumage ♂ has white border to black of neck, breast and flanks. **SV** Call is a plaintive whistled *peeuw* or *tüü*.

Pacific Golden Plover *Pluvialis fulva*

L 23–26 cm; WS 60–67 cm; WT 90–170 g

SD The commonest large plover in Japan. A common migrant (April/May and Aug–Oct) throughout coastal Japan from Nansei Shoto to Hokkaido and a locally common winterer in Nansei Shoto and Ogasawara Is. **HH** On migration occurs at grasslands, fields, lakeshores, rivers and coastal mudflats, in loose but often large flocks. **ID** Large, but somewhat slender, long-legged plover, with rather upright stance and small head. Adult in breeding plumage has face and underparts black, bordered white from forehead, supercilia merging into broad neck-stripe, which extends, though scalloped black, on flanks to vent. Upperparts spangled gold, white and black. Non-breeding adult and juvenile are duller, but with warmer buff or golden tones. Dark cap contrasts strongly with supercilia, ear-coverts have prominent grey spot. At rest, wings extend beyond tail tip when folded, but only 2–3 primary tips extend beyond tertials, which are longer than in American Golden Plover. In flight, faint white wing-stripe, dusky-grey underwing and axillaries; toes project beyond tail tip. **BP** Bill black, longer than American or Eurasian; eyes dark brown; legs long, greyish-black. **SV** Plaintive, somewhat soft, clear whistled *chu-vit* both in flight and on ground, and more drawn-out *tu-ee*, *kyo-bee* or *chu-veee* (second syllable clearly stressed); less commonly a trisyllabic *chu-ee-uh*. In display flight, gives slow series of well-spaced slurred whistles *chuvee chooeee*… **TN** Formerly considered conspecific with American Golden Plover as Lesser Golden Plover *P. dominica*.

American Golden Plover *Pluvialis dominica*

L 24–28 cm; WS 65–72 cm; WT 122–194 g

SD Accidental to Okinawa and C Honshu in spring and autumn, but may be overlooked among the large numbers of migrant Pacific Golden Plovers. **HH** Occurs on mudflats and grasslands. **ID** Large plover with long wings and legs, small head and rather upright stance; confusingly similar to Pacific. Adult in breeding plumage: ♂ has face and underparts solid black, ♀ slightly mottled on face and undertail-coverts; crown, nape and upperparts black spangled white and gold. Prominent white forehead and supercilia (more prominent than Pacific) merge into very broad neck-stripe, which terminates and is broadest at wing bend. Non-breeding adult and young are duller, with cool grey tones (see Pacific). Dark cap contrasts strongly with broad pale supercilia. At rest, wings long, extending well beyond tail tip (by 12–22 mm); tertials short, with usually 4–5 primary tips extending beyond them (Pacific only 2–3). In flight, feet do not, or very barely, project beyond tail tip (see Pacific), faint white wing-stripe, grey underwing and axillaries. **BP** Bill black, smaller than Pacific; eyes dark brown; legs greyish-black. **SV** Mournful whistled *kyuee* or *klee-i* (first syllable stressed), though often sounds shorter, monosyllabic *klee* or *kleep*; occasionally trisyllabic *dlu-ee-oo* given in flight; usually higher pitched than Pacific.

ad win
European Golden Plover
ad ♂
sum
juv
ad win
Pacific Golden Plover
ad ♂
sum
juv
ad win
American Golden Plover
ad win
juv
ad ♂
sum
ad win

Common Ringed Plover *Charadrius hiaticula* L 18–20 cm; WS 48–57 cm; WT 42–78 g

SD *C. h. tundrae* scarce migrant (Apr/May and Aug/Sep), occasional winter visitor; recorded Nansei Shoto, Ogasawara Is, north to Hokkaido. **HH** Coastal wetlands, mudflats, estuaries. **ID** Plump plover, deeper-chested than Little Ringed Plover, with broad black breast-band, obvious white supercilia behind eyes, white forehead, black forecrown, grey-brown crown and full white collar. Winter adult and juvenile have narrower, fainter, browner breast-bands and face markings, cheek patch rounded at bottom edge (see Semipalmated Plover). Flight fast, agile; prominent white bar on flight-feathers, tail plain, but darker at tip. **BP** Bill short, tip black, basal half orange (summer), or small yellow basal area (winter), or largely dark (juv); lores always black to gape (see Semipalmated Plover); eyes dark brown with distinct white supercilia in all plumages; legs dull ochre (juv) to bright orange (breeding ad), tiny web only between middle and outer toes. **SV** Mellow, whistled *pyuui*; *too-li* or *tu-wheep* (emphasis on first syllable) in flight; piping calls and sharp *skreeet* when agitated.

Semipalmated Plover *Charadrius semipalmatus* L 17–19 cm; WS 43–52 cm; WT 28–69 g

SD Vagrant, C Honshu (Chiba). **HH** Coastal wetlands, mudflats. **ID** Slightly smaller and more compact than Common Ringed Plover (CRP). Breeding ♂: lacks or has only faint white supercilia, black breast-band narrow at front. ♀: narrower breast-band than ♂. Winter adult: dark brown replaces black. Juvenile: as winter adult, but upperparts, coverts and tertials have dark subterminal bands and pale fringes. In flight, slightly shorter wingbar than CRP. **BP** Bill shorter, stubbier than CRP, more strongly tapered, black at tip, base orange (ad), or with hint of orange at base (winter ad and juv), often with white lores above gape; large black eyes with very narrow yellow eye-ring (usually absent in CRP); tarsi dull yellow-orange, webs between all three toes. **SV** A two-noted whistle *tew-it* or longer *tu-eet* (recalling Spotted Redshank) aids separation from CRP.

Long-billed Plover *Charadrius placidus* L 19–21 cm; WS 45 cm; WT 41–70 g

SD Scarce summer visitor Hokkaido; resident, partial migrant Honshu, Shikoku, Kyushu, rare winter visitor Nansei Shoto, Ogasawara Is. **HH** Rivers with gravel or rocky bars and banks, similar lakeside habitat; wetlands, wet fields on migration. **ID** Larger than Common Ringed Plover (CRP), but appears less plump, more elongated with longer tail. Plumage very similar to CRP, but whereas forehead bar is black, eyestripe is brown. Black collar narrower than CRP's. Non-breeder has less contrast on face and a brown collar with black only along the upper margin. Flights usually short; less prominent, narrower wingbar than CRP; long tail has black subterminal band and white tip. Superficially similar Little Ringed Plover (LRP) much smaller, with small head, lacks wingbar, less attenuated at tail/wingtips, shorter bill, and prominent yellow eye-ring when breeding. **BP** Bill long, black; narrow eye-ring pale yellow, irides dark brown; legs dull ochre to yellow. **SV** Calls include clear, piping *piwee* in flight; lower and flatter *pyiu* than LRP, and an explosive *sfreeit*. In display a duet of sharp *kip* notes in series, rising and falling in pitch, and a sharp, strong *pi pi pi pi…* in alarm.

Little Ringed Plover *Charadrius dubius* L 14–17 cm; WS 42–48 cm; WT 26–53 g

SD *C. d. curonicus* common summer visitor (Apr–Oct), Kyushu to Hokkaido, small numbers winter in S Japan; migrant through Nansei Shoto, rare visitor Ogasawara Is. **HH** Coastal, riverine and inland wetlands. Sociable, vocal, very active. **ID** Small, slim, sandy-brown plover with prominent black collar. Appears more slender, more elongated, more long-legged than CRP, thus structurally recalls larger Long-billed Plover. Broad white and narrow black collars separate brown of nape from mantle. Upperparts including rear crown mid-brown, flight-feathers darker, but very long tertials cover primaries. Face, lores and forecrown black (with white fringe above), and face patch extends to point below ear-coverts, forehead white. Juvenile is brown where adult is black, also has face patch extending in point below ear-coverts. Underparts white. Flight fast and agile, lacks (or has only very narrow) wingbar, tail plain, but paler at sides and darker at tip. **BP** Bill short, black with small orange base to lower mandible; bright yellow eye-ring prominent (ad) or less prominent (juv), irides dark brown; legs dull ochre (summer), or brown (winter). **SV** Gives soft, drawn-out downslurred *pee-oo* or more abrupt *peeu peeu*; when breeding gives various notes and in slow bat-like display flight gives a rapid, hard *pipipipipi*.

Common Ringed Plover
ad win
ad sum
juv
ad win
Semipalmated Plover
ad sum
juv
Long-billed Plover
ad sum
juv
ad win
Little Ringed Plover
ad sum
juv
ad win

Oriental Plover *Charadrius veredus* L 22–25 cm; WS 46–53 cm; WT 80–95 g

SD Accidental, Hokkaido to Nansei Shoto. HH Dry grasslands. ID Elegant medium-sized plover with long neck, long wings and long legs. Adult breeding: striking; head/face greyish-white, lower neck and band across chest orange to chestnut, deepening to black on upper belly. Adult winter and juvenile: like Mongolian Plover, with brown band on chest, rather plain face with pale forehead and supercilia, juvenile has prominent broad pale buff fringes to most of upperparts. In flight, lacks white wingbar; axillaries and underwing (coverts and flight-feathers) uniform brown; tail brown with white outer rectrices and white tips to all but central feathers. BP Bill black, longer than from bill base to eye; eyes dark brown; legs longish, yellow to pink. SV Repetitive loud chip-chip-chip in flight, also gives piping whistled kwink, a brief stony dzhup and a piping klink-klink-link.

Kentish Plover *Charadrius alexandrinus* L 15–18 cm; WS 42–45 cm; WT 32–56 g

SD *C. a. nihonensis* uncommon summer visitor Hokkaido, year-round N Honshu to Nansei Shoto. *C. a. alexandrinus* accidental Hokkaido, C & N Honshu, Izu and Okinawa Is. **HH** Beaches, rivers, marshes, favouring drier areas, but also mudflats. **ID** Small, short-billed plover, with sandy-brown upperparts. ♂: forehead, supercilia and underparts white; forecrown, eyestripe and narrow band at breast-sides black. ♀: lacks black on crown. Non-breeding ♂♀ have brown, not black, breast-sides. Flight rapid and agile, with prominent wingbar and white tail-sides, central rectrices brown, darker at tip. **BP** Bill black; eyes dark brown, legs greyish-flesh. **SV** Rattling trilled *trrrt*, soft *pi..pi..pi* or abrupt *pik*; *piru piru poi pirururu* calls from ground during breeding season and harder, rattling *geregeregeree* in bat-like display flight. **TN** Previously lumped with Snowy Plover (now *C. nivosus*).

Mongolian Plover *Charadrius (mongolus) mongolus* L 18–21 cm; WS 45–58 cm; WT 39–110 g

SD *C. m. stegmanni* common migrant Hokkaido to Nansei Shoto, occasionally winters S Japan. **HH** Coasts, sandy beaches, mudflats, estuaries, wetlands. **ID** Brightly coloured plover with black mask, extensive white forehead bisected by vertical black line, white chin and throat; broad rufous chest-band (with narrow black upper border) extends onto flanks and nape. Non-breeders overall duller brown, lack rufous band, face is less contrasting, with short narrow white supercilia. In flight, narrow but noticeable wingbar (narrower on primaries than Greater Sand Plover); tail has white sides, rump and central rectrices uniform mid-brown. **BP** Bill short, thick, black, blunt-tipped, length from tip to base equals base to eye centre (see Greater); eyes black; legs greyish-green. **SV** Soft trilled *puriri* or *prrrp* flight calls recall Ruddy Turnstone; also a sharper *kip-ip*.

Lesser Sand Plover *Charadrius (mongolus) atrifrons* L 18–21 cm; WS 45–58 cm; WT 39–110 g

SD *C. (m.) atrifrons* scarce migrant; *C. (m.) schaeferi* reported. **HH** As Mongolian Plover. **ID** Resembles Mongolian Plover, but has shorter wings, longer bill and tarsi, bolder mask, broader black forehead lacking white, and breeding ♂ lacks black border to rufous chest-band. **BP** Bill short, black; eyes black; legs greyish-green. **SV** Call as Mongolian Plover.

Greater Sand Plover *Charadrius leschenaultii* L 22–25 cm; WS 53–60 cm; WT 55–121 g

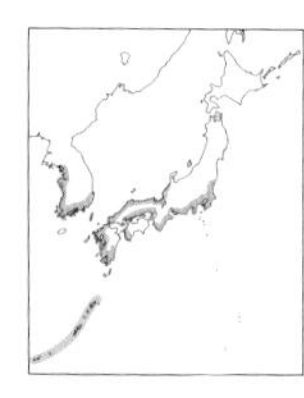

SD *C. l. leschenaultii* uncommon to scarce migrant throughout Japan (mostly mid-Apr–May; Aug–Sep), uncommon winter visitor Nansei Shoto. **HH** Coastal mudflats, frequenting drier, sandier areas. **ID** Very like Mongolian Plover (MP), with considerable variation and overlap, but generally larger, heavier, longer-legged with thicker, longer bill. Adult breeding: less black on head and narrower rufous chest-band (some with black upper margin), which does not extend far on flanks. Black mask mostly bordered above with rufous, reduced white above eye; small forehead patch, chin, throat and underparts white. Adult winter: lacks rufous band, face is less contrasting, white supercilia more prominent. Juvenile: confusingly like Mongolian Plover (MP), best separated on structure and bill size. In flight, faint narrow innerwing bar, conspicuous and broad on primaries; tail has white sides, rump and tail centre uniform mid-brown; feet protrude clearly beyond tail tip. **BP** Bill black, longer than from bill base to rear edge of eye, appears stronger, with more prominent gonys and sharper tip, than MP; eyes dark brown; legs longer than MP, dull yellow/green, not greyish. **SV** Trilling flight call, *kuriri, trrrt* or *prrrirt*, is very similar to, but slightly deeper and drier than, MP.

Oriental Plover
ad ♀
juv
ad ♂ sum
ad win
ad win
Kentish Plover
ad ♂ sum
ad ♀ sum
nihonensis
ad win
ad ♀ sum
juv
ad ♂ win
Mongolian Plover
ad sum
juv
Lesser Sand Plover
ad sum
ad win
Greater Sand Plover
ad win
ad sum
juv

Eurasian Dotterel *Charadrius morinellus* L 20–22 cm; WS 57–64 cm; WT ♂ 86–116 g, ♀ 99–142 g

SD Very rare or accidental migrant (spring and autumn) and winter visitor throughout Japan, with records from Hokkaido to Nansei Shoto. **HH** Usually found on dry grasslands, occasionally mudflats. **ID** Medium-sized, compact plover with long legs; deep-chested, small-headed, with prominent white supercilia meeting on nape in distinctive V, also has white band across chest. Adult in breeding plumage (♀ brighter than ♂) has dark blackish-grey crown contrasting with white supercilia, white throat, grey neck, narrow white chest-band bordered narrowly black above, with orange/chestnut breast, flanks and belly darkening to black; vent and undertail-coverts white. Non-breeding adult and juvenile are duller, greyish-brown with pale buff fringes to mantle, coverts and flight-feathers, underparts streaked greyish-brown, but long pale buff supercilia and white chest-band retained (albeit often faded). In flight, uniform upperparts lacking wingbar, but outermost primary shaft is white. **BP** Bill blackish-grey, slender; eyes large, black; legs greenish-yellow to ochre. **SV** Calls, given in flight, a deep rolling *brroot* and, in alarm, a clear whistled *weet-weeh* or soft *pee-u-ee*. **AN** Mountain Dotterel.

Greater Painted-snipe *Rostratula benghalensis* L 23–28 cm; WS 50–55 cm; WT ♂ 140–150 g, ♀ 170–180 g

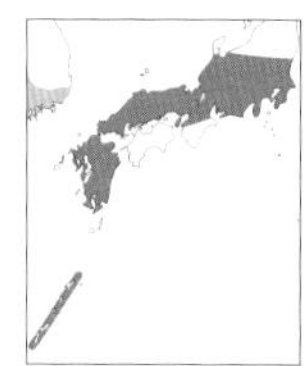

SD Now a scarce resident in Okinawa, Kyushu, Shikoku, and north to C Honshu; a rarer visitor further north to N Honshu and Hokkaido. **HH** Wet grasslands, especially wet ricefields and rushfields, from sea level to *c*. 900 m. Very secretive, crepuscular or nocturnal. **ID** Plump, short-tailed snipe-like shorebird with prominent 'spectacles' and 'braces', which (like Eurasian Dotterel) exhibits reverse sexual dimorphism. ♀ bright and boldly marked, with white eye-ring extending back from eye, contrasting with chestnut or maroon head and chest, and white stripe curving up breast-sides ('braces') from white underparts and extending into sandy-brown V on back. Mantle and wings greenish-brown. Often raises wings, revealing white underwing-coverts and pale brown spots on flight-feathers. ♂ considerably duller and smaller, mid-brown above with irregular dark markings, sandy eye patch and stripes on neck and back, and whitish underparts. Wings broader and rounder at tip than typical shorebirds. Flight typically short on rounded and arched wings, with feet dangling well beyond tail tip. **BP** Bill longish with slightly drooping tip, pinkish-orange (♀) or pinkish-grey (♂), with dark tip; eyes large, irides dark brown; legs greenish-grey. **SV** ♀ gives long series of low, slow, rhythmic, somewhat owl-like hoots, *hooo-hooo-hooo*, rising and falling slowly, or *koh koh koh uk uk* at night from ground or in circular flights. Also an explosive *tooick* and *twick-twick*.

Pheasant-tailed Jacana *Hydrophasianus chirurgus* L 31–58 cm; WT ♂ 126 g, ♀ 231 g

SD Occasionally straggles to Nansei Shoto (has bred), Kyushu and Honshu (mostly Jun–Mar), accidental Hokkaido. **HH** Well-vegetated ponds and lakes, and wet fields. **ID** Rail-like, but has long legs and extremely long toes. Attractive, boldly patterned breeding adult is dark chocolate-brown above, black below with white head and throat, yellow nape bordered black, white wings, and extremely long (23–35 cm) black tail. Non-breeding adult is white below, retaining only narrow chest-band, wing-coverts mottled brown, crown blackish with white supercilia, elongated tail-feathers lost. Juvenile is pale to mid-brown above, whitish below, with brown crown, yellowish neck and dark brown bar on neck-sides. Wings long and broad. In flight, wings almost all white, with narrow black tips, long trailing tail (♂) and prominent bundle of toes extending well beyond tail (♀) are all distinctive. **BP** Bill grey, legs greenish-grey; eye large, irides dark in adult, yellowish in young. **SV** Generally silent, but song consists of a bell-like *ku-wuuul*; calls include a purring *hrrrrrt*, a harder *chuu chuu* and a nasal mewing in alarm.

Eurasian Dotterel
juv
1st-win
ad win
ad ♀ sum
Greater Painted-snipe
ad ♂
ad ♀
ad ♂
ad ♀ display
Pheasant-tailed Jacana
(not to scale)
ad win
ad win
juv
ad sum

Little Curlew *Numenius minutus* L 28–32 cm; WS 68–71 cm; WT 108–240 g

SD Rare or scarce migrant throughout Japan from Nansei Shoto to Hokkaido. **HH** On migration and in winter typically found on short grassland or in dry crop fields, reclaimed land, sandy beaches and estuaries. **ID** Smallest curlew, with shortest, least-curved bill (see Common Whimbrel). Delicate; pale brown neck and breast with some dark streaking; upperparts darker with pale fringes; head prominently striped, like Whimbrel, with narrow, dark eyestripe, broad pale supercilia and two dark-brown lateral crown-stripes. At rest, primaries fall just short of tail tip. In flight, wings plain brown, underwing dark; rump and lower back pale brown, brown tail narrowly barred dark and white. **BP** Bill very short, slender, mostly straight, slightly decurved at tip, brown with pink basal half to lower mandible; eyes appear large, irides black; tarsi greenish-grey. **SV** Flight call a chattering three-note whistle, *pipipi* or *te-te-te*; shorter, higher, more metallic than Common Whimbrel.

Common Whimbrel *Numenius phaeopus* L 40–46 cm; WS 76–89 cm; WT ♂ 268–550 g, ♀ 315–600 g

SD Subspecies *N. p. variegatus* is a fairly common migrant (Apr/May, Aug/Sep) through Japan from Nansei Shoto, with some wintering in the south. **HH** On migration and in winter occurs at coastal mudflats, beaches, rocky shores, pastures, in flocks alone or with other species. **ID** Small curlew, with relatively short bill and somewhat short legs. Crown has two dark lateral stripes, separated by pale median stripe, prominent pale brown supercilia and narrow dark eyestripe. Upperparts dark brown; underparts buff. In flight, upperwing plain brown, axillaries and underwing-coverts white, barred dark grey-brown; rump and lower back pale greyish-brown, with narrow white stripe on lower back (recalling Spotted Redshank); toes do not protrude beyond tail. **BP** Bill decurved at tip, brown with pink basal half to lower mandible; eyes black; tarsi bluish-grey. **SV** Distinctive trilling seven-note whistle: *hwi pipipipipi* or *hu-hu-hu-hu-hu-hu-hu*, given commonly in flight year-round.

Hudsonian Whimbrel *Numenius hudsonicus* L 40–46 cm; WS 76–89 cm; WT ♂ 268–550 g, ♀ 315–600 g

SD Accidental or rare migrant in Japan. **HH** On migration occurs at coastal mudflats, beaches, rocky shores or pastures, typically with Common Whimbrel. **ID** Very closely resembles Common Whimbrel, but differs from Common in being overall richer buff with brown, barred underwing and axillaries, dark back, rump and uppertail-coverts concolorous with wings and tail, lacking white stripe. **BP** Bill decurved at tip, brown with pink basal half to lower mandible; eyes black; tarsi bluish-grey. **SV** Gives a series of short whistles and trilled notes, possibly stronger-sounding *quiquiquiquiqui* notes in flight cf. Common Whimbrel. **TN** Retained within Whimbrel as *Numenius phaeopus hudsonicus* by IOC.

Little Curlew
ad
ad
Common Whimbrel
ad
ad
ad
Hudsonian Whimbrel
ad
ad
ad

Bristle-thighed Curlew *Numenius tahitiensis* L 40–44 cm; WS 82–90 cm; WT ♂ 254–553 g, ♀ 372–796 g

SD Vulnerable. Accidental migrant (Mar–May, Jul–Sep) in Japan, with records from Hokkaido to Nansei Shoto. **HH** On migration generally occurs in drier habitats (including grassland) than Common Whimbrel, but also occurs in typical whimbrel habitats. **ID** Similar to Common Whimbrel in size and shape, but distinguished by flatter crown, large pale cinnamon-buff spots on mantle and wing-coverts, finely streaked breast abruptly demarcated from plain pale belly, and paler buffy-brown supercilia. In flight, wings plain brown, axillaries and underwing-coverts cinnamon-brown barred dark brown; most noticeably, rump pale buff and tail pale cinnamon-buff with dark brown bars; toes do not protrude beyond tail. Only in close views are thigh bristles visible. **BP** Bill, like Common Whimbrel's, long, decurved at tip, mostly brown with pink basal half to lower mandible; eyes black; tarsi bluish-grey. **SV** Calls include *chi-u-it; kwi; kuiiyo; piiyo*, whistled *whe-whe-whe-whe* and ringing *peeuu-pee* or *whee-wheeoo*.

Eurasian Curlew *Numenius arquata* L 50–60 cm; WS 80–100 cm; WT ♂ 410–1010 g, ♀ 475–1360 g

SD Subspecies *N. a. orientalis* is a fairly common migrant throughout coastal Japan, with some wintering (Oct–Apr) in SW Honshu, Kyushu and Nansei Shoto. **HH** On migration occurs in wet pastures and coastal grasslands, but most frequently at coastal wetlands and extensive mudflats; forages by deep probing. **ID** Large curlew with rather plain head and long bill. Overall mid- to pale brown with grey tones, especially on closed wings; neck and breast buff, streaked dark brown, belly and vent white; at long distance appears pale overall. In flight, plain brown wings contrast with rather black outer primaries and primary-coverts, white patch extends to point on back, white rump and pale brown tail barred dark brown, and whitish axillaries and underwing-coverts separate it from similar Far Eastern Curlew; feet protrude beyond tail; wingbeats slow. **BP** Bill very long (♀ longer, ♂/juv shorter), strongly arched, dark brownish-grey with pink basal half to lower mandible; eyes black; legs long, blue-grey. **SV** Haunting, somewhat cracked, oft-repeated rising *couer-leuw couer-leuw*, or *curr-lee* given by foraging and flying birds.

Far Eastern Curlew *Numenius madagascariensis* L 53–66 cm; WS 110 cm; WT 390–1350 g

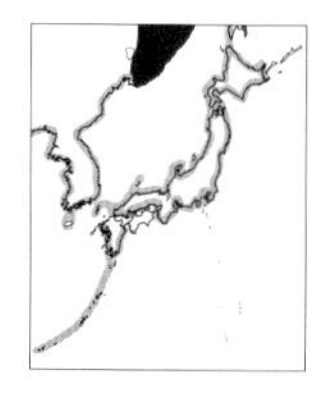

SD Endangered. Uncommon migrant (mid-Mar–early Jun, mid-Jul–Oct) throughout coastal Japan from Nansei Shoto to Hokkaido, often with Eurasian Curlew; local winter visitor in NW Kyushu. **HH** On migration occurs at coastal wetlands and mudflats. **ID** Largest curlew, with very long curved bill. Overall brown with warmer orange-brown tones than Eurasian; neck, breast, belly and vent warm buff or brown, streaked darker to belly and flanks; at long distance appears dark overall. In flight, plain brown wings, brown lower back, brown rump and tail barred dark brown, and dark axillaries and underwing-coverts separate it from similar Eurasian; toes protrude beyond tail. **BP** Bill very long (♀ longer, ♂/juv shorter), strongly arched, dark brownish-grey with pink basal half to lower mandible; eyes black; legs long, blue-grey. **SV** Similar to Eurasian, but flatter, deeper and longer *hoo ii nn* and more moaning single notes; in alarm a guttural *gurrr-wheeuh*.

Bristle-thighed Curlew
adults
adults
Eurasian Curlew
Far Eastern Curlew
adults

Eastern Black-tailed Godwit *Limosa (limosa) melanuroides*

L 36–44 cm; WS 70–82 cm; WT ♂ 160–440g, ♀ 244–500 g

SD Uncommon migrant (Apr–May; Aug–Oct) throughout Japan from Nansei Shoto to Hokkaido. **HH** Prefers fresh water. On migration and in winter occurs at coastal wetlands and mudflats, margins of rivers and lakes, also wet fields; typically feeds in quite deep water. **ID** Large, tall, long-legged, long-necked and long-billed shorebird. Breeding ♂ has rufous or chestnut head, with dark crown, rufous/chestnut neck and breast, prominent white supercilia from bill to eye, pale chin, heavy black barring on lower breast, flanks and belly, vent whitish, barred. Mantle has rufous, grey and black spots; wing-coverts rounded with pale fringes. ♀ is duller. Non-breeding adults are much greyer, with white on belly and vent. Juvenile has warm peach/orange-buff wash to breast and neck. In flight, wings more rounded than either Bar-tailed or Hudsonian; reveals blackish-brown forewing, with little contrast, narrow white wingbar, white rump, and black tail (legs extend well beyond). Underwing clean white (see Hudsonian). **BP** Very long bill straight, basal half pink, tip dark; eyes black; tarsi and toes black in breeding season, greenish-grey in non-breeder. **SV** A high, strident yapping *ki ki ki* or *kek kek kek*. **TN** Retained within Black-tailed Godwit *Limosa limosa* by IOC.

Hudsonian Godwit *Limosa haemastica*

L 36–42 cm; WS 74 cm; WT ♂ 196–266 g, ♀ 246–358 g

SD Accidental to Kyushu. **ID** Breeding adult has grey neck and dark rufous underparts; upperparts almost black. Non-breeding adult is dark, plain grey, with almost black crown. In flight, wings more pointed than Black-tailed, and readily distinguished by black axillaries and underwing-coverts, and narrow white underwing bar. From above, has dark flight-feathers and narrow white upperwing bars, largely black tail with narrow white band across uppertail-coverts; only the toes project beyond tail-tip. **BP** Very long, slightly upturned bill is pinkish-brown at base with dark tip (summer) or pinkish-based below, with dark upper mandible (winter). **SV** Call a high *kwidwid* or *kwehweh*.

Bar-tailed Godwit *Limosa lapponica*

L 33–41 cm; WS 70–80 cm; WT ♂ 190–400 g, ♀ 262–630 g

SD Two subspecies recorded on migration (Apr/May, Aug/Sep) throughout Japan from Nansei Shoto (some winter) to Hokkaido: *L. l. menzbieri* (accidental) and *L. l. baueri* (reasonably common). **HH** On migration, and in winter, coastal wetlands, mudflats, estuaries, where wades in shallow water and probes soft mud. **ID** Large, tall, long-legged and long-billed shorebird, *L. l. baueri* is slightly larger, but shorter-legged than Eastern Black-tailed Godwit, and stocky in comparison. Breeding ♂ has varying amounts of rufous on head, neck and breast, with pale supercilia, fine black streaking on neck, breast and flanks, and barring towards whitish vent. Mantle has dark brown, tawny and grey streaking; wing-coverts pointed, with very dark shaft-streaks. Larger ♀ typically has little rufous in breeding plumage. Subadult may migrate with little breeding plumage. Non-breeding adult is duller, upperparts more curlew-like with pale fringes to grey-brown mantle, scapulars and wing-coverts. Juvenile has dark brown upperparts notched pale buff, giving strongly patterned appearance to back. At rest, primaries extend beyond tail. In flight, grey-brown wings relieved only by darker primary-coverts and lack prominent wingbar; rump and lower back white, sparsely barred grey-brown in *L. l. menzbieri* and essentially appears grey-brown in *L. l. baueri* because heavily barred; tail variably barred grey-brown and white, but appears largely dark in both. **BP** Very long bill slightly upcurved, basal half pink, tip dark (culmen also dark in breeding season; bill noticeably longer in ♀); eyes black; tarsi black in breeding season, dark grey in non-breeding birds. **SV** Slower and lower pitched than Eastern Black-tailed, a strident *ke ke ke*, *kek kek* or *kirrik*.

Eastern Black-tailed Godwit
ad win
ad win
juv
ad win
ad sum
ad ♂ win
Hudsonian Godwit
ad ♂ sum
ad ♀ win
baueri
ad win
menzbieri
Bar-tailed Godwit
ad win
baueri
juv
baueri
ad ♂ sum
baueri

Spotted Redshank *Tringa erythropus*

L 29–32 cm; WS 61–67 cm; WT 97–230 g

SD Common migrant (Mar/Apr, Aug/Sep) throughout Japan from Nansei Shoto (some winter) to Hokkaido. **HH** Inland and coastal wetlands, including wet fields, pools, rivers, marshes and mudflats. **ID** Tall, elegant, long-legged and long-billed. Breeding plumage black with fine white spots on mantle, scapulars, wing-coverts and flight-feathers, white crescents above and below eyes, fine white barring on black flanks and vent. Non-breeding plumage pale grey, with prominent white supercilia, grey mantle, grey upperparts with fine white speckling, and grey on neck and chest but white on throat and belly. Juvenile like non-breeding adult, but browner above, more extensively grey below. In flight, plain black or grey wings lack wingbar, but contrast with narrow white rump and lower-back stripe, tail black or grey with fine barring; axillaries and underwing-coverts white; tarsi protrude beyond tail. **BP** Bill long, fine, black with red base; eyes black with narrow white ring; long, slender legs deep blackish-red (breeding), red-orange (non-breeding), or orange (juv). **SV** Short *chip chip chip* in alarm, but most distinctive is sharply whistled *chui* or *chew-ick* flight call (recalls Pacific Golden Plover, but sharper).

Common Redshank *Tringa totanus*

L 27–29 cm; WS 59–66 cm; WT 85–155 g

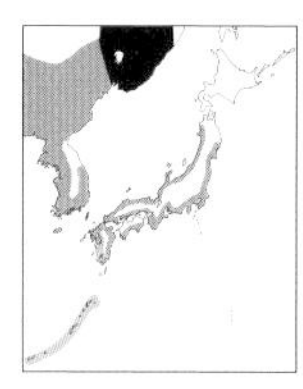

SD *T. t. ussuriensis* has bred (very scarce) in E Hokkaido; scarce migrant from Hokkaido to Nansei Shoto. **HH** Favours fresh and brackish marshes, wet fields, pools, rivers, marshes and mudflats. **ID** Less elegant than Spotted Redshank; neck and bill shorter. Adult breeding: brown above and on head; underparts white with prominent dark streaking/spotting on neck, breast and flanks. Non-breeding adult: greyish-brown above, buff on breast-sides with faint streaking. Juvenile: like non-breeding adult, but browner upperparts have pale buff fringes. In flight, prominent white panel on trailing edge of secondaries and inner primaries, white wedge from rump up back, tail pale grey with fine dark bars. *T. t. ussuriensis* larger and paler than races to west, and juvenile has paler legs, rendering them confusable not only with Spotted, but also even with yellowlegs. **BP** Bill orange at base with black tip; eyes black with narrow white ring; long legs red (breeding), reddish-orange (other seasons) or pale orange (juv); orange toes protrude beyond tail. **SV** Highly vocal, calling on ground, in flight and particularly during display flight, when circles on stiffly beating wings; typically gives a whistled, rather anxious, *chew-chew chew-hu-hu*, but also a longer, more drawn-out and plaintive *tyooooo* and excited *tyeeu*.

Common Greenshank *Tringa nebularia*

L 30–35 cm; WS 68–70 cm; WT 125–290 g

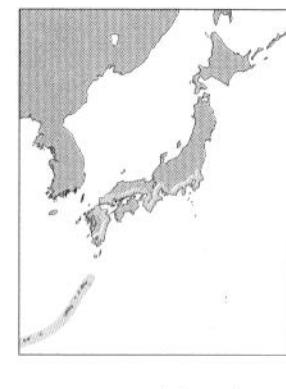

SD Fairly common migrant from Nansei Shoto to Hokkaido, with some wintering in S Japan. **HH** Wet fields and coastal wetlands. **ID** Heavy-set, long-legged, pale grey above and white below; heavier-looking than Marsh Sandpiper, with long, stout bill. Adult breeding: crown, face and neck finely streaked dark grey, upperparts grey-brown, many feathers with blackish centres and black marginal triangles. Lower neck and breast-sides heavily streaked grey. Adult non-breeding: paler with less prominent streaking on underparts. Juvenile: browner, with pale-fringed upperparts. In flight, wings dark, underwing dusky grey; long white wedge extends up back from rump, tail also white with fine dark bars; tarsi protrude beyond tail. **BP** Bill greyish at base, black tip slightly upturned; eyes black with narrow white ring; legs long, dull greenish-grey. **SV** On ground and in flight, gives loud, level, three- (or more) note whistle: *chew-chew-chew*.

Nordmann's Greenshank *Tringa guttifer*

L 29–32 cm; WT 136–158 g

SD Endangered. Very rare migrant from Nansei Shoto to Hokkaido. **HH** Mudflats. Feeding style is diagnostic as chases hurriedly after prey. **ID** Slightly smaller, stockier, with larger head and shorter, thicker neck than Common Greenshank (CG). Adult: recalls CG, but mantle, scapulars and wing-coverts blacker with pale fringes; head/neck heavily streaked, lower neck, breast-sides and flanks heavily spotted black; black spotting on crown, mantle and breast-sides may coalesce; underparts white with isolated black spots on belly. Non-breeding adult: upperparts more scaled and less streaked than CG, and pale-grey mantle and wings have even paler grey fringes. Juvenile: darker, browner on crown, upperparts and wings than non-breeding adult. In flight, underwing pure white; rump and tail like CG. Toes just protrude beyond tail. **BP** Bill thicker (particularly at base) than CG, bicoloured (black tip, yellowish base) and slightly upturned; eyes black; legs thicker, shorter and yellower than CG. All three toes webbed (only two in CG). **SV** Trilled *kee* or *kwee* and harsh *kwork* or *gwark* in flight. **AN** Spotted Greenshank.

Spotted Redshank
ad sum
juv
ad win
Common Redshank
ad sum
juv
ad win
Common Greenshank
ad win
juv
ad sum
ad win
juv
ad sum
Nordmann's Greenshank

Marsh Sandpiper *Tringa stagnatilis*

L 22–26 cm; WS 55–59 cm; WT 43–120 g

SD Uncommon migrant throughout Japan from Nansei Shoto to Hokkaido, with some wintering in S Nansei Shoto. **HH** Ricefields, marshes, mudflats and estuaries. **ID** Graceful, pale grey above, white below, with small head and long neck, differing from Green and Wood sandpipers by very long legs and white back, and from larger greenshanks in size. Breeding adult has pale brownish-grey mantle, scapulars and wing-coverts with black centres giving black-spotted appearance to back. Head and neck pale grey with pale supercilia; dark spotting extends to flanks, underparts otherwise white. Non-breeding adult is plain pale grey; face pale, though may show contrasting dark crown and ear-coverts, and pale supercilia, giving capped appearance. Juvenile is like non-breeding adult but has darker fringes to upperparts, face plain white. In flight, long white wedge extends up back from rump; tail white with fine dark bars, tarsi protruding beyond tip. **BP** Bill mid-length, needle-fine, black; eyes black; very long legs greenish-yellow. **SV** High-pitched single *kiu* or *pyoo*, sometimes repeated in greenshank-like series *kiu-kiu-kiu*, but faster, higher; also a repeated abrupt *yup* when flushed.

Greater Yellowlegs *Tringa melanoleuca*

L 29–33 cm; WS 70–74 cm; WT 111–235 g

SD Vagrant to Hokkaido, Honshu (has wintered), Shikoku and Okinawa. **HH** Freshwater and coastal wetlands. **ID** Large, elegant, with plain face marked by white eye-ring and white supraloral patch. Similar to Common Greenshank (CG), but has longer legs, more spotted mantle and square white rump. Breeding adult is darker, more heavily streaked on neck and breast than CG; mantle, scapulars and wing-coverts almost black, with narrow tips giving distinctly spotted appearance; underparts largely white, with extensive dark barring on flanks and some on vent. Non-breeding adult is like CG, but scapulars and wing-coverts more spotted than scaled, and head, neck and breast more heavily streaked. Juvenile resembles breeding adult, though less black above, with clean, fine grey streaking on breast. At rest, primary tips reach just beyond tail, tertials just beyond tail base. In flight, wings uniform dark above, white or pale grey underwing-coverts; white rump and tail diagnostic (like Lesser, lacks wedge on back); tail heavily barred dark grey; tarsi protrude beyond tail. **BP** Bill long, slightly upturned and more delicate than CG, thicker, more uptilted than Lesser, black tip, greenish-grey base; eyes black; long legs bright yellow. **SV** Three or more loud CG-like *pyuu* or *chew* notes, the final syllable lower pitched; also single, double and multiple calls; in alarm repeats single *tew* call.

Lesser Yellowlegs *Tringa flavipes*

L 23–25 cm; WS 59–64 cm; WT 48–114 g

SD Vagrant on migration and in winter to: Hokkaido, Honshu, Shikoku, Kyushu and Nansei Shoto. **HH** Freshwater and coastal wetlands. **ID** Slightly larger, slimmer and longer-winged than Wood Sandpiper, with only short, prominent supraloral patch (supercilia indistinct behind eye). Adult best separated from Greater Yellowlegs by smaller size, longer legs and wings, and voice. Juvenile is greyer, with less streaking on lower neck and upper breast. At rest, primary tips extend beyond tail, tertials halfway along tail. In flight, square white rump resembles Greater Yellowlegs; underwing-coverts white and pale grey; tail heavily barred dark grey; tarsi protrude beyond tail. **BP** Bill black at tip, greyish or brownish at base: shorter, thinner, straighter than Greater Yellowlegs; longer, thinner, darker than Wood Sandpiper; eyes black; legs long, bright yellow. **SV** Clear, high-pitched *tew* or *pyuu*, sometimes in quick series of 2–4 notes, rarely in distinct sets of 3 (typical of Greater Yellowlegs). In alarm a rising *kleet*.

Marsh Sandpiper
ad win
juv
ad sum
ad win
Greater Yellowlegs
ad win
juv
ad sum
Lesser Yellowlegs
ad win
juv
ad sum
ad win

Green Sandpiper *Tringa ochropus* L 21–24 cm; WS 57–61 cm; WT 53–119 g

SD Fairly common migrant throughout Japan, with some wintering from C Honshu to Nansei Shoto. **HH** Streams, rivers, freshwater wetlands, farmland drainage ditches; rarely coasts. **ID** Stocky, with blackish-brown upperparts and prominent white rump and belly. Recalls smaller Wood Sandpiper. Adult has greenish-brown upperparts with smattering of tiny white spots; head and neck streaked; heavy dark spotting on breast contrasts with clean white underparts; dark loral bar with white supraloral and narrow white eye-ring. Non-breeding birds are plainer and greyer on upperparts and breast. Juvenile has upperparts like breeding adult and underparts like non-breeding adult. At rest, wingtips reach tail tip; tertials fall just short of primary tips. In flight, wings are very dark (uniform with back); underwing almost black; square white rump very prominent; tail white with 2–3 black bars; toes protrude just beyond tail. **BP** Bill just longer than head, fine-tipped, but somewhat thick basal half, black; eyes black; legs dark greenish. **SV** Often calls explosively on flushing, *tluueet-veet-veet*. In alarm gives staccato series of *kwik* notes.

Wood Sandpiper *Tringa glareola* L 19–23 cm; WS 56–57 cm; WT 130–150 g

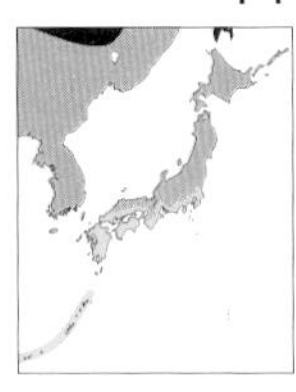

SD Common migrant throughout Japan with some wintering from C Honshu to Nansei Shoto. **HH** Inland freshwater and coastal brackish wetlands, wet fields, rivers and mudflats; often in small flocks. **ID** Medium-sized, rather slender sandpiper, similar to Green Sandpiper but more elegant, with longer legs. Adult is browner with prominent whitish supercilia, checkerboard back pattern, less contrasting rump and noticeably paler underwings. Breeding adult is brown, upperparts pale-fringed, giving overall spotted appearance. Non-breeding adult is browner, less spotted. Juvenile has warm brown upperparts and grey-brown wash to breast. At rest, wingtips reach tail tip; tertials fall just short of primary tips. In flight, wings and back brown; underwing pale grey; rump white; tail white with several narrow brown bars; toes protrude well beyond tail. **BP** Bill just longer than head, fine, straight, black; eyes black; legs pale, yellowish. **SV** Common alarm or flight call a high *chiff iff-iff*.

Grey-tailed Tattler *Tringa brevipes* L 24–27 cm; WS 60–65 cm; WT 80–170 g

SD Common coastal migrant throughout Japan, with some wintering in Nansei Shoto. **HH** Coastal wetlands, lakes, rivers, beaches and, principally, mudflats and estuaries, occasionally rocky shores. **ID** Medium to large, rather uniform ash-grey sandpiper, with mid-length bill and relatively short legs, prominent dark loral stripe and white supercilia extending beyond eye. Adult has unmarked grey upperparts, distinctive facial pattern and narrow grey bars on lower neck, breast, flanks and vent-sides, though central belly and vent are unbarred (see Wandering). Non-breeding adult plain grey above, white below, lacking barring on underparts, but has dusky wash over breast and flanks. Juvenile has pale-fringed upperparts and grey wash over chest and flanks, supercilia broad, diffuse behind eye, contrasting with black eyestripe that is particularly obvious between bill and eye; cheeks largely white. At rest primary tips reach tail tip. In flight, upperwing, rump and tail grey; underwing uniform dark grey. **BP** Black bill, may be yellowish at base of lower mandible; eyes black; legs short, yellowish. **SV** Clear double whistle, *pyu-ii* or *tuee-dee*, recalls Grey Plover, sometimes run in series: *tuee-dee-dee*. **TN** Formerly in genus *Heteroscelus*.

Wandering Tattler *Tringa incana* L 26–29 cm; WS 66 cm; WT 72–213 g

SD Very scarce local migrant and winter visitor from Hokkaido to Nansei Shoto. **HH** Almost exclusively along rocky shores, sometimes with Ruddy Turnstone and Rock Sandpiper. **ID** Slightly larger and longer-winged than very similar Grey-tailed Tattler (GTT). Adult has broader and more extensive dark barring on underparts. Non-breeding adult is darker than GTT, best distinguished by habitat and voice. Juvenile is like non-breeding adult, but upperparts are pale-fringed; supercilia short, narrow, only in front of eye, contrasting with diffuse black eyestripe between bill and eye; cheeks largely grey. At rest longer primary tips extend beyond tail. In flight, like GTT, but underwing blackish-grey, upperwing dark grey with blackish carpal and primaries. **BP** Bill dark grey, may be yellowish at base of lower mandible, lores black (bill shorter and darker than GTT); eyes black; legs short, yellowish. **SV** Flight call a series of short clear piping notes on even pitch: *pi pi pi pi*. **TN** Formerly in genus *Heteroscelus*.

Green Sandpiper
ad win
juv
ad sum
Wood Sandpiper
ad win
juv
ad sum
Grey-tailed Tattler
ad win
juv
ad sum
Wandering Tattler
ad win
juv
ad sum

Terek Sandpiper *Xenus cinereus*

L 22–25 cm; WS 57–59 cm; WT 50–126 g

SD Fairly common migrant (Apr/May; Jul–Oct) throughout Japan from Nansei Shoto to Hokkaido; usually among other shorebirds, rarely numerous on its own. **HH** Brackish or saltwater wetlands. Appears hunched; leans forwards when running; forages typically close to water or tide edge on wettest mud. **ID** Rather oddly proportioned shorebird; appears short-legged and stocky with distinctive long, upturned bill and steep forehead. Adult is brownish-grey with prominent black centres to coverts and scapulars, forming black bar on shoulder; head and neck grey with white streaking, underparts white. Non-breeding adult is paler, greyer brown and lacks black scapular line. Juvenile is darker and browner than adult with dark centres and pale buff fringes to coverts, creating scaled effect. At rest, blackish primary tips just visible beyond grey-brown tertials, and reach tail tip. In flight, grey-brown wing-coverts contrast with almost black leading edge, primaries and greater covert bar, and white secondaries form prominent white trailing edge; the rump and tail are both grey; toes do not protrude beyond tail. **BP** Bill long, thick and yellowish at base, with black tip; eyes black; legs short, yellowish-orange. **SV** Various whistled calls, in short series of clear, liquid notes, *pwee-wee-wee* or clattering *wick-a-wick-a-wick*.

Common Sandpiper *Actitis hypoleucos*

L 19–21 cm; WS 38–41 cm; WT 33–84 g

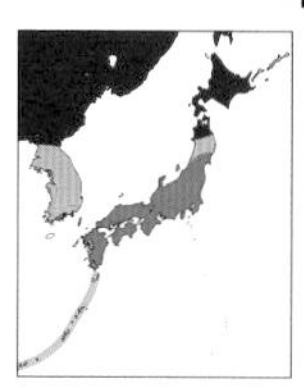

SD Breeds from Kyushu to Hokkaido; fairly common migrant throughout Japan; winters from C Japan south to Nansei Shoto and Ogasawara Is. **HH** Breeds around waterbodies, and along streams and rivers. On migration and in winter, generally solitary, at freshwater, brackish and coastal wetlands, along lake shores, streams and rivers, also beaches. **ID** Small brown and white sandpiper with rather short neck, bill and legs. Stance is distinctively horizontal combined with almost constant tail-bobbing. Adult is mid-brown above with brownish-grey breast patches and white wedge extending between closed wing and breast patch; white eye-ring and supercilia. Non-breeding adult is plainer, breast patches less distinct. Juvenile has scaled upperparts, the scapulars and wing-coverts have pale buff fringes. At rest, long-tailed, primaries fall well short of tail tip; tertial fringes have dark notches. Flight flickering, rapid wingbeats on down-angled wings interspersed with stiff-winged glides distinctive. Upperwing-coverts brown, primaries blackish-brown, with clear white wingbar on bases of flight-feathers to innerwing (also on underside); brown rump and tail has barred outer feathers; toes not visible beyond tail in flight. **BP** Bill short, dark grey; eyes black; legs short, olive or greyish-green to dull yellowish-brown. **SV** Calls readily on taking flight and in alarm, a thin, high-pitched and plaintive *wee-wee-wee*, or *chee-ree-ree* in quick series. Also a single, high-pitched, drawn-out *tweeeh*. Display flight, low on rapidly pumping wings, accompanied by fast twittering *sweedidee sweedidee* ....

Spotted Sandpiper *Actitis macularius*

L 18–20 cm; WS 37–40 cm; WT 19–64 g

SD Accidental to Hokkaido. **HH** As Common Sandpiper (CS). **ID** Almost identical to CS in size and structure, but tail distinctly shorter, projecting less far beyond wingtips. Breeding plumage adult is unmistakable with heavy black spotting on white throat, neck and breast; upperparts greyish-brown with bolder darker markings on mantle, scapulars and wing-coverts. Prominent blackish eyestripe, narrow white supercilia and eye-ring. Non-breeding adult is very like CS and could easily be overlooked, lacks spotting, but is greyer brown. Juvenile is also like CS, but has plainer, greyer lateral breast patches, and strongly barred median and lesser coverts (more prominent than in CS). Tail shorter and projects less beyond wing tips than CS. Tertial fringes lack faint dark notches of CS. Upperwing has similar pattern to CS, but wingbar short, narrower, reduced on innerwing, and underwing mostly white with dark flight-feathers and dark carpal bar; rump and tail like CS, but has less white on outer rectrices. **BP** Bill short, orange (breeding), or pale pinkish-horn (non-breeding), with dark tip and culmen (subtly thicker bill than CS, with tip slightly more drooping); eyes black; legs short, pale yellowish-flesh to bright yellow. **SV** Though vagrants often silent, separation from CS possible by voice, the calls being quieter, less resonant and lower pitched than CS, a single whistled *peet*, sometimes doubled, *peet-weet*, or in descending series like Green Sandpiper when flushed, *tueet-ueet-ueet*.

Terek Sandpiper
ad sum
ad win
ad win
Common Sandpiper
juv
ad sum
ad
Spotted Sandpiper
1st-win
ad sum
juv

Ruddy Turnstone *Arenaria interpres*

L 21–26 cm; WS 50–57 cm; WT 84–190 g

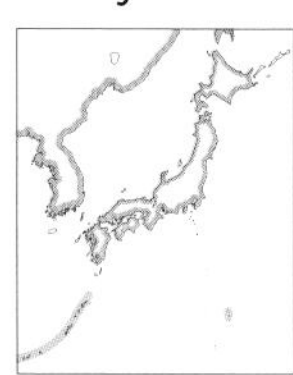

SD *A. i. interpres* is a common coastal migrant from Hokkaido to Nansei Shoto, with some wintering from Honshu southwards. **HH** Rocky shores, also beaches and occasionally coastal mudflats. May mix with other species, e.g. Sanderling, or may form dense flocks on mudflats, even foraging in short coastal grasslands. **ID** Small, stocky, with stubby bill and short legs. Breeding ♂ has bright rufous-orange upperparts and wings, with white face and underparts, and various complex and individually variable black markings through eye, on neck, on band across breast and on scapulars. ♀ similar, but more brown than orange on upperparts and less white, more brown, on head. Non-breeding adult retains same black markings, but lacks orange tones on upperparts, being duller grey-brown. Juvenile has blackish-brown upperparts with pale fringes, reduced face pattern and large blackish breast patch. At rest, primary tips just reach tail tip. In flight shows contrasting pattern of black, white and brown; back, scapular bar and bars at bases of flight-feathers white, rest of flight-feathers black, tail black with white base and tip; underwing white. **BP** Bill short, black, wedge-shaped, lower mandible angled slightly upwards; eyes black; legs short, orange (breeding) or pale orange (non-breeding). **SV** A low staccato, rattling *tuk tuk-i-tuk-tuk* when flushed or in flight.

Black Turnstone *Arenaria melanocephala*

L 23 cm; WS 53 cm; WT 120 g

SD Vagrant, Hegurajima and E Hokkaido. **HH** Splash zone of rocky shores, particularly where barnacles proliferate. **ID** Structure closely resembles Ruddy Turnstone (RT). Adult: almost entirely black upperparts, and black from head to upper breast; small areas of white below eye, forming large loral spot, and frosting on feathers of neck; rather long, loose scapulars and wing-coverts have narrow white fringes; underparts clear white. Non-breeding adult: similar, but lacks white on face; duller, slightly browner. Juvenile: extensively blackish-brown on head and upperparts. In flight, shows distinctive white back patch, white band at tail base, white wing-coverts patch and wingbar, on otherwise black upperwing and tail. **BP** Bill black; eyes black; legs short, dark orange-brown. **SV** Flight call a chattering *keerrt* (higher pitched than RT). In alarm, a long low rattle or clear nasal *weepa weepa weepa*… **TN** Not included by OSJ.

Great Knot *Calidris tenuirostris*

L 26–28 cm; WS 62–66 cm; WT 115–248 g

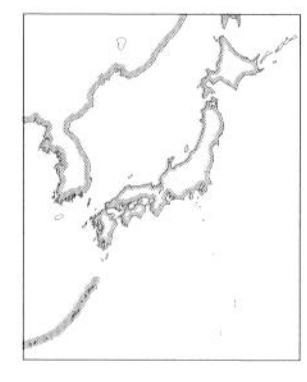

SD Endangered. Uncommon migrant (mostly Apr/May, Aug–Oct) throughout Japan from Nansei Shoto to Hokkaido. **HH** Forms tight flocks on intertidal mudflats. **ID** Large, grey sandpiper, with longish bill (longer than head); slightly larger, more attenuated rear, longer-necked and smaller-headed than Red Knot (RK). Adult: heavily streaked grey on head and neck, with prominent black spots/chevrons on breast/flanks, forming band of almost solid black on chest. Upperparts dark grey. Non-breeding adult and juvenile: plainer grey, lacking chest-band and with grey spots from neck to flanks. Belly and vent white at all seasons, but with scattered black spots in breeding plumage. Wings extend beyond tail tip, giving more elongated appearance than RK. In flight, appears grey with narrow white wingbar and white rump contrasting with grey tail. **BP** Bill long (longer than RK), blackish, thicker and greyer at base, slightly decurved to finer tip; eyes black; legs dull grey-green. **SV** Double whistle, *queet queet* or *nyut-nyut*, and distinctive *chucker-chucker-chucker* call.

Red Knot *Calidris canutus*

L 23–25 cm; WS 45–54 cm; WT 85–220 g

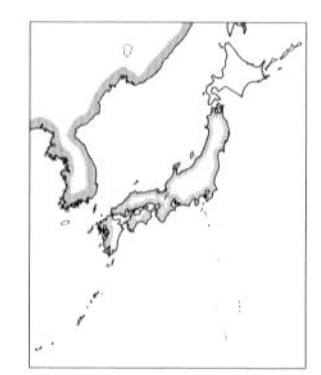

SD *C. c. rogersi* is a scarce migrant (mostly Apr/May, Aug–Oct) throughout Japan from Nansei Shoto to Hokkaido. **HH** Coastal intertidal mudflats, estuaries and occasionally beaches. **ID** Heavy-set grey sandpiper with long wings but shortish bill and short legs. Adult: reddish-orange on face, chest and belly; crown grey, streaked darker, upperparts grey with black centres and tips to many feathers (some orange), may have blue-grey appearance. Non-breeding adult and juvenile: largely plain grey above; grey feathers of mantle and wings have dark grey and white fringes, breast has grey wash, finely streaked black, belly and vent white with some dark streaking on flanks. In flight, grey with noticeable white wingbar contrasting with black flight-feathers and grey coverts; mostly white rump barred grey, showing little contrast with pale grey tail. **BP** Bill short (equals head), rather thick, straight, blackish; eyes black; legs dull greenish-grey. **SV** Flocks give steady chattering *kyo kyo kyo*, and in flight a low *knutt knutt*.

Ruddy Turnstone
ad win
juv
ad sum
ad win
Black Turnstone
ad win
ad ♂ sum
ad win
Great Knot
juv
ad sum
Red Knot
ad win
juv
ad sum
ad win

Sanderling *Calidris alba*

L 20–21 cm; WS 35–39 cm; WT 33–110 g

SD *C. a. rubida* migrates throughout Japan from Hokkaido to Nansei Shoto and also winters (Aug–May) in small numbers from Honshu southwards. **HH** Close-knit flocks forage on sandy beaches; follows tide, runs with fast, mechanical gait; occasionally on mudflats. **ID** Small, stocky, but larger than stints. Adult: rufous, black and white, but intensity variable. Head, face, neck, breast and upperparts largely rufous (recalling Red-necked Stint); mantle and wing-coverts grey with black shafts and tips (some with rusty-orange, others fringed white). Non-breeding adult: palest small shorebird, with prominent black patch on closed wing formed by black lesser coverts. Juvenile: white with black and silver-spangled upperparts. Wingtips reach tail tip or just beyond. In flight, broad white wingbar, black leading edge to wing with prominent carpal patch, black flight-feathers, black central tail with white sides. **BP** Bill short, black; eyes and tarsi black, foot lacks hind toe. **SV** In flight, a short hard *cheep cheep*; excited *twick twick* or liquid *pleet*; in alarm *veek-veek*.

Semipalmated Sandpiper *Calidris pusilla*

L 13–15 cm; WS 34–37 cm; WT 20–41 g

SD Accidental. **HH** Fresh, brackish and saltwater wetlands. **ID** Small, rather drab. Adult: uniform grey-brown, with weak supercilia, dark loral patch, pale forehead, grey-brown wing-coverts, scapulars black with pale fringes; crown and cheeks darker than supercilia, grey-brown to warmer rufous-brown. Non-breeding adult: largely uniform grey, with fine black centres to mantle feathers and black shaft-streaks to scapulars; underparts white, with grey-washed breast. Wingtips fall just short of tail tip, imparting plump look. Juvenile: dark cap as richly coloured as scapulars, dark ear-coverts, 'scaly' upperparts, black mantle and back with pale buff fringes, scapulars grey with black anchor marks and off-white fringes; recalls Little Stint, but lacks white V on mantle. In flight, long narrow white wingbar and white underwing. **BP** Bill short, straight, black (shortest in juv, longest in ♀), eyes black; tarsi black, with webbing between middle and outer toes (like Western, but unlike other stints). **SV** Flight call brief, a rather low-pitched, husky *chrup* or coarse *krrit*; sometimes a higher-pitched Western-like *kit* or *cheet*. **TN** Not included by OSJ.

Western Sandpiper *Calidris mauri*

L 14–17 cm; WS 28–37 cm; WT 18–42 g

SD Accidental in spring and autumn (Aug–Oct) to Honshu, Shikoku, Kyushu and Nansei Shoto. **HH** Coastal mudflats, estuaries and wetlands. **ID** Small stint with long bill, commonly appearing droop-tipped; structurally recalls Semipalmated Sandpiper (SS), but has longer legs. Adult: heavily streaked dark grey on neck; grey triangles on breast-sides/flanks; prominently rufous on crown-sides and ear-coverts; scapulars black and rufous. Non-breeding adult: pale grey (paler on face and breast than SS), but has less prominent black shafts to mantle/covert feathers, and grey-streaked breast. Juvenile: distinct rufous fringes to upper scapulars, forming stripe, also distinctive black anchors on grey lower scapulars; cap less richly coloured than scapulars. In flight, narrow white wingbar, tail has black centre and white sides; underwing mostly whitish, underside of flight-feathers grey. **BP** Bill length variable (♀ longer than ♂), but usually longer than SS, slightly decurved and fine-tipped, black; eyes black; legs short, black, front toes clearly webbed (like SS, unlike other stints). **SV** Raspy, snipe-like *jeet* or *krreep* in flight. Calls generally higher pitched and more drawn-out than SS.

Temminck's Stint *Calidris temminckii*

L 13–15 cm; WS 34–37 cm; WT 15–39 g

SD Scarce migrant (Apr/May, Aug–Oct) through Japan, and wintering in small numbers from Honshu to Nansei Shoto. **HH** Favours inland well-vegetated freshwater wetlands and wet fields; sometimes at mudflats and coastal wetlands. Creeps on flexed legs and pecks more slowly than Red-necked Stint. When flushed, usually flies off quickly, high and erratically. **ID** Small, dumpy, with rather horizontal stance and quite long tail. Adult: brown upperparts lack rusty tones, with rather rounded grey breast patches. Dark-centred scapulars, wing-coverts and tertials fringed brown and grey. Non-breeding adult: plain pale grey with grey wash on neck and breast, resembling small Common Sandpiper. Juvenile: grey, but with clear dark shafts, dark submarginal edges with pale fringes. In flight shows white wingbar, prominent white sides to dark-centred rump and tail. **BP** Bill short, slightly arched, dull greenish at base, blacker towards fine tip; eyes black; pale yellowish or greenish legs. **SV** Flight call is a purring trilled *tirrr* or prolonged *tirrr-r-r* (also given at night on migration) and when flushed.

Sanderling
ad win
ad sum
juv
Semipalmated
Sandpiper
juv
ad sum
Western
Sandpiper
juv
ad sum
juv
Temminck's Stint
ad sum
ad win
ad sum

Little Stint *Calidris minuta*

L 12–14 cm; WS 28–31 cm; WT 17–44 g

SD Very rare, Nansei Shoto (has wintered) to Hokkaido. **HH** Inland or coastal wetlands, mudflats. **ID** Slightly smaller than Red-necked Stint (RNS), non-breeders confusingly similar. Adult summer: reddish wash over cheeks and dark-spotted breast, chin and throat always white. Mantle, scapulars and wings concolorous, more orange than RNS; mantle, wing-coverts and black-centred tertials all fringed orange; prominent off-white or buff V on mantle. Central rectrices fringed orange (unlike RNS). Adult winter: pale grey, but with broader dark feather centres than RNS. Juvenile: darker cap, streaked breast-sides, prominent white 'braces', bright-edged dark grey-centred wing-coverts (coloration overlaps RNS and Semipalmated Sandpiper). In flight, prominent white wingbar; rump white with narrow black centre, tail grey. Underwing mostly whitish, underside of flight-feathers grey. **BP** Bill short, straight, black with fine tip, slightly longer and less blunt than RNS; eyes black; black legs slightly longer than RNS. **SV** A sharp, incisive *chit* or *stit*, and weak *pi pi pi* in flight.

Red-necked Stint *Calidris ruficollis*

L 13–16 cm; WS 29–33 cm; WT 18–51 g

SD Commonest migratory shorebird (Apr/May, Aug–Oct); some winter from Honshu southwards. **HH** Coastal/inland wetlands. **ID** Small, dumpy (bill slightly thicker, legs slightly shorter, body subtly longer than Little Stint, with longer primary projection creating slightly elongated, longer-bodied appearance). Adult summer: head, breast and throat have rufous-orange to rusty-red wash. Crown streaked; mantle/wing-coverts orange to chestnut with black centres, tertials paler, grey-brown centred, scapulars most rufous. Central tail-feathers not fringed orange. Adult winter: pale grey upperparts with narrow dark feather shafts, grey wash restricted to breast-sides. Juvenile: largely black mantle with rufous fringes, indistinct 'braces' on mantle, wing-coverts and tertials grey-brown with buff fringes; grey-brown wash on breast-sides (plumage overlaps with Little and Semipalmated, though dark cap typically has paler sides than either). At rest, tail tip projects slightly beyond wingtips; primary projection is as long as Little. Beware moult, when tail/wing measurements overlap with Little. In flight, prominent narrow white wingbar; rump mostly white with narrow black centre and grey tail; underwing mostly whitish, flight-feathers grey. **BP** Bill short, straight, blunt and black; eyes black; legs short, black. **SV** Flight call: rasping *quiit*, dry *churi*, chattering *chrit-chrit* or *chreek*.

Long-toed Stint *Calidris subminuta*

L 13–16 cm; WS 26–31 cm; WT 20–40 g

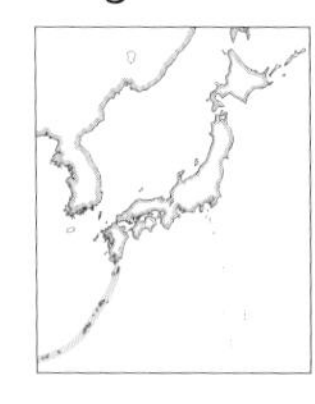

SD Scarce migrant (Apr/May, Aug–Oct), Nansei Shoto to Hokkaido; some winter, Kyushu, Nansei Shoto. **HH** Well-vegetated freshwater wetlands, muddy pools, rivers, wet ricefields, occasionally brackish wetlands. **ID** Small, slender, long-legged stint. Adult summer: dark-streaked rufous-brown cap, bordered by pale supercilia (often splits over eye). Cheeks, neck- and breast-sides finely streaked black. Upperparts blackish, but scapulars, coverts and tertials fringed warm rufous. Adult winter: greyer with grey-fringed dark-centred scapulars. Juvenile: dark ear patch, rufous-brown-fringed scapulars and tertials, but grey-fringed median/lesser coverts. Closed wing shows no primary projection (tertials equal primaries). In flight, as other stints (white wingbar, white rump-sides), but protruding toes diagnostic. Upright, long-necked stance recalls larger Sharp-tailed Sandpiper. **BP** Bill short, slightly curved, blackish with pale yellow (or orange-brown) base to lower mandible; eyes black; legs long (especially tibia), yellowish-brown or greenish-yellow. **SV** Flight call: soft, low, disyllabic purring *prrrp* and *chirrup*, recalls Curlew Sandpiper.

Least Sandpiper *Calidris minutilla*

L 13–15 cm; WS 32–34 cm; WT 17–33 g

SD Accidental. **HH** Freshwater/brackish wetlands, intertidal mudflats. **ID** Resembles Long-toed Stint (LTS), but crouches more, neck shorter, appears more compact, drabber overall. Adult summer: grey-brown, cap less rufous than LTS, pale supercilia usually join on forehead and contrast with broader, darker lores; breast streaked black on grey, upperparts and tertials narrowly fringed rufous, though these wear off in summer. Adult winter: grey with dark centres to grey-fringed scapulars less clearly marked than LTS. Juvenile: warm rufous above with narrow white V on scapulars (like Little Stint), with rufous-brown fringes to scapulars, tertials and wing-coverts. Closed wing as LTS. In flight, wings shorter and darker than other stints, white wingbar more prominent than LTS; toes do not extend beyond tail. **BP** Very fine black bill is short, straight or droop-tipped; eyes black; legs yellow or yellow-ochre (shorter than LTS), and toes short. **SV** Soft purring *prreet*, short series of shriller rising *kureee* or *brreeep* notes on take-off, thinner and higher-pitched than LTS. **TN** Not included by OSJ.

Little Stint
juv
ad sum
ad win
ad sum
Red-necked Stint
ad win
juv
ad sum
Long-toed Stint
ad win
ad sum
juv
juv
ad win
Least Sandpiper
ad sum
ad win

White-rumped Sandpiper *Calidris fuscicollis* L 15–18 cm; WS 36–38 cm; WT 30–60 g

SD Vagrant, C & N Honshu, Hokkaido. **HH** Coastal wetlands, wet fields. **ID** Long-bodied, slender, long-winged sandpiper with distinctive narrow white rump; appears slightly smaller, longer and lower than Dunlin. Adult: finely streaked head, neck, chest and flanks; crown and ear-coverts tinged rufous; mantle has rufous fringes, scapulars and wing-coverts dark-centred with broad grey-brown fringes. Non-breeding adult: grey with dark centres to grey-fringed scapulars; obvious white supercilia. Juvenile: brightly patterned with prominent supercilia, dark loral bar, and bright mantle and scapulars fringed rufous and white, forming prominent V. Closed wing is long, primaries project beyond tail, whilst tertials fall short of tail tip. In flight shows prominent white wingbar; entire rump white, contrasting with dark grey tail. **BP** Bill short, straight or droop-tipped, black with brown base to lower mandible; eyes black; short tarsi black. **SV** Flight call: thin, shrill insect-like or somewhat snipe-like *jeeeet* or *tzreet*, and shorter, clearer *tit* in rapid bat-like series.

Baird's Sandpiper *Calidris bairdii* L 14–19 cm; WS 36–46 cm; WT 32–46 g

SD Accidental migrant, Hokkaido to Nansei Shoto. **HH** Marshes, sandy beaches, mudflats, generally preferring open short grass and drier, upper shores. **ID** Very long-winged, long-bodied and short-legged sandpiper. Body has odd 'flattened oval' shape when viewed from head or rear. Adult: duller than other sandpipers, rather plain greyish-buff on head, neck and breast, upperparts similar, but silvery-grey with large black centres to pale scapulars. Non-breeding adult: grey-brown, warmer than White-rumped Sandpiper (WRS), with broader, more diffuse dark centres to scapulars/coverts. Juvenile: most brightly patterned plumage, with buffy breast-band and pale scaly pattern to mantle, scapulars/wing-coverts, rather than neater, more restricted white V of WRS. At rest, primaries extend well beyond tail, tertials fall well short of tip, accentuating elongated appearance. In flight, shows only weak white wingbar; rump dark brown with pale sides offering no contrast with dark brown tail. **BP** All-black bill finer at base and straighter than WRS; eyes black; short tarsi black. **SV** Purring trill, *kyrrp* or *krreep*, recalls Curlew Sandpiper, but softer. In alarm gives *veet-veet-veet* call.

Pectoral Sandpiper *Calidris melanotos* L 19–23 cm; WS 37–45 cm; WT ♂ 45–126 g, ♀ 31–97 g

SD A rare to scarce migrant (primarily Aug–Oct, occasionally spring) throughout Japan. **HH** Freshwater and coastal wetlands, wet ricefields, grassy marshes. **ID** Large sandpiper (♂ larger than ♀) with distinctive upright stance, resembling small Ruff. Adult: closely resembles Sharp-tailed Sandpiper; has warm rufous fringes to black-centred upperparts; cap, neck and breast streaked black on buff; however, breast streaks end abruptly and form clear division from otherwise white underparts, and form point in centre of chest. White supercilia weaker than in Sharp-tailed. Non-breeding adult: greyer, but retains clear demarcation between streaked chest and white belly. Juvenile: like warmly coloured adult with narrower rufous fringes to upperparts and prominent narrow white V on mantle. Primaries of closed wing reach tail tip. In flight, narrow white wingbar, rump and tail blackish with white rump-sides recalling Ruff, but less distinctive. **BP** Slightly decurved bill is dark at tip, grey or yellowish-brown at base; eyes black; legs longish, yellow or greenish-yellow. **SV** On take-off, rich, liquid trilling *kureep; prrit, kirrp* or *churrk* recalls Curlew Sandpiper but is deeper.

Sharp-tailed Sandpiper *Calidris acuminata* L 17–22 cm; WS 36–43 cm; WT ♂ 53–114 g, ♀ 39–105 g

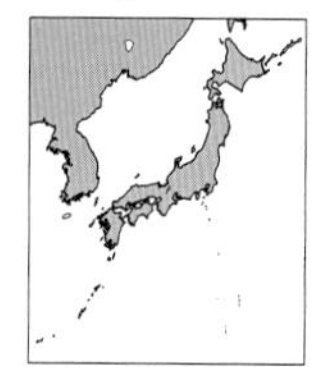

SD Fairly common migrant throughout Japan (mostly Apr/May, Aug–Oct). **HH** Intertidal mudflats, freshwater wetlands, including ricefields. **ID** Large sandpiper, recalling (but larger than) Long-toed Stint. Adult: streaked rufous cap, more prominent face pattern than Pectoral Sandpiper (PS), with pale supercilia that flare behind eyes (unlike PS), narrow white eye-ring; neck and breast boldly spotted and streaked black on buff wash (lacks clear demarcation on underparts of PS), streaks extend as bold crescents/arrowheads on flanks to vent, and generally brighter rufous than PS. Non-breeding adult: greyer, but retains clear rufous cap. Juvenile: less boldly streaked than adult, the streaks forming a necklace, below which there is a warm orange-buff wash to the breast, and narrower rufous-fringed upperparts. Closed wing shows no primary projection. In flight, pattern recalls PS and Ruff. **BP** Slightly curved bill is black, brown or pink at base of lower mandible; eyes black; legs longish, yellowish to green. **SV** A muffled, trilled *trrr*; in flight or when flushed a soft trilled *trrrp* or *purii*, and various low grunting noises, also a subdued, repetitive *ueep-ueep*.

White-rumped Sandpiper
ad win
ad win
ad sum
Baird's Sandpiper
ad win
juv
ad sum
ad win
Pectoral Sandpiper
juv
juv
ad ♂ sum
Sharp-tailed Sandpiper
ad win
juv
ad sum
ad win

Curlew Sandpiper *Calidris ferruginea* L 18–23 cm; WS 38–41 cm; WT 44–117 g

SD Uncommon or scarce migrant (mostly Apr/May, Aug–Oct) throughout coastal Japan. **HH** Muddy coastal wetlands, wet ricefields. **ID** Slender sandpiper, more elegantly proportioned than Dunlin, appearing longer-necked and more upright, with longish, curved bill. Adult: rusty-red head, neck and underparts, white undertail; patterned on back and wings with black, white and orange-brown. Non-breeding adult: rather plain grey with prominent pale supercilia, lightly streaked grey on head and neck, and white underparts. Juvenile: warmer, browner than non-breeding, with pale-scalloped fringes to mantle, scapulars and wing-coverts, unstreaked buff head, neck and breast, and narrow white supercilia. Closed wing long, primaries extending beyond tail and tertials almost to tail tip. In flight resembles Dunlin, but has distinctive white rump. **BP** Long curved bill black; eyes black; legs longish (toes extend beyond tail in flight, not in Dunlin), black. **SV** Flight call a distinctive soft purring *prrrp*, *prrriit* or *chirrup*, quite different from Dunlin's rasping call. **TN Cox's Sandpiper** *'C. paramelanotos'*, a rare hybrid of Curlew and Pectoral Sandpipers with intermediate characters of both, has been recorded several times in Japan.

Rock Sandpiper *Calidris ptilocnemis* L 20–23 cm; WS 43 cm; WT 80–132 g

SD *C. p. quarta*, rare winter visitor (Dec–Apr) mostly along Pacific coast of Hokkaido, N & C Honshu. **HH** Forages exclusively on rocky shores in splash zone. **ID** Dumpy, dark grey sandpiper. Adult: recalls Dunlin, with extensive pale rufous fringes to mantle and scapulars; head pale, greyish, throat pale, upper breast streaked; bold black belly patch extends from lower breast to legs (in Dunlin extends between legs). Non-breeding adult: dark grey on head, neck and breast, upperparts grey-fringed with dark brown shafts and centres. Juvenile: chestnut- and buff-fringed scapulars. Closed wing falls short of tail tip. In flight, mostly white underwing and conspicuous white wingbar. **BP** Bill short, black but yellow at base, drooping at tip; eyes black; legs short, ochre to green. **SV** Flight call a husky *cherk*.

Stilt Sandpiper *Calidris himantopus* L 18–23 cm; WS 43–47 cm; WT 40–68 g

SD Accidental (Jul–Sep) to Hokkaido, C Honshu, N Kyushu and Ogasawara Is. **HH** Freshwater wetlands; wades deeply, leaning well forward, probing mud rapidly with 'sewing machine' action recalling dowitchers. **ID** Elegant, long-billed and long-legged sandpiper, resembling large, slender Wood Sandpiper or small, slender dowitcher, but longer-legged. Adult is dark, heavily blotched black on mantle and wing-coverts, heavily streaked on head, neck and upper breast, and heavily barred on underparts; crown and cheeks rusty-orange, separated by prominent white supercilia. Non-breeding adult is paler and plainer grey above than winter dowitchers, retaining prominent supercilia. Juvenile has scaly brown upperparts and lightly streaked head and neck. Closed wings reach just beyond tail, tertials almost to tail tip. In flight, underwing largely grey with white centre; upperwing dark to pale greyish-brown; rump white, tail grey with long tarsi trailing obviously. **BP** Bill long, black, rather heavy and droops slightly towards swollen tip, resembling Curlew Sandpiper in shape; eyes black; long tarsi greenish-yellow. **SV** Usually silent, but in flight a rattling *kirrr* recalling Curlew Sandpiper, clearer whistled *feu* and husky *toof*, a wheezy *keewf* and clearer *kooowi*. **TN** Formerly *Micropalama himantopus*.

Dunlin *Calidris alpina* L 16–22 cm; WS 33–40 cm; WT 33–88 g

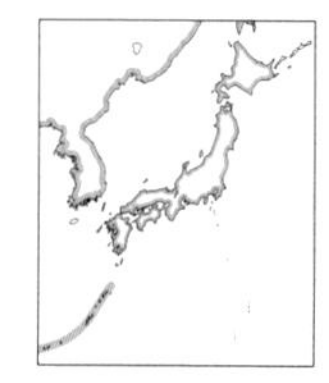

SD *C. a. sakhalina* is fairly common migrant throughout Japan, with small numbers wintering (Aug–May) from Hokkaido to Nansei Shoto. *C. a. arcticola* is rare migrant and winter visitor to Honshu. **HH** Beaches, coastal wetlands with muddy margins and inland freshwater wetlands, including wet ricefields. **ID** Stocky, somewhat large-headed sandpiper with long, droop-tipped bill. Adult: grey head and neck, with fine dark streaks; upperparts extensively dark rufous, underparts dominated by long black belly patch from lower breast back between legs (see Rock Sandpiper); vent and undertail-coverts white. Non-breeding adult: plain brownish-grey above, white below, resembling Curlew Sandpiper, but has shorter legs and wings. Juvenile: buffer than winter adult, with faintly streaked underparts, blackish mantle and scapulars with buff fringes. At rest, closed wings reach almost to tail tip. In flight, shows mostly white underwings and conspicuous white wingbars, rump has white sides but black centre. **BP** Bill black, but shorter, thicker and less curved than most Curlew Sandpipers; eyes black; legs medium to short, black or blackish-green. **SV** In flight and when flushed, commonly gives buzzing, whistled *skeeel* or slurred *screet*. In aggression or threat, a hoarse *gwrr-drr-drr-drr*.

Curlew Sandpiper
juv
juv
ad sum
ad win
Rock Sandpiper
ad win
juv
ad sum
Stilt Sandpiper
ad sum
juv
ad win
Dunlin
juv
ad sum
sakhalina
ad win
juv
ad sum
arcticola

Spoon-billed Sandpiper *Calidris pygmea* L 14–16 cm; WT 28–48 g

SD Endangered. Extremely rare migrant from Hokkaido to Nansei Shoto. **HH** Coastal lagoons, estuaries and tidal mudflats. Favours wet sand/mud, on beaches remains nearer waves, foraging in wet substrate in unique way with short jabbing action, back and forth and to sides. **ID** Small sandpiper with unique bill, though distinctive tip not always visible, especially in profile. Adult: brick red to orange head and neck, black feathers of upperparts fringed bright rufous. Non-breeding adult: plain grey above, white below, with rather prominent supercilia. Juvenile: brown-fringed back and wing-coverts, pale supercilia and very dark ear-coverts forming prominent patch. In flight, underwing largely white, upperwing dark with slight white wingbar, rump and tail mostly black with white sides. **BP** Short, black bill has spatulate tip; eyes black; legs medium to short, black. **SV** In flight gives a soft *puree*, *preep* or shrill *wheet*.

Broad-billed Sandpiper *Calidris falcinellus* L 16–18 cm; WS 34–37 cm; WT 28–68 g

SD *C. f. sibirica* is a very scarce or rare migrant from Nansei Shoto to Hokkaido. **HH** Beaches, ricefields and mudflats. Forages sluggishly, recalling snipe. **ID** Resembles large Long-toed Stint in breeding plumage, but small Dunlin in winter, with distinctive bill; often has conspicuous black carpal patch like Sanderling. Pale supercilia is double, splitting in front of eye. Adult: stint-like with heavily streaked cap, lightly streaked neck, upper breast and mantle, black scapulars, coverts and tertials broadly fringed orange-brown; breast streaks extend to sides, rest of underparts white. Non-breeding adult: plain grey above, the grey extending to upper chest, mantle feathers have dark centres, coverts white-fringed with black centres. Juvenile: like adult, with warm brown tones and warm buff/brown wash to lightly streaked breast. Closed wings reach just beyond tail, tertials almost to tail tip. In flight, underwing largely white, upperwing pale grey with slight white wingbar, central rump and tail mostly black with white rump-sides. **BP** Bill longish, straight, flattened slightly dorso-ventrally, but angles abruptly downwards at tip; eyes black; legs medium to short, greenish-grey. **SV** Dry trilling *ch-r-r-reep* or *tirr-tirr-terek* recalls Sand Martin.

Buff-breasted Sandpiper *Calidris subruficollis* L 16–21 cm; WS 43–47 cm; WT ♂ 53–117 g, ♀ 46–81 g

SD Accidental; recorded from Hokkaido south to Nansei Shoto, Ogasawara and Iwo Is. **HH** Prefers drier habitats (sandy beaches, short, dry grasslands, meadows, golf courses and airfields) than most shorebirds. **ID** Elegant, rather erect sandpiper with small rounded head and short bill. Adult: very plain orange-buff face, neck and underparts; crown darker, mantle and wing-coverts appear scaly (dark feather centres and pale buff/white fringes). Juvenile: less pronounced buff wash to underparts, browner upperparts. Closed wings long; tail long but primaries reach beyond tip, tertials almost to tail tip. In flight, upperwings plain brown, underwings largely white, with distinctive black crescent on primary-coverts; rump and long tail brown; tarsi hidden. **BP** Bill short, black; eyes prominent, black; legs long, yellow-ochre. **SV** Occasionally gives low, dry rattling flight call, *krrrt* or *pr-r-r-reet*, recalling Pectoral Sandpiper, and dry *chup* and *chitik* calls.

Ruff *Calidris pugnax* ♂ L 26–32 cm, WS 54–60 cm, WT 130–254 g; ♀ L 20–26 cm, WS 46–52 cm, WT 70–170 g

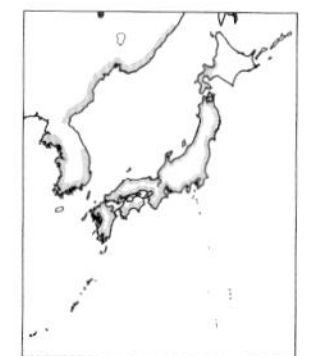

SD Uncommon migrant throughout Japan. **HH** Coastal and freshwater wetlands and wet grasslands. **ID** Large, long-legged shorebird, with long neck, small head and short bill, typically rather erect, but back hunched. Adults: sexually dimorphic in size and breeding plumage. ♂ (typically 20% larger than ♀) sports long, erectile ear-tufts and huge neck-ruff, individually variable from white to black, but may be orange, rusty or brown. Upperparts orange to black, with white fringes. Much smaller ♀ dark brown; noticeably scaled on upperparts; dark-centred mantle, scapulars and coverts have pale brown fringes, and tertials boldly barred. Non-breeding ♂ quickly loses ruff and resembles ♀. In winter, both sexes paler than summer ♀; upperparts retain scaly appearance, but feather centres greyer brown. Juvenile shares scaly upperparts with summer ♀, but has warm buff wash to head, neck and chest. Closed wings long; long tertials may completely cover primaries and tail tip. In flight, shows large white oval spots on sides of brown tail; underwing mostly white; upperwing dull brown with narrow white wingbar; toes extend beyond tail. **BP** Bill short, slightly curved, brown, pink or yellow, with yellow base (varying individually and with age and season); eyes black; legs long, yellow or green to orange-brown. **SV** Occasionally gives low croaking calls; single or double *kyuu*; *chuck-chuck* or *krit-krit* and shriller *hoo-ee* flight call.

Spoon-billed Sandpiper
ad win
ad sum
ad win
ad sum
juv
Broad-billed Sandpiper
juv
juv
ad win
ad sum
Buff-breasted Sandpiper
ad
juv
juv
juv
lekking males
Ruff
ad ♀ sum
ad ♂ sum
ad ♀ sum
ad ♂ win
juv ♀

Short-billed Dowitcher *Limnodromus griseus* L 25–29 cm; WS 45–51 cm; WT 65–154 g

SD Accidental (*L. g. hendersoni*) to Honshu and Shikoku. **HH** Coastal wetlands. **ID** Large, dark snipe- or godwit-like shorebird (very similar to Long-billed Dowitcher, from which best separated by flight call). Averages smaller and slimmer, with longer wings, shorter legs and bill than Long-billed, but considerable overlap in measurements. Eye located slightly higher on face and, combined with supercilia shape and bill structure, affords slightly different facial expression from Long-billed. Adult in breeding plumage differs from Long-billed in having pale/white belly, dense dark spots on neck and barred flanks. Upperparts dark; scapulars have pale fringes. Non-breeding adult is less plain than Long-billed, with arched supercilia, fine dark streaking on face, spotting on breast and paler grey flanks. Upperparts show more contrast between frostier pale grey and darker feather centres. Juv/1st-winter like juvenile Long-billed, but warmer orange wash on breast and brighter upperparts, also rufous fringes to, and bars across, dark tertials (Long-billed lacks bars). In flight, whitish secondary panel, dark tail and white wedge from rump onto lower back recall Spotted Redshank; axillaries and underwing-coverts darker than Long-billed; feet project just beyond tail. **BP** Bill long, thicker than snipe, shorter than Long-billed, with slightly drooping outer third (important distinction from Long-billed), blackish with slightly swollen tip; eyes black; tarsi toes greenish-yellow. **SV** Distinctive flight call a low, slurred, double or triple series of rattling notes: *kew chu-chu* or *too-dulu*.

Long-billed Dowitcher *Limnodromus scolopaceus* L 24–30 cm; WS 46–52 cm; WT 90–135 g

SD Rare migrant and winter visitor (Oct–Apr) from Hokkaido to Nansei Shoto. **HH** Favours muddy freshwater or brackish wetlands, occasionally on coastal mudflats. **ID** Large, stocky, dark snipe- or godwit-like shorebird (see Short-billed Dowitcher for structural and other differences). Adult in breeding plumage is largely rufous-brown, including belly. Dark barring on breast-sides/flanks; scapulars dark rufous with white tips. Non-breeding adult is pale grey, with clear division between grey breast and flanks and white belly; pale straight supercilia prominent; mantle/scapulars/coverts have dark shaft-streaks. Juvenile resembles non-breeding adult, but has warm buff wash to grey breast, rufous fringes to dark scapulars/coverts, and rusty-fringed grey tertials. Non-breeding Long-billed and Short-billed almost impossible to separate using plumage alone (but tertials of juv/1st-winter dark-centred with neat pale fringes; see Short-billed); calls always distinctive. Winter dowitchers in Japan all presumed to be this species. In flight, whitish secondary panel, dark tail and white wedge from rump onto lower back; feet project just beyond tail. **BP** Bill long, straight, thicker than snipes', longer than Short-billed, blackish from base to swollen tip; eyes black; tarsi greenish-yellow. **SV** Flight call a single high, sharp *keek* or sharp series, varying in length, of repeated chattering *keek-keek-keek* or *kyik-kyik-kyik-kyik*.

Asian Dowitcher *Limnodromus semipalmatus* L 33–36 cm; WS 59 cm; WT 127–245 g

SD Very rare migrant (Apr–May; Aug–Oct) throughout Japan from Nansei Shoto to Hokkaido. **HH** Grassy marshes, ricefields and coastal mudflats. Feeds with distinctive rocking and rapid vertical probing action. **ID** The largest dowitcher, close to Bar-tailed Godwit in size. From smaller Long-billed and Short-billed by dark back (no white rump) and black legs; from godwits by bill size and shape. Adult in breeding plumage is largely rufous-brown, face plain rufous, lacking pale supercilia of other dowitchers or godwits, but has dark loral stripe with small white spot at base of lower mandible. Upperparts dark brown, all feathers with narrow to broad warm rufous margins. Non-breeding adult is pale grey-brown, the upperparts with pale fringes to most feathers, underparts lightly barred, face very pale with dark lores and pale supercilia. Juvenile recalls non-breeding adult, but has warmer browner tones, buff fringes to upperparts and buff wash to breast, and bill extensively pinkish at base. In flight, wingtips rather black, inner primaries and secondaries paler, and has pale trailing edge to flight-feathers; pale, unmarked underwing (other dowitchers dark); rump and tail grey with dark bars (see Bar-tailed Godwit). Long legs trail beyond tail. **BP** All-black bill, long, straight and thicker than godwits, with broad base and prominent snipe-like swollen tip; eyes black; long tarsi blackish-grey. **SV** A plaintive yelping *tye chu* or *chep chep*, and soft *kru-ru kru-ru*.

Short-billed Dowitcher
ad win
juv
ad sum
Long-billed Dowitcher
ad win
juv
ad sum
ad win
Asian Dowitcher
ad win
juv
ad sum
ad win

Eurasian Woodcock *Scolopax rusticola*

L 28–35 cm; WS 56–60 cm; WT 200–446 g

SD Widespread summer visitor (May–Aug) Hokkaido, N & C Honshu. Winters (Nov–Apr) C Honshu south, including Nansei Shoto. **HH** Damp deciduous, mixed forest; winters at lower altitudes/latitudes near streams, in damp woodland, dry grasslands, sugarcane fields. **ID** Rotund, long-billed, short-legged 'shorebird'. Larger than snipe, with broader, more rounded wings. Forehead grey, crown and nape have broad dark brown and pale greyish-buff transverse bars. Upperparts warm brown, coverts, scapulars and particularly tertials with blackish-grey oval pale-centred spots and warm cinnamon-brown bands; underparts narrowly barred dark brown. In flight, squat and heavy; flight slow, straight on deeply bowed wings, head held high. Twilight roding display flight around margins of territory is very slow, with bill pointing down. **BP** Bill long, straight, deep-based, pinkish-grey with dark tip; eye very large, with split white eye-ring, irides black; short tarsi pinkish-grey. **SV** On take-off gives abrupt *chiki chiki chiki*. During display flight gives series of soft grunting *buu buu, buu buu* calls followed by louder, sibilant *tswissick*.

Amami Woodcock *Scolopax mira*

L 33–38 cm; WT 400–500 g

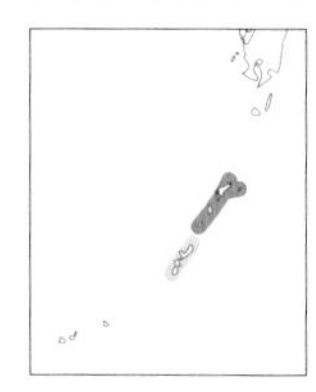

SD Vulnerable. Endemic, breeding only Amami-Oshima to Tokunoshima; some winter south to N Okinawa. **HH** Damp subtropical evergreen broadleaf hill forest; highly terrestrial. **ID** Resembles Eurasian Woodcock (EW), but upperparts darker, greyer brown, oval spots darker, lacking pale centres, with much narrower brown bands; distinctive triangular orange-brown patches separate dark spots at leading edge of flight-feathers, noticeable on closed wing. Displays on ground and, in March, during roding flight in 0.5–1 km circles over territory. If disturbed most likely to run, but may fly up and land on slopes or trees. Flight typically slow on deeply bowed wings, but can be fast and direct. **BP** Bill and tarsi as EW; distinctive pink and white crescents above and below eye, and diagnostic bare pink skin immediately behind it. **SV** On take-off gives sharp *je je* or *vett vet-vett*, snipe-like *jheet* and louder, duck-like *ghett!* in spring, as well as high *puu* or low *vuu* flight calls; when roding gives a low, burping *wart wart wart* similar to EW, interspersed with the loud *ghett!* call. On ground, strong *gu* and softer *ku* calls given during display.

Jack Snipe *Lymnocryptes minimus*

L 17–20 cm; WS 38–42 cm; WT 28–106 g

SD Rare or accidental migrant and winter visitor (Sep–Jan) throughout Japan, Hokkaido to Nansei Shoto. **HH** Solitary; dense wet vegetation, marshes, fields. Extremely skulking, only flushes at very close range. **ID** Small, dark, with rather short bill. Crown dark (lacks pale central crown-stripe of other snipe), bordered by broad, pale, split supercilia. Cheeks pale, with dark crescent below eye. Upperparts dark brown with distinct metallic purple-green gloss on mantle; two pale yellow-brown mantle-stripes. Juvenile has white undertail-coverts. In flight, very dark wings more rounded at tip than in other snipe, with narrow white trailing edge to secondaries, dark rump and black wedge-shaped tail (lacks white and rufous bands of most snipe), underwing-coverts and belly white; flight weak and slow, feet do not extend beyond tail tip. Bobs head while feeding; freezes until nearly trodden on. When flushed flies less erratically than other snipe then drops very quickly. **BP** Bill short, straight (c.1.5 times head length), deep-based, dark grey-brown with pale, pinkish-brown culmen; eyes black; legs short, greenish-yellow. **SV** Typically silent, but may give single soft *gah*, in series *gah gah gag gag*, or *gatch* when flushed.

Solitary Snipe *Gallinago solitaria*

L 29–31 cm; WS 51–56 cm; WT 127–245 g

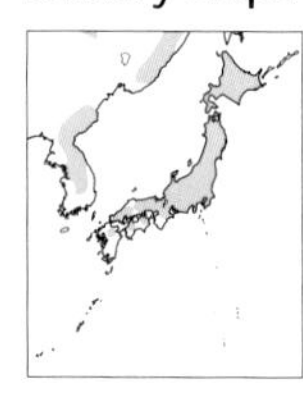

SD *G. s. japonica* uncommon to scarce winter visitor (mid-Oct–late Apr), Hokkaido, N & C Honshu, but may appear as far south as Nansei Shoto. **HH** Solitary. Winters even in snowy regions where wooded streams, springs or small marshes are ice-free; rarely in muddy ricefields. Bobs or rocks body steadily while feeding. **ID** Large, very dark; cold, milky blackish-brown or greyish-brown, with heavily barred underparts. Face appears whiter and back stripes broader and whiter than other snipe. Primaries/tertials extend almost to tail tip; feet do not project beyond tail in flight. Flies heavily and more slowly than smaller snipe, dropping at streamside; appears very dark and lacks white trailing edge to secondaries, with small white belly patch and much rufous in graduated or wedge-shaped tail. **BP** Bill very long, straight, black at tip becoming grey at base; eyes black; tarsi greenish-yellow. **SV** Harsh, Common Snipe-like *pench, kensh* or *jeht* when flushed.

Eurasian Woodcock
ad
ad
Amami Woodcock
ad
ad
ad
ad
Jack Snipe
ad
Solitary Snipe
ad

Latham's Snipe *Gallinago hardwickii*

L 23–33 cm; WS 48–54 cm; WT 95–277 g

SD Summer visitor (Apr–Sep) Hokkaido, C & SW Honshu, Kyushu. Scarce migrant elsewhere. **HH** Summer: wet meadows, grasslands with scrub, woodland edge, from sea level to 1,400 m. Perches prominently on treetops, posts or poles. Dry grasslands and rice stubble on migration. **ID** Larger, paler than Swinhoe's Snipe. Face pale, supercilia broad between eyes and bill. Mantle brown with broad buff fringes to scapulars; wing-coverts largely buff. Tail (visible only when fanned): warm orange-toned (Swinhoe's cooler grey), central feathers pale orange-buff to tip, narrow grey subterminal band; outer feathers grey-brown with narrow grey and white bars (Swinhoe's plain dark grey with white tips). Tail extends beyond wing tips; primaries entirely obscured by tertials. Longer-tailed than other snipe. Flies slowly, more directly, than other snipe; feet project beyond tail. Underwing dark; upperwing has prominent pale tawny panel; no white trailing edge to secondaries. **BP** Black-tipped bill has brownish base; eyes black; tarsi greenish. **SV** Call abrupt deep *geh geh* or *jek jek*. Territorial display flight spectacular (May–Jun only; climbs high before rushing dives and upward swoops), gives dramatic *tsupiyaku tsupiyaku tsupiyaku* calls followed by thrumming *gwo gwo gwo gwo-o-o* from stiff outertail feathers. **AN** Japanese Snipe.

Pin-tailed Snipe *Gallinago stenura*

L 25–27 cm; WS 44–47 cm; WT 84–170 g

SD Uncommon migrant; some winter Nansei Shoto. **HH** Wide range of wetland types. **ID** Smaller than Common Snipe (CS), narrow-chested, slightly larger head relative to body, shorter bill and tail, more pointed wings. Paler, cooler, greyer than CS and Swinhoe's; extensive white fringes to upperparts recall Solitary. Eyestripe narrows to bill base, where narrower than supercilia. Broad pale buff outer, and narrow inner, fringes (inner half width of outer) to rounded scapulars with bright, rufous centres. Underparts: flanks heavily barred, belly white. Outer four tail feathers very narrow. Wings more rounded than CS, tips fall short of tail tip, tertials mostly cover primaries. Flushes fast, but flight slower, less erratic than CS; feet prominent beyond tail tip. Very narrow white trailing edge to secondaries barely visible at close range. Underwing dark, lacking central white bar. **BP** Bill colour as others, but deep-based and relatively short, tapering evenly to tip (CS's is parallel-sided); eyes black; legs greenish-yellow. **SV** Calls similar to CS, but less urgent and rasping, though seldom in sequence; rarely gives high-pitched abrupt *jik*.

Swinhoe's Snipe *Gallinago megala*

L 27–29 cm; WS 47–50 cm; WT 82–164 g

SD Scarce migrant; may winter Nansei Shoto. **HH** As previous species. **ID** Very like Common (CS) and Pin-tailed (PTS), but larger, heavier; differs from Latham's in coloration. Buff-brown; saddle, wing-coverts, breast lack striking markings. Unlike Latham's, lacks contrast between dark saddle and pale coverts panel. Dark eyestripe extremely narrow at bill base, supercilia very broad. Crown peak behind, not in front of, eye (cf. PTS). Narrow outer tail feathers, intermediate between PTS and CS. Wings and tail short (much white on corners), primaries occasionally extend beyond tertials, but fall short of tail tip. Reddish-orange tail patch noticeable feature. Flushes heavily, slowly, flight less erratic than CS/PTS; feet protrude less than PTS. No white trailing edge to secondaries; underwing dark. **BP** Bill colour as others; eyes black; legs thicker and yellower-olive than PTS. **SV** Rises silently, rarely calling more than once, rasping, sneeze-like *jeht* or *chert*, higher pitched than CS; and repeated abrupt *skretch skretch*.

Common Snipe *Gallinago gallinago*

L 25–27 cm; WS 44–47 cm; WT 72–181 g

SD *G. g. gallinago* common migrant; winters (Oct–Apr) Honshu to Nansei Shoto. **HH** Wide range of wetlands, stream/river/lake margins, wet grasslands. **ID** Eyestripe broader near bill base, where wider than supercilia. Upperparts: broad pale buff outer fringes to rather pointed scapulars, inner fringes darker than Pin-tailed's. Underparts: flanks heavily barred, belly white. Wings short, tertials mostly cover primaries; primaries fall short of tail tip. Flushes abruptly, climbs with frequent, erratic zigzags, may drop quickly to cover. Dark underwing has white bars along covert tips; secondaries have broad white tips. **BP** Bill colour as others; eyes black; legs greenish-yellow. **SV** Calls harshly, rasping *jaak* or *j'yak*, *jeht-jeht* or *ca-atch*, often in rapid sequence.

Latham's Snipe
ad
ad
Pin-tailed Snipe
ad
ad
Swinhoe's Snipe
ad
ad
Common Snipe
ad
ad

Wilson's Phalarope *Phalaropus tricolor* L 22–24 cm; WS 35–43 cm; WT ♂ 30–110 g, ♀ 52–128 g

SD Accidental, C Honshu. **HH** Coasts, estuaries; swims less than other phalaropes, wades with characteristic crouching gait. **ID** Longer-necked, longer-legged and longer-billed than smaller phalaropes; more like *Tringa*. ♀: upperparts grey and chestnut with black band from lores and eyes on neck-sides; white eyebrow, chin, throat and underparts, with orange wash on sides of neck/breast. ♂: duller, showing less contrast and less distinct pattern on upperparts. Non-breeding adult: pale grey head, neck and upperparts, with white supercilia, throat and underparts. Juvenile: blackish-brown above, upperparts fringed rufous-brown, face and underparts white. At rest appears longer-tailed and longer-winged than other phalaropes. In flight, white rump contrasts with dark grey wings (no wingbar), mantle and mid-grey tail; underwing white. **BP** Bill needle-like, black; eyes black; legs longish, black (breeding) or pale yellow (non-breeding, juv). **SV** Occasionally gives short, sharp *chew* or *puu*, and muffled nasal grunts in flight.

Red-necked Phalarope *Phalaropus lobatus* L 16–20 cm; WS 30–38 cm; WT 20–48 g

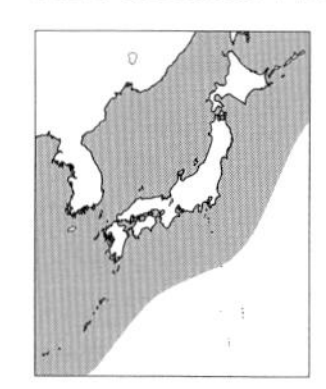

SD Common migrant off all coasts (Apr–Jun, Aug–Sep). **HH** Pelagic, sometimes abundant offshore during spring migration, also in bays, coastal wetlands, occasionally freshwater wetlands, wet fields. **ID** Small, delicate, elegant; often confiding. ♀: brightly coloured, with dark grey head and upperparts, orange-brown bands on mantle and scapulars, and bright red band on neck-side and upper breast; chin, throat and eyebrow white. Lower breast and flanks grey, grading into white on belly and vent. ♂: dull, less contrasting grey and red on head and neck, less bright on upperparts. Non-breeding adult: pale grey above (darker than Red Phalarope), white below, with blackish crown and black eye-patch reaching ear-coverts. Juvenile: back pattern like breeding ♂, but face pattern like non-breeding; more extensive grey on breast-sides. On water floats high, appears long-necked with small head; primaries reach tail-tip. In flight, black flight-feathers with narrow white wingbar, black rump and tail, with narrow white rump-sides. **BP** Bill fine, needle-like, black; eyes black; legs black, toes distinctly lobed. **SV** Gives chirping *kip*, *chep* or longer *kerrek* flight calls.

Red Phalarope *Phalaropus fulicarius* L 20–22 cm; WS 37–43 cm; WT 37–55 g

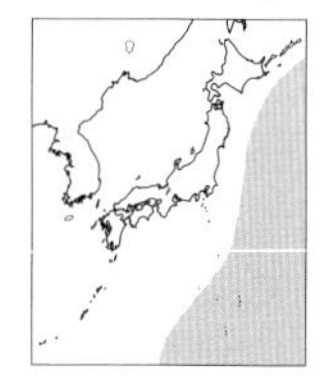

SD Uncommon migrant (rarely in winter), mostly along Pacific coast, Honshu to Nansei Shoto. **HH** Pelagic; occasionally in bays or offshore, coastal wetlands. **ID** Slightly larger and thicker-necked than Red-necked Phalarope (RNP). ♀: black cap and face, white cheeks, and deep rufous neck and underparts. Upperparts black with broad orange-rufous fringes to scapulars, wing-coverts and tertials. ♂: less cleanly marked, rufous of underparts more broken with white. Non-breeding adult: pale grey above, white below, with blackish crown and black eye patch extending to ear-coverts. Juvenile: back pattern like breeding ♂, with some grey scapulars, and face pattern like non-breeding, but more extensive dusky-grey on breast-sides; lacks mantle and scapular stripes of RNP. On water floats high; primaries reach tail tip. Slower, less erratic flight than RNP; black flight-feathers with narrow white wingbar, and grey rump and tail; in non-breeding plumage, very pale mantle contrasts with dark wings. **BP** Bill short, thicker than RNP, yellow with black tip (breeding), or black with pale yellow base; eyes black; short legs grey, toes distinctly lobed. **SV** Rather explosive, metallic *pik* or *wit* in flight or when flushed, higher-pitched and clearer than RNP. **AN** Grey Phalarope.

Oriental Pratincole *Glareola maldivarum* L 23–24 cm; WS 59–64 cm; WT 59–95 g

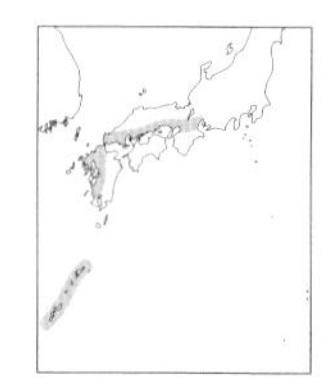

SD Uncommon summer visitor (May–Sep), breeding Honshu, Shikoku, Kyushu and Nansei Shoto. Migrant elsewhere, rarely overshoots beyond breeding range, accidental north to Hokkaido. **HH** Wetlands, grasslands; breeds colonially, flocks on migration. Agile aerial feeder, but also runs after terrestrial insects. **ID** Medium-sized, slim and tern-like. Lores and line bordering throat black; chin and throat warm buff, bordered at rear with white, then black. Flight-feathers and tail glossy black. Vent and undertail white, undertail-feathers with black tips. Young more uniform brown above and below, with narrow pale fringes affording scaly appearance. At rest, wings extend 2–3 cm beyond tail tip. Flight fast and agile, swallow-like, with long, narrow, dark wings (no white trailing edge), prominent white rump, short, shallow-forked black tail. Underwing-coverts rufous, contrasting with greyer underside to secondaries and darker primaries. Appears long-legged on ground, but toes barely reach tail-tip in flight. **BP** Bill short, black, red at base (ad) or all black (juv); eyes dark brown; legs grey. **SV** Harsh, sharp and shrill *kuriri* and staccato *shtick*; grating *tar-rak* or *kr-d-d-ik* calls are given only in flight.

Wilson's Phalarope
ad ♂ sum
juv
1st-win
ad ♀ sum
ad win
Red-necked Phalarope
ad ♀ sum
juv
ad win
juv
ad ♀ sum
ad win
Red Phalarope
ad ♀ sum
ad ♂ sum
ad win
juv
ad ♀ sum

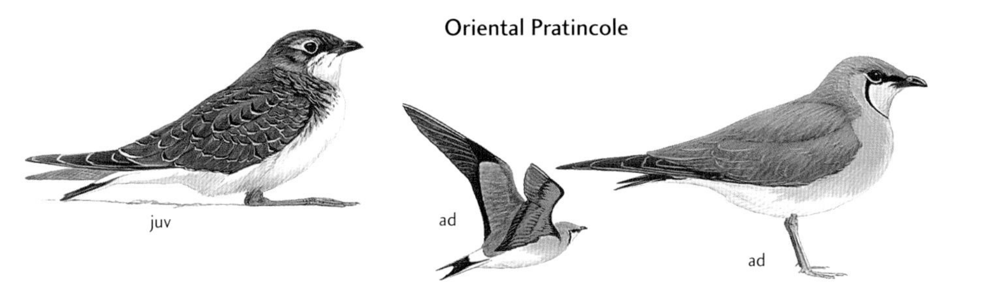
Oriental Pratincole
juv
ad
ad

Brown Noddy *Anous stolidus*

L 38–45 cm; WS 75–86 cm; WT 150–272 g

SD *A. s. pileatus* breeds as far north as Iwo and Ogasawara Is and S Nansei Shoto (Apr–Sep). Scarce further north in Nansei Shoto and a storm-blown accidental along Pacific coast north to Hokkaido. **HH** On and around isolated islets, where favours rocky crags with shady ledges. Dips to water surface to take food (does not plunge-dive like other terns). **ID** Large, elegant, dark, long-tailed tern. Adult is rather uniform sooty-brown, except forehead to nape, which is whitish or very pale grey on forehead becoming pale grey on rear crown; face blackish-brown with narrow white crescents above and below eye (less prominent at long range than Black Noddy). Juvenile resembles adult, but has sooty-brown crown. At rest, although wings are long and slender, tail is particularly long and extends beyond wingtips. Flight strong, on slightly arched wings with lazy 'rowing' action (somewhat gull-like); paler brown upperwing-coverts form noticeable panel and contrast with darker flight-feathers. Appears rather long-bodied in flight. Tail is somewhat broad and long, parallel-sided with notched tip, but when closed may appear pointed. **BP** Long slender bill is black; eyes black; tarsi dark brownish-black. **SV** At colonies makes odd buzzing and grunting noises, a rattled, growling *kwuwaa* or *garrrh*, a hoarse *gee-aaa*, and a rising croaking *brraak*. In courtship flight gives low *nek nek nek nek nek nekrrr*, and *geo geo* calls. Elsewhere rather quiet. **AN** Common Noddy.

Black Noddy *Anous minutus*

L 35–39 cm; WS 66–72 cm; WT 98–144 g

SD *A. m. marcusi* is a vagrant mainly to Iwo, Ogasawara and Nansei Shoto Is (Jul–Aug; perhaps formerly bred on Iwo Is). **HH** Oceanic islands, occasionally at Brown Noddy colonies; very rarely on coasts. **ID** Adult is smaller and blacker than Brown Noddy with much whiter forehead and crown, becoming grey on rear crown. Black face with prominent white crescent below eye. Juvenile resembles adult, but has clean white cap. At rest, wings reach or extend just beyond tail tip. Flight resembles Brown, but upper- and underwing all dark, and action more buoyant, with faster, shallower wingbeats than Brown. Tail somewhat broad, greyish, parallel-sided with notched tip, but when closed may appear pointed. **BP** Black bill is longer (longer than head), thinner and straighter than Brown; eyes black; tarsi dark brownish-black. **SV** Similar to Brown, but sharper and higher pitched, also a grating *keraa*, and *kuri kuri kuri* notes. **TN** Formerly considered race of Lesser Noddy *A. tenuirostris*. **AN** White-capped Noddy.

Blue Noddy *Anous ceruleus*

L 25–28 cm; WS 46–61 cm; WT 41–69 g

SD *A. c. saxatilis* has reached Minami-Torishima and Kita-iwo-jima, and could conceivably occur elsewhere following late summer and autumn typhoons. **HH** On and around remote oceanic islands, where forages by pattering at sea surface like storm-petrel. **ID** Small and pale. Adult is pale grey with whitish head, very pale blue-grey mantle and whitish-grey underparts; upperwing (including coverts and flight-feathers) is pale grey with darker trailing edge, underwing is almost white with darker trailing edge; tail has very shallow fork. Juvenile has mid-brownish-grey wash to upperparts. **BP** Black bill is fine and sharply pointed; black eyes rather prominent in pale face; tarsi and toes black with yellow webs. **SV** Sometimes gives a loud squealing call.

White Tern *Gygis alba*

L 25–33 cm; WS 76–80 cm; WT 92–139 g

SD *G. a. candida* is accidental to Nansei Shoto, Iwo and Ogasawara Is, and Pacific coast of main islands north to Hokkaido, though most records are old (pre-1950s). Could conceivably appear almost anywhere along Pacific coast following typhoons. **HH** On and around vegetated coral atolls. **ID** Adult is small, elegant, and all white with large dark eyes particularly prominent on plain face, and sharply pointed bill that appears slightly angled upwards. Juvenile has buff or pale-brown barring on mantle and spotting on crown, rump and upperwing-coverts. **BP** Bill largely black, but basally dull blue-grey; large eyes black; short tarsi blue-grey. **SV** Calls include guttural *juku juku juku*, *heech heech*, and a descending nasal chatter. **AN** Fairy Tern.

Brown Noddy
juv
ad
ad
ad
Black Noddy
ad
juv
Blue Noddy
ad
ad
juv
White Tern
ad
ad
juv

Black-legged Kittiwake *Rissa tridactyla*

L 37–43 cm; WS 91–105 cm; WT 305–512 g

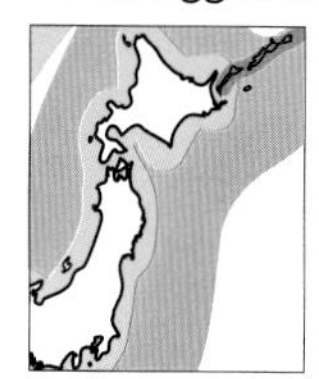

SD **Pacific Kittiwake** *R. t. pollicaris* migrates off Pacific and Sea of Japan coasts and is common off N Japan, especially Hokkaido in winter (mainly Nov–Mar), but has reached as far south as Izu Is and Nansei Shoto. **HH** Essentially pelagic, though also occurs along coasts and occasionally in harbours, especially after storms. **ID** Distinctive, clean-looking, medium-sized gull, with black-tipped wings and shallow-forked tail. Juvenile and 1st-winter have grey upperparts, dark outer primaries and prominent black carpal bar forming prominent dark M on upperwing; the shallow-notched tail has a narrow black terminal band; also a blackish smudge behind eye and black band on nape. At rest, sits partly upright with body at 45°; appears round-headed, primaries extend just beyond tail; adult is pale; 1st-winter is rather dark on closed wings. Flight light and buoyant on rather narrow wings. **BP** Bill short, pale yellow; eyes black; legs short, black (ad), rarely yellowish, orange-red or greyish (juv); legs usually, but not always, visible in flight. **SV** Occasionally gives strident, high-pitched, nasal *kittee-wayek* calls, even away from colonies.

Red-legged Kittiwake *Rissa brevirostris*

L 35–40 cm; WS 84–90 cm; WT 340–450 g

SD Vulnerable. Accidental to Pacific coast of Hokkaido and Honshu (mostly Jan–May, but also Aug and Nov). **HH** Essentially pelagic, but has occurred at river mouths or in harbours with other gulls. **ID** Superficially similar to Black-legged Kittiwake (BLK), but adult is slightly smaller, with larger, more rounded head, steeper forehead, larger and more prominent eyes. Mantle and wings are darker grey than BLK, white trailing edge is much broader and underside of primaries much darker grey. In winter, has dusky patch around eye and on ear-coverts. Juvenile and 1st-winter are like BLK, but nuchal bar is dark grey, not black, as are ear-coverts and eye smudges; white trailing edge of wings is even broader, recalling Sabine's Gull. Stance as BLK, but primaries extend well beyond tail. In flight, differs from BLK in its stronger, 'rowing' action; the darker upperwing (and darker underside to primaries) and broader, white trailing edge are distinctive; tarsi often not visible in flight. **BP** Bill shorter, more arched than BLK, yellow (ad) or black (juv); eyes black; legs very short, reddish (juv) or bright red (ad). Leg colour alone unreliable (see juvenile BLK). **SV** Similar to BLK, but also a much higher-pitched squealing *suweeer* call.

Ivory Gull *Pagophila eburnea*

L 40–47 cm; WS 94–120 cm; WT 520–700 g

SD Accidental in winter (Dec–Apr) to Hokkaido and N & C Honshu. **HH** Pelagic; rarely visits coasts or harbours; attracted to cetacean and seal carcasses. **ID** Unique stocky gull, with large rounded head, short neck, similar in size to Common Gull, with pigeon-like proportions. Adult: all white. Juvenile and 1st-winter: essentially white, but have dusky, blackish face and black spots on mantle, wing-coverts, flanks, primary and tail tips. At rest, primaries extend beyond tail. Flight buoyant and dove-like on rather broad wings. **BP** Bill short, greenish-grey or bluish-grey with yellow tip (ad), or grey with black tip (juv); eyes black, very prominent; very short tarsi black. **SV** Grating, tern-like calls *kyuui* or *kree-kree*, or harsher, recalling Black-headed Gull, and high, mewing whistle *wheeew* or *preeo*.

Sabine's Gull *Xema sabini*

L 30–36 cm; WS 80–91 cm; WT 135–225 g

SD Accidental to N & C Honshu. **HH** Pelagic; rarely along coasts. **ID** Small, elegant with forked tail and tricoloured upperwing. Adult has dark-grey hood, bordered at lower edge with black; mantle and wing-coverts are mid- to dark grey. Non-breeding adult has partial grey hood. At rest, adult has black primaries with white tips, extending well beyond tail. Juvenile appears scalloped, with dark greyish-brown nape, breast-sides, back and wing-coverts, all with black subterminal margins; tail white with narrow black terminal band. 1st-winter has paler wings, but retains prominent brown carpal patch, primary tips lack white, with adult winter-like head pattern. 1st-summer develops white primary tips and poorly defined grey hood. In flight, adult's grey mantle and wing-coverts contrast strongly with white secondaries and inner primaries, and black outer primaries; uppertail-coverts/tail all white, tail shallowly forked; juvenile and 1st-winter have browner grey mantle and wing-coverts, and narrow black tail-band. **BP** Bill short, black with yellow tip (ad), or all black (juv); eyes black; legs black, dull pink in juv/1st-winter. **SV** Occasionally gives harsh, grating, tern-like *kyeer* or *krrrree* calls.

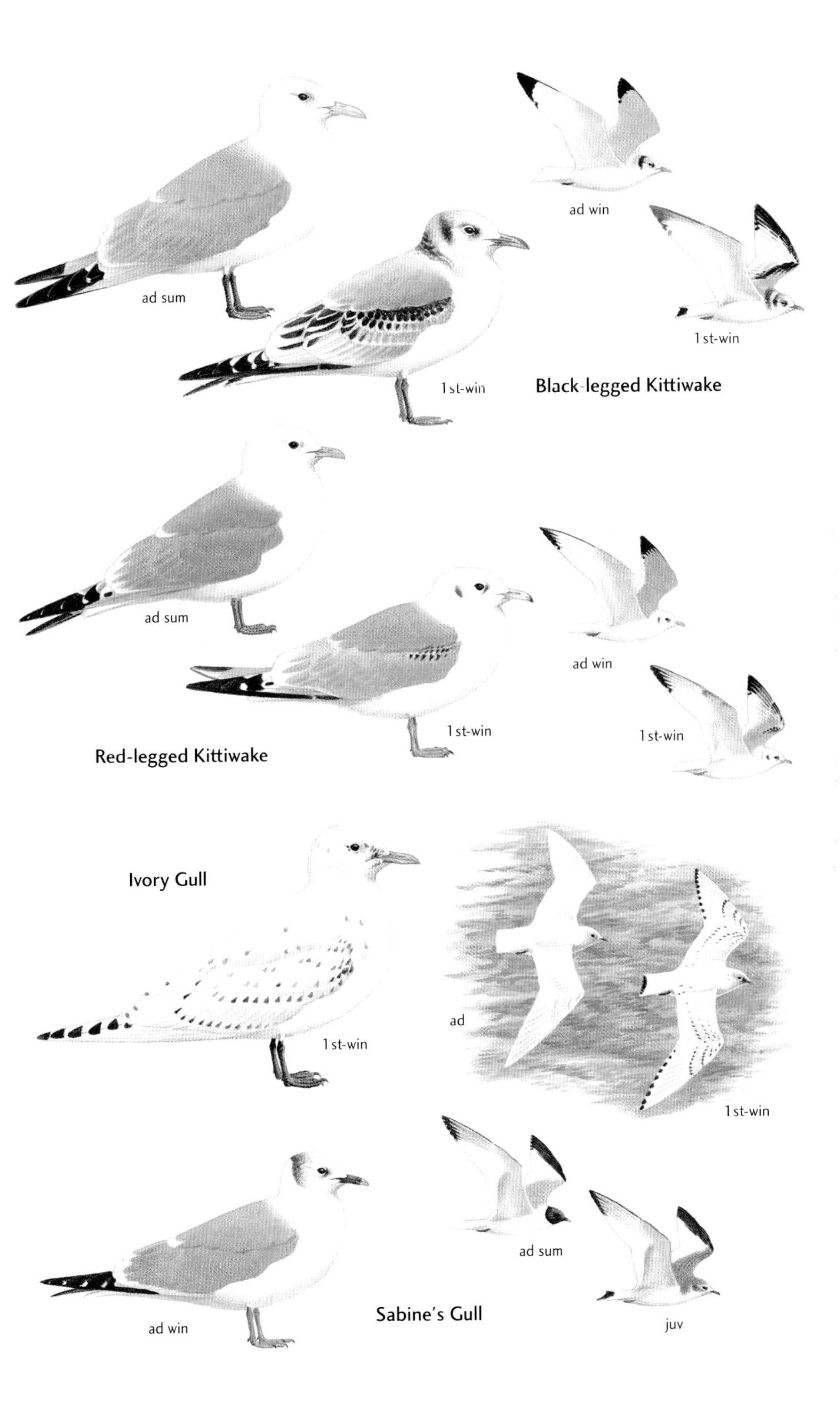
ad win
ad sum
1st-win
1st-win
Black-legged Kittiwake
ad sum
ad win
1st-win
1st-win
Red-legged Kittiwake
Ivory Gull
ad
1st-win
1st-win
ad sum
ad win
Sabine's Gull
juv

Slender-billed Gull *Chroicocephalus genei* L 42–44 cm; WS 102–110 cm; WT 220–350 g

SD Accidental to Kyushu. **HH** Estuaries and coastal lagoons. **ID** Elegant, marginally larger than Black-headed Gull (BHG), but longer-headed, longer-necked, longer-billed and lacks hood. Adult: white with grey upperparts and wings; underparts and even primaries may be suffused salmon-pink. Winter adult has faint grey spot on ear-coverts. Juvenile has dusky-brown wing-coverts and flight-feathers, but is more weakly patterned than equivalent-age BHG, and has slightly more prominent ear-coverts patch than adult. Flight graceful; upperwing plain grey with black-tipped primaries, and white leading edge (outer four primaries); young similar to BHG, but less heavily marked; also has white outer primaries in 1st-winter, and narrow black tail-band. **BP** Bill rather long, slender, blackish-red (breeding), red (non-breeding) or straw-yellow (1st-year); eyes white or yellowish-white (breeding), or pale brown (other plumages); legs somewhat longer than BHG, dull red (ad) or pale orange (juv). **SV** Similar to BHG, but calls include a lower and drier *aaaa*, excited *ka-ka-ka*, drawn-out *kraaah…* and nasal *krerrr-krerrr.* **TN** Species on this plate formerly placed in *Larus*.

Bonaparte's Gull *Chroicocephalus philadelphia* L 28–34 cm; WS 81–100 cm; WT 170–230 g

SD Accidental (Dec–May) to Hokkaido, C & W Honshu. **HH** Estuaries. **ID** Small, tern-like gull, superficially similar to larger Black-headed Gull (BHG). Adult has black hood and narrow white crescents above and below eye. Mantle and wings pale to mid-grey, wingtips at rest appear all-black and extend well beyond tail. Winter adult has dark ear-coverts spot and two faint grey bars on white crown. Juvenile resembles juvenile BHG, but has black ear-coverts spot and more pronounced, narrow, blacker M on upperwings. Wings narrow, flight light and graceful; upperwing like BHG, but underwing much paler, with almost white primaries, except for narrow black tips forming trailing edge. Tail white (ad), or with narrow black terminal band (juv). **BP** Bill fine, black; eyes black; tarsi dull pink. **SV** A more rasping or grating, rather tern-like *gerrr reeek* or *tee-er* than BHG.

Brown-headed Gull *Chroicocephalus brunnicephalus* L 41–45 cm; WT 450–714 g

SD Vagrant to C Honshu. **HH** Coasts, with tidal mudflats. **ID** Adult has dark chocolate-brown hood extending to rear crown, though paler on face, with prominent broken white eye-ring like Black-headed Gull (BHG). Non-breeding adult lacks hood, but has dark brown spot behind eye. Wings slightly broader with rather more rounded 'hand' than BHG, and flight not as light. 'Arm' and inner primaries pale grey. Primary-coverts and bases to outer primaries white, otherwise black with 2–3 mirrors. Underside of primaries largely black with mirrors, and underwing-coverts duskier grey than BHG. 1st-winter suggests BHG at rest, but undersides of folded primaries lack white. Differs in flight in that outer primaries and primary-coverts are black, while bases of inner primaries are white, almost reverse of BHG. **BP** Bill long, somewhat thicker than BHG, dark blood-red (breeding) or orange-red with black tip (non-breeding); orbital ring red; irides distinctly pale, yellowish, white or grey (ad), or dark (juv/1st-winter); legs dull orange-red, paler orange in winter/juv. **SV** Guttural *krreeah-kreeah*, a harsh *gek-gek* and wailing *ka-yek ka-yek*.

Black-headed Gull *Chroicocephalus ridibundus* L 37–43 cm; WS 94–110 cm; WT 210–385 g

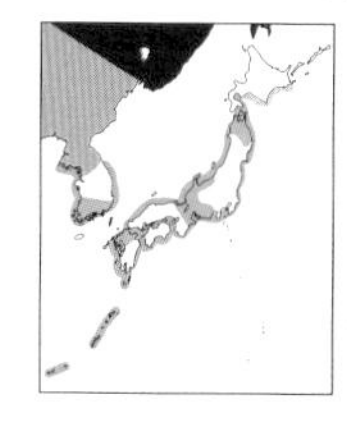

SD Common, even abundant migrant (Apr–May, Aug–Sep) from Nansei Shoto to Hokkaido. Winters fairly commonly around C & S Japan (Oct–Apr); occasionally occurs in Hokkaido in summer. **HH** Coasts, including bays, harbours and lagoons, also rivers and lakes. **ID** Small grey-and-white gull with pale-grey mantle and wings, dark chocolate-brown hood and distinctive white leading edge to primaries in flight, with only narrow black wingtip. Non-breeding adult lacks hood, but has blackish spot behind eye, and grey-smudged crown. Juvenile and 1st-winter resemble winter adult, but have brown tertials and wing-coverts, with grey midwing panel, black wingtips and narrow black terminal tail-band. In flight, wings narrow, somewhat tern-like, with pointed tip; mostly pale grey, but outer primaries white, forming broad white leading edge, though all outer primaries have small black tips; underwing has largely black primaries, with only outermost 1–2 white; tail white. **BP** Bill long, slender, dark blood-red, blackish-red (breeding) or orange-red with black tip (non-breeding); eyes black/brown; legs dull red, paler in winter, orange in juv/1st-winter. **SV** Call is typically a long, strident *kyaar* or *krreearr*, with shorter, sharper *kek* notes.

breeding
breeding
Slender-billed Gull
1st-win
ad sum
1st-win
ad win
Bonaparte's Gull
1st-win
breeding
non-breeding
Brown-headed Gull
non-breeding
breeding
non-breeding
1st-win
Black-headed Gull

Saunders's Gull *Chroicocephalus saundersi* L 29–33 cm; WS 87–91 cm; WT 200–215 g

SD Vulnerable. Scarce winter visitor (Nov–Mar) to SW Japan (particularly Kyushu), rare C Honshu; accidental north to Hokkaido. **HH** Mudflats, estuaries, river mouths, wet fields and ponds close to coast. Flight graceful; recalls marsh terns. Feeding style distinctive: drops suddenly from low level, quartering flight to snatch prey from ground, or settles briefly to feed before continuing to quarter. **ID** Like small Black-headed Gull (BHG), but more elegant. Adult has black hood, broad white crescents surrounding all but front of eye, and pale mantle and upperwing. Non-breeding adult has dusky-grey bar on crown, often eye to eye, and dark grey or blackish spot on ear-coverts. Juvenile has dark brown on head where adult is blackish, with brown wing-coverts, tertials and dark brown primary tips; tail pure white in adult, but has narrow black terminal band in juvenile. At rest, unlike BHG, black primaries show series of prominent white tips. Mantle and upperwing uniform pale grey, primaries have small black tips, and white outer primaries form white leading edge; in contrast, underwing shows black wedge formed by black bases to primaries; juvenile in flight shows black carpal spot, especially when seen head-on. Prominent white trailing edge often useful in separation from BHG. **BP** Bill short, thick, black; eyes brown/black; legs dull red (ad) or dull orange (juv/1st-winter). **SV** High-pitched, tern-like *teek-eek* or *kyi-kyi*. **TN** Formerly within genus *Larus* (e.g. OSJ), but also considered within monotypic *Saundersilarus*.

Little Gull *Hydrocoloeus minutus* L 24–30 cm; WS 62–69 cm; WT 88–162 g

SD Accidental; recorded from Hokkaido and Honshu, to Izu Is and Nansei Shoto. **HH** Coasts, bays and river mouths. **ID** Small, compact and elegant, with unique dark grey underwing. Adult has more extensive black (not brown) hood than Black-headed Gull (BHG), extending to nape; mantle/wings pale grey. Non-breeding adult has black on rear crown and spot on ear-coverts. Juvenile is dark, with blackish wing-coverts and flight-feathers and grey innerwing-panel, forming kittiwake-like dark M on upperwing. Mantle dark brown/black, moulting to grey in 1st-winter; tail white with narrow black terminal band. 1st-winter has paler wing but retains prominent black carpal bar and primary tips, and has adult winter-like head pattern. 1st-summer has poorly defined black hood, dark carpal bar and wingtips, but thereafter wings become steadily paler. At rest, primary tips rounded (though young have more pointed primaries), and protrude only just beyond tail. In flight, which is buoyant, wings slightly broader, shorter and more rounded than BHG. Wings (ad) pale grey and uniform with mantle, but underwing dark sooty grey, almost black, with narrow white margin formed by white tips to flight-feathers. **BP** Bill very short, fine, black or reddish-black; eyes black; short tarsi bright red (ad) or pale pink (juv/1st-winter). **SV** Commonly, a rather hard, nasal, tern-like *keck*, often run together in rapid series *kek-kek-kek*.... **TN** Formerly within genus *Larus* (e.g. OSJ).

Ross's Gull *Rhodostethia rosea* L 29–34 cm; WS 82–92 cm; WT 120–250 g

SD Accidental, usually singly, in winter to Hokkaido and N & C Honshu; however, flocks have occurred in NE Hokkaido (Dec–Feb). **HH** Visits coasts, river mouths and harbours. **ID** Small, very distinctive, with peaked head, long, narrow wings, wedge-shaped tail and unique plumage. Recalls Little Gull, but wings longer and more pointed, tail longer, also pointed. Adult has distinctive narrow black necklace (broadest on nape), rosy-pink flush to head and underparts, and diamond-shaped tail. In winter necklace lost, but has small blackish ear-coverts spot. Juvenile has brownish cap and nape, and dark-centred, buff-fringed scapulars; juvenile and 1st-winter have grey upperparts, but dark primaries and carpal bar, forming prominent dark M on upperwing, and clear secondaries (Little Gull typically has grey bar); long, diamond-shaped tail also has dark tip, and there is a dark smudge around eye and over ear-coverts, which may extend onto crown, nape and neck-sides. At rest, appears small-headed and elongated, somewhat tern-like, with primaries extending well beyond tail; adult extremely pale; 1st-winter has essentially black wings with white midwing panel. Flight buoyant and tern-like, upperwing grey with broad white trailing edge, and underwing darker grey, contrasting with paler belly, head and vent. **BP** Bill delicate, black; eyes black; legs red in adult, dull flesh-pink in young. **SV** Generally silent, but occasionally gives *kuwa kuwa* calls in flight.

ad sum
ad win
ad sum
1st-win
1st-win
Saunders's Gull
breeding
juv
non-breeding
breeding
Little Gull
ad sum
ad win
1st-win
1st-win
Ross's Gull

Laughing Gull *Leucophaeus atricilla* L 36–42 cm; WS 98–110 cm; WT 240–400 g

SD Accidental (subspecies uncertain), N & C Honshu, Iwo I. **HH** Beaches, harbours. **ID** Marginally larger than Black-headed Gull, but longer-winged, with smaller white primary tips, and longer bill has more drooping tip. Resembles Franklin's Gull, but eye-ring narrower and broken behind eye. Non-breeding adult: less hooded than Franklin's, with limited grey streaks or patches on rear crown. Upperparts uniformly dark grey, wingtips largely black, lacking mirrors (see Franklin's), underwing dusky-grey, black on primaries, unlike Franklin's. **BP** Bill relatively long, thick, dull red with drooping tip; eyes black; legs dull red. **SV** A disyllabic, nasal, laughing *kiiwa*, *kahwi* or *kee-agh*, and repetitive series of *ha ha hah* notes. **TN** All gulls on plate 83 were formerly in *Larus* (e.g. OSJ).

Franklin's Gull *Leucophaeus pipixcan* L 32–38 cm; WS 85–95 cm; WT 220–335 g

SD Accidental, N & C Honshu, S Nansei Shoto. **HH** Beaches, harbours. **ID** Dark-mantled gull, slightly smaller than Black-headed Gull (BHG). Adult: black hood with broad white crescents above and below eye joining at rear. Non-breeding adult: retains hood on rear crown and cheeks. At rest, primary extension long, with prominent white tips (see Laughing Gull). Wings slightly broader, shorter and blunter than BHG, dark grey, concolorous with back. Outer primaries subterminally black with white band separating black from basal grey. In flight, pale inner-primary window with white tips extends trailing edge from secondaries. White tail has black band, broadest in centre. Underwing and breast clean white. **BP** Bill short and thicker than BHG, bright red (breeding) or black (non-breeding); eyes brown/black; legs bright red (breeding), dull blackish-red (non-breeding). **SV** Calls include hollow laughing *kowii*, *queel*, and soft *krruk* or *kaa*, or shrill *guk*.

Relict Gull *Ichthyaetus relictus* L 39–45 cm; WT 540–700 g

SD Winter vagrant, C & W Honshu, N Kyushu. **HH** Mudflats, estuaries. **ID** Adult: white with pale to mid-grey mantle and wings, white tertial crescent and black primaries with white tips. Hood blackish-brown with white eye crescents, broad behind eye. Adult winter: lacks hood, has dusky-grey ear-coverts patch, some dark streaking on nape and sometimes on crown. In flight, black in outer primaries very variable, bases fade to white distally, with two conspicuous mirrors; upperwing resembles Franklin's Gull, but pale innerwing far less contrasting, some can appear surprisingly white-winged. Underwing almost entirely grey/white except small black primary tips. In flight, inner primaries and greater coverts grey, forming pale centre to wing, bordered above by dark brown carpal bar and below by prominent black subterminal spots on secondaries and inner primaries; primary-coverts and primaries black, forming bold wedge on leading edge. Can show one small mirror on outermost primary. Tail has narrow black subterminal band. Gait on ground almost plover-like. **BP** Bill dark red, relatively short with deep gonys, can be paler-based with dark tip in winter; eyes brown/black; legs dull, dark pink or red. **SV** Laughing *ka-kak ka-ka kee-a*, downturned *kyeu* and prolonged *ke-arr*.

Pallas's Gull *Ichthyaetus ichthyaetus* L 57–72 cm; WS 146–170 cm; WT 1100–2000 g

SD Accidental, C & W Honshu, Kyushu, Okinawa; several wintered almost annually (Oct–Apr) for many years in W Kyushu. **HH** Estuaries, mudflats. **ID** Very large four-year gull. Structure eye-catching: crown peak at rear, combining with long bill gives long-headed appearance, tertials bulky, long primary projection and long legs. Adult: full black hood, reduced in winter when may only be dusky around face and cheeks, but never entirely absent; white crescents above and below dark eye. Has mid-grey mantle and wings averaging paler than Vega, with white tertial crescent and conspicuous apical spots on primaries. In flight, front-heavy look due to large head and long, thick bill. Wings narrower than other large gulls, 'arm', inner primaries and primary-coverts mid- to pale grey, outer primaries and coverts white, creating broad wedge like Brown-headed, but with less black. Underwing white. **BP** Bill long, thick, yellow at base, red at tip (supposedly only when breeding, but commonly also in winter), with variable black band forward of gonys; eyes black; legs greenish-yellow. **SV** Generally silent; occasionally gives long deep, nasal crow-like *aaa*, *aagh* or *kra-ah* flight call. **AN** Great Black-headed Gull.

Descriptions of immature medium and large hooded gulls can be found in Appendix I (p 402)

ad sum
ad win
1st win
ad sum
1st-win
Laughing Gull
ad sum
ad win
1st-win
ad sum
1st-win
Franklin's Gull
breeding
1st-win
1st-win
non-breeding
Relict Gull
ad win
Pallas's Gull

Black-tailed Gull *Larus crassirostris* L 44–48 cm; WS 126–128 cm; WT 436–680 g

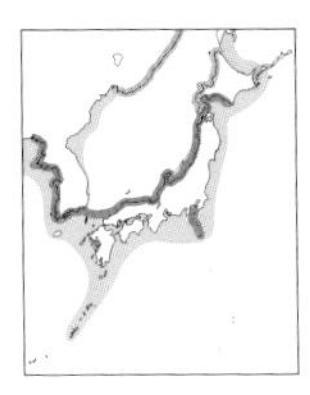

SD Commonest gull breeding around coasts and offshore islands from Hokkaido to Kyushu; winter visitor south to Nansei Shoto and Ogasawara Is. **HH** Breeds on rocky islets, coasts and cliffs; winters along coasts and at estuaries and harbours, rarely inland. **ID** Medium-sized, long, narrow-winged gull, with broad black tail-band. White head appears relatively flat-crowned, further accentuating long bill. Adult in breeding plumage is white and grey, with mid- to dark grey mantle and little contrast between mantle and primaries, white tertial crescent, black primaries with small white tips, and white tail with broad black subterminal band. White underparts may show pink flush in breeders. Winter adult is similar, but often dusky-grey on nape/rear crown, creating somewhat hooded appearance. In flight, has all-black wingtips, white trailing edge to dark-grey wings, and white outer tail-feathers and broad black subterminal band. Flight graceful relative to other larger gulls. **BP** Bill long, yellow, with black subterminal band and red tip; eyes yellow; legs greenish-yellow. **SV** Strong, though plaintive, nasal cat-like mewing: *aao* or *myaao*. Rather higher-pitched than larger gulls.

Common Gull *Larus canus* L 40–46 cm; WS 110–125 cm; WT 394–593 g

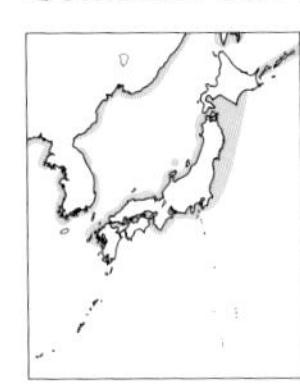

SD *L.* (*c.*) *kamtschatschensis* (**Kamchatka Gull**) winters (Oct–Apr) commonly around Japanese coasts from Hokkaido to Kyushu, rare south to Nansei Shoto and Ogasawara Is. *L. c. heinei* has also occurred in Hokkaido and C Honshu. **HH** Coasts, harbours, sometimes lakes and rivers. **ID** Resembles small, delicate Vega Gull, but has rounded head, plain face and rather gentle appearance. Adult in breeding plumage has mantle and wings mid-grey; prominent white tertial crescent separates grey of wings from black primaries. Head, neck, underparts and tail white, but in winter crown, ear-coverts, nape and neck-sides narrowly streaked or more broadly flecked brown; head streaking can be heavy. In flight, adult appears very white and grey, with prominent white mirrors in outermost black primaries. Flight more buoyant than larger gulls. **BP** Rather delicate bill varies from greenish- to bright yellow, lacks red spot of similar Vega Gull, generally paler in winter; subterminal markings range from complete black ring to plain, with dark smudge in winter adult; eyes dull yellow to brown/black, sometimes pale yellow; legs greenish to yellow. **SV** Generally a nasal mewing *kya kya kyaa* or *gyu gyu*, a longer *glieeoo*, and in alarm *gleeu-gleeu-gleeu*. **AN** North America: Mew Gull.

Mew Gull *Larus (canus) brachyrhynchus* L 40–46 cm; WS 110–125 cm; WT 394–586 g

SD Accidental to C Honshu. **ID** Separation difficult, but adult differs from Kamchatka Gull in having paler grey upperparts, different wing pattern, smaller size, shorter legs, 'gentler' appearance with larger eye and much shorter bill. In flight, less black in primaries, with prominent white 'tongues' separating black from grey feather bases extending to p8 or even p9, recalling Slaty-backed Gull's 'string of pearls'.

Ring-billed Gull *Larus delawarensis* L 41–49 cm; WS 112–127 cm; WT 400–590 g

SD Accidental. **HH** Coasts, estuaries and rivers. **ID** Slightly larger and bulkier than Common Gull, with paler grey upperparts and heavier, distinctively patterned bill. Adult has pale blue-grey mantle, scapulars and wing-coverts, black primaries with two white mirrors and small white tips. Adult in breeding plumage has white head, non-breeding has light brown flecking on crown, rear and sides of neck. In flight, wings somewhat narrower, more pointed than Vega. Adult has pale-grey inner primaries (paler than mantle), contrasting with black wingtips with small white mirrors above and below; tail white. **BP** Bill rather thick, yellow with broad black ring near tip; eyes pale yellow with red orbital ring, may be blackish in winter; tarsi yellow. **SV** Higher pitched, more nasal, than Vega Gull; also a soft *kowk*. **TN** Not included by OSJ.

Descriptions of immature medium and large gulls can be found in Appendix I (p 402)

ad sum
ad win
1st-win
1st-win
Black-tailed Gull
ad sum
ad win
1st-win
1st-win
Common Gull
ad sum
ad win
1st-win
1st-win
Mew Gull
ad sum
ad win
1st-win
Ring-billed Gull

California Gull *Larus californicus*

L 51–58 cm; WS 122–140 cm; WT 432–1045 g

SD Accidental; either *L. c. albertaensis* or *L. c. californicus*. **HH** Coasts, estuaries and tidal mudflats. **ID** Intermediate in size between Common and Vega Gulls. Slightly more rounded head than Vega, but has a relatively longer bill, and also rather long, narrow wings. Adult has mid-grey mantle and wings, white head, prominent white tertial crescent, with black in six outermost white-tipped primaries, the outer two with large white mirrors. Non-breeding adult has variable amount of dusky streaking around eye and on hindneck. In flight, appears very white and grey, with large black wingtips on both surfaces, clean-cut black broken only by prominent white mirrors in outermost black primaries. **BP** Bill appears quite long, yellow, with red gape line (spring/early summer), red gonys and, in winter, black subterminal band and white tip; black usually restricted to small area on gonys and tip yellow when breeding (see Ring-billed Gull (RBG)); narrow red orbital ring around usually dark eye (irides pale yellow in RBG); legs yellow or greenish-yellow, brighter when breeding. **SV** Deeper than RBG, but harsher and higher than American Herring; a deep *gaaal*. **TN** Not included by OSJ.

Glaucous-winged Gull *Larus glaucescens*

L 61–68 cm; WS 132–137 cm; WT 900–1250 g

SD Fairly common winter visitor to Hokkaido (mainly Nov–Mar; occasionally remains into summer) and N Honshu; scarce south to Nansei Shoto. **HH** Offshore, inshore and along rocky coasts, at river mouths, occasionally beaches and especially harbours. **ID** Large, stocky, four-year gull; resembles Glaucous Gull, but primaries always grey, never wholly white. Head white, rather flat-crowned, with especially large bill. Adult has mid-grey mantle and wings, duller than other gulls; in winter crown, face and nape streaked or faintly barred brown. At rest, exhibits less contrast than most large gulls, as upperparts and primaries are similarly mid-grey, wing-coverts largely framed by white trailing edge to secondaries; tertial crescent and smaller scapular crescent less conspicuous because mid-grey wings very similar shade to grey of primaries. Like Glaucous and Slaty-backed, rather short-winged, with wing projection beyond tail short, usually only three primaries. In flight, broad-winged and heavy; shows little contrast; white trailing edge very narrow, especially compared to Slaty-backed; outer primaries grey with narrow white tips and large white mirror near tip of outermost. Underwing shows little contrast between grey flight-feathers and wing-coverts. **BP** Bill long and heavier than other large gulls, yellow with pinkish gape and oval red spot at prominent gonys; pinkish orbital ring and dark brown eyes; tarsi deep pink. **SV** *Nyaao* or *kwa kwa*.

Glaucous Gull *Larus hyperboreus*

L 64–77 cm; WS 150–165 cm; WT 1070–2267 g

SD Eurasian *L. h. pallidissimus* winters (mostly Nov–Mar) along coasts of Hokkaido (common) and N Honshu (less common), scarce visitor south to Nansei Shoto and Ogaswara Is. Nearctic *L. h. barrovianus* also quite commonly reaches coasts of N Japan. **HH** Offshore, inshore, also along sandy coasts, at river mouths and especially harbours. **ID** Large, stocky, extremely pale four-year gull, with white primaries. Head white, rather flat crown bulging slightly at forehead, neck thick with large bill. Adult's mantle and wings are paler than all other large gulls; in winter nape streaked faintly brown. At rest, tertial crescent inconspicuous because primaries also white; primary tips extend just beyond tail. In flight, broad wings, thick neck and large head give front-heavy appearance; flight-feathers tipped white, and translucent from below (dark in other large gulls). Underwing shows little contrast between pale-grey flight-feathers and wing-coverts. *L. h. pallidissimus* is large and heavily built, whereas *L. h. barrovianus* is smaller, less bulky, longer-winged and shorter-billed; however, features vary individually and between sexes, and overlap between races. *L. h. barrovianus* tends to have rounder head, slimmer bill and longer wing projection (may be mistaken for Iceland Gull, but wings not as long as Iceland and head larger, less rounded with proportionately smaller eye and larger bill). Adding to confusion, hybrids of Glaucous with Glaucous-winged and American Herring could wander to Japan. **BP** Bill long and heavy, yellow with rather small oval red spot at gonys; yellow, rarely red, orbital ring, and clear yellow iris; tarsi deep pink. **SV** Similar to Vega Gull, but louder and coarser *myaaoo* or *kuwaa*.

Descriptions of immature large white-headed gulls can be found in Appendix I (p 403)

ad win
ad sum
1st-win
1st-win
California Gull
ad sum
1st-win
ad win
3rd-win
1st-win
Glaucous-winged Gull
ad win
pallidissimus
ad sum
juv
Glaucous Gull
ad win
2nd-win
barrovianus
ad win
juv
juv

Iceland Gull *Larus glaucoides* L 52–60 cm; WS 137–150 cm; WT 557–863 g

SD *L. g. glaucoides* vagrant to C Honshu and *L. g. kumlieni* accidental to Hokkaido, Honshu and Kyushu. **HH** Coasts and harbours. **ID** Four-year gull. *L. g. glaucoides* resembles larger Glaucous Gull at all ages (*L. g. kumlieni* is very variable) and separated by head and bill proportions, and wing projection; but note *barrovianus* Glaucous has fairly long primary projection, more rounded head and fairly thick-set bill. Overall, Iceland Gull has more gentle appearance than Glaucous. Primary projection of adult *glaucoides* long, entirely white and continuous with tertial crescent; *kumlieni* has primaries darker-centred than upperparts, though extremes only lightly marked or almost black, so may resemble Thayer's at rest, but in flight dark coloration far more restricted. In flight, wings narrower than Glaucous and more narrowly pointed. In flight both have pale undersides to primaries, but *kumlieni* has contrasting dark outer webs to upper surface of outermost feathers and often has dark subterminal markings on others; *glaucoides* more uniform, lacking dark markings. **BP** Pale yellow to yellowish-brown iris with purplish-red orbital ring, *kumlieni* often darker; legs proportionately shorter than Glaucous and feet deep pink. **SV** Similar to Glaucous but higher pitched.

Thayer's Gull *Larus (glaucoides) thayeri* L 56–64 cm; WS 130–148 cm; WT 846–1152 g

SD Accidental winter visitor (Nov–Mar) to Hokkaido and Honshu. Controversial taxon variously treated as race of American Herring or Iceland gulls, with which it hybridises. **HH** Coasts and harbours. **ID** Large, pale grey-mantled (slightly darker grey than American Herring), four-year gull, with rounded head and rather small bill. Adult has pale-grey mantle and wings, very similar to Iceland, but typically slightly darker, with conspicuous tertial crescent; in winter, head, nape and neck extensively, but variably, streaked/smudged brown, as if wearing milk-coffee cowl. Underside of primary projection has limited black, though some Vega look very similar. In flight, narrower-winged than other large gulls; black in primaries largely restricted to outer webs of three outermost, with white inner webs typically continuous with mirrors in outer pair, plus limited black subterminally on 2–3 others. This results in strikingly white underwing, frequently only showing black trailing edge to outer primaries and (not always) narrow blackish leading edge. Tail-band variable but always present, though indistinct in some. Underwing of adult almost entirely pale, with only narrow black primary tips visible. **BP** Bill long (averages longer than Iceland, but shorter than other large gulls), with gently curving culmen and weak gonydeal angle, yellowish-green small red spot; very dark yellowish-brown irides (some clear yellow), and purplish-red orbital ring; tarsi deep pink. **SV** Calls resemble American Herring, but higher pitched. **TN** Formerly part of Iceland Gull.

American Herring Gull *Larus smithsonianus* L 56–64 cm; WS 135–147 cm; WT 1150 g

SD Vagrant in winter to Hokkaido, N & C Honshu. **HH** River mouths, estuaries and fishing harbours. **ID** Adult is large mid-grey gull; smaller with longer primary projection than Vega Gull, saddle paler, closer to adult Glaucous. In flight, wings longer, thinner and darker, pale-inner primary window obviously darker and less contrasting, with surrounding dark feathers. Slaty-backed can be remarkably similar, but is heavily built, large-headed and stout-billed, with much shorter wing projection; primaries often brownish with pale fringes at tips (always black in American Herring). In flight, primaries have contrasting pale inner and dark outer webs like Thayer's. Tail is black to base (or nearly so). **BP** Bill pale to deep yellow with red gonydeal spot; eyes pale yellow with orange-yellow orbital ring; tarsi mid-pink. **SV** A high, cracked *klaaw klaaw klaaw klaaw* and deeper *gyow gyow gyow gyow*. **TN** Retained within Herring Gull *L. argentatus* by OSJ.

Descriptions of immature large white-headed gulls can be found in Appendix I (p 403)

Iceland Gull
glaucoides
ad win
juv
juv
ad sum
kumlieni
ad win
juv
ad sum
Thayer's Gull
ad win
juv
ad sum
ad win
juv
ad sum
juv
American Herring Gull

Vega Gull *Larus vegae* L 55–67 cm; WS 135–150 cm; WT 688–1775 g

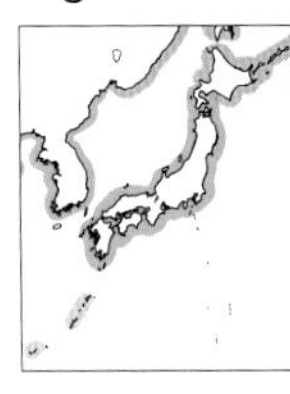

SD Common winter visitor to main Japanese islands, scarce south to Nansei Shoto. **HH** Coasts, estuaries, harbours. **ID** Large; variable, but large head and prominent bill are consistent. Mid-grey mantle and wings, prominent white tertial crescent and white tips to black primaries, outermost primaries show one large and one small white mirror. Non-breeding adult has dusky streaking on head and heavy blotching on hindneck and breast-sides. In flight, white and grey, with contrasting black wingtips and prominent white mirrors on outer two primaries, visible above and below. Underside of flight-feathers show through as pale to mid-grey. **BP** Bill deep, yellow with large red spot at prominent gonys; orange-red orbital ring, brownish-yellow irides; tarsi strong flesh pink. **SV** Rather vocal; long laughing display calls, and loud, guttural *guwaa; ao* or *gag-ag-ag* at other times. **TN** Formerly within Herring Gull *L. argentatus* complex.

Mongolian Gull *Larus mongolicus* L 55–68 cm; WS 140–155 cm; WT 1125 g

SD Uncommon or rare winter visitor (Oct–Apr) to Hokkaido and Kyushu. **HH** River mouths, estuaries, harbours. **ID** Large four-year gull, similar to Vega Gull. Neck long, tapers from broad base to head when stretched (more parallel-sided in Vega), and has high, full-chested appearance when relaxed, this combined with longer primary projection suggests a sleeker appearance. Adult: rounded head typically white, with winter streaking faint and restricted to lower hindneck. At rest, broad white tertial and scapular crescents; black primaries have 4–5 (usually four) small white spots at tips and extend just beyond tail (longer-winged than Vega). In flight, clean mid-grey and white with extensive black above and below, appearing clear-cut across wingtips with large mirror on outermost primary (p10) and smaller, sometimes inconspicuous one on p9. Underside of inner primaries and secondaries pale grey, similar to Vega. Separation of Mongolian from Caspian Gull *L. cachinnans* and 'Steppe' Gull *L.* (*c.*) *barabensis* unclear; all three perhaps recorded in Japan. **BP** Bill less heavy-looking than Vega; deep orange (spring) with large red gonys spot or yellow, often whitish at tip (non-breeder); red orbital ring; like Vega, iris yellowish, but variably flecked darker; legs pale flesh or greyish (winter), some becoming yellow (breeding). **SV** *Aa, aa* or *kwaa, kwaa*. **TN** Retained within Vega Gull (IOC), but also considered conspecific with Caspian Gull *L. cachinnans* (e.g. OSJ).

Slaty-backed Gull *Larus schistisagus* L 55–67 cm; WS 132–148 cm; WT 1050–1695 g

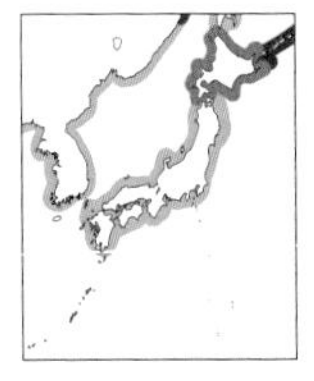

SD Breeds commonly around Hokkaido and N Honshu coasts; winters from Hokkaido to Kyushu, scarce further south. **HH** Breeds on isolated grassy islands, cliffs (locally on rooftops in Hokkaido), and is common on rocky/sandy coasts, at river mouths and harbours in winter. **ID** Very large, very dark four-year gull. Mantle and wings darker than most other gulls; at rest, broad, very conspicuous white tertial crescent, continuous with white trailing edge to secondaries, exposed below greater coverts. In flight, grey flight-feathers visible, creating contrasting underwing pattern. White trailing edge to secondaries and inner primaries broad and even. Continuing on outer primaries, a series of prominent white 'moons' on inner webs ('string of pearls') separates basal grey from subterminal black; eye-catching above and below. Outer primaries have 1–2 mirrors. **BP** Bill heavy, yellow with large oval red spot at gonys; reddish-pink orbital ring and yellow eyes; tarsi deep pink. **SV** *Kuwao* or *myaao*, but also longer series of notes *kwaau kwau kwau kwa a a a*.

Heuglin's Gull *Larus heuglini* L 51–65 cm; WS 124–150 cm; WT 550–1200 g

SD *L. h. heuglini* is accidental to Hokkaido, Honshu and Kyushu. Small numbers of *L. h. 'taimyrensis'* also migrate through W Honshu (Nov, Mar–Apr); some may winter. **HH** River mouths, estuaries and harbours. **ID** Large, well-proportioned gull with rounded head and strong bill. Looks long-winged, tail extension beyond tertials about one-third of primary projection beyond tertials. Following refers to *'taimyrensis'* which is distinctive at all ages: darker grey upperparts than Vega, but paler than Slaty-backed. Non-breeding has variable fine streaking on head and hindneck, and is often dusky around eyes. In flight, upperwing dark, outer primaries black, often with only one mirror; a second, if present, is small. Typically six, often seven feathers have black on both webs. **BP** Bill deep and parallel-edged with distinct gonydeal angle, washed-out yellow (winter), or brighter (breeding) with large oval red spot at gonys; red orbital ring and yellowish to whitish eyes, in winter variable flecked darker, thus can appear dark-eyed at distance; legs orange, becoming yellow when breeding. **SV** *Aa aa*. **TN** Retained within Lesser Black-backed Gull by IOC.

Descriptions of immature large white-headed gulls can be found in Appendix 1 (p 404)

Vega Gull
ad sum
ad win
1st-win
1st-win
2nd-win
Mongolian Gull
ad sum
ad win
1st-win
1st-win
2nd-win
1st-win
ad sum
3rd-win
Slaty-backed Gull
ad win
1st-win
ad win
taimyrensis
1st-win
Heuglin's Gull

Gull-billed Tern *Gelochelidon nilotica*

L 33–43 cm; WS 76–108 cm; WT 130–300 g

SD *G. n. affinis* is an uncommon or rare visitor mostly in SW Japan where most are post-breeding or typhoon-blown (Jul–Oct), but recorded north to N Honshu. **HH** Coasts, estuaries and rivers. **ID** Medium-sized, stocky tern with clean black cap, thick black bill and shallow-forked tail. Adult is white, with glossy black cap, grey wings and mantle, darker grey primaries with blacker bar on trailing edge. Winter adult is paler above, lacks black cap, but has black smudge through eye. Juvenile is pale brown on crown, hindneck and wing-coverts. Primaries extend well beyond tail. In flight, long-winged, buoyant with strong 'rowing' action; hovers and dives for fish, and hawks insects; upperwing plain grey, but may show dark trailing edge to primaries; underwing whitish with distinct black trailing edge to long primaries; slightly forked tail and rump concolorous with back. **BP** Bill differs from other black-capped terns in having a reddish-base (juv) or in being all-black (ad); eyes black; legs longer than other black-capped terns, black. **SV** In flight, gives nasal yapping *ga-wik*, *kay-wek* or chivvying *kewick-kewick*.

Caspian Tern *Hydroprogne caspia*

L 47–56 cm; WS 130–145 cm; WT 574–782 g

SD A scarce winter visitor (Oct–Mar) from Nansei Shoto to N Honshu. **HH** Coastal wetlands, estuaries and rivers. **ID** Gull-sized, black-capped tern with large head, thick neck and enormous red bill; unmistakable. Adult in breeding plumage is white, with glossy, flat black cap, pale-grey wings and mantle, and blackish primaries; tail short and forked. In winter, crown frosted with white tips and streaking. Juvenile has less clean, but more extensive, black cap, and faint brown scaling on wing-coverts, more noticeable on mantle, becoming paler grey in 1st-winter. At rest, primaries extend well beyond tail. In flight, which is buoyant, has strong 'rowing' action with rather stiff, shallow beats; essentially pale-grey upperwing and pale underwing with blackish primaries. **BP** Bill as long as head, bright red with small dusky tip in adult, dull orange in young; eyes black; legs short, black. **SV** A rasping *kaa kyaaa* or *krrr-aaaack*, and more prolonged *kerrrrsch*. Juvenile gives very different, whistled *wee-you*. **TN** This and following two species formerly placed in genus *Sterna* (e.g. OSJ).

Greater Crested Tern *Thalasseus bergii*

L 43–53 cm; WS 125–130 cm; WT 320–400 g

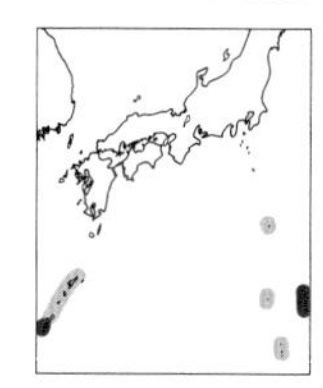

SD *T. b. cristatus* probably breeds (May–Sep) in Nansei Shoto and Ogasawara Is; rare further north, but has reached N Honshu. **HH** Coasts, islands, estuaries and river mouths. Forages in shallow inshore waters and at sea, resting on fishing buoys and floating platforms. **ID** Gull-sized, black-capped and crested tern. Adult is white, with black crest from just in front of eye to shaggy nape; forehead and lores white, mantle and wings mid-grey, primaries blackish; tail short and more deeply forked than Caspian Tern. Rump, uppertail-coverts and tail darkish grey, concolorous with mantle. Outer rectrices white, but inner ones grey. In winter has more extensive white on forecrown and around eye, retaining black only behind eye and on shaggy nape. Juvenile has less clean-cut black cap, and dusky blackish-brown mantle/wing-coverts, becoming paler grey in 1st-winter. At rest, primaries extend well beyond tail. Flight like light Caspian, with similar wing pattern; strong with quite deep flaps, also glides on outstretched wings on migration. **BP** Bill long, thin, greenish-yellow or pale yellow (ad), or dull orange (juv); eyes black; legs short, black (ad) or brown (juv). **SV** Calls alone or in duet. A coarse, purring *kr r ra a ar*, sharp rasping *kirrik* or *kurii kurii*, and hard rattling *skraach*.

Lesser Crested Tern *Thalasseus bengalensis*

L 35–43 cm; WS 88–105 cm; WT 185–242 g

SD Accidental to C Japan (presumably *T. b. torresii*). **HH** Coasts. **ID** Like diminutive Greater Crested Tern, but has sleeker, less shaggy crest and black forehead in breeding plumage. In flight, black of primaries more extensive on both surfaces. Mantle, rump, uppertail-coverts and tail concolorous grey (except white outer rectrices). **BP** Bill long, thin, orange-yellow to orange, paler at tip; eyes black; short tarsi black (ad) or yellow (juv). **SV** Flight call a raucous *kirrrik* or *kurii*.

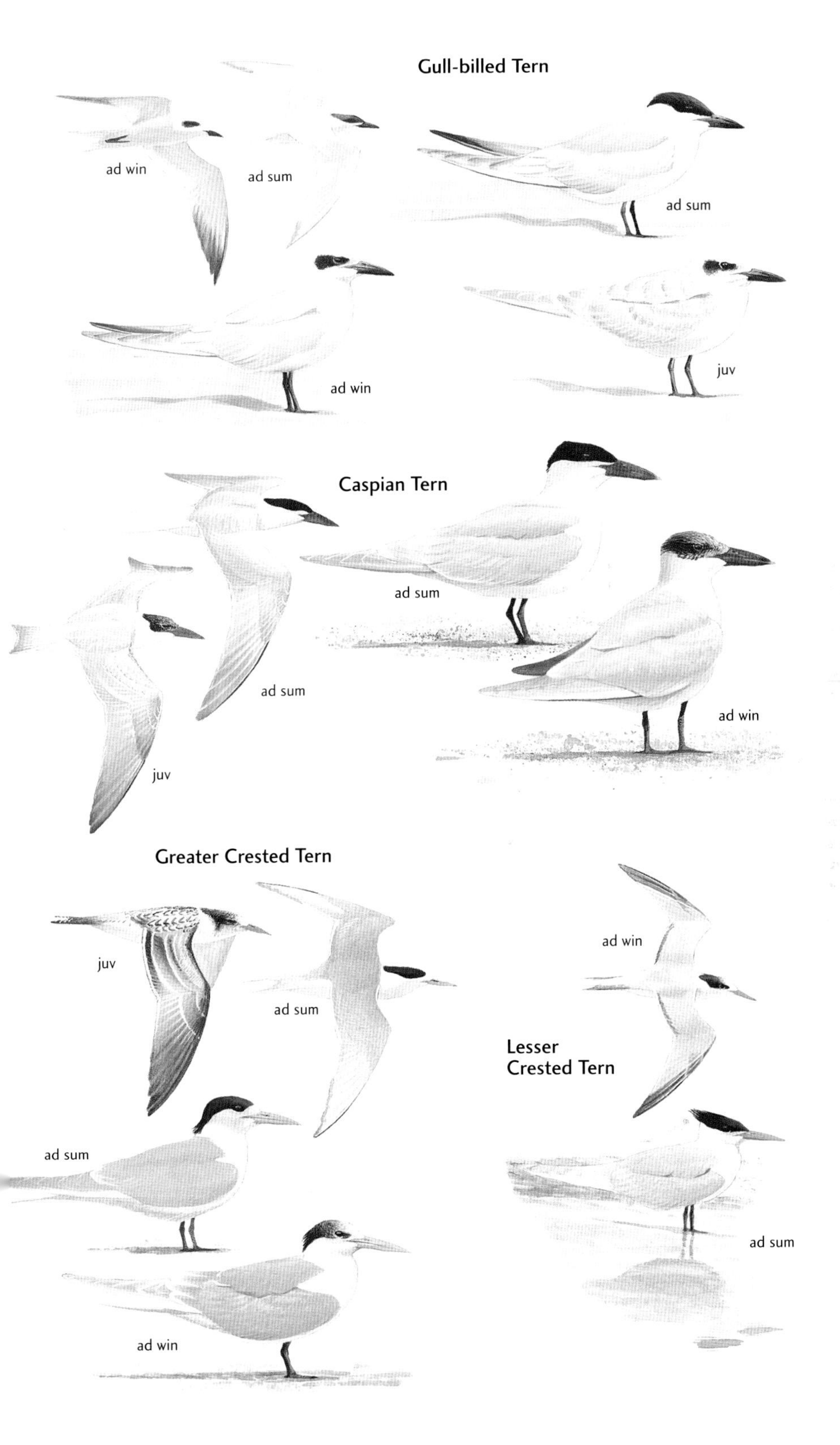
Gull-billed Tern
ad win
ad sum
ad sum
ad win
juv
Caspian Tern
ad sum
ad sum
ad win
juv
Greater Crested Tern
juv
ad sum
ad sum
ad win
ad win
Lesser
Crested Tern
ad sum

Little Tern *Sternula albifrons* L 22–28 cm; WS 47–55 cm; WT 47–70 g

SD *S. a. sinensis* summer visitor (mid-Apr–Sep), N Honshu to Nansei Shoto, strays north to Hokkaido. **HH** Breeds on sandy shores and shingle-bedded rivers. Visits coasts, coastal lagoons, tidal creeks. **ID** Small, delicate, pale grey tern. Adult breeding: upperparts, including wings, are pale grey, cap black with small white forehead patch extending to just above eye, lores black. Adult winter: more extensive white on forehead and white lores. Juvenile: resembles winter adult, but mantle and wing-coverts have scaled appearance. Appears large-headed, wingtips fall just short of tail streamers in summer, extending beyond at other times. Wingbeats fast, wings narrow, set well forward, flies as if front-heavy, commonly hovers, dips and plunge-dives, repeating latter rapidly. Outer 2–3 primaries black with white shafts; rump white, tail white, forked, with protruding tail-streamers. **BP** Long bill, pale yellow with small black tip (summer), or blackish (other seasons); eyes black; legs orange, duller outside breeding season. **SV** Rather noisy, sharp, high-pitched *kyi-kyi*, *ket* and rasping *kyik*. In display or alarm, more prolonged series of *kiri-kyik kiri-kyik*... calls. **TN** Terns on plate 89 formerly in *Sterna* (e.g. OSJ).

Least Tern *Sternula antillarum* L 22–24 cm; WS 50 cm; WT 39–52 g

SD Accidental, C Honshu. **HH** Coasts, harbours. **ID** Very similar to Little Tern. Differs in having only two dark outer primaries, and grey (not white) rump/tail. **BP** As Little Tern, but legs shorter, slimmer, darker. **SV** Calls rapid, sharp, *pideek-adik* or *kedeek*, also Little Tern-like *kweek* or *kwik*.

Aleutian Tern *Onychoprion aleuticus* L 32–34 cm; WS 75–80 cm; WT 83–140 g

SD Surprisingly scarce/rare (Hokkaido to Kyushu), given proximity to E Russian breeding grounds. Best looked for during Sea of Okhotsk pelagics (May–Jun, Aug–Oct). **HH** Forages offshore and in shallow inshore waters and bays; pelagic in winter. **ID** Adult breeding: recalls Common Tern *S. h. longipennis*, but smaller, black cap interrupted by white forehead extending to eye, black lores, dark-grey mantle and wings, and long black primaries; underparts grey, as in *S. h. longipennis*, but call always distinctive. Adult winter: more extensive white forehead and white lores, but retains black nape; underparts whiter, but upperparts dark grey. Juvenile/1st-winter: very dark, cap all blackish, reaching bill; upperparts dark grey, mantle, scapulars and coverts fringed bright cinnamon, neck and breast-sides also washed warm cinnamon. Adult in flight appears dark grey with white only on forehead and in narrow band from chin to cheeks; dark primaries extend beyond white tail. Flight light, agile; upperwing uniform dark grey, whilst underwing mainly pale grey with distinctive, prominent narrow black bar on trailing edge of secondaries and translucent inner primaries; outer primaries black from below; dark wings and mantle contrast clearly with white rump and forked tail; juvenile in flight has very dark wing-coverts with brown tinge, and cinnamon wash visible on breast-sides. See Arctic and Common Terns for identification of potentially confusing juveniles. **BP** Bill short, fine, black (ad), or black with slight yellowish cast to base (juv); eyes black; legs short, orange (juv) or black (ad). **SV** Short, sharp, *eek eek*, recalling Saunders's Gull.

Grey-backed Tern *Onychoprion lunatus* L 35–38 cm; WS 73–76 cm; WT 115–177 g

SD Accidental, north to Iwo Is (Kita Iwo-jima and Minami Torishima), perhaps formerly bred, but status now uncertain. **HH** Breeds on oceanic islands, on beaches, low cliffs. Pelagic at other times. **ID** Medium-sized, grey-backed tern. Resembles Bridled Tern, but has grey, not sooty-black upperparts, more like Aleutian, but with dark rump and white underparts. Adult breeding: cap and nape black, with white forehead extending beyond eye, eyestripe black; upperparts pale to mid-grey on mantle and back; primaries, secondaries, rump and tail blackish-grey. Underparts pure white. Adult winter: white-streaked forecrown. Juvenile: less distinct head pattern, buff-scaled upperparts and off-white breast-sides. **BP** Long slender bill, eyes and short tarsi all black. **SV** Generally silent away from colonies, where gives distinctive high-pitched screeching calls recalling Sooty, but softer and less harsh. **AN** Spectacled Tern.

Little Tern
non-breeding
ad win
juv
ad sum
ad sum
Aleutian Tern
ad sum
ad sum
juv
ad win
Grey-backed Tern
juv
ad win
ad sum
ad sum

Bridled Tern *Onychoprion anaethetus*

L 35–38 cm; WS 76–81 cm; WT 95–150 g

SD *O. a. anaethetus* breeds (May–Sep) in S Nansei Shoto (Okinawa and Yaeyama Is), but has strayed as far north as N Honshu and even Hokkaido. **HH** Breeds on uninhabited rocky offshore islets and forages inshore; at other times pelagic outside region. **ID** Medium-sized dark-backed tern (size of Common Tern, but longer-winged). Adult has charcoal grey-brown mantle/wings, black cap and nape (contrasting with paler mantle) with narrow white forehead band extending above eye to a point; black loral line broad and long (see Sooty). Face, neck and underparts white. Non-breeding adult has more extensive white forehead. Juvenile has dusky-grey rear crown, ear-coverts and nape, mid- to dark-brown upperparts prominently scaled on mantle and coverts with buff fringes. Appears strongly pied; plain dark wingtips reach just beyond tail in non-breeder, just short of tail tip when breeding; closed tail appears white from sides. Flight graceful, buoyant and agile, dipping down to pick food from sea surface; blackish-tipped flight-feathers contrast with white underwing-coverts. Rump and tail dark charcoal-grey in centre, tail deeply forked and outer sides of rump/tail white. Often perches on floating debris at sea. Adult Bridled differs from Sooty in having dark grey, not black back, white forehead extending in narrow point over eye, and streamers of closed tail long and all white (shorter and darker in Sooty). Juvenile Bridled is rather pale, whereas juvenile Sooty is mainly sooty-black with white spots. **BP** Long bill, eyes and short tarsi all black. **SV** Generally silent, except at colonies, where gives low barking *kuu* or *kuraa*; yapping *wup wup*; a rising mellow whistled *weeeep* and a quavering *nyaauw*, and *ke-eeeee* in courtship. **TN** Formerly *Sterna anaethetus* (e.g. OSJ).

Sooty Tern *Onychoprion fuscatus*

L 36–45 cm; WS 82–94 cm; WT 147–240 g

SD *O. f. nubilosa* breeds (Apr–Sep) in southernmost Nansei Shoto (Yaeyama Is), and *O. f. oahuensis* breeds on Ogasawara and Iwo Is. Storm-blown birds occasionally reach Pacific coast of Honshu, even SE Hokkaido. **HH** Breeds on rocky offshore, uninhabited islets and forages inshore; at other times pelagic outside region. **ID** Medium to large black-backed tern (nearly size of Greater Crested Tern), superficially similar to smaller Bridled Tern, but stockier with shorter tail. Adult is blacker on mantle/wings, and black cap more extensive, extending forward of eyes and not contrasting with mantle. White forehead band broader, but does not extend as a superciliary line; black loral line narrows from eye to bill base. Face, neck and underparts entirely white, appearing particularly bright in contrast with blacker upperparts. Non-breeding adult has more white on forehead, sometimes giving appearance of supercilia to eye; hind-collar paler, more like Bridled. Juvenile is almost entirely sooty, blackish-brown, including head, neck and underparts, except white vent, with white tips to mantle/wing-coverts creating slightly spotted appearance; underwing-coverts pale grey, paler in juvenile and darker in adult (see Bridled for differences in upperwing, underwing and tail). Wings broader, beats stiffer than Bridled; rump and tail black, tail deeply forked and only outermost rectrices are white. Rarely if ever perches on floating debris at sea (unlike Bridled, which does so frequently). **BP** Long bill, eyes and tarsi all black. **SV** Generally silent away from colony, where gives harsh, nasal *gii-ah* or *draaaaa* in threat, and nasal *wide-a-wake*, *ker-wacki-wack* or *ka weddy weddy* calls. **TN** Formerly *Sterna fuscata* (e.g. OSJ).

ad sum
ad sum
ad win
juv
Bridled Tern
ad win
Sooty Tern
ad sum
ad win
ad sum
juv
ad win

Roseate Tern *Sterna dougallii*

L 33–43 cm; WS 72–80 cm; WT 96–128 g

SD *S. d. bangsi* summer visitor (May–Sep), C & S Kyushu and Nansei Shoto, has bred Honshu and Shikoku; rarely typhoon-blown further north. **HH** Isolated, rocky offshore islets. **ID** Elegant, black-capped tern with rounded head, long, slender bill, and very deeply forked tail with greatly elongated outer tail-feathers. Adult: very pale-grey mantle and wings, primaries have black shafts and outer vanes; underparts white with faint rosy tinge; rump and tail white contrasting little with mantle. Winter adult: white forecrown. Juvenile/1st-winter: mottled brown crown and nape with dark forehead, grey upperparts (mantle/scapulars) have broad blackish fringes, giving heavily scalloped appearance, wing-coverts are mid-grey with dark fringes; tail shorter and unforked. At rest, despite long wings, tail extends well beyond wingtips, which appear blackish. Wings narrow, shorter than Common Tern; light flight with rapid, stiff, shallow wingbeats, differs from more graceful Common or Arctic Terns; hovers occasionally, often power-dives into water for prey; underwing white with some black near primary tips and in outermost primaries; lacks dark trailing edge to underside of primaries typical of Common/Arctic. **BP** Bill black (non-breeding/juv) or with deep-red base (breeding); eyes black; legs short, orange (ad), or black (juv). **SV** Flight calls raucous, grating: *krraahk* or *cherr-rrick*, distinctive *gyuii* or *chu-vee*, higher *skivvik*, also *keeer* (in alarm), and by juvenile *krrip*.

Black-naped Tern *Sterna sumatrana*

L 30–35 cm; WS 61–64 cm; WT 90–106 g

SD *S. s. sumatrana* summer visitor (May–Sep), Nansei Shoto; rarely typhoon-blown further north. **HH** As Roseate Tern. **ID** Slender, elegant, extremely pale greyish-white tern (can appear white), with black band from just forward of eye to nape. Juvenile/1st-winter is mottled brown on crown and nape; upperparts have buff to black subterminal marks; tail short and unforked. Wings long and slender; tail long and deeply forked. At rest, adult's long outer tail-streamers extend beyond wingtips. Flight buoyant; often hovers. **BP** Bill long, thin, entirely black; eyes black; legs short, black. **SV** Huskier, deeper *gui gui* call than Roseate, and various sharp notes.

Common Tern *Sterna hirundo*

L 31–39 cm; WS 72–83 cm; WT 90–146 g

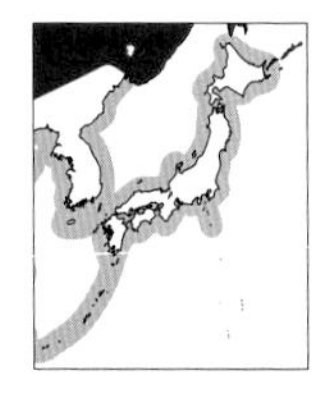

SD Siberian Tern *S. (h.) longipennis* (common migrant); **Common Tern** *S. h. minussensis* (rare/scarce migrant). **HH** Coasts; occasionally lakes, rivers, wet fields. **ID** Elegant, black-capped tern; crown slightly flat and head somewhat elongated. Adult **Siberian**: grey mantle, wings and underparts. Non-breeding adult: paler underparts and whiter forehead; black carpal bar prominent. Juvenile/1st-winter: cap like winter adult, but grey upperparts and wings with blackish fringes to mantle, coverts and scapulars. Long, blackish wingtips level with outer tail-streamers; outermost webs of outer tail-feathers dark-grey/black (white in Roseate Tern). Flight buoyant on long, narrow wings with long, deeply forked tail; hovers and plunge-dives; underwing mainly white, outer primary tips black, forming distinct dark panel, leaving only inner primaries translucent (see Arctic Tern); juvenile has dark carpal and secondary bars with paler midwing panel. **Common** has paler upperparts and upperwing than **Siberian**. **BP** Bill long, all black (**Siberian**) or crimson with blackish tip (**Common**); eyes black; legs short, usually black but sometimes blackish-red (**Siberian**), or noticeably red (**Common**), becoming black outside breeding season. **SV** Hard chattering *kyi kyi kyi* and harsh, descending, oft-repeated long *kree-arr* or *keeeyurr* with strong emphasis on first part, and screeching *kzrrssh*. In aggression, a hard, rattling *k-k-k-k*...

Arctic Tern *Sterna paradisaea*

L 33–39 cm; WS 76–85 cm; WT 86–127 g

SD Accidental, C Honshu. **HH** Coasts. **ID** Resembles slightly larger Siberian Tern (ST), but head rounder, bill smaller and legs shorter, and with relatively longer, narrower wings. Adult: black cap extends lower on lores (nearly to gape) than ST. Tail streamers longer than ST, extending beyond wingtips. Non-breeding adult: white forehead. Juvenile/1st-winter: cap like winter adult, but grey upperparts/wings have dark grey fringes to mantle, coverts and scapulars, and dark carpal bar (far less prominent than ST); outermost webs of outer tail-feathers dark grey/black (white in Roseate Tern). Flight as ST; upperwing uniform grey; underwing mainly white, translucent, with only narrow black tips to outer primaries (forming narrow trailing edge); juvenile has narrow, diffuse carpal bar, grey midwing panel and white secondaries, thus wing shades from dark at leading edge to pale. **BP** Bill short, fine, dark red (breeding), or black; eyes black; legs very short, red, duller in non-breeding/juv. **SV** Very similar to ST, but higher pitched and squeakier, a buzzy *gyii-errr* and *ki-ki-ki-ki-ki*, a rapid *titkerri titkerri*....

Roseate Tern
ad sum
ad sum
ad win
juv
Black-naped Tern
ad sum
ad sum
juv
ad sum
juv
Common Tern
longipennis
juv
ad win
ad sum
ad sum
Arctic Tern
ad sum
ad win
juv

Whiskered Tern *Chlidonias hybrida*

L 23–29 cm; WS 64–70 cm; WT 60–101 g

SD *C. h. hybrida* is scarce post-breeding migrant from Nansei Shoto to Hokkaido; rare in spring, and has occasionally wintered. **HH** Freshwater lagoons, lakes and pools, or flooded fields, where forages by dipping and hawking for food from surface or above. **ID** Small, grey tern, with shallow-forked tail and rounded wings. Adult has full black cap, grey upperparts, pale grey wings, and dark grey to blackish-grey underparts, with only chin/cheeks ('whiskers') white. Non-breeding adult is dark with extensive white forehead and white lores, black ear-coverts, rear crown and nape; and all-white underparts. Juvenile resembles winter adult, but mantle and wing-coverts have dark brown scalloping contrasting with paler grey rump and tail; flight-feathers blacker. At rest, appears slender, short-tailed, with wingtips extending beyond tail. Flight very light, changes direction frequently. Wingtips black, underwing pale grey or white, rump and short tail mid-grey. **BP** Short bill deep blood-red (breeding) or black; eyes black; tarsi (rather longer than other *Chlidonias*) blood-red. **SV** While foraging gives dry, metallic, rasping notes: *keh keh*; *ki-kitt*; *krche* or *kzzrt*.

White-winged Tern *Chlidonias leucopterus*

L 20–27 cm; WS 58–67 cm; WT 42–80 g

SD A scarce migrant (May–Oct) from Nansei Shoto to Hokkaido. **HH** Occurs along coasts, at coastal wetlands and at lakes. **ID** Adult has sooty-black head, neck and underparts, except white vent/undertail-coverts; black mantle, dark grey back, white wing-coverts, grey flight-feathers, white rump and tail. Non-breeding adult closely resembles Black Tern, but has much paler upperwing, less extensive and less distinct black on crown (diffuse streaking rather than cap), and distinct black ear-coverts patch; lacks dark patches on grey breast-sides just forward of wings. Juvenile is like winter adult, but mantle and wing-coverts have dark brown scalloping and lack conspicuous pale tertial tips. At rest, slender, short-tailed, with very long primaries extending well beyond tail, legs longer than Black. Flight very light, buoyant, frequently banking and changing direction, wings broader than Black. Primary tips black, outermost primaries have black shafts creating black leading edge to primaries, darker than rest of upperwing, which is pure white on forewing; underwing-coverts black, contrasting strongly with grey flight-feathers; dark mantle contrasts strongly with white rump. Juvenile appears very dark-backed in flight (giving 'saddle' effect), dark-scalloped mantle contrasts with grey innerwing and, especially, with white rump and grey tail; juvenile and non-breeding adult have dark carpal bar. **BP** Short bill, dark-blood red (breeding) or black; eyes black; tarsi orange (breeding) or dull orange/red. **SV** Calls include low, soft *kweek*, harder *kwek-kwek*, and Whiskered Tern-like short *kesch* and *kek*, rasping *giri giri* or crackling *gzzrk-gzzrk gzzrk*. **AN** White-winged Black Tern.

Black Tern *Chlidonias niger*

L 22–28 cm; WS 57–65 cm; WT 60–86 g

SD *C. n. niger* is accidental (mainly Jul–Oct) from Okinawa to Hokkaido. *C. n. surinamensis* is vagrant to C Honshu. **HH** Estuaries and marshes. **ID** Small, dark marsh tern, with shallow-forked tail, typically seen hawking low over wetlands. Adult is elegant, with sooty-black head, neck and underparts, except white vent/undertail-coverts; pale-grey mantle, wings and tail. Non-breeding adult has small neat black cap with teardrop extension behind eye; forehead, face and underparts otherwise white, but has dark grey breast-side patches just forward of wings (compare White-winged Tern). Juvenile resembles winter adult, particularly in black cap and breast patches, but mantle/wing-coverts have dark-brown scalloping with conspicuous pale tips, especially on tertials. At rest, slender, short-tailed, with very long primaries extending well beyond tail. Flight very buoyant, frequently banking and changing direction, with bill held down. Upperwing of breeder more uniform grey, whereas non-breeder has outer primaries black, darker than grey inner primaries and upperwing; underwing pale-grey, rump and short tail mid-grey (see White-winged); non-breeding adult has dark forewing and secondary tips, but pale grey midwing panel. Juvenile appears dark-backed in flight, the scalloped mantle contrasting with grey innerwing and grey rump/tail. **BP** Short bill is black (longer than White-winged); eyes black; short tarsi black (breeding) or dull orange/red. **SV** Contact calls *kii kii*; *klit klit*; *kleep* and *kweeer*.

Whiskered Tern
non-breeding
non-breeding
breeding
juv
breeding
White-winged Tern
non-breeding
breeding
juv
breeding

Black Tern
ad win
ad sum
juv
ad sum

South Polar Skua *Stercorarius maccormicki*

L 50–55 cm; WS 127–140 cm; WT 900–1600 g

SD Uncommon migrant past Pacific coast (mostly May–Aug, but also at other times) from Izu Is north to Hokkaido. To be looked for well offshore, primarily from coastal and inter-island ferries. **HH** Pelagic. **ID** Large skua resembling dark immature gull in coloration, with broad, rather blunt-tipped wings and heavy flight. Sexes similar, though ♀ larger than ♂. Adult is often considered dimorphic, but unlike morphs of smaller skuas, in South Polar there is complete gradation between extremes. Dark greyish-brown, with variable paler brown mottling on mantle, underparts and particularly head. Overall appearance a 'cool' brown bird, with pale, somewhat small head, lacking 'warmer', more rufous-brown tones, and dark-capped appearance of extralimital Great Skua or pale flecks of extralimital Brown Skua. Dark adult is extremely dark, but commonly has pale 'frosting' on dark nape and pale crescent at base of bill; paler adult may have sandier-brown underparts with pale fringes to mantle. Juvenile is like adult, typically with cold, grey-brown plumage. At rest (generally only on water, where floats rather high), primaries extend slightly beyond rounded tail. In flight, all ages show prominent white flashes at bases and along shafts of primaries, which are far more prominent than in smaller skuas; underwing-coverts black contrasting with paler body; uniformly unbarred underwing-coverts, axillaries and upper- and undertail-coverts distinguish it from young Pomarine Skua. 'Arm' broad, 'hand' short, with blunter wingtips than smaller species; tail broad, slightly wedge-shaped. **BP** Large, heavy bill is blackish-grey (ad); or has basal two-thirds blue-grey and tip black (juv); eyes black; short tarsi black. **SV** Occasional harsh gull-like *guaa* or *gwaa* calls, but generally silent in region. **TN** Formerly considered race of Great Skua *S. skua*. **AN** McCormick's Skua.

Pomarine Skua *Stercorarius pomarinus*

L 42–58 cm; WS 115–138 cm; WT 550–850 g

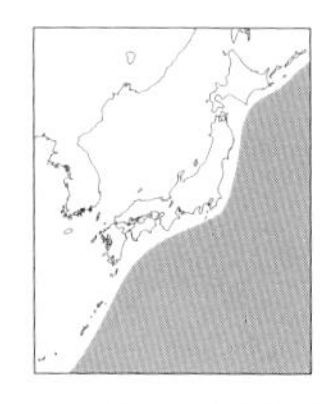

SD Uncommon migrant along Pacific coast and offshore in W Pacific, from Nansei Shoto to Hokkaido, recorded in all months but most commonly Nov–Apr. **HH** Occurs along coasts or well offshore; only very rarely inland (e.g. after typhoons). To be looked for off headlands and occasionally larger river mouths or coastal wetlands. **ID** Large dark skua (about size of Black-tailed Gull), adult and some subadults (not juvenile) deep-chested, with prominent elongated, twisted, spatulate central rectrices in breeding plumage. Adult sexes similar, and plumage similar year-round except for central rectrices, with two colour morphs. Light morph commoner (>80%); dark cap reaching below gape, dark, scaly breast-band (sometimes reduced or lacking), barred breast-sides and flanks; vent all dark. Dark morph (5–20%) all dark except white wing flashes. Juvenile most difficult to identify, ranging from very dark chocolate-brown to mid-brown with pale buff-brown barring. Appears large-headed, with obviously heavier, more distinctly two-toned bill than Arctic, and prominently barred vent. Much thicker bill with more restricted dark tip (or more extensive and obvious pale base) affords it a distinctly immature Glaucous Gull look. Head may appear large and dark, or large and grey with fine pale grey spotting. Blunt-tipped central rectrices barely protrude. At rest, although long-winged, primaries of adult do not reach tail tip; primaries of juvenile, however, extend beyond tail. In flight, which is steady and measured, appears rakish, but commonly heavy-chested; 'arm' appears evenly broad with comparatively slighter 'hand' (compare Arctic Skua). Small area of white in primary bases on upper- (4–6 primary shafts) and underwing, forming distinct 'flashes' (compare Arctic); adult has dark underwing; juvenile has pale-barred axillaries/underwing-coverts, and pale-barred rump/uppertail-coverts; central rectrices long (extending c. 5 cm), broad, with spoon-like tips, giving lumpy appearance to tail tip. **BP** Bill pinkish with black tip (summer), grey with black tip (winter), or prominently blue-grey with black tip visible even at long range (juv); eyes black; legs short, blackish-grey. **SV** Occasionally gives barking calls. **AN** North America: Pomarine Jaeger.

South Polar Skua
ad intermediate
ad dark
ad pale
juv intermediate
Pomarine Skua
juv dark
ad win pale
juv pale
ad sum pale
ad sum dark
juv intermediate
ad sum pale
ad sum pale
ad sum dark
juv intermediate

Arctic Skua *Stercorarius parasiticus*

L 37–51 cm; WS 102–125 cm; WT 330–610 g

SD Uncommon migrant (commonest Apr–Jul, but recorded all months), Nansei Shoto and Ogasawara Is north to Hokkaido. **HH** Along Pacific coast or well offshore; rarely inland after typhoons. Kleptoparasitic: pursues gulls and terns to steal food. Aerial engagements aerobatic and prolonged (cf. Pomarine Skua, which more frequently tackles larger seabirds and often kills smaller victims). **ID** Smaller and slighter than Pomarine Skua, less deep-chested, with elongated and narrowly pointed central rectrices (extending c. 5–8 cm). Adult (♂♀): plumage similar year-round except central rectrices. Two colour morphs common (much like Pomarine). Light morph predominates; dark cap does not enclose gape, usually has pale patch above bill base. Fewer have chest-band, and this lacks scaling, also lacks barred flanks. Dark morph all dark except white wing flashes, thus size, structure and flight pattern separate from Pomarine. Juvenile: appears small-headed; very dark chocolate-brown to mid cinnamon-brown with pale buff-brown head; upperparts have narrow rufous fringes and primaries have narrow rufous tips; little or no barring on vent of darker juvenile, less prominently barred in paler juvenile, which tend to appear 'warmer' rusty-brown, rather than 'cooler' grey-brown of pale Pomarine juvenile. Central rectrices barely protrude (1–3 cm), but are pointed, not blunt-tipped. At rest adult, though long-winged, has primaries that do not reach tail tip; in juvenile, however, primaries extend beyond tail. Flight fast, agile, rakish (falcon-like) and lighter than Pomarine. Wings long, narrow (including 'arm', so tail looks longer than Pomarine and wing base narrower), 'hand' appears longer, more pointed than Pomarine. Small area of white in primary bases on upper- (3–5 primary shafts) and underwing form distinct 'flashes' (like Pomarine); adult has very dark underwings; juvenile has pale-barred axillaries/underwing-coverts and more uniform rump/uppertail-coverts, either dark or mostly pale with little barring. **BP** Bill less heavy than Pomarine, gonydeal angle close to tip (mid-bill in Long-tailed) grey with black tip (ad), or blue-grey with black tip visible even at long range (juv); eyes black; legs short, blackish-grey. **SV** Usually silent. **AN** North America: Parasitic Jaeger.

Long-tailed Skua *Stercorarius longicaudus*

L 35–53 cm; WS 105–117 cm; WT 230–350 g

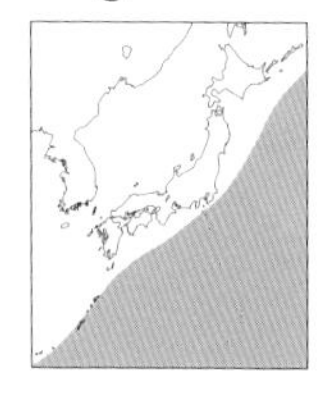

SD *S. l. pallescens* is scarce migrant (mostly Mar–Jun, but recorded all months), Nansei Shoto to Hokkaido. **HH** Along Pacific coast or well offshore; rarely inland after typhoons. **ID** Size of Black-headed Gull; smaller and slighter than Arctic Skua; flight more agile, buoyant and tern-like. Settles on sea more frequently than other skuas. Adult: brownish-grey mantle, upperwing-coverts and rump contrasting with black flight-feathers, black primary-coverts and tail. Central rectrices extending *c.* 12–24 cm, at least as long as tail, typically longer. Distinct cap is black. Cheeks and neck may have yellow wash like Pomarine or Arctic, but white lower neck/chest grade gradually into dusky-grey belly/vent – without sharp demarcation, although vent can appear quite dark. Non-breeding adult has indistinct cap, dusky face- and neck-sides, and barred upper- and undertail-coverts; lacks tail projections. Juvenile: like Arctic, ranges from mid-brown to paler grey-brown, but typically pale-headed with pale upper belly. Distinctly barred vent, like Pomarine, but very much slighter with slimmer body and longer, narrower wings even than Arctic. Tail projection of juvenile is short and bluntly rounded, not pointed. At rest adult, though long-winged, has primaries that do not reach tail tip; in juvenile, however, primaries extend beyond tail. Flight light and tern-like (lighter than Arctic), wings long, narrow and long-'handed'. Adult shows strong contrast between brownish-grey upperwing-coverts and blackish flight-feathers, forming distinct black trailing edge; white restricted to shafts of outer 2–3 primaries of upperwing only (distinct among skuas), appearing as obvious narrow stripes; juvenile has wing flashes above and below. Underwing is dark grey-brown (ad), or has finely barred axillaries/underwing-coverts, and narrowly barred rump/uppertail-coverts (juv). **BP** Bill short (about equal to distance from bill base to eye), shorter than Arctic, gonydeal angle not noticeable, nail covers about half of bill, blackish (ad); or basal half blue-grey with black tip (juv); eyes black; legs short, black above tarsus, bluish-grey below with black, 'dipped in ink', webbed toes. **SV** Usually silent. **AN** North America: Long-tailed Jaeger.

Arctic Skua
ad win pale
juv pale
ad 1st-sum pale
ad sum pale
juv intermediate
juv dark
ad sum dark
ad sum pale
ad sum dark
juv intermediate
Long-tailed Skua
juv intermediate
juv pale
2nd sum
ad win
juv dark
ad sum
juv dark
ad sum
juv pale
juv intermediate

Little Auk *Alle alle*

L 17–19 cm; WS 40–48 cm; WT 163 g

SD Accidental (presumably *A. a. polaris*), Hokkaido, Honshu, Kyushu and Okinawa. **HH** Pelagic; sometimes blown inshore. **ID** Small, dumpy, head large, neck thick, bill tiny. Adult: black hood and upperparts, 3–4 short white streaks on scapulars, prominent white secondary band; underparts white. Non-breeding adult: lacks black hood, but black crown extends to eye, on nape and in broad bar on lower neck-/breast-sides; white extends up behind eye. Juvenile: resembles winter adult, but duskier. Floats high on water, when white breast-sides are prominent; often drags wings on water between dives. In flight, short wings slightly rounded at tip whirr and blur, all black except white tips to secondaries forming trailing edge to innerwing; underwing dark grey. Most prominent feature of non-breeder in flight is dark neck-band; tail all black, very short. **BP** Bill black; eyes black; tarsi blue-grey. **SV** Generally silent. **AN** North America: Dovekie.

Brünnich's Guillemot *Uria lomvia*

L 39–43 cm; WS 65–73 cm; WT 810–1,080 g

SD *U. l. arra* is fairly common winter visitor (Nov–Apr) to Pacific coast of Hokkaido; scarce visitor farther south, as far as W Honshu. **HH** Largely pelagic, occasionally inshore, in channels, bays, harbours. **ID** Large, similar to Common Guillemot, but heavy-set, black and white, with distinctive bill shape. Blacker in all plumages than Common. Adult: black on head and neck, with clean border between strongly contrasting black and white underparts reaching point on mid-neck; upperparts and wings blackish. May show fine indented line curving back from eye as Common. Non-breeding adult: paler, but still blacker above than Common, from which separated by much darker head, black extending to lores, face and ear-coverts below level of eye and neck-sides. Underparts white, lacking dusky flank streaking of Common. At rest, adult has distinct white wingbar (tips of secondaries); wings short, pointed, fall short of tail tip. Flight like Common, but appears thicker-necked and shorter-beaked, thus squatter and heavier; darker upperwing relieved only by whitish trailing edge to secondaries; clean white underwing-coverts contrast with blackish flight-feathers, and white axillaries (dusky in Common); rump and tail narrower and blacker with white sides; toes project beyond tail. **BP** Bill, shorter, deeper, culmen more curved than Common, with gonydeal angle nearer midpoint rather than close to base, and variable white, grey or silver gape stripe extending back from base of black upper mandible; eyes black; tarsi blackish-grey, may stand on toes or rest on tarsi. **SV** Silent away from colonies. **AN** IOC: Thick-billed Murre.

Common Guillemot *Uria aalge*

L 38–43 cm; WS 64–71 cm; WT 945–1,044 g

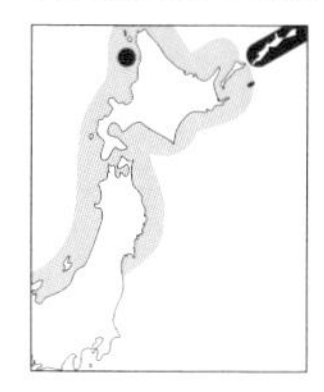

SD *U. a. inornata* was formerly a common breeder on offshore islands around Hokkaido, but extirpated; last few survive on Teuri I off W Hokkaido. A fairly common winter visitor (Nov–Apr) to Pacific coast; less common in Sea of Japan, recorded south to W Honshu. **HH** Rocky islands with cliffs; usually pelagic in winter, but occasionally inshore, in channels, bays and harbours. **ID** Large, heavy-set, blackish-brown and white alcid confusable only with Brünnich's Guillemot. Adult: blackish-brown head and neck, with clean contrasting border between black and white underparts on lower neck; upperparts and wings blackish-brown. May show fine indented line curving back from eye, like crease in feathering. Non-breeding adult: much whiter, crown to lores and nape blackish-brown, with fine black line curving back from eye on head-sides; white extends to level of eye on rear head-sides. Underparts white with dusky brownish or blackish streaks on flanks. Juvenile is like winter adult, but blunter-ended and fluffier. At rest, adult has distinct white wingbar (tips of secondaries); wings short, pointed, fall short of tail tip. In flight, broad-based, pointed wings whirr rapidly; dark upperwing relieved only by whitish trailing edge to secondaries; dusky-white underwing-coverts contrast with blackish flight-feathers and dusky axillaries; rump and tail appear broad and dark; toes project beyond tail. **BP** Bill, long, straight, black, narrowly pointed with gonydeal angle close to base; eyes black; tarsi blackish-grey, may stand on toes or rest on tarsi. **SV** Rolling, nasal *orrrrr* at colonies. **AN** IOC: Common Murre.

Razorbill *Alca torda*

L 38–43 cm; WS 60–69 cm; WT 505–890 g

SD Vagrant. **HH** Pelagic. **ID** Smaller, blacker than Common Guillemot, with thick neck, distinctive, laterally flattened bill, and long pointed tail. In flight, white axillaries and underwing resemble Brünnich's Guillemot. **BP** Bill black with white vertical line near tip and white loral line from bill to eye (absent in winter). **SV** Generally silent.

Little Auk
ad sum
ad win
ad sum
ad win
Brünnich's Guillemot
ad sum
ad win

Common Guillemot
Brünnich's
Common
ad sum
ad win

Razorbill
ad sum
ad win

Pigeon Guillemot *Cepphus columba*

L 30–37 cm; WS 58 cm; WT 450–550 g

SD *C. c. kaiurka* is rare winter visitor (Dec–Mar) to N Japan, mostly E Hokkaido, rarely Honshu; many records likely mistaken for Snow's Guillemot. **HH** Winters at sea, but occasionally encountered around coasts and in habours. **ID** Medium-sized, very dark auk. In summer all black with prominent white wing patch partially divided by dark bar at base of greater coverts, visible at rest but more prominent in flight, when also reveals dull to dark-grey underwing. Juvenile/1st-year and non-breeding adult: white mottled with black/ brown above, white below; has grey underwing. **BP** Bill black, slightly upturned, head held level or slightly uptilted; eyes black; tarsi/feet bright red. **SV** Silent at sea.

Snow's Guillemot *Cepphus (columba) snowi*

L 30–37 cm; WS 58 cm; WT 450–550 g

SD Breeds only in the Kuril Islands and a scarce winter visitor (Dec–Mar) to N Japan, mostly E Hokkaido, rarely south to C Honshu. **HH** Breeds along rocky coasts with scree and boulder talus slopes. Pelagic in winter. **ID** Medium-sized, black auk. Breeding adult: appears intermediate between Pigeon and Spectacled Guillemots, with all-black wings, variable white barring on coverts, usually as series of narrow white bars; also shows small pale area around eye, recalling first-summer Spectacled. More likely than Pigeon Guillemot in Hokkaido in winter because of much closer proximity to breeding range. **BP** Bill black, slightly upturned, head held level or slightly uptilted; eyes black; tarsi/feet bright red. **SV** High-pitched sibilant twittering at colonies; otherwise silent.

Spectacled Guillemot *Cepphus carbo*

L 37–40 cm; WS 65.5–69 cm; WT 490 g

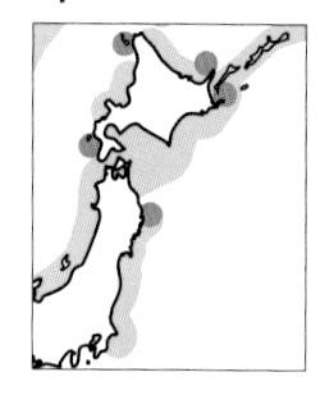

SD Essentially a Sea of Okhotsk endemic, which breeds also around E Hokkaido and on islands off northernmost Honshu, but has declined considerably in recent decades. Disperses south in winter, when commoner in Hokkaido and along Pacific shores of N Honshu; has strayed south to Izu Is. **HH** Rocky coasts, breeding among rock piles just above tideline. Winters in ice-free areas off rocky coasts and headlands, occasionally bays and harbours. **ID** Larger than Pigeon Guillemot. Sooty blackish-brown, except white patch around eye and curving back from it, and smaller white patches at bill base. White patches at tail-sides may reflect moult or individual variation. Non-breeding adult upperparts blackish-brown, underparts from chin, throat, neck-sides, breast to vent white. Face blackish, grading into white throat, reduced white ring around eye, head- and neck-sides dusky-grey, not black like forehead/crown. Forehead usually steep (see winter Long-billed Murrelet). Wings all black; whirr in flight like other guillemots; tail all black, very short, toes often protrude beyond tip. **BP** Bill long, thin, black, reveals bright red mouth lining when calling; eyes black; tarsi/feet bright red (often visible). **SV** Gives high-pitched, rather tremulous whistles: *piii piii* or more rapid *pi pi pi* or *chi chi chi* near colonies.

Cassin's Auklet *Ptychoramphus aleuticus*

L 23 cm; WS 38 cm; WT 150–200 g

SD *P. a. aleuticus* is accidental to E Hokkaido in winter. **ID** Stocky, large-headed grey auklet with short bill. Overall dark grey, darker on upperside, somewhat paler below. In flight, note pale central stripe on otherwise dark underwing, paler belly and pale grey patch just behind base of wings. At long range, deceptively similar to larger, non-breeding Rhinoceros Auklet, but latter has larger dull yellow bill and uniform underwing. **BP** Very short bill is triangular, angled upwards, lower mandible has pale horn base, otherwise dark grey; eyes dull off-white or yellowish-white in adult, making eye very conspicuous, dark grey in juvenile (Aug–Feb); all ages have white crescent above and in front of eye; tarsi blue-grey. **SV** Silent away from colonies. **TN** Not included by OSJ.

Pigeon Guillemot
ad sum
ad sum
ad win
ad win
juv
Snow's Guillemot
ad sum
ad sum
ad sum
ad win
ad win
Spectacled Guillemot
ad sum
ad sum
ad win
ad win
ad moulting to
summer plumage
Cassin's Auklet
ad
ad

Long-billed Murrelet *Brachyramphus perdix*

L 24–26 cm; WS 43 cm; WT 196–269 g

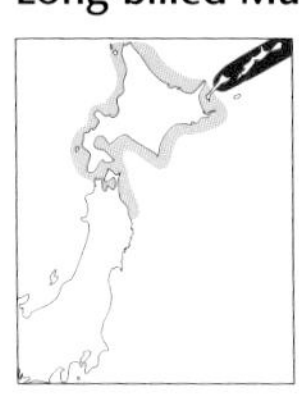

SD Scarce East Asian endemic, rare breeder Hokkaido. Scarce winter wanderer to Hokkaido, also south to Kyushu, Nansei Shoto. **HH** At sea off forested regions (presumably tree-nester). **ID** Small, dumpy murrelet with hunched appearance, elongated profile and slender bill. Adult (breeding): dark brown, with pale brown throat and narrow white crescents above and below eye. Non-breeding adult: resembles small, winter Spectacled Guillemot (size assessment difficult at sea), gently sloping profile, white crescents above and below eye, black crown extends on nape and neck-sides, back blackish-grey, upperwings have prominent white scapular bar; pale-grey underwing-coverts. Juvenile: resembles winter adult, but flanks duskier. Floats high, tail short, often cocked, wingtips extending beyond tail. Flight usually low, fast and direct; wings narrow, pointed, beat rapidly; underwing-coverts pale. **BP** Bill long, appearing more so due to gently sloping profile, black; eyes black; tarsi black. **SV** Thin, whistled *fii fii*. **TN** Formerly within Marbled Murrelet.

Kittlitz's Murrelet *Brachyramphus brevirostris*

L 22–23 cm; WS 43 cm; WT 224 g

SD Vagrant. **HH** Pelagic. **ID** Slightly smaller than Long-billed Murrelet; essentially similar, but with much shorter bill. Adult: mid- to pale golden brown, upperparts and flanks speckled, belly and undertail-coverts white. Suggestion of 'pale face' becomes obvious in non-breeding plumage. Non-breeding: narrow, dark-grey crown, grey nape and upperparts, but appears almost black. Face very white, eye prominent, with white lores, and white above eye, on rear head-sides and foreneck; grey patches extend onto lower-neck-/breast-sides, forming near-complete collar, underparts white; prominent white scapular bar. Juvenile: resembles winter adult, but duskier on flanks. Floats high, tail short, often cocked. In flight, dark wings narrow, pointed and contrast with somewhat golden-brown body; underwing dark in all plumages. **BP** Bill very short, black; eyes black; tarsi black. **SV** Generally silent. **TN** Not included by OSJ.

Ancient Murrelet *Synthliboramphus antiquus*

L 24–27 cm; WS 40–43 cm; WT 177–249 g

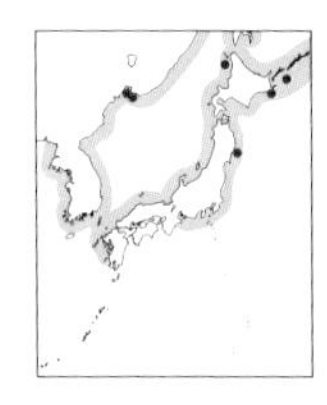

SD *S. a. antiquus* scarce breeder on islands off Hokkaido, winter visitor off Hokkaido and N Honshu, scarce/rare south to Nansei Shoto. **HH** Winters along Sea of Japan and Pacific coasts. Pelagic, occasionally bays, harbours. **ID** Stocky, appearing large- and rather flat-headed, with black, grey and white plumage. Contrast between grey back and black crown an excellent field mark in all plumages. Adult: plain mid-grey above and on wings and rump, folded wing appears almost black, tail short and black, wingtips extend just beyond tail. Black of head reaches throat, face-sides below eye and lower neck-sides, contrasting with grey mantle. Narrow white line of hoary feathers from behind eye to nape. Underparts to undertail-coverts white, flanks streaked grey. Non-breeding adult: duskier head, lacks hoary 'crest', black on throat less extensive. Lacks white scapular bar of other murrelets (except Japanese). Juvenile: resembles winter adult. On water floats low, tail short, often cocked, neck hunched, as if leaning forward. In flight, underwing white with almost vertical white patch extending onto neck-sides. On landing, simply stops flying and splashes into water breast-first from height of *c.* 1 m or more. Flocks often fly short distance then splash down together. **BP** Bill short, stout, conical, pale horn, ivory or even yellow; eyes black; tarsi blue-grey. **SV** Occasionally gives abrupt high-pitched chipping *chi chi*, or a whistled *teep*.

Japanese Murrelet *Synthliboramphus wumizusume*

L 24–26 cm; WT 183 g

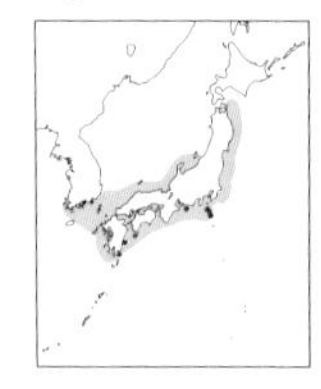

SD Vulnerable. Rare/scarce breeder (Feb–Apr) on isolated offshore islands, mainly from Izu Is southwest to Kyushu, accidental Nansei Shoto. Disperses north after breeding, some reach N Honshu, E Hokkaido. **HH** Rocky islets, headlands, isolated stacks during Feb–May breeding season; close to shore in summer, otherwise pelagic, dispersing away from breeding areas. **ID** Recalls Ancient Murrelet, but prominent white stripes on black crown-sides meet on nape, has slightly loose black crest and larger bill. General appearance is of horizontal black and white bands on head-sides, and broad black band from head to flanks, whereas Ancient has vertical white and black bands on neck. Adult: plain mid-grey upperparts, folded wing appears almost black, tail short and black. Black of head extends only to upper throat, but extends from face down sides in continuous band. Underparts white, flanks blackish-grey. Non-breeding adult: like Ancient, lacks white scapular bar, has less conspicuous crest. Juvenile: resembles winter adult. Posture on water like Ancient Murrelet. In flight, underwing white. **BP** Bill short, conical, pale blue-grey; eyes black; tarsi blue-grey to yellowish-grey. **SV** Abrupt, bunting-like *chi chi chi chi* and, at colonies at night, a distinctive bubbling *byubyubyu*. **AN** Crested Murrelet.

Long-billed Murrelet
ad sum
ad win
juv
Kittlitz's Murrelet
ad sum
ad sum
ad win
juv
Ancient Murrelet
ad sum
ad sum
ad win
ad win
ad sum crest raised
Japanese Murrelet
ad sum
ad sum
ad win
ad win

Parakeet Auklet *Aethia psittacula* L 23–25 cm; WS 44–48 cm; WT 297 g

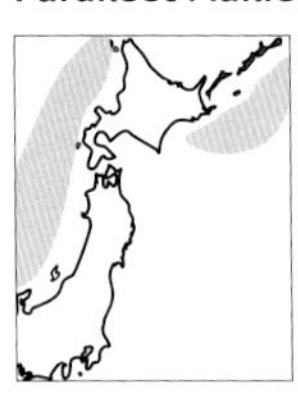

SD Rare winter visitor (Dec–Mar) straying occasionally to Hokkaido and Honshu south to Izu Is. **HH** Pelagic, usually alone, but may be within Crested or Least Auklet flocks; occasionally inshore. **ID** Dumpy, similar in size to Crested Auklet. Adult in breeding plumage is mostly dark grey above, but breast to vent bright white, upper breast and flanks smudged dark grey and white; single white plume extends behind eye. Non-breeding adult is all dark above, but white of underparts extends on throat and even chin is pale. On water floats quite high, tail short, often cocked, neck hunched. In flight, all-dark wings, dark head, white belly and prominent bill distinctive; head appears raised, wings whirr. Juvenile resembles adult; in flight has narrow pale line on central underwing, resembling Least; has dusky flanks and neck, and lacks white scapular bar. **BP** Bill stubby, upturned and bright orange (breeding), dull orange (non-breeding) or grey (juv); eyes white; legs pale horn, webs dark blackish-grey. **SV** Silent at sea.

Least Auklet *Aethia pusilla* L 12–15 cm; WS 33–36 cm; WT 85 g

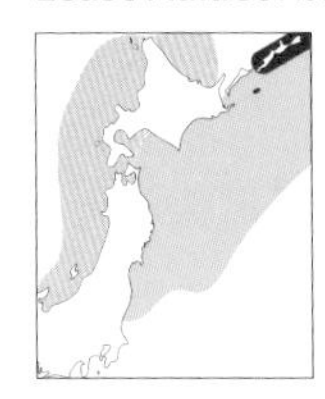

SD Common winter visitor (Oct–Apr) to N Japan, particularly off E Hokkaido, but also N Honshu; scarce in Sea of Japan and has strayed as far south as Kyushu. **HH** Pelagic, occasionally inshore, even in harbours. At sea forms dense compact flocks, flying just above wave height (even flying through wave tops), that may appear like distant smoke drifting across water. **ID** Tiny, dumpy auklet: dark and scaly in summer, pale and pied in winter. Breeding-plumage adult is mostly slate-grey, variably mottled white on throat, chest and vent (some have very dark chests and flank barring, others only lightly barred below); white throat patch well defined and conspicuous, even in flight. Forehead has hoary white streaks, and similar streaks extend behind eye. Non-breeding adult has dark upperparts and whitish scapular bar on closed wing; white underparts, including flanks, to chin. Face dark grey and white stripe behind eye less prominent. On water floats quite high, tail short, often cocked, neck hunched. In flight, upperwing uniformly dark and underwing mostly so, but has pale bar on centre of wing; flight whirring. **BP** Bill tiny, black with red tip (breeding), black with dull orange tip (non-breeding), or all dark (juv); eyes white; legs pale grey, webs dark blackish-grey. **SV** Flocks sometimes chatter at sea.

Whiskered Auklet *Aethia pygmaea* L 17–22 cm; WS 36 cm; WT 99–136 g

SD Extremely rare (accidental) in Hokkaido in winter (Feb–Apr) despite proximity to central Kuril Is breeding colonies; accidental south to N & C Honshu. **HH** Pelagic outside breeding season, but occasionally seen off rocky headlands. **ID** Similar to Crested Auklet, but size is closer to Least. Adult is stunning, with seven fine, wispy facial plumes, those extending from bill base forming white V on face. Non-breeding adult loses upper white facial plume and other plumes less prominent. Juvenile has paler grey underparts and face with dark eyestripe and facial bar. On water usually floats quite high, tail short, often cocked, neck hunched or stretched up. In flight, wings dark above and below; undertail paler grey than Crested; whirrs low over water. **BP** Bill tiny, bright orange (breeding), dull orange (non-breeding), or grey (juv); eyes white; tarsi blue-grey. **SV** Silent at sea.

Crested Auklet *Aethia cristatella* L 23–27 cm; WS 40–50 cm; WT 285 g

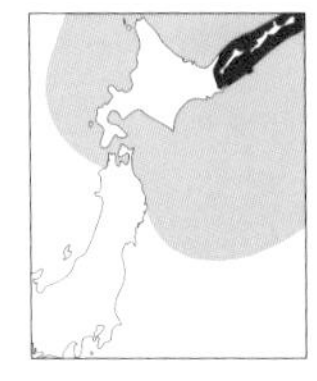

SD Common winter visitor to N Japan, especially E Hokkaido and NE Honshu; rare in Sea of Japan. **HH** Pelagic outside breeding season, but occasionally seen within sight of land off rocky headlands and occasionally in harbours. Forms dense flocks low above waves, often with Least Auklet; flocks may appear like distant smoke drifting across water. **ID** Size as Ancient and Japanese murrelets, but dumpier, with sooty grey-black plumage. Adult has short shaggy black crest curling forwards, prominent beak and gape, and short white plume behind eye. Non-breeding adult has thinner (or absent) crest, white cheek plume less prominent, bill inconspicuous. On water floats low, tail short, often cocked, neck hunched. In flight, pot-bellied; wings dark above and below, rather long; wings whirr; undertail-coverts and vent dark grey (pale in Whiskered). **BP** Bill stubby, bright orange with swollen upcurved gape (breeding), dull orange-black bill (non-breeding), or grey (juv); eyes white; tarsi blue-grey. **SV** Silent at sea.

Parakeet Auklet
ad sum
ad win
Least Auklet
juv
ad sum
ad win
ad sum
ad sum
Whiskered Auklet
ad sum
ad win
juv
ad sum
Crested Auklet
ad sum
ad sum
ad sum
juv
ad win

Rhinoceros Auklet *Cerorhinca monocerata*

L 32–38 cm; WS 56–63 cm; WT 520 g

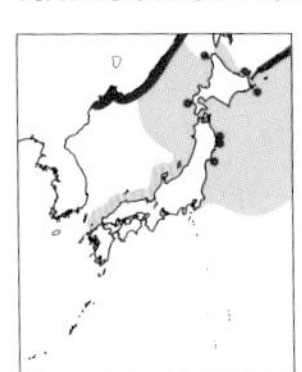

SD Common (locally abundant) breeder off Hokkaido (Teuri I hosts world's largest colony, c. 400,000); feeds far from colonies off NW, SW and E Hokkaido and Kuril Islands, thus found widely around Hokkaido coasts. Outside breeding season it is pelagic, dispersing along coasts of Sea of Japan and Pacific, rarely as far as Kyushu and Izu Is. **HH** Burrow-nester on islands with deep clifftop soil, feeding relatively near colonies. Returns at dusk and scurries rapidly to burrow. **ID** Large, size of Horned Puffin but predominantly blackish-grey upperparts, with only belly and vent whitish and not clear-cut from grey of flanks or breast. Head angular, with flat crown merging into long, heavy bill, white plumes behind eye and prominent white whiskers in breeding plumage. Long profile like guillemot, but bill more like winter puffin. Non-breeding adult lacks or has reduced facial plumes, is duller overall and resembles juvenile Tufted Puffin, which has deeper orange bill, more rounded head, all-dark belly and orange toes. Less upright than N Pacific auklets, more horizontal and neck more stretched. On water floats quite high like other puffins, tail short, often cocked, but may swim with only head and shoulders above surface. In flight, all-dark wings, upperparts and head (appears raised), contrast with dull white belly/vent; flight heavy on whirring wings with bend at 'wrist'. **BP** Bill dull orange with grey culmen, sporting bizarre off-white horn only when breeding, or duller and yellower with culmen grey (non-breeding) or dark grey (juv); eyes orange; legs pale grey, webs dark blackish-grey. **SV** Gives deep throaty gurgling *gugu gugu* and moaning *woo woo* in rising and falling series on returning to colony.

Tufted Puffin *Fratercula cirrhata*

L 33–41 cm; WS 64–66 cm; WT 780 g

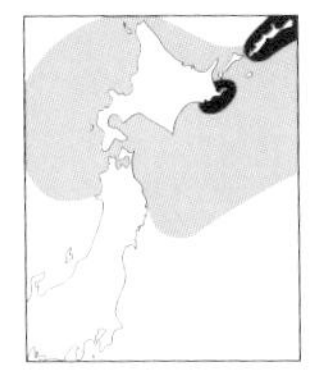

SD Several pairs breed in extreme SE Hokkaido, where species is at southwestern limit of range. Scarce elsewhere in winter, but has occurred off N & C Honshu. **HH** Colonial, nesting in deep burrows in thick soil. Feeds diurnally close to breeding sites; thereafter disperses at sea, but nomadic rather than migratory. **ID** Largest puffin. All-black with large, clownish head. Adult is blackish-grey, offset by large, triangular white face patch, and long yellow plumes behind ear-coverts. Non-breeding adult has only faint outline of face patch and plumes absent or indistinct. Juvenile is browner with less conspicuous bill. Stands very upright at colonies. On water floats high, neck short, head very rounded. Flight heavy and direct, wings whirring, tail short, toes extend beyond tip. Longer wings with bend at 'wrist' and slightly rounded tips visible in flight (recalls Rhinoceros Auklet, but differs from most auklets and murrelets). **BP** Bill very deep and short, largely red-orange with yellow-orange base, grey at base of lower mandible (breeding), smaller, grey-based orange bill (non-breeder sheds outer sheath), or smaller and duller (juv); eyes yellowish-white (ad) or brown (juv), narrow eye-ring red; tarsi bright orange (ad), or pale grey (juv). **SV** Rather quiet, even at colonies, a low, groaning *kurrr*; silent at sea.

Horned Puffin *Fratercula corniculata*

L 32–41 cm; WS 56–58 cm; WT 620 g

SD Disperses from breeding colonies (some as close as N Kuril Is) only short distances at sea; reaches Hokkaido occasionally in autumn and winter, accidental south to C Honshu. **HH** Pelagic after breeding, but occasionally occurs in inshore waters. **ID** Large, dumpy alcid with large, clownish head. Adult's white face and enormous bill are distinctive; eye prominent, appearing triangular due to fleshy horn above eye; fine black line extends behind eye. Non-breeding adult has dusky to dark-grey face, bill less prominent. Juvenile is similar to non-breeding adult, but has less conspicuous bill. On water floats quite high, neck appears short. In flight, all-dark wings and blackish upperparts contrast with white belly and face; flight heavy and direct, wings whirring. **BP** Bill is very deep and short, with high culmen, yellow at base and gape but red at tip (breeding), smaller, grey-based reddish-orange (non-breeding), or less deep and duller (juv); eyes black with narrow red/orange crescents above and below, and small conical, blue-grey 'horn' above eye (lacking in juv, reduced in winter ad); tarsi bright orange (usually visible in flight). **SV** Silent at sea.

Rhinoceros Auklet
ad sum
juv
ad sum
ad win

Tufted Puffin
ad sum
ad sum
ad win
juv
Horned Puffin
ad sum
ad win
juv
ad sum

Pallas's Sandgrouse *Syrrhaptes paradoxus* L 27–41 cm; WS 63–78 cm; WT ♂ 250–300 g, ♀ 200–260 g

SD Accidental, Honshu, Kyushu, Nansei Shoto. **HH** Dry grasslands, agricultural land. Walks quickly, pecking like dove. **ID** Pigeon-sized, with small yellowish or orange-buff head, neck and breast grey, upperparts barred buff, grey and black, shoulders and breast buff, belly patch black. Short legs, long, narrow grey primaries and long, pin-tail plumes all conspicuous. ♂: black barring on mantle and rump extends to lower neck and breast as narrow gorget, with limited spotting on wing-coverts. ♀: narrow black necklace, barring on mantle/rump, spotting on wing-coverts. In flight, underwing pale with black trailing edge to primaries and secondaries forms dark wingbar, long pointed wings with attenuated needle-like outer primaries and elongated central tail feathers also prominent. **BP** Bill very short, grey; eyes orange/brown; tarsi feathered, whitish-buff. **SV** Flight call is a rolling *por-r-r*. Narrow outer primaries thrum in flight.

Feral Pigeon *Columba livia* L 29–35 cm; WS 60–71 cm; WT 180–355 g

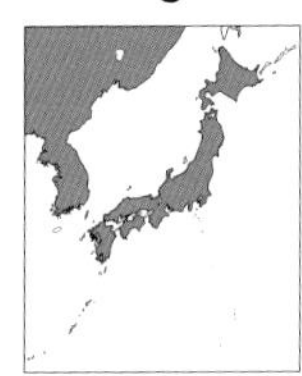

SD Widespread resident, Hokkaido to Nansei Shoto. **HH** Commensal, urban, suburban, rural. Survives locally even in regions with harsh winters, in urban areas or farms with livestock or grain stores. **ID** Plumage extremely variable. Wild-type: blue-grey with metallic green and purple sheen on neck, blackish-grey primaries and tail tip, and two black bars on wing-coverts. Tail grey, with white outer feathers, narrow black subterminal band and grey tip. In flight, long-winged, with pointed wingtips; underwing pale with dark border (flight-feather tips dark), and pale grey to white lower back and rump contrasting with mid-grey tail. Flight fast; whirls in tight flocks around feeding/roosting sites. Wings often held in steep dihedral. Extremely variable from brown and white to almost black. Four forms common: *all dark*, blackish; *pied*, bold black and white markings; *checkered*, like wild form, but with fine white bars or spots; and *brown*, largely brown except for flight-feathers and tail. **BP** Bill short, narrow, black, with raised grey cere; eyes orange-brown; tarsi orange-red. **SV** Burbling or moaning cooing *bru-u-oo-u*, or *oo-oo-oo* chorus of several birds together. In display, gives rattling clatter of wingbeats on take-off. **AN** Rock Dove.

Stock Dove *Columba oenas* L 32–34 cm; WS 60–69 cm; WT ♂ 303–365g, ♀ 286–290 g

SD Accidental (subspecies uncertain), islands off W Honshu, Kyushu, Nansei Shoto. **HH** Woodland edge, farmland. **ID** Compact, pale blue-grey, with purplish, green and pink sheen on neck, vinous breast and otherwise grey underparts. Mostly plain grey, with two short black bars on closed wing, black flight-feathers, grey rump and broad black terminal tail-band. In flight shows black flight-feather tips, paler primary bases and wing-coverts. Also note back/rump/tail pattern. **BP** Bill short, narrow yellowish tip, pink base; eyes dark reddish-brown; tarsi dark pink. **SV** Migrants generally silent.

Japanese Wood Pigeon *Columba janthina* L 37–43 cm; WT 402 g

SD *C. j. janthina*, islands off C & S Honshu, Kyushu, N Nansei Shoto; *C. j. nitens* (endangered, 30–40? birds), Ogasawara and Iwo Is; and *C. j. stejnegeri*, Yaeyama Is, S Nansei Shoto. Supposedly resident, yet mysteriously appears annually during spring/autumn on islands in Sea of Japan, and occasionally even mainland Japan. **HH** Mature broadleaf evergreen subtropical and temperate forest; feeds on berries in canopy, often seen in display flight over canopy, also in pines in Nansei Shoto. **ID** Largest, darkest pigeon. Brownish-black with metallic green gloss on neck and purple gloss on shoulders. *C. j. stejnegeri* appears smaller, shorter-tailed than nominate. *C. j. nitens*: reddish-violet or purplish-brown on head and neck. In flight, uniformly dark, crow-like, with long neck, broad wings and long fanned tail; flight slow, heavy with deep beats. **BP** Bill longer than other pigeons, narrow, black, horn-coloured at tip; eyes dark reddish-brown; tarsi deep red (ad), or pink (juv). **SV** Prolonged continuous deep moaning or growling *u wuu*... or *u uu*... like lowing cow; also dry *gnerrr* like bleating goat. Foraging birds move heavily and audibly in canopy. Single, loud wing clap on take-off. **AN** Black Woodpigeon.

Eastern Spotted Dove *Spilopelia chinensis* L 27–34 cm; WS 53 cm; WT 128–160 g

SD Vagrant, S Nansei Shoto. **HH** Farmland, woodland edge. **ID** Ground-foraging dove with prominent dark-grey neck patch covered with fine silvery spots. Long, narrow, graduated tail mainly blackish-brown with white tips to outer feathers forming contrasting white corners, visible in flight. **BP** Bill dark grey; eyes orange; tarsi dull dark pink. **SV** A purring crooning.

Pallas's Sandgrouse
ad ♂
ad ♀
ad ♂
ad
ad
Feral Pigeon
Japanese Wood Pigeon
ad nitens
ad janthina
ad janthina
Stock Dove
ad
ad
Eastern Spotted Dove
ad

Oriental Turtle Dove *Streptopelia orientalis*

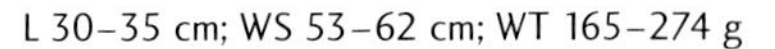
L 30–35 cm; WS 53–62 cm; WT 165–274 g

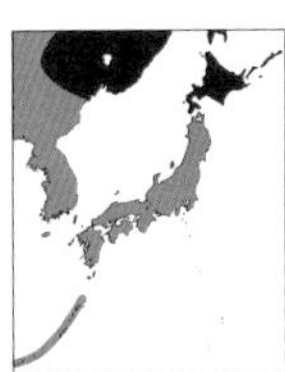

SD *S. o. orientalis*, Hokkaido (summer visitor May–Oct), resident throughout Honshu, Shikoku, Kyushu, accidental Ogasawara. *S. o. stimpsoni* resident Amami-Oshima south through Nansei Shoto. **HH** Boreal, temperate, subtropical forests; in temperate zone around woodland edges, farmland, parkland, large suburban and even urban gardens; commonly forages on ground. **ID** Medium-sized dove with prominent neck bars. Forehead blue-grey, head and face pale pinkish-brown, grading into blackish-brown upperparts. Mantle, scapulars, and upperwing-coverts dark with extensive blackish-brown centres, with rounded, rather broad rufous fringes, giving strongly scaled appearance. Lower back, rump and uppertail-coverts grey; slightly rounded blackish tail has pale grey tips forming narrow terminal band. Underparts pale pinkish-brown, whiter on belly and vent. Flight slow, appears dark with little contrast, except on undertail, which is largely black with broad pale-grey terminal band. *S. o. stimpsoni* rather dark, especially on neck and head, but forehead appears whiter than in nominate. **BP** Bill slender, dark grey; eyes orange; tarsi dull pink. **SV** Soft, deep *kuu*. In breeding season gives soft, repetitive hollow crooning: *or-doo doo-doo hoo-hoo hoo hoaw* or *der-der-pou-pou der-der-pou-pou*. **AN** Rufous Turtle Dove.

Eurasian Collared Dove *Streptopelia decaocto*

L 28–33 cm; WS 47–56 cm; WT 120–260 g

SD *S. d. xanthocycla*: accidental Sea of Japan islands and Nansei Shoto. *S. d. decaocto:* introduced, established, but scarce, C Honshu. **HH** Farmland and villages. Moves quietly amongst vegetation and on ground; relatively tame and approachable. **ID** Rather delicate, elegant and small-headed dove. Mostly pale, tan or pinkish-grey, with browner wings, wing-coverts and tail, black flight-feathers; white-bordered black hind-collar is distinctive. Flight action light and agile, with pale mantle and shoulder contrasting with grey wing-coverts and secondaries, and blackish primaries. Uppertail buffish-brown with black bases and white tips to outer tail-feathers, underwing-coverts pale and flight-feathers grey, with broad black base to underside of tail, which has broad white tip. **BP** Bill black; eyes dark reddish-brown; tarsi dull pink. Hybrids with domestic strains are typically paler overall, with paler undertail-coverts, and shorter, two- (not three-) syllabled calls. **SV** Song is a soft, repetitive three-note crooning: *coo-coooo-coo*.

Red Turtle Dove *Streptopelia tranquebarica*

L 20.5–23 cm; WT 104 g

SD *S. t. humilis* is a rare winter visitor (Oct–May) to S Japan (mainly Kyushu and Nansei Shoto), and an accidental visitor to all main islands. **HH** Scrub, woodland edge, farmland with hedges and isolated stands of trees. Moves quietly in trees when foraging; sometimes on ground. **ID** Small, compact, grey-headed dove, with rather dark plumage and black hind-collar. Adult ♂ has pale grey head, narrow, all-black hind-collar, deep brownish-pink upperparts (darkest on wing-coverts) and pale-grey rump; flight-feathers and tail blackish-grey with white tips to black outer tail-feathers. Underparts pale brownish-pink. ♀ is generally duller, less pinkish-brown. Juvenile has buff-fringed wing-coverts, affording overall scaled appearance recalling Oriental Turtle Dove, but single broad black neck bar distinctive. In flight, wing action is light and agile; appears somewhat dark with contrasting dark primaries, grey head and white corners to tail. **BP** Bill mid-grey to greyish-black; pale-grey orbital skin, irides brown to blackish-brown; tarsi dull grey to dark purplish-red. **SV** Soft *go goroo*, a *croo-croo-croo*, and purring *gurr gurr-gr-gurr*. **AN** Red Collared Dove.

Grey-crowned Emerald Dove *Chalcophaps indica*

L 23–27 cm; WT 108–160 g

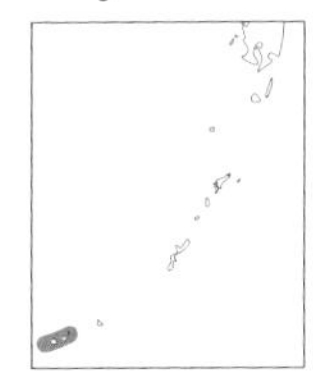

SD *C. i. indica* resident only in S Nansei Shoto (Yaeyama Is). **HH** Forages alone or in pairs on ground in dark subtropical broadleaf forest. **ID** Small, short-tailed dove. Adult is rather dark, with white or silver-grey forehead and band above eye, grey crown and nape (♂ extensive, ♀ restricted to forecrown); mantle dark greyish-pink, scapulars and wing-coverts iridescent green, ♂ has white and grey on carpals. Underparts dark greyish-pink, paler on belly. Juvenile is darker and browner, lacking grey crown, with rufous wingbar formed by tips to greater coverts, and extensively barred belly. Moves slowly and hesitantly; clatters on take-off, flies fast and low. In flight, narrow white band on forewing, two white bars across otherwise dark-grey lower back; rump and tail dark blackish-grey, with pale grey sides. **BP** Bill bright red or orange-red; eyes large, black; tarsi red. **SV** A very deep, rhythmic mellow cooing, almost humming, repeated several times, *whooo-whooo…* or *tuc-cooo*, the *tuc* often inaudible. **TN** Considered as *C. i. yamashinai* by OSJ. **AN** Common Emerald Dove.

Oriental Turtle Dove
orientalis
ad
ad
juv
ad
stimpsoni
Eurasian Collared Dove
ad
ad
ad ♂
ad ♀
Red Turtle Dove
ad ♀
ad ♂
Grey-crowned Emerald Dove
ad ♂
ad ♂
ad ♀

White-bellied Green Pigeon *Treron sieboldii*

L 31–33 cm; WT 180–270 g

SD *T. s. sieboldii* is a fairly common summer visitor (May–Sep) to Hokkaido and N Honshu, occurs year-round (residents supplemented by winter visitors) through C and W Honshu, Shikoku, Kyushu and Tanegashima, and rare visitor to Izu, Ogasawara, Iwo Is and Nansei Shoto. **HH** Broadleaf evergreen forest with fruiting trees; in north, deciduous forest with fruiting trees and vines; feeds quietly and inconspicuously in canopy, bursting into flight when disturbed. Bizarrely, flocks visit coasts to drink saltwater. **ID** Colourful, with creamy flanks, vent and undertail-coverts. ♂ head, neck and breast yellowish-green, mantle grey, wing-coverts and secondaries dull dark green, but broad scapular patch maroon. ♀ plain green, except pale flanks and vent. Dark patches or scaling on rear flanks and vent of ♂♀, far less extensive than in Ryukyu Green Pigeon. Wings rounded at tip, flight lazy but fast; usually singly or pairs, but flocks outside breeding season. **BP** Bill blue-grey at base, horn-coloured at tip; orbital skin blue-grey, irides have blue and orange rings; tarsi dull reddish-pink. **SV** Song a long, drawn-out, strongly inflected, mournful *oh aooh* and slightly more fluty *ooaa aaoo*. **TN** Formerly *Sphenurus sieboldii*. **AN** Japanese Green Pigeon.

Taiwan Green Pigeon *Treron formosae*

L 25–26 cm

SD *T. f. formosae* is accidental in S Nansei Shoto (Yaeyama Is). **HH** Subtropical evergreen forest, typically feeding on fruits in canopy, but shy and difficult to observe. **ID** Smallest of three green pigeons. Rather plain. Head yellowish-green, with golden cap from forehead to nape. Upperparts dark green, scapulars deep brownish-maroon (♂) or greenish-brown (♀), wings blackish-brown with very narrow yellowish-green fringes to greater coverts and secondaries. Underparts green, vent pale yellowish-green, each feather with dark blackish-green centre, undertail-coverts long with dark blackish-green centres and yellow fringes. Tail broad, long and rounded. Wings somewhat rounded at tip, flight heavy but fast above canopy. **BP** Bill blue-grey, rather stout-based; irides dark orange-brown with dark blue ring; tarsi dull dark pink. **SV** Song a long, fluty, mournful note, suddenly rising and wavering near end, *po-aa-poaaoo*, deeper than, but not as inflected as, White-bellied Green Pigeon. **TN** Retained, along with Ryukyu Green Pigeon, as Whistling Green Pigeon *Treron formosae* by IOC.

Ryukyu Green Pigeon *Treron permagnus*

L 33–35 cm; WT 250–270 g

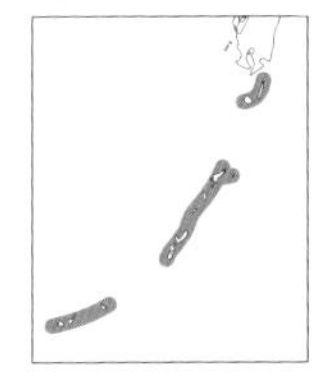

SD Endemic to Nansei Shoto: *T. p. permagnus* endemic in N, from Yakushima to Okinawa; *T. p. medioximus* from Miyako to Yonaguni. **HH** Not uncommon in subtropical forest, even suburban parks and gardens. Can be very tame and approachable, or shy and secretive. **ID** Larger and bulkier than White-bellied Green Pigeon, and much larger than similar Taiwan Green Pigeon; rather plain, but with distinctive undertail pattern. Deep green head, upperparts and underparts; scapulars deep brownish-maroon, wings blackish-brown with very narrow greenish fringes to greater coverts and secondaries. Lesser wing-coverts have slight reddish-violet tone (♂) or are deep greenish-brown (♀). Tail broad, long and rounded, flanks green, but vent feathers blackish-green with yellow fringes. Undertail-coverts long with dark blackish-green centres, narrowly fringed yellow, and extending almost to tail tip (slightly shorter with much broader fringes in Taiwan Green Pigeon). Wings somewhat rounded at tip, flight heavy but fast over canopy. *T. p. permagnus* larger than *T. p. medioximus*, but otherwise similar. **BP** Bill blue-grey, rather stout-based; irides have deep scarlet and dark blue rings; tarsi dull pink. **SV** Song a long, fluty mournful note, suddenly rising and wavering near end, *po-aa-poaaoo*, deeper, but not as inflected or as mournful as White-bellied. Also a staccato *puppupupupu*. **TN** Retained, along with Taiwan Green Pigeon, as Whistling Green Pigeon *Treron formosae* by IOC..

Black-chinned Fruit Dove *Ptilinopus leclancheri*

L 26–28 cm; WT ♂ 174g, ♀ 153–159 g

SD *P. l. taiwanus* accidental to Yaeyama Is. **HH** Lowland subtropical forest, where shy. **ID** Adult ♂ small with pale grey hood extending to nape and upper breast. Chin black, band bordering hood on lower breast purple, belly greyish-green and vent cinnamon. Mantle, scapulars, wing-coverts, tertials and rump bright green, flight-feathers and tail blackish-brown with green tone. ♀ has green head and neck, and dull purple pectoral band. Juvenile lacks pectoral band. Both ♀ and juvenile have face to vent considerably darker grey than ♂ (and Emerald Dove). In flight, flight-feathers appear black, contrasting with green upperparts and wing-coverts. Birds overhead can look very dark. **BP** Bill bright yellow with red base to lower mandible (♂), or dull yellow (♀); eyes red (♂) or dark brown (♀); tarsi dark reddish-pink. **SV** A deep, rather drawn-out *brrrrooooo*, easily lost in forest cacophony.

ad ♂
ad ♂
White-bellied
Green Pigeon
ad ♀
Ryukyu Green Pigeon
medioximus
ad ♀
Taiwan Green Pigeon
ad ♂
ad ♂
ad ♂
Black-chinned
Fruit Dove
ad ♀
ad ♂

Lesser Coucal *Centropus bengalensis* L 31–42 cm; WT 88–152 g

SD *C. b. lignator* has strayed to S Nansei Shoto (Sakishima Is) and Tsushima. **HH** Scrub, farmland, grassland and marsh edges. **ID** Large, heavy-set cuckoo, with rather short, rounded wings and long graduated tail. Very similar to extralimital Greater Coucal, but smaller, bill and tail shorter, and underwing-coverts chestnut (not black). Adult in breeding plumage is dull or dirty black, with dull brown back and warmer rufous-brown wings. Non-breeding adult has pale straw-coloured streaking on crown, mantle, face and upper breast, underparts otherwise rufous-white, barred dusky. Juvenile resembles non-breeding adult, but has dark barring on brown wings and tail, tawny head and neck with dark streaks, and tawny underparts. Flight typically low, laboured, with slow flaps. **BP** Bill thick, arched, slightly hooked, black in adult, greyish-horn in young; eye-ring dull blue, irides reddish-brown; tarsi blackish. **SV** Song a series of double, hollow notes followed by staccato phrases, *huup huup huup-uup tokalok tokalok*.

Chestnut-winged Cuckoo *Clamator coromandus* L 45–47 cm; WT 70–77 g

SD Accidental to Nansei Shoto, Sea of Japan islands, and NW Honshu. Secretive. **HH** Favours scrub, broadleaf forest and forest edge. **ID** Large, long-tailed cuckoo, proportions somewhat magpie-like. Adult has black head, with prominent erectile nuchal crest, sides of neck and collar white; mantle, rump and long graduated tail black; latter with white tips; underparts white with warm orange wash to chin, throat and upper breast; scapulars, upperwing-coverts and flight-feathers all chestnut. Vent and undertail-coverts black. Juvenile has rufous-scaled upperparts, lacks orange wash on underparts. Flight rather slow and heavy, like coucal. **BP** Bill arched, sharply pointed, black; eyes red; tarsi black. **SV** A loud hoarse *kurii kurii*, harsh *creech-creech-creech*, series of double metallic whistles *breep breep* and a cackling rattle *ghee ghe-ghuh-ghuh-ghuh-ghuh*. **AN** Red-winged Cuckoo.

Asian Koel *Eudynamys scolopaceus* L 39–46 cm; WT 190–327 g

SD *E. s. chinensis* is accidental to S Nansei Shoto (Sakishima Is) and as far north as C Kyushu, W Honshu and Izu Islands. **HH** Skulking but vocal bird of dense primary and secondary forest, open forest, plantations, orchards, scrub and gardens. **ID** Large, heavy-set cuckoo, with somewhat long, broad tail. ♂ glossy greenish-black. ♀ blackish-brown with numerous fine buff spots on wings, back and rump, buff-barred tail, buff streaks on throat and barring across entire underparts. **BP** Bill heavy, arched and slightly hooked, dark grey-green or dull-green; eye-ring dull blue, irides red; tarsi blue-grey. **SV** Name derives from voice; shrill, fast, oft-repeated slurred whistles *ko-el* rising in pitch and frequency; a loud repetitive *kow-wow*, by day or at night. Also a wide range of other sweet to harsh notes. **AN** Western Koel.

Pacific Long-tailed Cuckoo *Urodynamis taitensis* L 40 cm; WT 125 g

SD Vagrant to C Honshu. **HH** Favours dense forests. **ID** Large, heavy-set cuckoo, with prominent pale supercilia and long, broad tail. The upperparts are brown with transverse rufous bars, while the underparts are buff with longitudinal dark brown streaks. **BP** Bill heavy, arched, yellowish-brown; eyes pale brown; tarsi brownish. **SV** Calls include a piercing, rising *zzhweeesh*, and a strident *pe-pe-pe-pe-pe-pe-pe*.

Lesser Coucal
ad breeding
ad non-breeding
juv
Chestnut-winged Cuckoo
ad
juv
Asian Koel
ad ♂
ad ♀
Pacific Long-tailed Cuckoo
ad
juv

Fork-tailed Drongo-Cuckoo *Surniculus dicruroides* L 25 cm; WT 35 g

SD Accidental (Apr/May) to Okinawa and Kyushu. **HH** Uncommon and secretive, at forest edge and in scrub. **ID** Small to medium, slim, black cuckoo (drongo-like, but behaves like cuckoo). Adult is glossy blue-black (some have white thighs and nuchal patch), with long, deeply notched (drongo-like) tail. Vent/undertail-coverts are black with narrow white bars that continue on underside of outer tail-feathers. Juvenile has white-spangled wing-coverts, rump and tail tip. **BP** Bill arched, black; eyes brown; tarsi blue-grey. **SV** Ascending series of 4–7 piercing, rising whistles, *pii pii pii...*, by day or night. **TN** Retained as Square-tailed Drongo-cuckoo *S. lugubris* by OSJ.

Large Hawk-Cuckoo *Hierococcyx sparverioides* L 38–40 cm; WT 150 g

SD Accidental to NW Honshu, NW Kyushu and Nansei Shoto. **HH** Open deciduous woodland. **ID** Large; can appear confusingly like sparrowhawk, best separated using jizz. Adult has dark grey crown and face and black chin; upperparts dark grey-brown, upper breast rufous, rest of underparts white with heavy streaking on upper breast and barring on lower breast, vent white. Tail, long, full, grey with 4–5 broad blackish bars and grey/white tip. Juvenile has finely-barred mantle, more broadly barred back, rump and wings. Underparts white, with rufous wash on neck-sides, vertical dark gular stripe, bold vertical flecks on breast, narrow horizontal dark bars on belly and flanks; vent white. **BP** Bill short, arched, blackish with yellow gape line; eye-ring yellow, irides yellow (ad) or brown (juv); tarsi yellow. **SV** Shrill series of loud and piercing whistled notes, rising in pitch *pee-pee-ah pee-pee-ah pee-pee-ah...*, with hysterical crescendo. Calls at night, during the day, and often in flight. ♀ gives short, more tuneful, purring whistles *turr durr durr* (rising in volume).

Northern Hawk-Cuckoo *Hierococcyx hyperythrus* L 32–35 cm; WT 100–150 g

SD Summer visitor (May–Aug) to all four main islands of Japan; migrant through Nansei Shoto. **HH** Coniferous, mixed and deciduous broadleaf forest on mountain slopes. Not uncommon, but elusive and very secretive. Brood parasite of flycatchers. **ID** Medium-sized cuckoo that may appear confusingly like sparrowhawk. Adult has mid-grey crown, cheeks and chin, and white throat, neck-sides and nuchal crescent; upperparts plain grey with prominent white scapular crescent. Underparts washed warm rufous from neck-sides and breast to flanks. Tail, long, quite broad, grey with 3+ narrow blackish bars, a very broad blackish band near tip bordered above with rufous and tipped rufous. Juvenile has brown wings with grey bars, and blackish streaks on lower neck, breast and flanks. **BP** Bill short, arched, grey above, greenish-yellow at base and tip; eye-ring yellow, irides reddish-brown; tarsi yellow. **SV** Highly vocal, calls by day and night from perch and in flight; a far-carrying frenetic, shrill *ju-ichi*, beginning weakly, but accelerating and becoming stronger and higher pitched: *ju-ichi ju-ichi ju-ichi*. **TN** Formerly known as Hodgson's Hawk Cuckoo *H. fugax*, and Rufous Hawk Cuckoo.

Fork-tailed
Drongo-Cuckoo
ad
juv
ad
Large Hawk-Cuckoo
ad
juv
Northern Hawk-Cuckoo
ad
juv
ad

Lesser Cuckoo *Cuculus poliocephalus*

L 22–28 cm; WT 50–52 g

SD Common summer visitor (May–Aug), Nansei Shoto to SW Hokkaido; accidental C & E Hokkaido, Ogasawara and Iwo Is. **HH** Elusive, deciduous and evergreen broadleaf forest, lowlands and hills. Brood parasite of *Cettia* warblers. **ID** Slimmer, more compact than other cuckoos, hood variable, but sometimes less extensive, only to upper neck. Blackish barring on underparts wider spaced even than Oriental Cuckoo, so appears whiter, enhanced by unbarred vent and buffy-grey undertail-coverts; undertail blackish with white spots, uppertail grey with narrow white tip. Hepatic ♀ is bright rufous with indistinct barring or blotches on crown and nape. Narrow white panel on underwing, the white coverts quite strongly barred dark, and rump/uppertail-coverts relatively darker than Oriental, contrasting less with tail. **BP** Bill short, arched, grey above, yellowish below and at gape; eye-ring yellow, irides brown; tarsi yellow. **SV** Highly vocal in early morning and late afternoon, also at night, and in flight over canopy. Loud six-note whistled *tep-pen-kaketaka* with emphasis on *kake*, falling on final slurred double syllable. ♀ gives high-pitched piping *pipipipipipipi* in flight.

Indian Cuckoo *Cuculus micropterus*

L 32–33 cm; WT 119–120 g

SD *C. m. micropterus* accidental or rare summer visitor (Apr–Jun), Nansei Shoto and Kyushu north to N Honshu and Teurijima (Hokkaido). **HH** Elusive, lowland forest, forest edge. **ID** Resembles Common Cuckoo; smaller, with darker eyes, mantle colour and distinctive tail pattern. Adult: hood mid-grey (♂) or brownish-grey (♀); upperparts dark grey (♂ slaty, ♀ dark brown), rump and tail darkest. Underparts white, with narrow to broad slate bands across breast, flanks and undertail-coverts. Tail long, dark grey (concolorous with rump) with broad blackish subterminal band, prominent narrow grey/white tips and white marginal spots (often concealed when tail closed); pale to dark grey underneath with bands of white spots. Juvenile: whitish or buff scaling on head and back. **BP** Bill short, arched, grey above, yellowish below and at gape; eye-ring yellow or grey, irides brown; tarsi yellow. **SV** Repetitive, loud, four-syllable call *kwer-kwah-kwah-kurh*, the last syllable lowest and longest.

Oriental Cuckoo *Cuculus optatus*

L 30–34 cm; WT 99–100 g

SD Common summer visitor (May–Aug), all main islands, migrant Nansei Shoto, accidental Ogasawara and Iwo Is. **HH** Secretive, boreal forests in the north and at high altitude, mature mixed forest further south; favours canopy; rarely in open habitats. Brood parasite of *Phylloscopus* warblers. **ID** Closely resembles Common Cuckoo. Many have distinctly yellowish-buff undertail-coverts, lacking bars, but sometimes with distinct spots. Hepatic ♀ has barred rump. Juvenile like Common. Flight rapid and direct; underwing shows bold white barring on inner primaries and outer secondaries, and has barred underwing-coverts. **BP** Bill slightly shorter than Common; eye-ring yellow, irides orange/brown, or dark (juv); tarsi yellow. **SV** ♂ calls from high canopy, far-carrying, deeply resonant and rhythmic; even, double notes in series: *po-po…po-po…po-po…* or *boop-boop…boop-boop…boop-boop*, sometimes preceded by hoarse intake *gua*. Commonly gives a very rapid multisyllabic *po-po-po-po-po-po-po* before settling into typical monotonous pattern of 10–20 bisyllabic notes. **TN** Formerly *C. saturatus*. **AN** Horsfield's Cuckoo.

Common Cuckoo *Cuculus canorus*

L 32–36 cm; WS 54–60 cm; WT 70–130 g

SD *C. c. canorus*, common summer visitor (May–Aug), all main islands, migrant Nansei Shoto, accidental Ogasawara and Iwo Is. **HH** Often conspicuous in open grassland, farmland, reedbeds, marshes, parkland, low woodland, open boreal forest. Brood parasite of *Acrocephalus* warblers, accentors and pipits. **ID** Adult: hood and upperparts mid- to dark grey. Underparts white, greyish-black bars on breast and flanks narrower than Oriental; vent and undertail-coverts white (not buff). Long uppertail-coverts as back, but tail darker blackish-grey than upperparts, with large white tips, undertail dark with white spots on outer feathers and large white tips to all. ♀ as ♂, though may have rufous wash to upper breast, or hepatic (rufous-brown with narrow black bars, palest on breast and belly, but rump unbarred). Juvenile: finely barred brown and grey across upperparts, rump and tail, with white nape patch. Flight heavy with shallow beats; underwing uniform, coverts whitish, lightly barred; broader-based silvery-white underwing panel, so appears much whiter than Oriental, with less contrasting, shorter central stripe, reaching only to p5–6. **BP** Bill short, arched, grey above, yellowish below and at gape (bill usually longer than Oriental, but overlaps); eye-ring yellow, irides yellow/orange (ad) or dark (juv); tarsi yellow. **SV** Loud repetitive disyllabic *cuk-kooo* call given frequently from post, bush or treetop; ♂ cocks tail and droops wings when calling. In flight, ♂ gives typical call or guttural chattering; ♀ may give descending series of bubbling or cackling *squip quip quipurrrr…* calls.

Lesser Cuckoo
ad ♂
ad ♀
hepatic
juv
Indian Cuckoo
ad ♂
juv
Oriental Cuckoo
ad ♀
hepatic
juv
ad
ad ♂
ad ♂
ad ♂
Common Cuckoo
ad ♀
hepatic
juv

Japanese Scops Owl *Otus semitorques*

L 23–25 cm; WS 55–59 cm; WT 100–200 g

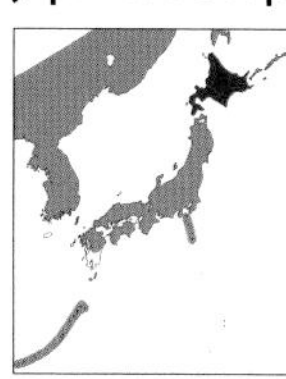

SD *O. s. semitorques* is widespread, but scarce resident of Japan's four main islands and main offshore islands (Tsushima, Oki, Sado, Izu), though perhaps only a summer visitor/migrant in Hokkaido; *O. s. ussuriensis* has strayed to Honshu. **HH** From lowlands to low mountains: farmland, tree-lined streets, parks, woodland edge and forest (deciduous/mixed in N, subtropical evergreen in S), where hunts mainly terrestrial insects, reptiles and small mammals, occasionally birds. Crepuscular/nocturnal. **ID** Rather large scops owl with particularly large head and conspicuous ear-tufts. Generally greyish-brown or dull brown mottled black and buff, with pale-brown nuchal collar; upperparts browner, face and underparts greyer, face rimmed blackish. **BP** Bill short, hooked, grey; eyes reddish-orange, pupil generally appearing large; tarsi feathered brown, toes yellowish. **SV** Very variable, regionally and sexually. Includes a frog-like *whuk* and whistled *pew*, also *kwooo*, *kwaa*, *kuui* and *wowowo* calls. Dog-like barking calls in breeding season and cat-like *myau-myau* calls year-round. **TN** Previously within Collared Scops Owl *O. bakkamoena*/*O. lempiji* (e.g. OSJ).

Pryer's Scops Owl *Otus (semitorques) pryeri*

L 23–25 cm; WS 55–59 cm; WT 100–170 g

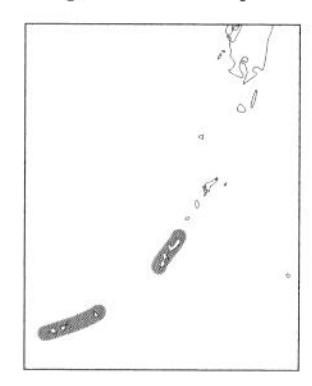

SD Endemic resident of C & S Nansei Shoto (Okinawa to Iriomote). **HH** Subtropical evergreen forest, where hunts mainly terrestrial insects, reptiles and small mammals, occasionally birds. Crepuscular/nocturnal. **ID** Very similar to Japanese Scops Owl, but smaller and redder and lacking toe feathers. **BP** Bill short, hooked, grey; eyes reddish; tarsi unfeathered, toes yellowish. **SV** On Okinawa: *pew pew pew*; *kyo kyo kyo* or *woffu-woffu-woffu-woffu*. **TN** Previously within Collared Scops Owl *O. bakkamoena*/*O. lempiji* (e.g. OSJ).

Oriental Scops Owl *Otus sunia*

L 18–21 cm; WS 50.5–52.6 cm; WT 75–95 g

SD *O. s. japonicus* is summer visitor (Apr–Sep) throughout Japan, but scarce in Hokkaido and absent from Nansei Shoto. **HH** Parks, large gardens, woodland edge and montane forest (deciduous and mixed in N and evergreen broadleaf in S). Crepuscular/nocturnal. **ID** Small scops owl with two colour forms, grey (common) and rufous (scarce), with prominent ear-tufts. Grey morph overall mid- to dark greyish-brown, with black spotting on crown, fine black streaking on mantle, prominent white spots on scapulars (forming bar) and white spots in primaries. Facial disc grey with whiter brows and blacker margin; grey-brown underparts finely vermiculated with strong dark streaks. Rufous morph is reddish-brown, with more prominent scapular bar. Wings rather short, only 4–5 primaries extending beyond tertials. Best distinguished from similar species by voice. **BP** Bill pale grey-horn; eyes yellow to pale orange; lower tarsi unfeathered, feet grey to greyish-flesh. **SV** Soft, monotonous, three-note phrase, *bu-po-so*, or *buk-kyok-koo* (first syllable sometimes too soft to hear), often repeated at night, occasionally calls during day, especially on spring migration.

Ryukyu Scops Owl *Otus elegans*

L 19–22 cm; WS 60 cm; WT 94–125 g

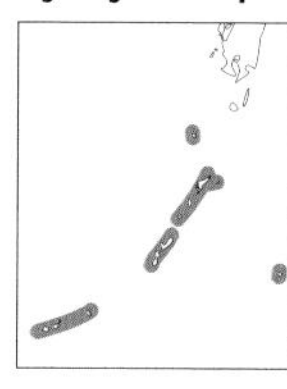

SD *O. e. elegans* is widespread in Nansei Shoto from Amami Is south to Yonaguni; also Okinoshima (offshore Kyushu); *O. e. interpositus* is resident on Daito Is. **HH** Subtropical evergreen broadleaf forest from sea level to hill tops. Crepuscular/nocturnal. **ID** Small, dark rufous-brown scops owl with short (often not visible) ear-tufts; lacks collar of Collared Scops, and is more spotted than Oriental. Dark spotting on crown, fine vermiculation and dark streaks on mantle, and distinct white scapular bar. Prominent facial disc with white brows and chin/lower face. Underparts finely barred and strongly streaked. **BP** Bill dark grey; eyes yellow; tarsi feathered, feet rather large, toes grey. **SV** Highly vocal: ♂ gives very repetitive and rather resonant coughing whistle, *ko-ho ko-ho*; or *u-hu* or *pu-wu*; ♀ sometimes responds with a nasal *nnya* or *niea*, also a high-pitched chittering recalling fledgling kestrels. **AN** Elegant Scops Owl.

Japanese Scops Owl
Pryer's Scops Owl
ad brown form
ad grey form
ad

Oriental Scops Owl
ad

Ryukyu Scops Owl
elegans
ad

Snowy Owl *Bubo scandiacus* ♂ L 55–64 cm; WT 700–2500 g; ♀ L 60–70 cm, ♂♀ WS 125–166 cm; WT 708–2950 g

SD Very rare visitor, mostly in winter, to Hokkaido, also recorded in N, C & W Honshu. **HH** Open habitats, forest edge, coastal grasslands or alpine regions. Commonly diurnal. **ID** Very large white owl, with rather small head lacking ear-tufts. ♂ has some black spotting on wing-coverts and sparse black bars on tertials. ♀ generally larger, appears greyer, because of extent of black streaking on crown and nape, and narrow black barring on mantle, wings, underparts and tail; face, neck and upper breast white; at close range retains overall appearance of being white. In flight, ♂ ghostly; ♀ appears white with heavy grey barring on tail and finer barring on wings. **BP** Bill greyish-black and mostly concealed by facial feathering; eyes large, black-rimmed lids contrast with bright golden-yellow irides; tarsi feathered grey-white, toes large, claws black. **SV** Generally silent away from breeding grounds. **TN** Formerly *Nyctea scandiaca*.

Eurasian Eagle-Owl *Bubo bubo* L 48–75 cm; WS 138–170 cm; WT ♂ 1500–2800 g; ♀ 1750–4200 g

SD *B. b. borissowi* is extremely rare resident of N Hokkaido and S Kuril Is; *B. b. kiautschensis* is accidental to Izu, Goto and Amami Is. **HH** Forested hills with rocky outcrops and cliffs. Crepuscular/nocturnal. **ID** Very large; upperparts dark brown and tawny with black and grey mottling, underparts creamy brown to tawny with heavy blackish-brown spotting on breast and fine barring and more elongated streaking on belly and flanks; large facial disc has black rim and long ear-tufts also black-edged. In flight, appears rather plain, rusty brown and wings extremely broad. **BP** Bill dark grey; eyes deep orange; legs feathered, toes yellow. **SV** Very deep, hoarse coughing *uh-hoo* or *whoohuu* repeated infrequently, far-carrying; clicks beak if disturbed or gives hard barking *ka ka-kau*.

Blakiston's Fish Owl *Bubo blakistoni* L 60–72 cm; WS 180–190 cm; WT ♂ 3100–3550 g, ♀ 3600–4600 g

SD Endangered. Extremely rare resident of E & C Hokkaido and S Kuril Is. **HH** Mature, mixed boreal riparian forest in hills and lowlands: requires rivers, lakes or springs that do not freeze in winter, and large cavities for nesting. Crepuscular/nocturnal. **ID** Enormous. More uniformly greyish-brown than Eurasian Eagle-Owl, lacks black outline to facial disc and ear-tufts are broader, looser. Has white chin and throat, especially noticeable when throat bulges during calling. Upperparts cool, mid-brown with blackish-brown shaft-streaking to mantle and back, scapulars more broadly streaked blackish-brown, closed wings heavily barred dark brown and pale sandy brown; tawny-buff underparts have many narrow elongated shaft-streaks and fine dark crossbars. **BP** Bill dark greyish-horn; eyes yellowish-orange; tarsi feathered, pinkish-grey toes have only very short feathering or none. **SV** Very deep, echoing duet: ♂ gives deep *boo-boo*, immediately followed by ♀'s more sonorous single *bu*; this three-note duet is repeated in short or long series at *c.*one-minute intervals. **TN** Retained in genus *Ketupa* by OSJ.

Ural Owl *Strix uralensis* L 50–62 cm; WS 124–134 cm; WT ♂ 500–950 g, ♀ 570–1300 g

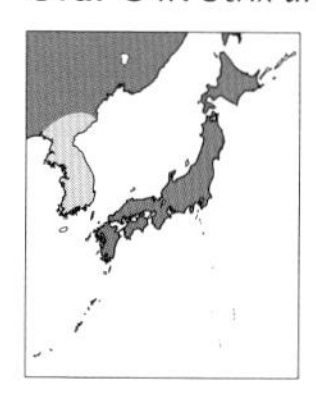

SD Resident throughout main Japanese islands: *S. u. japonica* (Hokkaido); *S. u. hondoensis* (N Honshu); *S. u. momiyamae* (C Honshu); and *S. u. fuscescens* (W & S Honshu, Kyushu and Shikoku). **HH** Mature mixed forest from northern cool temperate to semi-subtropical. **ID** Large, greyish-brown owl with large head; pale facial disc radially streaked brown, rimmed narrowly white and black. Upperparts cool greyish-brown, heavy blackish-brown streaking on head and mantle; wings and tail dark greyish-brown with paler and darker bars and prominent off-white scapular bar. Underparts pale buff with dark blackish-brown shaft-streaks, heaviest on neck and breast, more widely spaced on belly. Tail long, somewhat wedge-shaped, barred, extending well beyond wings. *S. u. japonica* is very pale greyish-brown with very pale face, white spots bordering facial disc, and largely white underparts. The other main island races are doubtfully separable in the field, but are smaller than *japonica*, darker dusky-brown, with heavier streaking on back and breast and adjoining facial disc. Flight slow and *Buteo*-like on broad wings. **BP** Bill dull yellow; eyes small, irides black; tarsi feathered whitish. **SV** Deep, gruff *guhu … hoo huhu hoo-hoooh* or *gouhou … guroske go ho*, with clear pause between introductory call and sequence of hoots that dies away at end; mainly autumn and late winter. Also *goh goh goh*, a harsh *gyaa gyaa* or *schrank* (♀ only), similar to Grey Heron, and loud barking given by nesting ♀.

Snowy Owl
ad ♂
ad ♀
Blakiston's
Fish Owl
Eurasian
Eagle-Owl
Ural Owl
ad
japonica
ad
hondoensis

Little Owl *Athene noctua*

L 21–23 cm; WS 54–58 cm; WT ♂ 167–177g, ♀ 166–206 g

SD Accidental, or escapee (subspecies uncertain). **HH** Farmland and open woodland, isolated tree rows and windbreaks. Diurnal or crepuscular. **ID** Medium-sized owl with long legs. Broad-headed, lacking ear-tufts, but has prominent dark-rimmed facial disc with pale eyebrows, whisker lines and chin bar. Flat crown is mid-brown finely spotted white; back, wings and tail sandy to dark brown with paler spots on mantle and scapulars, tail has broad pale bars. Underparts buff, broadly streaked mid-brown, but lower belly/vent whitish. Undulating flight on very rounded wings; appears short-tailed. May perch prominently on posts, bobbing when excited. **BP** Bill yellow-horn; eyes large, irides lemon-yellow; legs and toes feathered pale buff or white. **SV** Calls (day or night) somewhat wigeon-like, plaintive high-pitched whistled *quew*, *kee-you* or *kaaaooh*; also a low, mellow hooting in slow series, and high-pitched staccato *kir-rik-kir-ik*.... **TN** Not included by OSJ.

Boreal Owl *Aegolius funereus*

♂ L 21–25 cm; WS 50–62 cm; WT 90–115 g;
♀ L 25–28 cm; WT 120–200 g

SD *A. f. sibiricus* is scarce; but possibly widespread resident in Hokkaido; accidental to N Honshu. **HH** Mature boreal forest, using old woodpecker holes (particularly Black Woodpecker) for nesting. Nocturnal. **ID** Small, but very large-headed, spotted owl. Prominent white and grey facial disc, with almost complete black border and raised black eyebrows affording 'surprised' look; chin and lower disc rim brownish-black. Crown spotted grey, nape, mantle and wings dark brown with large white spots, especially on scapulars; underparts whitish with large brown spots especially heavy in band across upper breast. Wings and tail both broad, rounded, brown, spotted with grey in five rows across primaries, three on tail. **BP** Bill yellowish-horn; eyes large, irides yellow; tarsi feathered buff. **SV** Territorial ♂ gives far-carrying repetitive series of short, soft hoots, in bouts lasting many minutes: *po-po-po-po-po*... rising slightly in pitch and becoming clearer, but ending rather suddenly; also a sharp whistled *skiew*. **AN** Tengmalm's Owl.

Northern Boobook *Ninox japonica*

L 27–33 cm; WS 66–70 cm; WT 172–227 g

SD Japanese Hawk-Owl *N. (j.) japonica* (possibly a full species) is summer visitor (May–Sep) to main islands of Japan north to Hokkaido (where uncommon), and scarce visitor to Nansei Shoto (breeds in N), Ogasawara and Iwo Is. **Ryukyu Hawk-Owl** *N. (j.) totogo* (possibly full species) is resident in Nansei Shoto from Amami Is south to Sakishima Is. *N. j. florensis (ex macroptera)* is accidental to Sakishima Is, Daito Is, Izu Is, N Honshu and Hokkaido. **HH** Gardens, parks, secondary and primary forest, temperate to tropical, from lowlands to c.1,500 m. Mainly nocturnal, hunting large insects in flight; often drawn to streetlights. **ID** Medium-sized, 'elongated' owl with no facial disc or ear-tufts. Small, grey-brown, rounded head and long barred tail give distinctive shape. **Japanese** is largely dark chocolate-brown on head and upperparts, with heavy, brown streaking on whitish underparts; white spot above bill, between eyes; chin and vent white. **Ryukyu** is even darker, with darker face and more heavily streaked underparts. **BP** Bill greyish-black; eyes oversized, irides yellow-orange; legs brown, toes yellow. **SV** Call given frequently by **Japanese** on territory consists of deep, paired hoots repeated for many minutes at a time: *hoho hoho hoho* .... whereas **Ryukyu** gives more evenly spaced *ho ho ho ho* notes, trailing away. **TN** Retained within Brown Hawk Owl *N. scutulata* by OSJ.

Eastern Grass Owl *Tyto longimembris*

♀ L 32–36 cm; WS 100–116 cm; WT 265–450 g

SD Vagrant to Iriomotejima (subspecies uncertain). **HH** Open areas with tall grassland. Crepuscular. **ID** Distinctive heart-shaped facial disc and long narrow wings. Upperparts dark brown and tawny, with some fine silvery spots on crown, mantle and wings (lacks heavy streaking on chest of Short-eared Owl, which may occur in similar habitat), flight-feathers barred tawny, grey and smudgy blackish-brown; underparts creamy buff with fine black spots, belly and vent whitish. Facial disc grey-buff with tawny rim, blackish-brown vertical line on forehead and smudges between eyes and bill. Broad wings have golden-buff patch at base of primaries; tail short, pale, with dark bars. **BP** Bill whitish; eyes appear relatively small, black; tarsi white to whitish-pink. **SV** Various shrieking and screaming sounds in flight.

Little Owl
Boreal Owl
Northern Boobook
ad japonica
ad
totogo
Eastern Grass Owl
ad japonica
ad
ad

Long-eared Owl *Asio otus* ♂ L 35–38 cm, WT 220–305 g; ♀ L 37–40 cm, WT 260–435 g; WS 90–102 cm

SD *A. o. otus* uncommon resident N Japan, winter visitor C Japan to Kyushu, rare Nansei Shoto, Ogasawara Is and Iwo Is. **HH** Coniferous and mixed forests, windbreaks, woodland. Northern birds migratory/irruptive. Nocturnal/crepuscular; roosts communally in winter. Erects long ear-tufts when alert, then upright camouflaged posture if disturbed. **ID** Facial disc orange-buff; eyebrows and whiskers form white X. Upperparts dark greyish-brown and tawny, with heavy streaking on mantle and wings, white scapular spots and strong grey barring on flight-feathers; extensive tawny-buff panel at base of primaries. Underparts buff, narrow streaking, with some side bars, continues on belly. Flight slow, wavering, on long narrow wings, 'rowing' wingbeats interspersed with glides, very similar to Short-eared Owl (SEO), but wings shorter, broader, orange-buff with dark bars; tail has narrow grey barring, upperwing dark with dark carpal patch, orange-buff primary base panel, *4–5* narrow bands across grey flight-feathers (see SEO); underwing has broad black carpal crescent, and *3–5* blackish bands on grey primary tips; undertail brown narrowly barred grey. **BP** Bill grey; eyes orange; tarsi feathered buff. **SV** ♂ gives slow series of low moaning *boo boo boo*; *oo oo oo oo* or *hooom hooom* notes, occasionally in duet; ♀ gives higher, softer *sheoof* and sighing *hnyauu*. Nasal, barking *wrack wrack-wrack* in alarm. Juvenile gives high, metallic squeaking *kee-kee*.

Short-eared Owl *Asio flammeus* L 35–41 cm; WS 94–110 cm; WT ♂ 200–450g, ♀ 280–500 g

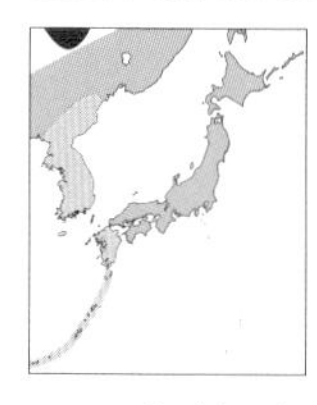

SD *A. f. flammeus* uncommon/scarce winter visitor (Oct–Apr), Hokkaido to Nansei Shoto, accidental Ogasawara Is. **HH** Open farmland, grassland, reedbeds, marshes. Crepuscular, sometimes diurnal, hunts in open, roosts on ground, may perch in open. **ID** Large head, prominent pale facial disc, with darker radial streaking and dusky patches around eyes; short ear-tufts rarely visible. Upperparts heavily mottled, some have fairly prominent scapular bar; buff panel at base of primaries. Darker on breast than belly, creamy to buff or pale brown with heavy streaks concentrated on upper breast, with long narrow streaks on lower breast (lacking side bars), unpatterned belly/vent. Flight typically low, quartering like harrier, may hover or stall then drop onto prey; upperwing has black carpal patch, *2–3* black bands on pale buff-brown primaries and *3–4* narrow black bands on secondaries. Underwing very pale, almost white, with broad blackish bands on primary tips, broad black carpal crescent, and black line to rear of axillaries formed by dark tertials; buff tail broadly barred black above, undertail narrowly barred black. **BP** Bill dark greyish-black; eyes yellow; tarsi feathered, buff. **SV** Typically silent.

Grey Nightjar *Caprimulgus jotaka* L 27–32 cm; WT 60–113 g

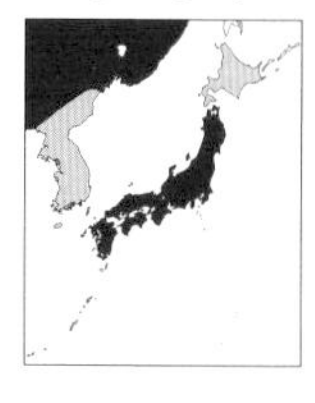

SD *C. j. jotaka* uncommon summer visitor (May–Oct) to all four main islands, rare visitor Nansei Shoto, Ogasawara and Iwo Is. **HH** Forested areas with clearings, at treeline in mountains; crepuscular/nocturnal. **ID** Highly cryptic; heavily barred and streaked blackish-brown and grey. Crown flat, face dark with white malar and broad white chin. Flight erratic and lazy; ♂ shows white bases to outer primaries, ♀ buffish-brown, broad, white, subterminal band on undertail (absent in ♀). **BP** Bill grey; eyes black; tarsi grey. **SV** Monotonous, repetitive *chuckchuckchuckchuck* or *kyokyokyokyokyo* lasting several minutes, at dusk, dawn and by night, from high perch or ground. Sharp wing-clapping in flight. **TN** Formerly within Jungle Nightjar *C. indicus* (e.g. OSJ).

Oriental Dollarbird *Eurystomus orientalis* L 27–32 cm; WT 109–186 g

SD *E. o. cyanocollis* very uncommon widespread summer visitor (May–Sep), Honshu, Shikoku and Kyushu; migrant Nansei Shoto, accidental Hokkaido, Ogasawara and Iwo Is. **HH** Forest, woodland edge in river valleys. Sits upright on prominent perch; sallies for large insects. **ID** Stocky, with large head, long wings and short tail. Adult: dark blackish-brown to dark green and cobalt blue. Flight loose and floppy, wings long, broadly rounded with whitish or pale-blue patches near base of primaries. Juvenile: darker with poorly defined wing patch. **BP** Bill short, broad-based, red (ad) or black above, reddish-orange below (juv); narrow eye-ring red, irides brown; toes red. **SV** Harsh, guttural *khya khya-a*, a hoarse, noisy *shraak* or *grek*, and in flight a cackling *ge ge gegegeegegege* or shorter *cher-cher*. **AN** Broad-billed Roller.

ad
Long-eared Owl
ad
Short-eared Owl
Grey Nightjar
ad ♀
ad ♂
ad ♂
Oriental Dollarbird
ad
ad

Himalayan Swiftlet *Aerodramus brevirostris*

L 13–14 cm; WT 12–13 g

SD Has strayed to Hokkaido, Honshu, Kyushu and Nansei Shoto (subspecies uncertain). **HH** Over forests and lowland cultivation. **ID** Small, blackish-brown swiftlet, with long, blunt-tipped wings, white outer-primary shafts; tail short with shallow fork. Generally uniform brown, but broad greyish- to brownish-black rump band contrasts with darker mantle and blackish-brown tail; underparts (especially throat) paler greyish-brown, scaled paler on undertail-coverts, and blackish-brown underwing-coverts contrast with paler flight-feathers. **BP** Bill black; eyes large, irides brown; toes black. **SV** Silent away from breeding range.

White-throated Needletail *Hirundapus caudacutus*

L 19–21 cm; WS 50–53 cm; WT 101–140 g

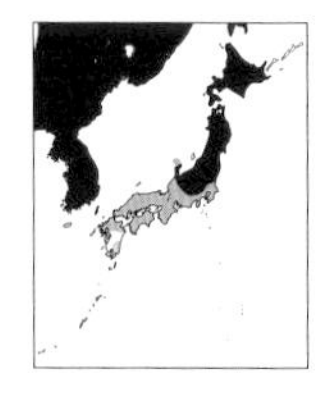

SD *H. c. caudacutus* is a summer visitor (Apr–Sep) to N Honshu and Hokkaido, migrating through C & S Japan. **HH** Montane regions with mature forest. Generally high overhead; sometimes descends to lakes to drink, or over flooded fields or agricultural land to feed. **ID** Very large, with long scythe-shaped wings, bulky, rather long body, and short blunt tail (needle-fine tips visible only at close range). Adult: blackish-brown, with sharply defined white throat and large U-shaped vent patch extending forwards on flanks to rear of wings; forehead and supraloral also narrowly white. Upperparts dark brown with conspicuous pale silvery-grey 'saddle', wings and tail glossed metallic green, white on inner tertial tips; has metallic blue-green patch on innerwing-coverts and outer tertials. Juvenile: duller with less contrasting mantle. **BP** Bill short, black; eyes brown; toes black. **SV** A high-pitched, shrill 'screaming' *tsuiririri juriri* recalls Pacific Swift; wings make audible *swoosh* when low overhead.

Silver-backed Needletail *Hirundapus cochinchinensis*

L 19–20 cm; WT 76–86 g

SD Vagrant to Yonagunijima and Tairajima, Tokara Is. **HH** Typically high over mature forest. **ID** Like White-throated Needletail, but appears shorter-bodied and slimmer. Weakly defined greyish-white throat has diffuse edge, more diffuse but brighter 'saddle' visible at long range; lacks white on tertials. **BP** Bill short, black; eyes brown; toes black. **SV** Generally silent, but wings audible. **TN** Not included by OSJ.

Common Swift *Apus apus*

L 16–19 cm; WS 40–44 cm; WT 36–52 g

SD *A. a. pekinensis* is a very rare spring overshoot from NE China to S Nansei Shoto (Yaeyama) and islands in Sea of Japan (e.g. Hegura). **HH** Over coastal lowlands. **ID** Uniform dark blackish-brown swift with all-dark rump and only slightly forked tail; lacks contrast on upperwing. Throat white, forehead pale grey. **BP** Bill black; eyes brown; very short tarsi black. **SV** Sometimes utters shrill buzzing screams: *vzz-vzz vzzzz*, or *sriiirr*. **TN** Not included by OSJ.

Pacific Swift *Apus pacificus*

L 17–20 cm; WS 43–54 cm; WT 43–50 g

SD *A. p. pacificus* is a fairly common summer visitor (Apr–Oct) to Hokkaido. *A. p. kurodae/kanoi* breeds from N Honshu to Amami Is, and is a rare visitor to Ogasawara and Iwo Is. **HH** Coasts (with cliffs) and high mountains; nests colonially in cliff crevices, also under roofs of buildings; often forages in flocks. **ID** Rather long, slender-bodied swift, with long, narrow sickle-shaped wings. Plain blackish-brown (usually appears black) with narrow, but very conspicuous white rump band and deeply forked tail; tail and primaries blackest, mantle and wing-coverts slightly browner, tertials and secondaries paler still. Throat whitish, with some paler, browner scaling on flanks, belly and vent, most marked in young birds. **BP** Bill black; eyes brown; very short tarsi black. **SV** Flocks close to breeding sites are highly vocal, giving shrill, high-pitched, trilling screams: *tsiririri* or *juririri* and harsh *spee-err*; calls are more sibilant, less buzzy than Common Swift. **AN** Asian White-rumped Swift.

House Swift *Apus nipalensis*

L 12–15 cm; WS 28–35 cm; WT 20–35 g

SD *A. n. kuntzi* is a locally common resident in SW Honshu, Shikoku and Kyushu; also reaches Nansei Shoto, Ogasawara and Iwo Is. **HH** Colonial; favours montane and coastal cliffs and caves, but also nests on buildings in coastal towns. **ID** Small, rather stocky, blackish-brown swift (usually appears black) with broad white rump band wrapping onto flanks, and short, slightly notched tail, the notch disappearing when fanned in rather fluttering flight. Wings shorter, broader and broader-tipped, less scythe-like than other swifts, and trailing edge to wing often appears straight. Throat greyish or whitish. **BP** Bill black; eyes brown; toes black. **SV** High-pitched twittering trill, *chiiririririri* or *juririri*, and soft screaming *vzz-vzz* like weak Common Swift. **TN** Formerly within Little Swift *A. affinis*. OSJ considers this *A. n. kuntzi*, but IOC *A. n. nipalensis*.

Himalayan Swiftlet
ad
White-throated Needletail
ad
Common Swift
ad
Silver-backed
Needletail
ad
Pacific Swift
pacificus
ad
House Swift
ad

Ruddy Kingfisher *Halcyon coromanda*

L 25–28 cm; WT 60–92 g

SD *H. c. major* is a summer visitor (May–Aug) to Japan's main islands north to SW Hokkaido; *H. c. bangsi* is resident throughout Nansei Shoto. **HH** Scarce, solitary and rather secretive, but vocal; favours mature deciduous or dense broadleaf evergreen forest, with lakes, rivers and streams. **ID** Large, ruddy-orange kingfisher. Upperparts orange or rufous-brown, with violet sheen on upper back and bright, narrow, turquoise lower back/rump. Underparts paler rufous-orange, chin/throat almost white and vent pale. *H. c. bangsi* is darker with more extensive violet or purplish sheen to upperparts, neck and chest than *H. c. major*, with larger pale-blue rump patch. **BP** Bill very large, especially deep at base, orange-red; eyes brown; toes orange-red. **SV** Mostly silent, but breeding ♂ sings (mainly early morning) from concealed perch in canopy, but also during day when raining. Song a high-pitched descending, rolling whistled trill: *pyorrrr* or *kyororoଓ*; also an explosive rattle.

White-breasted Kingfisher *Halcyon smyrnensis*

L 27–28 cm; WT 75–108 g

SD Vagrant to S Nansei Shoto (Yaeyama Is; subspecies uncertain). **HH** Freshwater and coastal wetlands. **ID** Large. Adult: deep chocolate-brown head and underparts, with extensive white patch from chin to centre of breast; mantle, back, wings, rump and tail bright blue. Juvenile: duller with paler bill and dusky breast markings. In flight, contrasting dark brown wing-coverts, blue secondaries, and white primaries with black tips. **BP** Bill very large, especially deep at base, bright red; eyes brown; toes red. **SV** Sharp, woodpecker-like *kyo*, *kya*, *chik* or *kit*, thin, short *pi* and angry rattling *krich-krich*.... **AN** White-throated Kingfisher.

Black-capped Kingfisher *Halcyon pileata*

L 28–30 cm; WT 64–118 g

SD Rare spring migrant (Apr–Jun) in S Japan, has bred W Honshu, accidental north to Hokkaido. **HH** Found at wide range of wooded and wetland habitats. **ID** Large. Adult: black head with white chin, collar and upper breast; mantle, rump and tail deep blue, as are secondaries and primary-coverts (mantle and upperwing have purple-violet sheen); remaining wing-coverts black; primaries white with black tips, but hidden at rest. Lower breast, belly, flanks and vent rufous-orange. Juvenile: duller (including bill) with buff collar and dusky scaling on breast. In flight, contrasting black wing-coverts, blue secondaries, white primaries with black tips. **BP** Bill very large, especially deep at base, dull red; eyes brown; toes dark red. **SV** A short *ki ki*, and in breeding season a louder, fast, hard rattle, *kyoro kyoro*... or *kikikikikikiki*, recalling White-breasted, but less grating.

Collared Kingfisher *Todiramphus chloris*

L 23–25 cm; WT 51–100 g

SD *T. c. collaris* is vagrant to S Nansei Shoto. **HH** Coastal wetlands, especially mangroves. **ID** Upperparts, from crown to tail, iridescent greenish-blue, with distinctive white collar; underparts white. Broad black band from base of bill to nape separates white underparts from green-blue crown; also has white patch between eye and base of bill. **BP** Bill very large, especially deep at base, upper mandible and tip black, lower mandible whitish/horn; eyes brown; toes dark grey/black. **SV** Calls include strident *krek-krerk*. **TN** Formerly *Halcyon chloris*. **AN** Mangrove Kingfisher.

Oriental Dwarf Kingfisher *Ceyx erithaca*

L 14 cm; WT 14–21 g

SD *C. e. erithaca* vagrant to Okinawa. **HH** Forested streams and pools. **ID** A tiny, bright rufous and black kingfisher, with large head and very short tail. ♂ largely rufous-orange, but with black forehead, blue-black mantle, black wings and violet sheen to crown and to rump (although rufous-backed morph also occurs). ♀ similar, but lacks violet sheen to crown. Juvenile is duller version of adult. **BP** Bill long, red; eye dark brown, surrounded by black eye-patch; toes red. **SV** Call consists of very high-pitched, shrill *tsriet-tsriet* or *tseet* and softer *tjie-tjie-tjie* notes given when perched and in flight. **AN** Black-backed Dwarf Kingfisher.

Ruddy Kingfisher
ad *major*
ad *bangsi*
ad *bangsi*
White-breasted Kingfisher
ad
Black-capped Kingfisher
ad
Collared Kingfisher
ad
Oriental Dwarf Kingfisher
ad ♂

Common Kingfisher *Alcedo atthis* L 16–20 cm; WS 24–25 cm; WT 19–40 g

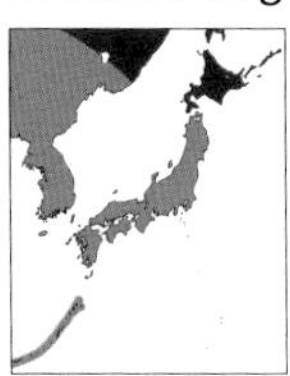

SD *A. a. bengalensis* is fairly common resident through most of Japan from Nansei Shoto to N Honshu, but summer visitor in Hokkaido, winter visitor in Izu Is, and accidental to Ogasawara Is. **HH** Wetlands, lakes, ponds, wooded streams and rivers, where flow gentle or non-existent. On migration and in winter also on coasts, at harbours and estuaries. **ID** Adult has bright metallic green head and wings, scaled dark green and pale blue on crown and spotted turquoise on upperwing-coverts; upper back, rump and short tail shining blue. Orange spot on lores and band across ear-coverts, white neck-sides and chin; otherwise entire underparts and underwing-coverts bright orange. Juvenile is duller with dark breast-band and black toes. Flight low, fast and direct; also hovers and plunge-dives after prey. **BP** Bill long, black (♂), or orange-based (♀); eyes brown; toes red. **SV** Often calls in flight, a strongly whistled *tiii*, *tjii* or *peeet*; repeats calls rapidly or gives series of hard *chit-it* or *tee titi titi titi* notes when agitated. **AN** River Kingfisher.

Crested Kingfisher *Megaceryle lugubris* L 37–43 cm; WT 230–280 g

SD *M. l. lugubris* widespread but scarce resident of S & C Japan, from Yakushima to N Honshu; *M. l. pallida* is local resident in Hokkaido. **HH** Cold, fast-flowing rivers and streams in forested mountains; moves downriver, rarely to coasts, in winter. **ID** Very large, stout, grey and white kingfisher, with overly large, crested head and erectile plumes from forehead to nape. Overall, black above and white below; upperparts narrowly barred white on shaggy crest, back and wings, and more broadly barred white on rather long tail. Largely white underparts have band of grey streaks from malar region to breast-sides, and broader band, similarly grey with white, on upper breast. ♂ has some rusty-orange in malar stripe and chest band, and white underwing-coverts. ♀ lacks orange, but has rusty underwing-coverts. Wings broad, flight steady, direct. *M. l. pallida* is larger and paler grey overall than *M. l. lugubris*. **BP** Bill long, largely black, but blue-grey at base and horn-coloured at tip; eyes brown; toes grey. **SV** Loud, grating, chattering *kyara kyara* given by both sexes; powerful *chek chek* and wader-like *wick* or *pik pik-wik* in flight. **TN** Formerly *Ceryle lugubris*. **AN** Greater Pied Kingfisher.

Rainbow Bee-eater *Merops ornatus* L 19–28 cm; WT 20–33 g

SD Vagrant to S Nansei Shoto. **ID** Resembles larger Blue-tailed Bee-eater, but has rusty-brown on crown, yellow and black on throat, and rump and vent azure-blue, with shorter black tail. ♂ has long, narrow tail-streamers with spatulate tips. ♀ has shorter, broader central rectrices. **BP** Bill long, slender, curved, black; eyes dark red (♂) or reddish-brown (♀); toes black. **SV** A melodious, fluty *piru*. **AN** Australian Bee-eater.

Blue-tailed Bee-eater *Merops philippinus* L 29–36 cm; WT 29–43 g

SD Vagrant to Okinawa. **ID** Crown, nape and mantle are green, lower back, rump and tail are blue. Black eyestripe is bordered with blue; chin yellow, foreneck brown. Breast to belly green, but undertail-coverts blue. **BP** Bill long, slender, curved, black; eyes red (ad) or brown (juv); short tarsi greyish-black. **SV** Gives *cheer-it* call singly or in trilled or rattled series in flight.

Eurasian Hoopoe *Upupa epops* L 25–32 cm; WS 44–48 cm; WT 47–89 g

SD *U. e. epops* is a scarce, early spring overshoot migrant to Japan (Feb–Jun; has bred Honshu) from Nansei Shoto to Hokkaido, accidental to Ogasawara and Iwo Is. **HH** Open woodland, forest edge, groves and thickets, especially in river valleys, and in parks and gardens. Commonly forages for invertebrates in dry soil or sandy ground. **ID** Small head, large erectile crest and long decurved bill give strange hammer-headed appearance. Adult is overall pinkish-buff, with black and white barred wings; crest longer than head, usually held flat, comprises long loose graduated feathers each tipped black, forming barring across crown. Juvenile is duller with shorter crest and bill. In slow, undulating flight reveals broad, barred, square-ended wings, white lower back, and black tail with one broad, curving white band across middle; erects fan-like crest on alighting (and in aggression). **BP** Bill long (5–6 cm), thin, decurved, black, greyish-pink at base; eyes brown; toes black. **SV** Harsh *guwaai* call, but territorial song a muted series of hollow trisyllabic hoots, *oop-oop-oop oop-oop-oop*....

Common Kingfisher
ad ♀
juv
ad diving
for fish
ad ♂
ad ♀
lugubris
Crested Kingfisher
ad ♂
lugubris
ad ♂
ad ♀
ad ♂
pallida
Rainbow Bee-eater
ad
ad
juv
Blue-tailed Bee-eater
ad
juv
ad
ad
ad
Eurasian Hoopoe

Eurasian Wryneck *Jynx torquilla*

L 16–18 cm; WT 30–50 g

SD *J. t. japonica* is scarce summer visitor (May–Sep) to Hokkaido and N Honshu, scarce migrant and occasional winter visitor (Oct–Apr) from C Honshu to Kyushu, rare in Nansei Shoto. **HH** Open deciduous woodland, forest edges, riparian thickets, hedgerows and clumps of trees in cultivated land; in winter also in reedbeds. Usually feeds on ground. **ID** Small, highly cryptic, atypical woodpecker. Overall grey-brown, upperparts greyer with broad blackish-brown band on crown and back, also from lores to ear-coverts, neck and scapulars, and malar region. Underparts warmer buffy-grey with narrow dark brown bars from chin to flanks. Wings rusty-brown with blackish spotting, and blackish barred flight-feathers; tail long, grey and rounded at tip, with 3–4 narrow blackish-brown bars. **BP** Bill conical, short, pointed, horn-coloured; eyes brown; toes grey-brown. **SV** High-pitched, repetitive ringing *quee-quee-quee* recalls Lesser Spotted Woodpecker, but lower and hoarser. When disturbed at nest writhes neck and hisses.

Rufous-bellied Woodpecker *Dendrocopos hyperythrus*

L 20–25 cm; WT 53–74 g

SD Migrant *D. h. subrufinus* is vagrant to Sea of Japan islands off W Honshu and Hokkaido. **HH** Mixed broadleaf and coniferous forests. **ID** Rufous, black and white woodpecker. ♂ has bright red cap and nape, white face, black back, rump and tail (mantle barred white), wing-coverts tipped white and flight-feathers barred white (no white shoulder patch). ♀ has white-spotted black crown. Underparts rufous-orange, pale red on vent. Juvenile is black above, spotted white, with dark buff underparts heavily mottled black. **BP** Bill long, dark grey upper mandible, yellow below; eyes reddish-brown; tarsi grey. **SV** Silent away from breeding range.

Japanese Pygmy Woodpecker *Yungipicus kizuki*

L 13–15 cm; WT 18–26 g

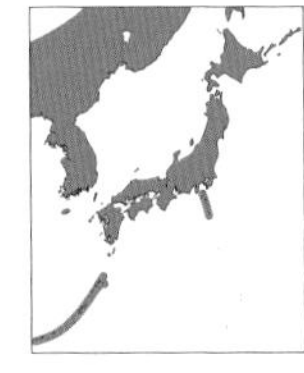

SD Ranges throughout Japan: *Y. k. seebohmi* (Hokkaido); *Y. k. nippon* (N & C Honshu); *Y. k. shikokuensis* (SW Honshu, Shikoku); *Y. k. kizuki* (Kyushu); *Y. k. matsudairai* (Yaku-shima, Izu Is); *Y. k. kotataki* (Tsushima, Oki Is); *Y. k. amamii* (Amami Is); *Y. k. nigrescens* (Okinawa); *Y. k. orii* (Iriomotejima). **HH** Lowland to subalpine (to 2,100 m) forests, also riparian thickets, scrub, urban parks and gardens; especially forages on thinner branches; often with mixed woodland bird flocks. **ID** Small, dusky, ladder-backed woodpecker. Upperparts dusky-brown, greyer on crown, mantle plain, but back narrowly barred blackish-brown and white, tail black. Face dusky-brown with pale supercilia merging into whitish patch on sides of hindneck; malar region, chin/throat and upper breast also whitish, lateral throat-stripe dusky-brown merging into dark neck-sides and dusky underparts, which have darker spotting. Underparts off-white streaked grey-brown in northern races, buff with heavy dark brown streaking elsewhere. Becomes smaller and darker in N–S cline, southern populations also having heavier streaked underparts. ♂ has tiny red spot on sides of hindcrown, visible only when wind ruffles feathers or in territorial disputes. **BP** Bill short, sharply pointed; eyes brown to reddish-brown (age-related); short tarsi blackish-grey. **SV** Calls frequently, sharp *khit-khit-khit* notes, more frequently a highly distinctive buzzy *kzzz kzzz* or an agitated *kikikiki*. Drumming extremely faint; feeding taps can be confused with foraging Varied Tit.

Lesser Spotted Woodpecker *Dryobates minor*

L 14–16 cm; WS 24–29 cm; WT 16–26 g

SD *D. m. amurensis* is scarce and local resident of Hokkaido. **HH** Deciduous and mixed lowland woodland (often oaks or alders), near rivers, wetlands or at forest edge. Quiet, unobtrusive; commonly forages at mid-level in trees, on underside of larger branches and thin snags. **ID** Small rounded head and fine bill contribute to gentle appearance. Smaller and less sharply pied than Great Spotted Woodpecker. ♂ forehead off-white, crown red, with buff cheeks and black T-bar on face-sides reaching neither nape nor bill. ♀ has more extensive off-white forehead and black rear crown; black T-bar reduced. Upperparts resemble White-backed Woodpecker, with broad white transverse bars on folded wing; black back is barred white, but rump and tail black. Underparts white to buff, streaked finely with black. In flight, white-barred black wings and back distinctive, flight deeply undulating. **BP** Bill fine, grey; eyes brown; tarsi grey. **SV** Very vocal when breeding, otherwise rather silent: high-pitched gee-geegeegee, or *ki ki* notes, weaker than Great Spotted, and Wryneck-like (but less querulous) or falcon-like *kee-kee-kee-kee*. Drumming rarely heard, but comprises brief, weak high-pitched rattling, often in two parts.

Eurasian Wryneck
ad
Rufous-bellied Woodpecker
ad ♂
ad ♀
Japanese Pygmy Woodpecker
nigrescens
ad ♂
ad ♀
Lesser Spotted Woodpecker
ad ♂
ad ♀

White-backed Woodpecker *Dendrocopos leucotos* L 25–30 cm; WT 92–158 g

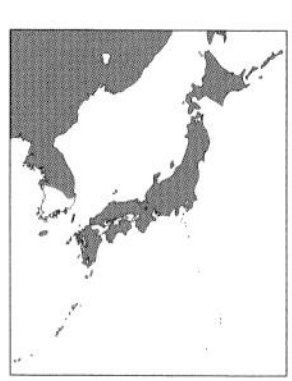

SD Resident: *D. l. subcirris* (Hokkaido); *D. l. stejnegeri* (N & C Honshu and Sado I); and *D. l. namiyei* (C & W Honshu, Shikoku, Kyushu, Oki Is). **HH** Mature deciduous woodland, often in damp areas, with dead and dying trees. Often feeds at base of trunks or on ground. **ID** Large pied woodpecker superficially like Great Spotted Woodpecker (GSWP). ♂ has red crown, ♀ black crown. Black face bar reaches bill base, connects to neck bar, but not to nape. Upperparts black with broad white transverse bars on folded wing; lower back/rump white (especially obvious in flight). Forehead, cheeks, neck- and throat-sides whitish, but underparts buffier, with narrow black streaks from chest to flanks; rear underparts suffused buffish-pink and vent pale red. Tail black with large white spots at sides. In flight, resembles GSWP, but lacks scapular patch; white lower back/rump distinctive. Races become darker from north to south, with more extensive black on chest, heavier black streaking on deeper red underparts. **BP** Bill long, grey; eyes brown; tarsi grey. **SV** Hard contact *kyo kyo* and weak *wick* calls perhaps inseparable from those of GSWP. Pairs, and ♀ with young, sometimes give cackling series of harsh *sketchekekeke* notes. In late winter/early spring ♂ drums powerfully for up to two seconds; the normally resonant roll accelerates from middle onwards, fades at end, rather like a dropped table-tennis ball bouncing to a halt.

Owston's Woodpecker *Dendrocopos owstoni* L 25–30 cm; WT 92–158 g

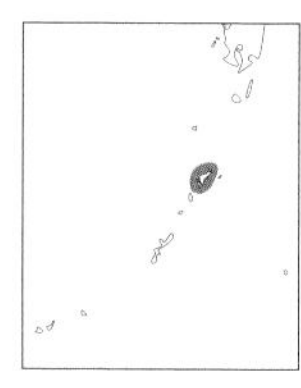

SD Uncommon resident on Amami-Oshima. **HH** Mature subtropical forest, where often feeds at base of trunks or on ground. **ID** Structure and plumage recall White-backed Woodpecker (WBWP), but appears larger and very much darker, with broad black stripe on neck-sides to upper breast and back, almost entirely black upperparts. So heavily streaked on underparts as to appear almost all black, and lower belly and vent dark red. **BP** Bill long, grey; eyes brown; tarsi grey. **SV** As White-backed Woodpecker. **TN** Retained within *D. leucotos* by IOC, but not others. **AN** Amami Woodpecker.

Great Spotted Woodpecker *Dendrocopos major* L 20–24 cm; WS 38–44 cm; WT 62–98 g

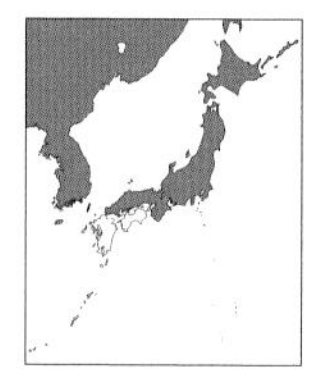

SD Largely resident *D. m. japonicus* is common and widespread in Hokkaido. *D. m. hondoensis* is resident in Honshu, Sado and Tsushima, but accidental in Shikoku and Kyushu. *D. m. brevirostris* is vagrant, occasionally reaching Sea of Japan islands. **HH** Very wide range of woodland/forest types, including gardens and riparian scrub. Agile, forages on trunks, limbs, even among fruits on outer twigs, occasionally on ground. **ID** The commonest pied woodpecker; ♂ has black crown with small, bright red nape patch, ♀ lacks red nape. Boldly black and white with large white shoulder patches, black bar from nape to base of bill, and large, deep red vent patch. Tail black with large white spots at sides. Juvenile like White-backed Woodpecker, but has less distinct white shoulder, more diffuse red vent and all-red crown (but black rim). *D. m. brevirostris* has larger white scapular patches, and whiter face and underparts. In flight, wings black with white patches on innerwing, four narrow bands of spots on flight-feathers, and white bars on sides of otherwise black tail. **BP** Bill dark grey, chisel-shaped (short and thick in *brevirostris*); eyes grey (nestlings) becoming dark brown then reddish-brown (ad); short tarsi blue-grey. **SV** Abrupt *kick* or *chick*, rather loud, sometimes given in rapid series *ke-ke-ke-ke* in alarm. Drumming brief (< 1 second), very rapid, ending abruptly, but repeated frequently, especially by ♂, in early spring.

Pryer's Woodpecker *Dendrocopos noguchii* L 31–35 cm; WT 155 g

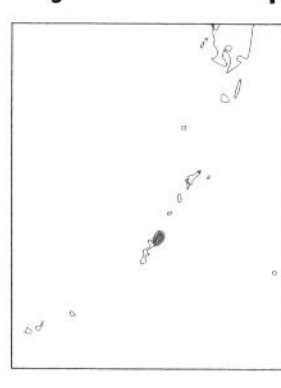

SD Critically Endangered. Endemic to Yanbaru, N Okinawa. **HH** Mature, subtropical broadleaf evergreen forest; feeds on ground and in canopy. **ID** Large, dark, with deep red belly and vent, and some red on breast and mantle. ♂ brighter than ♀, with deep red crown and nape; ♀ has brown crown contrasting with paler brown head-sides. Wings blackish-brown with several white spots in outer primaries; tail blackish-brown. **BP** Bill pale greyish-horn; eyes dark reddish-brown; strong tarsi blackish-grey. **SV** Highly vocal year-round; a sharp *kwe kwe kwe*, whiplash-like *pwip* or *whit*, hard *kyo* or *kyu-kyu-kup* in contact and more rattling *kyararara*. 'Drum rolls' (three per minute) vary in length, but accelerate. **TN** Formerly *Sapheopipo noguchii*. **AN** Okinawa Woodpecker.

White-backed Woodpecker

Owston's Woodpecker

Great Spotted Woodpecker

Pryer's Woodpecker

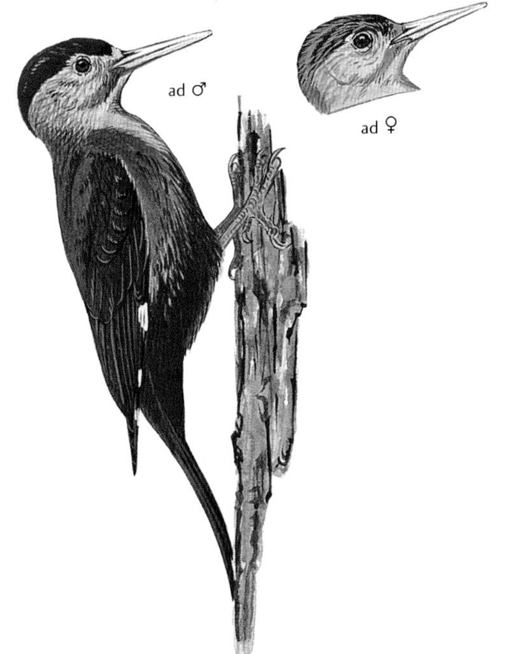

Eurasian Three-toed Woodpecker *Picoides tridactylus* L 20–24 cm; WS 32–38 cm; WT 46–76 g

SD *P. t. inouyei* rare local resident, C Hokkaido. **HH** Boreal and subalpine forest above 650 m; favours dead and dying spruce. Quiet, shy. **ID** Blackish-grey woodpecker with white back and ochre-yellow (♂) or grey-streaked crown (♀). Underparts white with black malar extending into heavy streaking on breast-sides, and barring on belly/vent. In flight, distinctive, wings largely dark (with narrow rows of white spots), back white. **BP** Bill grey; eyes black; tarsi grey. **SV** Call: abrupt *pwick* or *kip*, softer than Great Spotted, a short shrill rattled alarm *kri-kri-kri-kri* and short powerful drumming (> 1 second), accelerating and trailing off at end; given in paired bouts.

Black Woodpecker *Dryocopus martius* L 45–55 cm; WS 67–73 cm; WT 250–370 g

SD *D. m. martius* uncommon, widespread resident Hokkaido, very rare resident N Honshu. **HH** Mature mixed forest, sometimes in pure conifer stands (if not dense); wanders in winter to more marginal habitat. Forages low on large trees, often near ground. Excavates distinctive, deep vertical oval cavities. **ID** Glossy black, crow-sized, with thin neck and large head (♂ crown red; ♀ red hindcrown). Juvenile: sooty-black, dull red crown. Flight direct, but slow, appears clumsy with head raised until last few metres before landing, when typically undulating. **BP** Bill large, pale ivory with grey tip; white irides; strong tarsi dark grey. **SV** Call: loud, vibrant *kyoon kyoon*, far-carrying ringing *kweeoo kweeoo* and *kree-a kree-a kree-a* territorial call; in flight, rapid *kyorokyorokyoro* or *krry-krry-krry*. Song: strident series of loud whistles *kwee kvi-kvi-kvi-kvi*…or *kree-kree-kree*. Powerful irregular taps when foraging; powerful drumming sounds like distant heavy gunfire, very loud and rather long (up to three seconds), up to four rolls per minute.

Japanese Green Woodpecker *Picus awokera* L 29–30 cm; WT 103–138 g

SD Endemic resident. *P. a. awokera* Honshu (and associated offshore islets), Tobishima, Awashima, Sado, Oki; *P. a. horii* Shikoku, Kyushu; *P. a. takatsukasae* Tanegashima, Yakushima. **HH** Mixed deciduous and broadleaf evergreen forest; commonest at 300–1,400 m. **ID** Distinctive green and grey woodpecker with heavily marked underparts. Head, face and breast grey, lores black. ♂: bright red crown, nape and malar patch. ♀: grey crown, red nape and red centre to black malar. Mantle, scapulars, wing-coverts, secondaries and tertials green, primaries blackish-brown with white spots; rump bright green, tail darker green with faint dark grey barring on outer feathers. Off-white belly, flanks and undertail-coverts all covered with rows of black chevrons. Populations decrease in size and become increasingly dark N–S. **BP** Bill grey above with black tip, yellow below; eyes black; tarsi grey. **SV** Call: strong, whistled *piyoo piyoo piyoo*, whiplash-like *pwip pwip* and frog-like *kere kerere*; also a hard, abrupt *ket ket*; flight call harsh chattering *jerrrrerrerr*, downslurred and indignant in tone. Drum roll is fast and rather long. **AN** Japanese Woodpecker.

Grey-headed Woodpecker *Picus canus* L 26–33 cm; WS 38–40 cm; WT 110–206 g

SD *P. c. jessoensis* widespread resident Hokkaido; accidental N Honshu. **HH** Mature deciduous and mixed broadleaf forest from lowlands to foothills. Forages on trunks and larger limbs, commonly resting conspicuously high in trees. **ID** Large greyish-green woodpecker, with small, rounded grey head with black loral stripe and narrow black malar; small forehead patch bright red (♂), or black-streaked (♀). Greyish-green mantle and back, somewhat stronger olive-green on wing-coverts, flight-feathers blackish-brown with white spots; rump bright green (prominent in flight), tail dull blackish-green and unbarred. Whitish chin/throat, and dull pale grey throat to vent, latter lightly scaled darker. Closed wings have black and white bands on primaries. In flight, primaries and outer secondaries largely black with transverse rows of white spots. **BP** Bill mid-length, dark grey, blacker at tip and base of upper mandible, pale horn at base of lower; eyes brown, becoming blood-red in older birds; tarsi grey. **SV** Call: (very vocal) single *kik* and strongly whistled descending series of up to 20 *pyoo pyopyopyopyo* notes, slowing after fast start. Drumming can be loud, but mostly a short, quiet roll lasting 1–1.5 seconds, rather even-pitched, neither fading nor slowing.

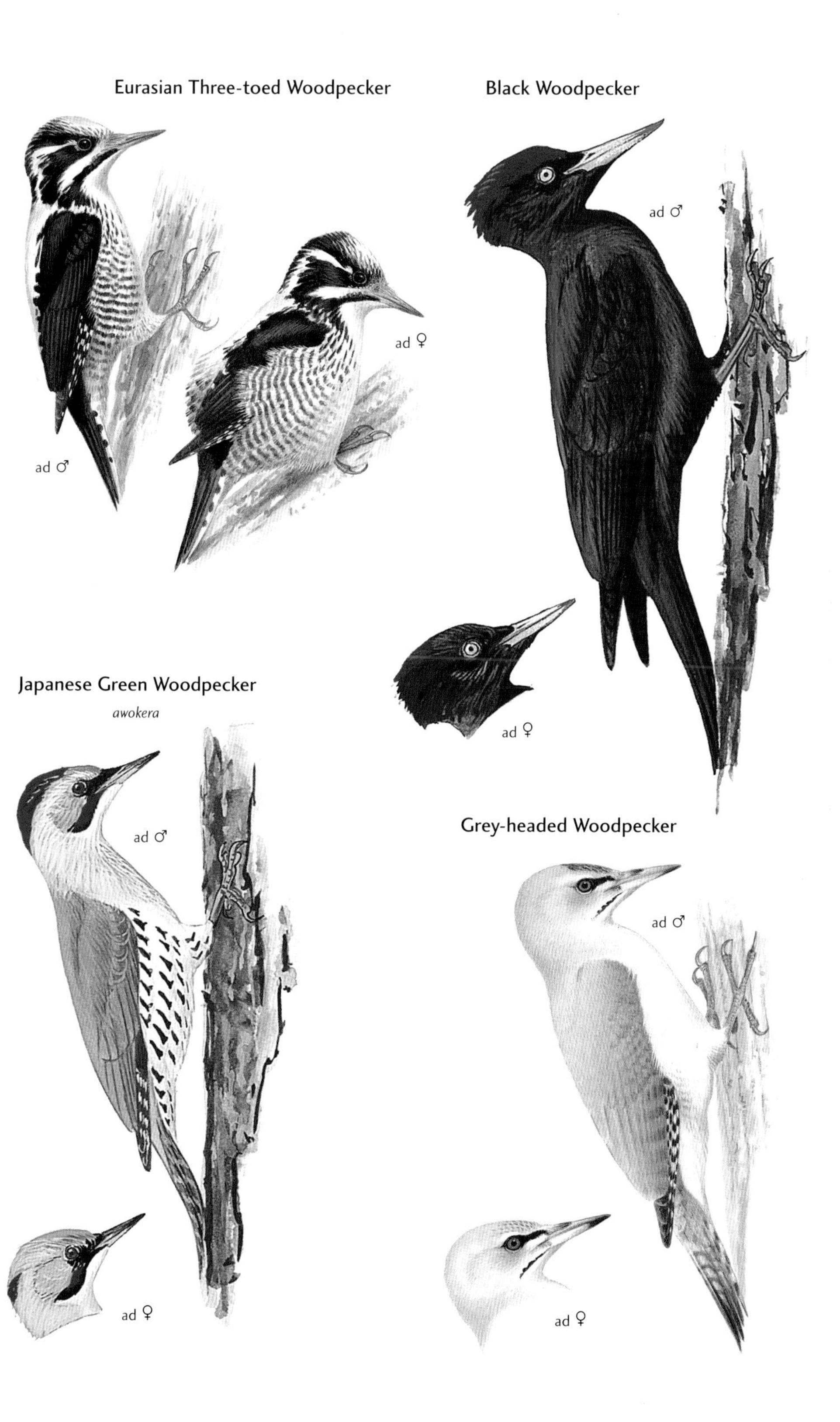
Eurasian Three-toed Woodpecker
ad ♂
ad ♀
Black Woodpecker
ad ♂
ad ♀
Japanese Green Woodpecker
awokera
ad ♂
ad ♀
Grey-headed Woodpecker
ad ♂
ad ♀

Lesser Kestrel *Falco naumanni* L 31–34 cm; WS 62–73 cm; WT ♂ 90–172 g, ♀ 138–208 g

SD Vulnerable. Accidental, Honshu, Tsushima and Yaeyama Is. **HH** Wooded hills, grasslands, cultivation. **ID** Slimmer and slightly smaller than Common Kestrel. ♂: plain grey head and face. Upperparts plain rufous-brown, greater coverts blue-grey forming panel on innerwing; flight-feathers black. Underparts deep buff-orange with small black spots. ♀/juvenile: paler than Common, with plain face. At rest, wingtips almost reach tail tip. Flight fast, agile, quick beats, stiffer and shallower than Common; hovers less than Common, circles and soars more. Compared to Common, appears shorter-bodied, wings more pointed, tail more wedge-shaped (central rectrices often protrude). Underwings: ♂ very pale, primaries almost unmarked white contrasting with black tips, underwing-coverts only slightly spotted; ♀ pale grey with darker grey barring on flight-feathers, spotting on axillaries and underwing-coverts, markings less conspicuous than Common. **BP** Bill very short, yellow with dark grey tip; eye-ring yellow, irides dark brown; tarsi yellow, claws white. **SV** Generally silent, but may give a shrill, chattering trisyllabic flight call *kyi kyi kyi*, or *jhee jhee jhet*.

Common Kestrel *Falco tinnunculus* L 27–39 cm; WS 57–79 cm; WT 191–299 g

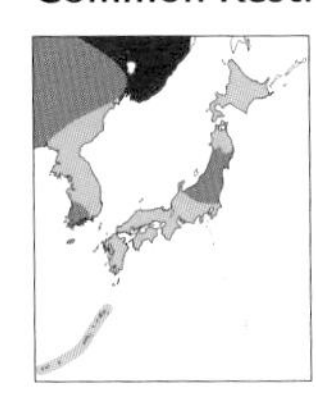

SD *F. t. interstinctus* breeds locally, C Hokkaido, C Honshu; mostly in winter, Hokkaido to Nansei Shoto. *F. t. perpallidus* reported in winter. **HH** Coastal areas with short vegetation, agricultural land. **ID** Mid-sized falcon with long, narrow wings, with rather rounded tips; tail long with rounded tip. ♂: head grey with diffuse dark eyestripe and moustachial stripe. Upperparts rufous-brown with black 'anchor' spots on mantle and wing-coverts; primaries and primary-coverts black. Underparts buff-orange with many black streaks. ♀/juvenile: noticeably streaked rufous-brown crown and nape, dark eyestripe and moustachial stripe; tail rufous with many narrow dark bars and bold band on tip. Occasionally sandy-brown birds recorded, either pale morph or *F. t. perpallidus*. At rest, perches upright, wingtips reach just beyond mid-tail. Flight fast, agile, graceful with shallow beats; soars on flat wings with tail fanned; commonly hovers into wind or with fast, shallow wingbeats when hunting. Underwings: pale, heavily barred on underside of flight-feathers. **BP** Bill very short, yellow with dark grey tip; eye-ring yellow, irides dark brown; tarsi yellow with blackish-grey claws. **SV** When breeding noisy, uttering piercing, high-pitched screams, sharp *kyi kyi kyi* or *klee-klee-klee* notes, and chittering series of hard *stik stik stik* notes; otherwise silent.

Amur Falcon *Falco amurensis* L 27–30 cm; WS 63–71 cm; WT ♂ 97–155 g, ♀ 111–188 g

SD Rare overshoot migrant, Nansei Shoto and Kyushu to Hokkaido. **HH** Open agricultural areas; perches on trees and wires. **ID** Dark falcon with long, narrow wings and tail. ♂: grey with darker eyestripe, moustachial and upperparts; thighs, vent and undertail-coverts rufous-orange; underwing white. ♀: recalls Eurasian Hobby; dark grey above, narrowly barred black, with white cheeks, short blunt moustachial, blackish spots on breast and bars on flanks; thighs and vent buff; tail grey barred black, with broad band at tip; young ♂ intermediate between ♀ and adult ♂. Juvenile: strongly streaked blackish-brown below, with rufous-brown crown; upperparts have rufous-buff fringes. At rest, wingtips extend to or just beyond tail tip. Flight fast, dashing, in pursuit of large insects, frequently hovers. **BP** Bill grey with reddish-orange cere; eye-ring reddish-orange, irides dark brown; tarsi orange-red (ad) or yellow-orange (juv), claws white. **SV** Generally silent.

Merlin *Falco columbarius* L 24–34 cm; WS 53–73 cm; WT ♂ 140–193 g, ♀ 205–274 g

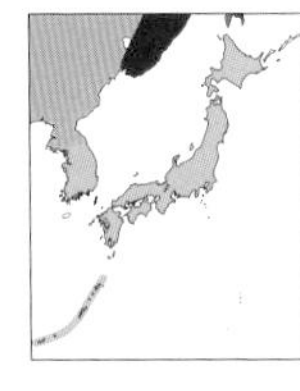

SD *F. c. insignis*, uncommon winterer (Oct–Apr), Hokkaido to Nansei Shoto. *F. c. pacificus*, rare visitor, N Japan. **HH** Coastal lowlands, agricultural land, wetlands. **ID** Small, compact falcon with short, broad-based, pointed wings, and short tail. Recalls larger Peregrine, but has pale cheeks, narrow supercilia, weak moustachial, and pale hind-collar. ♂: pale blue-grey upperparts, rufous nape-sides, pale orange-buff underparts with dark streaks, plain grey tail with broad dark subterminal band, white at tip. ♀/juvenile: mottled brown above with pale supercilia, brown streaking on pale buff underparts, and narrowly-barred brown uppertail with broad subterminal band and whitish tip. At rest, wingtips fall just short of tail tip. In flight, ♂ grey above with darker primaries and tail-band; ♀ brown with broadly banded tail. Flight extremely fast, changing direction rapidly; wingbeats fast, flickering, interspersed with short glides; soars on flat wings with tail partly spread. *F. c. pacificus* is larger and darker than very similar *F. c. insignis*. **BP** Bill black with yellow cere; eyes large, dark brown with narrow yellow eye-ring; tarsi yellow. **SV** Generally silent, but may give alarm calls: *quik-ik-ik-ik*.

Lesser Kestrel
ad ♂
ad ♀
ad ♂
ad ♀
ad ♀
imm ♂
imm ♂
Common Kestrel
ad ♀
ad ♂
ad ♂
ad ♂
ad ♀
ad ♀
Amur Falcon
ad ♂
ad ♀
juv
ad ♂
ad ♀
imm ♂
imm ♂
Merlin
♀ pursuing Snow Buntings
ad ♂
ad ♀
ad ♂
ad ♀

Eurasian Hobby *Falco subbuteo*
L 32–37 cm; WS 68–84 cm; WT ♂ 131–232g, ♀ 141–340 g

SD *F. s. subbuteo* breeds (May–Sep) locally in Hokkaido and N Honshu. Occurs widely on migration. **HH** Forested and open areas, agricultural and suburban areas with scattered woodlands; often near water. **ID** Dark falcon with long, narrow, scythe-like pointed wings and mid-length square-tipped tail. ♀ resembles illustrated ♂, but has brown-tinged upperparts and dark-streaked thighs. Juvenile is largely dark brown with buffy-orange thighs and vent. Extremely active low-level pursuit flight after large insects (especially dragonflies) or small birds, on powerful stiff wingbeats interspersed with short glides, occasionally soars on flat wings angled back at carpal with tail spread. **BP** Bill dark grey with yellow cere; eye-ring yellow, irides dark brown; tarsi yellow. **SV** Repetitive, agitated shrill *klee-klee-klee*... or scolding *kew-kew-kew* on territory; vocal with young, post-breeding and on autumn migration.

Saker Falcon *Falco cherrug*
L 47–57 cm; WS 97–126 cm; WT ♂ 750–990 g, ♀ 975–1150 g

SD Vagrant (subspecies uncertain) to Yaeyama Is. **HH** Open areas with woodland. **ID** Large, *Buteo*-sized falcon. Adults variable, but generally head pale with whitish supercilia, poorly marked narrow moustachial stripes and somewhat darker crown; upperparts warm brown, underparts buff with dark streaks/bars, typically broadest and blackest on sides/thighs (dark 'trousers'). Juv/1st-year like adult, but moustachial more prominent, supercilia whiter, underparts boldly streaked with all-dark 'trousers'. At rest, tail extends just beyond wingtips. Flight powerful, beats slower, lazier than Peregrine, on long, broad-based, blunt-tipped wings; occasionally hovers; upperwing 'hand' dark blackish-brown, 'arm' paler brown, dark covert band on underwing contrasts with greyer remiges; upper tail has numerous pale oval spots. **BP** Bill pale grey, tip blackish-grey, base pale, cere yellow (ad) or dull greyish-green (juv); eye-ring yellow, irides dark brown; feet yellow (ad) or dull blue-grey (juv). **SV** Generally silent away from breeding grounds.

Gyrfalcon *Falco rusticolus*
L 50–63 cm; WS 105–131 cm; WT ♂ 800–1320 g, ♀ 1130–2100 g

SD Very rare winter visitor to Hokkaido, Honshu, Kyushu and Tsushima. **HH** Favours coastal areas, cliffs, and large rivers. **ID** Very large, barrel-chested, broad-bodied falcon recalling large *Accipiter* or *Buteo*. Adults range from white to dark grey; mid-grey morph most common and widespread. Juv/1st-year darker than adult, upperparts brown-tinged, underparts heavily streaked. At rest, third of tail extends beyond wingtips. Flight extremely powerful, apparently leisurely, but deceptively fast, with stiff shallow beats; also glides and soars on flat wings. In flight, underwing-coverts darker than flight-feathers in all but white morph, which has all-white underwing; tail long, broad-based, with prominent undertail-coverts. **BP** Bill grey with yellow (ad) or blue-grey (juv) cere and gape; eye-ring yellow, irides dark brown; tarsi yellow (ad) or blue-grey (juv). **SV** Usually silent, but may give gruff calls recalling Peregrine, but slower, more nasal and drawn-out *kak kak kak*... and rattling *keeak keeak keeak*.

Peregrine Falcon *Falco peregrinus*
L 38–51 cm; WS 84–120 cm; WT ♂ 588–740 g, ♀ 825–1330 g

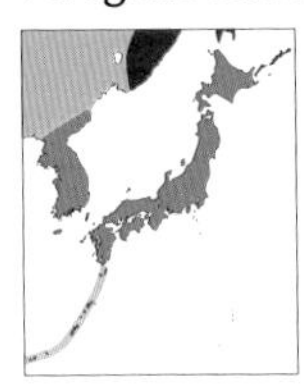

SD *F. p. japonensis* is a scarce breeder from Kyushu to Hokkaido, more commonly encountered in winter from Hokkaido to Nansei Shoto; *F. p. furuitii* is an endangered (extinct?) endemic resident of Iwo Is; and *F. p. pealei* is a rare visitor to Japan from Kuril Is. **HH** Breeds on rocky cliffs and remote islands; in winter found along coasts, at wetlands and rivers, but also in mountains, open country and cities. **ID** Large, compact falcon (♀ larger than ♂), dark above, pale below; large head with striking dark moustache (all ages/races); long, broad-based wings and mid-length, broad-based tail. Sexes/ages variable; subspecific ID difficult, but *pealei* is large, heavy, generally dark brown with broad moustachial. At rest, wingtips extend nearly to tail tip. Flight powerful, fast; smooth, shallow beats interspersed with short glides on flat wings; soars on flat wings (leading edge angled, trailing edge straight); often makes spectacular high-speed stoops in pursuit of avian prey. In flight, head and rump appear broad, wings triangular (broad-based 'arm', 'hand' narrowly pointed), tail tapers slightly; upperwing lead grey, may contrast with paler rump and tail; uniformly barred underwing lacks contrast. **BP** Bill short, deep, mostly grey; cere yellow; eye-ring yellow, irides dark brown; tarsi yellow to yellowish-orange (ad) or bluish-grey to bluish-green (juv). **SV** Generally silent away from territory, but can be very noisy on territory, giving harsh, scolding chatter or screaming *kyek-kyek-kyek* or *rehk rehk rehk* in alarm, and a whining *shri-shreee-shreeee*.

Eurasian Hobby
ad
juv
ad
juv
hunting a dragonfly
Saker Falcon
ad
ad
ad
Gryfalcon
ad white
morph
ad grey
morph
ad white
morph
ad grey
morph
white morph hunting Harlequin Duck
Peregrine Falcon
japonensis
ad
ad
ad
juv

Red-breasted Parakeet *Psittacula alexandri* L 33–38 cm; WT 133–168 g

SD A feral population of *P. a. fasciata* has become established in Tokyo. **HH** Well-wooded suburban and urban parks, and tree-lined streets. **ID** A large, green and pink parakeet; head grey with narrow black band from just above bill to eyes, and black chin and sides to lower face. ♂ upperparts green, yellowish-green on wing-coverts, with elongated blue central rectrices with greenish-yellow tips. Deep vinous-pink from throat to lower breast, but belly, flanks and undertail-coverts green. ♀ has duller pink underparts. **BP** Bill large, upper mandible deep red with yellow tip, lower mandible blackish-pink or black; eyes pale yellow; tarsi grey. **SV** Honking *yaink yaink* and wailing *knyaouw* calls are very different from other parakeets.

Rose-ringed Parakeet *Psittacula krameri* L ♂ 39–42 cm, ♀ 27–36 cm; WS 42–48 cm; WT 95–143 g

SD Widespread in cage-bird trade. A population of *P. k. manillensis* has become established in C & W Honshu (Chiba to Hiroshima). The wide range of other escapee Asian parakeets that may also be encountered in warmer parts of Japan is beyond the scope of this guide. **HH** Well-wooded suburban and urban parks, and tree-lined streets, where noisy and conspicuous. **ID** Somewhat large-headed, long-tailed green parakeet (lacks red shoulders of larger Alexandrine). Almost entirely pale yellowish-green. ♂ has black chin patch, narrow black collar, below which is a narrow rose-pink hind-collar. ♀ lacks chin patch and collars. In flight, very long narrow tail highly conspicuous, wings green, beats rapid. **BP** Bill large, upper mandible deep red, lower mandible black; eye-ring pale green/grey, irides black; tarsi grey. **SV** Noisy, commonly chattering loudly in trees and squawking in noisy groups in flight; a piercing *kyik kyik kyiek*, or noisy squealing *keeew* and grating *krech-krech-krech*. **AN** Ring-necked Parakeet.

Alexandrine Parakeet *Psittacula eupatria* L 50–62 cm; WT 198–258 g

SD Established feral population in C Honshu (probably nominate subspecies). **HH** Cultivated areas, wooded parks and suburbs. **ID** Large, pale green parakeet (like large Rose-ringed) with green crown and upper face, and grey-green nape and lower face; distinctive red shoulders and very long, largely blue tail with pale yellowish-white tip. ♂ has black chin and fore-collar, with turquoise and pink hind-collars. ♀ lacks chin patch and collar. **BP** Bill very large, deep red; eye-ring pink, irides pale grey; tarsi grey. **SV** Squawking or screeching *tskraau* or *skyurt*.

Budgerigar *Melopsittacus undulatus* L 18–19 cm; WS 30 cm; WT 26–29 g

SD Very common cage-bird; escapes occur widely and survive in warmer regions of C & SW Honshu, and Kyushu. **HH** Rural and suburban lowlands with woodland, also reed marshes; often mixing with sparrows and finches. **ID** Small-headed, long-tailed small 'parrot'. Wild types largely green with yellow head and upperparts, black spots on throat, narrow black barring on crown and face, and black scallops on mantle and wing-coverts. Rump and underparts green; long, pointed tail deep blue. Domesticated varieties may be almost any colour or combination of colours, from yellow to blue. Wings pointed, with pale yellow wing-stripe above and below contrasting with blackish flight-feathers, long central rectrices entirely dark green. Flight rapid, whirring. **BP** Bill very short, face flat-looking, horn-coloured with blue cere (♂) or grey with rusty-orange cere (♀); eyes white; tarsi grey. **SV** Dry chattering, soft warbling, and chirruping with scratchy notes, also a distinctive high-pitched screech in alarm.

Monk Parakeet *Myiopsitta monachus* L 28–31 cm; WS 48 cm; WT 100 g

SD A feral population (subspecies uncertain) has become established in SW Honshu (Hyogo). **HH** Cultivated and residential areas; sociable and communal nester. **ID** Upperparts and tail bright green, face and throat pale grey, belly greenish-yellow, wings blue. **BP** Bill dull orange, eyes brown, legs and feet greyish. **SV** Rapid chattering of short notes when perched or louder squawking in flight.

Red-breasted Parakeet
ad ♀
ad ♂
juv
Red-breasted
Parakeet ad ♂
Rose-ringed
Parakeet ad ♂
ad ♂
Alexandrine
Parakeet
Rose-ringed
Parakeet
ad ♀
ad ♀
ad ♂
ad ♂
Budgerigar
'blue'
'yellow'
'natural'
Monk Parakeet

Hooded Pitta *Pitta sordida*

L 16–19 cm; WT 42–70 g

SD Vagrant (*P. s. cucullata*) to S Nansei Shoto. **HH** Forest. **ID** Deep green upperparts with a black hood and brown crown; underparts paler apple-green with deep red lower belly, vent and undertail-coverts. Lower back and rump pale blue. Wings blue with white patches, sky-blue lesser and median coverts, primaries and tail black. **BP** Bill short, black; eyes dark brown; tarsi flesh-pink. **SV** An explosive bisyllabic whistled *wieuw-wieuw*.

Fairy Pitta *Pitta nympha*

L 16–20 cm; WT 67–155 g

SD Vulnerable. Scarce (declining) and local summer visitor (May–Aug) to Kyushu (and offshore islands), Shikoku and C & SW Honshu. Accidental to Nansei Shoto and islands in Sea of Japan north to Hokkaido. **HH** Inhabits dark broadleaf evergreen, subtropical and tropical forests, including secondary forest, mainly in lowlands to 1,200 m, foraging on ground, but singing high in trees. **ID** Brilliantly coloured, with large head, long, broad wings and very short tail (primaries extend beyond tip); rather erect. Adult: upperparts and wings bright apple-green; crown chestnut with black median stripe, and broad black mask from bill through eye and around nape, bordered above by broad yellow supercilia. Pale-yellow chin, throat, neck and breast, bright red on belly, vent and undertail-coverts, bright blue on scapulars and rump/tail. Juvenile: duller, with large white spots on median coverts. In flight, black outer coverts and primaries, with white panel at base of primaries; blue tail has black subterminal band. **BP** Bill large, black (ad) or dark brown with scarlet-orange tip (juv); eyes large, irides black; long tarsi dull pink. **SV** Quadrisyllabic, whistled song delivered as two paired notes, variously transliterated as: *pee-yu pee-yu*, *hoo-hee hoo-hee* and even *shiropen-kuropen*; also a cat-like scolding call.

Black-winged Cuckooshrike *Coracina melaschistos*

L 19–24 cm; WT 35–42 g

SD *C. m. intermedia* is an accidental spring migrant to Nansei Shoto, Kyushu and W Honshu. **HH** Coastal and lowland forests. **ID** Medium-sized with a long, graduated tail. Overall grey with black wings (no contrast between coverts and flight-feathers) and tail, latter with white tips to outermost feathers above and broad white tips below forming bars. ♂ dark ash-grey, blacker on face, paler near vent. ♀ paler with less black on face, white crescents above and below eye, and underparts grey to mid-chest, below that white with grey-barred undertail-coverts. In flight from below shows white patch at base of primaries. **BP** Bill thick, black with slight hook; eyes reddish-brown; tarsi dark grey. **SV** A magpie-like chattering and raptor-like squealing. Song a descending series of 3–4 high-pitched whistles: *wii wii jeeow jeeow*.

White-breasted Woodswallow *Artamus leucorynchus*

L 17–19 cm; WT 36–50 g

SD Vagrant (*A. l. leucorynchus*) to SW Honshu and Sakishima Is. **HH** Open areas, including agricultural land with isolated trees. **ID** Starling-like in proportions and flight, with rather straight-edged, triangular wings and short, broad tail. Adult: hood and upperparts blackish-grey, blackest on face and chin; underparts, underwing, lower rump and uppertail-coverts white. Juvenile: lacks black hood, has buff scaling on brown crown, neck, mantle and back, and orange-buff wash on chest. **BP** Bill deep at base, sharply pointed, dull blue (brownish in juv); eyes black; short legs and small feet dark grey/black. **SV** Call, often given in flight, a harsh, rather hoarse *geet geet* or *pert pert*; also chatters and gives softer *ku ku ku* calls.

Hooded Pitta
ad
singing in canopy
Fairy Pitta
ad
Black-winged Cuckooshrike
ad ♀
ad ♂
juv
White-breasted
Woodswallow
ad
ad

Ashy Minivet *Pericrocotus divaricatus*

L 18–21 cm; WT 20–22 g

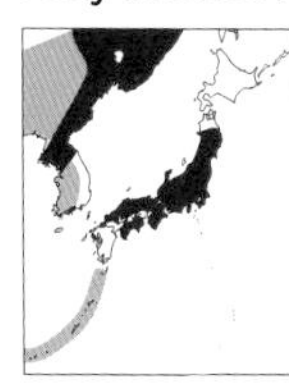

SD Locally common, declining summer visitor (Apr–Oct), Kyushu to N Honshu; migrant Nansei Shoto; rare Hokkaido, Ogasawara and Iwo Is. **HH** Mixed broadleaf forest and woodland. **ID** Grey and white, upright posture with long tail. ♂: white forehead, black hindcrown, thick black eye-stripe merges with post-auricular patch and black nape. Upperparts grey, flight-feathers black with pale fringes to primaries, tail long with white outer rectrices. ♀: black lores, soft grey upperparts, underparts off-white. Juvenile: like brownish-grey ♀. In flight, white underparts, white underwing-coverts, broad wingbars and call diagnostic. **BP** Bill thick, black, slightly hooked; eyes black; short tarsi black. **SV** High-pitched, metallic, cicada-like trill: *hirihirihirin* rapidly ascending, with hesitant, tinkling quality, *tsure re re... reee* especially on taking flight; drier, more quavering than Ryukyu Minivet.

Ryukyu Minivet *Pericrocotus tegimae*

L 18–21 cm; WT 21 g

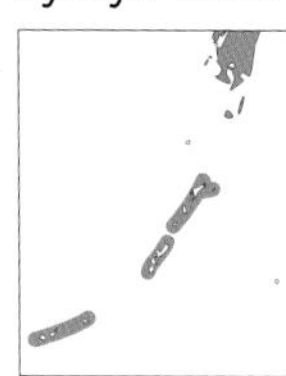

SD Resident Nansei Shoto; expanding northwards through Kyushu, W Honshu and Shikoku (breeding reported); has reached C Honshu. **HH** Evergreen forest and suburban gardens in Nansei Shoto; in Kyushu, resident to 1,700 m in evergreen and mixed deciduous forest, and sometimes in adjoining cedar plantations. **ID** Shorter wings than similar Ashy Minivet. Adult: ashy-black crown and ear-coverts concolorous with upperparts (♂), or paler (♀), but still darker than ♀ Ashy. White forehead and supercilia narrow, with split white eye-ring (usually lacking on Ashy). Dark grey wash extends across breast. Juvenile: differs markedly from Ashy; upperparts dark grey (crown pattern is 'ghost' of ad) with slight pale mottling, and more white-spotted appearance due to neat white spots on scapulars. Underparts dirty white, with fine dark streaking on breast and flanks. All plumages: tail less extensively white on outer rectrices than Ashy; fringes of closed primaries dark. Primary projection slightly shorter than length of longest tertial (longer in Ashy). **BP** Bill and eyes like Ashy; tarsi short, dark greyish-flesh to black. **SV** Call: like Ashy, but a deeper, harder, rather strained *schree... schree... schree...*, either ascending or on same pitch, often given as two consecutive trills; also soft, whispery *tseet* in contact. Song: comprises call followed by a high tinkling *schreee... ti ti ti tititititi!* **TN** Formerly within Ashy Minivet; retained by OSJ.

Tiger Shrike *Lanius tigrinus*

L 18–19 cm; WT 25–33 g

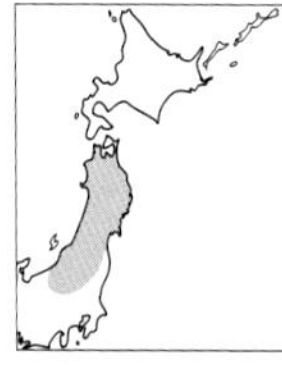

SD Scarce summer visitor (May–Aug) C & N Honshu; scarce migrant or accidental Nansei Shoto to Hokkaido. **HH** Lowland forests, woodland edges, open country with bushes. **ID** ♂: blue-grey crown, nape and upper mantle, broad black mask from forehead to ear-coverts; wings, rump and tail rufous-brown/chestnut, with black scaling (tail less marked). Underparts white. ♀: resembles dull ♂, but blue-grey limited to crown and nape (not upper mantle), upperparts less rufous, crown and nape duller, mask more restricted, barred from cheeks to flanks. 1st-winter (♂♀): upperparts yellowish-brown with more black scaling on wing-coverts; confusable with juvenile Red-backed and Brown shrikes, but note large head and eyes, large bill, characteristic vermiculation and pale spotting on upperparts. **BP** Bill stout, appears slightly oversized, strongly hooked, black (ad) or flesh pink with small dark tip (1st-winter); eyes large, black; tarsi black. **SV** Harsh chattering *gyun gyun gichigichigichigichi*. **AN** Thick-billed Shrike.

Bull-headed Shrike *Lanius bucephalus*

L 19–20 cm; WT 31–54 g

SD *L. b. bucephalus* summer visitor (Apr–Sep) Hokkaido, year-round C & W Japan, winter visitor Nansei Shoto; resident Tokara Is and Daito Is. **HH** Thickets and brush in open country, forest edge. Some breed very early; beware confusion between young fledgings in May and rarer migrants. **ID** Wings appear short, because of short primary projection and long thin tail. ♂: crown/nape dark rufous-brown; mantle, wing-coverts and rump grey; mask, wings and tail black. Mask not over bill (as in Tiger/Brown), narrower at lores, broader at rear. White patch at base of primaries is prominent. Underparts white, with orange wash on flanks, sometimes scaled on breast. ♀: upperparts grey washed brown; lacks white primary patch; underparts buff with narrow scaling; face 'gentler' than other similar shrikes, lacks black mask, brown behind eye, lores pale (see Brown). 1st-winter: like adult ♀ (1st-winter ♂ has white patch at base of primaries), but retains some juvenile feathers, thus tips of primary-coverts buff. **BP** Bill thick, short, well-hooked, black, with pale base to lower mandible; large eyes black; tarsi black. **SV** Call: harsh chattering *ju ju ju*, also *chi-chi-tyo-tyo*. Song: rasping, coarse *kyiikyiikyiikyii chikichikichiki gyun gyun*; also mimics other passerines.

Ashy Minivet
ad ♀
ad ♂
Ryukyu Minivet
ad ♀
ad ♂
ad ♂
ad ♂
Bull-headed
Shrike
Tiger Shrike
ad ♂
juv ♂
ad ♀
juv
ad ♀
ad ♂ fresh
juv

Brown Shrike *Lanius cristatus*

L 17–20 cm; WT 30–38 g

SD *L. c. lucionensis* is a scarce migrant in Kyushu and Nansei Shoto; **Japanese Shrike** *L. (c.) superciliosus* is a summer visitor to Hokkaido (rare) and N & C Honshu (scarce), occurring regularly on migration in Honshu, Kyushu and Nansei Shoto. **HH** Thickets, forest edge, plantations, parks and gardens, and open country, including farmland, with isolated trees. **ID** Rather plain brown and somewhat slender; sexes very similar, though ♀ usually duller, with less distinct mask and dark-scaled underparts (see Bull-headed Shrike); usually little or no contrast between nape and mantle, but stronger between back and rump/tail (see Isabelline). Wings dark brown, with no (or slight) wing patch at base of primaries. ♂ *superciliosus* has warm rufous-brown upperparts, broad black mask from forehead to ear-coverts bordered by broad white supercilia joining on forehead; chin and cheeks white, underparts have rich orange-buff wash to breast-sides and flanks. ♀ less bright, supercilia do *not* meet, greater wing-coverts fringed buff, and has dark brown scalloping on flanks. *L. c. lucionensis* duller, ash-grey on forehead, with variable white (sometimes none) above black mask, crown and nape grey, mantle greyish-brown; chin/throat/cheeks white, but underparts extensively buff-washed. *L. c. cristatus* is like pale *superciliosus* with colder, sandy-brown crown, mantle and rump, tail largely blackish-brown, white supercilia less contrasting, forehead narrower. *L. c. confusus* resembles *lucionensis*, but white forehead broader and head browner. *L. (c.) superciliosus* has most rufous upperparts and broadest supercilia. White supercilia and forehead usually broader in ♂ than ♀. Separated from Red-backed by short primary projection, from Isabelline by darker tail (♀ red-brown, not orange-brown) with more graduated tip, slightly heavier bill and yellowish-buff underparts. **BP** Bill thick, short, well-hooked, black; eyes large, irides dark brown; tarsi black. **SV** Harsh chattering *che che che che* or *gichigichigichi* in alarm.

Red-backed Shrike *Lanius collurio*

L 17–19 cm; WT 25–35 g

SD Vagrant (*L. c. collurio*) to Yonagunijima, Kyushu, Shikoku, C Honshu and Hegurajima; has overwintered in Kyushu. **HH** Open country with low bushes. **ID** ♂ pale grey crown and nape contrast with bold black mask bordered above by narrow white supercilia, and narrow black forehead. Warm reddish-brown mantle/scapulars and fringes to wing-coverts, secondaries and tertials. Tail long, round-tipped and almost pure black, but white sides broadest from base to mid-tail. White cheeks, chin, flanks and breast may be suffused warm peach. Flight-feathers black fringed pale brown with small white patch at base of primaries. ♀ has less boldly marked face, brown forecrown, grey hindcrown, off-white lores, broad brown patch behind eye, and distinct dark scaling formed by narrow tips to feathers of breast and flanks; tail dark brown with narrow white edges. Juvenile/1st-winter like ♀, but crown brown to dark grey with fine black stripes, upper back boldly barred and scaled black on brown. Underparts essentially off-white, but breast and flanks finely scalloped black. **BP** Bill grey; eyes dark brown; legs/feet black. **SV** Harsh grating *schak-schak* and a tongue-clicking *tschek*.

Isabelline Shrike *Lanius isabellinus*

L 16–18 cm; WT 25–34 g

SD Vagrant (subspecies uncertain) to Hegurajima, Kyushu and Okinawa. **ID** Paler, more sandy-brown than Red-backed Shrike, with longer rufous tail recalling Brown. ♂ sandy with reddish-brown forehead and narrow black mask broadening from eye to ear-coverts, with narrow white border above lores and eye. Pale grey-brown nape, mantle, scapulars, and fringes to lesser/greater coverts, secondaries and tertials. Primary-coverts and primaries black, with small white patch at base of latter. Long tail with rounded tip is warm rusty-red, with darker, browner tips especially to central rectrices. Underparts white, with creamy cast to cheeks, breast-sides and flanks. ♀ face mask less bold, and often faintly vermiculated on breast and flanks. Juvenile/1st-winter like greyish-buff young Red-backed, but little or no scaling on much plainer grey-buff mantle and back; pale buff fringes to blackish-brown wing-coverts and flight-feathers. Underparts essentially off-white, with fine grey scaling on breast and flanks. **BP** Bill grey with paler base to lower mandible (ad) or pinkish-grey with pink base (juv); eyes dark brown; legs/feet dark grey. **SV** As Red-backed.

Brown Shrike
ad ♂
superciliosus
ad ♀
superciliosus
juv
ad ♂
superciliosus
ad ♂
cristatus
ad ♂
lucionensis
ad ♂
Red-backed Shrike
ad ♀
juv
ad ♂
Isabelline Shrike
ad ♂
ad ♂
ad ♀
juv

Long-tailed Shrike *Lanius schach*

L 21–27 cm; WT 50–53 g

SD Accidental (*L. s. schach*) visitor to C & W Honshu, Kyushu, Tsushima and Nansei Shoto. **HH** Clumps and thickets, forest edge and open country, with isolated trees and plantations. **ID** Rather large, black, grey and rufous shrike with long, graduated tail (lacking white) and rounded tip. Black mask extends high onto forehead, crown and mantle grey, wing-coverts, lower back and rump rufous, wings black with white patch at base of primaries (conspicuous in flight), rufous fringes to tertials and outer rectrices. White chin, face-sides and breast, washed rufous on flanks, darker rufous on belly/vent. **BP** Bill short, well-hooked, black; eyes large, irides black; tarsi black. **SV** Harsh screeching and chattering calls: *gidigidi*, *giiitt*, *gijigiji...*, *gyiip*, and a warbling song mimicking other birds. **AN** Rufous-backed Shrike.

Northern Shrike *Lanius borealis*

L 24–27 cm; WT 48–81 g

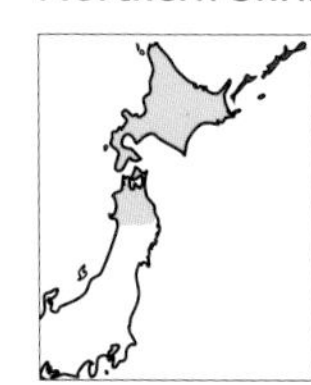

SD *L. b. bianchii* is an uncommon/scarce winter visitor to Hokkaido, which has straggled south as far as Kyushu. *L. b. mollis* has occurred as vagrant in Honshu and Kyushu **HH** Forest edges, wetland margins, open country, including agricultural land with isolated trees. **ID** Large, grey, black-and-white shrike. Adult: pale grey from crown to lower back, rump paler or white, particularly noticeable in flight (see Chinese Grey). Black mask from lores (narrow) across ear-coverts (broad); wings black with broad white band at base of primaries (prominent on closed wing), secondaries and tertials black, latter with white tips; tail black with white outer feathers, and white tips to all but central feathers. Underparts white or pale grey with clear barring. Juvenile/1st-winter: like washed-out adult, with less clearly marked black mask, weak to strong brown tones to face and underparts, and strongly vermiculated flanks and breast, latter generally more diffuse. In flight, white wing patch restricted to primary bases on both surfaces. **BP** Bill slender, short, well-hooked, black, pale pink base in young; eyes large, irides black; tarsi black. **SV** Typically silent outside breeding season, but occasionally gives coarse chattering *gijigijigiji* or harsh *check-check* calls. **AN** Northern Grey Shrike *Lanius borealis*.

Chinese Grey Shrike *Lanius sphenocercus*

L 28–31 cm; WT 80–100 g

SD *L. s. sphenocercus* is very rare winter visitor/accidental to Japan, with records from Hokkaido to Nansei Shoto. **HH** Scrub, thickets, meadows, wetlands, marshes and wet agricultural land. **ID** Very large, grey, black-and-white shrike; larger and longer-tailed than Northern Shrike. Upperparts pale to mid-grey from crown to lower back, rump darker grey than Northern, less contrasting with tail, which is dark greyish-black. Black mask somewhat narrower on ear-coverts than Northern, with narrow white supercilia from bill to ear-coverts; wings black with large white patch at base of primaries, narrower band across secondaries, connecting quite broad white outer fringes to tertials, which are also prominently tipped white. Appears short-winged, tips falling near tail base, but primaries extend well beyond tertial tips. In flight, very prominent white bar on primaries, narrower white bar on secondaries, narrow white bar at edge of wing-coverts and white trailing edge to tertials, thus much whiter in wing than Northern. Underparts white. Tail graduated, with longer central and shorter outer feathers; tail-length longer than wing-length (Northern has shorter tail, with tail-length rather shorter than wing-length). **BP** Bill thicker than Northern, short, well-hooked, black (base pale in 1st-winter); eyes large, irides black; tarsi black. **SV** Harsh, chattering *ga-ga-ga* and harsh *check-cherr* resembling Northern.

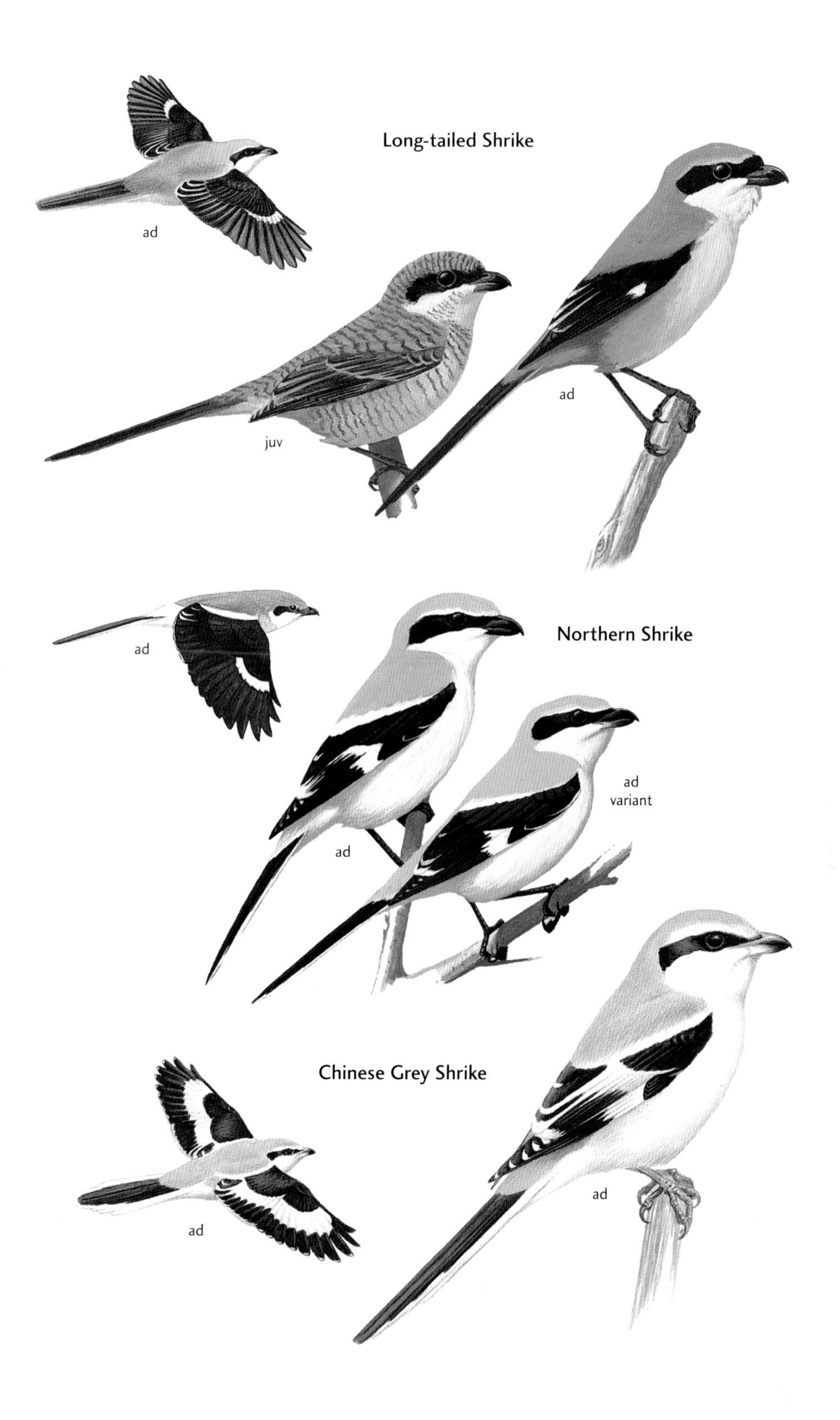

Long-tailed Shrike
ad
ad
juv
Northern Shrike
ad
ad
variant
ad
Chinese Grey Shrike
ad
ad

Black-naped Oriole *Oriolus chinensis*

L 24–28 cm; WT 81–101 g

SD Migrant *O. c. diffusus* is a rare visitor, mostly in spring, occasionally autumn, from Nansei Shoto to Hokkaido (has bred in Honshu), primarily to islands in Sea of Japan. **HH** Lowland deciduous woodland, plantations and parkland, where secretive and best found by voice. **ID** Unmistakable, the only large yellow bird to occur in Japan. ♂ bright golden-yellow with broad black 'bandana' from lores to nape, black wing-coverts, and yellow-fringed black flight-feathers; tail black with yellow corners. ♀ more lemon-yellow, greener on wings and has narrower black 'head scarf'. Juvenile/1st-winter greenish-yellow, lacks head scarf, but has blackish-streaked white breast and belly, black areas are grey; by spring has brownish nape-band and prominent black streaking on underparts. **BP** Bill large, bright flesh-pink (ad) or greyish above, pink below (juv); eye appears large, with narrow pink eye-ring, iris pale brown; tarsi dark grey/black. **SV** Call harsh, nasal and somewhat jay- or cat-like, *niiie, myaa* or *gyaa*. Song a clear fluty whistling, *lwee wee wee-leeow*, recalling Japanese Grosbeak, but more powerful.

Black Drongo *Dicrurus macrocercus*

L 26–32 cm; WT 42–65 g

SD Rare migrant (subspecies uncertain) occasionally reaching Japan from Nansei Shoto to Hokkaido, mostly to offshore islands in Sea of Japan in spring. **HH** Open country with trees, agricultural fields and urban parks, frequently perching on poles, wires and treetops. **ID** Large, all-black with long tail. Entire plumage black, but gloss variable, having a blue cast on breast and back. Tiny white spot may be visible at corner of gape. Long tail is deeply forked and tips curve upwards and outwards. Juvenile/1st-winter has duller wings and tail, rather less forked tail (uncurved), and whitish-scaled uppertail-coverts, breast and undertail-coverts. **BP** Bill heavy, black with prominent rictal bristles; eyes reddish-brown to black; tarsi black. **SV** Harsh, rasping calls: *zyee; shyaa*.

Ashy Drongo *Dicrurus leucophaeus*

L 24–29 cm

SD Rare migrant *D. l. leucogenis* occasionally reaches Japan in spring and autumn from Nansei Shoto to C Honshu. **HH** Forest edge and open woodland, but also in parks. **ID** A pale, washed-out version of Black Drongo. Entire plumage ash-grey, darker on wings and tail, and black at base of bill, especially lores, with dusky ear-coverts, though some have pale grey lores and white facial patch (unclear whether individual, age-related or subspecific variation). Underparts paler ash-grey, becoming even paler on belly. Long tail more deeply forked than Black, but also has outward-curved tips. **BP** Bill heavy, black, with short rictal bristles; eyes reddish-brown to black; tarsi grey. **SV** Chattering calls recall Bull-headed Shrike and sometimes imitates other passerines; song is a simple phrase: *chochobyuui*.

Hair-crested Drongo *Dicrurus hottentottus*

L 31–32 cm

SD Accidental migrant *D. h. brevirostris* occasionally reaches Nansei Shoto and north to Hegurajima. **HH** Favours forests and open areas with trees. **ID** A large, velvety black version of Black Drongo. Entire plumage black, with dark green gloss on head, breast, back and wing-coverts, strongest on wings and tail; some feathers of crown and breast have iridescent blue sheen (spangles). Long, loose crest of filament feathers rising from forehead. Long tail is broader at tip, barely forked and tips curl upwards and outwards. **BP** Bill heavy, grey, strongly arched to fine tip, with short bristles on forehead; eyes reddish-brown to black; tarsi black. **SV** Various harsh screeching calls and melodious notes.

Black-naped Oriole
ad ♂
ad ♀
juv
Black Drongo
ad
juv
ad
Ashy Drongo
ad
ad
juv
Hair-crested Drongo
ad
ad
juv

Black-naped Monarch *Hypothymis azurea*

L 15–17 cm; WT 9–13 g

SD Vagrant to Yonagunijima (subspecies uncertain, but likely *H. a. oberholseri* of Taiwan). **HH** Favours middle and lower levels of broadleaf forest and woodland thickets; also secondary forest and urban parks. **ID** Slender, small-headed and long-tailed flycatcher superficially resembling slightly larger Blue-and-white Flycatcher. ♂ almost entirely deep azure-blue, except sooty-black tufts at base of upper mandible and on rear crown, and narrow black half-collar on throat; breast grades from blue to bluish-grey on lower breast and belly, to white on vent. Wings blue with black flight-feathers; tail blackish-blue with blue fringes to outer rectrices, tip rounded. ♀ has blue head and chest, but grey underparts, becoming whiter below tail. Mantle, wings, back and tail dark grey-brown with blue fringes to outer tail-feathers. Juvenile is like ♀. **BP** Bill small, slender, dark blue-grey; eye appears small, irides black; tarsi black. **SV** Contact call: harsh *chee chweet*, also series of three or more whistles, *treet-treet-treet*.

Amur Paradise Flycatcher *Terpsiphone incei*

L ♂ 47–48 cm, ♀ 20–21 cm; WT 20–22 g

SD Vagrant to Nansei Shoto. **HH** Shady, mature mixed deciduous broadleaf forest in hills and along coast. **ID** Distinctive, long-tailed flycatcher. ♂ is brown with glossy black hood and nuchal crest (hood bluer than Japanese Paradise Flycatcher), with dark grey hind-collar and breast-band; upperparts (mantle, wings and tail) mainly plain rufous-brown, belly and vent white. Tail long, but extremely elongated central feathers of adult ♂ (young ♂ lacks full tail) project up to 30 cm, and may be more than twice tail-length. Rare white morph ♂ shares black hood and crest, but is otherwise all white. ♀ resembles typical ♂, but is duller with smaller crest, black of head tinged blue and lacks elongated tail-feathers (very closely resembles ♀ Japanese, but has warmer, brighter chestnut-brown mantle and wings, and grey of breast, all more contrasting with black hood). **BP** Bill blue; eye large, with blue eye-ring, irides black; tarsi black. **SV** Harsh, nasal and abrupt: *chet-trkh-chettr* or *dzh-zee dzh-zee*; also a loud *chee-tew* in contact. **TN** Formerly within Asian Paradise Flycatcher *T. paradisi*. Not included by OSJ.

Japanese Paradise Flycatcher *Terpsiphone atrocaudata*

L ♂ 35–45 cm, ♀ 17–18 cm; WT 17–22 g

SD Local and uncommon summer visitor (May–Sep). *T. a. atrocaudata* breeds through most of Kyushu, Shikoku and Honshu, but is only accidental in Hokkaido. *T. a. illex* is a locally common summer visitor throughout Nansei Shoto. **HH** Shady mature deciduous or evergreen broadleaf forest in temperate areas, and dark subtropical evergreen forest in south. **ID** Slightly smaller than Amur Paradise Flycatcher. ♂ has black hood with purplish-blue gloss, becoming blackish-grey on chest, off-white to white on belly and vent. Mantle, wings and rump dark purplish-chestnut, tail (including extremely long central feathers) black. No white morph. Immature ♂ is like adult, but has shorter central tail-feathers. ♀ closely recalls ♀ Amur, but is duller, darker brown on mantle, wings and tail, generally lacking rufous tones, though some are confusingly rufous. *T. a. illex* is smaller and darker. **BP** Bill blue, short, broad-based; eye large, with broad blue eye-ring, irides black; tarsi black. **SV** A coarse *gii* or *bii* and querulous *jouey*. Song a somewhat rasping, whistled *tski-hi-hoshi hoi-hoi-hoi*; or *fi-chii hoihoihoi*. **AN** Black Paradise Flycatcher.

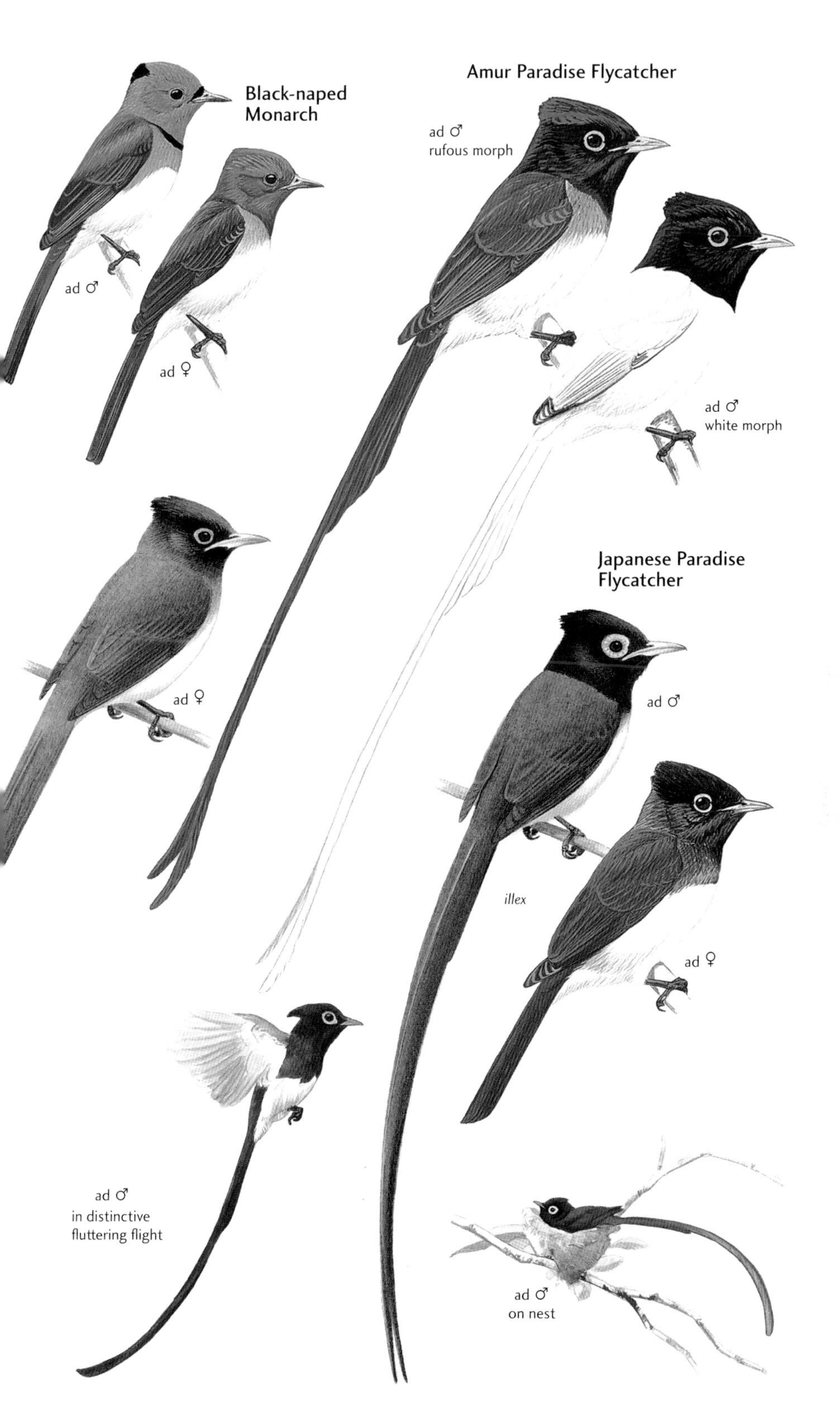
Black-naped
Monarch
ad ♂
ad ♀
ad ♀
Amur Paradise Flycatcher
ad ♂
rufous morph
ad ♂
white morph
Japanese Paradise
Flycatcher
ad ♂
illex
ad ♀
ad ♂
in distinctive
fluttering flight
ad ♂
on nest

Eurasian Jay *Garrulus glandarius* L 32–37 cm; WS 52–58 cm; WT 140–190 g

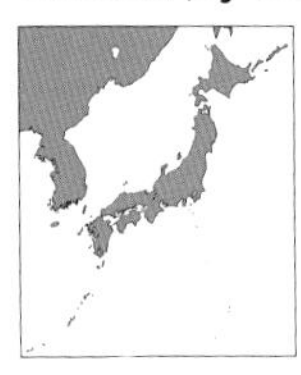

SD **Brandt's Jay** *G. (g.) brandtii* of Hokkaido is common, partly sedentary, but shows strong seasonal NE-SW migratory movements through Hokkaido. **Japanese Jay** *G. (g.) japonicus* is resident: *japonicus* (Honshu, Shikoku, Tsushima and Izu Is), *tokugawae* (Sado I), *hiugaensis* (Kyushu) and *orii* (Yakushima). **HH** Deciduous and evergreen forests, and woodland patches in open country. Often solitary (when skulks) or in family parties, but flocks on migration and sometimes in winter. **ID** Large, big-headed, colourful corvid. **Brandt's Jay** has dark cinnamon head and wash to breast, face generally plain with broad black lateral throat-stripes; mantle and scapulars pale grey-brown, rump white, tail black; wings largely black, but has white fringes to primaries and broad white patch at base of secondaries, wing-coverts turquoise-blue barred black and white. Underparts grey with cinnamon wash to breast, white on vent and undertail-coverts. **Japanese Jay** subspecies probably inseparable in field. All have pale grey forehead streaked black, black face, head uniform with back. In flight, **Brandt's** and **Japanese** have broad, rounded wings, broad tail and characteristic somewhat laboured, erratic flight, often at some height over forest. **BP** Bill strong, blunt, black; eyes reddish-brown (**Brandt's**) or white (**Japanese**); tarsi grey-brown. **SV** Generally silent, but can be very vocal, responding quickly and loudly to intrusion; mostly gives rasping, harsh *gsharrr*, but also soft sweet whistles. Commonly imitates other birds.

Lidth's Jay *Garrulus lidthi* L 38 cm; WT 170–196 g

SD Vulnerable. Endemic resident on Amami Is. **HH** Mature subtropical broadleaf evergreen and coniferous forest, forest edges and gardens. Forages largely on ground. Forms social roosts outside breeding season. **ID** Beautiful combination of deep cobalt-blue hood, wings and tail, and deep vinaceous-brown mantle, back, rump, breast, belly and vent. Face black, the chin with fine white streaking; wings largely deep blue with fine black barring on coverts; primaries, secondaries and tertials largely black with cobalt outer fringes and fine white spots at tips; tail broadly tipped white, particularly on underside. **BP** Bill blunt, thick, very pale straw-yellow, bluish-grey at base of lower mandible; eyes black with pale orbital ring; tarsi grey. **SV** Calls varied, harsh, but drier and slightly thinner than Eurasian Jay: deep *gyaa*, *pyuui*, also *skerr skerr*. No true song, but sometimes gives a soft murmuring *kyuh kyukyu kuku*.

Azure-winged Magpie *Cyanopica cyanus* L 33–37 cm; WS 38–40 cm; WT 65–79 g

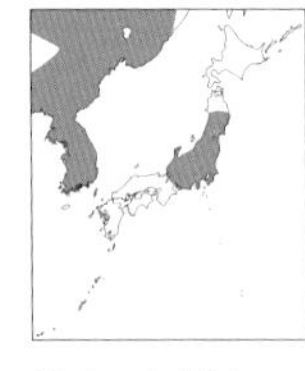

SD Locally common resident *C. c. japonica* is restricted to N & C Honshu; formerly N Kyushu; accidental Shikoku. **HH** Sociable, often in noisy groups, in deciduous hill forests, riverine thickets, orchards and large urban parks. **ID** Slender and pale. Upperparts cleanly marked, with black cap, grey mantle and rump, pale to deep powder-blue wings and tail; primaries black with blue outer fringes, long graduated tail has broad white tip; underparts and collar clean white. In flight, short rounded wings and long tail, and rapid flapping interspersed by long glides distinctive. **BP** Bill slender, short, black; eyes black; tarsi dark-grey/black. **SV** Various calls, a screeching *ray-it wit-wit-wit*; harsh, repetitive *zhreee*, *geh*, *kyururuRu* and *zweep zweep zweep*.

Oriental Magpie *Pica (pica) serica* L 40–51 cm; WS 52–60 cm; WT 182–272 g

SD Local and restricted range in S Japan (essentially N Kyushu), where presumed introduced in 17th/18th centuries from Korea, also recorded C Honshu and Shikoku; has recently colonised SW Hokkaido. **HH** Open wooded habitats, thickets, agricultural land with scattered trees, suburban and urban parks and gardens; messy domed nest conspicuous on poles, pylons and trees. **ID** Large, pied corvid. Hood and upperparts largely black with variable purple, blue and green iridescence; scapulars and inner webs of primaries white (visible in flight), primaries have black fringes and tips; black chest, white belly, black vent. Long tail is graduated, broadest at mid-point. Flight laboured, with frequent wingbeats. **BP** Bill strong, pointed, black; eyes black; tarsi black. **SV** Various harsh chattering *kasha kasha* and cackling calls that are higher and more 'tinny' than European birds. **AN** Eurasian Magpie; Korean Magpie.

Taiwan Blue Magpie *Urocissa caerulea* L 64–69 cm

SD Introduced in SW Honshu (Hyogo). **HH** Broadleaf evergreen forest and forest edge. **ID** Extremely long-tailed, large, colourful magpie. Almost entirely deep cobalt-blue; hood, breast and underwing-coverts black, wings blue with white tips to tertials. Tail long and graduated, with black and white tips to each feather; underparts somewhat paler blue, paler still on belly and white on vent. **BP** Bill strong, arched and chilli-red; eyes pale yellow; tarsi bright red. **SV** Cackling, metallic *kyak-kyak-kyak-kyak*, and various softer and harsher calls and whistles.

Eurasian Jay
brandtii
ad
ad
japonicus
ad
japonicus
Lidth's Jay
ad
ad
ad
ad
Taiwan Blue Magpie
Azure-winged Magpie
ad
ad
ad
juv
Oriental Magpie
ad

Spotted Nutcracker *Nucifraga caryocatactes*

L 32–38 cm; WS 52–58 cm; WT 145–213 g

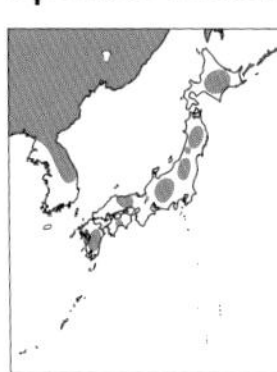

SD *N. c. japonica* is fairly common resident of montane regions of Hokkaido, Honshu; uncommon Shikoku and Kyushu; accidental Izu Is. *N. c. macrorhynchos* vagrant to N Kyushu. **HH** Pure coniferous boreal and lowland mixed forests, and alpine conifers, including stone pine forest in south; some (numbers vary greatly between years) descend to lower elevations in winter, when may also occur in small flocks. Actively caches seeds during autumn as winter food store. **ID** Dark brown, broad-winged, short-tailed corvid. Entirely mid-brown to dark chocolate-brown, heavily spotted white on face, neck, mantle and underparts. Lores whitish, eye-ring white, cap and nape blackish-brown, wings and tail also dark blackish-brown, tail has white corners. In flight, broad wings, white vent and short tail very noticeable; flight undulating. **BP** Bill slender and rather long, sharply pointed, black; eyes black; tarsi black. **SV** Recalls Eurasian Jay, but deeper, more growling *graarr* or *zhrrerr*, also given in brief series, *zhree-zhree-zhree*, sometimes higher-pitched; also a range of whistles and mimicry. **AN** Northern Nutcracker.

Western Jackdaw *Coloeus monedula*

L 33–34 cm; WS 67–74 cm; WT 180–260 g

SD Vagrant (subspecies uncertain) to E Hokkaido, Teuri I and Kyushu (Kumamoto). **HH** Open wooded areas with crags, cliffs or settlements. Typically sociable, highly vocal and gregarious, but solitary as vagrant. **ID** Small black corvid with rather rounded head and short wings. Adult is generally black with metallic-blue sheen to scapulars, but distinctly pale grey nape and head-sides. Juvenile lacks silver-streaked ear-coverts (see Daurian Jackdaw). Wings rather short and pointed, with fast, pigeon-like wingbeats and on ground gait is pigeon-like. **BP** Bill short, slender, black; eyes white; tarsi black. **SV** Highly excitable and vocal in flocks, giving abrupt, loud but quite pleasant *chyak*. **TN** Formerly in genus *Corvus*. **AN** Eurasian Jackdaw.

Daurian Jackdaw *Coloeus dauuricus*

L 33–34 cm; WS 67–74 cm; WT 154–275 g

SD Local and scarce winter visitor (Nov–Mar) to Kyushu; rare winter visitor elsewhere, mainly in Sea of Japan coastal prefectures, from Nansei Shoto north to Hokkaido. **HH** In winter, very sociable and frequently found among Eastern Rook flocks on agricultural land, typically ricefields with wooded areas nearby for roosting. **ID** Small, black and white (or pale grey) corvid. Adults are somewhat variable; extremely pale form has black hood and upperparts (including wings, tail and vent) and white nape, collar, breast and belly. Darkest forms have more grey, less white. Juvenile/1st-winter largely black, closely resembling Western Jackdaw, but has variable grey or silver on sides of head and nape, and dark eye. **BP** Bill short, slender, black; eyes black; tarsi black. **SV** Highly excitable and vocal, giving abrupt, loud *chyak* calls, probably indistinguishable from Western Jackdaw. **TN** Formerly in genus *Corvus*.

House Crow *Corvus splendens*

L 41–43 cm; WS 76–85; WT 252–362 g

SD Vagrant (possibly ship-assisted; subspecies uncertain). **HH** Human habitation, agricultural land and rubbish dumps in coastal areas. **ID** Medium-sized grey and black crow, slightly smaller than Oriental, with strongly peaked crown. Forecrown, face and throat black; nape, neck, breast and flanks grey, shading to black on back, wings, tail and lower belly. **BP** Bill slightly arched, quite thick, black; eyes black; tarsi black. **SV** Highly social and vocal, giving range of calls, including dry, flat *kaaa-kaao*. **TN** Not included by OSJ.

Spotted Nutcracker
ad macrorhynchos
ad japonica
ad japonica
Western Jackdaw
ad
ad
Daurian Jackdaw
ad
juv
House Crow
ad
Daurian Jackdaw flock feeding

Eastern Rook *Corvus (frugilegus) pastinator* L 44–47 cm; WS 81–99 cm; WT 325–516 g

SD Locally common winter visitor (Nov–Mar), particularly to W Kyushu and W Honshu; marked migration through Sea of Japan coastal prefectures north as far as W Hokkaido, recorded south as far as S Nansei Shoto. **HH** Typically forages on agricultural land, often in large flocks, often with other crows, roosting in woodland. **ID** Large corvid with rather small head, slender neck and broad tail. Black with bluish-purple iridescence; thigh feathers shaggy, like baggy trousers. In display, blunt-ended broad tail is fanned. In flight, head protrudes more than Oriental Crow, primaries distinctly 'fingered', wing bases narrow, tail full. **BP** Bill slender, sharply pointed, black with greyish-white base; eyes black; tarsi black. **SV** Dry, flat, nasal *kaak*, weaker and harsher than Oriental Crow. **AN** Rook.

Oriental Crow *Corvus (corone) orientalis* L 45–50 cm; WS 93–104 cm; WT 320–686 g

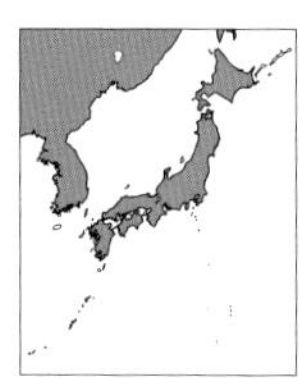

SD Widespread and common resident throughout the main and offshore islands of Japan, accidental to Nansei Shoto, Ogasawara and Iwo Is. **HH** Mountains and coasts, also cities (especially winter); flocks in winter, foraging over agricultural land. Commonly walks, like Eastern Rook. **ID** Large, all-black with slight metallic-blue sheen. Similar size to some small races of Japanese Crow, but separated by low, continuously sloping profile – from bill tip to slightly rounded crown. In flight, primaries 'fingered', but each primary broader than Eastern Rook's. **BP** Bill slender, slightly arched, pointed, but not as slender or pointed as rook, nor as blunt and deep as Japanese Crow, black; eyes black; tarsi black. **SV** Harsh rolling *caw* repeated 3–4 times. Calling posture differs from Japanese – tail often depressed, body hunched, head thrust forward. **AN** Carrion Crow.

Japanese Crow *Corvus (macrorhynchos) japonensis* L 46–59 cm; WS 100–130 cm; WT 600–750 g

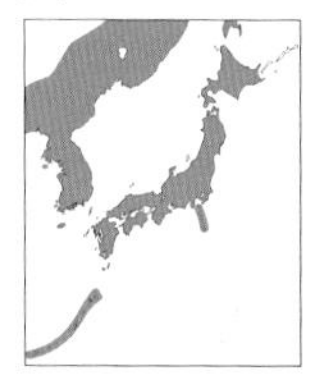

SD Widespread and common resident and partial migrant, with some northern birds moving south in winter. Largest races in north, smallest in south: *C. (m.) japonensis* (most of Japan, Hokkaido to Ogasawara Is); *C. (m.)/j. connectens* (Amami Is to Miyako); *C. (m.)/j. osai* (Yaeyama Is); *C. (m.)/j. mandshuricus* is resident on Tsushima. Subspecies of very large birds arriving to winter in Hokkaido undetermined. **HH** In both urban and rural areas also associated with woodlands, margins of cultivated land, even montane forest. Gathers at large roosts (often with Oriental Crow) during much of year; in winter, typically forages in large mixed flocks. Aggressive, will harass raptors, and even attacks pedestrians near nests. Commonly moves on ground using bouncing hop; also walks. **ID** Very large, all-black, with noticeable, but variable, purple/blue sheen, especially on scapulars and wings. Head large with flatter crown than Oriental, more vertical forehead emphasised when forehead-feathers erect. Chin-feathers also sometimes erected, giving shaggy-throated appearance resembling Northern Raven (for which it is sometimes mistaken). Beware small *osai* of Yaeyama Is; close to Oriental in size, with typical bill shape, but less prominent forehead and distinctive, rook-like call. In flight, primaries distinctly 'fingered', slightly more widely than Oriental, far more so than Northern Raven. **BP** Bill, black, deep, bluntly curved to tip, so upper mandible distinctly arched (with steep forehead, giving different profile from Oriental); eyes black; tarsi black. **SV** Almost laughing *awa-awa-awa* to harsh, clear *kaaw*, *gwarr* or *kaa kaa*, hoarser than Oriental, sometimes intermixed with throaty rattling sounds. When calling, tail usually raised and body often horizontal. **AN** Large-billed Crow; Thick-billed Crow; Jungle Crow.

Northern Raven *Corvus corax* L 54–69 cm; WS 120–150 cm; WT 800–1560 g

SD *C. c. kamtschaticus* is a scarce winter visitor (Oct–Apr) to E Hokkaido, accidental elsewhere; accidental to N & W Honshu. **HH** Favours rugged terrain: forested mountains, river valleys, rocky coasts, also volcanoes and calderas. Almost invariably in pairs, or family parties in winter; larger groups may gather at food sources. Powerful flier, even playful, engaging in impressive aerobatics. **ID** Large corvid with long, narrow-tipped wings, long, wedge-shaped tail and distinctive vocalisations. All black with metallic purplish-blue gloss; throat-feathers shaggy, giving bearded appearance. Profile recalls Oriental Crow, lacks steep forehead of Japanese Crow. Wings long, primaries less noticeably 'fingered' than other large black corvids. **BP** Bill large, deep, black; eyes black; tarsi black. **SV** Highly vocal; distinctive honking and croaking calls, e.g. *prrok-prrok-prrok*; sometimes with high-pitched fluty notes and almost musical *kapon kapon*.

Eastern Rook
ad
ad calling
juv
flock
Oriental Crow
ad
ad calling
Japanese Crow
ad *japonensis*
ad *connectens* calling
ad *japonensis*
ad
Northern Raven

Bohemian Waxwing *Bombycilla garrulus*

L 19–23 cm; WS 32–35 cm; WT 50–75 g

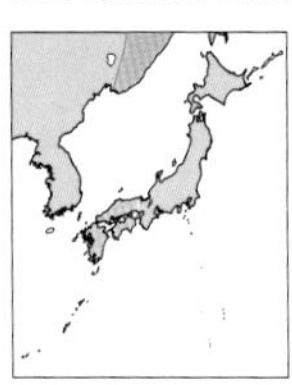

SD *B. g. garrulus* irruptive and nomadic winter visitor (Oct–May), all main islands, accidental Nansei Shoto, Izu, Ogasawara and Iwo Is. **HH** Forests, woodlands, parks, gardens, roadside trees, wherever there are berries. **ID** Overall buffy, grey-brown, with chestnut/orange vent. Narrow black mask from forehead to nape (below crest), chin also black (less extensive in ♀). Erectile, swept-back crest orange- to pinkish-brown. Flight-feathers and primary-coverts black with broad white tips (forming bars) to primary-coverts and secondaries, yellow outer and white inner tips to primaries; secondaries have elongated red, wax-like tips. Tail black with yellow terminal band (broader in ♂). Flight starling-like – fast and erratic; pale, pinkish-buff upperparts contrast with black primaries/secondaries. **BP** Bill short, black with yellow-horn to blue-grey base to lower mandible; eyes dark brown; tarsi dark grey/black. **SV** Highly vocal, uttering pleasant high-pitched sibilant trills: *ssirrreee ssirrreee* with bell-like quality, often given by whole flock before take-off.

Japanese Waxwing *Bombycilla japonica*

L 15–18 cm; WS 27–30 cm; WT 54–64 g

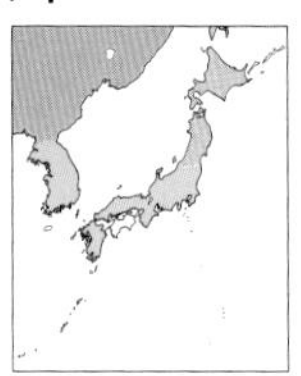

SD Uncommon, irruptive and nomadic winter visitor (Oct–May) throughout Japan; accidental Nansei Shoto, Izu, Ogasawara and Iwo Is. Autumn and spring migrations rather late (Nov/Dec, May). **HH** Winters in same habitats, and often joins Bohemian Waxwing flocks, though also forms monospecific groups. **ID** Smaller, plainer and greyer than Bohemian, with distinctive pale belly and dull, orange/red undertail-coverts. Grey-brown of mantle/back lacks warmer tones, with more extensive grey on wings and tail. Black mask continues to rear and tip of erectile crest (does not extend to crest in Bohemian). Largely grey secondaries and outer webs of primaries, with broad red scapular band and narrow red line at tips of secondaries; lacks yellow tips to primaries and waxen tips of Bohemian, but has broader white tips to both webs of primaries. Tail has narrower black band and dull red terminal band. Underparts pinkish-buff, with distinctive yellow patch on central belly. In flight, look for narrow red wingbar; yellow belly patch and red tail-band. **BP** Bill short, black; eyes dark reddish-brown; tarsi grey/black. **SV** Much like Bohemian, but trills higher pitched, more silvery and shorter: *chiri chiri chiri or hiiii hiiii,* also high-pitched whistles.

Marsh Tit *Poecile palustris*

L 11–14 cm; WT 9–13 g

SD Common resident of Hokkaido (*P. p. hensoni*). **HH** Occurs in mature deciduous and mixed forest, woodland edge, riverine thickets, scrub, urban parks and gardens, commonly forming mixed flocks with woodland birds in winter. **ID** Small and pale, with structure of Japanese Tit: head rather small, tail rather long and square-tipped. Crown and nape glossy black, small, rather neat black bib, mantle, wings, rump and tail uniform dull ash-grey brown; underparts, cheeks and head-sides white, breast and belly off-white, with grey/buff wash on flanks. Wings often have pale fringes to secondaries, thus very similar to Willow (criteria for separation, such as call and wing patterns, of western subspecies less helpful in E Asia). **BP** Bill short, stubby (thicker and blunter than Willow), black with paler bluish-grey cutting edges. Eyes large, black; tarsi dark grey. **SV** Various calls include thin *tseet*, and hard churring *chichi jeejee*. Strongly whistled spring song *pew-pew-pew* is reminiscent of Eurasian Nuthatch and very like Willow. Song is also similar to Willow, but stronger. **TN** Formerly *Parus palustris*.

Willow Tit *Poecile montanus*

L 11–14 cm; WT 8–14 g

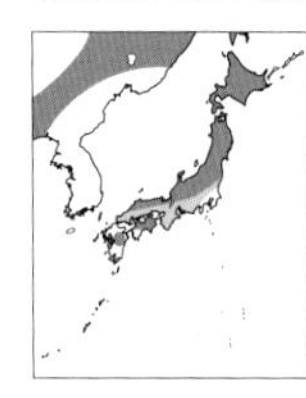

SD *P. m. restrictus* is a common resident of Honshu, Kyushu and Shikoku and an uncommon resident of Hokkaido; *P. m. sachalinensis* is former vagrant to Hokkaido and N Honshu. **HH** Coniferous and mixed mature deciduous forest, woodland edge, scrub and urban parks and gardens, but favours areas with dead trees more than Marsh Tit. **ID** Very similar to Marsh, but structure differs slightly; appears larger-headed and thicker-necked; shorter tail has more rounded tip. Crown and nape duller black than Marsh, lacking gloss; bib less neat, generally more extensive than Marsh; and pale fringes to tertials and secondaries form somewhat more prominent wing panel. **BP** Bill short, stubby, but finer, more pointed than Marsh, black; eyes large, black; tarsi dark grey. **SV** Calls closely resemble those of Marsh. Call a harsh, nasal *chichi jeejee*. Song a high, strident *tsupii tsupii pipii pipii* or *cho cho cho*, slightly more metallic than Marsh. **TN** Formerly *Parus montanus*.

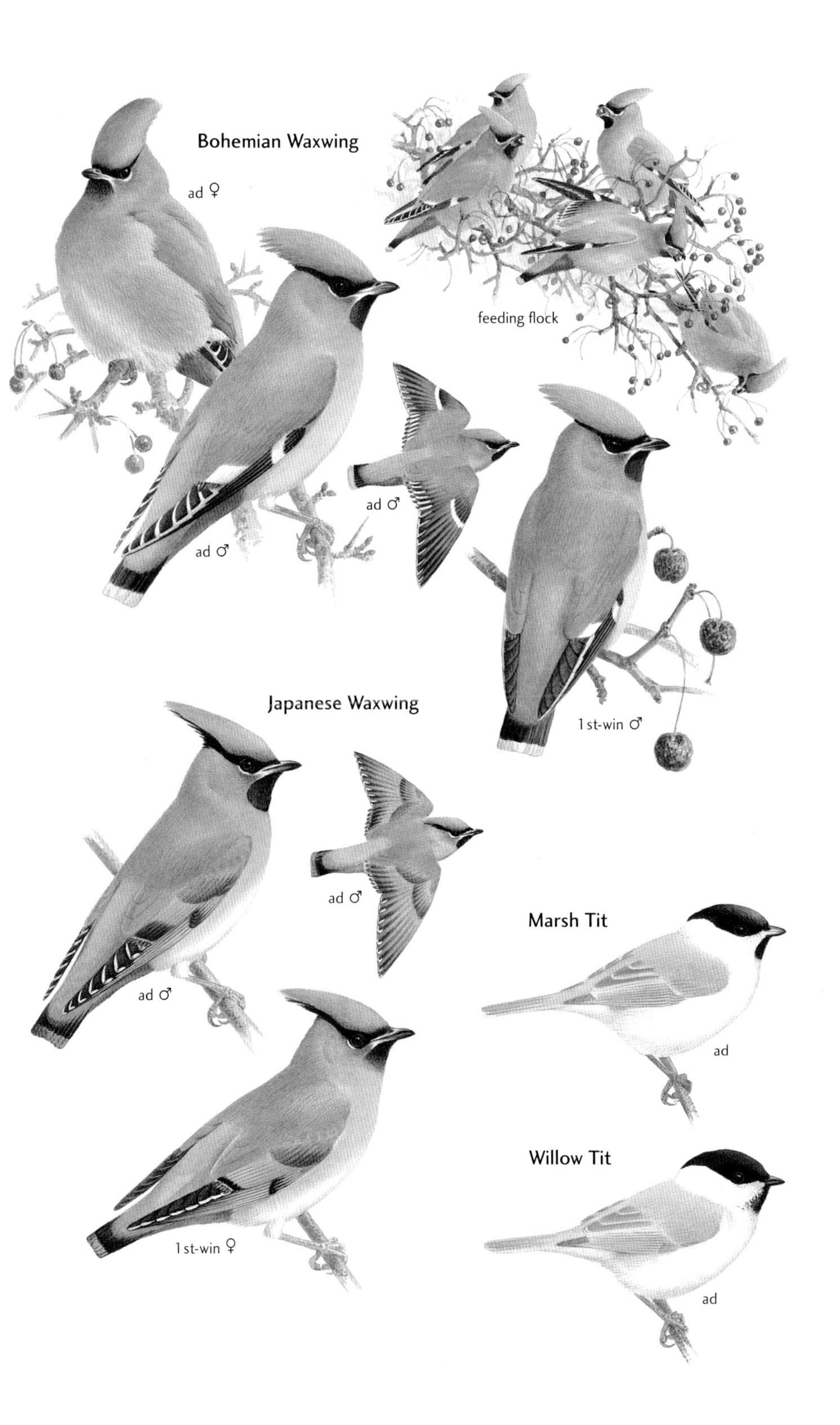
Bohemian Waxwing
ad ♀
feeding flock
ad ♂
ad ♂
1st-win ♂
Japanese Waxwing
ad ♂
ad ♂
1st-win ♀
Marsh Tit
ad
Willow Tit
ad

Varied Tit *Sittiparus varius*

L 14–16 cm; WT 17–22 g

SD Resident from Hokkaido to Nansei Shoto. *S. v. varius* Hokkaido, Honshu, Shikoku, Kyushu; *S. v. namiyei* (N Izu Is); *S. v. sunsunpi* (Tanegashima); *S. v. yakushimensis* (Yakushima); *S. v. orii* (extinct Daito I); and *S. v. amamii* (Nansei Shoto from Tokara to Okinawa). **HH** Deciduous and evergreen broadleaf forests, woodland, also scrub, parks and gardens in winter, when readily joins mixed flocks. **ID** Large, noisy, blue-grey and pale chestnut tit. Forehead, lores, cheeks and small nape patch off-white or creamy yellowish-white; rest of head, crown, face-sides to eye level, chin, and throat black. Hind-collar and most of underparts deep rufous or pale to mid-chestnut, with buff upper breast. Mantle, wings, rump and tail plain blue-grey. Populations become progressively darker from north to south. **BP** Bill strong, black; eyes black; tarsi strong, black. **SV** Calls include a nasal *nii nii* or *tsuee tsuee*, rasping *vay vay vay* and weak *tsuu tsuu tsuu*, also a thin, high *see see see*, recalling Goldcrest; in alarm a loud *tsutsu bee bee bee*. Song is slow thin *tsuu tsuu pee tsuu tsuu pee* and repetitive *tsi-turrr*, with much regional and local variation. **TN** Formerly *Parus varius*.

Owston's Tit *Sittiparus owstoni*

L 14–16 cm; WT 17–22 g

SD Endemic to S Izu Is (Miyake, Mikura and Hachijo Is). **HH** Evergreen broadleaf forests, woodland, scrub and gardens. **ID** Larger and darker than Varied Tit, with pronounced rusty-orange forehead, small nape patch and cheeks, more extensive black bib; chestnut of cheeks continuous with all-chestnut underparts. Upperparts darker brownish blue-grey. Differs also in breeding ecology. **BP** Bill rather deep, strong, black; eyes black; tarsi rather strong, black. **SV** Vocalisations very similar to Varied Tit. **TN** Formerly within *Parus varius*; retained by OSJ. **AN** Izu Tit.

Orii's Tit *Sittiparus olivaceus*

L 11–15 cm; WT 16–18 g

SD Endemic to Yaeyama Is (Ishigaki Is, where scarce, and Iriomote Is). **HH** Evergreen broadleaf forest. **ID** Smaller and duller than Varied Tit, with rusty-orange forehead, pale-orange cheeks and small nape patch. Upperparts blue-grey, tinged olive on the mantle; underparts dull pale orange. **BP** Bill rather deep, strong, black; eyes black; tarsi rather strong, black. **SV** Vocalisations recall Varied Tit, but high-pitched *tsee-tsee* notes paired with harsh *jee-jee-jee* notes. **TN** Formerly within *Parus varius*; retained by OSJ. **AN** Iriomote Tit.

Coal Tit *Periparus ater*

L 10–12 cm; WT 6–10 g

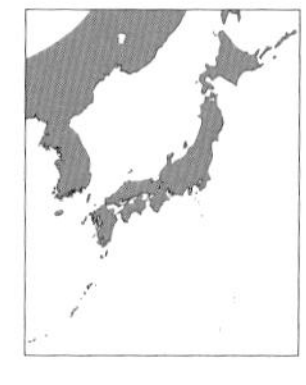

SD Common and wide-ranging resident throughout mainland Japan: *P. a. ater* in Hokkaido; *P. a. insularis* from N Honshu to Yakushima. **HH** Mature coniferous and mixed forests, in montane and lowland regions, less often in parks and gardens; readily joins mixed-tit flocks in winter. Favours coniferous trees more than other tits. **ID** Very small, rather slim black-and-grey tit, with rather large head and short tail. Black head has distinct, fine crest, white nape and white cheeks. Mantle, rump and tail dark bluish-grey, wings blacker with pale fringes to coverts forming two narrow wingbars, and white tips to tertials. Black bib broadens widely across upper chest, diffusing into grey of neck and buff or off-white of breast and belly. **BP** Bill slender, finely pointed, black; eyes large, irides black; tarsi dark grey. **SV** Call thin, Goldcrest-like *see-see-see* and *tsuu tsu-tsu-tsu-chi-ririri*. Song is rather repetitive, high and fast, *tse tse peen tse tse peen*… and a ringing *s'pee, s'pee, s'pee*, clearer and higher than Japanese Tit. **TN** Formerly *Parus ater*.

Yellow-bellied Tit *Pardaliparus venustulus*

L 10 cm; WT 9–12 g

SD Vagrant to N Kyushu, C Honshu, and Hegurajima. **ID** Resembles colourful Coal Tit, with more rounded head (lacks crest) and shorter, thicker bill. Cap, chin and throat black, contrasting strongly with broad white nape and narrow white cheeks; mantle dark grey with black streaking, wings blackish with double row of white spots (tips of coverts) on dark wing; tail blackish with white outer tail-feathers. Underparts yellow. **BP** Bill short, thick, black; eyes black; tarsi dark grey. **SV** Call a high-pitched, nasal *si-si-si-si*. **TN** Formerly *Parus venustulus*.

Varied Tit
ad
varius
juv
ad *amamii*
Orii's Tit
Owston's Tit
ad
ad
Coal Tit
insularis
ad
juv
Yellow-bellied Tit
ad
juv

Japanese Tit *Parus minor* L 14–15 cm; WT 14–17 g

SD Common resident from Hokkaido to Nansei Shoto. *P. m. minor* Hokkaido south to N Kyushu and Izu Is; *P. m. kagoshimae* Goto Is and S Kyushu; *P. m. amamiensis* on Amami Is; and *P. m. okinawae* on Okinawa. **HH** Temperate and subtropical forests; from mixed deciduous to broadleaf evergreen, scrub, suburban gardens and parks. **ID** Distinctive black and grey tit with black belly stripe (broadest in ♂, reaching undertail-coverts; narrow in ♀), and yellowish-green only on mantle; back, wing-coverts and rump blue-grey, tail black (with white outer feathers), underparts off-white or buff, lacking yellow tones. Wings have white fringes to blackish tertials. Tail largely white below, black at base and narrowly down centre. **BP** Bill black; eyes black; legs rather strong, tarsi dark grey/black. **SV** Typically demonstrative and repetitive *bee-tsu bee-tsu bee-tsu....*; *tea-cher-tea-cher*, also *tsupi tsupi*. Song contains repeated call notes: *tsutsupii tsutsupii, tsupii tsupii, tsupi tsupi tsupi*. **TN** Formerly within Great Tit *P. major*. **AN** Eastern Great Tit.

Ishigaki Tit *Parus (minor) nigriloris* L 13–17 cm

SD Endemic to Yaeyama Is. **HH** Broadleaf evergreen forest and mangroves; also gardens. **ID** Very dark, grey tit. Head black, cap extends to nape and below eye, black chin/throat patch extend neck-sides, leaving only small white cheek patch. Mantle, back and scapulars mid-grey, wing-coverts and wing-feathers black with narrow grey fringes and faint greater covert bar, tertials have white fringes. Tail long, greyish-black with white outer feathers. Black of throat and neck-sides reaches upper chest and central belly as broad black stripe (broader in ♂); underparts dull mid-grey, dark grey on flanks. **BP** As Japanese Tit. **SV** Distinctive electric jarring quality: *zerr zerr zerr*. Song a jaunty, repetitive two-note whistle. **TN** Formerly within Japanese Tit *P. minor* (retained within *P. major* by OSJ).

Azure Tit *Cyanistes cyanus* L 12–14 cm; WT 10–16 g

SD Vagrant to Rishiri, Hokkaido (*C. c. yenisseensis*?). **HH** Woodlands and thickets close to water. **ID** Small, pallid blue-grey and white tit with somewhat long tail. Pale whitish-grey crown and nape, with dark blue-grey eyestripe which joins broader, blacker hind-collar; mantle, scapulars and rump pale blue-grey, tail deeper blue with white outer tail-feathers and rounded white tip; wings largely deep blue with broad white bar on greater coverts and prominent white tips to tertials. **BP** Bill very stubby, black; eyes black; legs black. **SV** Call a thin repetitive *chi chwee chi chwee chi chwee..., jii jii* or *tsee-tsee-tserrr de-de-de*. **TN** Formerly *Parus cyanus*.

Chinese Penduline Tit *Remiz consobrinus* L 9–12 cm; WT 7–12 g

SD Very localised and scarce winter visitor (Oct–May) from C Honshu south to S Kyushu; accidental north to N Honshu and south to Okinawa. **HH** Reedbeds, marshes, tall grasses, thickets and open woodland near wetlands; winter numbers and movements erratic. **ID** Rather pale, with short, notched tail. ♂: grey crown and nape contrast strongly with black mask from forehead to ear-coverts, bordered above with white; upperparts warm rufous-brown, especially on neck-sides and mantle, to grey-brown back and rump. Wings and tail black, former with chestnut wing-coverts forming wingbar in flight. Creamy white chin/throat, grading to off-white and buff on belly. ♀: duller than ♂, with brown mask and lacks warm rufous tones. **BP** Bill finely pointed, conical, grey; eyes black; tarsi black. **SV** Call a very thin, high-pitched, but descending, drawn-out *tseeooo*; also a ringing *tsi* or *chii-chii-chii* (similar to Japanese White-eye, but thinner). **TN** Formerly within Eurasian Penduline Tit *R. pendulinus* (retained by OSJ).

Bearded Reedling *Panurus biarmicus* L 14–17 cm; WT 12–18 g

SD Vagrant (*P. b. russicus*) in winter to NW, C & W Honshu. **HH** Reed and cattail beds fringing rivers, lakes and marshes. **ID** Rather plain cinnamon-brown bird with long (c. 7 cm) graduated tail with rounded tip. ♂ has plain pale blue-grey head with prominent black lores and drooping black 'moustaches'; mantle, back, tail and flanks warm tawny-brown; underparts off-white suffused pink, except undertail-coverts, which are black; wing-coverts, tertials and primary tips black, folded primaries appear largely white. ♀ lacks grey hood, black 'moustaches' and black undertail-coverts. Flight rather weak on rapid whirring wingbeats. **BP** Bill short, finely pointed, yellow-orange; eyes small, white (♂), or orange (♀); tarsi dark-grey to black. **SV** Metallic *ching ching* while foraging or in flight. **AN** Bearded Tit.

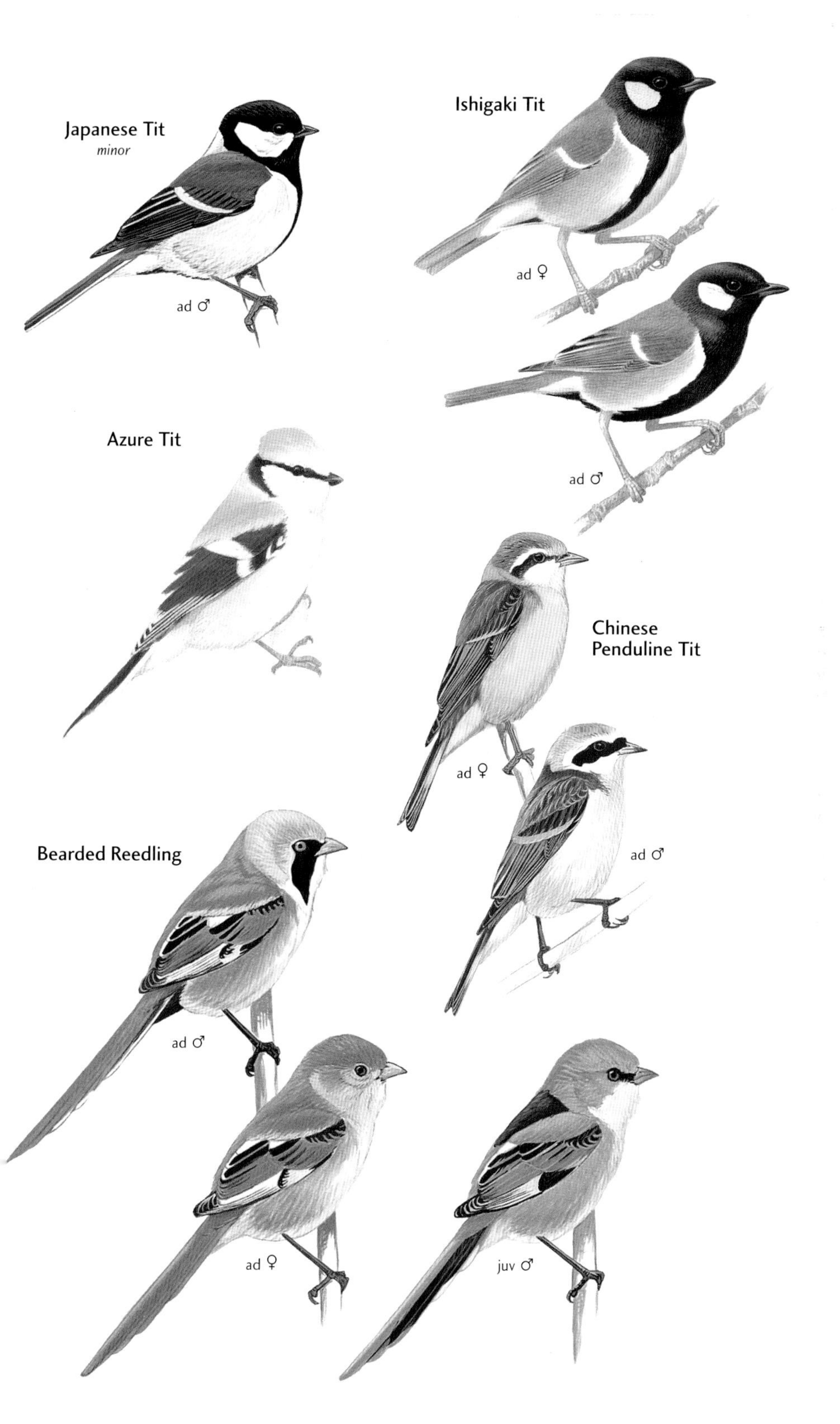

Japanese Tit
minor
ad ♂
Ishigaki Tit
ad ♀
ad ♂
Azure Tit
Chinese
Penduline Tit
ad ♀
ad ♂
Bearded Reedling
ad ♂
ad ♀
juv ♂

Eurasian Skylark *Alauda arvensis*

L 16–19 cm; WT 26–50 g

SD Common and widespread from Hokkaido to Nansei Shoto; *A. a. lonnbergi* is scarce visitor with records from Hokkaido to Izu Is, and *A. a. pekinensis* is scarce visitor wintering in Kyushu and with records from Hokkaido south to Nansei Shoto and Izu Is; however, subspecies are doubtfully separable in the field. *A. a. japonica* (sometimes considered separate species, **Japanese Skylark** *A. (a.) japonica*, but also considered within Oriental Skylark) is summer visitor to Hokkaido and resident from N Honshu south to Kyushu, with records as far south as Nansei Shoto. **HH** Agricultural land and short grassland; mostly present year-round, but northern birds migratory and wintering ranges unclear. **ID** Medium-sized, buffy-brown lark with distinct, broad, rounded crest and obvious display flight. Overall brownish-grey with buff, even orange, tones. Crown finely streaked blackish, crown-feathers may be raised in distinct crest; face appears gentle, with broad whitish supercilia and brown ear-coverts patch; mantle and coverts have dark-centred grey-brown feathers, and dark flight-feathers broadly fringed rusty-brown (paler when worn). Slightly smaller *japonica* has somewhat darker upperparts, more rufous-brown lesser covert patch. Underparts have band of short, fine black streaks across upper breast and neck-sides, contrasting with white belly with hardly any streaking on flanks, whereas *pekinensis* has less contrasting underparts pattern and streaks extending well onto flanks. At rest, primary projection beyond tertials long. Tail short, dark brown with paler central and white outer feathers. Upperwing has variably distinct or indistinct white or buff trailing edge, underwing grey-brown. **BP** Bill short, upper mandible grey, lower horn; eyes black; tarsi dull grey-pink; hindclaw longer than toe. **SV** Call, typically given on take-off, a repeated, rolling *chirrup*, *chrr-ik*, *byuru* or *prreet*. May sing from perch, but typically in high display flight (wings fluttering while hovering, tail fanned); a very prolonged torrent of rapid chirrups, whistles and complex phrases interspersed with calls.

Oriental Skylark *Alauda gulgula*

L 15–18 cm; WT 24–30 g

SD Has strayed to S Japan (race uncertain). **HH** Dry agricultural land. **ID** Very similar to Eurasian Skylark, from which best distinguished by slightly smaller size, paler upperparts, short primary projection, short tail with buff, not white, edges; buff, not white, trailing edge to wing (but see *A. a. japonica*), more prominently white behind eye (fresh plumage), and slightly longer, finer bill. Indistinct rufous wing-panel formed by fringes to primaries. May also raise small crest. **BP** Bill short, fine, upper mandible grey, lower pink/horn; eyes black; tarsi dull grey-pink; hindclaw longer than toe. **SV** Call, typically given at take-off, *swit switswit* or a dry buzzing *drzz*, or *bazz bazz*, with Eurasian Skylark-like notes. **TN** Not included by OSJ.

Horned Lark *Eremophila alpestris*

L 14–17 cm; WT 26–46 g

SD *E. a. flava* is rare migrant and rare winter visitor (Nov–Mar) to Hokkaido, Honshu and Tsushima. **HH** On migration and in winter occurs in short-grass areas, fallow cultivation, coasts and on beaches. **ID** Distinctive, slender, medium-sized lark, with prominent black mask, black breast-band and fine, black horns; may have yellow on face. Upperparts rather plain mid- to sandy brown, more rufous on nape and rump, with fine streaking on mantle. Underparts white to buff, with broad buff streaking on flanks. ♂ smartly attired, ♀ similar but less boldly patterned. In flight, long-winged, upperwing plain, lacks pale trailing edge, underwing off-white, tail long, blackish with pale grey or brown central, and white outer feathers. **BP** Bill stubby, grey at base, blackish at tip; eyes black; tarsi black. **SV** Calls high, weak and thin, *seeh*; *see-tu* or *chit chit-see*, sometimes a harsher *prsh* or *tssr*, and liquid *tur-reep*. Song, given in flight or from rock perch, includes rapidly repeated short tinkling phrases and rippling trills followed by short chatter. **AN** Shore Lark.

Eurasian Skylark
ad
ad
ad song flight
ad lonnbergi
ad japonica
juv
Oriental Skylark
Horned Lark
ad ♂
ad ♀
juv

Bimaculated Lark *Melanocorypha bimaculata* L 16–17 cm; WT 47–62 g

SD *M. b. torquata* is accidental in winter to C Honshu, Izu Is, N Kyushu, Nansei Shoto. **HH** Open agricultural land. **ID** Large, heavy-set, heavy-billed, short-tailed lark. Upperparts sandy-brown with dark centres to most feathers, crown finely spotted dark, wing-feathers dark brown with sandy fringes; most prominent feature is black patch forming narrow collar on foreneck and streaking on sides of upper breast. Head large, strongly patterned, with prominent white supercilia, darker crown, dark ear-coverts, dark line through eye, white crescent below eye forward to bill, and white chin with narrow malar stripe. Tail short, blackish-brown, including sides, but has broad white band at tip. In flight, upperwing lacks white trailing edge, and shows little contrast between upperwing-coverts and remiges; tail short (often fanned), white-tipped, and underwing brownish-grey. **BP** Bill large, heavy, rather blunt, grey culmen, otherwise yellow; eyes black; strong legs dull orange. **SV** Calls generally harsh and drawn-out, also recalling Eurasian Skylark – a chirruping *biru*, but with drier, rasping *tchur* and *ju ju* notes recalling Asian Short-toed.

Mongolian Lark *Melanocorypha mongolica* L 18–22 cm

SD Vagrant to Hokkaido (Teurito), NW Honshu (Tobishima) and Okinawa (Zamamijima). **HH** Open grassland. **ID** Large, pale lark with very large bill. Face plain, pale sandy-brown, with broad eye-ring and stripe extending back from eye. Upperparts warm brown on crown and nape, somewhat greyish on hindneck; mantle grey-brown with black streaking, blackish-brown rump and tail, with white outer tail-feathers. Broad black band across neck-sides to throat and breast. Wings blackish-brown, with buff fringes to coverts and tertials, and broad white or pale fringes to flight-feathers. Underparts: chin white, breast to vent off-white with warmer rusty wash on flanks. Juvenile lacks rufous and black neck-band. **BP** Bill pale pink or yellow with grey culmen and tip; eye appears small, irides dark brown; tarsi pale pinkish-grey. **SV** Various harsh and high-pitched calls.

Greater Short-toed Lark *Calandrella brachydactyla* L 14–15 cm; WT 20–26 g

SD Rare migrant and winter visitor (*C. b. longipennis*), which has occurred widely from Nansei Shoto to Hokkaido. **HH** Open areas with sparse vegetation, including agricultural fields. **ID** Small, plain lark with unstreaked breast and variable black patches on upper-breast/neck-sides. Upperparts sandy-brown, crown somewhat darker, appearing slightly capped, with dark streaking; broad pale supercilia and eye-ring, mantle and back sandy-brown with darker streaks, wings blackish-brown with broad pale fringes to coverts and tertials (very long, reaching primary tips). Underparts generally white, with warm rufous-buff wash to breast-sides and black patch. **BP** Bill stout, rather round-tipped, grey above, horn below; eyes black; tarsi flesh-pink. **SV** Often calls on take-off. In flight, a dry sparrow-like *tjrip* or *dreet*, but also has *prrt* call similar to next species. Other calls skylark-like *jiru jiru*, or sparrow-like *chun chun* or *pyu pyu*.

Asian Short-toed Lark *Alaudala cheleensis* L 13–14 cm; WT 20–27 g

SD *A. c. cheleensis* is very rare winter visitor from Nansei Shoto to Hokkaido. **HH** Open areas with short, dry vegetation. **ID** Small, compact, rather dark sandy-brown lark, closely recalling Greater Short-toed, but lacks black neck patches. Instead has necklace of narrow streaking on upper breast. Upperparts sandy-brown heavily streaked dark brown; face rather plain with narrow buff supercilia, eye-ring and lores, darker narrow malar on otherwise off-white chin; wings blackish-brown with paler fringes to coverts and tertials; tertials short, *not* covering primary tips; tail blackish-brown with white outer feathers. Underparts off-white with buff lower neck and flanks, and dark necklace of streaks. **BP** Bill stubby, greyish-horn; eyes black; tarsi brownish-pink. **SV** Dry, buzzy *drrrrd* recalling Sand Martin, and *chirrick*, *puri*, *chui* or *pichu*. In flight, a purring *prrrt* or *prrr-rrr-rrr*. **TN** Sometimes considered within Lesser Short-toed Lark *A. rufescens*. Retained in genus *Calandrella* by OSJ.

Bimaculated Lark

Mongolian Lark

Greater Short-toed Lark

Asian Short-toed Lark

Red-whiskered Bulbul *Pycnonotus jocosus*

L 18–21 cm; WT 25–31 g

SD Common cagebird. Escapees/feral population in C Japan (subspecies uncertain). **HH** Wooded areas near habitation. **ID** Dark, medium-sized, rather slender bulbul with distinctive head pattern and crest. Adult has black head with erect spiky crest; ear-coverts red above white, separated from white chin/throat by narrow black malar. Upperparts largely dusky grey-brown, but nape and neck-sides black. White of throat/face separated from rest of underparts by black neck bar, below which grades to dusky grey-brown on flanks and breast-sides; centre of breast and belly white, vent contrastingly red. Juvenile has shorter, browner crest, lacks red post-ocular patch, and vent duller orange or buffish-pink. **BP** Bill slender, black; eyes dark brown; tarsi black. **SV** Calls include *queee-kwut* and musical *per'r'p*. Song rich and complex: *wit-ti-waet queep kwil-ya queek-kay*. **TN** Not included by OSJ.

Light-vented Bulbul *Pycnonotus sinensis*

L 18–19 cm; WT 75 g

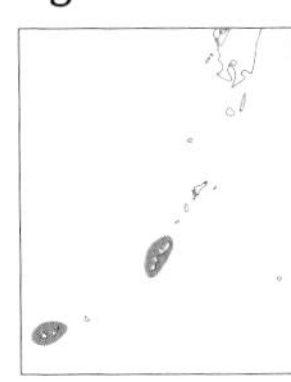

SD *P. s. orii* is resident in S Nansei Shoto and expanding northwards, now to northern Okinawa; accidental visitor (or escapee) to Kyushu and W & C Honshu. **HH** Lightly wooded habitat, open cultivated areas and gardens near habitation. Sociable and noisy, often perching conspicuously on treetops, poles or wires. **ID** Pale bulbul with black head and broad white 'bandana' from eye to nape (where broadest), bordered below with black, also has tiny white spot on lores and larger spot on rear ear-coverts; chin and throat white, bordered by black malar. Mantle and back greyish-green, rump plain grey, tail dark grey with green outer fringes to feathers; wings greyish-brown with yellowish-green outer fringes to flight-feathers; greyish-buff breast and flanks seasonally variable (perhaps more extensive in winter), off-white belly, vent white. **BP** Bill black; eyes dark brown; tarsi black. **SV** Generally coarse and shrill, but song includes more melodious tones. Vocalisations somewhat subdued *ju ju*, sometimes a continuous *piyopiyopiyopiyopiyo* and somewhat nasal *vyer*. Song a strident, whistle-warble: *chip-chop-chop-twee*; also *plit prilyor trilor* often repeated. **AN** Chinese Bulbul. **TN** Perhaps synonymous with *P. s. sinensis*, but current taxonomy unclear.

Black Bulbul *Hypsipetes leucocephalus*

L 24–27 cm; WT 44–61 g

SD Vagrant to Yonagunijima. **HH** Broadleaf evergreen and mixed deciduous forests. **ID** Medium to large black bulbul with rather loose, ragged 'crest' on rear crown and long, square-ended or slightly notched tail. May have black head, or white hood, and white tips to grey belly and vent feathers. **BP** Bill prominently orange; eyes dark brown; tarsi bright orange or red. **SV** Noisy, calling while perched and in flight. A whining, plaintive *keer* and cat-like *meow* or *nyeeer*; flight call a strident *tsit* or *tseesp*. **TN** Not included by OSJ.

Brown-eared Bulbul *Hypsipetes amaurotis*

L 27–29 cm; WT 60–86 g

SD Common resident, or year-round visitor, throughout Japan from Hokkaido to Nansei Shoto, but with marked local movements. *H. a. amaurotis* Hokkaido to Yakushima and Izu Is, winters to Nansei Shoto; *H. a. ogawae* resident Tokara and Amami; *H. a. pryeri* resident Okinawa and Miyako Is; *H. a. stejnegeri* resident on Yaeyama Is; *H. a. nagamichii* resident on Yonagunijima; *H. a. squamiceps* resident on Ogasawara Is; *H. a. magnirostris* on Iwo Is; and *H. a. borodinonis* on Daito Is. **HH** Deciduous, mixed and evergreen broadleaf forest, from lowlands to montane foothills (to c.1,600 m). In winter also in rural/agricultural areas with scattered trees and in suburban and urban gardens and parks. **ID** Large, drab bulbul, with long tail and strongly undulating flight. Adult *M. a. amaurotis* is overall dark ash-grey with fine paler 'frosting' on head, slightly shaggy feathering on rear crown (sometimes raised as crest) and larger pale grey spots on chest, with diagnostic dark chestnut crescent on ear-coverts. Upperparts plain grey, browner on wings and tail. Underparts have brown wash on flanks and undertail-coverts black with white fringes. Juvenile is duller, browner and lacks silvery wash. Underwing-coverts dark brown; long tail broadens towards square tip. Southern races e.g. *pryeri* and *stejnegeri* are smaller, darker, with dark brown (not grey) mantle and more extensive chestnut ear-patch joining dark chestnut-brown of neck, breast and underparts. **BP** Bill sharply pointed, black (larger in southern races); eyes dark reddish-brown; tarsi dark grey. **SV** Noisy; highly social and vociferous. Calls varied, but almost invariably loud, harsh, shrill and drawn-out, including *wheesp*; *whee-eesp*; *shreep shreeeep*; *pii-hyara*, *piyopiyopiyo* and *hiihii*.

Red-whiskered
Bulbul
ad
Light-vented Bulbul
ad orii
ad sinensis
juv
Black Bulbul
ad
Brown-eared Bulbul
ad amaurotis
ad pryeri

PLATE 132: MARTINS AND SWALLOWS I

Grey-throated Martin *Riparia chinensis* L 10–13 cm; WT 9–17 g

SD *R. c. chinensis* is vagrant to Yaeyama Is and Okinawa. **HH** Wetlands and open grassland habitats. **ID** Closely resembles Sand Martin, but underparts duskier, off-white to buff on chin/throat, lacks contrast between throat and ear-coverts, and has less clear demarcation between upperparts and underparts; lacks Sand Martin's distinctive brown breast-band, instead has grey-brown wash on chest. In flight, underwing rather dark. **BP** Bill tiny, black; eyes black; tarsi brown/black. **SV** Calls include distinctive Long-tailed Tit-like rasping *chitrr* and ringing *chit-it*, in addition to quiet twittering calls very similar to Sand Martin. **TN** Formerly within Brown-throated Martin *R. paludicola*.

Sand Martin *Riparia riparia* L 12–13 cm; WS 26–29 cm; WT 11–19 g

SD *R. r. ijimae* is locally common summer visitor (May–Aug) breeding only in Hokkaido, and a migrant through all areas south to Nansei Shoto. **HH** Almost exclusively near water; along rivers, at lakes, wetlands and coasts, nesting in colonies in sand cliffs or banks. **ID** Small, compact, slender hirundine. Adult is mid grey-brown above with pale underparts and distinctive, clearly defined, narrow brown breast-band. Head small, 'face' dark, with white crescent on neck curving up behind auriculars. Young have paler fringes to mantle and wing-covert feathers, grey-buff face and throat, and less clearly marked breast-band. At rest, wingtips reach tail tip; in flight, wings appear rather broad in 'arm'; dark on upper surface, dusky on underwing; tail short, clearly notched. **BP** Bill tiny, black; eyes black; tarsi brown/black. **SV** Common flight calls dry and scratchy: *chirr-chirr*, also *ju ju ju* or *juku juku juku ju ju*; around colonies, flocks give excited harsh chattering including typical *trrrsh*. **AN** North America: Bank Swallow.

Barn Swallow *Hirundo rustica* L 17–19 cm; WS 32–35 cm; WT 16–22 g

SD *H. r. gutturalis* is common summer visitor (Apr–Oct) from Kyushu to Hokkaido, later arriving in N, and migrant through Nansei Shoto, with some wintering in Kyushu. *H. r. saturata* is scarce visitor, with records from Nansei Shoto to N Honshu, which has bred locally. **HH** Generally in lowland habitats from urban to rural areas, often near water, particularly in areas with domestic livestock. Nests under eaves of buildings. Congregates in roosting flocks, especially on or prior to migration, sometimes in trees, reedbeds, or on wires. **ID** Adult *gutturalis*: glossy steely-blue upperparts and largely white underparts. Forehead, chin and throat deep brick-red, bordered below by *narrow* blue-black band on upper chest, then white to vent, but some have buff cast to underparts; underwing-coverts clean white (see Pacific Swallow). Tail long, deeply forked, outer tail streamers (2–7 cm) are longest in ♂ and very short in juvenile. Juvenile: duller, dusky below, with dull orange throat and indistinct chest-band. Adult *saturata*: underparts, including underwing coverts, have light to strong rusty orange cast. Flight-feathers blue-black; subterminal band of white spots revealed when tail spread. Highly active insectivore; flight fast, aerobatic, either high, or low over ground or water. **BP** Bill short (gape wide) black; eyes black; tarsi black. **SV** Short, hard twittering *chubi* or *veet-veet*. Song: rapid, rambling squeaky or scratchy twittering *pichi kuchu chiriri*.... Alarm call: sharp and agitated *vitveet*, *siflitt* or *flitt*!

Pacific Swallow *Hirundo tahitica* L 13 cm; WT 11–16 g

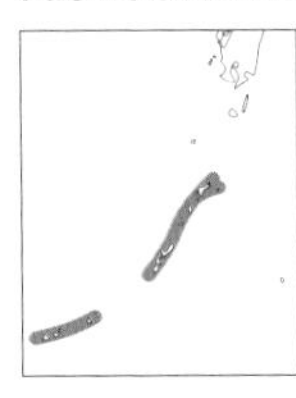

SD *H. t. namiyei* (may be split as **Small House Swallow** within *H. javanica*) is locally common resident of Nansei Shoto, from Yonaguni I to Amami Is, some breed Takara and Yakushima, vagrant north to N Kyushu and NW Honshu. **HH** Various lowland habitats, from suburban to rural areas, often near water. Nests under eaves or bridges. **ID** Small swallow with glossy, steely blue upperparts, and largely grey or buff underparts. Adult: forehead, chin and throat patch deep brick red; lacks blue-black chest-band of Barn Swallow, underparts dusky grey-buff; undertail-coverts dark with pale fringes, creating distinctive hatched pattern. Tail short, slightly forked with subterminal row of white spots, without streamers. Juvenile closely resembles juvenile Barn Swallow, but duller, duskier below and lacks chest-band. Flight-feathers blue-black; underwing-coverts dusky-grey. Flight fast and aerobatic, often low over ground or water. **BP** Bill short (gape wide), black; eyes black; tarsi black. **SV** Similar to Barn, but shriller. Calls frequently in flight, *je je je* or *ju ju ju* and a starling-like *skreet* or *vitt*. Song a rapid rambling series also resembling Barn Swallow *juku juku tsiriri*....

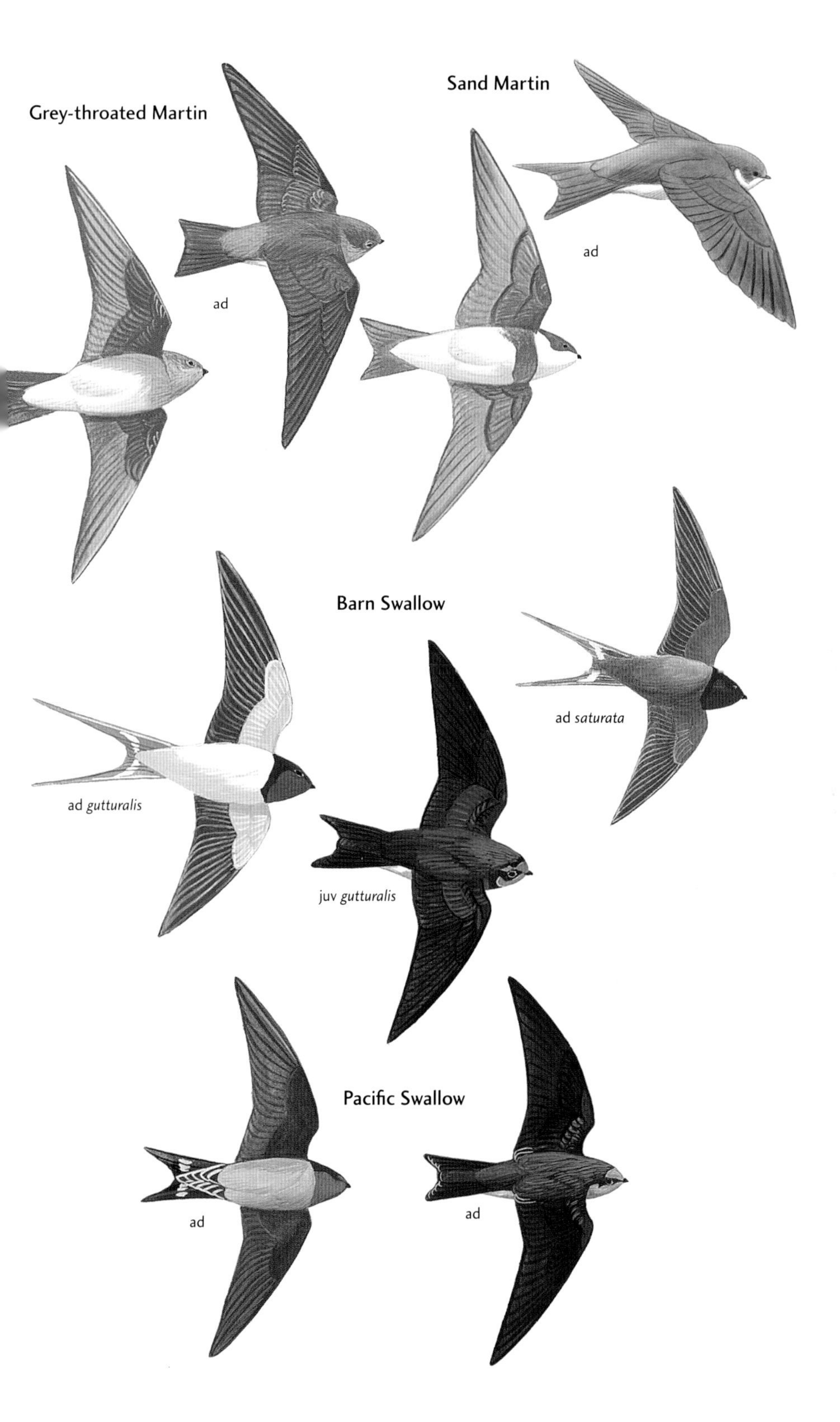
Grey-throated Martin
ad
Sand Martin
ad
Barn Swallow
ad *saturata*
ad *gutturalis*
juv *gutturalis*
Pacific Swallow
ad
ad

Tree Swallow *Tachycineta bicolor* — L 12 13 cm; WS 34 37 cm; WT 17 25 g

SD Vagrant to S Hokkaido. **HH** Wetlands and open areas. **ID** Very contrasting, rather stocky, between Barn Swallow and Sand Martin in size, with broad wings and short, barely notched tail. Upperparts very dark. Underparts from chin to vent clean white. Adult: ♂ has distinctive blue-green sheen on upperparts. ♀ has less distinctive green cast to otherwise blackish plumage, and white tertial tips. Young: uniform grey-brown above with white tertial tips, and may show incomplete dusky breast-band leading to confusion with Sand Martin. At rest, wingtips reach or extend just beyond tail. In flight, from above appears uniformly dark, almost blackish, with white crescents visible at rump-sides at all ages; from below, dark underwing contrasts with white body. **BP** Bill tiny, black; eyes black; tarsi pinkish-grey. **SV** Twittering and soft chirping notes, *quuii*, *tsuwi* and scratchy *tzeev*.

Eastern House Martin *Delichon lagopodum* — L 13–14 cm; WS 26–29 cm; WT 15–23 g

SD An accidental migrant, with records from Nansei Shoto, Amami Is, islands off NW Honshu and SW Hokkaido. **ID** Very clean black and white, typically larger, longer-tailed with deeper fork, and more glossy upperparts than Asian House Martin. More sharply defined black cap does not extend to cheeks or chin. Adult: upperparts steel blue-black, often glossy, strong contrast with *large*, broad white rump, uppertail-coverts and lower back; underparts, from chin to vent, clean white. Juvenile: duskier, more closely resembles Asian. Wings broader based and shorter than swallow; underwing-coverts whitish-grey; tail short, sharply forked (see Asian), undertail-coverts white. **BP** Bill short, black; eyes black; legs feathered (white), feet grey-pink. **SV** Calls frequently in flight: a steady pleasing twittering *juriri juriri*, a stronger *prrit* or *brit*, very similar to Asian, but lower-pitched. **AN** Previously within Northern House Martin *D. urbicum*.

Asian House Martin *Delichon dasypus* — L 13 cm; WT 18–24 g

SD *D. d. dasypus* is summer visitor (May–Sep) throughout Japan from Kyushu to Hokkaido, scarce winterer in south, and scarce migrant to Nansei Shoto, Ogasawara and Iwo Is. **HH** In montane or coastal regions with cliffs, nesting on crags, under bridges or in tunnels; in lowlands on migration and in winter. **ID** Small, compact, dusky martin; much like Eastern House Martin but less neat. Black cap extends onto face and ear-coverts, and just below bill on chin. Upperparts dull steel blue-black, contrasting with rather *small*, grey-streaked, white rump. Throat and neck-sides grey-white, breast, flanks and belly dusky grey-white, even buff, often with narrow streaking; underwing-coverts black, undertail-coverts usually dusky off-white. In flight, uppertail-coverts glossy bluish-black, tail fork shallower than Northern; when tail fanned, appears square-ended. **BP** Bill short, black; eyes black; legs feathered (white), toes grey-pink. **SV** *Juriri juri* or *ju ju piriri*.

Red-rumped Swallow *Cecropis daurica* — L 16–19 cm; WS 32–34 cm; WT 19–29 g

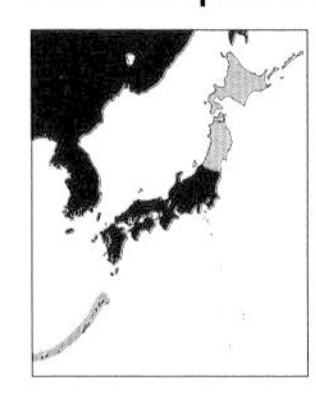

SD *C. d. japonica* is fairly common, local summer visitor (May–Sep) from Kyushu to Hokkaido (scarce), with migrants passing through Nansei Shoto and also reaching Ogasawara Is. **HH** Lowland habitats typically close to water. Nest a mud bottle attached under eaves, bridges or cliffs. **ID** Slightly larger than similar Barn Swallow. Adult: ♂ upperparts glossy blue-black, rump patch brick-red; tail blue-black with very long outer tail-feathers (5–6 cm). Supercilia, head-sides to rear of ear-coverts and nape-sides dusky brick-red; many have rufous extending quite far around neck like a hind-collar. Face and underparts heavily marked with narrow, dark-grey streaks. Vent white, undertail-coverts black. ♀ has shorter tail. Juvenile: duller browner above, paler rufous areas and less distinct streaking; short tail. In flight, flight-feathers blue-black, underwing-coverts creamy buff; pale rump and white vent contrast with black undertail-feathers, giving tail oddly detached look. Flight fast and aerobatic. **BP** Bill short-black; eyes black; tarsi black. **SV** Barn Swallow-like *jubi chibi* notes, but also a nasal *tveyk*. Song a rapid, complex series of twittering notes: *jubitt-juru-juri-churujuri*, slower, lower and harsher than Barn Swallow; in alarm a sharp *kiir!* **TN** Formerly in genus *Hirundo*.

Tree Swallow
1st-win
ad
ad
Eastern House
Martin
ad
Asian House Martin
ad
ad
ad
Red-rumped Swallow
ad

Japanese Bush Warbler *Horornis diphone* L 14–18 cm; WT 10–22 g

SD Common. Considerable size variation between sexes and subspecies; perhaps multiple species. *H. d. riukiuensis* (= *sakhalinensis*) migrates via Japan, recorded Hokkaido to Okinawa, winter visitor C & SW Honshu and Nansei Shoto; *H. d. cantans* main and offshore islands south to Yakushima, migratory northern birds winter Honshu/Kyushu; *H. d. restrictus* (presumed extinct Daito Is) resident Amami and Okinawa Is, probably Tokara; *H. d. diphone* endemic to Ogasawara and Iwo Is possibly merits specific status. **HH** Dense forest, riparian scrub, wooded parks; skulks in low vegetation, sometimes sings in open. **ID** Variable. Greyish-brown to warm brown, paler grey-brown below to white on face and throat, greyish-buff on flanks; long prominent tail has rounded tip. Island races smaller, darker and greyer. *H. d. cantans* (commonest bush warbler in Japan) upperparts yellowish-brown or olive-tinged, with warm chestnut-brown fringed remiges, supercilia pale buffish-brown; underparts dirty white. *H. d. riukiuensis* plain greyish-brown, with darker brown crown than *cantans*. *H. d. diphone* very similar to *cantans*, but smaller-bodied, with more elongated profile; forehead and crown rufous-brown, supercilia yellowish-white, flight-feathers rufous fringed; underparts yellowish-white with buffish wash to breast. *H. d. restrictus* smaller, darker, browner than other races, with strong red-brown tone to forehead, wings and tail. **BP** Bill somewhat blunt (notably much longer in *C. d. diphone*), brown or blackish above, yellowish-pink below; eyes black; tarsi long, brownish-pink. **SV** Extremely vocal. Call: hard dry *tchak* or *chek*. Song: varied and rich-toned, long whistle then explosive burst of three notes *pheeuw hou-ke-kyo*, also *hoo-hokekyo hii-hikekyo* or continuously *pipipipi kekyo kekyo kekyo*.... Also descending staccato series of trisyllabic notes, with a rippling precursor in alarm: *tirrrrrrrr chepi chepi chepi che-pichew che-pichew che-pichew.* ♀ utters descending *hee-hee-hee* when breeding (until chicks fledge).

Korean Bush Warbler *Horornis canturians* L 14–17 cm

SD *H. c. borealis* accidental, NW Hokkaido to S Nansei Shoto, some winter Yaeyama Is. **HH** As Japanese. **ID** Compared with previous species, Korean is more earth-brown or even chestnut on upperparts/wings, with distinctive orange-rust forehead, more prominent pale grey supercilia, and strongly buff-washed underparts. Beware considerable size difference between sexes. **BP** Bill heavier, more stub-tipped than Japanese, blackish above, yellowish below; eyes black; tarsi (sturdier than Japanese) orange-brown to pink. **SV** Extremely vocal. Call: rolled *chrek* or stronger, Oriental Reed Warbler-like *trrrek!*, also a vaguely Radde's Warbler-like *trrt* or *prrrt*. Song: less rich, weaker than Japanese with a shorter opening whistle, chuntering *ho hokeryon* or *pu-hu-hu* followed by a short *chirweeu*. **TN** Retained in Japanese Bush Warbler by OSJ. **AN** Manchurian Bush Warbler.

Asian Stubtail *Urosphena squameiceps* L 9–11 cm; WT 7–11 g

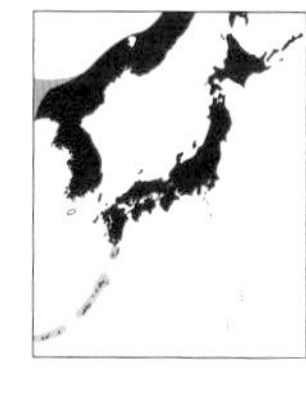

SD *U. s. squameiceps* summer visitor (May–Oct), Yakushima to Hokkaido, migrants recorded Nansei Shoto (some wintering north to S Kyushu), accidental Ogasawara and Iwo Is. **HH** Coniferous boreal to mixed temperate and broadleaf evergreen forests; skulks in dense ground cover, including dwarf bamboo. **ID** Tiny, dark, warm brown, with long off-white supercilia wrapping round onto nape, and long blackish eye stripe. Very short tail is sometimes cocked. Underparts off-white, undertail-coverts buff. **BP** Bill fine, black, with pinkish-yellow base to lower mandible; eyes black; tarsi pale pink. **SV** Call high-pitched *tchick*, wren-like *tyutt* or *kyip*, and Japanese Bush Warbler-like *tchak*, but slightly 'wetter'. Song: rapid, repetitive insect-like 'white noise', rising steadily in pitch and volume, pulsating *tsitsutsatsitsutsatsitsutsa*...; *see-see-see-see-see-see-see* or *shiri-shiri-shiri-shiriri*. Migrants give a penetrating *sti-titit!*

Long-tailed Tit *Aegithalos caudatus* L 13–17 cm; WT 6–10 g

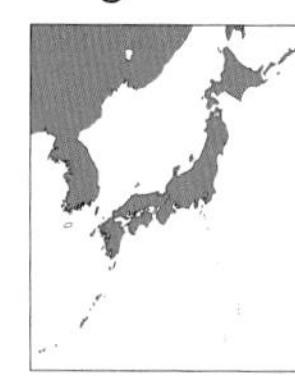

SD Common resident: *A. c. caudatus* Hokkaido, accidental Honshu; *A. c. trivirgatus* Honshu, Sado; *A. c. kiusiuensis* Shikoku, Kyushu; and *A. c. magnus* Tsushima. **HH** Mixed and deciduous forest, woodland edge, and in winter also scrub, often in small flocks, sometimes with other species. **ID** Small, pale, long-tailed bird, with short rounded wings; tail of up to 9 cm. Adult: *A. c. caudatus* has entirely white head; other races have broad dark bands from lores to mantle and are generally darker. Band of dull pink extends across scapulars to lower back. Underparts whitish, sometimes with pink wash on flanks, brighter on vent. Juvenile: shorter-tailed, duskier and lacks pink. **BP** Bill short, stubby, black; eyes small, black; tarsi black. **SV** Range of thin, high-pitched trisyllabic *sree-sree-sree* calls and deeper, stronger churring *cherrrr cherrrr* or softer *prrrr prrrr* notes. Song a complex, thin soft twittering *chii-chii-chii-tsuriri-juriri*.

Japanese Bush Warbler
ad *cantans*
ad *riukiuensis*
Korean Bush Warbler
ad ♀
ad ♂
Asian Stubtail
ad
ad
caudatus
Long-tailed Tit
ad
trivirgatus

Willow Warbler *Phylloscopus trochilus* L 11–12 cm; WT 6–15 g

SD Accidental (*P. t. yakutensis*) to Yonagunijima, Amami-Oshima, N Kyushu, W Honshu, Tsushima and Hegurajima. **HH** Woodland and scrub. Regularly wags tail downward, recalling Siberian Chiffchaff. **ID** Plain, resembling grey-brown Arctic Warbler, but with shorter, off-white supercilia. Upperparts greyish-brown, hint of green only on rump; wings and tail darker brown with faint green outer fringes, and long primary projection. Underparts dusky-olive to greyish-white, with some streaking on breast-sides, and yellow underwing-coverts. Pale supercilia above dark eyestripe, lack of wingbars and leg colour distinguish it from very similar Siberian Chiffchaff. **BP** Bill fine, blackish-brown with pink-based lower mandible; eyes black; tarsi pinkish-brown to warm brown. **SV** Sweet, slightly hesitant upslurred *phwee*, sharply pitched *hewit* or *hoowee*.

Siberian Chiffchaff *Phylloscopus tristis* L 11–12 cm; WT 6–11 g

SD Rare migrant and winter visitor to Yaeyama Is, Kyushu, W, C & N Honshu. **HH** Dry thickets and reedbeds. **ID** Plain brown, buff and white. Pale greyish-brown upperparts, weak olive on back and rump, flight-feathers fringed olive. Yellow restricted to small area at bend of wing. Pale buff supercilia and strong dark eyestripe; ear-coverts, neck- and breast-sides, and flanks cool buff, lacking any hint of yellow. White chin and throat, off-white to cream below. Primary projection short (about half of tertial length). In worn plumage may show short, pale wingbar (see Greenish Warbler). **BP** Bill short, fine, predominantly black; eyes dark brown; legs black or blackish-brown. **SV** Mournful, high-pitched, monosyllabic *heet* or *viip*; similar to Daurian Redstart, but slightly longer and softer. **TN** Sometimes included in Common Chiffchaff *P. collybita*, e.g. OSJ.

Wood Warbler *Phylloscopus sibilatrix* L 11–13 cm; WT 6–15 g

SD Accidental to Hokkaido, Tobishima, Hegurajima and C Honshu in autumn. **HH** Bushes and woodland. **ID** Cleanly marked with bright yellowish-green upperparts. Supercilia, chin/throat and upper breast bright lemon-yellow, belly and vent are pure white. Wings long, with long primary projection, but tail fairly short. **BP** Bill dark brown above, pale yellowish-pink below; eyes dark brown; legs brownish- or yellowish-pink. **SV** A powerful *jii*, sharp *zip* or soft, sad *hwui* or *tyouyou*.

Dusky Warbler *Phylloscopus fuscatus* L 10–13 cm; WT 6–13 g

SD *P. f. fuscatus* is scarce migrant and scarce winter visitor, recorded from Nansei Shoto to Hokkaido. **HH** Skulks in dense vegetation, scrub, bushes or thickets near streams/ditches, rivers or ponds; very active and vocal, often flicking tail and wings. **ID** Recalls Siberian Chiffchaff, but darker greyish-brown upperparts lack any green tones and tail rather short. Resembles Radde's Warbler, but slightly slimmer, smaller-headed, shorter-tailed and thinner-billed. Eyestripe clear, dark, especially from bill to eye. Supercilia narrow, white between bill and eye, off-white or buff behind; white arc below eye. Wings rather short, primary projection short, tail quite long. Off-white chin/throat, breast and flanks grey-white, rear flanks and vent have warmer buff-brown wash. **BP** Bill short, fine, blackish above, paler horn at base and sides of lower mandible; eyes dark brown; thin legs and small feet brownish-pink to dark orange-brown. **SV** Calls (like Japanese Bush or Eurasian Wren) hard, dry, but somewhat muffled *tak tak tak*, *tchak*, *chett* or slightly wetter *chett-chett*, often repeated rapidly; sometimes a rolled *trrac*.

Radde's Warbler *Phylloscopus schwarzi* L 12–14 cm; WT 8–15 g

SD Rare migrant recorded from Nansei Shoto to Hokkaido. **HH** Deciduous thickets, scrub, and forest with dense undergrowth near water; usually active near forest floor. **ID** Large-headed, dark *Phylloscopus* with rather stout bill and tarsi. Long, prominent supercilia extend to nape-sides; broad, buff and diffuse between bill and eye, narrower, cleaner and creamy-white behind (in Dusky, supercilia broad and diffuse behind eye). Upperparts dark olive-brown, slightly greener on rump. Underparts dusky, off-white on throat, with buff wash to chest and flanks, and distinctive cinnamon-buff undertail-coverts. Belly may be yellow-tinged in autumn. Larger, generally more dark olive-green than Dusky, with longer, broader eyestripe and supercilia, heavier bill, stouter legs and larger feet. In fresh plumage Radde's has greener cast to upperparts and yellowish cast to supercilia and underparts, differing from overall browner appearance of Dusky. **BP** Bill rather short and thick, with dark brown upper mandible and yellowish or pink at base of lower mandible; eyes dark brown; legs vary from dark orange-pink to pale brown. **SV** Call a strong, bush warbler-like *check check*, *chrep* or *pwek* with softer, more throaty quality than Dusky, often with stuttering delivery; scolding alarm is *trrr-trick-trr*.

Willow Warbler
1st-win
ad
Siberian Chiffchaff
ad
Wood Warbler
ad
Dusky Warbler
ad
Radde's Warbler
breeding
non-breeding

Tickell's Leaf Warbler *Phylloscopus affinis* L 10–11 cm; WT 6–8 g

SD Vagrant, Okinawa, Hegurajima. Subspecies uncertain. **HH** Skulks in low scrub. **ID** Small to medium-sized compact warbler resembling Siberian Chiffchaff in form, but brighter. Mid- to dark smoky-olive from crown to tail, with long, pale yellow supercilia, broad, distinct eyestripe (weak on lores, stronger behind eye, extending well onto ear-coverts). Face yellowish-olive. Chin, throat and breast rather bright lemon-yellow, fading to buff on breast-sides, grey/olive on flanks and whiter on belly. *No* wingbars. Outer tail-feathers have inner vanes and narrow tips white. **BP** Bill short, dark greyish-brown above, pale pinkish-brown below; eyes dark brown; tarsi quite bright brownish-pink. **SV** Sharp, husky *chup* or *chep* and repetitive *tak-tak*.

Pallas's Leaf Warbler *Phylloscopus proregulus* L 9–10 cm; WT 5–8 g

SD Rare, but annual, migrant recorded from Nansei Shoto to Hokkaido. **HH** On migration occurs in lowland scrub and woodland. **ID** Very small, bright, often hovers, revealing distinctive pale yellow coronal stripe, lemon-yellow rump and short tail. Prominent lemon-yellow supercilia contrast with long black eyestripes and dark crown sides. Wings brownish-grey with two deep-yellow wingbars; tertials blackish broadly fringed white (contrast variable). Underparts greyish-white, to pale yellow on vent. **BP** Bill fine, blackish-brown above, paler horn at base below; eyes black; legs dark brownish-pink or brownish-grey. **SV** Calls infrequently, a strong, nasal *chuii*, *dju-ee*, or *hueet*, softer, quieter and deeper than Yellow-browed, and rising less.

Yellow-browed Warbler *Phylloscopus inornatus* L 10–11 cm; WT 5–9 g

SD Rare migrant from Nansei Shoto to Hokkaido, scarce winter visitor S Kyushu to Nansei Shoto, and accidental to Ogasawara Is. **HH** In broadleaf deciduous woodland. Appears agitated, frequently flicking wings. **ID** Small, pale olive-green, but variable. Well-marked birds tend to have greener tones, others much paler and greyer; wingbars either prominent or partly obscured. Poorly defined pale rear crown stripe, prominent long, pale (yellowish/whitish) supercilia, and weak black eyestripe. Two creamy wingbars on median and greater coverts, the latter usually broad with prominent dark border; primaries fringed green; tertials black broadly fringed cream or whitish (though contrast often lacking), secondaries finely tipped white. Underparts creamy white. **BP** Bill fine, blackish-grey above, paler yellowish-horn at base below; eyes dark brown; tarsi pinkish-brown. **SV** Calls frequently, a rather loud, distinctive upslurred *tsweeoo*, *chuii* or *chiiii* (recalling Japanese White-eye), rising terminally; or penetrating *sweest*.

Hume's Leaf Warbler *Phylloscopus humei* L 10–11 cm; WT 5–9 g

SD Accidental (most likely *P. h. mandellii*, possibly distinct **Mandelli's Leaf Warbler**) to offshore Japan. **HH** Woodlands and gardens. **ID** Small, dull grey-green, very like Yellow-browed Warbler; plumage-based ID not always possible. In autumn (fresh), greyer, more 'washed-out' than Yellow-browed; lesser coverts wingbar less distinct, but greater coverts wingbar broad and white. Cheeks appear paler, supercilia more buff or dull yellowish-white, crown lacks green tone; tertials less contrasting, with greyer (less black) centres; wingbar slightly buff; underparts mostly dull off-white with yellowish tone to flanks. **BP** Bill darker than Yellow-browed's, mostly black; eyes dark brown; tarsi dark blackish- or orange-brown. **SV** Call forceful, whistled *dsweet*, *tsui* or *weesoo*, drier sparrow-like *chirp* and clearly disyllabic, rasping *juwheet* (Yellow-browed call more slurred and whispery). **TN** Formerly within Yellow-browed Warbler. **TN** Not included by OSJ.

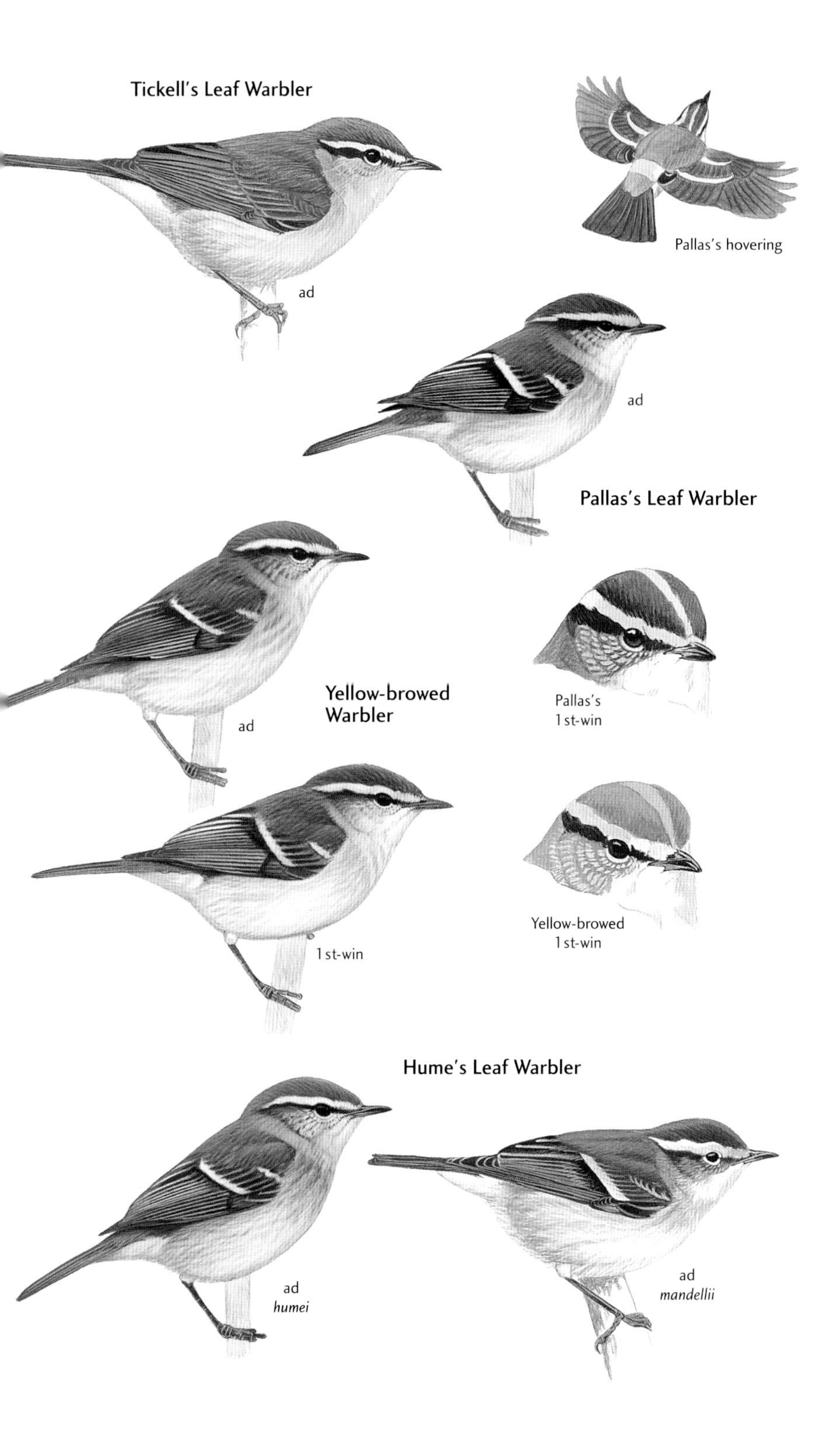
Tickell's Leaf Warbler
ad
Pallas's hovering
ad
Pallas's Leaf Warbler
ad
Yellow-browed
Warbler
Pallas's
1st-win
1st-win
Yellow-browed
1st-win
Hume's Leaf Warbler
ad
humei
ad
mandellii

Arctic Warbler *Phylloscopus borealis* L 11–13 cm; WT 8–15 g

SD *P. b. borealis* accidental, Honshu, Tsushima. *P. b. kennicotti* on migration and in winter in Yaeyama Is. **HH** Deciduous, coniferous and mixed forests, wintering in evergreen forests, mangroves. **ID** Large, dark green, with long head, broad dark eyestripe from bill base to nape-side, long white supercilia reach only to lores, not bill. Upperparts rather dark olive-green; underparts off-white, breast yellow-tinged (obvious in many juv, lacking in most ad), vent white. Two very narrow, whitish wingbars; upper bar sometimes obscure; worn spring individuals may show almost no wingbars. Primary projection long. *P. b. kennicotti* differs from *P. b. borealis* in having finer bill, shorter and less broad-based, slightly brighter green upperparts and brighter yellow underparts. **BP** Bill rather heavy, dark brown above, orange/pink at base of lower mandible, typically with dark tip; eyes dark brown; tarsi dull orange-brown to yellowish-pink, toes paler and brighter in juvenile. **SV** Hard, dipper-like *dzit*, *dzik* or *bjjt*, a softer *vit*, and whistled *ryu ryu*. Song: repetitive, mechanical, insect-like *zirirriri...*, *drree-ree-ree-ree*, or *chirrit-chirrit chirrit-chirrit*.

Kamchatka Leaf Warbler *Phylloscopus examinandus* L 11–13 cm; WT 7–15 g

SD Scarce migrant through Japan, Nansei Shoto to Hokkaido, may breed Shiretoko Peninsula. **HH** Deciduous, coniferous and mixed forests. **ID** Very similar to Arctic and Japanese Leaf Warblers, field characteristics poorly known; slightly larger than *P. b. xanthodryas* with heavier bill and less yellowish underparts. **BP** As Arctic. **SV** Very similar call to Arctic, *dzirit dzirit*. Song: rapid, monotonous *chichori chichori chichori...* **TN** Formerly within *P. borealis*.

Japanese Leaf Warbler *Phylloscopus xanthodryas* L 11–13 cm; WT 10–12 g

SD Common summer visitor (May–Sep), Honshu, Shikoku, Kyushu, and migrant through Japan from Yaeyama Is to N Honshu. **HH** Deciduous, coniferous and mixed forests <2,500 m in summer, at lower elevations on migration. **ID** Very like Arctic Warbler, but brighter green above, with broader, yellower wingbars and yellowish underparts (especially flanks), whiter on belly. **BP** As Arctic. **SV** Hard, dipper-like deep *dzeet*. Song: same rhythm as Arctic Warbler, but softer *jup chorichori chorichori*, *chi-chirra chi-chirra chi-chirra*, *ji-ji-ro ji-ji-ro* becoming louder. **TN** Formerly within *P. borealis*.

Greenish Warbler *Phylloscopus trochiloides* L 10–12 cm; WT 6–10 g

SD Accidental, offshore Japan (*viridanus* or *obscuratus*). Greenish and Two-barred represent rare example of avian ring species; treated separately here because their populations in E Asia appear to behave as distinct species. **HH** Lowland scrub, thickets, woodland. **ID** Small, dark-green warbler recalling Siberian Chiffchaff, but has very long whitish supercilia to nape, broader behind eye, above long dark olive eyestripe, with off-white crescent below eye; head appears rather large and rounded. Upperparts plain dark olive-green, underparts off-white. Primaries and secondaries dark brown with narrow pale-green fringes and a very narrow, yellowish-white greater coverts wingbar; but in fresh autumn plumage may have pale yellow tips to median coverts, suggesting second bar (more common in *obscuratus*); primary projection of Greenish/Two-barred shorter than in Arctic. **BP** Bill fine, dark brown above, pale horn or yellow to pinkish-orange below; eyes dark brown; tarsi dull dark brown to brownish-pink. **SV** Loud, slightly disyllabic *psueee*, *tisli* or slurred *chli-wee*; in alarm a sharp *si-chiwee* or persistent *tsit tsit*. **TN** Not included by OSJ.

Two-barred Warbler *Phylloscopus plumbeitarsus* L 11–12 cm; WT 9 g

SD Vagrant, Hegurajima, Hokkaido. **HH** Scrub, secondary growth. **ID** Resembles Greenish, Arctic and Yellow-browed, but is cleaner, darker green above, and whiter below than Greenish, with double wingbars (greater coverts bar broader and longer than Greenish, that on lesser coverts narrower, yellow-white, but distinct). Supercilia almost reach bill base, unlike in Arctic. Primary projection of Two-barred/Greenish shorter than Arctic. **BP** Bill fine, dark brown above, pink or yellow below; eyes dark brown; tarsi blackish-grey to dull reddish-brown. **SV** Flat, trisyllabic *chi-wi-ri* or *chururi*, similar in tone to White Wagtail and Eurasian Tree Sparrow, but can also recall disyllabic call of Greenish Warbler, making separation on voice extremely difficult and potentially unreliable.

Arctic Warbler
1st-win
Kamchatka
Leaf Warbler
ad
Japanese
Leaf Warbler
ad
Greenish Warbler
ad fresh
(spring)
1st-win
Two-barred Warbler
ad
ad

Pale-legged Leaf Warbler *Phylloscopus tenellipes*

L 10–11 cm; WT 13 g

SD Accidental or very rare spring migrant, Sea of Japan islands to W Hokkaido. **HH** Lowland thickets, woods, montane forests. **ID** Small, olive-brown warbler with pale legs, and long creamy-white supercilia (narrow, sometimes buff between bill and eye, broader behind), over broad, dark eyestripe. Plain, dark grey-brown crown contrasts little with dark nape/mantle, olive-brown cast especially on rump; underparts off-white. Wings brown, with green fringes to flight-feathers, may show two faint wingbars. Primaries short, 5–6 primaries extend beyond tertials. Tail brown with olive-brown fringes, commonly pumped downwards. Browner with more olive upperparts than Eastern Crowned and Ijima's warblers. **BP** Bill moderately fine, with dark brown culmen, pale pink edges to upper mandible, and pale pinkish-horn below; eyes dark brown; tarsi typically whitish-pink, sometimes pale blue-grey. **SV** Call: hard *tit, tit, piit*, or *tink*, is higher-pitched than that of Sakhalin Leaf. Song: harsh, shivering, cricket-like in short rapid phrases *chi chi chi chi chi chi chi...* or *see see see si si si si si...*, tones recall Lanceolated Warbler and Asian Stubtail, with greater emphasis at beginning and slight upward inflection.

Sakhalin Leaf Warbler *Phylloscopus borealoides*

L 11–12 cm; WT 11 g

SD Summer visitor (Apr–Oct), breeds Hokkaido, C & N Honshu mountains; migrant or accidental south to S Nansei Shoto. **HH** Mixed montane boreal forest with strong conifer element, to treeline; also lowland woodland on migration. **ID** Closely resembles Pale-legged (PL), but supercilia perhaps wider behind eye and legs marginally darker. Strong contrast between greyish-toned crown/nape, and greenish (or brownish) mantle, brown back, and somewhat rufous-brown or rusty rump, brown wings and tail; flight-feathers and tertials fringed greenish-olive. May show faint wingbars. Primaries marginally longer than PL, 7–8 primaries extends beyond tertials. Tail like PL, but appears rather short and square-cut, with narrow whitish border to inner webs of outermost three feathers; often wagged downwards. **BP** Bill moderately fine, dark brown above, pale horn or pink at base of lower mandible, extreme tip very pale horn; eyes dark brown; tarsi dull pinkish-brown. **SV** Call: see PL; on breeding grounds gives louder, more emphatic *tsit tsit*. Song: repetitive high-pitched, three-note whistle – *hee-tsoo-kee hee-tsoo-kee hee-tsoo-kee*. **TN** Formerly included in *P. tenellipes*.

Eastern Crowned Warbler *Phylloscopus coronatus*

L 11–13 cm; WT 7–12 g

SD Common migrant, summer visitor (Apr–Oct), Kyushu to Hokkaido, scarce migrant Nansei Shoto. **HH** Mixed broadleaf forest. **ID** Large olive-green warbler. Adult: dark crown sides contrast with prominent paler coronal stripe (does not reach forehead), long, whitish supercilia are narrow and yellowish in front of eyes, broader behind and almost join at nape. Upperparts have strong green cast, brownish olive-grey upper mantle, yellowish-green fringes to flight-feathers, and often a single, narrow, yellowish-white wingbar. Underparts clean, off-white, with pale yellow wash to vent. Juvenile: browner upperparts, duller yellow undertail-coverts, and less well-defined crown-stripe. **BP** Bill thick, broad-based, long, dark grey/brown above, pale orange or bright yellow below, lacks dark tip; eyes dark brown; tarsi dark pink to greyish-brown. **SV** Call: (rarely) strong *chi* or *chiu* (similar to Ijima's *chiu*, but more strident and cheery), soft *phit phit*, or harsher, nasal *dwee*. Song: (frequently) simple, strong 3–4-note phrase, *pichew pichew bwee* (the final note very distinctively nasal).

Ijima's Leaf Warbler *Phylloscopus ijimae*

L 10–12 cm

SD Vulnerable. Summer visitor (May–Sep), Izu and Tokara Is (Apr–Sep); rare migrant Honshu, Shikoku, Kyushu, Nansei Shoto. **HH** Subtropical deciduous and evergreen broadleaf forest. Migrants visit mixed, evergreen forest, bamboo, scrub, alder thickets. **ID** Recalls larger Eastern Crowned Warbler (ECW), but lacks coronal stripe. Head pattern least contrasting of this group. Supercilia long, buffish-white above dark olive-brown lores and eyestripe; appears whitest above and below eye, as if 'spectacled', contributing to large-eyed look; eyestripe narrower than eye (same as eye in Arctic/ECW). Pale-grey crown and mantle, latter and back with green tinge; flight-feathers grey-brown with bright green outer fringes, one indistinct wingbar. Grey-brown outer tail-feathers also show green tone. Underparts off-white to pale grey with variable yellowish-green wash on vent. **BP** Bill fine, marginally heaver/longer than ECW, upper mandible solid dark brown to tip; lower mandible dull yellow, orange or pinkish-orange, narrower based than ECW; eyes dark brown; tarsi medium flesh-grey, perhaps darker than ECW. **SV** Call: (frequent) soft *pee*, *hu-eet*, a downslurred *se-chui*, *chiu*, or *twee* reminiscent of Coal Tit and ECW, but with melancholy ring. Song: variable, Coal Tit-like *chubi chubi chubi chui chui chui pii chobi chobi*, very sibilant *shiri-shiri-shiri fisisisisi*, wavering *swisswisswisswisswiss*, occasionally slowing into more enunciated *tsu wiss tsu wiss tsu wiss tsu wiss*. Occasionally a repeated *tseeoo tseeo tseeo* between song bursts.

Pale-legged Leaf Warbler
fresh
worn
Sakhalin Leaf Warbler
fresh
worn
Eastern Crowned Warbler
fresh
worn
Ijima's Leaf Warbler
fresh
worn

Oriental Reed Warbler *Acrocephalus orientalis* L 17–19 cm; WT 22–30 g

SD Summer visitor (May–Sep) throughout much of Japan from Kyushu to SW Hokkaido, migrant and occasional winter visitor in Nansei Shoto, accidental to Ogasawara Is. **HH** Reedbeds, riparian thickets and agricultural areas from sea level to c. 1,000 m. **ID** Face pattern weak; broad supercilia are whitish from bill to eye and indistinct pale brown to rear, bordered only below by weak, narrow blackish-brown eyestripe. Overall olive-brown with grey cast to crown, back, and paler, greyer rump; tail rather long and somewhat square-ended. Underparts off-white on throat and belly, with indistinctly dark-streaked breast, warm buff wash on flanks and vent. Primary extension shorter than length of visible tertials. When singing, reveals bright orange-red mouth lining. In flight thrush-like, with plain wings and long tail rounded at tip, with whitish tips to outer feathers. **BP** Bill long and rather thick, dark grey-brown above and at tip, yellowish- or pinkish-brown on most of lower mandible; eyes brown; strong tarsi pinkish-grey, toes grey. **SV** A deep, thick *turrr* or *chichikarr*, loud arresting *tack!* sharp *tick* and slurred *trek*, *krak*, *kirr* or *ge*. Noisy song, often delivered from conspicuous perch atop reeds/bushes or wires, a series of loud, ratcheting gravelly calls and dry chuckles: *kawa-kawa-kawa-gurk-gurk-eek-eek-kawa-gurk*; *kiruk kiruk kiruk jee jee jee*. **TN** Formerly within Great Reed Warbler *A. arundinaceus*.

Black-browed Reed Warbler *Acrocephalus bistrigiceps* L 13–14 cm; WT 10–15 g

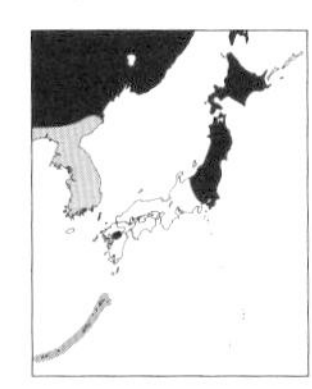

SD Locally common summer visitor (May–Sep) from Kyushu to Hokkaido, migrant through Nansei Shoto. **HH** Reedbeds, scrubby grassland, woodland fringes near wetlands and rivers, particularly with willows to 1,500 m. **ID** Often shares habitat with Oriental Reed Warbler, but readily distinguished by much smaller size, distinctive face pattern and voice. Adult has prominent white supercilia that broaden behind eyes, ending rather squarely and bordered above by long, narrow black brows and below by fine black eyestripes. Generally mid-brown above, warmer and more rufous on rump, and whitish below with white chin/throat contrasting with brown ear-coverts, and warm buff or pale-brown wash to sides and flanks. Juvenile/1st-year has distinctive yellowish-buff wash to upper- and underparts, and broader, less-defined brow. **BP** Bill fine, short, dark blackish-grey above, paler at base of lower mandible; eyes dark brown; tarsi dark brownish-pink. **SV** Harsh churring *kurr*, hard *jat jat* and low *trruk*. Song: prolonged jumbled mixture of notes given from conspicuous perch atop reeds or bushes, *chi chi chi chur jee jee jee jurr chi-ur chi-ur chi-ur chi-ur* interspersed with dry rattles, harsh trills and mimicry; also *kirikiri-pi gyoshi kyoriri-piririri....*; reveals bright yellowish mouth lining when singing.

Sedge Warbler *Acrocephalus schoenobaenus* L 11–13 cm; WT 12 g

SD Vagrant, Tsushima, Hokkaido. **HH** Reedbeds and scrub. **ID** Recalls Black-browed Reed Warbler, but broad buff supercilia contrast with dark crown and cheeks. Overall olive-brown; mantle has diffuse dark streaking, rump is yellowish-brown. Adult is unmarked on chest, whereas immature has fine dark streaks. **BP** Bill grey above, pinkish below; eyes brown; legs brownish-pink. **SV** Gives sharp *tsek* in alarm, or dry rattling *errrr*.

Speckled Reed Warbler *Acrocephalus sorghophilus* L 12–13 cm

SD Endangered. Accidental to S Japan (Yonagunijima). **HH** Reedbeds and agricultural crops. **ID** Similar to Black-browed Reed Warbler (BBRW) in size, structure and black lateral crown-stripes, but distinguished by fine black streaking on crown, narrower black margins to crown, broader pale creamy-buff supercilia behind eye, paler brown nape and mantle, with narrow black streaking on mantle; wings show broad pale fringes to dark greyish-brown coverts and tertials, and narrow pale fringes to flight-feathers; rump uniform mid-brown, tail dark brown with buff fringes and tips; white chin/throat with buff wash on flanks. **BP** Bill fine (somewhat stronger than BBRW), culmen dark blackish-brown, with pale ochre edges, lower mandible entirely pale ochre; eyes dark brown; tarsi grey. **SV** Calls undescribed. **AN** Streaked Reed Warbler.

Black-browed Reed Warbler
Oriental Reed Warbler
1st-win
ad
ad
1st-win
Sedge Warbler
Speckled Reed Warbler
ad
aut/1st-win
juv
ad spring

Paddyfield Warbler *Acrocephalus agricola* L 12–14 cm; WT 8–11 g

SD *A. agricola* ssp. is vagrant to Hegurajima and N Honshu. **HH** Reedbeds, tall grasses, willows and birches fringing wetlands. **ID** Unstreaked *Acrocephalus* closely resembling Black-browed Reed Warbler (BBRW), but has more prominent white supercilia, broadest behind eye and bordered above by narrow, black margin to crown and below by short dark eyestripe, though has less clearly defined black lateral crown-stripes than BBRW; appears to have rounded head due to erectile crown feathers; neck-sides pale. Upperparts warm sandy to mid-brown, darker on crown, and contrastingly rusty-brown on rump and uppertail-coverts; whitish from chin to vent with buff wash on sides and lower belly; tertials typically dark with paler fringes. Tail rather long and distinctly rounded. **BP** Bill rather thick, sharply pointed, greyish-brown upper mandible, pale yellowish- or pinkish-buff lower mandible with dark tip; eyes dark brown; tarsi pinkish-brown. **SV** Hard *check* or *tack*, rolling *cherrr* or *trrr*, and harsh *cheeer*.

Blyth's Reed Warbler *Acrocephalus dumetorum* L 12–14 cm; WT 8–16 g

SD Vagrant to Hokkaido, Hegurajima, Niigata, and Okinawa Is. **HH** More arboreal and less associated with wetlands than most *Acrocephalus*; in lightly wooded country, riparian and flooded deciduous forests, also forest edge. **ID** A plain, 'cool', even drab greyish-brown, unstreaked reed warbler; rather slim, short-winged and long-billed. From crown to tail rather uniform cool olive-brown, short, rounded wings somewhat browner; face pattern distinct, with short white supercilia prominent only between bill and eye, eyestripe dusky dark brown. Underparts plain, off-white from chin to vent, with buff flanks. **BP** Bill rather long, thick, greyish-brown upper mandible, with pale pinkish-brown base to lower mandible; eyes dark brown; legs/feet pinkish-brown. **SV** Hard, jarring and scraping calls: *thik*, *chak* and *cherr* interspersed with sweet whistles.

Thick-billed Warbler *Iduna aedon* L 18–19 cm; WT 22–31 g

SD *I. a. rufescens* is vagrant to C Honshu and Hegurajima. **HH** Woodland/forest edge, dense thickets, scrub and bushy areas. **ID** Large, plain, short-winged and long-tailed, superficially resembling Oriental Reed Warbler (ORW), but more shrike-like proportions and plainer face appears 'gentler' with larger eye, and lacks supercilia and eyestripes of ORW, with distinctive, pale lores. Upperparts rusty-brown, slightly greyer on face and crown, warmer on lower back and rump. Underparts off-white, whitest on chin/throat, with buff wash to flanks and vent. Tail long and graduated. Primary projection short. **BP** Bill large, thick (shorter, thicker, blunter than ORW, with more curved upper mandible), dark greyish-brown above, paler yellowish- or pinkish-horn below; large eyes, dark reddish-brown; strong tarsi bluish-grey. **SV** Low muffled *tuc*, sometimes in rolled series when agitated, *tuc tuc tuc trruc trruc trrrc* (recalling Dusky Warbler), a wheezy *wep* or *jep*, strong, hard *chack*, *chock* or *tack*, often repeated; and occasionally *skeesh* sounding like air escaping from a pump. Alarm call is a loud *jah jah* or *bzee bzee*. **TN** Formerly *Phragmaticola aedon rufescens* and also in genus *Acrocephalus*.

Booted Warbler *Iduna caligata* L 11–12 cm; WT 7–11 g

SD Vagrant to Hegurajima and Tairajima (Tokara Is). **HH** Scrub. **ID** Shape and size recall *Phylloscopus*, but plumage like *Acrocephalus*. Small, very plain, greyish-brown, with distinctly rounded crown, rather prominent supercilia, and somewhat short, square-ended tail. White supercilia, long and broad, but diffuse behind eye, contrasting with rather dark forecrown, narrow black eyestripe and narrow, darker border to crown. Upperparts pale, sandy, grey-brown from crown to rump, including scapulars; wings and tail blackish-brown with pale, grey-brown fringes to coverts and secondaries, and whitish fringes to tertials; may suggest a pale wing-panel. Wingtips just reach tail base, with short primary projection about half of longest tertial; tail greyish-brown, rather square-tipped, with off-white fringes to outer feathers, undertail-coverts short. **BP** Bill very short, slender, blunt, dark upper mandible, pale lower mandible with dark tip; eyes black; tarsi pinkish-grey. **SV** Harsh, hard *chet*, *chek* or *chat*, and short, dry trills: *tr'r'rk*.

Paddyfield Warbler
ad worn
ad
1st-win
ad worn
Blyth's Reed Warbler
ad
juv/1st-win
Thick-billed Warbler
ad
Booted
Warbler
ad
juv/1st-win

Lanceolated Warbler *Locustella lanceolata*

L 11–13 cm; WT 9–13 g

SD *L. l. hendersonii* scarce, declining, summer visitor (May–Sep), E Hokkaido and N Honshu, accidental south to Nansei Shoto. **HH** Wet meadows, damp grassland with scattered bushes, abandoned fields; moves mouse-like through vegetation. **ID** Smallest *Locustella;* mid olive-brown very finely streaked black on crown, heavily on mantle and finely on underparts. Supercilia long, but faint. Underparts whitish to buff/brown, with prominent narrow streaking on breast-sides and flanks, and fine teardrop spots on vent and long undertail-coverts. Dark tail is short and rounded at tip. **BP** Bill has dark grey culmen and tip, with yellowish-pink lower mandible; eyes dark brown; tarsi pale brownish-pink. **SV** A short, hard *chu chu*, fainter *tack*, metallic *pit* or *chit* (similar to Pallas's Grasshopper Warbler, but quieter and slightly drier and squeakier), and harsh, scolding series of *cheek-cheek* notes. Day song comprises short bursts of very fast, high, insect-like churring or metallic reeling, *chiririririririri*; nocturnal song similar, but continues for many minutes.

Middendorff's Grasshopper Warbler *Locustella ochotensis*

L 13–16 cm; WT 16–23 g

SD Locally uncommon summer visitor (May–Sep) to Hokkaido, scarce migrant south to Nansei Shoto. **HH** Wetland margins with bushes, woodland fringes, headlands with dwarf bamboo. **ID** Large, plain, with low-sloping head/bill profile and longish tail. More richly coloured and more contrasting than Styan's. Adult: brown overall, pale creamy white or pale buff supercilia, weak before eye, but extend well back to ear-coverts; mantle more olive with rather darker, reddish-brown centres, forming diffuse streaks; rump/uppertail-coverts more yellowish- or rufous-brown. Tail long, rounded, often fanned slightly in flight, showing subterminal black spots and white tips. Juvenile: yellow-tinged face and underparts, dark-streaked breast, and warmer olive-brown flanks than adult. Differs from Pallas's in having weakly streaked upperparts, tail typically has less contrasting dark subterminal band, and from Styan's by shorter bill, browner upperparts, paler underparts and darker, more prominent eyestripe. **BP** Bill short, dark grey upper mandible, yellowish- or pinkish-grey base to dark-tipped lower mandible; eyes dark brown; tarsi brownish- or flesh-pink. **SV** Call: an abrupt *tit tit tit....* Song: dry rattling: *che-tit che-tit che-tit-chewee-chewee-chewee-chewee* from bush or in song-flight. **AN** Middendorff's Warbler.

Styan's Grasshopper Warbler *Locustella pleskei*

L 15–17 cm; WT 18–29 g

SD Vulnerable. Breeds (May–Sep) on small islands off W & C Japan east to Izu Is, scarce migrant south to Nansei Shoto. **HH** Grasslands and dwarf bamboo. **ID** Very like Middendorff's; separated on distribution, larger bill and subtle colour differences. Styan's has shorter, more greyish-buff supercilia, dark lores (darker than crown) and weak eyestripe (thin or absent behind eye). Upperparts uniform greyish olive-brown. Only mantle shows subtle broad dark streaks; wing-coverts and tertials olive with pale buff fringes, flight-feathers have olive-brown fringes. Underparts dusky pale grey (slightly darker than Middendorff's), darkest on breast-sides; tail like Middendorff's, but dark brown with narrow off-white tips to outer 3–4 feathers, undertail-coverts buff. **BP** Bill long (longer than distance from rear of eye to bill base), dark grey with pale tip and greyish- or yellowish-pink lower mandible; pale eye-ring, irides dark brown; tarsi sturdy, brownish-pink, strong short hindclaw. **SV** Call: abrupt, hard *stit it it* or *tschup-tschuptschup*. Song: breezy, slightly electric 3–4-part wavering phrase *swee swee swee swee* (slower and harder than Ijima's Warbler's song, which sounds similar at distance) from exposed perch. Also dry chirping: *tski tski tski...; chitti chuichuichui*. **AN** Pleske's Warbler.

Pallas's Grasshopper Warbler *Locustella certhiola*

L 13–14 cm; WT 13–22 g

SD *L. c. rubescens* very rare migrant, S Nansei Shoto to Hokkaido. **HH** Wetlands, wet meadows. Extremely skulking. **ID** Generally mid-brown; almost black crown with fine grey-brown streaking, usually heavy dark streaking on brown mantle, scapulars/wing-coverts and tertials blackish-brown with pale fringes; rump contrastingly more rufous- or rusty-brown, with dark centres to uppertail-coverts. Long, broad grey-white supercilia. Underparts grey-buff with browner wash to breast-sides, flanks and vent. Dark rusty-brown tail has rounded tip, with blackish subterminal band and greyish-white tips (best seen from below); vent and undertail-coverts unstreaked. Juvenile: yellowish wash to chest and flanks, fine streaking across throat extends to flanks, clear white tips to tertials. **BP** Bill blackish-grey above with dark-tipped yellowish-pink lower mandible; eyes dark reddish-brown; tarsi pink. **SV** Calls range from ticking *pit*, dry clicking *chat* and dry rolling rattle *trrrrrrrt*; also abrupt, explosive *dt dt dt* in alarm. **AN** Rusty-rumped Warbler.

Lanceolated Warbler
ad
1st-win
Middendorff's
Grasshopper Warbler
ad
1st-win
Styan's
Grasshopper Warbler
ad
1st-win
Pallas's Grasshopper Warbler
ad
1st-win

Marsh Grassbird *Locustella pryeri*

L 12–14 cm; WT 9–17 g

SD Near Threatened. *L. p. pryeri* is very local and restricted in range and habitat in N, C & W Honshu, accidental Shikoku. **HH** Occurs year-round in reedbeds and rank grassland near rivers or swamps. Like Zitting Cisticola, can balance while grasping separate reed stems with each foot. Sings from atop tall reed or in distinctive arcing display flight up and over territory. **ID** Medium-sized warbler, resembling rather plain Zitting Cisticola, but with longer tail. Generally mid- to rufous-brown on upperparts, including wings and tail, with fine black streaking on crown, unstreaked nape and bold black scaling on back; tertials also blackish. Underparts whitish with brown wash to breast-sides and flanks. Lores and ear-coverts pale grey-brown, supercilia broad but extends only from eye, as does indistinct eyestripe. Tail long, rounded, typically fanned in flight. **BP** Bill short, somewhat thick, black above with pink base to lower mandible; eyes black; tarsi dull brownish-pink. **SV** Alarm call: a hard *jutt jutt* or *chut chut*, lower than Japanese Bush Warbler and recalling Siberian Rubythroat's low *jut* call. Song: *churuchuruchuru chochiri chohiri* and *jukukuku kyururu${ru}$*, given during display flight. In autumn and winter gives hard *chak chak chak* and fast repetitive *chur-chur-chur-chur* contact calls. Also a dry, slightly rising *trrik* or *trrrrett*, occasionally louder and even thrush-like in tone, *churrrrek!* **TN** Formerly within genus *Megalurus*. **AN** Japanese Marsh Warbler; Japanese Swamp Warbler.

Sakhalin Grasshopper Warbler *Locustella amnicola*

L 16–18 cm; WT 22–33 g

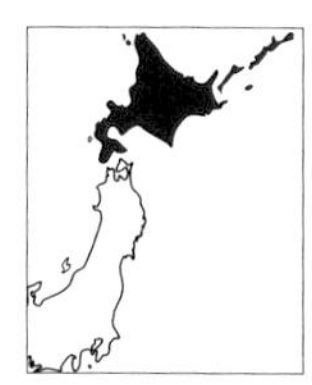

SD A widespread summer visitor (Jun–Sep) in Hokkaido, scarce migrant further south as far as Nansei Shoto. **HH** Extremely skulking in undergrowth of lowland forest, and bushes near streams. **ID** Largest *Locustella*; entirely unstreaked. Adult: upperparts warm, dark olive-brown. Face grey or greyish-white, with dark eyestripe and long greyish-white supercilia extending to nape. Greyish-white chin/throat and face with grey-brown wash to breast-sides and buff wash on flanks more extensive than in other *Locustella*. Tail rusty-brown, long, rounded, with rusty-brown rump and long, rusty undertail-coverts. Juvenile: warmer brown upperparts and yellower or olive, rather than grey, tones to face and underparts. **BP** Bill long, slightly decurved, dark grey, base of lower mandible yellowish or pinkish; eyes dark brown; strong tarsi pinkish-brown. **SV** Vociferous: call is a guttural *gu gu gu*; song is a very loud and repetitive *chot-pin chot-pin-kake-taka*; also *choppin chipicho*, hurried and accelerating, given from deep cover day and night. **TN** Formerly within Gray's Grasshopper Warbler *L. fasciolata*, e.g. OSJ. **AN** Sakhalin Warbler.

Siberian Bush Warbler *Locustella davidi*

L 12 cm; WT 10 g

SD Vagrant to Hokkaido; possibly overlooked accidental. **HH** Extremely skulking, poorly known species. Occurs in streamside thickets, reedbeds, tall grasslands and scrub. **ID** Generally dark brown with short, broad wings and long, graduated tail. Pale, buffy supercilia, grey ear-coverts, grey-white chin, throat and breast, with necklace of fine black streaks (more prominent in ♂). Underparts rufous-brown, long undertail-coverts dark brown with white crescentic tips; tail rounded. In non-breeding plumage throat spotting less distinct (even completely obscured) and underparts and supercilia yellow-toned. **BP** Bill dark grey with black tip (lower mandible pale in non-breeding season); eyes dark brown; tarsi pinkish-brown. **SV** Rasping *tschuk* and low *tuk*. **TN** Formerly within Spotted Bush Warbler *Bradypterus thoracicus*. **AN** Père David's Bush Warbler; Baikal Bush Warbler. **TN** Not included by OSJ.

Marsh Grassbird

Sakhalin Grasshopper Warbler
ad
1st-win

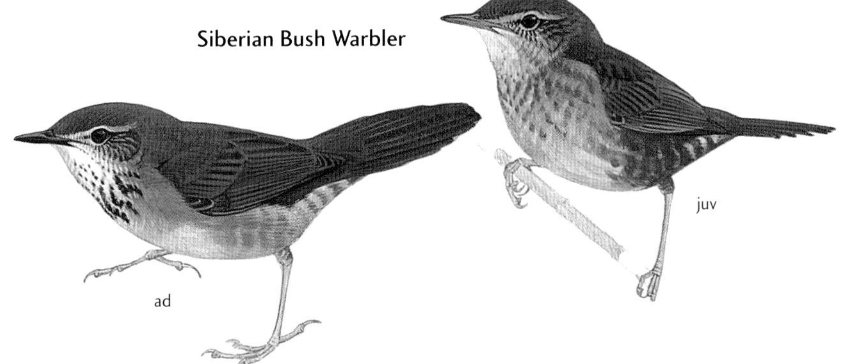
Siberian Bush Warbler
juv
ad

Zitting Cisticola *Cisticola juncidis*

L 10–14 cm; WT 8–12 g

SD *C. j. brunniceps* is summer visitor (Apr–Sep) to N & C Honshu, and year-round (resident?) from C Honshu to Izu Is and Nansei Shoto. **HH** Locally common in grasslands and reedbeds, typically at wetland margins, but also in grassy fields, rice and sugarcane fields. Performs distinctive display flight. **ID** Small, generally brown, noticeably darker on crown, more rufous on back and rump, with off-white underparts, browner on flanks; supercilia broad and pale in front of eye, buff on head-sides behind eye, otherwise face rather plain. Mantle, tertials and coverts black fringed buff. Tail graduated, typically fanned in flight, with black subterminal band and white tip; from below tail appears broadly banded black and grey. In winter, dark crown more streaked, supercilia broader, paler, more prominent. **BP** Bill sharp, arched, grey with blackish tip; eyes black; tarsi flesh-pink. **SV** Loud, hard *zit zit zit*, or in flight a high, weak *tsiek*, slightly broken in tone. During courtship, ♂ calls while rising, hovering and circling in undulating display flight over territory; when rising it gives metallic *chin chin chin* or *dzip dzip dzip* notes, while descending it gives harder *chat chat chat* notes. **AN** Fan-tailed Warbler.

Plain Prinia *Prinia inornata*

L 11 cm; WT 6–9 g

SD Accidental (*P. i. flavirostris*) to Tokashiki, Okinawa. **HH** Tall grasses, reeds, cropfields and scrub. **ID** Rather dull, unstreaked with plain greyish earth-brown upperparts, short, pale buff supercilia, buff lores and buffish-brown ear-coverts, affording pale-faced appearance. Tail long, graduated, with pale tips; wings short, earth-brown, with greenish tone to outer webs of primaries. Buffy-brown throat and chest grades to pale yellowish-buff belly and vent. **BP** Bill black; eyes pale brown; tarsi pink. **SV** Calls varied, including a nasal *beep*, plaintive *tee-tee-tee* and buzzing *bzzp* and *zzpink*. **TN** Not included by OSJ.

Chinese Hwamei *Garrulax canorus*

L 21–24 cm; WT 49–75 g

SD Introduced, now well-established (subspecies uncertain) from N Honshu to Kyushu. **HH** Favours low montane forest, dwarf bamboo or dense vegetation on hillsides, and is especially fond of narrow stream valleys. Often located by noisy habit of hopping amongst or turning leaf litter on forest floor. Very active when feeding, but often hard to see in dense foliage. **ID** Thrush-like earth-brown bird with short wings and long, full tail. Distinctive grey-white 'spectacles' comprising prominent white eye-rings and brows extending across head-sides. Crown and nape reddish-brown, ear-coverts and chin earth-brown, neck slightly paler, rest of upperparts dark brown with narrow black streaking on crown, nape and mantle; wings dark brown, as tail but latter narrowly and indistinctly barred blackish-brown. Underparts rufous-brown with fine streaking from chin to lower breast. **BP** Bill pale horn; eyes pale grey-brown, with bluish-grey orbital skin; tarsi yellowish-brown. **SV** Very soft contact call, a slurred thrush-like *trrrrrr*, which can be difficult to hear. Song comprises four loud melodic whistles introduced by a mimicked phrase (e.g. call of Japanese Sparrowhawk). Highly prized as cagebird for its rich song. **AN** Melodious Laughingthrush.

Zitting Cisticola
ad fresh
ad worn
Plain Prinia
ad
Chinese Hwamei
ad
ad

Moustached Laughingthrush *Garrulax cineraceus*

L 21–24 cm; WT 43–55 g

SD Introduced (subspecies uncertain), now widespread on Shikoku (Ehime and Kochi). **HH** Scrub, bamboo thickets and broadleaf forests and plantations above 200 m, sometimes near habitation. **ID** Rather small, boldly marked brown laughingthrush. Black from forehead to nape, but otherwise warm earth-brown from back to tail. Face white, with narrow black line behind eye, black malar and black-streaked neck-sides. Wings brown with black primary-coverts, pale blue-grey primaries, tertials and secondaries terminally black with narrow white tips; tail long, brown with broad black subterminal band and white tip. White chin and throat with narrow grey streaks merging with black-streaked face- to neck-sides; breast, flanks and vent orange-brown. Laughingthrushes typically have short wings and long tails, flight consists of series of rapid wingbeats followed by long glide. **BP** Bill strong, grey above, yellow below; eyes yellow with narrow black ring; strong tarsi brownish-pink. **SV** Musical notes and thrush-like chattering; song a loud *diu-diuuid*.

Masked Laughingthrush *Garrulax perspicillatus*

L 28–32 cm; WT 100–132 g

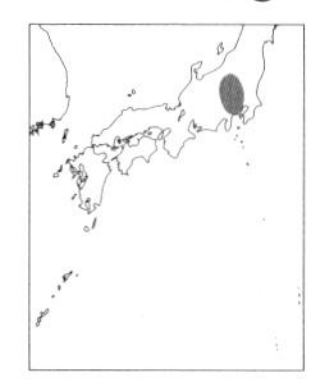

SD Introduced and established in C Honshu. **HH** Forages on ground in broadleaf and mixed forests, scrub, dense grass and bamboo thickets, commonly in small noisy parties. **ID** A large, plain laughingthrush. Upperparts drab ashen grey-brown from crown to tail, though latter blacker towards tips of outer feathers. Forehead, face, ear-coverts and chin black. Underparts ash-brown, paler on belly and grading to rufous on vent. **BP** Bill strong, black; eyes black; tarsi strong, brownish-pink. **SV** Calls include harsh chattering and loud *jhew* or *jhow* notes.

White-browed Laughingthrush *Garrulax sannio*

L 22–24 cm; WT 52–83 g

SD Introduced (subspecies uncertain) and established in C Honshu (Gunma and Ibaraki prefectures). **HH** Favours scrub, woodland edges, forest and bamboo thickets. **ID** Mid-sized, brown laughingthrush with white face pattern. Dark earth-brown forehead to nape; mantle, back and rump mid grey-brown, short wings warm brown, as is full, graduated tail. Face largely creamy white with broad creamy supercilia from lores to nape-sides and creamy white ear-coverts, rest of face including dark post-ocular stripe warm earth-brown. Underparts warm brown to grey brown from throat to belly, cinnamon on vent. **BP** Bill blunt, dark grey; eyes black; strong tarsi brownish-pink. **SV** Cackling, buzzing and harsh ringing notes.

Red-billed Leiothrix *Leiothrix lutea*

L 13–15 cm; WT 18–25 g

SD Introduced (subspecies uncertain), now naturalised and locally common in Kyushu, Shikoku and central Honshu. **HH** Highly social, in groups in dense undergrowth of dark secondary forest, *Cryptomeria* plantations and montane bamboo scrub to above 1,000 m. **ID** A grey-brown babbler with olive-green crown and bright orange breast. Face plain, 'gentle', with large pale yellow eye patch, dark blackish-grey malar streak and grey ear-coverts. Adult: upperparts rather plain olive-grey (except greener olive crown and nape), darker on wings and tail, grey wing-coverts contrast with yellow/orange outer fringes to base of primaries and orange outer fringes to secondaries; tail blackish-brown, broad and square-tipped, slightly notched. Chin and throat yellow, breast deeper yellow/orange, belly to vent pale yellow, flanks grey. Juvenile/1st-year: slightly duller markings and reduced orange-red fringes on folded wing. **BP** Bill short, red, black at base; black eyes appear large; tarsi orange-pink. **SV** Call: similar to Japanese Bush Warbler, but slightly thicker *chwet*, also buzzy rattling *zye zye* or *fii-fii-fii* in alarm. Song: rich, mellow, rather rapidly warbled phrase, recalling Japanese Thrush. **AN** Pekin Robin.

Lesser Whitethroat *Sylvia curruca*

L 12–14 cm; WT 9–18 g

SD Accidental migrant and winter visitor (subspecies uncertain but presumably *S. c. curruca* = including '*blythi*') recorded from Hokkaido to Amami Oshima. **HH** Woodland edges, thickets and scrub. Usually skulks in dense vegetation. **ID** Small and compact; grey-brown upperparts with darker grey crown, somewhat blacker wings and tail. Lores and ear-coverts black contrasting with crown and, particularly, white chin and throat. Underparts white with grey-brown wash to breast-sides/flanks. Tail rather long with prominent off-white inner webs to outer rectrices, recalling buntings. **BP** Bill rather short, black; narrow pale grey eye-ring, irides dark reddish-brown with black ring; tarsi black. **SV** Short, hard and abrupt *tek*, *chett*, *tac* or *cha*.

Moustached
Laughingthrush
ad
Masked Laughingthrush
ad
White-browed
Laughingthrush
ad
Red-billed
Leiothrix
ad
Lesser Whitethroat
breeding
1st-win

Vinous-throated Parrotbill *Sinosuthora webbiana*

L 12–13 cm; WT 10–13 g

SD Accidental to offshore Japan (subspecies uncertain). **HH** Scrub, riparian thickets, woodland edges and fringes of reedbeds. **ID** Small and plain. Overall mid sandy- or pinkish-brown, darker and more chestnut on crown and wings, with paler buffy-brown underparts. Long tail is darker, with grey-brown outer feathers and squarish tip. **BP** Bill very short and stubby, grey with pale/horn tip; eyes small, black, very prominent on plain face; tarsi grey. **SV** Flock members give thin chattering *chii chii chii chii*. **AN** Webb's Parrotbill. **TN** Not included by OSJ.

Bonin Honeyeater *Apalopteron familiare*

L 12–14 cm; WT 15 g

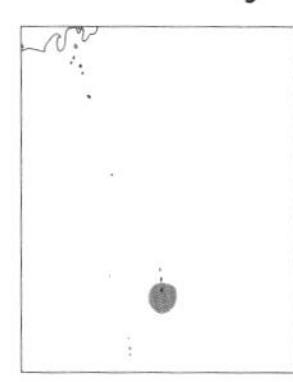

SD Vulnerable endemic. Ogasawara Is: *A. f. familiare* extinct on Mukojima, Nakodojima and Chichijima; *A. f. hahasima* extant on Hahajima, Mukoujima and Imotojima. **HH** From gardens with tall bushes to plantations, woodland edge and open subtropical forest. **ID** Superficially resembles large white-eye (often treated as congeneric), being yellowish-green and grey overall, but has unique black face pattern. Forecrown, central forehead stripe reaching bill, small patch above rear of eye and elongated triangle pointing down face below eye, are all black; sides of forehead, rear ear-coverts, chin and throat bright yellow, neck-sides and flanks greyish-yellow. Crown, mantle and back olive-green, wings brighter with yellow outer fringes to flight-feathers; tail dark grey-olive. **BP** Bill rather long, arched, black; eyes appear large, with white crescents above and below, irides dark reddish-brown; tarsi black. **SV** Soft *pee-yu*, *chui*, *weet* and *pit* notes, a loud explosive *tit-tit*, and when mobbing gives harsher calls, *weet-weet* and *zhree-zhree*.... Song, given from high perch and occasionally in flight, is melodious warbling *tu-ti-ti ti-titu-tuoo*; also *chui churiripyuuyo* and *fiyo chui chuchee feeyo*. **TN** Sometimes placed in *Zosterops*. **AN** Bonin White-eye.

Chestnut-flanked White-eye *Zosterops erythropleurus*

L 10–12 cm

SD Rare migrant from Yonagunijima to Hokkaido, mostly on offshore islands. **HH** Migrants occur in any type of woodland. **ID** Small, bright green rather warbler-like bird, very similar to Japanese White-eye. Hood and upperparts bright yellow-green. Yellow chin/throat and vent, and clear white belly, but usually has distinct broad chestnut patch at sides (fainter in young, making separation from *Z. j. japonicus* tricky). Primary projection 75–100% length of exposed tertials (longer than Japanese White-eye). **BP** Bill finely pointed, grey above and at tip, pink below and at base; eyes appear large, surrounded by prominent broad white eye-ring, broken at lores, irides black; tarsi grey. **SV** *Chii chii* or *tsee-plee*, similar to Japanese but less powerful and less clear.

Japanese White-eye *Zosterops japonicus*

L 10–12 cm; WT 11 g

SD Widespread and common throughout Japan, though only summer visitor to N Honshu and Hokkaido; resident C & S Japan. Various subspecies: *Z. j. yesoensis* Hokkaido; *Z. j. japonicus* Honshu, Kyushu, Shikoku and Tsushima, winter visitor to Nansei Shoto; *Z. j. stejnegeri* Izu Is and introduced to Ogasawara Is; *Z. j. alani* Iwo Is and introduced to Ogasawara; *Z. j. insularis* Yaku-shima, accidental to Okinawa; *Z. j. loochooensis* Nansei Shoto from Amami Is to Yaeyama Is; *Z. j. daitoensis* Daito Is. **HH** Deciduous and evergreen broadleaf forests, especially with flowers and fruits, but on migration and in winter in any type of woodland, gardens and parks. **ID** Small, bright green rather warbler-like bird. Hood and upperparts bright yellow-green, with prominent broad white eye-ring; yellow breast. Underparts off-white to buffy-grey, darker on flanks, but lacks clear contrast between white belly and chestnut of Chestnut-flanked; breast and flanks have reddish-brown wash, undertail-coverts yellowish. *Z. j. japonicus*, in particular, often has rather brown, even maroon, tone to flanks, making separation from Chestnut-flanked more difficult. *Z. j. loochooensis* and *daitoensis* smaller-bodied than *japonicus*, with greyish-white breast and flanks. Rare migrant small race, with yellower upperparts than *japonicus* and greyish-white breast and flanks, may refer to *simplex*. **BP** Bill slightly arched and fine-pointed, dark grey above and at tip, paler blue-grey below and at base; eyes orange to orange-brown; tarsi grey/black. **SV** Call: high, thin twittering *tsee tsee*, *chii chii puu chii chii*, *chu*. Song: rapid and complex *chuichui chochopiichui*.

Vinous-throated Parrotbill
ad
ad
Bonin Honeyeater
hahasima
ad
Chestnut-flanked White-eye
ad ♂
ad ♀
Japanese White-eye
ad simplex
ad japonicus

Goldcrest *Regulus regulus* L 9–10 cm; WT 3–6 g

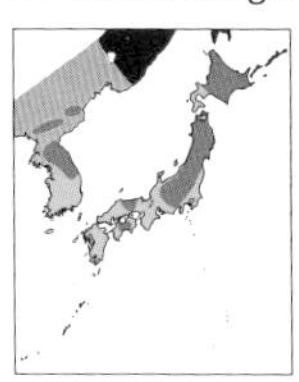

SD *R. r. japonensis* (possibly distinct **Asian Goldcrest**) resident Hokkaido, N & C Honshu, and winter visitor to Izu Is, SW Honshu, Shikoku and Kyushu, rare Nansei Shoto. **HH** Coniferous and mixed forests, and various woodland types on migration and in winter. **ID** Tiny; large-headed and short-tailed, with plain olive-green upperparts. Crown yellow, bordered by broad black lateral crown-stripes that do not merge on forehead, ♂ has orange central crown with yellow margins; short, narrow black malar, white lores and spectacles, grey head-sides, ear-coverts and nape; wings largely black with two broad white bars, yellowish fringes to primaries, and white-fringes to tertials. **BP** Bill fine, short black; black eyes appear especially large in broad pale eye-ring; tarsi dull brownish-pink or brighter orange-yellow (breeding ♂). **SV** Call: thin, high-pitched *sree-sree-sree*, shorter, less insistent than Eurasian Treecreeper, and quiet *seech* and *zick*. Song: complex series of thin, sibilant notes in a rapid trill *chiichiichii chiririri tsutsutsutsu-tjii-tsitsi-chocho*, and alternating high and low notes *tee-de-dee tee-de-dee*.

Eurasian Wren *Troglodytes troglodytes* L 9–11 cm; WT 7–13 g

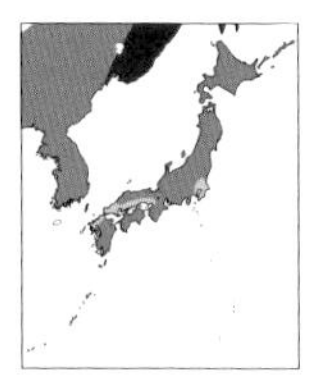

SD Resident: *T. t. fumigatus* Hokkaido to Kyushu and N Izu Is, rare winter visitor to Nansei Shoto; *T. t. dauricus* vagrant to W Honshu and Okinawa Is, possibly resident Tsushima; *T. t. mosukei* S Izu Is; *T. t. ogawae* Yakushima; *T. t. orii* Daito Is (extinct). **HH** Favours shady woodland, stream sides, rocky areas and well-vegetated damp gullies; winters in almost any riparian habitat. **ID** Tiny, cock-tailed bird. Appears dark brown, but finely barred black and grey, and has long, narrow brownish-white supercilia. Wings short, rounded, tail short and habitually cocked. Flight fast, whirring. Distinctive *T. t. fumigatus* is very dark brown with longer, darker bill and longer tail than other races. **BP** Bill slender, sharply pointed, blackish-brown with grey/horn base to lower mandible; eyes dark brown; tarsi pinkish-brown. **SV** Call: indignant chatting *chet chet chet*, recalls Japanese Bush Warbler, but higher. Song: astonishingly loud, far-carrying, easily heard over rushing water, rapid and complex *pipipi chui chui chiyo chiyo churiri*.

Eurasian Nuthatch *Sitta europaea* L 12–17 cm; WT 18–21 g

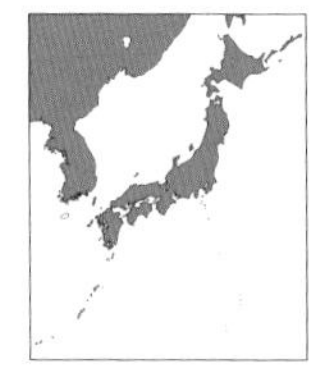

SD Common resident: *S. e. clara* Hokkaido; *S. e. amurensis* Honshu, Shikoku and N Kyushu; *S. e. roseilia* S Kyushu. **HH** Deciduous and evergreen broadleaf forests, sometimes in conifers, also woodland, scrub, parks and gardens in winter, readily joins mixed flocks. Acrobatic, foraging on trunks and larger branches. **ID** Large-headed, stub-tailed and vociferous. Very long thick black eyestripe extending to nape-sides, bordered above from forehead to just behind eyes by narrow supercilia; wings blackish-grey, tail grey in centre, black at sides with white patches near tips. Underparts largely white or off-white, with variable chestnut, from lower belly and flanks to vent (*amurensis* and *roseilia*), *asiatica* is much paler blue-grey above, all-white below with very limited chestnut scalloping on undertail-coverts. From below, wings show black and white carpal patches, and tail is largely black with white corners. **BP** Bill very strong, wedge-shaped, black; eyes black; legs strong, feet large, black. **SV** Calls: loud, liquid *plewp plewp plewp*, drawn-out *ziit*, forceful *twett* and high-pitched mouse-like *spee tee tee tee*. Song: loud and penetrating, comprises whistled series of loud, high, clear trilled or rippling notes *pipipipipipi* or *fififififi*.... and *jujujuju*....

Eurasian Treecreeper *Certhia familiaris* L 12–15 cm; WT 7–9 g

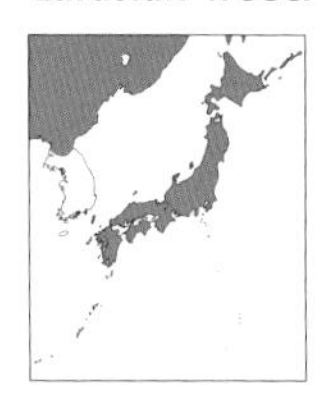

SD Fairly common resident: *C. f. daurica* in Hokkaido, and *C. f. japonica* in Honshu, Shikoku and Kyushu. **HH** Mixed deciduous broadleaf and coniferous forests to warmer evergreen broadleaf forest. May join mixed-species flocks in winter, when may also disperse lower, even visiting urban parks. Creeps mouse-like up tree trunks and larger limbs, then flies to base of another tree. **ID** Slender, dark-mottled grey-brown bird. Supercilia and underparts creamy white, except buff-washed flanks and vent. Long tail, serves as support when climbing upwards. In flight, distinct pale wingbar on mid-underwing. **BP** Bill long, fine, arched, blackish above, pink below; eyes black; tarsi large, pinkish-brown, with long hindclaw. **SV** Call: very high-pitched sibilant and slightly buzzy *tsee tsee* or *tsuu tsuririri* recalling Goldcrest, but more prolonged. Song: *pichi pii pii chii chii chiririri* falling in pitch to final flourish.

Goldcrest

ad ♂

ad ♀

Eurasian Wren

fumigatus

ad

Eurasian Nuthatch

asiatica

ad

ad

Eurasian Treecreeper

japonica

Asian Glossy Starling *Aplonis panayensis* L 17–20 cm; WT 50–60 g

SD Accidental in winter and early spring to Yaeyama Is; race unknown. **HH** Woodland and forest edges. **ID** Mid-sized, plain, black starling. Adult: entirely deep glossy black with metallic green-glossed face, neck and breast, and purple gloss to remaining plumage. Juvenile: blackish-brown above with some green gloss, buff below with heavy dark streaking. **BP** Bill more crow-like than starling-like, blunt, black; eyes large, irides bright red (ad) or dull orange (juv); tarsi blackish-grey. **SV** Common Starling-like *chank* and shrill *sreep*. **TN** Not included by OSJ, but established introduction in Taiwan.

Crested Myna *Acridotheres cristatellus* L 26–27 cm; WT 108–140 g

SD *A. c. cristatellus* has become established locally in Tokyo, elsewhere in central Honshu and Shikoku. **HH** Open areas with scrub, around cultivation and suburban parks. **ID** Large, mostly black, starling-like bird with unusual short bushy crest at base of bill. Entirely black except white panel at base of primaries, white scalloping on vent (albeit rather indistinct and difficult to see), white corners to rounded tail and narrow tips to rectrices. In flight shows short, broad white primary bar. **BP** Bill pale, ivory-coloured or even pale greenish-straw, with orange base to lower mandible; eyes prominent in black face, irides bright orange; legs dull yellow-orange. **SV** Hard *kyuru kyuru* or *kyutt kyutt* notes.

Javan Myna *Acridotheres javanicus* L 23–25 cm; WT 100 g

SD Introduced and established in C Honshu (Tokyo); recorded Yonagunijima. **HH** Agricultural land, parks and gardens. **ID** Dark-grey myna, with bright orange bill and legs, and short, curly black crest above bill. Head, neck and wings black; underparts, mantle, back, scapulars, rump and tail dark grey; white ventral area small. Wings have broad white bases to primaries, and broad white tips to outer tail-feathers. In flight, white on wings, vent and tail diagnostic. Slightly smaller than Crested Myna, with shorter crest, greyer body, larger white tail patches, narrower white wing spots and yellower bill. **BP** Bill bright orange; eyes white to pale yellow (ad) or pale blue (juv); tarsi yellowish-orange (ad) or pale yellowish-flesh (juv). **SV** Call: a guttural chattering *kyuru kyuru*. Song: complex *gyugyu kirurikirurukyororii*. **AN** White-vented Myna.

Bank Myna *Acridotheres ginginianus* L 23–25 cm; WT 64–76 g

SD Introduced locally in C Honshu (Tokyo). **HH** Villages and towns with trees, parks and gardens. **ID** Blue-grey with black cap and cheeks. Resembles Common Myna, but black of head extends only to face, and has short crest on forehead. Chin, throat, breast, mantle, scapulars, back and rump all dark grey, while belly and vent are buff-brown. Wings and tail black and outer tail tips yellowish-buff. In flight, shows orange-buff patch at base of primaries, yellowish-buff tail tips and border, and orange-buff underwing. **BP** Bill dull yellow; bare skin around eyes reddish-orange, eyes brown; tarsi dull dark yellow. **SV** Croaks, clucks and screeching notes as well as whistles, warbles and mimicry.

Common Myna *Acridotheres tristis* L 23–25 cm; WT 106 g

SD A frequent cagebird escapee that has become established in C Japan, and recorded on Ishigakijima (*A. t. tristis*). **HH** Agricultural areas and villages, also gardens and parks in towns, where forages on ground. **ID** Fairly large brown myna, with blackish-brown hood, wings and tail. Underparts grey-brown, except white lower belly, vent and undertail-coverts. In flight, shows prominent broad white patch at base of primaries, white tail tips and white underwing. **BP** Bill yellow; bare skin around eyes yellow, irides orange-brown; tarsi orange-yellow. **SV** Both weak and harsh scolding notes (*chake chake*), while song combines skilled mimicry with tuneless chattering, gurgling and whistling notes: *hee hee chirk-a chirk-a chirk-a*.... **AN** Indian Myna.

Asian Glossy Starling
ad
imm
Crested Myna
ad
Javan Myna
ad
ad
Bank Myna
ad
Common Myna
ad

Red-billed Starling *Spodiopsar sericeus*

L 22–24 cm; WT 65 g

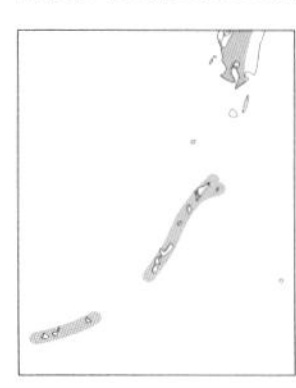

SD Rare to scarce migrant and winter visitor (Nov–Apr) in Nansei Shoto and S Kyushu (sometimes in small flocks or with Common Starling). Accidental north to N Honshu; vagrant north to Hokkaido. **HH** Lowland agricultural areas and open areas with scrub. **ID** A large starling. ♂ has distinctive pale hood, yellowish on crown, face and head-sides, and white on chin, throat and upper breast; upperparts mid slate-grey, blackest at edge of pale hood, rump pale grey, wings black with white panel at base of primaries, black tail slightly rounded at tip. ♀ pale buffy-grey, white on chin/throat, darker on mantle, very pale on rump; wings and tail as ♂. In flight note pale head, white wing patch and contrast between pale rump and black tail. **BP** Bill long, slender and sharply pointed, red with grey culmen and black tip; eyes black; legs bright red-orange (♂) or dull orange (♀). **SV** Chattering *jree-eep or zhree-eep*. **AN** Silky Starling.

White-cheeked Starling *Spodiopsar cineraceus*

L 24–25 cm; WT 75–90 g

SD Common resident (or local migrant) throughout much of Japan; summer visitor to Hokkaido, and winter visitor to Nansei Shoto. **HH** Favours deciduous forest fringes, groves of trees and habitation, often in urban areas, also agricultural land. Highly gregarious pre- and post-breeding, and in winter. **ID** Large, dark-grey and brown starling. ♂ hood blackish, but forehead, chin and cheeks white with some dark streaking; upper- and underparts, wings and tail mid-brown, with white rump, white fringes to secondaries and tips to tail-feathers. ♀ slightly duller, young plainer still and greyer but has pale, off-white cheeks. In flight, distinctive starling structure combined with white rump, tail tips and underwing-coverts, and pale panel in secondaries diagnostic. Some adults have much whiter head. **BP** Orange bill is black-tipped (ad) or all dull orange (juv); eyes distinct on white face, irides black; legs deep orange (ad) or dull brownish-orange (juv). **SV** Highly social and vocal bird, with families and flocks maintaining contact using various throaty chattering, even creaking sounds: *chir-chir-chay-cheet-cheet*, *gyuru*, *gyee* and *chi chi*, but commonest call a harsh *jah*. **AN** Grey Starling.

Pied Myna *Gragupica contra*

L 20–25 cm; WT 76–90 g

SD Introduced and established in C Honshu (Tokyo). **HH** Agricultural areas with trees, damp grasslands and around habitation. Also parks and gardens in residential areas. **ID** Mid-sized black and pale-buff starling. Adult: upperparts glossy black from crown to lower back, also tail and wings (with white band across scapulars), rump and uppertail-coverts pale greyish-buff; lores and ear-coverts dusky off-white; chin, throat and upper breast/neck-sides glossy black, with green-glossed head; breast, flanks and undertail-coverts pale greyish-buff. Juvenile: dull brown where adult is black, with paler bill. **BP** Bill long, sharply pointed, yellow with red at base of lower mandible; large bare red orbital patch, irides off-white (ad) or pale brown (juv); tarsi yellow. **SV** Various high-pitched musical notes, a chattering *cheek-cheurk* and descending *treek-treek-treek*. **AN** Pied Myna.

Daurian Starling *Agropsar sturninus*

L 18–19 cm; WT 100 g

SD Rare migrant to offshore Japan from S Nansei Shoto to NW Hokkaido. **HH** Typically in groves of trees, woodland and forest edges, also rural and semi-rural areas, around cultivation and villages. **ID** Small, rather neat, grey, black and buff starling. ♂ has plain face with head and entire underparts mid-grey; rear crown patch and mantle black with metallic violet/purple iridescence, wings and tail black with green gloss; at rest, broad white bar on scapulars, white tips to median coverts and orange-brown bases to primaries; rump, vent and undertail-coverts cinnamon-buff; belly greyish-buff. ♀ has less distinct wing pattern, is browner where ♂ is black, and lacks gloss. Juvenile is very similar to Chestnut-cheeked, but usually has white scapular bar and pale tips to tertials. **BP** Bill fine-pointed, black; eyes prominent in plain face, irides black; tarsi dull greyish-brown. **SV** A guttural *kyuru kyuru*, similar to Chestnut-cheeked Starling. **AN** Purple-backed Starling.

Red-billed Starling
ad ♂
ad ♀
ad ♂
juv
White-cheeked Starling
ad
ad
ad
juv
Daurian Starling
ad ♂
ad ♂
ad ♀
Pied Myna
juv
ad
ad

Chestnut-cheeked Starling *Agropsar philippensis* L 17–19 cm; WT 47 g

SD Uncommon summer visitor (May–Sep) breeding from C Honshu north to Hokkaido, migrating through W Honshu, Kyushu and Nansei Shoto (where some winter). **HH** Groves of trees in rural and semi-rural areas, cultivation and villages. **ID** Small, rather dusky, grey, black and buff starling. ♂ has creamy white head with plain face, but reddish-chestnut patch on ear-coverts and neck-sides; nape grey, mantle and scapulars black, with violet- or purple-glossed scapulars, mantle and upper back; wings strongly green-glossed; grey lower back and buff rump contrast with black tail. Underparts creamy on throat and upper breast, dark to pale grey from breast to vent. Grey-white scapular bar and grey-white panel near base of primaries. ♀ much plainer grey-buff, head/face plain, mantle brown, wings brown with indistinct pattern, lower back and rump buff. **BP** Bill fine-pointed, black; eyes prominent in plain face, irides black; legs blackish-grey. **SV** Harsh *jee* and throaty *gyuru gyuru*. Song a rapid and complex series of notes: *pyuu-kirurip-kyuru-kyuru-gyiip*. **AN** Violet-backed Starling; Red-cheeked Starling

White-shouldered Starling *Sturnia sinensis* L 18–20 cm; WT 61 g

SD Rare migrant from S Kyushu and Shikoku north to C & N Honshu, and scarce winter visitor from S Kyushu to S Nansei Shoto. **HH** Mostly in dry farmland with isolated stands of trees; often perches on wires. **ID** Pale, grey, black and white starling. ♂ almost white-headed, becoming pale grey from nape and ear-coverts to darker grey on back; lower back pale grey, rump pale buff; chin/throat white grading to grey on underparts; wings and tail black, with prominent white shoulder patch and band on tail tip. ♀ has darker brownish-grey head and upperparts, wings and tail browner with reduced white shoulder and only white corners to tail. White shoulders and tail pattern distinctive in flight. Juvenile: like ♀, but lacks white shoulders. **BP** Bill fine-pointed, whitish-grey; eyes appear small and indistinct in plain face, irides white or bluish-white; legs blue-grey. **SV** A throaty chattering *kyuru kyururii*, *kaar* or *gi gi* similar to Chestnut-cheeked Starling, and soft *preep* when flushed. Calls generally higher-pitched than other starlings of region. **AN** Chinese Starling; Grey-backed Starling.

Rosy Starling *Pastor roseus* L 19–24 cm; WT 67–88 g

Accidental visitor to S Japan, from S Nansei Shoto and Ogasawara Is to C Honshu. **HH** Agricultural land with scattered trees or scrub. **ID** Adult ♂'s unique shaggy crest and glossy black and pink breeding plumage make it unmistakable. Crest, hood, wings, vent, rump and tail all glossy black (purplish on head, blue-green on wings), remaining plumage pale buffy-pink. Non-breeding and 1st-winter duller, with much of pink obscured by buff fringes. ♀ similar to ♂ but duller. Juvenile in autumn (more likely to wander out of range), plain sandy-brown, paler than juvenile Common Starling, with broad pale fringes to wing-feathers, and stout bill. **BP** Bill rather thick, pink with black base (breeding ad) or yellow-horn with grey culmen (juv/1st-winter); eyes black; tarsi pink (ad) or dull yellowish-orange (juv). **SV** Rather variable calls, but generally short, harsh and rasping, some similar to Common Starling: *kyururi*, *chit*, or *baaht*.

Common Starling *Sturnus vulgaris* L 22–24 cm; WT 55–100 g

SD *S. v. poltaratskyi* is scarce winter visitor (Nov–Apr) from S Nansei Shoto north to Hokkaido, but especially in S Kyushu. **HH** Habitation, often urban areas, also agricultural land; highly social, often in dense flocks. **ID** A generally dark, monomorphic starling. Adult breeding: black with strong metallic purple/green iridescence, especially on neck/breast; wings and tail black with brown fringes to feathers; some fine spotting, buff or grey-brown tips to scapulars, and some spots on nape, mantle and flanks. Non-breeding adult moults into fresh plumage, largely with pale-buff tips, so in winter appears heavily spotted, forehead almost entirely pale buff, head with tiny spots, lores black, underparts finely spotted white, upperparts more coarsely so with buff; mantle in winter has green sheen in sunlight. Juvenile: drab, mid-brown with pale throat; differs from Rosy Starling in less prominently fringed wing-feathers and duller, grey bill. In flight, broad-based rather triangular wings and shortish blunt tail give distinctive shape. **BP** Bill straight, fine-pointed, yellow in breeding season, dull grey-black at other times, brownish in young; black eyes indistinct in dark face; tarsi dark orange in summer, dull brown-orange in winter. **SV** Varied guttural chattering notes *gyaa*, *gyuru* and *gyeee*. Often gives high-pitched 'radio-tuning' whistles as sub-song during winter. **AN** European Starling.

Chestnut-cheeked Starling
ad ♀
ad ♂
ad ♂
White-shouldered Starling
ad ♂
ad ♀
ad ♂
ad ♂
non-breeding
breeding
Rosy Starling
juv
non-breeding
Common Starling
juv
non-breeding
breeding

Siberian Thrush *Geokichla sibirica*

L 21–24 cm; WT 60–80 g

SD *G. s. davisoni* summer visitor (Apr–Sep) Hokkaido, N & C Honshu, scarce migrant south to Nansei Shoto. **HH** Boreal and montane coniferous and mixed deciduous/evergreen broadleaf forest. **ID** Adult ♂: blue-black with silver-white supercilia and narrow white tips to undertail-coverts. 1st-year ♂: duller dark grey overall, yellow-buff supercilia, some buff on ear-coverts and throat. ♀: dark olive-brown with pale, yellowish-buff supercilia, submoustachial and chin. Upperparts plain brown, underparts pale buff, but heavy dark-brown scaling gives dark appearance. In flight, shows white corners to tail and two white bars on slaty-black underwing (more contrasting than White's Thrush). **BP** Bill black (♂) or grey-tipped with yellow base (♀); eyes dark brown; tarsi bright yellow. **SV** Call: high pitched *tsi*, or sharper *zit*, in flight a wavering sibilant *siiiiih*. Sometimes a loud *chirr*, rattling *chrssss* in alarm, or *jack*. Song: from high perch, simple, slow, two-note whistle, given hesitantly and commonly followed by faint sibilant, high-pitched note: *kiron-tsee*, *kyoro tsuii* or *kyoron chii*. Occasionally includes other wavering notes: *tyui'i – tss yui'i-tss* or *tss sss ss*. **TN** Formerly in *Zoothera*.

Orange-headed Thrush *Geokichla citrina*

L 20–23 cm; WT 47–67 g

SD Vagrant to Tairajima, Kagoshima (Tokara). **HH** Dense thickets, evergreen forest. **ID** Brightly coloured; ♂: head and chest warm orange, face paler orange-buff with two vertical dark black-brown sub-ocular and auricular bars. Mantle, wings and tail bluish-grey. White median coverts form wing patch; belly and vent white. ♀: duller with olive-brown upperparts and warm brown wings. **BP** Bill dark grey; eyes large, irides black; tarsi brownish-pink. **SV** A thin *tzeet*, subdued *tjuck*, and screeching *teer-teer-teer* in alarm.

White's Thrush *Zoothera aurea*

L 24–30 cm; WT 88–130 g

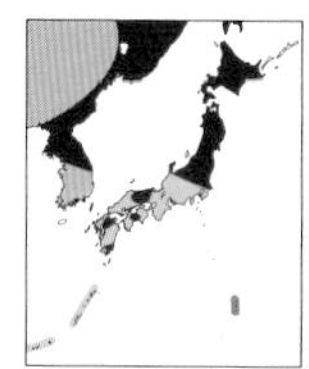

SD *Z. a. toratugumi* fairly common migrant and summer visitor Kyushu, C & N Honshu, Hokkaido, resident Ogasawara and Iwo Is, winter visitor Kyushu and Nansei Shoto. **HH** Dark boreal forest, and mature mixed and montane forests (500–1,600 m). Winters in forest, wooded parks, gardens. Feeds quietly in damp shady areas; unlike other thrushes walks rather than hops; has curious double-bobbing creeping gait. **ID** Large with proportionately short tail. Golden olive-brown covered with black, rounded scales. Face varies from pale and 'open' to distinctly barred, with pale lores and eye-ring, and black malar, sub-ocular 'teardrop' and strong auricular crescent. Primary-coverts black-tipped, median/greater coverts buff-tipped, affording pattern to otherwise plain wings. In flight shows white axillaries, boldly barred black-and-white underwing and white corners to tail. **BP** Bill rather long, stout, dark grey at tip, white to flesh-pink at base; eyes large with strong white orbital, irides black; tarsi flesh-pink. **SV** Hard *ga ga*, *gyororururu* or raspy *rraattchh* in alarm, low chuckling note on flushing. Sings at night or dawn, a slow, soft, mournful and drawn-out whistle, repeated after several seconds, and may solo or duet two whistled notes, one significantly higher pitched: *hyeeee jeweeee* or *twooo-chuooo*. **TN** Retained within *Z. dauma* by OSJ.

Amami Thrush *Zoothera major*

L 29–30 cm

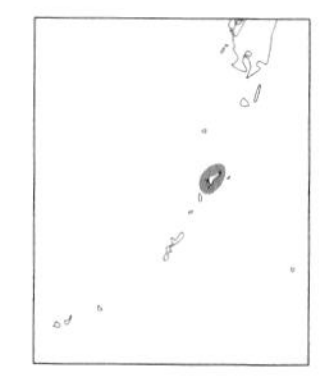

SD Near Threatened. Amami-Oshima and Kakeromajima. **HH** Dark, broadleaf evergreen primary forest at 100–400 m; crepuscular. Lacks White's Thrush's curious double-bobbing creeping gait, instead moves like *Pluvialis* plover – fast runs interspersed with abrupt pauses. **ID** Resembles White's Thrush, but face paler with subtly whiter malar, darker narrow throat-stripe, more prominent black bar below eye and at rear of ear-coverts, large gold spots on crown. Has 12 (not 14) tail-feathers, and distinctive song. **BP** Bill long, stout, dark grey at tip, yellow at base of lower mandible; eyes large, surrounded by bare pink skin, particularly at rear, irides black; tarsi brownish-orange or brownish-pink. **SV** Call: thin flat *tsih*, lower and more piercing, less wavering than Pale Thrush, also whispery *sih* and very high, thin, descending *tseeooo* in alarm. Song: mainly before or at dawn (especially late Feb–Mar), is pleasantly musical resembling Japanese Thrush, 3–4-part series of melodic whistles ending in flourish, *chieli... cheelü... tridüli-tsi!* or *tsuii chee kyoronchee*. Terminal flourish sounds like speeded-up Siberian's song. Occasionally a breezy, high *treer* note is inserted. **TN** Retained within *Z. dauma* by OSJ.

Scaly Thrush *Zoothera dauma*

L 24–30 cm; WT 88–103 g

SD *Z. d. iriomotensis* rare resident Yaeyama Is (Iriomotejima). **HH** Dark subtropical evergreen forest. **ID** Smaller and darker than White's or Amami Thrushes, with more crescentic scaling, slightly shorter bill and slightly weaker auricular crescent. **BP** Bill dark grey at tip, horn at base; eyes large with narrow white orbital, irides black; tarsi flesh-pink. **SV** Undescribed.

Siberian Thrush
ad ♀ foraging
in leaf litter
ad ♀
ad ♂
ad ♂
ad ♂
1st-year
♂
ad ♂
juv
Orange-headed
Thrush
melli
White's Thrush
ad
ad ♀
ad foraging
ad ♂
ad
toratugumi
ad
Scaly Thrush
ad
ad
Amami Thrush

Grey-cheeked Thrush *Catharus minimus*

L 17–19 cm; WT 26–50 g

SD Vagrant (*C. m. minimus*) in autumn to offshore Japan (Hegurajima). **HH** Wooded areas, shrubs. **ID** Small, greyish olive-brown thrush with very plain, cold grey face, broken pale grey eye-crescents and pale throat bordered below by loose necklace of dark spots extending to breast. Tail, often cocked, long, dull brown. In flight, two white bars contrast with blackish central underwing bar and dark flight-feathers. **BP** Bill yellowish-brown below with dark grey tip and culmen; black eyes appear large in plain face, with indistinct pale eye-ring; long tarsi dull pinkish-brown. **SV** A shrill, drawn-out *tsiiew* or thin seee; flight call high-pitched, a penetrating, nasal *jee-er*.

Grey-backed Thrush *Turdus hortulorum*

L 18–23 cm; WT 54–70 g

SD Rare migrant, S Nansei Shoto to Hokkaido. **HH** Thickets, open mixed deciduous forest, broadleaf evergreen forest, riparian woodland. **ID** Adult ♂: pale blue-grey hood and upperparts, wings and tail darker grey. Underparts orange brown, belly to vent white. Immature ♂: streaked upper breast. ♀: pale to mid olive-brown head and upperparts; underparts creamy white, spotted on throat and breast-sides, with orange-brown wash on breast and flanks. On take-off reveals orange-brown underwing-coverts. **BP** Bill yellow (♂), or yellowish-brown (♀); narrow yellow eye-ring, irides black; tarsi pinkish-yellow. **SV** Various *duiitt*, *zwiip* and *shiriniip* notes. Chuckling *chuck-chuck* and *tsee* in alarm recall Japanese Thrush.

Japanese Thrush *Turdus cardis*

L 21–22 cm; WT 50–70 g

SD Summer visitor (Apr–Sep), breeding from Hokkaido to Kyushu, scarce migrant through Nansei Shoto. **HH** Mature deciduous and evergreen broadleaf forest, from sea level to 1,200 m. **ID** Small, compact thrush. Adult ♂: almost entirely glossy black, except for white belly and flanks covered with black arrowhead spots, vent clear white. 1st-winter ♂: similar to adult, but dark grey rather than black, has brownish-black head and breast, and white flecking on breast. 1st-summer is dimorphic, recalling adult ♂ or like ♀. ♀: plain brown above, creamy white below with buffy-orange wash from neck-sides to flanks (and on underwing-coverts), and narrow black malar stripe merging with small black spots on breast to flanks. **BP** Bill yellow; ♂ has prominent yellow eye-ring, irides black; tarsi dull orange or pale pinkish-yellow. **SV** A thin *tsweee* or *zwii*, a *tsuuu*, hollow *chuk* and chuckling *kyokyokyo*. Song, from high perch, very attractive, comprising varied mix of rich fluting whistles and warbles: *kyoroi kyorokyoro kyokokyoko kokiiko kiiko* or *kyoroon-kyoroon kyoko-kyoko*, with phrases often repeated several times in quick succession.

Chinese Blackbird *Turdus mandarinus*

L 24–29 cm; WT 80–120 g

SD Very rare visitor, Nansei Shoto to Hokkaido, mainly S and W Japan. **HH** Deciduous woodland, parks. **ID** Adult ♂: sooty-black. 1st-year ♂: dark blackish-brown, but may show rufous tone to throat-sides. ♀: dark sooty blackish-brown, with paler underparts, narrow buffish-white throat and rust-brown tinge to breast and flanks; generally lacks spots on lower throat and breast. Juvenile: dark rufous-brown with some buff streaking and mottling. Long primary projection and broad-based wings differ from western forms. Flight heavy and undulating, with head and neck prominent. **BP** Bill yellow (♂) or dull dark grey-brown with yellow base to lower mandible (♀); narrow eye-ring pale yellow (♂ only), irides black; tarsi black. **SV** Alarm a loud chattering *plik plik plik*, persistent *twink twink twink*, also chuckling *pyuck pyuck* while feeding, and buzzy *dzeeb* and high thin *sri* flight calls. **TN** Retained within Common Blackbird *T. merula* by OSJ.

Eyebrowed Thrush *Turdus obscurus*

L 21–23 cm; WT 58–117 g

SD Common spring and autumn migrant, Honshu, Hokkaido; some winter Shikoku, Kyushu, Nansei Shoto. **HH** Dark boreal and montane forest, mature deciduous and evergreen forest, open woodland and parkland in lowlands. Shy and flighty. **ID** Resembles slim Brown-headed Thrush. ♂: blue-grey hood with prominent white supercilia, black lores, narrow white streak below eye and short white malar streak. ♀: crown, ear-coverts and neck grey-brown, with blackish-grey malar and extensive white on chin/throat; orange-brown of underparts less bright than ♂. 1st-year ♂: like ♀ but with more grey on head and less white on chin/throat. In flight, pale brownish-grey axillaries and underwing-coverts; white spots at tail corners. **BP** Bill, culmen dark, tip blackish, lower mandible yellow; narrow yellow eye-ring, irides black; tarsi dull brownish-yellow. **SV** Contact and flight call a thin *seee*, *tsuii* or *seep*, also thin *sip-sip* or *zip-zip*, and occasional deeper chuckling *tuck-tuck* or *kyott-kyott* notes similar to Brown-headed Thrush, but thinner, sharper and stronger; also a rattled *turrr*.

Grey-cheeked Thrush
1st-year
ad
Grey-backed Thrush
1st-year ♂
ad ♂
ad ♂
ad ♀
ad ♂
Japanese Thrush
1st-win ♂
ad ♀ 1st-sum
ad ♀
ad ♂ /1st-year
1st-sum ♂
1st-sum ♂
ad ♂
Chinese Blackbird
ad ♂
ad ♀
Eyebrowed Thrush
ad ♂
ad ♂
ad ♀
1st-year
ad ♂

Pale Thrush *Turdus pallidus*

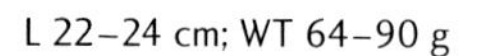
L 22–24 cm; WT 64–90 g

SD Common winter visitor (Oct–May) and migrant from Nansei Shoto to N Honshu; scarce migrant in Hokkaido; scarce breeder Tsushima. **HH** Open deciduous and coniferous woodland, including parks and gardens, where forages on ground. **ID** Superficially drab, like dull Brown-headed Thrush. ♂ has grey hood and mid-brown upperparts; underparts pale brown to brownish-buff on belly and sides, central belly and vent white. ♀ paler, with white of submoustachial separated from throat by dark malar. In flight, rather plain, except for diagnostic white corners to tail. **BP** Bill has dark-grey tip and culmen, dull-yellow base to lower mandible; narrow yellow eye-ring, irides black; tarsi pale brownish-yellow. **SV** Alarm- and contact calls include a discordant thin *tzeee* or *tsuii* in flight; stronger *shi-ri-riip* and deep, chuckling *kyott kyott* or *gyo-kyo-kyo* when disturbed.

Brown-headed Thrush *Turdus chrysolaus*

L 23–24 cm; WT 55–90 g

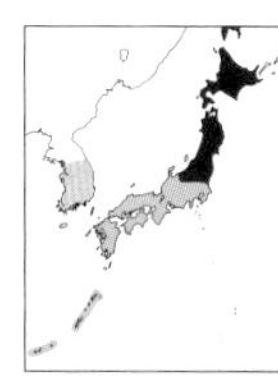

SD Common summer visitor *T. c. chrysolaus* breeds in Hokkaido and N & C Honshu and winters from C Honshu southwards to Nansei Shoto. *T. c. orii* breeds in Kuril I and is rare visitor in C Honshu. **HH** Mature deciduous broadleaf forest from sea level to 1,200 m in Hokkaido, to 2,400 m in Honshu; also parks, gardens and agricultural areas in winter and on migration. **ID** ♂ has blackish-brown hood and mid olive-brown upperparts. ♀ has head concolorous with upperparts, throat pale and lightly streaked. Juvenile has indistinct supercilia, dark spotting on neck, throat and chest, orange-brown wash to flanks. *T. c. orii* is slightly larger than nominate, and has darker (sootier) crown, not concolorous with dark olive-brown back; face and throat blacker (more closely resembling Izu Thrush, but lacks clear contrast between head, breast and hindneck, and tail is not black). On take-off reveals pale-grey underwing-coverts and orange-brown axillaries. **BP** Bill dull yellow with dusky-grey tip and culmen (ad) or all grey (juv); thicker and longer in *T. c. orii*; narrow yellow eye-ring, irides black; tarsi pinkish-yellow. **SV** Alarm call a harsh *chuck-chuck*, deep chuckling or bubbling notes, and thin *tsurii* or *zeeee* flight call. Song a pleasant, simple three-part *kiron...kiron..tsee*; or *kyoron...kyoron...tsureep*; less varied than Japanese Thrush, resembling Siberian Thrush.

Izu Thrush *Turdus celaenops*

L 23 cm; WT 80 g

SD Vulnerable. Endemic to Izu Is and Tokara Is; scarce winter visitor to C Honshu and Yakushima; rare migrant Shikoku, Kyushu and Okinawa. **HH** Shady deciduous and evergreen broadleaf forest, and nearby agricultural land and gardens on Izu Is; also mixed juniper/rhododendron forest to treeline on islands SW of range. **ID** Very dark-headed, brown thrush. Adult ♂ has black hood reaching upper breast; upperparts warm, dark rufous-brown. Breast-sides, flanks and belly-sides warm orange-chestnut; central underparts and vent white or largely white with 4–5 deep rufous spots (as in confusingly similar *orii* Brown-headed Thrush, BHT, which occurs, for example, on Tokara Is on migration). 1st-year can look confusingly similar to nominate BHT. 1st-winter ♂ resembles adult, but has greyer head and breast with some streaking on throat. ♀ like ♂, but grey-brown on head, not black, and has off-white chin narrowly streaked grey and extensive streaking on undertail-coverts (lacking in BHT). **BP** Bill bright orange-yellow (♂), with dark tip and culmen (♀) (grey with yellow base in young); eye-ring bright yellow, irides black; tarsi brownish-orange. **SV** Throaty *kyop kyop* or *quwatt quwatt* notes, and thinner, more sibilant *tsuii* or *tyii*; bubbling alarm is deeper, more guttural than Pale Thrush or BHT. Song, from low perch, a brief *gyororott jiitt* or *kyoro-ruru jiip*, alternatively described as like a deeper, more thrush-like version of Japanese Robin's 3–5 buzzing trills *tsurrrrrr...turrrrrr... tzurrrrrrr...tsizi*.

Fieldfare *Turdus pilaris*

L 22–27 cm; WT 76–141 g

SD Accidental winter visitor (Oct–Feb), with records from Tsushima, C Honshu and Hokkaido. **HH** Visits open agricultural land with isolated trees and wooded countryside. **ID** Large, grey and brown thrush, with distinctive blue-grey head, nape, lower back, rump and uppertail-coverts. Underparts off-white with warm buff-orange wash to breast, narrow dark streaks on throat-sides becoming larger, darker spotting and scalloping on breast-sides and flanks. Rather upright stance; appears deep-chested. 1st-winter less clearly and brightly marked. Flight strong, undulating, flashes pure white axillaries and underwing-coverts. **BP** Bill large, brownish-yellow; eyes dark brown; long tarsi blue-grey. **SV** Alarm and flight calls generally loud and hard, 2–3 notes, *tchack-tchack*, but also thin, nasal *zreep* or squeaky *gih*.

Pale Thrush
ad ♂
ad ♂
ad ♂
ad ♀
Brown-headed Thrush
chrysolaus
ad ♂
1st-year
ad ♀
ad ♂
Izu Thrush
ad ♂
ad ♂
ad ♂
ad ♀
Fieldfare
ad
ad
1st-win ♀
ad

Black-throated Thrush *Turdus atrogularis*

L 24–27 cm; WT 54–110 g

SD Accidental migrant and winter visitor to Nansei Shoto, Kyushu, Honshu and Hokkaido. **HH** Forest, thickets, scrub and gardens. **ID** Adult ♂ has dark ash-grey upperparts from forehead to rump, somewhat darker wings and tail, with face to breast black and contrasting strongly with mainly white underparts. Winter/1st-winter ♂ has greyer face and white fringes to black feathers of throat/breast. ♀ recalls 1st-winter ♂, but has largely white chin/throat and more white streaking in malar region. 1st-winter ♀ very like Red-throated Thrush, but lacks red in tail, and like Naumann's and Dusky thrushes, but greyer and lacks rufous in wings, tail or flanks. **BP** Bill tip and culmen black with yellow base to lower mandible; eyes black; tarsi dark brownish-pink. **SV** Alarm and flight calls closely resemble Naumann's and Dusky, a thin *tseep*, harsh *chack-chack* and soft chuckling. **TN** Retained within *T. ruficollis* by OSJ.

Red-throated Thrush *Turdus ruficollis*

L 24–27 cm; WT 63–103 g

SD Very rare migrant, which has reached Nansei Shoto, Kyushu, Honshu and Hokkaido. **HH** Forest, woodland, scrub and orchards. **ID** Grey, red and white thrush, with ashy-grey upperparts, black lores and dull red outer tail. Adult ♂ has deep red supercilia, neck-sides, chin/throat and breast, and white underparts; in winter red of throat narrowly fringed white. 1st-winter ♂ less bright; pale to deep orange-red supercilia, lower cheek, malar, throat and breast, with variably streaked submalar and upper breast. ♀ has paler supercilia, white chin, black-streaked throat-side, and pale rufous breast; 1st-winter ♀ like Black-throated Thrush, but has rufous outer tail; also recalls 1st-winter Naumann's/Dusky Thrush, but lacks rufous in wings and flanks. Underwing-coverts pale orange-brown. Occasional birds appear intermediate between Red-throated and Naumann's, but age/sexual differences remain unclear in this complex. **BP** Bill has blackish tip and upper mandible with yellow base to lower mandible; eyes black; tarsi dull brownish-pink. **SV** Alarm and flight calls as Black-throated Thrush.

Naumann's Thrush *Turdus naumanni*

L 23–25 cm; WT 63–81 g

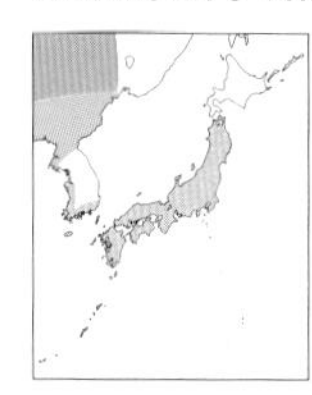

SD Very scarce winter visitor from N Honshu to Nansei Shoto and scarce migrant to Hokkaido. **HH** Mid-elevation to lowland mixed forest, parks, agricultural land and gardens, often foraging in open. Sometimes joins Dusky Thrush flocks. **ID** Variable, but adult generally mid grey-brown from forehead to back, with rusty-red or brick-orange lower back, base and outer tail (always lacking in Dusky). ♂ has face buff or orange, with brick-orange supercilia, neck-side and malar, throat bordered by grey-brown lateral throat-stripes. Underparts variably rufous-orange, with white scaling from lower chest to vent, and white central belly. ♀ has more dark streaking on throat-side, little or no rufous-orange on face and less red on underparts. 1st-winter has throat streaking extending to neck- and breast-sides. In flight, outer tail-feathers distinctly rufous-orange, wings showing only limited (or no) rufous-brown panel on secondaries. **BP** Bill has blackish tip and culmen with yellow lower mandible; eyes black; tarsi dull brownish-yellow. **SV** Shrill, nasal *cheeh*, harsh *shak* or *chack* in alarm, which is commonly repeated, sometimes in series. **AN** Rufous-tailed Thrush.

Dusky Thrush *Turdus eunomus*

L 23–25 cm; WT 65–107 g

SD Common to abundant migrant and winter visitor (Oct–May) from Hokkaido to Nansei Shoto. **HH** As Naumann's Thrush. **ID** Extremely variable, but generally dark with much black on face and underparts, extensive rusty-red in wings (coverts, primary bases, tertials) and rump, but none in tail. More contrasting than Naumann's Thrush, though can be confusingly similar. ♂ has prominent creamy white supercilia, chin, throat, breast and neck bar, with blackish-brown lores and ear-coverts, narrow dark-brown lateral throat-stripe, black breast-band and heavy black scaling on breast and flanks. Upperparts olive-brown to dark-brown; wings appear bright rufous-brown. ♀ is poorly marked and less contrasting than ♂, but also has dark-brown tail and distinct rufous wing-panel. In flight, tail lacks rufous, but wings appears bright rufous-brown; also has rusty-red axillaries. **BP** Bill has blackish tip and culmen with yellow lower mandible (brighter than Naumann's); eyes black; tarsi dull brownish-yellow. **SV** Varied sibilant and chattering calls: *kii kii*, *chirii*, *tsuii* or *shrree* and *quwatt quwatt*, also strident *chek-chek-chek-chek* and staccato alarm *chuck*. **TN** Lumped with *T. naumanni* by OSJ.

Black-throated Thrush
ad ♂
ad ♂
ad ♂
ad ♀
1st-win ♂
Red-throated Thrush
ad ♂
ad ♂
1st-win ♂
ad ♂
ad ♀
Naumann's Thrush
ad ♂
ad ♀
ad ♂
ad ♂
Dusky Thrush
ad ♂
ad ♂
ad ♀
1st-win ♂

Redwing *Turdus iliacus* L 20–24 cm; WT 46–88 g

SD *T. i. iliacus* is an accidental winter visitor, which has reached Hokkaido, N, C & W Honshu, and Okinawa. **HH** Woodland, agricultural and suburban areas with berry- or fruit-bearing trees/shrubs; sometimes with other thrushes. **ID** Small, slender, resembling Naumann's Thrush or unstreaked Eyebrowed Thrush, but has prominent supercilia and deep rusty-red flanks and underwings. Upperparts drab earth-brown. Ear-coverts dark brown, bordered by long creamy supercilia; chin to belly off-white with narrow dark streaks forming malar and merging into heavy streaks on breast-sides and somewhat weaker streaks on belly; flanks and underwing distinctively rusty-red. **BP** Bill brown with lower mandible mostly pale yellow with dark tip; eyes black; tarsi yellowish- or pinkish-brown. **SV** Flight call a long, thin high-pitched buzzing tseee or *shirii*; an abrupt *chup* or *chittick*; alarm a harder, rattling *trrt-trrt-trrt* or *chet-chet-chet*.

Song Thrush *Turdus philomelos* L 20–23 cm; WT 50–107 g

SD Vagrant in winter (likely *T. p. nataliae*). **HH** Open woodland and parks in lowlands and hills, foraging in open on ground. **ID** Medium-sized dark olive-brown thrush. Upperparts olive-brown, face plain with faint malar of black spots (lacks prominent supercilia of Redwing); underparts off-white, with warm buff wash to breast, fine dark spotting on throat-sides, larger spots on breast and fainter browner spots on flanks. In flight, yellowish-buff underwing-coverts (reddish in Redwing). **BP** Bill dark blackish-grey above and at tip, paler at base of lower mandible; eyes dark brown; tarsi pinkish-brown. **SV** Call, commonly given on take-off or when flushed, a sharp, anxious *tsui* or *tseeu* and soft but sharp *tip* or *tsipp* or *zit* similar to, but softer than, Rustic Bunting. Alarm call is series of sharp, scolding *tix-ix-ix-ix* or *stuk-stuk-stuk* sounds, or an explosive chatter *tikikikikikik*. **TN** Not included by OSJ.

Mistle Thrush *Turdus viscivorus* L 27–28 cm; WT 93–167 g

SD Accidental winter visitor (Oct–Feb; most likely *T. v. bonapartei*) with records from Kyushu, W Honshu and E Hokkaido. **HH** Open deciduous woodland and parkland. Rather vigilant and wary. **ID** Large, greyish olive-brown thrush. Upperparts and face plain grey-brown, paler on rump; tail long with white tips to outer three feathers. Underparts off-white with buff wash to breast and heavy dark spotting, small and concentrated on throat-sides and upper breast, larger on belly, blackest and largest on flanks and lower belly. Lacks golden tones of White's Thrush. In flight, note pale rump, whitish underwings and white tail-corners (compare with smaller, plainer Song Thrush). **BP** Bill large, blackish-brown with pale base to lower mandible; eyes dark brown; tarsi yellowish-brown. **SV** Flight and alarm call a dry rattling *trrrrk* or *zer'r'r'r'r*; also an abrupt *tuc* or *kewk*.

Redwing
ad
ad
1st-year
1st-year
Song Thrush
ad
ad
ad
ad feeding by
smashing snail shell
Mistle Thrush
ad
ad
ad
juv

Spotted Flycatcher *Muscicapa striata*

L 14–15 cm; WT 11–25 g

SD Vagrant (*M. s. mongola*), Hegurajima. **HH** Forest edge, gardens. Upright; frequently flicks tail. **ID** Resembles Grey-streaked Flycatcher (GSF), but with shorter wings (reaching halfway to tail tip). Head less rounded and profile more elongated than other grey/brown flycatchers. Ash-grey, with fine black streaking on pale forehead and crown. Weak eye-ring, faintly pale lores and faint dusky malar stripe. Wings dark grey-brown with narrow pale fringes to coverts, inner secondaries and tertials. Pale greyish-brown streaks on white breast and flanks. **BP** Bill fine, black; eyes black, smaller than GSF; tarsi black. **SV** Call a short *seep*, harsh *tek-tek*, slightly longer *zee zeet-eet*, harder *eez-tuk-tuk* or rattling alarm *ch-r-r-r-r-rer*.

Grey-streaked Flycatcher *Muscicapa griseisticta*

L 13–15 cm; WT 15–22 g

SD Uncommon migrant, Sea of Japan coast, Nansei Shoto to Hokkaido (rare breeder). **HH** Mixed broadleaf forest, larch forest, open upland and lowland habitats. **ID** Plain ash grey-brown, face plain, with prominent whitish lores and indistinct pale eye-ring. More heavily streaked below than Spotted Flycatcher (SF), with almost plain crown. Chin, throat broad submoustachial stripe and neck bar all white. Dark malar broadens, merging into dark streaking on breast and flanks. Narrow dark streaking on lower breast/upper belly distinguishes it from similar Dark-sided Flycatcher (DSF) and SF. Undertail-coverts white. Long wings blackish-brown, with narrow off-white fringes to tertials; narrow white fringes to greater coverts form a single distinct pale wingbar. Primary extension longer than in DSF or Asian Brown Flycatcher (ABF), primaries reaching close to tail tip. **BP** Bill blackish, slightly longer and thicker than DSF; eyes large (less so than ABF), irides black; tarsi blackish-grey. **SV** Call: whispery, slightly rising, thin *heest*, a thin *tsuii* or *speet-teet-teet*; in alarm a plaintive *tsr tsr*. Song: formless high twittering. **AN** Grey-spotted Flycatcher.

Dark-sided Flycatcher *Muscicapa sibirica*

L 13–14 cm; WT 9–16 g

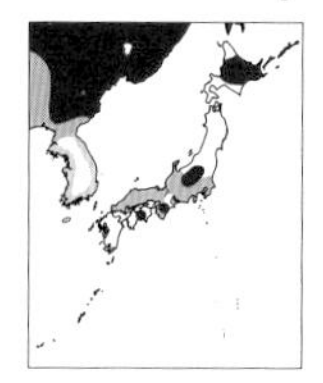

SD Summer visitor (*M. s. sibirica*; May–Oct), C & N Honshu, Hokkaido; migrant Sea of Japan coast, offshore islands south to Nansei Shoto. **HH** Montane mixed taiga forest, mixed broadleaf forest. On migration and in winter, lowland habitats from urban parks to woodland. **ID** Shares large-headed appearance and upright stance with GSF and ABF. Plain, with shorter wings than GSF, primaries reaching only to mid-tail. Upperparts dark grey-brown; face plain, sooty-grey lores (less distinct than ABF), prominent pale eye-ring. Dark malar contrasts strongly with white chin/throat and pale or white partial collar. Underparts dirty white (darker than ABF or GSF), with dusky grey-brown wash and broad, diffuse streaks on breast and flanks. Pale buffy-brown wingbar; pale fringes to tertials form prominent wing-panel. Primary length intermediate between ABF and GSF, exposed primaries 15–20% longer than tertials. **BP** Bill shorter, less deep-based than GSF, shorter than ABF, blackish base to lower mandible slightly paler; eyes large, black; tarsi black. **SV** Call: thin *tsuii or chii* and downslurred *feeeer*; flight call a thin, straight *siht*. Song: weak series of high-pitched notes, trills and whistles, easily overlooked and very similar to ABF, but usually includes *tsichiriri* or *tsee-tsee-tsee* notes. **AN** Sooty Flycatcher; Siberian Flycatcher.

Asian Brown Flycatcher *Muscicapa dauurica*

L 12–14 cm; WT 8–16 g

SD Common summer visitor (*M. d. dauurica* (May–Sep), Kyushu to Hokkaido, common migrant further south. **HH** Mature mixed broadleaf forest, larches and birches in northern areas, wide range of wooded and open habitats on migration. **ID** Small, plain, with large head and *short* tail. Upperparts plain greyish-brown; face plain with prominent pale lores, narrow band above bill and prominent off-white eye-ring. Lacks bold malar and half-collar of Dark-sided Flycatcher (DSF), but may show indistinct malar. Underparts off-white with grey-brown wash, but far less heavy than DSF; sometimes faintly streaked on breast; undertail-coverts unmarked white. Wings plainer than either DSF or GSF, with very indistinct whitish wingbar and faint wing-panel formed by pale tertial fringes (more prominent in 1st-winter). Primaries shorter than other related flycatchers, exposed primaries shorter (*c.* 80–90%) than tertials. **BP** Bill blackish, with prominent pale base to lower mandible, longer than DSF; eyes largest of grey/brown flycatchers, irides black; tarsi black. **SV** Call: hard *trrr* followed by *dit tit it* notes, or *chuck*; also thin *tsuii* or *chee*. Flight call: thin *siht* sounding identical to DSF. Song: subdued, but varied, drawn-out jumble of complex chatters, warbles and chuckles, *tsii-chiriri-chopiriri* at high pitch that is easily overlooked, slower than DSF. **TN** Formerly *M. latirostris*.

Spotted Flycatcher
ad worn
ad fresh
Grey-streaked Flycatcher
ad worn
ad fresh
Dark-sided Flycatcher
1st-win
ad
Asian Brown Flycatcher
ad worn
ad fresh

Ferruginous Flycatcher *Muscicapa ferruginea*

L 12–13 cm; WT 9–17 g

SD Rare migrant, recorded from Nansei Shoto to N Honshu. **HH** Woodlands. **ID** Small, warm-coloured *Muscicapa*. Broad head of adult is grey, with pale buff lores and prominent white eye-ring, chin/throat and neck-sides white, bordered by narrow dark malar; underparts dull to bright orange-brown, brightest on flanks and vent, belly whitish. Upperparts warm mid-brown to warm orange-brown. Wings blackish-brown with orange fringes to greater coverts forming distinct orange wingbar; tertials and secondaries also fringed orange. Juvenile like adult, but has spotted grey head and large pale orange-buff spots on mantle and underparts. **BP** Bill short, dark grey with yellow base to lower mandible; eyes appear large, with white eye-ring, irides black; tarsi black. **SV** Very high, sibilant *tsiiiii*, ending abruptly.

European Pied Flycatcher *Ficedula hypoleuca*

L 12–14 cm; WT 9–22 g

SD Accidental (*F. h. sibirica*) autumn migrant to Hegurajima and N Honshu. **HH** Open woodland. **ID** ♂ is boldly pied. *F. h. sibirica* also has grey morph, in which head, face and mantle are dark grey, rather than black. ♀ warm brown on head, face and upperparts, whitish on chin, but pale ash-brown on underparts; wings show similar but less boldly marked panel than ♂. **BP** Bill black; eyes black; tarsi black. **SV** Soft tongue-clicking *teck*, a more metallic and more repetitive alarm note *pik pik pik* and *whee-tic* when excited.

Yellow-rumped Flycatcher *Ficedula zanthopygia*

L 13–14 cm; WT 12–15 g

SD Rare migrant, mostly on Sea of Japan islands, recorded from Nansei Shoto to Hokkaido. **HH** Mature mixed broadleaf forest, often near water; also woodlands, parks and scrub on migration. **ID** Small, very bright *Ficedula*. ♂ largely black, white and yellow, with broad white supercilia, prominent white wing patch (on inner greater coverts) and white tertial fringes. Lower back, rump and underparts bright lemon-yellow. ♀ plainer, lacking contrast; olive-green above and off-white below; wings largely olive with white greater-covert bar and tertial fringes forming fairly prominent patch on folded wing; and prominent bright lemon-yellow rump. In flight, white innerwing patch and white tertial fringes of ♂ contrast with black wings and yellow back/rump; ♀ in flight has prominent rump and less distinct wing patches (see Narcissus). **BP** Bill black; eyes black, ♀ has narrow white eye-ring; tarsi black. **SV** Call resembles Taiga Flycatcher, but deeper, harder rattling *trrrt*; also a more rippling *prrrip-prrrip*. Song (sometimes heard from migrants) similar to Narcissus, but shorter, more thrush-like whistling: *tji tji tjiririri*... **AN** Tricoloured Flycatcher.

Narcissus Flycatcher *Ficedula narcissina*

L 13–14 cm; WT 14–17 g

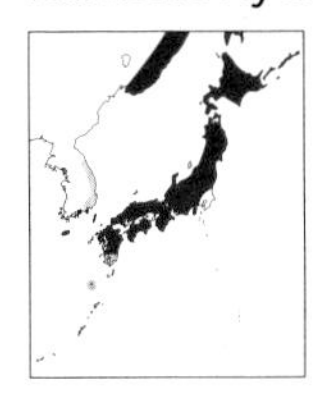

SD Common summer visitor (May–Sep) throughout mainland Japan from C Kyushu to Hokkaido; accidental to Ogasawara and Iwo Is. **HH** Mature mixed broadleaf deciduous forest with some conifers in north, and broadleaf evergreen forest in south; prefers shady areas. On migration appears in wide range of habitats, including urban parks. **ID** Adult ♂ has black upperparts, with long yellow supercilia; wings black, with small but prominent white innerwing patch (tertials lack white or present only at bases); lower back and rump bright, rich yellow, the rump feathers often erected prominently in display. Underparts grade from bright, deep orange on chin/throat to bright yellow on breast and flanks, and white on lower belly/vent. 1st-winter ♂ resembles adult, but frequently has much of nape and mantle dark olive- or greyish-green, often bordered black, and has greyer mantle and wings. ♀ plain olive-brown or olive-green (closely resembling ♀ Blue-and-white Flycatcher), with faint pale supercilia before eye; lacks yellow rump patch and white wing patch of Yellow-rumped; rump dull green or yellowish-olive, uppertail-coverts and tail fringes somewhat richer brown; wing-coverts and tertials darker grey than ♀ Blue-and-white, from which best separated by size. Underparts off-white; breast-sides and flanks brownish-white, throat and belly slightly yellow. In flight, ♂ has small white innerwing patch and bright yellow rump; ♀ plain. **BP** Bill slate-blue or black; eyes black; tarsi slate-blue to bluish-grey. **SV** Soft *tink-tink* and bubbling, rising *brrrut* (thicker in tone than Ryukyu or Mugimaki flycatchers). On migration, series of plaintive, upslurred whistles, *puee puee puee*, or series of downslurred plaintive *piu piu piu* notes interspersed with quite deep tutting *tchuk* notes. Highly vocal, song extremely varied, including mimicry, a 3–4-part series of warbled or whistled notes; the motif *cho-tee-cho-turr* with second syllable higher is common; and a distinctive *pi-pe-poi* is frequently incorporated. ♂ gives an urgent subsong full of metallic *zink* and whistled notes in defence of territory.

Ferruginous Flycatcher
ad
European Pied Flycatcher
1st-win
ad ♀ breeding
ad ♂ breeding
Yellow-rumped Flycatcher
ad ♀
ad ♂
Narcissus Flycatcher
ad ♂
ad ♀

Green-backed Flycatcher *Ficedula elisae*

L 13–14 cm

SD Vagrant, Shimane Prefecture. **HH** Broadleaf forest, preferring shady areas. **ID** Resembles Narcissus, but has shorter wings. Furthermore, ♂ has dull greenish-olive head, but bright yellow supraloral stripe to just above eye and narrow eye-ring (lacks broadening yellow supercilia of Narcissus); dark greyish-olive mantle and scapulars; rump pale or bright yellow; wings greyish-black with larger white coverts patch than Narcissus; tail dark greyish-black; underparts plain yellow (lacks orange throat of Narcissus). ♀ has olive-green upperparts, pale yellow patch above lores and dull yellow or yellowish-buff underparts. **BP** Bill black; eyes black; tarsi black. **SV** A low *tok tok tok*, purring *tchook tchook* and sharp *tek tek*. **TN** Formerly within Narcissus Flycatcher. **AN** Elisa's Flycatcher; Chinese Flycatcher. **TN** Not included by OSJ.

Ryukyu Flycatcher *Ficedula owstoni*

L 13–14 cm

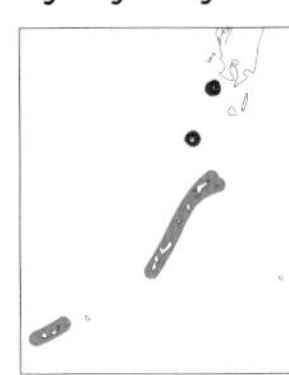

SD Endemic to Nansei Shoto: Kuroshima, Yakushima, Tokara Is and Amami-Oshima south to Yaeyama Is, where largely resident, but northern population summer visitor; reported north to SW Honshu. **HH** Primary and secondary broadleaf evergreen subtropical forest (even gardens on Yaeyama Is), preferring shady areas. **ID** Similar to Narcissus Flycatcher, but slightly smaller with shorter wings and primary projection. Adult ♂ is less black than Narcissus, with dark olive-green crown, mantle and upper back, and orange-yellow lower back and rump, fairly prominent but small wing patch (formed by white tertial fringes); supercilia less golden-yellow than Narcissus and underparts pale yellow, *lacking* orange-tinged throat. 1st-year ♂ (may breed and sing in this plumage), closely resembles ♀; rather plain olive-brown, with blackish- or greenish-brown crown, upper ear-coverts and eyestripe, lacks supercilia; face and underparts to mid-belly yellowish-brown (lacking strong orange suffusion of adult ♂ Narcissus, and paler than 1st-year ♂ Narcissus), vent and lower belly off-white; mantle, nape and lower ear-coverts dark moss-green. Wings blackish-brown, with paler brown fringes to coverts and tertials. In 1st-year ♂, first feature to develop is white on tertial webs. ♀ perhaps inseparable from ♀ Narcissus, but upperparts tinged green (somewhat browner in Narcissus), immature frequently has yellowish eye-ring. **BP** Bill black, but heavier than Narcissus, may appear slightly upturned; eyes black; tarsi dark lead-grey. **SV** Piping, downslurred but insistent *piu...piu...piu...* sometimes interspersed with a low *tuc tuc* or low, strong *chuc*, recalling Dusky Warbler. Similar to some Narcissus calls, but lacks latter's distinctive *prrit*. Song comprises short, simple phrases (closer to Yellow-rumped than Narcissus), a rather constant three-part warbling phrase, with 1–2-second intervals between each part: *chur-lee.... tridlee... chidlee....* (lacks mimicry of Narcissus). Like Narcissus, has aggressive subsong given near ground in presence of intruders, a complex series of metallic churrs and rattles, some very high-pitched. **TN** Retained within Narcissus Flycatcher by IOC.

Mugimaki Flycatcher *Ficedula mugimaki*

L 13–14 cm; WT 10–13 g

SD A scarce migrant, recorded mostly in spring, from Nansei Shoto north to W Hokkaido, more frequently on offshore islands than main islands. **HH** Favours shady mature mixed broadleaf forest, damp montane and lowland boreal forest, and wider range of habitats on migration, including conifers. **ID** Small, brightly marked flycatcher, appearing plump, round-headed and short-billed. Adult ♂ is largely black, with short white streak above and behind eye, bright orange underparts and white belly. Black wings have large patch formed by white median coverts, and narrow white fringes to tertials and basal sides to tail, making it very distinctive in flight. First year resembles adult, but is dark grey instead of black, and orange of underparts is less bright. ♀ less contrasting, mid-brown where ♂ is black, with narrow greater-covert bar and tertial fringes, lacking white in tail base; underparts washed pale orange. **BP** Bill short, black; eyes large, irides black; tarsi grey or black. **SV** *Beerirri* calls similar to, but softer than, Narcissus; also a rattling *turrt*, low *chuck* and soft *tyu*. Song consists of loud trills.

Green-backed Flycatcher
ad ♂
ad ♀
Ryukyu Flycatcher
ad ♂
ad ♀
Mugimaki Flycatcher
1st-year ♂
ad ♂
ad ♀

Red-breasted Flycatcher *Ficedula parva*

L 11–13 cm; WT 9–12 g

SD Very rare winter visitor (Oct–Apr), mostly to C Honshu, but also to Shikoku and Kyushu. **HH** Woodlands, parks and forest edges. **ID** Small, closely resembling Taiga Flycatcher, but wings marginally shorter, and uppertail-coverts paler than or concolorous with tail. ♂ has extensive warm rusty-orange throat and upper breast, merging into white belly. Retains red bib throughout winter. 1st-summer ♂ resembles ♀. ♀ lacks red throat patch, being more creamy buff below with larger, more diffuse white throat. **BP** Bill quite broad-based, black above with reddish-brown lower mandible tipped darker (compare Taiga); eyes large and prominent on plain face, narrow off-white eye-ring, irides dark brown; tarsi black. **SV** Slurred, rattled *serrrt* or wren-like *drrrrrr* (softer and slower than Taiga).

Taiga Flycatcher *Ficedula albicilla*

L 11–13 cm; WT 8–14 g

SD Scarce migrant and rare winter visitor (Oct–May) recorded from Nansei Shoto to Hokkaido. **HH** Woodlands, parks and forest edges. **ID** Small, with large head and typically cocked tail. Crown brown, giving 'capped' appearance, otherwise upperparts plain ash-brown with dark brown wings (some pale fringes to coverts and tertials), black or dark blackish-brown tail with prominent white basal patches, and uppertail-coverts blacker than tail in both sexes. ♂ has warm rusty-orange on very restricted area of chin and throat, bordered broadly at sides and below with grey, grading into off-white underparts with pale peach suffusion. Face plain, lores, malar and ear-coverts grey. Acquires ♀-like winter plumage. 1st-summer ♂ already resembles adult ♂. ♀ lacks red throat, being more uniform grey-buff below with small white throat patch. **BP** Bill quite broad-based, almost entirely black, deeper than Red-breasted Flycatcher; eyes prominent in plain face, irides dark brown; tarsi black. **SV** A rolling but hard fast, dry trilling or clicking *trrrt* or *trrrrr* (faster than Red-breasted), recalls quiet Mistle Thrush. Also a softer *tic* and hard *tzit*.

Blue-and-white Flycatcher *Cyanoptila cyanomelana*

L 16–17 cm; WT 20–26 g

SD *C. c. cyanomelana* is fairly common summer (May–Sep) visitor to main islands from Kyushu to Hokkaido, and fairly common migrant including through Nansei Shoto; accidental to Ogasawara and Iwo Is. Vagrant *C. c. intermedia* has reached Kyushu and N Nansei Shoto (Danjo Is). **HH** Lowlands to *c.* 1,200 m in forested mountains, generally in mature mixed broadleaf forest with dense undergrowth, often near streams, rivers or waterfalls; on migration also in parks. **ID** Adult ♂ has shining, deep-blue upperparts from crown to tail, including wing-coverts, with blue outer fringes to tertials, secondaries and primary bases; forehead may appear silvery blue. Face, throat, breast and sides black, belly, vent and sides to tail base pure white. 1st-winter/1st-year ♂ resembles ♀, but has blue wings, rump and tail. ♀ is plain, generally warm, pale to mid-brown above, rather rufous on rump and tail, with rufous-brown fringes to tertials and inner flight-feathers, and very plain face; olive-grey on neck and breast, and off-white belly and vent. ♂ *C. c. intermedia* has turquoise or azure-blue crown and upperparts (cobalt-blue in *C. c. cyanomelana*) with tinge of green, and deep greenish-blue or aquamarine face to breast and flanks (instead of black), throat has greenish gloss; neck and mantle lack purple tinge of *C. c. cyanomelana*, flanks pale grey, and has white centre to tail base (rather than sides). ♀ *intermedia* closely resembles ♀ *cyanomelana* but is generally darker or more rufous-brown with less white on throat. **BP** Bill black; eyes large, appearing particularly so in plain face of ♀/juv, irides black; tarsi black. **SV** A strong *tchuck* or *chik chuk*. A persistent songster, typically from high perch, giving a varied, short fluty warble with a slightly cracked and melancholic tone: *hi-hwi-pipipipi tsi tsi tsi* or *piii hii hii piii chuichui*, ending with a soft *jitt jitt*, or *hii-rii-rii-chichin*. ♀ occasionally gives short version of ♂'s song.

Verditer Flycatcher *Eumyias thalassinus*

L 15–17 cm; WT 15–20 g

SD Vagrant to Ishigakijima, S Nansei Shoto and Kagoshima Prefecture, Kyushu (subspecies uncertain, but most likely *E. t. thalassinus*). **HH** Mixed woodland. **ID** Large, rather plain turquoise flycatcher, with longish tail and upright stance. ♂ entirely greenish-blue except black lores, black ventral streaking and black wings and tail (heavily fringed turquoise). ♀ similar to ♂ but has dusky-grey lores. Juvenile is duller, grey-brown with turquoise wash, and buff and black spotting/scaling. **BP** Bill blackish-grey; eyes large, irides black; tarsi black. **SV** Short, plaintive *pseeut* and longer, drier *tze-ju-jui*.

Red-breasted Flycatcher
ad ♂
ad ♀
Taiga Flycatcher
ad ♂
ad ♀
Blue-and-white Flycatcher
ad ♀ cyanomelana
ad ♂ cyanomelana
ad ♀ intermedia
ad ♂ intermedia
Verditer Flycatcher
ad ♂
ad ♀

European Robin *Erithacus rubecula* L 14 cm; WT 14–25 g

SD Vagrants (subspecies uncertain) have reached Hokkaido, C Honshu, Tobishima and Hegurajima. **HH** Shady woodlands, parks and gardens, where forages on ground. **ID** Upright stance and rather plump appearance resemble Japanese Robin, but darker earth-brown from crown to tail, and face and breast orange-red bordered with grey; belly off-white. **BP** Bill fine, sharply pointed, blackish-brown; eyes large, irides black; tarsi blackish-pink. **SV** Call a sharp *tic*, often repeated in excited rapid-fire series, *tic-tic-tic-tit*, even *tic tic tikerititit*. In alarm a high-pitched thin *tsiih*.

Japanese Robin *Larvivora akahige* L 14–15 cm; WT 20–25 g

SD Summer visitor (Apr–Oct): breeds from Kyushu to Hokkaido, with small numbers reaching Nansei Shoto on migration. **HH** Mature montane (600–2,500 m) broadleaf (deciduous and evergreen) forest, also with fir and spruce, often in shadier areas, where difficult to see. Perky and upright, foraging on ground. **ID** ♂ upperparts warm rufous-brown, but lores, face, neck and breast bright reddish- or orange-brown, and tail bright rufous-brown. Grey of underparts darkest where meets orange of breast, and may appear as blackish border. Paler grey on belly becoming yellowish-white in centre and on vent. ♀ less bright, with less contrasting breast markings and lacks black border to orange breast. **BP** Bill black; eyes black; tarsi yellowish-pink. **SV** A hard, tacking *tun tun* or *tsu*, or high-pitched straight *hiii* and thin metallic *tsip*. Song a loud, distinctive and quite far-carrying drawn-out trill, commencing with a single high note followed by a somewhat rattling trill: *peen-karakarararara*. Repetitions occur at different pitches in series: *tyurrrrrr.... pyorrrrrrr... tyurrrrrr* etc. **TN** Formerly in genus *Luscinia*.

Izu Robin *Larvivora tanensis* L 14–15 cm; WT 20–25 g

SD Resident on Izu Is. **HH** Mature lowland broadleaf (deciduous and evergreen) forest. **ID** ♂ as Japanese Robin but lacks black border to orange breast, and has paler grey belly and flanks. **BP** Bill black with yellowish base; eyes black; tarsi yellowish-pink. **SV** Slightly slower trills and notes are harder than previous species. **TN** As yet retained with preceding species by OSJ.

Ryukyu Robin *Larvivora komadori* L 14–15 cm; WT 23–27 g

SD Endemic to Nansei Shoto, breeding on islands off SW Kyushu and Tokara Is and Amami Oshima to Tokunoshima in N Nansei Shoto, and wintering in Yaeyama Is of S Nansei Shoto; has strayed north to Goto Is. **HH** Understorey of shady evergreen forest, often in gullies or near streams, below 600 m. Forages on ground; often at forest edge or on tracks in early morning. **ID** Perky, black-breasted orange robin. ♂ has bright orange-rufous upperparts (including wings), black forehead, face and chest, and white or greyish-white from belly to vent, with blackish flank patches. ♀ often has some black spotting on breast. **BP** Bill black; eyes black; long tarsi yellowish-brown. **SV** A high-pitched, rising whine *swiiii* or *hii-hii*, hard warning *gu gu*, and *kirrick* alarm-note accompanied by tail-flicking and wing-quivering. Song a series of melodious yodelling whistles, changing in pitch with each repetition, typically given around dawn: *pyolololo.... trelulululu.... tyulululululu....* tending to stop after three repetitions, then starts again; similar to Japanese Robin, but more musical. **TN** As yet retained with following species by IOC.

Okinawa Robin *Larvivora namiyei* L 14–15 cm; WT 23–27 g

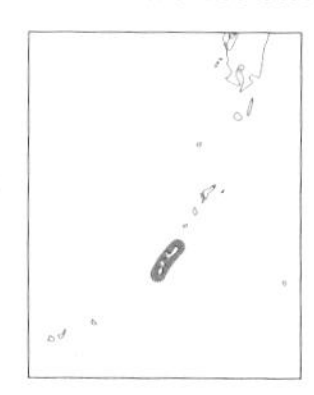

SD Endemic to Nansei Shoto, resident on Okinawa Is. **HH** As northern Ryukyu Robin. **ID** Okinawan Robin differs from Ryukyu Robin in having rufous-orange forehead and more uniform dark grey belly and flanks. ♀ very similar to Ryukyu Robin, but is pale greyish-buff on breast and grey-white below. **BP** Bill black; eyes black; long tarsi yellowish-brown. **SV** Very similar to Ryukyu Robin.

European Robin
ad
Japanese Robin
ad ♂
ad ♀
Izu Robin
ad
Ryukyu Robin
ad ♂
ad ♀
Okinawa Robin
ad ♂

Siberian Blue Robin *Larvivora cyane* L 13–14 cm; WT 11–18 g

SD *L. c. nechaevi* is summer visitor (Apr–Sep) to Shikoku, C & N Honshu and Hokkaido, and migrant or accidental visitor south to Nansei Shoto. **HH** Mixed taiga forest, forest edge or clearings; often around gullies and streams or fallen trees. Generally skulking, close to forest floor, often in dwarf bamboo or dense cover. On migration and in winter in scrub and forest. Stance rather horizontal, ducks its head and pumps tail. **ID** ♂ upperparts uniform deep blue, wings and tail somewhat blue-black, with bright white underparts. Lores and line from bill base to breast-sides jet black. Young ♂ browner on face and wings (lacking black), but has variable blue on rump, uppertail-coverts and tail. ♀ very pale to mid olive-brown with very plain face, but often has dull, dark blue uppertail-coverts/tail base, with few distinguishing marks except tarsi. Some lack dark blue uppertail-coverts and have slight scaling on chest, recalling Swinhoe's Robin, but stance of latter usually erect. **BP** Bill black, sometimes showing pink gape; eyes appear large (especially ♀), irides black, with very narrow white eye-ring; long tarsi very pallid pink. **SV** A thin *chip chip*, a se-*ic*, low *chuck-chuck-chuck* and, in alarm, hard *tak tak* or *dack*. Song similar to Japanese Robin's but more varied, and starts with series of hard call-like notes: *zit zit zit* or *chitt chitt chitt* followed by rapid, explosive trilling rattle *lololololo* or *hichohichohicho chochocho*, or *tsutsutsutsu hin-kararara*. **TN** Formerly in genus *Luscinia*.

Swinhoe's Robin *Larvivora sibilans* L 13–14 cm

SD Very rare spring migrant through Japan from Nansei Shoto to W Hokkaido. **HH** Damp well-wooded or forested areas (deciduous and coniferous), typically in dense undergrowth, often in gullies or near streams, to 1,200 m. Commonly skulks in dense vegetation. Stance rather erect; shivers tail and rear body. **ID** Rather plain brown upperparts, with bright rufous uppertail-coverts and tail (resembling Japanese Robin, but deeper, less bright). Pale supraloral and eye-ring. Underparts greyish-white with greyish-brown scaling on throat-sides, chest and flanks, where brownest. **BP** Bill black; eyes appear large in rather plain face, irides black; long tarsi reddish-pink. **SV** A low *tuc-tuc*. Song (heard from spring migrants) a strong, erratic rattling trill, more drawn-out than Japanese Robin, varied trilling phrases with falling intonation: *shu-rururuṙu, hin-rururun, hyururururuṙu, hichochochocho*. Similar to Siberian Blue Robin, but less powerful. **AN** Rufous-tailed Robin. **TN** Formerly in genus *Luscinia*.

Red-flanked Bluetail *Tarsiger cyanurus* L 13–15 cm; WT 10–18 g

SD Fairly common migrant; common summer visitor (Apr–Sep) to Hokkaido and to upper elevations in C and N Honshu, scarce in Shikoku and Kyushu. Winters from C Honshu to Kyushu and Nansei Shoto. **HH** Subalpine evergreen or mixed forests at lower latitudes, sometimes to sea level, and typically in lowland taiga at higher latitudes. In winter, various woodland types, even suburban parks. Quite confiding, often sings from obvious perch at mid-levels. Forages on ground. Restless, often flicks tail and wings. **ID** Plump and rather large-headed. ♂ unmistakably blue, orange and white. Blue extends onto face, throat- and breast-sides. Supraloral spot extends over eye as narrow supercilia, variable but often silvery-white. Underparts largely clean white, with narrow white throat and distinctive large orange-red flank patches. ♀ appears 'open-faced' with very prominent eye in pale eye-ring, and distinctive narrow white throat; upperparts olive-brown, greyer on rump and blue-grey on tail. Immature ♂ (also defends territory) much like ♀, but has brighter orange flanks, bluer tail and often some blue in wings. Juvenile heavily spotted pale brown, but also has blue tail. **BP** Bill black; eyes, especially of ♀, appear large, irides black; long tarsi black. **SV** Calls frequently, a soft *tuc tuc-tuc* or *heet katt-katt* (first note high-pitched, latter two hard). Song rapid, cheerful: *hichuri churiririchurochii* or *hyoro-hyurururip*.

White-tailed Robin *Myiomela leucura* L 17–19 cm; WT 24–30 g

SD Vagrant to offshore Kyushu (Danjo Is) (subspecies uncertain). **HH** Shady forest and bamboo. **ID** Large blue-black robin recalling Blue-and-white Flycatcher. ♂ generally black, with shining blue forehead, scapulars and wing-coverts, and outer fringes to flight-feathers. Black tail is long, round-tipped, with prominent white 'lozenges' at base of lateral (but not outermost) feathers, revealed as tail is fanned or flicked, and in flight. ♀ mostly dark olive- to earth-brown, with diffuse white throat and similar tail pattern to ♂. **BP** Bill dark grey; eyes black; tarsi black. **SV** A hard *chut*, low *tuc-tuc-tuc* and a high-pitched, straight whistled *sweet*. **TN** Not included by OSJ.

Siberian Blue Robin
ad ♀
ad ♂
juv
Swinhoe's Robin
ad
Red-flanked Bluetail
ad ♂
ad ♀
White-tailed Robin
ad ♂
ad ♀

PLATE 161: SHORTWING, BLUETHROAT AND RUBYTHROAT

White-browed Shortwing *Brachypteryx montana* — L 12–13 cm; WT 28 g

SD Vagrant (Hegura-jima) likely *B. m. sinensis*. **HH** Secretive in dense, shady forest. **ID** ♂ overall dark, slaty blue-grey, with prominent, short white supercilia, narrowly white-fringed carpal, and paler blue-grey underparts, with central belly and vent being almost white. ♀ dull brown above with rufous-brown wings and tail; face plain dull brown, lacks ♂'s supercilia, but has pale eye-ring; underparts, pale brown on face, throat, breast and flanks, whiter on central belly. **BP** Bill fine, black; eyes black; tarsi blackish-brown. **SV** A hard *tack* and rattled *tt-tt-tt* in alarm accompanied by wing-flicking. Song a series of single silvery notes quickening to plaintive, formless babbling before terminating abruptly. **AN** Blue Shortwing. **TN** Not included by OSJ.

Bluethroat *Luscinia svecica* — L 13–15 cm; WT 12–25 g

SD Very scarce migrant or winter visitor with records from Hokkaido, N, C & W Honshu, Shikoku, Kyushu to Nansei Shoto and even Ogasawara Is (subspecies uncertain, but possibly nominate *L. s. svecica* – **Red-spotted** or **Arctic Bluethroat** – but *L. s. przevalskii* winters close to Japan in E China). **HH** Rather secretive and skulking on migration and in winter, when favours scrub and grassy areas near water. **ID** Face, chest and tail pattern distinctive. Adult ♂ in breeding plumage has prominent white supercilia, blue chin and throat, with central red spot, and unmistakable chest pattern – banded orange, blue, black, white and orange. Upperparts plain olive-brown, with some dark streaking on mantle. Underparts creamy white with buff flanks. Immature and winter adult ♂ have more washed-out face and chest, and have blue restricted to lower throat/upper breast. ♀ lacks blue and orange of chest, instead has white supercilia and throat, contrasting with black malar and chest band of black streaks. Tail of both sexes short, but distinctive, even in brief flight views: brown centre and black tip with bright rufous patches at sides of base. Stance rather upright, when droops wings and cocks tail. Subspecies indistinguishable in winter. **BP** Bill fine, black; eyes black; long tarsi black. **SV** A hard dry *tatt* or *chack*, subdued *turrc* and *shtik-shtik*, also sharp *trac*, and whistled *heett* or *hueet* (rather *Phylloscopus*-like) when surprised, a hoarse *bzrew* and in winter *skwink*.

Siberian Rubythroat *Calliope calliope* — L 14–16 cm; WT 16–29 g

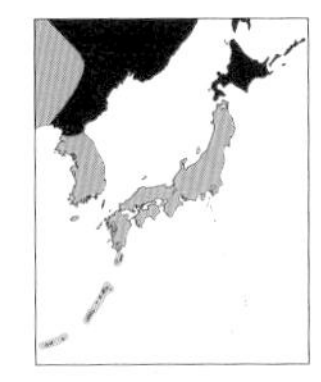

SD *C. c. camtschatkensis* is widespread, but declining, summer visitor (May–Aug) in Hokkaido; migrant through Honshu, Shikoku and Kyushu, some wintering in Nansei Shoto; accidental to Ogasawara and Iwo Is. **HH** Conspicuous on breeding grounds; scarce and rather secretive on migration and in winter. Favours treeline/alpine zone in mountains, or lowland boreal habitats with bushes. In winter skulks in grassy areas with bushes and near wetlands with reeds. **ID** Face pattern distinctive and ♂ simply stunning. Upperparts largely plain mid olive-brown, with paler brown chest (greyer with wear), greyish-brown on flanks and whitish on belly and vent. ♂ unmistakable; short, clear white supercilia separated from broad white malar by bold black lores, with black lateral throat-stripe and blackish-grey face, but outstanding feature is brilliant metallic ruby chin/throat, which pulsates when singing. Young ♂ less boldly marked. ♀ has less boldly marked face, and white chin/throat, though some have pale pink wash to chin. When flushed, appears chunky, short-tailed and plain brown. **BP** Bill fine, black; eyes black; long tarsi yellowish-pink. **SV** A deep, gruff, muffled *vehp* or *jütt*, and Fieldfare-like *schak* in alarm, or a combined *huitt-tak-tak* (recalling Red-flanked Bluetail). ♂ gives whistled *cue-ee*, *ti-lui* or *feeyoou(eet)* on territory, on migration and in winter. Song sweet, complex, penetrating but slightly melancholic warbling, mixing clear whistles and harsh notes: *kyoro-kiri hyogori kii-kyorochirii*; and *choichoi chorori chuichui chiichirichiri*.

White-browed Shortwing
ad ♂
ad ♀
Bluethroat
ad ♂
ad ♀
1st-win ♀
ad ♂
1st-win ♂
Siberian Rubythroat
ad ♂
ad ♂
ad ♀ showing red throat
typical ad ♀

Eversmann's Redstart *Phoenicurus erythronotus* L 15–16 cm; WT 15–22 g

SD Vagrant to Hokkaido (Rishirito). **HH** Dry scrubby areas; behaves like flycatcher, flicking tail and wings. **ID** ♂ has grey crown and nape, and rufous-orange throat, chest and mantle. Mask, wings and centre of tail black; has white panel across wings and rufous orange sides to tail. ♀ is very much plainer, pale ashy-brown with two buff wingbars and buff tertial edges. **BP** Bill fine, black; eyes black, those of ♀ especially prominent in plain face; tarsi black. **SV** Call is a soft croaking *gre-er*.

Eastern Black Redstart *Phoenicurus (ochruros) rufiventris* L 14–15 cm; WT 12–20 g

SD Accidental visitor with records from Hokkaido, C & W Honshu, various islands in Sea of Japan and south to Yonagunijima. **HH** Sparse vegetation in open, rocky areas. **ID** ♂ sooty-black, blackest on face and chest, greyer on mantle with brown cast to wings; grey on forehead (white in ♂ Common Redstart). Underparts and tail bright brick-orange. Tail especially distinctive, with orange rump and sides to black-centred tail. ♀ much plainer, warm mid-brown above and paler below, especially on chin, where nearly white, very similar to Daurian Redstart, but both sexes lack white wing patches; darker overall than Common. Rump and tail resemble ♂ but less bright. **BP** Bill fine, black; eye of ♀ especially prominent in plain face, irides black; long tarsi black. **SV** A sharp *tsip*, harder *tuc* and combination of hard tacking and thin, almost whistled, notes: *gatt hee* or *gap gap hee*. **TN** Retained within Black Redstart *P. ochruros* by IOC.

Common Redstart *Phoenicurus phoenicurus* L 14–15 cm; WT 11–23 g

SD Vagrant *P. p. phoenicurus* has reached Hegurajima. **HH** Open woodland, parks and gardens. **ID** ♂ bright; black, grey and orange. Upperparts range from white on forehead to mid ash-grey on crown, nape, mantle and back; rump, uppertail-coverts and tail-sides bright rusty-red, tail itself blackish-brown. Face, from above bill to ear-coverts, chin and throat sooty-black; breast brick-orange, becoming white on belly, flanks and vent. Wings plain, lack white. ♀ plainer, with mid-brown face, head and upperparts; rump and tail bright rusty-red; off-white throat, breast and belly washed dull orange-brown (closely resembles ♀ Black Redstart, but paler). **BP** Bill fine, black; eyes dark brown; tarsi dark brown. **SV** A strong, liquid, somewhat Willow Warbler-like, plaintive *hueet* commonly repeated, or in combination as *hueet-hueet hueet-tick*, and harder, scolding *tchak*.

Daurian Redstart *Phoenicurus auroreus* L 14–15 cm; WT 11–20 g

SD *P. a. auroreus* is fairly common winter visitor (Nov–Apr) throughout Japan south of Hokkaido; scarce migrant Hokkaido; has bred in Hokkaido and Honshu; accidental to Ogasawara and Iwo Is. **HH** Open hillsides, open forest with rocky areas; in winter at woodland edges, agricultural margins, in parks and large gardens. **ID** Adult ♂ largely black and orange, with silver-grey forehead and crown-sides, grey crown and nape, jet-black face and chin. Mantle and wings largely black, but has prominent white patch on secondaries and tertials; lower back, rump and tail-sides orange, central rectrices black. Immature ♂ resembles adult, but less cleanly marked. ♀ largely brown and orange, much plainer, warm mid-brown above, paler below with conspicuous white wing patch and orange rump and tail-sides. **BP** Bill fine, black; eye of ♀ especially prominent on plain face, irides black; long tarsi black. **SV** Call combines high sharp notes with harder notes; typically gives strong double *hit wheet*, *heett katt* or *tuc tuc peet* similar to Red-flanked Bluetail, but straighter and louder.

Blue-fronted Redstart *Phoenicurus frontalis* L 15–16 cm; WT 12–19 g

SD Vagrant to Yamagata and southern Nansei Shoto. **HH** Scrub and bushes. **ID** ♂ has blue head, throat and upperparts; underparts chestnut-orange. Tail centre and tip black, but rump and tail sides bright orange. ♀ has ashy-brown head, breast and upperparts, and orange wash to belly. Tail pattern as in ♂, but less bright. **BP** Bill fine, black; eyes black; long tarsi black. **SV** Calls include clicking *tik* and a thin *ee-tit*, *ee-tit-tit*. **TN** Not included by OSJ.

Eversmann's Redstart
♂ fresh
(autumn)
ad ♀
♂ worn
(summer)
Eastern Black Redstart
ad ♂
ad ♀
Common Redstart
ad ♂
ad ♀
1st-win
♂
ad ♂
Blue-fronted Redstart
ad ♂
ad ♂
ad ♀
ad ♂
ad ♀
1st-win ♂
Daurian Redstart

Common Rock Thrush *Monticola saxatilis* L 16–19 cm; WT 40–65 g

SD Vagrant to Iriomote-jima, Yaeyama Is. **HH** Forested montane slopes. **ID** ♂ has greyish-blue head, neck, mantle and back, with white across middle of back; wings dark blackish-brown with grey fringes/tips to most feathers, tail blackish-brown with redstart-like orange-red uppertail-coverts and fringes to outer tail-feathers. Chin/throat and face grey-blue, sharply delineated from warm rusty-orange of entire underparts. ♀ duller greyish-brown, but shares tail pattern; upperparts grey-brown with buff spotting and scaling, underparts grey-brown on face, buff-brown below, with orange wash to chest and dark scalloping over much of rest. Reddish tail distinguishes ♀ from ♀ Eastern Blue Rock Thrush. **BP** Bill fine, sharply pointed, quite long, grey/horn; eyes dark brown; tarsi black. **SV** Varied including a hard *chack-chack*, shrike-like *ks-chrrr*, whistled *feweet* and thin *he-he hee*. **AN** White-backed Rock Thrush. **TN** Not included by OSJ.

Eastern Blue Rock Thrush *Monticola philippensis* L 20–26 cm; WT 75 g

SD Summer visitor to Hokkaido, but resident around coasts of much of Japan from N Honshu south to Nansei Shoto. **HH** Locally common on rocky coasts, especially where there are cliffs and crags, but also around harbours and in coastal towns, where often perches prominently. **ID** ♂ has deep-blue hood, upperparts, rump and thighs, blackish-brown wings with blue outer fringes, blue-grey tail and deep chestnut underparts. Immature resembles adult, but has narrow scaling over blue and chestnut areas. ♀ is drabber, grey-brown with blue-grey cast to upperparts; underparts are spotted/scaled pale grey-brown on face, throat and upper breast, and barred on lower chest, belly and vent. **BP** Bill strong, rather long, black; eyes black; tarsi black. **SV** Varied, but unremarkable range of harsh calls: *tak-tak*, *ka-tchuc-tchuc*, *hee* or *chin*. Song (both sexes), given from perch or in flight, comprises sweeter, melodious whistled notes in short series of varied phrases: *hee choicho peechiyo, hiyochee pee pipipi chuu* or *tju-sri tjurr-titi wuchi-trr-trrt-tri*, and includes mimicry of other passerines. **TN** Included within *M. solitarius* by IOC.

Western Blue Rock Thrush *Monticola solitarius* L 21–23 cm; WT 37–70 g

SD *M. s. pandoo* is very rare visitor to offshore Japan from Nansei Shoto and Ogasawara Is north to N Honshu. **HH** Rocky areas. **ID** ♂ like Eastern Blue Rock Thrush (EBRT), but smaller and almost entirely blue (some may have restricted chestnut on vent); ♀ and immature probably indistinguishable. **BP** As EBRT. **SV** Varied but unremarkable range of harsh calls: *tak-tak*, *ka-tchuc-tchuc*, *hee* or *chin*.

White-throated Rock Thrush *Monticola gularis* L 15–19 cm; WT 32–37 g

SD Very rare overshoot migrant to Japan, mostly in spring, with records from Nansei Shoto north to Teuri I. **HH** Migrants appear on coasts and in coastal forests. **ID** ♂ is beautiful mix of cobalt-blue, black and orange; has shining deep-blue crown, shoulders and tail-sides, black mask, mantle and wings (last with conspicuous white patch), and orange lores, malar and neck-sides. Underparts from breast to vent, also back and rump, bright rufous-orange; white throat patch noticeable when face-on. ♀ generally plainer, cooler brown, but has black-centred, buff-fringed feathers on back giving barred or scaled appearance, and black-fringed pale buff feathers to chest and flanks; malar, rear ear-coverts and throat distinctly white. Very upright stance. **BP** Bill short, thick, black, faintly yellow at gape; eyes large, irides black; tarsi pinkish-brown. **SV** A soft *tsip* or *tseep* in flight, and harsh *chak* or *tack-tack*; song comprises various beautiful drawn-out rising whistles *swee wee lalee lu lu lu*. **AN** White-breasted Rock Thrush.

Common Rock Thrush
ad ♂ sum
ad ♂ sum
1st-year ♂
ad ♀ sum
ad ♂ sum
Eastern Blue
Rock Thrush
ad ♂
ad ♂
Western Blue
Rock Thrush
ad ♂
ad ♀
White-throated Rock Thrush
ad ♂ sum
ad ♀ sum
ad ♂ sum
1st-year ♂

Whinchat *Saxicola rubetra*

L 12–15 cm; WT 13–26 g

SD Vagrant, with records from Okinawa and Hegurajima. **HH** Open grassland habitats with bushes. **ID** Small brown chat with prominent supercilia. Upperparts dark brown with paler stripes on crown and fringes to feathers of mantle and back, rump buffy-orange heavily streaked with black, tail dark blackish-brown with distinct white flashes at sides of base. Wings have narrow white patch on scapulars and square white patch on greater coverts. ♂ has contrasting face, with long pale supercilia from lores to rear of ear-coverts and dark blackish-brown ear-coverts. Chin/throat white, but has strong orange wash from chin to lower breast, rest of underparts white. Non-breeding ♂ and ♀, duller, with weaker face pattern, differing from ♀ Stejneger's Stonechat in having darker ear-coverts, pale supercilia, more defined eyestripe and more distinct malar. **BP** Bill fine, sharply pointed, grey/horn; eyes dark brown; long tarsi pink. **SV** Call combines short whistled *phew* and hard clicking: *phew-tak phew-tak-tak*....

Stejneger's Stonechat *Saxicola stejnegeri*

L 12–13 cm; WT 13–17 g

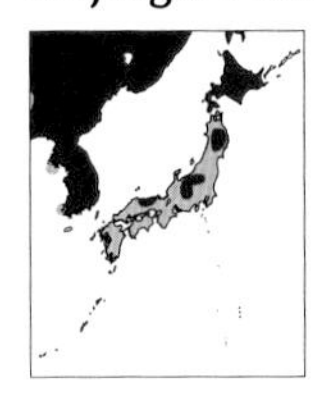

SD Common summer visitor (Apr–Aug) to C & N Honshu and Hokkaido, uncommon migrant elsewhere south to Nansei Shoto. **HH** Favours dry grasslands with bushes, damp meadows and agricultural land, in lowlands and hills. Perches prominently on bushes and grass stems. **ID** ♂ has strongly contrasting pattern of largely black and white with some orange; black hood, upperparts and tail, with bold, broad white neck and scapular patches and large clear white uppertail-coverts/rump patch; underparts clean white with small, bright orange upper-chest patch. Winter ♂ resembles ♀, but retains only ghost of black hood, particularly on face. ♀ rather drab plain sandy orange-brown, with grey-brown head, mantle and wings, more orange-brown on underparts with plain orange-buff rump, tail blackish; white scapular patch less prominent than in ♂. In flight, short black tail, white (or pale) rump patch and bold white scapular patches unmistakable. **BP** Bill fine, short, black; eyes black; tarsi black. **SV** Call a hard, stony, *ja ja*, *jat* or *hit*, like pebbles being knocked together, given in combination with sharp whistle: *wist jat-jat*. Song a clear, but rather thin, weak and rather formless chattering: *hii-hyoro-hiri-hii* or *hiichu hichii chii pii chochii*. **TN** Formerly within Siberian Stonechat *S. maurus*, but included within Common Stonechat *S. torquatus* by others.

Pied Bush Chat *Saxicola caprata*

L 13–14 cm; WT 14–26 g

SD Accidental in winter and spring to S Japan, most records from Nansei Shoto, but recorded north to Awashima; subspecies uncertain. **HH** Occurs in agricultural land, damp meadows and grassland, often near water. **ID** ♂ almost entirely glossy black, with white only on wing-coverts, rump, lower belly and vent; 1st-winter ♂ less black, feathers narrowly fringed buff. ♀ plain, mid- to dark brown above, more rufous sandy-brown below, with rusty, rufous-orange rump. **BP** Bill fine, black; eyes dark brown; tarsi black. **SV** A plaintive *hweet* and hard, insistent *chek-chek*.

Grey Bush Chat *Saxicola ferreus*

L 14–15 cm; WT 14–16 g

SD Accidental to Nansei Shoto, Kyushu and Sea of Japan islands north to Tobishima. **HH** Dry, open areas with scrub, also agricultural land. **ID** Small pale chat; recalls Stejneger's Stonechat in structure, but longer-tailed. ♂ grey, with prominent white supercilia, white chin and throat contrasting with black mask; upperparts mid-grey streaked blacker, white bar on lesser coverts (partly obscured at rest but conspicuous in flight), pale grey rump and outer tail-feathers, with black central rectrices, and underparts plain mid-grey. ♀ warm orange-brown, with white chin/throat, orange-buff supercilia contrast slightly with darker brown crown and ear-coverts, mantle orange-brown streaked black, rump and outer tail-feathers plain orange-brown, central tail black, and wings blackish-brown with orange-brown outer fringes to flight-feathers but no white wing patch. Underparts dull orange-brown, whiter on belly. **BP** Bill fine, black; eyes black; tarsi dark-grey. **SV** A soft *zizz*, insect-like *jijijijijit* and harder *jahi jahi* and *tak-tak-tak* notes.

Whinchat
ad ♂ worn
1st-win
Stejneger's Stonechat
ad ♂
ad ♀
1st-win
Pied Bush Chat
ad ♂
ad ♀
Grey Bush Chat
ad ♂
ad ♀

Isabelline Wheatear *Oenanthe isabellina*

L 16–17 cm; WT 22–38 g

SD Accidental migrant, with records from Nansei Shoto north to Hokkaido. **HH** Dry open areas and agricultural land. **ID** Large, upright, sandy, grey-brown or sandy-brown and buff wheatear lacking contrast between head, mantle and wings; head and bill rather large, tail rather short. Face plain, relieved by buff supercilia. Black lores and alula diagnostic, in combination with dark-centred median coverts always paler than alula (unlike Northern Wheatear). Adult ♂ generally has blacker lores than ♀ or 1st-winter ♂, but otherwise similar. Rump, uppertail-coverts and basal half of outer tail white, rest of tail blackish-brown; tail is shorter than Desert Wheatear, with more extensive white at base and sides. **BP** Black bill appears rather large; eyes black; long tarsi black. **SV** A hard *chack* or *chek-chek*, and whistled *wiiu*.

Northern Wheatear *Oenanthe oenanthe*

L 14–17 cm; WT 18–33 g

SD *O. o. oenanthe* is an accidental visitor, with records from Nansei Shoto to Hokkaido, and even Ogasawara and Iwo Is. **HH** Dry, open grassy areas and agricultural land with short vegetation. **ID** Pale grey or grey-brown with short tail, long legs, strongly contrasting plumage and much white in tail. Very upright, bobs and flicks wings frequently. ♂: has pale ash-grey or blue-grey upperparts with narrow white forehead band; lores and ear-coverts black; rump, uppertail-coverts and two-thirds of basal part of outer tail-feathers white, central rectrices and band across tip black, wings also black. Underparts off-white with variable peach wash to throat and breast. In autumn, upperparts tinged brownish and black mask is narrower and slightly duller. ♀: browner overall, lacks mask, instead has pale supercilia above dark eyestripe, wings strongly contrast with back, tail pattern as ♂ but duller (larger Isabelline Wheatear is similar, but lacks contrast between wings and body). Juvenile: more richly coloured, with russet-brown upperparts and greater/median coverts, and rich, warm, orange-buff wash over much of underparts (Isabelline very similar, but not as richly coloured, lacks contrast between wings and body). **BP** Bill black; eyes black; tarsi black. **SV** Sharp whistles, *wheeet*, and hard *tchak tchak* notes.

Pied Wheatear *Oenanthe pleschanka*

L 14–16 cm; WT 16–22 g

SD Accidental, with records from Tsushima, C & N Honshu and Sea of Japan islands from Mishima to Rishiri. **HH** Dry, open habitats, including cultivated areas. **ID** ♂ breeding boldly patterned black, grey and white. Crown and nape grey-white, mantle and upper back black, lower back, rump and most of tail-sides white (though outer feathers have black edges), central rectrices and narrow band across tail tip black. Black face, chin and throat are connected to black upperparts, creamy white breast, belly and vent, with buff wash to breast-sides. Winter ♂ retains black face and throat, but upperparts brown, wings blackish-brown with buff fringes to feathers. ♀ drabber, brown and white; upperparts and breast pale to mid-brown, wing-coverts and flight-feathers blackish, contrasting with paler upperparts; has faint pale supercilia, clean white rump, tail pattern like ♂ and white belly. 1st-winter (♂♀): pale fringes to feathers of mantle, back and scapulars, while ♂ has faintly indicated dusky throat patch. **BP** Bill fine, sharply pointed, black; eyes black; long tarsi black. **SV** Harsh *tschak*, nasal *chep* and buzzy *brsche*.

Desert Wheatear *Oenanthe deserti*

L 14–15 cm; WT 15–34 g

SD *O. d. oreophila* is accidental visitor with records from Nansei Shoto to N Honshu, and has even reached Ogasawara Is. **HH** Dry agricultural land. **ID** Pale sandy-brown with considerable contrast between pale body and black wings and tail; tail all black, contrasting with white or buff tail base and rump. Upperparts pale sandy-brown. Underparts off-white with buff wash strongest on breast. ♂ has black face, chin/throat and neck-sides. Winter ♂ has black face/bib scaled orange-buff (white in 1st-winter) and wing-feathers broadly fringed orange-buff. ♀ paler and greyer-brown overall, with pale lesser wing-coverts, rufous-tinged cheeks, lacks black bib, and has brownish-black tail and wings; wing-coverts and tertials have black centres. Winter ♀ has paler wings; all feathers more extensively fringed orange-buff, alula black but does not contrast with rest of wing (see Isabelline Wheatear). **BP** Bill black; eyes dark brown; tarsi black. **SV** A whistled *swii*, hard clicking *tsak* and muffled, rattled *tk-tk-tk*.

Northern Wheatear
ad ♂
ad ♂
ad ♂
ad ♀
ad ♀
Isabelline
Wheatear
ad ♂
ad ♀
1st-win
Pied Wheatear
ad ♂
ad ♀
♂ 1st-win
ad ♂
♀ 1st-win
ad ♂
(worn)
Desert Wheatear
ad ♂
ad ♂
fresh
aut/win
ad ♀
(worn)
ad ♀
fresh
aut/win

Taiwan Niltava *Niltava (vivida) vivida* L 18–19 cm; WT 17 g

SD Vagrant, Okinawa and Yonagunijima. **HH** Evergreen and mixed deciduous forest. **ID** Large, upright, large-headed flycatcher with high-peaked crown and long, round-tipped tail. ♂: shining deep-blue hood and upperparts, black or blue-black lores and face, and deep orange upper breast to vent; young ♂ has speckled brown head and dull grey-blue upperparts, wings and tail. ♀: superficially resembles ♀ Blue-and-white Flycatcher, but has greyer head with buffy-orange forehead, lores, face and throat; underparts plain grey; upperparts grey-brown, paler on rump, blackish-brown tail has rufous fringes to outer feathers, but rounded tip (square in Blue-and-white). **BP** Bill slightly hook-tipped, black with prominent rictal bristles; eyes appear large on plain face, irides dark brown; tarsi black. **SV** Call is clear whistled *yiyou-yiyou* and hard, penetrating *pit* with metallic ring. **TN** Retained within Vivid Niltava by IOC.

Brown Dipper *Cinclus pallasii* L 21–23 cm; WT 60–90 g

SD Widespread resident (*C. p. pallasii*), Yakushima to Hokkaido. **HH** Strongly territorial along fast-flowing montane streams and rivers (to *c.* 1,800 m); descends in winter to ice-free areas, including river mouths. **ID** Plump, uniformly dark, chocolate-brown, resembling large, dark wren. Bobs on waterside rocks, flicking tail upwards. Flight very fast, direct and low over water. **BP** Bill short, thrush-like, black; irides dark brown, but white nictitating membrane commonly flicked over eye; stout legs and large, oversized feet dark grey/ black. **SV** Repetitive, hard *dzzeet* or *cheet* or buzzing *zzit zzit* in flight; very loud song, extremely varied rich warbling, *chityiijoijoi*, including trills, rattles and buzzing notes; audible even above the sound of fast water. **AN** Pallas's Dipper.

House Sparrow *Passer domesticus* L 14–17 cm; WT 24–38 g

SD Accidental (*P. d. domesticus*), Hokkaido, Hegurajima, Mishima. **HH** Human habitation. **ID** Large, grey and brown sparrow, with large head. ♂: dull grey crown, black lores and extensive black bib, broad chestnut eyestripe and nape. ♀: cold, ashy grey-brown with pale supercilia (♀ Russet Sparrow is brighter and neater). **BP** Bill stout, blackish-grey (breeding ♂), yellowish (non-breeding ♂), or yellow below with grey culmen (♀ and juv); eyes black; tarsi pinkish-grey. **SV** Hard *chup*, similar to Eurasian Tree Sparrow.

Russet Sparrow *Passer rutilans* L 13–14 cm; WT 20 g

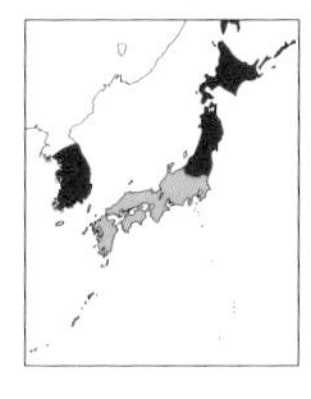

SD Summer visitor (Apr–Sep) (*P. r. rutilans*), C & N Honshu, Hokkaido; winter visitor (Oct–Mar) SW Honshu to Kyushu; scarce visitor south to Nansei Shoto. **HH** Breeds in mature forest, riparian woodland, also around rural villages; winters in agricultural areas, often in large flocks, only rarely mixing with Eurasian Tree Sparrow (ETS). **ID** Paler, neater, brighter than ETS. ♂: rich rufous-brown crown, nape, mantle and scapulars, streaked black on mantle; wings black with broad brown fringes to flight-feathers, white tips to coverts forming clear double wingbar; tail shorter than ETS. Chin and lores black, cheeks off-white; underparts off-white to grey. Winter ♂: less richly coloured, has pale patch on rear crown-sides. ♀: sandy-brown with prominent broad supercilia contrasting with dark forecrown and dark eyestripe; upperparts brown with black and cream stripes on chestnut mantle; underparts pale sandy-brown. Closed wing shows white median-coverts bar, pale fringes to greater coverts and pale panel at base of primaries. **BP** Bill more slender and pointed than ETS, greyish-black (summer ♂), with yellow/ horn base to lower mandible (winter ♂ and ♀); eyes dark brown; legs dull pink. **SV** Calls include hard *chup* and high *cheet*. Song: hurried *chee tsuri pyo piriri*. **AN** Cinnamon Sparrow.

Eurasian Tree Sparrow *Passer montanus* L 14–15 cm; WT 18–27 g

SD Common resident (*P. m. saturatus*) from Nansei Shoto to Hokkaido. **HH** Habitation, from dense urban areas to rural villages, in gardens, parks and agricultural land; may nest in loose colonies and commonly flocks in winter. **ID** Monomorphic; neatly marked, brown and white sparrow. Cap and nape chestnut; cheeks, throat and neck-sides white, with contrasting black lores, chin and cheek spot forming diagnostic head pattern, with complete off-white or grey neck-band. Upperparts warm brown with dark streaking on mantle; wings brown with white fringes to coverts forming two narrow wingbars, primaries and secondaries black, fringed warm brown; rump and tail grey-brown. Underparts off-white with buff-washed flanks. Young lack black chin and ear-coverts patch. **BP** Bill stubby, black in summer, yellow-horn at base of lower mandible in winter; eyes black; legs dull pink. **SV** Commonly gives an abrupt *chun chun*, also a cheery, nasal *twuweet*, and dry rattled *tett-ett-ett* in flight. Song is little more than a hurried series of calls.

Taiwan Niltava
ad ♀
ad ♂
Brown Dipper
ad
juv
House Sparrow
ad ♂
ad ♀
juv
Eurasian Tree Sparrow
ad ♀
ad ♂
ad
Russet Sparrow

Lesser Masked Weaver *Ploceus intermedius* L 13 cm; WT 17–27 g

SD Introduced and established in C Honshu (subspecies uncertain). **HH** Favours open woodland, agricultural land and parks. **ID** ♂ has black mask and forehead, with contrasting pale eyes; rear crown, neck and underparts bright yellow, upperparts yellow with black streaking on mantle and back, wings black with broad yellow fringes to coverts and flight-feathers; tail short, black with yellow fringes to feathers. ♀ (and non-breeding ♂) has yellowish olive-green upperparts from forehead to rump, with prominent yellow supercilia and pale eyes, mantle heavily streaked black, wings as ♂ but slightly duller, underparts dull yellow. **BP** Bill strong, long and conical, black; eyes pale yellow to white (♂), pale yellow (♀) or dark brown (juv); tarsi grey. **SV** Mixes liquid and nasal calls into accelerating series of notes for song.

Southern Red Bishop *Euplectes orix* L 13 cm; WT ♂ 21–30 g ♀ 17–26 g

SD A common cagebird; introduced or escapees (subspecies uncertain) establish local populations, sometimes viable in warmer regions of C Honshu. **HH** Grassland near water. **ID** A small, large-headed finch, with short wings and tail. Tail frequently flicked open. ♂ (breeding) has black forehead and cheeks, black belly, brown wings and tail, and otherwise bright orange plumage. ♀ (and non-breeding ♂) is plainer, mid-brown above with pale streaking, and pale sandy-buff below. **BP** Bill deep, stubby, black (breeding ♂) or pinkish with grey culmen (♀ and non-breeding ♂); eyes dark brown; tarsi dull pinkish-brown. **SV** Dry chipping *cheet-cheet* notes. Song a tuneless buzzing chirping.

Orange-cheeked Waxbill *Estrilda melpoda* L 9–10 cm; WT 6–10 g

SD Introduced and established in C Honshu (subspecies uncertain). **HH** Dry grassland and open waste ground. **ID** Small brown waxbill with red bill and orange cheeks. Crown and nape grey, mantle and wings warm chestnut, rump deep red, tail black. Underparts from chin to vent off-white. **BP** Bill deep-based, short, waxy red; eyes black; tarsi black. **SV** Sibilant twittering: *shirii shirii shi shi shii shii*.

Black-rumped Waxbill *Estrilda troglodytes* L 9–10 cm; WT 7–9 g

SD Introduced and established locally in C Honshu. **HH** Favours dry vegetation, grasslands and edges of riverine reedbeds and marshes. **ID** Pale, neat waxbill; rather pale plain brown above, with prominent black rump and tail; underparts very pale whitish-buff with broad red stripe through eye and variable pink wash or red stripe on centre of belly. **BP** Bill stout, bright pink (ad) or black (juv); eyes black; tarsi dark grey. **SV** Loud metallic *chip*; song includes both loud chipping and long upslurred *soyiiiii* notes.

Red Avadavat *Amandava amandava* L 9–11 cm; WT 10 g

SD Introduced and established locally in C & W Honshu, Shikoku and Kyushu Japan (subspecies uncertain). **HH** Dry grasslands, including reedbed fringes, scrub and agricultural fields, where moves in restless flocks. **ID** Small dark red (♂) or pale sandy-brown (♀) finch. ♂ has deep red forehead, crown, cheeks, rump and uppertail-coverts; wings and short tail are black, with small silver spots on wing-coverts, tips of tertials and outer tail-feathers; lores and around eye black; underparts orange-red from chin to belly, with white spots on breast-sides and flanks, vent black. ♀ upperparts dull grey-brown, but bright red on rump and uppertail-coverts; wings and tail like ♂ but fewer spots on coverts, face plain grey with black lores and around eyes, white chin and throat, buff flanks and belly, vent paler. Juvenile lacks red and has buff double wingbars. **BP** Bill sharply pointed, orange; eyes red; tarsi pink. **SV** Calls weak and thin, *teei* or *zsi*, in flight a short, soft *chick-chick*. Song comprises a series of call-like notes, but includes a motif like an un-oiled sign creaking in wind, and ends in a short trill.

Java Sparrow *Lonchura oryzivora* L 13–16 cm; WT 20–25 g

SD Vulnerable. Introduced and established locally in C & W Honshu and Kyushu. **HH** Urban and rural areas, in gardens, fields and woods. **ID** Stocky grey finch with massive bill and distinctive face pattern. Adult: black head with large white cheek patch, upper- and underparts largely grey, pinkish-grey on belly, white on vent and black on tail. Juvenile: dull greyish-brown above, greyish-buff below, with dusky-brown cap. **BP** Bill massive, blunt, red; eye-ring red, eyes black; tarsi pink. **SV** Hard *tup*, *t'luk* or *ch'luk* notes. Song: bell-like soft chattering notes accelerate into a trill interspersed with both higher and deeper notes, ending with a prolonged whistled *ti-tui*.

Lesser Masked Weaver
ad ♂
juv
ad ♀
Orange-cheeked Waxbill
ad
juv
Southern
Red Bishop
ad ♂ sum
Black-rumped
Waxbill
ad
juv
Red Avadavat
ad ♂
ad ♀
Java Sparrow
juv
ad

White-rumped Munia *Lonchura striata* L 10–11 cm

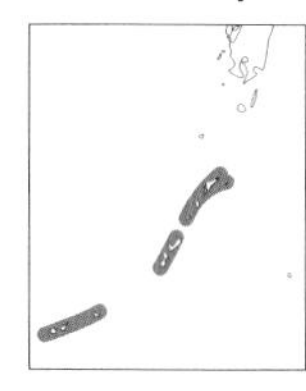

SD Uncommon resident in Okinawa, where perhaps a natural colonist (subspecies uncertain, but most likely *L. s. swinhoei*). **HH** Gardens, agricultural areas, scrub and forest edge, in small noisy flocks. Often occurs together with Scaly-breasted Munia. **ID** Small brown finch with white lower back and rather pointed tail. Dark, almost black upper breast and head impart hooded appearance. Mostly dark brown with fine, off-white; streaking on head, breast, mantle and back; lower back white, rump plain brown, pointed tail black. Wings dark blackish-brown with paler fringes to many feathers. Underparts off-white. **BP** Bill large, upper mandible blackish-grey, lower mandible pale blue-grey; eyes black; tarsi dark grey. **SV** Thin twittering *chee chee*, *peet peet* and high-pitched, rolling *prree* or *breeet* flight call.

Long-tailed Paradise Whydah *Vidua paradisaea* L ♂ 38 cm; WT 15–29 g

SD Introduced and established locally in C Honshu. **HH** Dry ricefields and other cultivation with associated grassland or reeds. **ID** ♂ has black face, cap and throat, black mantle, back and wings, and extremely elongated tapering tail; cheeks and breast golden-yellow to chestnut and rest of underparts yellowish-buff to off-white. ♀ and non-breeding ♂ are generally nondescript mid-brown with dark blackish-brown streaking on upperparts and breast, but with striking head pattern. Black crown with buff central crown-stripe, prominent white supercilia and black eyestripes extending as two black crescents, one behind eye, the other bordering ear-coverts. **BP** Bill short, deep-based, black; eyes black; tarsi pink. **SV** Combination of hard chipping, nasal, squeaking and chattering notes.

Scaly-breasted Munia *Lonchura punctulata* L 10–12 cm

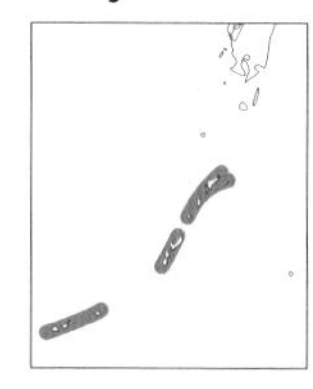

SD Resident (*L. p. topela*) occurs widely in Nansei Shoto from Yaeyama to Amami Is, either natural colonists or derived from cagebird trade. **HH** Dry grasslands, gardens, fields and scrub, in flocks, often with other species. **ID** Small, rather drab finch. Adult: largely mid-brown, becoming blackish-brown on chin, throat and tail. Underparts off-white with brown centres to most feathers affording distinctive scaled appearance; belly and vent off-white. Juvenile: plain brown above, pale buff below. **BP** Bill large, dark grey upper mandible with paler culmen, lower mandible pale grey; eyes black; tarsi dark grey. **SV** Plaintive, slightly nasal *weh weh* and a *pee yu*. **AN** Spotted Munia; Nutmeg Mannikin; Spice Finch.

Chestnut Munia *Lonchura atricapilla* L 10–12 cm

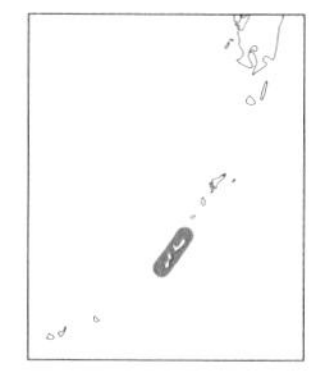

SD Introduced and established locally in Nansei Shoto, Kyushu, Shikoku, and W & C Honshu (subspecies uncertain). **HH** Scrub, grasslands and ricefields in single-species flocks, or mixed with Scaly-breasted Munia. **ID** Small finch with dark plumage and very large bill. Adult: hood black, as is central belly to vent. Rest of plumage plain dark chocolate-brown from neck to tail, wings, lower breast and flanks. Juvenile: paler brown, lacks black hood. **BP** Bill massive, pale blue-grey; eyes black; tarsi dark grey. **SV** Three-note *chirp chirp chirp* in flight, and high-pitched reedy *pwi-pwi*. Song comprises quiet musical notes interspersed with long whistles and bill-clicking.

White-headed Munia *Lonchura maja* L 10 cm

SD Introduced and established locally in Shikoku, and W & C Honshu. **HH** Frequents ricefields and reedbeds. **ID** Small chestnut-brown munia with a white head, bordered with buff on sides and back of neck. **BP** Bill massive at base, tapering to sharp point, blue-grey; black eyes appear large in white face; tarsi dark blue-grey. **SV** High-pitched piping *pee-eet*. Song a repetitive, tinkling *weeeeee heeheeheeheehee* interspersed with bill-clicking.

Tricoloured Munia *Lonchura malacca* L 11–12 cm

SD Introduced in C & W Honshu and Nansei Shoto. **HH** Damp fields with tall grasses or reeds. **ID** Adult: hood, upper breast, centre to belly and vent all black, contrasting with white lower breast and flanks. Juvenile: plain brown above, pale buff below. **BP** Bill large, grey; eyes black; tarsi dark grey. **SV** Calls include chirping and a nasal *tay*.

White-rumped Munia
ads
Long-tailed
Paradise Whydah
ad ♂ sum
ad ♂ win
Scaly-breasted
Munia
ad
juv
Chestnut Munia
juv
ad ♂
White-headed Munia
ad
juv
Tricoloured
Munia
ad
juv

Alpine Accentor *Prunella collaris*

L 15–19 cm; WT 33–45 g

SD Resident in high mountains of C & N Honshu, where *P. c. erythropygia* is short-distance altitudinal migrant; as an accidental it has reached north to Hokkaido and south to Kyushu. **HH** Generally above treeline (usually above 1,800 m), on rocky crags and alpine meadows in summer. Forages quietly and secretively on ground. Descends in winter, when favours rocky areas in forest; quietly confiding, moving methodically across snow-free banks, or near streams and damp areas. **ID** Grey and brown thrush-like bird, larger than other accentors, with distinctly grey-hooded appearance with fine silver spotting on chin, and white crescents above and below eyes. Upperparts dark, streaked chestnut and black; scapulars chestnut, wings black and rufous with wingbars formed by white tips to coverts; rump and uppertail-coverts rufous, tail blackish-rufous with white tip. Grey chest, rufous/chestnut belly, flanks and vent, with dark grey chevrons on flanks and lower belly. **BP** Bill strong; tip and upper mandible black, lower mandible and base pale yellow; eyes dark reddish-brown; tarsi dark pinkish-grey or brown. **SV** Short *kyon* or *kyo*, lark-like *drip*, *truiririp* or *tschirr*, and loud chirruping flight call. ♂ song, given from rock or in short display flight, is soft but powerful musical warbling, *kyichichi-jiri-jiri* or *chuchuri churuchurubyurirupitti* and *kyorikyori, kyorikyorichi*. ♀ song is a simpler series of trills.

Siberian Accentor *Prunella montanella*

L 13–15 cm; WT 15–20 g

SD Rare winter visitor and occasional migrant (likely *P. m. badia*) from Kyushu to Hokkaido. **HH** Thickets, shrubs near streams, sometimes in dry forest and grassland on hillsides. **ID** Generally drab brown, but has distinctive mask-like head pattern with black of crown, lores and ear-coverts contrasting with long, broad yellow-ochre supercilia and yellow-ochre ear-spot; chin, throat, breast and flanks deep ochre-yellow, with diffuse rufous flank streaks; belly and undertail-coverts buff to off-white. Neck-sides grey, mantle rich chestnut, upperparts warm brown streaked black; wings brown with single prominent, white greater-covert bar; rump brownish-grey, tail blackish-brown. **BP** Bill fine, sharply pointed, black with ochre base to lower mandible; eyes dark brown; tarsi pinkish-brown or orange-brown. **SV** Trisyllabic, insect-like *ti-ti-ti*; *tiriri* or *see-see-see*.

Japanese Accentor *Prunella rubida*

L 14–16 cm; WT 15–23 g

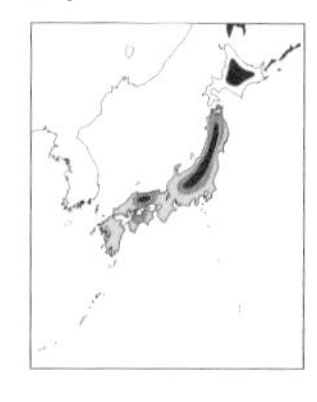

SD Summer visitor to Hokkaido and high mountains of N Honshu, resident elsewhere in Honshu and Shikoku. Altitudinal and latitudinal migrant, descending lower and to south in winter. Winters from C Honshu and Izu Is west to NE Kyushu. **HH** Stone pines and dense thickets of Rowan near treeline in summer; deciduous forests at middle elevations, often near rivers/streams, in thickets and scrub in winter. **ID** Dark accentor. Crown brown, nape greyish-brown, mantle and wings dark chestnut-brown with heavy blackish-brown and paler brown streaking; underparts, head and face dark grey, but face 'frosted' paler grey, flanks and vent have some rufous streaking. **BP** Bill fine, sharply pointed, blackish-grey; eyes dark reddish-brown; tarsi brownish-pink. **SV** Call: thin *tsuririri* or *chiririri*. Song: rapid, clear and tinkling *tsee-tsee-syuu tsee-tsee-syuu*; *chiri chirichiri* or *chuririri chuuchii hirihichiririri*, typically from top of stone pine.

Forest Wagtail *Dendronanthus indicus*

L 16–18 cm; WT 13–18 g

SD Rare migrant and winter visitor, which has been recorded from Nansei Shoto to Hokkaido; has bred in SW Honshu and N Kyushu, and occasionally winters in Kyushu. **HH** Breeds around open glades and paths, near streams/rivers, in broadleaf evergreen and deciduous forest. Winters in woodland, orchards and plantations. Well-camouflaged against leaf litter; when flushed may alight quickly on ground or in trees. **ID** Distinctive brown, black and white wagtail with long slender tail equal in length to body. Upperparts drab olive-brown, with prominent white supercilia, black wing-coverts with broad yellowish-white fringes forming double wingbar; long tail brown with white outer rectrices. Underparts whitish with central black breast patch extending as narrow collar, and second black bar on sides of lower breast. In flight, distinctive black median coverts bordered above and below with white, and black wingtips unmistakable. On ground commonly, and distinctively, sways rear and tail from side to side. **BP** Bill grey above, pinkish below; eyes dark brown; legs pink. **SV** Call: a single *pink* or double metallic *pink-pink*, occasionally a very quiet *tsip* while foraging. Song: a simple repetitive disyllabic *tsi-fee*, or a husky *chuchupii chuchupii* recalling Japanese Tit.

Alpine Accentor
ad
juv
Siberian Accentor
fresh
worn
Japanese Accentor
ad
Forest Wagtail
fledgling
ad

Western Yellow Wagtail *Motacilla flava* L 16–18 cm; WT 11–26 g

SD Vagrant *M. f. thunbergi* (includes *plexa*), *M. f. leucocephala* and *M. f. beema* have reached Okinawa, Tokara Is, NW Kyushu, Tsushima, and W & C Honshu. **HH** Wet meadows and wetland margins. **ID** Adult: upperparts plain olive-green, wings blackish with white fringes to coverts (narrow wingbars in flight), long, slender, blackish tail with white outer feathers. Pale yellow chin, brighter yellow from throat to belly, slaty blue-grey crown and nape, with slight white supercilia behind eye; lores and cheeks black. Non-breeding adult: upperparts grey-brown, flanks off-white to buff, pale yellow lower vent and undertail-coverts; white supercilia do not wrap around ear-coverts as in Citrine Wagtail. Tail approximately same length as body. **BP** Bill black (summer), or dark grey above, horn below (winter); eyes dark brown; tarsi black. **SV** A thin buzzy *tsweep*, *bizi* or *zi*.

Eastern Yellow Wagtail *Motacilla tschutschensis* L 16–18 cm; WT 11–26 g

SD **Green-headed Wagtail** *M. (t.) taivana* (sometimes treated specifically) breeds locally in northernmost Hokkaido (May–Aug), and winters in Nansei Shoto (Oct–Apr). *M. t. tschutschensis* (includes *simillima*) and *M. t. macronyx* are rare migrants from Nansei Shoto to Hokkaido. **HH** Wet meadows and wetland margins. **ID** Adult: broad yellow supercilia, olive-green face, crown and upperparts, blackish wings with prominent white fringes to coverts (narrow wingbars in flight), bright yellow underparts from chin to belly, and long, slender, blackish tail with white outer feathers (approximately same length as body). Non-breeding adult: upperparts brown, flanks off-white to buff, some with pale yellow lower vent and undertail-coverts; white supercilia do not wrap around ear-coverts as in Citrine Wagtail. **BP** Bill black (summer), or dark grey above, horn below (winter); eyes dark brown; tarsi black. **SV** A thin buzzy *tsweep*, *bizi* or *zi*. Song, from perch, a very short series of twittered notes *srii-sriiit*. **TN** Also included within *M. flava* (e.g. OSJ).

Citrine Wagtail *Motacilla citreola* L 17–20 cm; WT 18–25 g

SD *M. c. citreola* is accidental visitor from Nansei Shoto to Hokkaido; *M. c. calcarata* is vagrant (Haboro, Hokkaido). **HH** Margins of grassy wetlands. **ID** Large, plain, long-tailed wagtail. Breeding ♂ has bright yellow head and underparts, becoming whiter towards vent. Broad blackish bar on hindneck, grey mantle, black and white wings, long black tail with white outer feathers. ♀ is rather plain, but upperparts generally grey, with uniform grey crown, nape and mantle; face yellow, pale yellow supercilia (which continues around ear-coverts) and malar region, darker grey on cheeks; underparts off-white with grey-washed flanks. Juvenile resembles ♀, but with brownish-grey upperparts, lacks yellow wash on face, supercilia (with dark border above) and ear-coverts surround buff, forehead and lores also buff. 1st-winter much greyer than yellow wagtail, with white supercilia and ear-coverts surround, pale lores and white undertail-coverts. In flight, black wings and pale grey coverts with white fringes form broad double wingbar, distinctive in all plumages. **BP** Bill all black (summer), or all dark (winter); eyes black; tarsi black. **SV** Call like Eastern Yellow, but slightly sweeter, *tsuili*, a loud, ripping *tsreep*, also *biju biju*, *ju ju* and *chui*.

Grey Wagtail *Motacilla cinerea* L 17–20 cm; WT 14–22 g

SD *M. c. cinerea* is widespread throughout Japan; summer visitor in Hokkaido and winter visitor in south (including Nansei Shoto); year round in Kyushu, Shikoku and Honshu. **HH** Along fast-flowing rocky streams and rivers; also at wetlands and coasts in winter. **ID** Largest and longest-tailed wagtail (tail longer than body). Upperparts plain dark grey, wings black, tail black with white outer feathers. Breeding ♂ has prominent white supercilia, black chin and throat, and white malar/submoustachial stripe contrasting with dark grey ear-coverts; underparts bright lemon-yellow from chest to vent. Non-breeding ♂ has white chin and throat, and buffy supercilia. ♀ has less distinct supercilia, white chin/throat mottled black, and generally paler underparts, white suffused pale yellow, particularly on vent/undertail-coverts. Non-breeding ♀ paler with more buff on breast. Juvenile is like non-breeding ♀, but dark parts more olive, pale parts more buff. In flight, grey back, black wings with single white wingbar, bright yellow rump and very long tail diagnostic. **BP** Bill black (♂) or dark grey (♀); eyes dark brown; legs flesh-pink. **SV** Calls: variable, hard metallic *tzit, tzit-tzit, tzit-zee, chichin chichin*, or sharp *chittick*; stronger, clearer and higher than White Wagtail. Song: display flight ends in parachuting to ground; song is long, complex and sibilant, with various phrases, including *si-si-si* and *see-see-swee*, usually ending in a trill: *tzii-tz-tzi-tzi-tzee-ree-ree-ree*.

Western Yellow Wagtail
thunbergi
ad ♂
ad ♀
Eastern Yellow Wagtail
ad ♂ spring macronyx
ad ♂ spring taivana
ad ♀ tschutschensis
ad ♀ macronyx
ad ♂ spring tschutschensis
ad ♂
lcarata
Citrine Wagtail
ad ♀ breeding
ad ♂ citreola
1st-win
juv
Grey Wagtail
ad ♀ breeding
ad ♂ breeding
ad ♂ non-breeding

White Wagtail *Motacilla alba*

L 17–21 cm; WT 18–30 g

SD Black-backed Wagtail *M. a. lugens* common, widespread year round, mostly summer in Hokkaido (scarce in winter), resident Honshu, Shikoku, Kyushu, winter visitor south to Nansei Shoto, Ogasawara Is. **Amur Wagtail** *M. a. leucopsis* scarce breeder SW Japan; rare visitor Ogasawara, Nansei Shoto to Hokkaido; **East Siberian Wagtail** *M. a. ocularis* rare visitor Nansei Shoto to Hokkaido; **Masked Wagtail** *M. a. personata* rare visitor Nansei Shoto to Kyushu; **Baikal Wagtail** *M. a. baicalensis* accidental Nansei Shoto to Honshu; **Himalayan Wagtail** *M. a. alboides* vagrant Yaeyama Is; **White Wagtail** *M. a. alba* (includes *dukhunensis*) vagrant Yaeyama Is. **HH** Rivers, cultivated and suburban areas to coasts. **ID** All subspecies: pied, with grey/black backs, largely white wings, long black tail with white outer feathers. **Black-backed** ♂: black upperparts, broad black throat patch connected to mantle; wing-coverts broadly fringed white; in winter grey mantle with reduced black chest patch. ♀: grey upperparts, narrow black chest band connects to collar. **Amur** ♂: black above, forehead, face and chin white, black chest patch unconnected to black of neck/mantle. ♀: grey upperparts, small black chest patch. ♂♀ plain white face from forehead and chin to ear-coverts. **Baikal** closely recalls **Amur**, but ♂'s mantle grey not black, black chest patch extends to throat and to neck-sides. **East Siberian** (♂ resembles winter-plumaged **Black-backed**): mantle and rump grey, black of crown broad at rear and connected to black eyeline; chin, throat and chest patch black, not connected to mantle or neck patch. **BP** Bill black; eyes black; legs black. **SV** Call: clearly bisyllabic *chuchun chuchun*, *chichin chichin* or *chizzick chizzick*. Song: simple *tsutsu tsutsu zuizui* or much more complex, fast chirping series of slurred, warbled notes.

Japanese Wagtail *Motacilla grandis*

L 18–21 cm; WT 25–31 g

SD Summer visitor Hokkaido, locally common and largely sedentary resident Honshu, Shikoku, Kyushu, winter visitor or scarce visitor south to Nansei Shoto; some local seasonal altitudinal and latitudinal movements. **HH** Fast-flowing montane streams and rivers, broad shingle-bedded lowland rivers; occasionally ponds, lakes, coastal areas. **ID** Adult: black hood, upperparts and broad chest patch, white forehead, supercilia and chin patch. ♂: jet black. ♀: paler greyish-black. Juvenile: grey where adult is black, may lack white supercilia. At rest has extensive white wing patch (larger than White), white-fringed tertials, and very long black tail with white outer feathers. In flight, wings largely white, but with extensive black tips to primaries. **BP** Bill black; eyes dark brown; legs black. **SV** Call: buzzy *jiji jiji*, *bjee* or *bjeen*. Song: complex, recalls White Wagtail, *chichii joijui* and *tsutsuchiiichiii juu juu* and, more fully, as *tz tzui tztzui, pitz pitz tztzui pitz pitz bitz, bitzeen bitz bitzeen bitz bitzeen, tztzui tzigi chigi jijijiji*.

White Wagtail
ad ♂
lugens
spring ♀
spring ♂
juv
1st-win ♂
ad ♀ win
baicalensis
spring ♀
spring ♂
♀ win
1st-win ♂
leucopsis
spring ♂
spring ♀
juv
Japanese Wagtail
ad ♂
ad ♂
ad ♀
juv
ocularis
spring ♂
spring ♀
ad ♂ win
spring ♂
personata
spring ♂
alboides

Richard's Pipit *Anthus richardi*

L 17–18 cm; WT 21–40 g

SD Rare migrant, Hokkaido to Nansei Shoto, occasionally winters in south. **HH** Dry grassland, cultivated areas. **ID** Large, bulky, deep-chested pipit; upright stance, long tail, stout legs and pale, well-streaked appearance all distinctive. Upperparts mid-brown with darker streaks. Prominent pale supercilia, lores, chin and throat; narrow, blackish malar stripe broadens to form patch then merges with narrow dark streaking on lower neck and upper breast. Underparts buffy-brown to off-white. Median coverts, have blackish centres and broad buff/whitish fringes, tertials and secondaries blackish, fringed buff. 1st-winter: cleaner, with narrow white fringes to median and greater coverts and tertials. In deeply undulating flight, long tail very conspicuous, tail-sides white; when flushed typically gains height and distance quickly. **BP** Bill longish, grey above, pink below, heavy and arched; eyes dark brown; long tarsi pink, hindclaw very long. **SV** Call: loud, harsh, sparrow-like and explosive *rreep*, *chree-eep* or *schreep*, commonly given on take-off and in flight.

Blyth's Pipit *Anthus godlewskii*

L 15–17 cm; WT 23–24 g

SD Accidental migrant, Nansei Shoto to Hokkaido. **HH** Dry cultivated habitats, sometimes wetter areas. **ID** Resembles Richard's Pipit, from which best distinguished by smaller size (more compact), less upright stance, shorter tail and shorter legs; finer, more sharply pointed bill, and vocalisations. Overall pale like Richard's, but plumages of both variable. Median coverts, with squarer blackish centres and broader pale fringes, form more prominent wingbars than in Richard's, but only in adults. Upperparts more neatly streaked, and underparts more extensive and plainer buff than Richard's. **BP** Bill grey above, pale pink below; eyes dark brown; tarsi pale or yellowish-pink, tarsi shorter and hindclaw shorter and more arched than Richard's. **SV** Call: wheezy or buzzing *spzeeu* or *pscheeo* (similar to Richard's, but higher, more shrill and descending), a mellow, low *chip-chup*, shorter and higher pitched than Richard's; also harsh *bzrp* or *brzi* in alarm.

Meadow Pipit *Anthus pratensis*

L 15 cm; WT 15–22 g

SD Accidental Nansei Shoto to W Honshu (subspecies uncertain). **HH** Damp grasslands, meadows. **ID** Small, dark, olive-brown; upperparts narrowly streaked black, rump plainer/unstreaked. Face plain, supercilia faint, eye-ring narrow, chin/throat off-white with narrow lateral throat-stripe extending as gorget of dark streaks to flanks. Breast streaking weaker, flank streaking stronger, than Tree or Olive-backed pipits; belly buff. **BP** Bill fine, blackish-brown; eyes dark brown; tarsi yellowish-brown, hindclaw longer than hindtoe, only slightly curved (longer than Tree or Olive-backed). **SV** Call: thin, sibilant *sip-sip-sip*, similar to Buff-bellied, but squeakier, and more insistent *spip-spip-spip* or *ist ist ist*.

Richard's Pipit
1st-win
juv
ad
ad
Blyth's Pipit
1st-win
ad
ad
Meadow Pipit
ad
ad
1st-win

Tree Pipit *Anthus trivialis*

L 14–16 cm; WT 19–25 g

SD Accidental *A. t. trivialis*, Nansei Shoto to N Honshu. **HH** Woodland, open areas with trees. **ID** Resembles Olive-backed Pipit (OBP), but smaller, browner, with weaker face pattern (supercilia least distinct before eye, strongest above eye, lacking black border above); generally lacks OBP's prominent post-auricular creamy spot and black crescent. Upperparts more heavily streaked than OBP. Median coverts have black centres extending to tip, fringes off-white. Underparts buff-tinged white, breast heavily streaked, flanks have narrower, elongated dusky streaks. **BP** Bill strong, somewhat long, heavy-based, culmen tip slightly decurved, dark brown above, pale horn/pink at base; eyes dark brown; tarsi pale or pinkish. **SV** Call: yellow wagtail-like *tseep*, *teez* or *spihz*, and *bzzt*, also *duii* (very like OBP); alarm *syt*.

Olive-backed Pipit *Anthus hodgsoni*

L 15–17 cm; WT 17–26 g

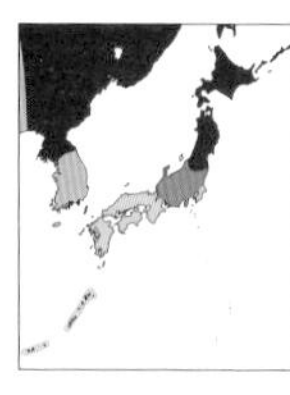

SD *A. h. hodgsoni*: summer visitor (May–Sep) Hokkaido, N Honshu, resident C & SW Honshu, has bred Shikoku and Kyushu, winter visitor south to Nansei Shoto. *A. h. yunnanensis*: accidental Hokkaido, N Honshu, Kyushu. **HH** Boreal/montane forest in summer; winters in lowland forest, woodland, parks. **ID** Olive-green and off-white; head rounded and well marked; face distinctive, with prominent two-tone supercilia, buffish before eye, pale cream behind eye, bordered above by narrow blackish line; distinct white post-auricular spot (like extension of supercilia), above blackish crescent. Chin/throat whitish, split by narrow black malar stripe, merging into broad black streaks on breast, narrowing only slightly on flanks. Upperparts mid- to dark olive-green, mantle unstreaked, or with faint narrow dark streaking in spring; wings and tail have greenish fringes, wings with double clear wingbars, and median coverts have dark, rounded centres with unbroken pale fringes. *A. h. hodgsoni* more uniform olive with broader stripes on back, scapulars, breast and flanks than *A. h. yunnanensis*; those breeding in Japan have indistinctly streaked upperparts, thus are closer to *A. h. yunnanensis*. Primaries extend further beyond tertial tips in Japanese population than elsewhere. **BP** Bill short, narrow-based, with fine, sharp tip, dark grey above, dark horn below; eyes dark brown; tarsi pale or yellowish-pink. **SV** Call: thin *dzzt*, *tseez*, *zii* or *duii*, similar to Tree Pipit (usually inseparable); alarm *sit*. Song: fast, complex, somewhat skylark-like, *tsui-tsui-choi-choi zizizi*, but delivered from treetop, or in descending display flight; song frequently terminates in calls.

Pechora Pipit *Anthus gustavi*

L 14–15 cm; WT 20–26 g

SD Rare migrant (*A. g. gustavi* May; Sep–Oct), Nansei Shoto to Hokkaido; *A. g. menzbieri* accidental Yaeyama Is. **HH** Wet grassland, forest edges. **ID** Resembles 1st-winter Red-throated Pipit (RTP), but darker, more heavily streaked. Face pattern more distinct, with subtle supercilia from bill to just rear of eye, blackish loral stripe from eye to bill (absent in RTP). Narrow malar does not reach bill, but joins dark neck patch and merges into heavy breast and flank streaking. Upperparts warmer brown-olive, more boldly marked than RTP, with more prominent, contrasting, black and white 'braces', and double wingbars (slightly bolder than RTP), greater coverts usually blacker than RTP, creating contrasting wing pattern. Underparts creamy-white (chin/throat), with yellowish-buff wash on breast/flanks, and whitish belly. Tertials noticeably shorter than primaries, 2–3 primary tips extend slightly beyond tertials (in 1st-winter RTP all primaries cloaked by tertials). In flight, 'braces' and wingbars prominent. **BP** Bill short, thickish, grey above, pink below and at base; eyes dark brown; tarsi pale pinkish. **SV** Typically silent, even when flushed (RTP usually calls). Call: abrupt, hard 1- or 2-syllable *pwit*, *chi*, *chu* or *tsep*; or squeaky, but emphatic, *dit dit dit* to more Grey Wagtail-like hard *tsip*.

Tree Pipit
ad
1st-win
ad
Olive-backed Pipit
1st-win
yunnanensis
ad *hodgsoni*
ad *yunnanensis*
ad *yunnanensis*
Pechora Pipit
ad *gustavi*
ad sum
ad *gustavi*

Rosy Pipit *Anthus roseatus*

L 15–17 cm; WT 17–25 g

SD Vagrant to N Kyushu (Fukuoka) in winter. **HH** Wet grasslands and ricefields. **ID** Resemblies Meadow and Buff-bellied pipits, but has more strongly streaked mantle and bolder supercilia (pale and broad with black brow above); lores and ear-coverts dark. Adult has rather grey head, with pink supercilia, distinct black eyestripe and bold black malar; underparts plain with pale pink flush, flanks lightly streaked dark. Non-breeding adult has buffy-pink supercilia, greyer mantle, boldly streaked black; underparts lack pink with narrow black malar merging into more extensive spotting on breast-sides to flanks with buff wash. **BP** Bill short, fine; grey above, horn/pink below; eyes dark brown; tarsi pale or pinkish. **SV** A weak *tseep* or *seep-seep*.

Red-throated Pipit *Anthus cervinus*

L 14–15 cm; WT 19–21 g

SD Scarce migrant through Japan from Hokkaido southwards, and an uncommon winter visitor (Nov–Apr) to SW Kyushu and Nansei Shoto. **HH** Favours wet grasslands and marshy edges. **ID** Compact pipit, with short tail, and plain face. Resembles Buff-bellied Pipit, but upperparts sandy-brown with more distinct black streaking. Two parallel pale lines ('braces') on mantle (cf. also Pechora). Extent of red individually and seasonally variable; summer ♂ brightest, pale orange to deep brick red, head and upper breast, forming distinct hood in some, more diffuse with paler orange wash to belly and flanks in others; sides heavily streaked (streaks do not narrow on flanks, as in Tree or Olive-backed). 1st-winter more contrasting, with distinct supercilia, bolder mantle streaking, and thin, bold lateral throat-stripes extending into more extensive streaking on breast/flanks. Unlike similar Pechora, tertials cover primaries. **BP** Bill short, fine, grey at tip, yellowish-horn at base; eyes dark brown; tarsi pinkish. **SV** Call: clear, thin *teeze*, a yellow wagtail-like *pssiih*, or *chuirii* when flushed; alarm call is a harder *chyup*.

Buff-bellied Pipit *Anthus rubescens*

L 14–17 cm; WT 21–25 g

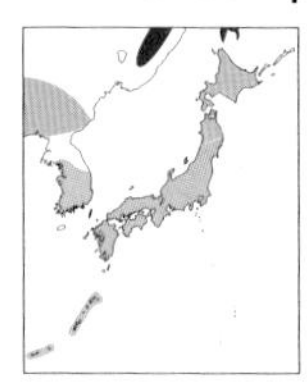

SD Common migrant (*A. r. japonicus*) through Hokkaido and a winter visitor (Oct–Apr) from Honshu to Nansei Shoto (likely specifically distinct from **American Pipit** *A. r. rubescens*, which may also reach Japan in winter). **HH** Damp grasslands, fields, wetland and woodland edges. **ID** Rather drab and featureless. Face weakly marked, with pale supercilia, plain pale lores, cream chin/throat with prominent black malar forming black neck mark, and merging with breast and flank streaks. Upperparts dull, indistinctly streaked; underparts buff with variable streaking from breast to flanks. Adult breeding orange-buff or pale rufous-cinnamon below (pink-toned in Water Pipit), with lighter black streaking; upperparts grey-brown. Non-breeding browner above with dark streaking, underparts whiter with heavier black streaking and more distinct lateral throat-stripe. *A. r. japonicus* averages slightly darker above, more heavily streaked below, with bolder dark malar, and brighter, fleshier legs than *rubescens*. Also resembles Meadow Pipit, but upperparts greyer-brown, only faintly streaked, crown only lightly streaked (crown streaking prominent in Meadow). **BP** Bill blackish-brown, grey-tipped, horn-coloured base (shorter and finer than Water); eyes dark brown; tarsi dull, pale yellowish-pink (*japonicus*) or dark blackish-brown (*rubescens*). **SV** A sharp, clear *pit*; *pi-pit* or squeaky *tseep* or *speep-eep*, recalling Meadow, sometimes rapidly repeated, *si-si-si-si-sif*, and in alarm a rising *pwisp*.

Water Pipit *Anthus spinoletta*

L 15–17 cm; WT 19–23 g

SD *A. s. blakistoni* is an accidental in winter to S Japan. **HH** Wetlands, from coastal salt marshes to inland marshes, rivers, lakes and wet fields. **ID** Pale, somewhat colourful pipit. Adult breeding: head largely grey, crown lightly streaked black, broad creamy supercilia behind eye and pale crescent below it, lores largely dark, breaking eye-ring; mantle dark greyish-brown streaked lightly black, wings blackish-brown, tail long, blackish-brown with prominent white outer feathers. Underparts creamy, even peach, or buff from chin to lower breast/flanks; very narrow dark lateral throat streak not linked to fine streaking on breast-sides and flanks (less heavily streaked below than Rosy or Buff-bellied pipits), belly and vent white. Non-breeding: more streaked, head less grey, with less distinct supercilia, lacks extensive dark malar, and has fine brown rather than coarse dark underparts streaking. Has less distinct breast streaking than Asian Buff-bellied and generally cleaner white underparts. Lacks buffy wash to underparts of American Buff-bellied. **BP** Bill fine, sharp, largely dark grey or blackish-brown, pink at base of lower mandible; eyes small, black; tarsi dark grey or blackish-brown. **SV** A single or double, thin *weest*, also *psri* and *pheet*. **TN** Not included by OSJ.

Rosy Pipit
ad win
ad sum
ad win
Red-throated Pipit
ad win
ad sum
ad win
Buff-bellied Pipit
ad win rubescens
ad sum japonicus
ad win japonicus
Water Pipit
ad win

Common Chaffinch *Fringilla coelebs*

L 14–16 cm; WT 18–29 g

SD Vagrant (*F. c. coelebs*) to Rishirito, Hokkaido. **HH** Woodland. **ID** A rather colourful, sparrow-sized finch. ♂ has blue-grey crown and nape, brown cheeks and mantle, olive lower back and rump, and dull, pinkish-buff underparts. Wings black, with blue-grey shoulders and broad white wing-panel and wingbar; tail long, notched, blackish, with white outer feathers. ♀ is rather plain greyish-brown, with very plain face, but has white shoulder patch and white tips to wing-coverts forming second wingbar. **BP** Bill rather thin, conical and sharply pointed, grey; eyes black; tarsi dull grey-brown. **SV** Sharp, explosive *spink*, *fink* or *chink*, and in flight a soft *yupp* or *chup* recalling Brambling's flight call.

Brambling *Fringilla montifringilla*

L 14–16 cm; WT 17–30 g

SD Common spring migrant (May); winters (Oct–Apr) commonly, even abundantly, but erratically throughout Japan from Hokkaido to Kyushu, scarce further south. **HH** Winters in forests, woodlands, parks and agricultural land, in spring in mature wooded habitat. **ID** Largely orange and black finch. Breeding plumage ♂ has black head, mantle and back, orange throat, breast and shoulders, white rump and black tail. Orange from chin to breast and flanks; belly to vent white, with some black streaking on flanks. Orange scapulars, tips of greater coverts and outer fringes of secondaries. Winter ♂ is paler, with browner head and mantle, and orange of underparts less bright. ♀ resembles winter ♂, but has dusky grey-brown ear-coverts with broad grey crescent on head-sides to rear of ear-coverts; breast, scapulars and greater coverts all tinged orange or rusty-buff. In flight, relatively long-winged, orange and black wing pattern and contrasting white rump and black tail distinctive. Tail quite long and obviously notched. **BP** Bill dull horn-coloured with (♂) or without (♀) dark grey tip; eyes black; legs dull pink. **SV** Call: strong nasal *dzwee* and in flight an oft-repeated soft *chup* or *tk-tk-tk*. Song: by migrants on temporary territory, rather monotonous and slow, incorporating distinctive buzzing *rrrrrhew* and strong nasal *byeen* notes.

Hawfinch *Coccothraustes coccothraustes*

L 16–19 cm; WT 45–70 g

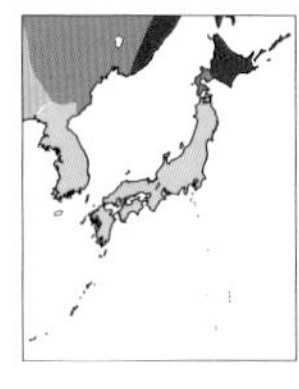

SD *C. c. japonicus* is a widespread, and sometimes very common migrant through Hokkaido and N Honshu. Some breed in Hokkaido and N Honshu; winters commonly from C Honshu to Kyushu, scarce winter visitor to Nansei Shoto. *C. c. coccothraustes* is vagrant to Hokkaido, N & W Honshu. **HH** In montane and lowland deciduous and mixed forests in summer, also woodlands, parks and gardens in winter. **ID** Large, compact, bull-headed, but short-tailed, finch. Sexes very similar, but ♂ somewhat brighter. Head warm orange-brown, with black lores, eye surround, narrow forehead bar and chin patch; grey nape and neck-sides. Upperparts dark brown, mid-brown on rump; underparts buffy-brown, but white on vent. Scapulars and coverts brown, with broad white bar on greater coverts, primaries and secondaries glossy blue-black, the inner primaries with strangely crinkled broad spatulate tips; rump and uppertail-coverts brown, short, slightly notched tail black with broad white tip. In deeply undulating flight, wings and tail flash much white – showing a white panel at base of primaries, broad bar across coverts and broad tail tip. **BP** Bill deep and massive, grey at base with blackish tip (summer), or horn-coloured (winter/juv); eyes small, irides mid-brown; tarsi pink. **SV** Call: explosive *tsi*, *tzick* or *tic* given at rest, or repeatedly in flight. Song: comprises various harsh chattering sounds: *tsutsutsu chuu-pip-pip-tsiriri*.

Common Chaffinch
ad ♂
ad ♀
ad ♀
Brambling
ad ♂ sum
ad ♀ win
ad ♂ win
ad ♀ win
Hawfinch
ad ♀
juv
ad ♂ sum

Chinese Grosbeak *Eophona migratoria*

L 15–19 cm; WT 47–50 g

SD Uncommon to rare migrant and winter visitor (*E. m. migratoria*) to C Honshu (has bred), Shikoku, and Kyushu; rare north to Hokkaido and south to Nansei Shoto. **HH** Montane and lowland deciduous forest, woodlands, parks and gardens. **ID** Large, highly vocal and boldly marked finch, superficially resembling Japanese Grosbeak, but smaller. ♂ has fuller black cap, extending to ear-coverts and chin; upperparts brown, pale grey-brown on rump; underparts pinkish-brown, strongly washed rufous or cinnamon on flanks and vent. Wings glossy blue-black, with small white patch at base of primaries and all-white primary and secondary tips; tail glossy black and deeply notched. In flight, narrow white primary bar, trailing edge and wingtips, and pale grey rump contrasting with black tail all diagnostic. ♀ lacks black hood with duller upperparts and less glossy black wings and tail. **BP** Bill large, dull yellow with blackish tip and bluish base (bill of Japanese much yellower); eyes red-brown; tarsi dull pink. **SV** Call: a loud *tek-tek* or *dek-dek*. Song: a loudly whistled *chee chee choree kirichoo*, similar to Japanese. **AN** Yellow-billed Grosbeak.

Japanese Grosbeak *Eophona personata*

L 22–24 cm; WT 60–85 g

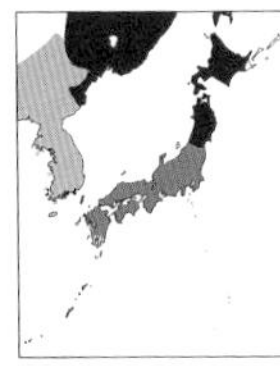

SD Partly migratory, partially resident. *E. p. personata* is a fairly common summer visitor to Hokkaido (May–Sep) and N Honshu, but occurs year-round and winters throughout rest of main Japanese archipelago; scarce migrant south to Nansei Shoto. **HH** In montane and lowland deciduous boreal forest, also mixed lowland broadleaf forest, in summer; in forest and woodland, parks and gardens in winter. **ID** Very large, highly vocal, boldly marked finch. Adult is readily recognised by very large bill, glossy black face and cap, and generally mid-grey plumage, lightly tinged brown on tertials, grey on vent. Wings glossy black to tip, with bold white patch midway along primaries; long tail is glossy black and deeply notched. Juvenile has black lores and margin to bill, but otherwise head, back and underparts brownish-grey, with same wing and tail pattern as adult. **BP** Bill massive, bright rich yellow; eyes dark brown; tarsi brownish-pink. **SV** Call: deep, hard *tuk-tuk*. Song: simple, comprising 4–5 strongly whistled notes, rising and falling and ending in longer note, *tsuki-hi-ho-shi*.

Pine Grosbeak *Pinicola enucleator*

L 19–24 cm; WT 40–62 g

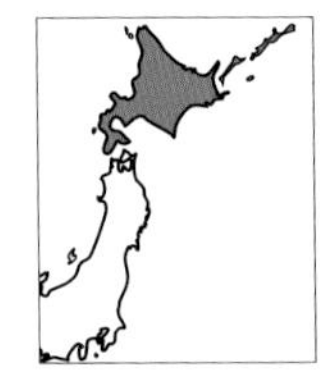

SD *P. e. sakhalinensis* is an uncommon resident of Hokkaido, breeding at high altitudes and wandering to lower altitudes in winter; accidental south to N, C & W Honshu. *P. e. kamtschatkensis* is vagrant to Hokkaido, N Honshu and Hegurajima. **HH** Favours taiga forest, preferring deciduous areas with alder and birch, but also found in low pine forest and alpine stone pines in summer, visiting similar habitats at lower elevations in winter, when occasionally also visits berry-bearing shrubs or trees, even in towns and villages, sometimes mixing with waxwings. **ID** Very large, heavy-set finch with rather small rounded head. Adult ♂ generally dark pink with black lores and eye patch, and mantle, back and wings largely black, but mantle-feathers fringed deep pink, scapulars with grey, coverts with white, forming double white wingbar; rump red with some black scaling, and notched, rather long tail is black. Underparts deep reddish-pink grading to dark grey on flanks, belly and vent. Juvenile ♂ orange on head, breast and rump. ♀ has yellow-green head and breast, upperparts and much of underparts grey. Flight slow and undulating. **BP** Bill large and stubby, greyish-black; eyes black; tarsi black. **SV** Calls: soft, somewhat bullfinch-like, sweetly whistled: *pee-u*, *pyüru pyüru* or *pyou-you lee*. Song: soft, fast and high-pitched, *pyuru pyuru pyuro ruriri*, similar to pattern of Red-flanked Bluetail.

Chinese Grosbeak
ad ♂ sum
ad ♂ win
ad ♀
Japanese Grosbeak
ad
juv
Pine Grosbeak
ad ♂
ad ♀

Grey-bellied Bullfinch *Pyrrhula (pyrrhula) griseiventris* L 14–18 cm; WT 21–34 g

SD Resident in Hokkaido, N & C Honshu; winter visitor south to Izu Is and Kyushu; scarce elsewhere south to Nansei Shoto. **HH** Fairly common in montane and lowland mixed and coniferous forests in summer, also woodland edge, scrub and gardens in winter. **ID** Large, plump, bull-necked finch with prominent white rump. ♂ has glossy black cap, black lores and eye patch and very narrow black bib contrasting with bright pink cheeks and throat. Upperparts grey, wings black with narrow white lesser-covert bar, and broad white greater covert bar, vent and rump, tail black. Underparts entirely mid- to dark grey. ♀ shares same pattern of black and white, but upperparts plain grey-brown, and underparts grey. Juvenile resembles ♀, but lacks black cap. **BP** Bill short, stubby, dark greyish-black; eyes small, black; tarsi dull dark pink. **SV** Call: soft, melancholic, repetitive piping: *teu teu teu* or downslurred *pheew pheew pheew*. Song: a softly whistled *fiyo fiyo fee*. **TN** Included within following species by IOC.

Eurasian Bullfinch *Pyrrhula pyrrhula* L 14–18 cm; WT 27–38 g

SD *P. p. rosacea* is an uncommon winter visitor from Hokkaido south to Honshu, Izu Is, Shikoku and Kyushu. *P. p. cassinii* is a rare winter visitor from Hokkaido to Kyushu. **HH** Forests, woodland edges, scrub and gardens. **ID** As Grey-bellied Bullfinch, but smaller. *P. p. rosacea* is more pink, and pink of cheeks less intense than in Grey-bellied, contrasting less with pinkish-brown underparts; mantle brownish-grey, white spots in outer tail. *P. p. cassinii* is pinkest race, colour extending from cheeks over entire underparts, only lower belly and vent white; more extensive white in outer tail. ♀ shares same pattern of black and white, but upperparts plain grey-brown, and underparts pinkish-brown. **BP** As in Grey-bellied. **SV** Call: soft, melancholic, repetitive piping: *teu teu teu* or downslurred *pheew pheew pheew*.

Asian Rosy Finch *Leucosticte arctoa* L 16–19 cm; WT 30 g

SD Winter visitor (*L. a. brunneonucha*; Nov–Apr) locally in Hokkaido and N & C Honshu, occasionally south to Kyushu; scarce breeder in C Hokkaido. **HH** Above treeline in mountains in summer; in winter in low mountains and forests, also lowlands and snow-free coasts and headlands. **ID** Large, rather dull, but rather long-winged finch. ♂ blackish, particularly on forehead, face, underparts, wings and tail. Pale-brown crown and nape grade into brown mantle streaked dark grey, lower back and rump dark brown. Underparts blackish-brown spotted pale grey on throat and breast, with raspberry-pink flanks; scapulars and wing-coverts fringed and tipped brighter pink; undertail-coverts also pink. ♀ has pink restricted to scapulars, covert tips and flanks. Flight strong but undulating, wings long, tail long and notched. **BP** Bill yellow/horn with dark grey tip; eyes dark brown; tarsi dark grey/black. **SV** Call: sparrow-like *iyuu* and dry *peut*. Song: given from exposed rock, is range of twittering notes. **AN** Arctic Rosy Finch.

Common Rosefinch *Carpodacus erythrinus* L 13–15 cm; WT 19–33 g

SD Rare migrant (*C. e. grebnitskii*; Apr–May) through Japan, with records from Nansei Shoto to Hokkaido, mainly along Sea of Japan coast and on islands. **HH** Forests, thickets and woodland edges. **ID** Medium-sized, rather plain finch. ♂ has deep-red head, chin/throat and breast, pinkish-white on rest of underparts; reddish-grey mantle and scapulars, bright red rump; wings and tail blackish, with broad grey-brown fringes, tinged pink. Young ♂ has red confined to head, rest of body grey-brown like ♀. ♀ very plain, especially face, with no distinguishing features, except dark eye in pale unmarked face. Upperparts dark olive-brown streaked darker; underparts pale grey-brown with diffuse streaking on breast and flanks. Flight strong but undulating, tail rather long and notched. **BP** Bill stout with rounded tip, dull grey; eyes black; tarsi greyish-pink. **SV** Call: strongly whistled *vüi* or *chüi*, or *chooee-ee* commonly given in flight; also quiet, short *zik* before take-off and in flight. Song: a simple, sweetly whistled combination of call-like notes: *vidyew-vui vidyew-vui vidyew-vidyew-vui*, typically given from high song post or treetop. **AN** Scarlet Rosefinch.

ad ♂
ad ♂
Grey-bellied Bullfinch
ad ♀
ad ♂
Eurasian Bullfinch
Asian Rosy Finch
ad ♂
ad ♀
ad ♂ in song
Common Rosefinch

Long-tailed Rosefinch *Carpodacus sibiricus*

L 13–18 cm; WT 14–16 g

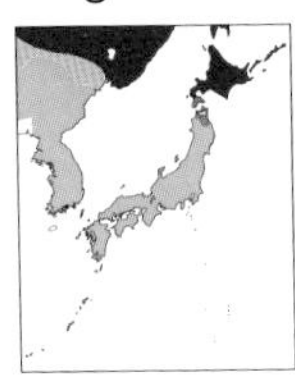

SD *C. s. sanguinolentus* is a fairly common summer visitor (May–Sep) breeding in Hokkaido and occasionally N Honshu, wintering (Oct–Apr) south to Kyushu; accidental in Izu and Ogasawara Is. **HH** Forest and wetland fringes, riparian scrub, open woodland and agricultural land with bushes or trees. **ID** Small-bodied but long-tailed. ♂ deep pink with silvery crown and cheeks, mantle dark pink with black streaking, lower back and rump unstreaked deep pink, and tail black with white outer rectrices. Forehead and lores dark pink, underparts deep pink, silvery on flanks, greyer on belly. Wings largely black, with two prominent wingbars and pale panel formed by white fringes to tertials. Winter ♂ duller, less pink, browner above. ♀ plainer brown with very plain face, but wing pattern similar to ♂. First-winter similar. Flight rather weak and fluttering. **BP** Bill stubby, pale greyish; eye of ♂ set in dark patch, but that of ♀ prominent in plain face, resembling Common Rosefinch, irides black; tarsi dull dark pink. **SV** Call: soft, plaintive fluty, commonly double or triple whistles: *hwit-hwot*, *fee fee*, *pee popo* and distinctive ringing *stip*. Song: a hurried *churu churu chee fee fee fee*.

Pallas's Rosefinch *Carpodacus roseus*

L 15–18 cm; WT 21–35 g

SD *C. r. portenkoi* is scarce and irregular winter visitor (Oct–Apr) to Hokkaido and N & C Honshu, and rare visitor south to Kyushu and Nansei Shoto. **HH** Forest edges, scrub and agricultural land with trees, also wooded parks. **ID** Heavy-set finch with rather large head and prominent eye. ♂ is dark raspberry-pink with forehead and chin/throat covered in silver spots. Mantle and back dark pink streaked black; underparts deep pink grading to white on belly and vent; lower back and rump plain pink; wings black with pink scapulars, white fringes to wing-coverts forming double wingbar, and white-fringed tertials and pale pink outer fringes to primaries and secondaries; notched tail black, also with pale pinkish outer fringes. Young ♂ resembles ♀, but has variable pink on head, breast and rump. ♀ generally brown with rather heavily streaked upperparts and warm rusty-brown tone to breast, with fine dark streaking; crown and nape greyish-brown, wings have pale fringes to coverts and flight-feathers, and dark pink rump is unstreaked. **BP** Bill short, deep, dull grey; eyes small, irides black; legs pinkish-grey, feet grey. **SV** Soft whistled *fee*, a metallic *tsuiii*, a quite loud, discordant, bunting-like *dzih* and strong *chek-chek*, slightly deeper and softer than Hawfinch.

Oriental Greenfinch *Chloris sinica*

L 13–17 cm; WT 17–30 g

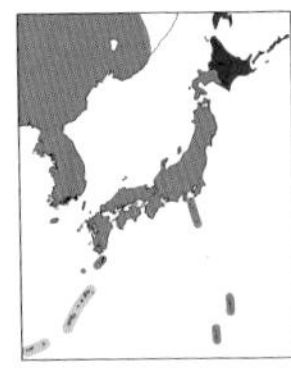

SD Widespread and common year round in Japan, but with complex interchange of subspecies on migration, in summer and winter. *C. s. minor* is largely resident in Hokkaido, Honshu and Izu Is, Kyushu and Tsushima, but scarce visitor south to Nansei Shoto. Larger *C. s. kawarahiba* breeds in Hokkaido, wintering from Honshu southwards, including to Nansei Shoto. Small *C. s. kittlitzi* is resident on Ogasawara and Iwo Is. **HH** Mixed coniferous and deciduous forests and agricultural areas in summer; woodland, forest edge, riverine scrub, agricultural land and gardens in winter. **ID** Large, dark, olive-brown finch with prominent, bright-yellow wing and tail patches. ♂ has olive-grey head, black around eye and bill, and grey nape; upperparts dark olive-brown; underparts slightly paler olive-brown. ♀ is browner, and young birds duller with heavy streaking above and below. Wing-feathers mostly black, but yellow bases to primaries form bold yellow flash on closed wing, and has grey-white fringes to tertials; rump grey-brown, tail black with yellow vent and basal tail-sides. Tail rather broad with shallow notch. In flight shows broad yellow wingbar; flight typically finch-like, undulating deeply, but display flight is loose-winged and slow, somewhat butterfly-like. *C. s. kittlitzi* is small, generally dark olive-green, with little yellow on underparts except vent, and larger bill than *C. s. minor*; *C. s. kawarahiba* is much larger with broader white tertial fringes. **BP** Bill strong, conical, pink; eyes black; tarsi pink. **SV** Call: a very nasal *djeeeen*, *djuwee* or *dzweee*. Song: a slightly sweet chattering comprising *kirr korr* and *kirikiri-korokoro-been* notes given from high perch or in slow song-flight. Song is interspersed with or preceded by calls. **AN** Grey-capped Greenfinch.

Long-tailed Rosefinch
ad ♀ sum
ad ♂ sum
ad ♂ win
ad ♂ win
Pallas's Rosefinch
ad ♂
1st-sum ♂
ad ♀
Oriental Greenfinch
ad ♂
ad ♀
juv

Common Redpoll *Acanthis flammea*

L 11–14 cm; WT 12–16 g

SD Irregular irruptive winter visitor (*A. f. flammea*; Oct–Mar) to Hokkaido, locally common in some winters; scarce or rare winter visitor south to Honshu, Shikoku, Kyushu and Nansei Shoto. **HH** Montane and lowland forest with birches and alders, also parks, gardens and fieldside vegetation. **ID** Small, greyish-brown, highly variable, rather streaky finch. ♂: forehead deep red, lores and chin spot black. In flight shows double white wingbar and plain grey-brown rump. Underparts off-white or buff with variable amounts of streaking. Lower face, throat, breast and rump of ♂ variably washed pale to deep pink, brightening during winter. ♀ lacks pink. Juvenile lacks red forehead and black on face/throat and is slightly darker and more heavily streaked, but this plumage rarely seen south of breeding range. Tail dull black with obvious notch. Flight buoyant, undulating; flocks active, 'dancing' in air. **BP** Bill fine, sharply conical, yellow/horn; eyes black; tarsi dark grey/black. **SV** Call: nasal *dsooee* when perching, flight notes recall Eurasian Siskin, but longer and harder *ju ju chueen* or reverberating, chattering *che che che che* or *chett-chett-chett* with hard metallic edge. **AN** North America: Mealy Redpoll. **TN** Formerly within *Carduelis*.

Arctic Redpoll *Acanthis hornemanni*

L 12–16 cm; WT 10–16 g

SD Very rare winter visitor (*A. h. exilipes*; Oct–Mar) to Hokkaido, and an accidental visitor to N & W Honshu, and Sado I. **HH** Forest and grasslands. **ID** Paler and less streaked than Common Redpoll; mantle paler grey-brown with whitish fringes, or almost white with darker brown streaks; lower back and rump *unstreaked* white (♂ with variable pale pink tone); underparts white only lightly streaked on flanks; vent and undertail-coverts white, unstreaked (longest feathers may have dark central shaft-streak). ♂ suffused pink on cheeks and breast, though sometimes buff wash on breast. ♀ lacks pink flush. Wings whiter on secondaries and coverts, with prominent white wingbar and tertial fringes. Obviously notched tail is blackish with pale outer fringes, contrasting strongly with white rump. In flight, white wingbars, white vent and unstreaked rump are all useful features. **BP** Bill stubby, short, deep, with straight culmen, pale yellow/horn; eyes black; tarsi dark grey/black. **SV** Calls slightly softer and higher than Common Redpoll. **AN** North America: Hoary Redpoll, Coues's Redpoll. **TN** Formerly within *Carduelis*.

Red Crossbill *Loxia curvirostra*

L 17–19 cm; WT 28–53 g

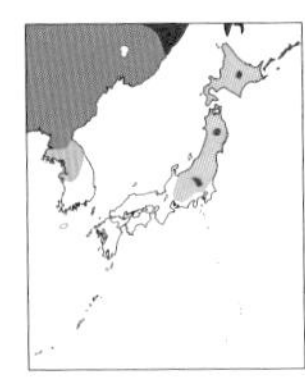

SD Uncommon winter visitor (*L. c. japonica*; Oct–May) to Hokkaido and Honshu, a scarce, or rare, migrant elsewhere south to Nansei Shoto, Ogasawara and Iwo Is. A scarce breeder in Hokkaido and N & C Honshu. Irruptive, varying greatly in numbers between years. **HH** Taiga and temperate forests, often in mountains, sometimes in lowlands. **ID** Large colourful stocky finch, with largish rounded head. ♂ variably bright brick- or orange-red on head, underparts, mantle and rump, mantle with some brown, wings and tail black, sometimes with white on vent. ♀ olive to yellowish-green, greyer on head and face, brighter green on rump, with dark wings and tail; juvenile resembles ♀, but is heavily streaked; 1st-year ♂ greenish-brown with orange or rusty tinge to back and underparts. In flight, often vocal, appears bull-headed, tail clearly notched; flight deeply undulating. **BP** Bill deep, stubby (though size variable) with unusual crossed tips, blackish-grey; eyes black; tarsi dark grey/black, pinkish-grey in young. **SV** Call: in flight or from treetop perch, deep, explosive, even metallic, *chup chup chup* or *glipp-glipp-glipp*. Song: a loud mixture of trills and twittering *chu chui chu pyuu pee pee*. **AN** Common Crossbill.

Two-barred Crossbill *Loxia leucoptera*

L 14–16 cm; WT 25–40 g

SD Rare winter visitor (*L. l. bifasciata*) to Hokkaido, Honshu and Kyushu. **HH** Deciduous taiga, especially larch, birch and rowan, but also fir and pine. **ID** Resembles Common Crossbill, but has thinner bill, smaller head, prominent wing pattern and longer tail. ♂'s combination of bright raspberry-red head, underparts and mantle, and prominent double white wingbar on otherwise black wings, is diagnostic. ♀ dull olive-green, streaked darker greyish-brown on crown and, especially, mantle and scapulars, and underparts rather paler yellow-olive, streaked dark grey; rump greenish-yellow. Juvenile resembles ♀, but more heavily streaked, and 1st-year ♂ is pale, orange-red. In flight, more slender than Common, all plumages show white wingbars, tail clearly notched; often vocal. Flight deeply undulating. **BP** Bill longer, more slender than Common, but similarly scissor-like, blackish-grey; eyes black; tarsi dark grey/black. **SV** Call: softer and higher pitched than Common: *chip-chipp-chipp* or *glib glib*, scratchier and somewhat redpoll-like, and discordant piping *tviiht*. **AN** North America: White-winged Crossbill.

Common Redpoll
ad ♀ win
juv
ad ♂ win
ad ♂ win
ad ♂ sum
Arctic Redpoll
ad ♂ win
ad ♂ sum
ad ♂ sum
Red Crossbill
Two-barred Crossbill
ad ♂
ad ♀
juv
ad ♂
ad ♀
juv

European Goldfinch *Carduelis carduelis*

L 12–15 cm; WT 14–19 g

SD Vagrant. Both **European Goldfinch** *C. c. carduelis* and **Grey-crowned Goldfinch** *C. c. caniceps* recorded S & W Japan (Feb, May, Oct). **HH** Mixed forest, woodland, parks and gardens. **ID Grey-crowned Goldfinch** is colourful, with bright red face, black lores, grey-white head-sides and underparts, darker grey mantle and flanks, black wings with yellow bases to primaries, secondaries and outer tertials, forming broad golden-yellow band, white fringes and tips to tertials, white rump and short, notched black tail with white spots near tip. **European Goldfinch** has deeper, more extensive bright red forehead and chin, black crown and hind-collar, white head-sides and underparts, dark grey-brown mantle and breast-sides, blacker wings with broad golden-yellow band, and only white tips to tertials. **BP** Bill sharply conical, pale pinkish-horn; eyes black; tarsi dull pink. **SV** Call: a musical tinkling *kiri kiri* or *tickelitt*; flight call a lilting, liquid *tilili* or *tulilit*. **TN** Not included by OSJ.

Eurasian Siskin *Spinus spinus*

L 11–13 cm; WT 9–17 g

SD Widespread, fairly common winter visitor (Oct–May) from Hokkaido to Nansei Shoto. Irruptive, winter numbers varying greatly between years. Scarce breeder in Hokkaido and N Honshu. **HH** Mixed taiga forest with birch and alder, riparian woodland, parks and gardens. **ID** Small yellow-green finch with bright yellow wing, rump and tail patches. ♂: black forehead and chin, contrasting with yellow face; olive-green mantle streaked black, yellow rump, black tail with yellow bases to outer feathers; shallowly notched tail is narrower and shorter than in Oriental Greenfinch. Underparts yellow, whiter on belly and flanks, with dark-grey streaking on flanks. Wings black with broad yellow tips to coverts and outer fringes to flight-feathers. ♀: duller, lacks black forehead and chin, less yellow below. **BP** Bill fine, sharply conical, pink with grey culmen and tip; eyes black; tarsi blackish-pink. **SV** Call: varied, rising or falling, either thin *tsuu-ee*, *chueen* (clearer than Oriental Greenfinch) or *tilu*; or hard, dry rattling *tet-tet*. Song: prolonged, rambling and complex, many thin twittering notes interspersed with trills *tseen jukuku tsupyee*...

Myrtle Warbler *Setophaga coronata*

L 12–14 cm; WT 12 g

SD Vagrant in winter to C Honshu (Kanagawa Prefecture). **HH** Open woodland. **ID** Distinctive yellow patches on rump and breast-sides in all plumages. ♂ breeding blue-grey, blacker on ear-coverts, white on throat and underparts, with black streaking on mantle, across chest and sides; yellow on crown, broken white supercilia, two white wing-covert bars. ♀ is like a dull ♂, with dark ear-coverts, whitish throat, but browner-grey mantle and chest. 1st-winter browner than adult. ♀ with dark ear-coverts bordered above by narrow dark eyeline and below by pale off-white or buff-white throat wrapping around rear of ear-coverts. **BP** Bill slender, black; prominent white crescents above and below black eyes; tarsi black. **SV** Call: a low, flat *chep* or *tep* and in flight a clear, rising *svit*. **TN** Previously Yellow-rumped Warbler in genus *Dendroica*.

Wilson's Warbler *Cardellina pusilla*

L 11–13 cm; WT 8 g

SD Vagrant to Japan (Hegurajima; subspecies uncertain). **ID** Very small, very active, bright-yellow bird, the size of Japanese White-eye, with rounded wings and long, thin tail. Adult bright, plain olive-green above and yellow below. Face very plain, yellowish-olive, with distinct black cap (♂) or forehead patch (♀), yellow forehead and head-sides in ♂ and dull green crown in immature ♀. **BP** Bill very fine, short, grey-pink; eyes appear large on plain yellow/olive face, irides black; tarsi dull pink. **SV** Call: flat *timp*, and (in flight) clear, abrupt *tilk*. **TN** Previously in genus *Wilsonia*.

European Goldfinch
juv
ad caniceps
ad
carduelis
Eurasian Siskin
juv
ad ♂
ad ♂
ad ♀
Myrtle Warbler
ad ♂
ad ♀
juv
Wilson's Warbler
1st-win ♀
ad ♂ sum

Crested Bunting *Emberiza lathami*

L 16–18 cm; WT 20–26 g

SD Vagrant to S Nansei Shoto (Iriomotejima). **HH** Dry grassland. **ID** Large, dark bunting with prominent pointed crest (♂♀). ♂ is largely black and rufous-brown. ♀ is brown, pale-throated, darkest on chest with narrow blackish streaks, and has warm dull rufous-brown wings and fringes to dark-brown tail. **BP** Bill large, dusky greyish-pink; eyes large, dark brown; tarsi dull brownish-pink. **SV** Hard *chi*.

Yellowhammer *Emberiza citrinella*

L 15–18 cm; WT 14–36 g

SD Accidental in winter and spring (*E. c. erythrogenys*; Oct–May) to N, C & W Honshu, Kyushu and Tsushima. **HH** Thickets, woodland edge and agricultural land with scattered trees. **ID** Large, long-tailed, yellow-headed bunting. ♂ has essentially yellow head and underparts, with dusky patch at rear of crown abutting rear ear-coverts. Upperparts brown with heavy black streaking on mantle, bright rufous on rump. Rufous-brown also in band across breast and streaking on flanks. Tail long, notched, often flicked, showing white-fringed outer feathers. ♀ duller, with mainly brown head, somewhat yellower on supercilia, malar and throat, but also has rufous-brown rump and streaking on belly; palest ♀ very similar to ♀ Pine Bunting, but never white on belly. Yellowhammer x Pine Bunting hybrids are potential identification pitfall. **BP** Bill stubby, grey; eyes pale brown; tarsi greyish-pink. **SV** Calls include *tsui*, *tsik-tsik* and a liquid, clicking *pt..pt..pt..pittlitt*.

Pine Bunting *Emberiza leucocephalos*

L 16–18 cm; WT 24–35 g

SD *E. l. leucocephalos* is a scarce or rare winter visitor (Oct–Apr) to Japan from Hokkaido to Nansei Shoto. **HH** Mixed deciduous forest, woodland edge and agricultural land with trees. **ID** A large, dark, rufous bunting. Breeding ♂ has distinctive head pattern of white crown and ear-coverts (both bordered black), broad chestnut supercilia, chestnut chin/throat and head-side. Nape grey, mantle rufous-brown streaked black; lower back, rump and uppertail-coverts plain rufous-brown; tail blackish-brown with white outer feathers. Underparts rufous-brown, with narrow grey-white collar and neck patch separating chestnut throat from rufous breast; belly and vent white; wings blackish-brown with rufous-brown fringes to most feathers. Winter ♂ duller, greyer brown above and below, with only 'ghost' of summer head pattern, though cheek patch still prominent. ♀ (see similar Yellowhammer) is generally greyish-brown, with paler supercilia, off-white malar bordered above by black moustachial and below by dark lateral throat-stripe, which extends as heavy dark-grey streaking on breast and sides; lacks yellowish tones of Yellowhammer. 1st-winter resembles adult of respective sex. **BP** Bill sharp-pointed, blue-grey with dark culmen; eyes black; tarsi brownish-pink. **SV** Calls are mostly identical to Yellowhammer, but also gives hard *tsick* and downslurred *chüeh*.

Meadow Bunting *Emberiza cioides*

L 15–18 cm; WT 20–26 g

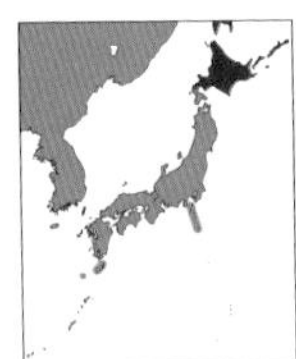

SD *E. c. ciopsis* is fairly common and widespread resident throughout most of Japan from Hokkaido to Yakushima, only a summer visitor to Hokkaido, and a scarce visitor to Ogasawara and Nansei Shoto. **HH** Open wooded areas, thickets, cleared forests and agricultural areas in lowlands and low hills. **ID** Large, dark, warm rufous-brown bunting. ♂ has distinctive black-and-white head pattern, with white supercilia joining collar, which runs to chin, black lores and black ear-coverts, white malar and black lateral throat-stripe, and crown is dark chestnut bordered laterally with black. Upperparts warm, dark rufous-brown from crown to tail, distinctly streaked on mantle and back but plain rufous on lower back, rump and uppertail-coverts; tail blackish and rufous-brown with white outer fringes to outer feathers. Chin and throat white, upper breast orange-brown, then plain dark rufous-brown grading to off-white on belly. ♀ generally paler, sandy- rather than rufous-brown, with broad white supercilia, mainly white chin and throat, and brown ear-coverts; otherwise like washed-out ♂. **BP** Bill dark grey; eyes black; tarsi brownish-pink. **SV** Call: differs from other buntings in being uttered in series, often three *zit-zit-zit* notes (sometimes 2–4), not singly. Song *cho-pizt-two-chirr* or *tsui chocho tsuryi cho tsupitchi richipi*.

Crested Bunting
ad ♂
ad ♀
Yellowhammer
1st-win
ad ♂ win
ad ♂ sum
ad ♀
Pine Bunting
1st-win
ad ♂ win
ad ♂ sum
ad ♀ sum
Meadow Bunting
ad ♂
ad ♂
ad ♀

Grey-necked Bunting *Emberiza buchanani*

L 15–17 cm; WT 17–26 g

SD Vagrant in autumn (Sep–Oct; subspecies uncertain) to Hegurajima and Tobishima. **HH** Rocky areas with sparse vegetation. **ID** Rather plain bunting, resembling Ortolan. ♂ has dull blue-grey head, face and neck, distinctive pale buff malar, grey lateral throat-stripe and whitish throat; underparts warm rufous-buff (lacks Ortolan's grey upper breast), whiter on belly; upperparts, wings and tail mid-brown with darker streaking and white outer tail-feathers. ♀ is less clearly marked, and 1st-winter and juvenile only have slight grey cast to head and buffish underparts, with light streaking on mantle and breast. **BP** Bill pinkish-orange; eye-ring white, eyes black; legs dull pink to brownish-pink. **SV** Call is rather strong *chi*.

Ortolan Bunting *Emberiza hortulana*

L 15–17 cm; WT 20–28 g

SD Vagrant (Jun–Oct) to Hegurajima, Tokunoshima, Kumejima and Teurijima. **HH** Open dry habitats with thickets. **ID** Rather large bunting. ♂ has olive-grey head, neck and breast, yellow malar stripe, chin and throat patch. Upperparts brown with heavy dark streaking, underparts rufous-brown on belly. Lesser wing-coverts blackish in Ortolan (grey in very similar Grey-necked). ♀ lacks olive-grey of ♂, being brown, with whitish-ochre throat, breast and belly, and brown streaking on breast (unmarked in ♀ Grey-necked). 1st-winter and juvenile heavily streaked on mantle, breast and malar, with yellow tinge to buff submoustachial stripe and chin/throat. **BP** Bill pink; eyes rather prominent, with narrow white ring, irides dark brown; tarsi pink or brownish-pink. **SV** Varied calls include soft, clicking *plett* or *tsupitt tsupitt*, harder *chu* and disyllabic *sli-e*.

Tristram's Bunting *Emberiza tristrami*

L 14–15 cm; WT 14–21 g

SD Rare migrant from Nansei Shoto to Hokkaido. **HH** Favours shady areas of mixed taiga forest, particularly beneath stands of fir; shy and nervous. **ID** Distinctive, small, but rather stocky, compact bunting with very heavily striped head. ♂ has black head and chin, with grey-white coronal stripe, supercilia and malar, and white spot on rear ear-coverts. Greyish-brown on mantle with black streaking, rufous-brown to chestnut on lower back, rump and tail; underparts white, with extensive dull rufous-brown wash on breast and flanks with dark streaking. ♀ less contrasting, greyish-brown instead of black on head, but shares similar striped pattern, with buff supercilia and ear-coverts, and has whitish chin/throat with dark lateral throat-stripes. **BP** Sharply pointed bill is grey above and at tip, pink below; eyes black; tarsi deep pink. **SV** Call is slightly metallic *tsip*, resembling calls of Rustic and Elegant buntings.

Chestnut-eared Bunting *Emberiza fucata*

L 15–16 cm; WT 14–29 g

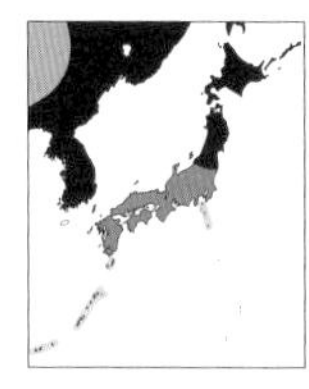

SD *E. f. fucata* is an uncommon and declining summer visitor (May–Sep) to Hokkaido, an uncommon and local resident from N Honshu to Kyushu, and an uncommon winter visitor south to Izu Is and S Nansei Shoto. **HH** Open grassy habitats with thickets, including rank meadows and wetland fringes; winters in open agricultural land. **ID** Large, well-patterned bunting with distinctive chestnut ear patch (see Little Bunting) and double breast-band. ♂ has grey crown and nape, bright chestnut ear-coverts, and contrasting face pattern of black moustachial, white malar and chin/throat, and black lateral throat-stripe extending as necklace of black streaks. Mantle grey-brown with black streaking; scapulars, lower back, rump and uppertail-coverts plain rufous-brown; tail blackish-brown. Underparts white on chin/throat with black, white and chestnut breast-bands, then warm orange-brown wash on sides grading to white on belly; wings blackish-brown with mid-brown feather fringes. ♀ less cleanly marked, but has chestnut ear-coverts patch, lacks contrast of ♂, but also has dark lateral throat-stripe extending as streaking on breast and flanks. **BP** Bill grey above, pinkish-grey below; prominent narrow white eye-ring, irides black; tarsi brownish-pink. **SV** Call is rather spitting, staccato *pit* or *pt*. Song recalls Meadow Bunting, but is deeper, shorter, weaker, less clear, ending in three-part phrase *chip chip chil-ri-wit chi chi tsiririri* or *che chitsu chirinju*. **AN** Grey-headed Bunting.

Grey-necked Bunting
ad ♂
1st-win
Ortolan Bunting
ad ♂
1st-win
Tristram's Bunting
ad ♂ sum
ad ♀
ad ♂ win
Chestnut-eared Bunting

ad ♂ win
ad ♂ sum
ad ♀ sum
ad ♂ sum
1st-win ♂

Little Bunting *Emberiza pusilla*

L 12–14 cm; WT 13–19 g

SD Rare or scarce migrant from Hokkaido to Yakushima, rare winter visitor to Kyushu and Nansei Shoto, and accidental to Ogasawara Is. **HH** Scrub, woodland fringes and dry agricultural land with tall grasses or reeds. **ID** Small, compact bunting with distinctly chestnut face (see Chestnut-eared Bunting) and striped head. ♂ mostly chestnut head, face and lores with black lateral crown-stripes, narrow eyestripe and outer border to ear-coverts, narrow moustachial and lateral throat-stripes merging into prominent but narrow black streaking on sides of otherwise clean white breast and flanks. Upperparts greyish-brown with black streaking on mantle and scapulars; wings blackish-brown, with white tips to coverts forming faint wingbars, and rufous fringes to secondaries. ♀ and 1st-winter ♂ resemble adult ♂, but lateral crown-stripes less clear and face less distinctly chestnut, but still fairly bright. **BP** Bill rather small, grey; distinctive narrow white eye-ring around black eye; tarsi dull orange/pink. **SV** Short, clipped, slightly metallic *zip*, somewhat wetter-sounding than other buntings.

Yellow-browed Bunting *Emberiza chrysophrys*

L 14–16 cm; WT 20 g

SD Rare migrant to Japan, recorded from Nansei Shoto to Hokkaido. **HH** Taiga forest, woodland edges, thickets and agricultural land with trees. **ID** Small, compact, with unique head pattern; superficially resembles Tristram's Bunting, but less dark overall and less striped on head. ♂ has black head, but grey nape (not chestnut), broad yellow supercilia from just above eyes becoming white at rear, white spot on otherwise black ear-coverts, white malar, black lateral throat-stripe and narrow black streaking on chin, breast-sides and flanks; underparts otherwise off-white with brown-washed flanks. Upperparts brown on neck and mantle with heavy streaking, plain mid-brown lower back and rump, and brownish-black tail with white outer feathers. White-tipped coverts form two narrow wingbars. ♀ has less boldly marked head, but longer supercilia are yellow from bill base to above eye, then white behind. **BP** Bill grey above and at tip, pinkish-grey below; eyes black; tarsi pink. **SV** A thin, metallic *tzip*, recalling Little Bunting, but less 'wet'.

Rustic Bunting *Emberiza rustica*

L 13–14 cm; WT 14–26 g

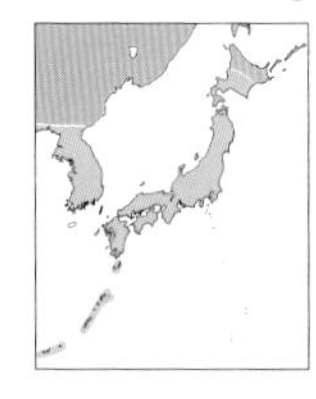

SD Vulnerable. Widespread winter visitor and spring migrant (Oct–May) throughout Japan south of Hokkaido (where scarce migrant) to Nansei Shoto. **HH** Taiga forest, forest edge, dry lowland woodland, riparian thickets and margins of agricultural land with rank vegetation. **ID** Smallish compact bunting with distinct crest and striking head pattern. Breeding ♂ has black head, with erectile crest, white lateral crown-stripe from above eye to nape, and white chin and throat with black lateral throat-stripe. Upperparts chestnut on hindneck, brown on back but heavily streaked black, lower back and rump dull chestnut, tail long, blackish with white outer feathers. Underparts white, with chestnut band on upper breast and chestnut streaking on flanks. Winter ♂ less contrasting, generally lacking black on head, but does have black outline to brownish ear-coverts, and crown still appears crested, whilst dark lateral throat-stripe blends into chestnut of upper breast. ♀ resembles winter ♂, but paler and less boldly marked, lacking any black on ear-coverts. White-tipped coverts form two narrow wingbars, most prominent in summer ♂. **BP** Bill grey above and at tip, pink at base (summer ♂), or pinkish-grey (♀/winter ♂); eyes black; tarsi dull pink. **SV** Strong *tsip* or *fuchip*.

Elegant Bunting *Emberiza elegans*

L 15–17 cm; WT 15–24 g

SD Uncommon visitor (*E. e. elegans*) wintering (Nov–Apr) from Nansei Shoto to Hokkaido (where scarce); some breeding records from Tsushima and W Honshu. **HH** Open deciduous woodland, woodland edges, often on low hillsides. **ID** Breeding ♂ has black crown and short erectile crest, black mask from supraloral to ear-coverts and black chest shield; remainder of head is bright lemon-yellow. Grey half-collar on nape, mantle pale brown heavily streaked rufous-brown, rump greyish-brown, and tail ash-grey and blackish-brown. Underparts largely white with chestnut streaking on sides; wings blackish-brown with white fringes to coverts, brown fringes to flight-feathers and broad rusty-brown fringes to tertials. Winter ♂ similar, but with duller, less contrasting head pattern. ♀ less contrasting, lacking black on head or underparts, but has distinct yellow wash to supercilia, head-sides and chin/throat; lack of malar stripe makes separation from ♀ Rustic easy. **BP** Rather stout bill, grey above, pinkish-grey below; eyes black; tarsi pink. **SV** Call: a clear, somewhat moist-sounding *tsi* or *tsi-ti tsip*. Song: a long, slurred trilling *chichi churichuri churiri chichi*. **AN** Yellow-throated Bunting.

Little Bunting
ad ♂ sum
ad win
Yellow-browed Bunting
ad ♂
1st-win ♀
ad ♀
Rustic Bunting
ad ♂
ad ♂ sum
1st-win
ad ♀ sum
Elegant Bunting
ad ♂
ad ♀

Yellow-breasted Bunting *Emberiza aureola*

L 14–16 cm; WT 17–26 g

SD Endangered. Once abundant, *E. a. ornata* has undergone a catastrophic decline. Until 1980s it was common and widespread summer visitor to Hokkaido (where now extinct); now it is very rare migrant from Nansei Shoto to Hokkaido. **HH** Breeds in wetland fringes, reedbeds, rank meadows and riparian grasslands; on migration also in dry agricultural land with scrub, grasses and reeds. **ID** A quite large, somewhat stout bunting. Breeding ♂: very boldly marked, dark chocolate-brown above, bright yellow below, with broad black mask, chocolate-brown chest-band and streaks on flanks, conspicuous white scapulars and bold white wingbar. Winter ♂ and immature ♂ lack mask and chest-band and are greyer on ear-coverts bordered narrowly below with black. ♀: resembles winter ♂, but has broad pale supercilia, dark border to ear-coverts, prominent white median-covert bar and brighter yellow underparts. Juvenile heavily streaked on breast and flanks. Lacks chestnut coloration on rump of Chestnut Bunting. **BP** Bill heavy, pink (breeding ♂), or otherwise grey above and at tip, pink below and at base; eyes black; tarsi pink. **SV** Call: soft *tip-tip* or *tzip*. Song: loud, clearly whistled, ascending series of notes until final one, which descends: *tsyu tsui tee-e tee-e tsee-tee*; *fee hyo hyui chui churee* or *filyou-filyou-filee-filee-filee-tyou-tyou*.

Chestnut Bunting *Emberiza rutila*

L 12–15 cm; WT 16–19 g

SD Rare migrant from Nansei Shoto to Hokkaido, most frequently on islands in Sea of Japan. **HH** Scrub, woodland fringes and dry agricultural land with trees/shrubs. **ID** Distinctively colourful small bunting. Breeding ♂: has bright chestnut hood and upperparts, with bright-yellow underparts, becoming grey only on sides; wings blackish-brown, broadly fringed chestnut on coverts, secondaries and tertials; tail blackish-brown. Winter ♂: has less bright chestnut hood and mantle flecked with yellow. ♀: recalls ♀ Yellow-breasted Bunting, but smaller; head to back greyish-brown with heavy streaking on mantle and scapulars, lower back, rump and uppertail-coverts quite bright chestnut, tail blackish with white outer feathers. Face rather nondescript with weak yellowish-buff supercilia; malar, throat and underparts yellowish-buff with dark lateral throat-stripe merging into fine streaking on flanks. **BP** Bill delicate, grey; eyes black; tarsi dull pink. **SV** Short, hard *tsip* or *zit*.

Black-headed Bunting *Emberiza melanocephala*

L 15–18 cm; WT 23–33 g

SD Rare migrant from Nansei Shoto to Hokkaido, mostly to offshore islands, and very rare winter visitor to S Nansei Shoto. **HH** Thickets and woodland edge near agricultural land. **ID** Large, bulky, bull-headed bunting. Breeding ♂: unmistakable, with black head, face and neck-sides contrasting with rufous-brown or chestnut upperparts, and bright-yellow underparts. Non-breeding ♂: has pale buff fringes to feathers of head and mantle. ♀ (very closely recalls ♀ Red-headed Bunting) has plain sandy-brown head, breast and upperparts, strong yellow tinge to throat, breast, belly and undertail-coverts, and narrow streaking on sides. Both sexes have white fringes to wing-coverts, forming two wingbars, and broad pale fringes to tertials. Most records involve ♀s or juveniles; these are best separated from similar Red-headed by rufous fringes to mantle and back, slightly stronger contrast between grey-buff ear-coverts and paler off-white chin/throat, and more uniformly yellow underparts. **BP** Large bill rather long, bulbous, sharply pointed, with straight culmen, dark grey; eyes brown, often with white eye-ring; tarsi quite bright pink. **SV** Varied and similar to other large buntings, strong *jüp*, *zrt*, *tsit* and clicking *ptr'r'r*.

Red-headed Bunting *Emberiza bruniceps*

L 16–17 cm; WT 18–31 g

SD Accidental to Tobishima, Hegurajima, Tsushima and Yonagunijima. **HH** As Black-headed Bunting. **ID** Large, bulky, bull-headed bunting. Breeding ♂: unmistakable, with bright chestnut head and chest, yellow-olive upperparts, streaked black, yellow rump and bright yellow underparts. Non-breeding ♂: has less clearly marked chestnut head and breast, yellow malar stripe and yellow flecks in chestnut. ♀ (often inseparable from ♀ Black-headed): plain sandy-brown on head, breast and upperparts, yellowish on flanks and belly, bright yellow on vent and greenish-yellow on rump/uppertail-coverts; wings blackish, feathers fringed buff. **BP** Large dark-grey bill is rather sharply pointed, with straight culmen, but shorter and more triangular than Black-headed; eyes prominent in plain face, irides black; tarsi quite bright pink. **SV** Calls indistinguishable from Black-headed.

Yellow-breasted Bunting

ad ♂ win

ad ♂ sum

ad ♀

imm / 1st-win

Chestnut Bunting

ad ♂

ad ♀

1st-sum ♂

1st-win ♀

Red-headed Bunting

ad ♂ win

ad ♂ sum

ad ♀

Black-headed Bunting

ad ♂ win

ad ♂ sum

ad ♀

Yellow Bunting *Emberiza sulphurata*

L 13–14 cm; WT 17–22 g

SD Vulnerable. Scarce, local summer visitor (May–Sep), C & N Honshu; scarce/rare migrant Nansei Shoto to Hokkaido. **HH** Mixed, but mainly deciduous, forest edge and shrubby grasslands at mid-elevations (600–1,500 m). **ID** Superficially resembles larger Masked Bunting, but cleaner, with plainer face and more prominent wingbars; quieter, less active. ♂ has head, face, nape and neck-sides plain greyish-olive; black lores contrast with narrow, but noticeable, white eye-ring. Upperparts greyish-olive with black-streaked mantle and scapulars, lower back and rump plain yellowish-olive. ♀ lacks black lores, but has white eye-ring and yellowish wash to creamy-buff underparts from chin to vent, with some contrast in malar region. Prominent white tips to median and greater coverts form distinct double wingbars (slightly less distinct in ♀). **BP** Bill blue-grey; eyes particularly noticeable due to white crescents above and below, irides black; tarsi dull pink. **SV** Call: a metallic *tsip*, softer than Masked but very similar to Tristram's and Chestnut. Song: recalls Masked, but softer and faster: *chip-in chin-chin chee-chee-chee che-rui* or *chichon pipi chiichii chiichii*.

Masked Bunting *Emberiza personata*

L 13–16 cm; WT 21 g

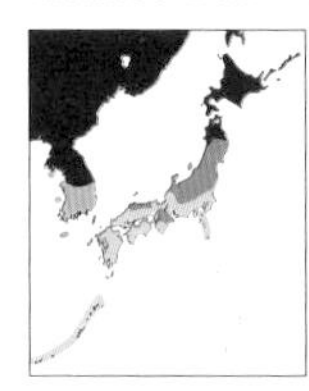

SD Common and widespread summer visitor (Apr–Oct), breeding throughout Hokkaido, N & C Honshu, wintering (Oct–Apr), Honshu south to Nansei Shoto; accidental Ogasawara Is. **HH** Mixed, but mainly deciduous, lowland forests and river valleys, to mid-elevation mountains in summer, and in forest, woodland fringes, scrub, parks, gardens and agricultural land in winter, particularly in areas with dwarf bamboo ground cover. **ID** Note double wingbar, white outer tail-feathers, and nervous behaviour, often flicking tail. ♂ has strong black mask, olive crown, nape and ear-coverts, bright-yellow underparts, with dark olive-green neck-sides and streaking on breast-sides/flanks, upperparts paler brown and wings also paler brown than Black-faced. White fringes to lesser and greater coverts form faint wingbars. ♀ resembles Black-faced ♀, but supercilia, malar and underparts washed variably dull to pale yellow. **BP** Bill greyish-pink with grey tip and culmen; eyes black; tarsi dull brownish-pink. **SV** Call a hard, forced, slightly discordant, *tsip* or *jit*. Song a slow *tsip-chee-tree phirrr* or *choppiichott pii chiriri*. **TN** Also included within Black-faced Bunting (e.g. IOC).

Black-faced Bunting *Emberiza spodocephala*

L 13–16 cm; WT 21 g

SD *E. s. spodocephala* (including '*extremi-orientis*') is a rare migrant, reported Nansei Shoto to N Honshu. **HH** Deciduous woodland, scrub, parks, gardens, agricultural land. **ID** Shares double wingbar, white outer tail-feathers, calls and behaviour with Masked Bunting, but *E. s. spodocephala*, the common continental form, is rather dull and dark, recalling Grey Bunting. ♂ has dark greenish-grey or greyish-olive (even blackish-grey) hood, with extensive black lores and narrow black chin; upperparts dark brown with black and grey streaking, rump plain brown; underparts pale yellow on belly, browner and streaked on flanks. ♀ lacks black of lores and chin, and dark-hooded appearance, instead has dull grey-brown supercilia, broad pale malar bordered darker on moustachial and lateral throat-stripe, breast dusky olive-brown heavily streaked, and rest of underparts off-white. ♂ *E. s. sordida* is plainer, with dark olive-green hood sharply demarcated from bright-yellow underparts; ♀ resembles ♀ Masked, but browner crown and ear-coverts, buff not yellow supercilia. **BP** Bill greyish-pink with grey tip and culmen; eyes black; tarsi dull brownish-pink. **SV** Hard, forced, slightly discordant, *tsip* or *jit*.

Grey Bunting *Emberiza variabilis*

L 14–17 cm; WT 20–38 g

SD *E. v. variabilis* is an uncommon and local summer visitor (May–Sep), Hokkaido, N & C Honshu, Shikoku; winter visitor (Oct–Apr) N Honshu to Nansei Shoto; *E. v. musica* also winters in Japan. **HH** Favours mixed deciduous and coniferous forests of mid-elevations, with undergrowth and thickets of dwarf bamboo, preferring dense, shady cover, where quite skulking; in winter in shady forest, woodland and parks. **ID** Rather plain, dark grey bunting; lacks white in tail. ♂ slate-grey, with black-streaked mantle, black wing-feathers with broad slate-grey fringes to wing-coverts and tertials. Immature ♂ has face and underparts like dull ♂, upperparts like ♀. ♀ is generally dark grey-brown with black streaking, with grey-brown ear-coverts bordered below by blackish moustachial stripe, pale grey malar and dark-brown lateral throat-stripe; chin/throat whitish. Underparts dark dusky-brown with quite heavy darker streaking. In flight, plain dark rufous-brown rump is particularly noticeable. **BP** Bill pink with grey culmen and tip; eyes black; tarsi pink. **SV** Call: a fine, thin *tsi*. Song: slow, slightly sweet and somewhat flycatcher-like, with 3–5 distinct notes: *swee swee chi-chi-chi*; also *huiiii tsi-tsi tsu-chi hee hee* or *fee choichoi*.

Yellow Bunting
ad ♂
ad ♀
1st-win ♀
Masked Bunting
ad ♂
ad ♀
Black-faced Bunting
ad ♂
ad ♂
ad ♀
Grey Bunting
variabilis
ad ♂
1st-win ♂
ad ♀

Pallas's Reed Bunting *Emberiza pallasi*

L 13–14 cm; WT 14–16 g

SD *E. p. polaris* is very rare winter visitor to Kyushu and accidental migrant recorded from Tsushima to N Honshu and Hokkaido; nominate *E. p. pallasi* is vagrant to N Kyushu, and *E. p. minor* may occur. **HH** Dry agricultural land with scrub, grasses and reeds. **ID** Smaller, paler, more delicate than other reed buntings, with small head and fine bill. ♂ has glossy black hood broken by broad white malar stripe; nape, neck-sides and underparts clear white, unstreaked (or with some very fine streaking on flanks and thin dusky streaks on breast-sides) and lacking grey on sides; upperparts pale tawny-brown with contrasting black streaking on mantle and back; lower back, rump and uppertail-coverts sandy or pale buff; and long tail ashy-black with white outer feathers. Wings lack rufous on lesser coverts of Common Reed Bunting (CRB), instead has pale blue-grey lesser wing-coverts and sandy fringes to rest of wing-feathers. Winter ♂ lacks black hood, has prominent buff supercilia and malar, and dusky lateral throat-stripe; underparts pale buff, but remain unstreaked. Lacks pale median forecrown-stripe of CRB. ♀ resembles winter ♂, but has distinct narrow lateral throat-stripe and whiter underparts, still with some faint dusky streaking. **BP** Bill short, sharply pointed, with straight culmen, lower mandible much slighter than CRB, black in breeding ♂, otherwise greyish-black with mostly dull pinkish-horn lower mandible (in CRB entirely dark or grey); eyes appear small, irides black; tarsi dull brownish-orange. **SV** Somewhat sparrow-like *chep* and *tschirp*, as well as more typical bunting-like *tsip* and occasional CRB-like *dsiu*.

Japanese Reed Bunting *Emberiza yessoensis*

L 14–15 cm; WT 13–14 g

SD *E. y. yessoensis* is uncommon and very local in N & C Honshu and Kyushu (Kumamoto). In winter, very local in S & W Honshu and Shikoku. Accidental elsewhere from Danjo Is to Hokkaido. **HH** Marshy habitats, wetland fringes with bushes, reedbeds, and tall-grass meadows; in winter, coastal marshes and open agricultural land near water. **ID** The most richly coloured reed bunting. ♂ has unbroken, glossy black hood extending only to lower neck at front, otherwise mostly warm rufous/orange-brown; mantle heavily streaked black and white, lesser wing-coverts show some blue-grey, otherwise wings mostly rufous with prominent black tertials. Winter ♂ retains strong 'ghost' of black hood, with prominent orange-buff supercilia. 1st-winter ♂ resembles adult ♀ from Dec onwards, head darkens Feb onwards. ♀ resembles winter ♂, but has distinct orange-buff malar and narrow distinct lateral throat-stripe contrasting with off-white throat. Lower back, rump and uppertail-coverts warm rufous-brown in both sexes, readily distinguishing them from Common or Pallas's. **BP** Bill rather sharply pointed with straight culmen, lower mandible heavier than Pallas's, black in breeding ♂, grey above and at tip, bright pink below, especially at base, in winter ♂/♀; eyes black; tarsi quite bright pink. **SV** Hard *tsu tsu cho* or *chi*. Song like repetitive Meadow Bunting: *chui-tsui-chirin, choppi churiri pi* or *cho pichu piichuu picho*. **AN** Ochre-rumped Bunting.

Common Reed Bunting *Emberiza schoeniclus*

L 13–19 cm; WT 16–25 cm

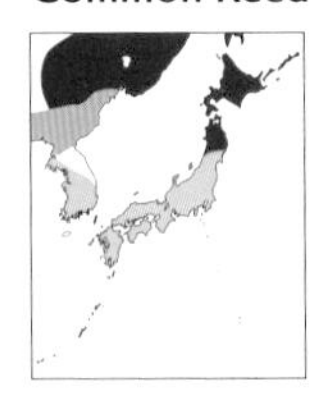

SD *E. s. pyrrhulina* is a fairly common summer visitor (May–Sep) to Hokkaido and N Honshu. Winters (Oct–Apr) in C & W Honshu to Kyushu, and very rare Nansei Shoto. **HH** Wetland fringes, reedbeds, thickets and tall grasses, rank meadows and riparian grasslands; winters in similar habitats, but also in dry agricultural land with scrub, grasses and reeds. **ID** Largest of the three reed buntings; long-tailed. ♂: has glossy black hood to breast, broken by bold white malar stripe; nape, neck-sides and underparts white, somewhat grey-white at sides; upperparts pale rufous-brown heavily streaked black on mantle, back and scapulars, but lower back, rump and uppertail-coverts ashy grey-brown, tail ashy-black with white outer feathers. Winter ♂: duller, lacks black hood, but has weak median forecrown-stripe, pale ashy-brown supercilia, brown lores, crown and ear-coverts, and black lateral throat-stripe forming prominent neck patch and merging into narrow streaking on flanks. Often has stronger grey tone to rump. ♀: resembles winter ♂, but lateral throat-stripe less prominent and supercilia continue to base of bill. **BP** Bill heavy, culmen slightly arched, lower mandible robust, greyish-black; eyes black; tarsi dull brownish-orange. **SV** Rather plaintive, sibilant *siooo*, harsher *bjee* and *chuiin*. Song a rising *chii chuichui chi chui jurin* or *shree-shree-teeree-teeree*.

Pallas's Reed Bunting
polaris
ad ♂ win
ad ♂ sum
ad ♀
1st-win ♀
Japanese Reed Bunting
ad ♂ win
ad ♂ sum
1st-win ♀
ad ♀
Common Reed Bunting
ad ♂ sum
ad ♂ win
ad ♀

Sooty Fox Sparrow *Passerella unalaschcensis* L 16–19 cm; WT 27–49 g

SD Accidental in winter (subspecies uncertain). **HH** Favours brushy habitats. **ID** Large, dark-brown sparrow with plain head, face and unstreaked upperparts. Tail tinged warmer brown or reddish-brown. Underparts white with extensive, heavy dark streaking or mottling on throat, breast and flanks, somewhat whiter with less streaking on belly. **BP** Bill rather large, short, straw yellow or orange-yellow base to lower mandible, with dark-grey culmen; eyes dark brown; tarsi dull brownish-pink. **SV** Call: a loud, low *tschup*, also described as *chi*, *cha* or *check*, a sharp *smack* or *chap*, and in flight a sharp, rising *seeep*. **TN** Formerly within *Passerella (Zonotrichia) iliaca* (e.g. OSJ).

Song Sparrow *Melospiza melodia* L 13–16 cm; WT 20 g

SD Vagrant to Mishima (subspecies uncertain). **HH** Low vegetation and scrub. **ID** Fairly large, round-headed and long-tailed dark sparrow, with short, rounded wings; rather coarsely streaked, thus superficially recalls various ♀ *Emberiza* but, like similar Savannah Sparrow, lacks white in outer tail-feathers. Adult: dull grey with heavy brown streaks often converging to central breast spot; crown-sides, ear-coverts and lateral throat-stripe brown; mantle and breast heavily streaked brown; wings and tail largely plain dark brown. Buffish-grey supercilia lack yellow. Juvenile: more heavily streaked with colder, darker blackish-brown. **BP** Bill sharply pointed, grey; eyes dark brown; tarsi dull greyish-pink. **SV** Call is a husky *jimp*, hard, high *tik* (in alarm) and in flight a thin, level *seeet*.

White-crowned Sparrow *Zonotrichia leucophrys* L 16–19 cm; WT 25–33 g

SD *Z. l. gambelii* is extremely rare winter visitor (Oct to Apr), with records from Hokkaido, N & C Honshu, Shikoku, Mishima and Hegurajima. **HH** Favours brushy and weedy, not wooded, habitats, and agricultural and coastal areas. **ID** Adult breeding unmistakable, with narrow white crown bordered by broad black lateral crown-stripes, grey lores, white supercilia broad behind eye to nape, and black eyestripe from eye to nape. Face, chin/throat and breast plain grey, flanks brown; upperparts grey-brown with black streaking, tail rather long and plain brown. Wings brown with two white bars formed by tips to coverts, and rufous fringes to tertials. 1st-winter (most likely vagrants): head pattern much weaker than adult, with brown crown, dull grey supercilia, brown eyestripe from eye, grey to grey-brown face and throat separated by dark brown lateral throat-stripe, nape streaked and grades into dull grey-brown back streaked blackish-brown; underparts dusky grey-brown, browner on flanks. **BP** Bill pale pink or pale yellow; eyes black with white crescents above and below; tarsi yellowish-brown. **SV** Call is rather strong, sharp *pink* or metallic *pzit* and in flight a high, thin, rising *seeet*.

Golden-crowned Sparrow *Zonotrichia atricapilla* L 17–18 cm; WT 29 g

SD Extremely rare winter visitor and migrant to Honshu, Hokkaido and various Sea of Japan islands. **HH** Favours brushy areas and woodland edge. **ID** Large, plain-faced sparrow with long tail and two-toned bill. Adult breeding generally similar to White-crowned, but has golden-yellow forecrown, whiter at rear, and broad black band across head-sides to eye and bill, face plain grey, underparts dull grey with rufous-brown wash to flanks. Non-breeding adult has reduced black and yellow on head, and is greyer. 1st-winter has little or no black on head, and only small area of often dingy yellow on forehead. **BP** Bill yellowish-horn below and grey above (ad), or all grey (young); eyes black; tarsi flesh-pink. **SV** Call is sharp, flat *pink* and in flight a thin *seet*.

Sooty Fox Sparrow
ad
Song Sparrow
ad ♂
White-crowned Sparrow
ad sum
1st-win

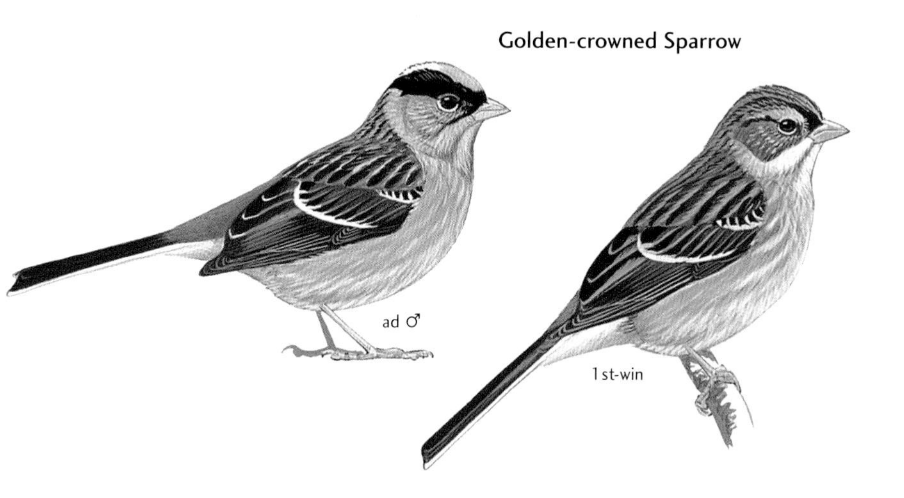
Golden-crowned Sparrow
ad ♂
1st-win

Savannah Sparrow *Passerculus sandwichensis*

L 14–16 cm; WT 20 g

SD *P. s. sandwichensis* is very rare, but regular, winter visitor mainly to Kyushu, but recorded from Okinawa to E Hokkaido. **HH** Grassy areas, fallow fields, open grasslands and coasts. **ID** Small, neat sparrow, with clean streaking and characteristic yellow patch on lores (limited or lacking in some imms). Recalls several ♀ buntings, but lacks white outer tail-feathers. Face striped, with pale buff supercilia becoming prominently yellow in front of eye, dark eyestripe broadening at rear, brown ear-coverts, blackish moustachial and lateral throat-stripe. Narrow whitish lateral crown-stripe. Upperparts grey-brown with dark streaking; underparts off-white with heavily streaked breast and flanks, clean white belly and undertail-coverts. In flight, wings quite long, tail quite short, square or slightly notched, outer feathers may appear pale. Quite similar to slightly larger Yellow-browed Bunting, but yellow confined to supraloral area, rather than extending behind eye, and has less contrasting head pattern. **BP** Bill small, sharply pointed, dull pink with grey culmen and tip; eyes black with narrow white eye-ring; tarsi dull pink. **SV** Call: sharp, slightly metallic *tsui*, *ji* or *tsip*, and (in flight) thin, weakly descending *tsiw*. **TN** Formerly *Ammodramus sandwichensis*.

Red-crested Cardinal *Paroaria coronata*

L 18–19 cm

SD Common in cagebird trade, and feral populations established in C & W Honshu. **HH** Favours areas with shrubs and bushes, or woodland edge. **ID** Large finch-like bird with entire head, erectile crest, face and throat bright red; upperparts, wings and long tail grey, underparts white. **BP** Bill pale whitish-pink; eyes brown; tarsi black. **SV** Song: consists of thrush-like whistled phrases *tsilewp-jewp tsilewp-jewp…* or *dew-dewe-duh-dew-diuh*.

Lapland Longspur *Calcarius lapponicus*

L 15–17 cm; WT 20–31 g

SD *C. l. coloratus* is rare winter visitor (Oct–Mar) to Hokkaido, and rare or accidental winter visitor to Honshu, Shikoku, Kyushu and Nansei Shoto. **HH** Beaches and dunes, open agricultural land or wasteland. Commonly adopts hunched posture resembling larks. **ID** Stocky, medium-sized bunting with large head. Wings quite long, reaching beyond uppertail-coverts, with long primary projection, brownish-black with distinctive rufous fringes to greater coverts and tertials in all plumages; tail long, notched, with white outer feathers. Breeding ♂: has black head and chest, white supercilia curve down neck- to breast-sides, and nape/hindneck bright chestnut. Upperparts brown, streaked black. Winter ♂: has plainer face, usually with 'ghost' of black pattern on throat and chest, retains chestnut nape and has chestnut on wing-coverts and tertials. Breeding ♀: is buff on breast and flanks, with white belly. Non-breeding ♀: generally pale brown on upperparts and breast, wing-coverts and tertials warm brown; face pale with dark corners to ear-coverts, white malar and dark lateral throat-stripe. **BP** Bill yellowish-horn with grey tip; eyes black; tarsi blackish-brown, hindclaw longer than hindtoe. **SV** Call: distinctive dry rattled *prrrt* (like Snow Bunting) and whistled *tleuw*, or run together as *ticketick-tleuw*. **AN** Lapland Bunting.

Snow Bunting *Plectrophenax nivalis*

L 15–18 cm; WT 28–34 g

SD *P. n. vlasowae* is very uncommon and local winter visitor (Oct–Mar) to coastal Hokkaido, and rare or accidental winter visitor elsewhere from Honshu to Nansei Shoto. **HH** Open ground, along snow-free beaches, riverbanks and grassy capes. Restless winter family parties and flocks flutter in 'dancing' flight, then drop suddenly to settle, recalling rosyfinches. **ID** Large, unmistakably black and white bunting with long wings reaching beyond uppertail-coverts. Flight buoyant and flickering, may circle repeatedly before settling; wings largely white with extensive black tips; tail largely black with broad white outer panel and base. Breeding ♂: jet black and white; head, entire underparts, lower back, rump and much of wings white (primary tips black). Upperparts black, as is short, notched tail. Winter ♂: has warm orange-brown crown and ear-coverts, back mottled brown and black, and warm brown breast-sides and flanks. Breeding ♀: resembles winter ♂ but has dusky grey-black streaks on mantle, is not as cleanly pied, and head less clean white with dusky streaking, especially on crown and ear-coverts. Winter ♀: resembles winter ♂. **BP** Bill rather small, black in summer ♂, yellow with grey tip in ♀/winter ♂; black eyes prominent in plain face; tarsi black. **SV** Various calls: similar to Lapland Bunting, but more liquid, rippling *prrrp*, rattled *tiriririt* and softer *tew* or *pyeuw*, often given in flight; also a jarring *jrrt* given occasionally while feeding.

Savannah Sparrow
ad
ad
ad ♂
Red-crested
Cardinal
ad
Lapland Longspur
ad ♂ win
ad ♀ sum
ad ♂ sum
1st-win ♀
ad ♀ win
Snow Bunting
ad ♀ sum
ad ♂
sum
ad ♂ sum
juv
ad ♂ win

PLATE 189: EXTINCT OR PRESUMED EXTINCT SPECIES

Species recorded from Japan that are now either locally or globally extinct.

Crested Shelduck *Tadorna cristata* L 60–64 cm

SD Extinct; vagrant winter visitor. **HH** Coastal wetlands. **ID** Striking dark shelduck with black cap, pale face and neck, and black breast and collar; ♀ similar, with white 'spectacles'. **BP** Bill waxy red; eyes dark brown; tarsi orange.

White-browed Crake *Porzana cinerea* L 15–20 cm; WS 27 cm; WT 40–62 g

SD Locally extinct resident of Iwo Is; extinct since 1911. **HH** Swamps. **ID** Distinctive facial pattern. Straw-buff and dark brown upperparts with grey underparts. **BP** Bill slender, yellowish-orange; eyes deep red; tarsi pale yellowish-olive. **TN** Formerly *Poliolimnas cinereus*. **AN** Ashy Crake.

Slender-billed Curlew *Numenius tenuirostris* L 36–41 cm; WS 80–92 cm; WT 255–360 g

SD Critically Endangered; probably extinct. Rare visitor in early 20th century. **ID** Plumage resembles Eurasian Curlew, but size closer to Common Whimbrel. Distinguished by short black streaks on breast, large heart-shaped spots on lower breast/flanks, and unmarked belly and vent. **BP** Bill slender, short, mostly straight, black with pink base to lower mandible, fine and slightly decurved at tip; eyes black; legs shorter than curlew, dark grey.

Ryukyu Woodpigeon *Columba jouyi* L 45 cm

SD Extinct; endemic to Okinawa, Kerama and Daito Is; last recorded 1904 (Okinawa) and 1936 (Daito Is). **HH** Subtropical forest. **ID** More uniformly black than close relative Bonin Woodpigeon, with purple-glossed head, green-glossed neck and underparts, and distinctive silvery crescent on upper back. **BP** Bill and cere dark blue; legs red.

Bonin Woodpigeon *Columba versicolor* L 45 cm

SD Extinct; endemic to Nakoudo-jima and Chichi-jima, Ogasawara Is. Discovered on Chichi-jima, June 1827, by Beechey; two collected on Chichi-jima, May 1828 (Kittlitz), and one on Nakoudo-jima, 15 Sep 1889 (Holst). Not recorded since. **HH** Subtropical forest. **ID** Larger than extant Black Woodpigeon. Dark grey, darkest, almost slate-grey, on wings and tail, with maroon, or green and purple gloss to back and rump, green tinge to flanks, with paler crescentic patch on neck/breast. **BP** Bill and cere dull yellow; legs red.

Miyako Kingfisher *Todiramphus (cinnamominus) miyakoensis* L 20 cm

SD This previously considered endemic taxon was collected only once on Miyako I (in 1887), an island perhaps unlikely to have supported such a species. Perhaps a local subspecies of Micronesian Kingfisher *H. cinnamominus*, or an accidental stray, ship-assisted, or collected elsewhere. **ID** Largely brownish-orange, with blue-green stripe from bill base across face to back; wings, back and tail blue-green with cobalt-blue rump and uppertail-coverts. **BP** Specimen lacks bill sheath, hence colour unknown; legs red.

White-bellied Woodpecker *Dryocopus javensis* L 40–48 cm; WT 197–347 g

SD *D. j. richardsi*: locally extinct resident of Tsushima, last recorded 1920. **HH** Lowland and hill forest. **ID** Enormous, black with white rump, primary bases, lower breast, flanks and belly. ♂ crown and narrow malar region bright red; ♀ head all-black. **BP** Bill long, blackish-grey; eyes white or pale yellow; large tarsi dark grey.

Kittlitz's Thrush *Zoothera terrestris*

SD Extinct; endemic on Ogasawara Is (Chichijima); extinct since 1880s. Quite common when discovered and four specimens collected on Chichi-jima in May 1828 by Baron F. H. von Kittlitz; captive in Ueno Zoo until 1885. **HH** Ground-dwelling and perhaps ground-nesting inhabitant of subtropical woodland. **ID** A small, dark-streaked brown thrush with white areas on underparts. **BP** Bill dark grey; legs dull ochre. **TN** Sometimes within genus *Cichlopasser* (e.g. OSJ). **AN** Bonin Thrush.

Bonin Grosbeak *Carpodacus ferreorostris* L 18 cm

SD Extinct, since 1830s; endemic to Ogasawara Is. Discovered 1827 (Beechey); also collected in 1828 (Kittlitz), but never again. Size variation of specimens suggests possibility of two different island populations. **HH** Subtropical forest. **ID** Large, dimorphic, grosbeak-like bird, brown with red forehead, supercilia, lower face and neck (♂), or plain brown (♀). **BP** Massive dark grey bill; legs dull brownish-pink. **TN** Formerly within genus *Chaunoproctus*.

Crested Shelduck
White-browed Crake
Ryukyu Woodpigeon
Slender-billed Curlew
Bonin Woodpigeon
Miyako Kingfisher
White-bellied Woodpecker
Kittlitz's Thrush
ad ♂
ad ♀
Bonin Grosbeak

APPENDIX 1
IDENTIFICATION OF NON-ADULT LARGE GULLS

MEDIUM AND LARGE HOODED GULLS

Laughing Gull *Leucophaeus atricilla* L 36–42 cm; WS 98–110 cm; WT 240–400 g

ID 1st-winter: from Franklin's by darker grey mantle, grey-brown hindneck, grey breast-sides to flanks; juvenile, brown upperwing-coverts retained, but lacks white apical spots on closed wing (Franklin's can lose spots due to wear). In flight, shows dark axillaries and grey-mottled underwing coverts (pale in Franklin's), blackish inner primaries (cf. pale inner primary window in Franklin's). Tail has grey-white base with broad black terminal band. 1st-summer: may retain faded juvenile coverts and very worn primaries. 2nd-winter: closely resembles adult. **BP** Bill long, thick, blackish with red tip in juv/1st-winter; legs black in juv/1st-winter.

Franklin's Gull *Leucophaeus pipixcan* L 32–38 cm; WS 85–95 cm; WT 220–335 g

ID 1st-winter: clearly demarcated partial blackish hood, white neck and underparts. Neat grey saddle contrasts with juvenile wing-coverts. Tail basally white with narrower black terminal band. Uniquely, undergoes complete moult into 1st-summer plumage, after which appears more adult-like, but has more black in primary tips and some may show dark feathers in tail and secondaries until 2nd-winter. **BP** Bill shorter and thicker than Black-headed Gull, black; legs black.

Relict Gull *Ichthyaetus relictus* L 39–45 cm; WT 540–700 g

ID 1st-winter: white-headed with streaked hindneck, grey saddle and wings with brown lesser coverts and tips to grey median coverts; black primaries lack white tips. **BP** Bill grey-brown in 1st-winter; eyes brown/black; legs blackish-grey.

Pallas's Gull *Ichthyaetus ichthyaetus* L 57–72 cm; WS 146–170 cm; WT 1100–2000 g

ID Juvenile: eye-catching structure of adult, but with pale-fringed brown mantle, scapulars and wing-coverts, and fairly uniform greater coverts lacking checkered pattern typical of most large gulls. Assumes adult-like grey mantle and scapulars early in first winter, though lower hindneck and wing-coverts mainly brown, rump and tail white with broad black terminal band. In flight, plain greyish-brown greater coverts form pale midwing panel. 2nd-winter: similar to 3rd-winter Vega Gull, but retains bold black tail-band. **BP** 1st-year has black-tipped pinkish-yellow bill; eyes black; legs greenish-yellow.

Black-tailed Gull *Larus crassirostris* L 44–48 cm; WS 126–128 cm; WT 436–680 g

ID Juvenile: extremely dark brown, with pale fringes to saddle, wing-coverts and tertials; could be confused with dark-morph skua. 1st-winter: brown-winged, with grey wash to underparts, palest on head, face typically whitish, with clear white vent and rump, and all-black tail. 2nd-winter: grey mantle and less grey wash to underparts, mainly on neck-sides; tail white with broad black terminal band. **BP** Bill long, pink with black tip (juv/1st-winter), or dull yellow or flesh-coloured with black tip (2nd-winter); eyes brown/black until at least 2nd-winter; legs pink until 1st-winter, thereafter becoming pale yellow.

Common Gull *Larus canus* L 40–46 cm; WS 110–125 cm; WT 394–593 g

ID Juvenile: very dark, coffee-coloured, mantle and scapulars dark brown with broad pale fringes; dark carpal and secondary bars, and pale grey midwing bar; blackish outer primaries and greyer inner primaries; rump and tail mostly white with broad black terminal band. **Kamchatka Gull** matures more slowly than *heinei* and retains this plumage into mid- or even late winter, only gradually replacing juvenile feathers with grey. 2nd-winter: frequently retains smudgy brownish-grey secondary-coverts, traces of secondary bar and underwing coverts can have dusky tips; more often has black in tail. Most *heinei* resemble adult at this age; though some retain immature lesser and median secondary-coverts, signs of immaturity usually restricted to primary-coverts and, in some cases, black in tail. In flight, 1st-winter appears dark, with much brown on upper surfaces and all-dark primaries. **BP** Rather delicate bill is dull with blackish spot near tip of lower mandible.

Ring-billed Gull *Larus delawarensis* L 41–49 cm; WS 112–127 cm; WT 400–590 g

ID 1st-winter: pale-grey mantle and greater coverts, contrasting with dark brown, black-centred, lesser and median coverts, and in flight has grey panel in inner primaries, grey bar across middle of upperwing and pale underwing with broad dark-brown border above and below; tail white with brown flecks and black subterminal band. 2nd-winter: similar, but lacks white primary tips and is duskier on head. Notched pattern on tertials and coverts can assist separation from Kamchatka Gull. **BP** Bill pink with black tip (1st-winter).

LARGE WHITE-HEADED GULLS

California Gull *Larus californicus* L 51–58 cm; WS 122–140 cm; WT 432–1045 g

ID Very dark juvenile resembles young Black-tailed, but rump barred brown and tail dark brown, not black. Scapulars and wing-coverts of 1st-year have chocolate-brown centres with silvery-white edges, imparting overall scalloped appearance. By 2nd-winter develops grey mantle, legs bluish-grey, bill grey with blackish band near tip.

Glaucous-winged Gull *Larus glaucescens* 61–68 cm; WS 132–137 cm; WT 900–1250 g

ID 1st-winter: rather uniform mid grey-brown, upperwing-coverts have pale fringes, giving scaled appearance, but primaries same colour as body. By 2nd-winter mantle mid-grey, rump white (often with heavy grey-brown wash), tail coffee-coloured, wing-coverts and primaries grey-brown, secondaries dark brown. In flight, broad-winged and heavy; 1st-winter appears uniform mid-brown. **BP** Bill long and heavy, black (juv/1st-winter), then with pink base (2nd-winter); tarsi deep pink.

Glaucous Gull *Larus hyperboreus* L 64–77 cm; WS 150–165 cm; WT 1070–2267 g

ID Juvenile/1st-winter: recalls Glaucous-winged Gull, but paler, uniform tan or coffee-coloured with white-fringed wing-coverts, primaries always paler, lacks tail-band. 2nd-winter: entire plumage mostly white with some brown flecks on wing-coverts, mantle and tail, but some still quite brown. At rest, primary tips extend just beyond tail. In flight, broad wings, thick neck and large head give front-heavy appearance; flight-feathers buff-white in rather uniform 1st-winter. **BP** 1st-winter bill basal two-thirds dull pink, tip black, 2nd-winter has pink bill with dark band and pale tip; juv/1st-winter has dark brown iris, 2nd-winter variably coloured (whitish and grey-green to brown); tarsi dull pink.

Iceland Gull *Larus glaucoides* L 52–60 cm; WS 137–150 cm; WT 557–863 g

ID 1st-winter: similar to Glaucous, though often greyer, primaries of *kumlieni* variable, from as pale as *glaucoides* to as dark as Thayer's. Whilst both can show subterminal arrowhead markings to primary tips, *glaucoides* is often uniformly white, and *kumlieni* shows dark centres to outer primaries, lacking in *glaucoides*; with wear, *kumlieni* becomes less distinctive as winter progresses. Base of bill becomes paler during 1st-winter in *glaucoides* but never as extensive as in Glaucous and is more diffuse towards gonys, with less 'dipped-in-paint' appearance. However, *kumlieni* more likely to retain mostly black or all-black bill until late winter. 2nd-winter: *glaucoides*' primaries tend to be paler than upperparts, whereas *kumlieni*'s are darker. In flight both have pale undersides to primaries, but *kumlieni* has contrasting dark outer webs to upper surface of outermost feathers and often has dark subterminal markings on others; *glaucoides* more uniform, lacking dark markings. Rump and tail of *kumlieni* differ from more uniform *glaucoides* in having broad dark tail-band with contrasting white rump. **BP** Dark iris of juvenile often becomes paler in 2nd-winter in *glaucoides*, less often in *kumlieni*; legs and feet dull pink.

Thayer's Gull *Larus (glaucoides) thayeri* L 56–64 cm; WS 130–148 cm; WT 846–1152 g

ID 1st-winter: rather plain, mottled tan-brown, with dark-centred tertials and pale-fringed dark brown primaries. 2nd-winter: mantle often grey but wings like younger birds and underparts paler. Usually exhibits contrast between pale rump and mostly blackish-brown tail. In flight, narrower winged than other large gulls. Beware of small juvenile and 1st-winter Slaty-backed, which can show very similar primary pattern, though its wings look broader, more paddle-shaped, and it has narrow, slightly darker terminal band on primary tips, distinguishing it from *kumlieni* Iceland Gull. **BP** Bill long, black in 1st-winter, develops pink base by 2nd-winter; juvenile to 2nd-winter has dark brown eyes, 3rd-winter has very dark yellowish-brown irides; tarsi dull pink.

American Herring Gull *Larus smithsonianus* L 56–64 cm; WS 135–147 cm; WT 1150 g

ID Care is needed to separate juvenile and 1st-winter from dark Vega and very variable Slaty-backed. From Vega, combination of smaller size, slightly longer primary projection and solidly dark outer greater coverts bar distinctive at rest (but Vega can show dark outermost greater coverts, usually hidden by breast-feathers, though typically checkered). Slaty-backed can be remarkably similar, but is heavily built, large-headed and stout-billed, with a much shorter wing projection. **BP** Bill basally dull pink, largely black (1st-winter), increasingly pink with smaller black tip (2nd-winter), dull yellow with black band near tip (3rd-winter); eyes brown (juvenile), to pale yellow (3rd-winter); tarsi greyish-flesh at first, becoming pale to mid-pink from 2nd-winter.

Vega Gull *Larus vegae*

L 55–67 cm; WS 135–150 cm; WT 688–1775 g

ID Juvenile or 1st-winter can be very dark, with barred scapulars and checkered wing-coverts, broad dark tail-band and narrowly barred rump and uppertail-coverts; underparts dusky-brown. Upperwing has pale-grey inner primaries and blackish-brown outers; secondaries dark brown. By 2nd-winter, mantle grey, wing-coverts paler brown almost grey, and underparts cleaner. **BP** Bill deep, black (juv/1st-winter), thereafter pale pink with dark tip; brownish-yellow irides; tarsi strong flesh pink.

Mongolian Gull *Larus mongolicus*

L 55–68 cm; WS 140–155 cm; WT 1125 g

ID Large four-year gull, similar to Vega. Juvenile has dark-brown upperparts, all feathers pale-fringed giving scaled appearance, head typically almost white, contrasting with black bill and brown-streaked neck and breast. Separation of 1st-/2nd-winter from Vega is beyond scope of this guide. **BP** Bill not normally as heavy looking as Vega, black in juv/1st-winter, becoming pink-based with age; legs greyish to whitish in juv/1st-winter.

Slaty-backed Gull *Larus schistisagus*

L 55–67 cm; WS 132–148 cm; WT 1050–1695 g

ID Very large, very dark four-year gull. Juvenile is very dark brown, gradually becoming paler, especially on head, in 1st-winter when mantle and scapulars have dark shaft-streaks. Greater coverts often more solidly dark, suggesting American Herring, as does all-dark tail and heavily barred rump/uppertail-coverts. Primary projection blackish to brownish, often with pale fringes, thus can recall Thayer's, but Slaty-backed much larger, bulkier with shorter wing projection than either Thayer's or American Herring. In flight, suggests American Herring due to tail, rump/uppertail-coverts, greater coverts pattern, and dark underwing, but inner primary window paler, primaries often brownish not black, with obviously pale inner webs creating 'Venetian blind' pattern, like Thayer's; also structurally different, bulkier with broader, shorter wings. From late winter, increasingly very worn and bleached, with white coverts, brown primaries and irregular dark grey on mantle; similar-age Glaucous-winged uniformly pale grey. By 2nd-winter, saddle more adult-like. **BP** Bill heavy, black in juv/1st-winter, thereafter pale pink with dark tip; tarsi deep pink.

Heuglin's Gull *Larus heuglini*

L 51–65 cm; WS 124–150 cm; WT 550–1200 g

ID Large, well-proportioned gull with rounded head and strong bill. Looks long-winged, tail extension beyond tertials about one-third of primary projection beyond tertials. Following refers to '*taimyrensis*', which is distinctive at all ages. Juvenile has dark saddle, lesser and median wing-coverts with narrow pale fringes, greater coverts mainly uniformly dark as American Herring Gull. Juvenile scapulars replaced by darkish grey 1st-winter feathers with darker anchors; grey fades to whitish during winter to give much paler overall appearance, with darker internal anchors prominent. Head becomes much whiter, and by late March may be moulting median wing-coverts, unlike Vega. Retained juvenile tertials largely blackish and contrast with increasingly pale body. In flight, juvenile is very dark, inner-primary window dull, less contrasting than Vega, and with dark greater coverts bar creates darker, more uniform upperwing, like American Herring. Shares largely black tail with latter, but rump and especially tail-coverts spotted rather than barred. In 2nd-winter dark adult feathers visible in saddle, thus darker than Vega, more elegant than Slaty-backed. **BP** Bill dark in juvenile, becoming pale-based with dark tip in winter.

APPENDIX 2
ADDITIONAL, UNDOCUMENTED OR DOUBTFULLY RECORDED SPECIES

The following species have also been reported from Japan, but are not currently accepted:

American Black Duck	*Anas rubripes*	Record uncertain.
Velvet Scoter	*Melanitta fusca*	Reported, but not published.
Grey-backed Storm-Petrel	*Garrodia nereis*	Reported, but not published.
White-bellied Storm-Petrel	*Fregatta grallaria*	Reported, but not published.
Wandering Albatross	*Diomedia exulans*	Identification of record under review.
Least Storm-Petrel	*Oceanodroma microsoma*	Reported, but not published.
Murphy's Petrel	*Pterodroma ultima*	Reported, but not published.
Trinidade Petrel	*Pterodroma arminjoniana*	Reported, but not published.
Townsend's Shearwater	*Puffinus auricularis*	Reported, but not published.
Tropical Shearwater	*Puffinus bailloni*	Reported, but not published.
Indian Pond Heron	*Ardeola bacchus*	Publication pending.
Christmas Island Frigatebird	*Fregata andrewsi*	Previously accepted, but identification of record now doubted.
Brahminy Kite	*Haliastur indus*	Reported, but not published.
Xantus's Murrelet	*Synthliboramphus hypoleucus*	Reported, but not published.
Philippine Cuckoo Dove	*Macropygia tenuirostris*	Reported, but not published.
Jacobin Cuckoo	*Clamator jacobinus*	Reported, but not published.
Uniform Swiftlet	*Aerodramus vanikorensis*	Reported, but not published.
Edible-nest Swiftlet	*Aerodramus fuciphagus*	Reported, but not published.
Alpine Swift	*Tachymarptis melba*	Reported, but not published.
Eurasian Crag Martin	*Ptyonoprogne rupestris*	Reported, but not published.
Yellow-streaked Warbler	*Phylloscopus armandii*	Reported, but not published.
Claudia's Warbler	*Phylloscopus (reguloides) claudiae*	Reported, but not published.
Sulphur-breasted Warbler	*Phylloscopus ricketti*	Reported, but not published.
Chinese Leaf Warbler	*Phylloscopus yunnanensis*	Publication pending.
Common Whitethroat	*Sylvia communis*	Reported, but not published.
White-eared Sibia	*Heterophasia auricularis*	Reported, but not published.
Blunt-winged Warbler	*Acrocephalus concinens*	Reported, but not published.
Manchurian Reed Warbler	*Acrocephalus tangorum*	Publication pending.
Icterine Warbler	*Hippolais icterina*	Reported, but not published.
American Robin	*Turdus migratorius*	Reported, but not published.
Varied Thrush	*Ixoreus naevius*	Reported, but not published.
Swainson's Thrush	*Catharus ustulatus*	Reported, but not published.
Plumbeous Water Redstart	*Rhyacornis fuliginosa*	Wild status questioned.
White-tailed Robin	*Myiomela leucura*	Wild status questioned.
White-throated Bush Chat	*Saxicola insignis*	Reported, but not published.
Rufous-bellied Niltava	*Niltava sundara*	Reported, but not published.
Tawny Pipit	*Anthus campestris*	Reported, but not published.
Dark-eyed Junco	*Junco hyemalis*	Reported, but omitted by OSJ.

The Ornithological Society of Japan (OSJ) maintains the list of avian species recorded in Japan, and publishes a checklist in book form at irregular intervals, and *The Journal of Japanese Ornithology* twice annually. Records may not have been accepted by OSJ for various reasons, including: record not supported by specimen or photograph, insufficient detail, lack of publication (in scientific form), concerns over identification, or concerns over likely origin. The key to inclusion in the OSJ list is prior publication in an academic journal. Anyone with details suitable for publication of any of the above species is advised to submit them to OSJ.

The following species have also been reported, but are considered to be escapees without established populations:

Egyptian Goose	*Alopochen aegyptiacus*
Wood Duck	*Aix sponsa*
Scarlet Ibis	*Eudocimus ruber*
Black Crowned Crane	*Balearica pavonina*
Greater Flamingo	*Phoenicopterus roseus*
Purple Swamphen	*Porphyrio porphyrio*
Yellow-crowned Bishop	*Euplectes afer*
Zebra Finch	*Taeniopygia guttata*

APPENDIX 3
SPECIES THOUGHT LIKELY TO OCCUR IN THE FUTURE

Spectacled Eider	*Somateria fischeri*
Black-browed Albatross	*Thalassarche melanophris*
Atlantic Yellownosed Albatross	*Thalassarche chlororhynchos*
Great-winged Petrel	*Pterodroma macroptera*
Collared Petrel	*Pterodroma brevipes*
Beck's Petrel	*Pterodroma becki*
Tahiti Petrel	*Pseudobulweria rostrata*
White Stork	*Ciconia ciconia*
Red-tailed Hawk	*Buteo jamaicensis*
White-bellied Sea Eagle	*Haliaeetus leucogaster*
Surfbird	*Aphriza virgata*
Purple Sandpiper	*Calidris marítima*
Killdeer	*Charadrius vociferus*
Black Oystercatcher	*Haematopus bachmani*
Chinese Crested Tern	*Thalasseus bernsteini*
Atlantic Puffin	*Fratercula arctica*
Marbled Murrelet	*Brachyramphus marmoratus*
Hill Pigeon	*Columba rupestris*
Great Grey Owl	*Strix nebulosa*
Northern Hawk Owl	*Surnia ulula*
European Roller	*Coracias garrulus*
Bronzed Drongo	*Dicrurus aeneus*
Crested Lark	*Galerida cristata*
Golden-headed Cisticola	*Cisticola exilis*
Barred Warbler	*Sylvia nisoria*
Wallcreeper	*Tichodroma muraria*
Black-collared Starling	*Gracupica nigricollis*
American Robin	*Turdus migratorius*
Hermit Thrush	*Catharus guttatus*
Orange-crowned Warbler	*Oreothlypsis celata*
American Yellow Warbler	*Setophaga petechia*
Common Yellowthroat	*Geothylyptis trichas*
Northern Waterthrush	*Parkesia noveboracensis*
American Tree Sparrow	*Spizella arborea*
Lincoln's Sparrow	*Melospiza lincolnii*

References for Appendices 2 and 3

Brazil, M. A. 2009. *Field Guide to the Birds of East Asia.* Christopher Helm, London.

Ikenaga, H., Kawakami, K. & Yanagisawa, N. 2014. Check-list of Japanese Birds 7th Revised Edition species and subspecies presently unaccepted. *Japanese Journal of Ornithology* 63 (1): 134-149 [in Japanese].

Maki, H., Onishi, T. & Iozawa, H. 2014. *A Photographic Guide to the Birds of Japan.* Nihon no Chorui 650. Heibonsha; Tokyo.

Shimba, T. 2013. *A Photographic Guide to the Birds of Japan and North-east Asia.* Seitai-kagaku Shuppan, Tokyo.

The Ornithological Society of Japan. 2012. *Check-list of Japanese Birds*, 7th revised edition. The Ornithological Society of Japan, Sanda.

INDEX

Page numbers in **bold** refer to plates.